SURVEY
OF
SOCIAL
SCIENCE

SURVEY
OF
SOCIAL
SCIENCE

SOCIOLOGY SERIES

Volume 3
903-1386

Horticultural Economic Systems—The Police

Edited by

FRANK N. MAGILL

Consulting Editor

HÉCTOR L. DELGADO
UNIVERSITY OF ARIZONA

SALEM PRESS

Pasadena, California   Englewood Cliffs, New Jersey

∞ The paper used in these volumes conforms to the
American National Standard for Permanence of Paper for
Printed Library Materials, Z39.48-1984.

Library of Congress Cataloging-in-Publication Data
Survey of social science. Sociology series / [edited by]
Frank N. Magill; consulting editor, Héctor L. Delgado.
    v. cm.
    Includes bibliographical references and index.
    1. Sociology—Encyclopedias.   I. Magill, Frank
Northen, 1907-   . II. Delgado, Héctor L., 1949-   .
HM17.S86   1994   94-31770
301'.03—dc20   CIP
ISBN 0-89356-739-6 (set)
ISBN 0-89356-742-6 (volume 3)

PRINTED IN THE UNITED STATES OF AMERICA

CONTENTS

SOCIOLOGY

CONTENTS

SURVEY
OF
SOCIAL
SCIENCE

HORTICULTURAL ECONOMIC SYSTEMS

Type of sociology: Major social institutions
Field of study: The economy

Horticultural economic systems are based on cultivation without the use of plows. In preindustrial horticulture, human labor supplies all the energy that goes into cultivation. This imposes some limits, but horticulture is not merely a primitive forerunner of plow agriculture; it has supported dense populations and states and still feeds hundreds of millions.

Principal terms
> CHIEFDOM: a polity that lacks full-time politicians or bureaucrats; a few individuals, however, control political power and the flow of wealth
> MATRIARCHY: a society ruled or otherwise under the control of women, as men rule a patriarchy
> POPULATION PRESSURE: a population's demand for resource exploitation—not a simple function of population density, because resources and technology vary; the amount of population pressure that can be absorbed through technological advances is a controversial subject
> SETTLEMENT PATTERN: the arrangement of habitation
> SOCIAL EVOLUTION: regular change from one form of society to another, following general laws or principles; often associated with progress and with progression through a sequence of stages
> STATE: a polity that includes strong, centralized rule, including a professional bureaucracy that administers it; associated with moderate to high degree of social stratification
> SUSTAINABLE: capable of being continued indefinitely without degrading nonrenewable resources

Overview

Many authorities subsume horticulture under agriculture, but others reserve "agriculture" for systems in which draft animals or tractors pull plows and do other tasks. In preindustrial horticulture, the availability of labor limits the size of the operation. for that reason some authors write of horticultural "gardens" but agricultural "fields," although a horticultural landscape can consist of contiguous areas in grain or any crop.

There are relatively "extensive" forms of horticulture—that is, those in which inputs of labor, material, or capital are few—and more "intensive" forms, in which inputs are greater. Preindustrial horticulturists make few energy investments, since they do not exploit the energy of animals in cultivation. The object of intensification is to raise yields. Gains may be in the current season, such as those from drainage.

One of the most widespread forms of horticulture is used extensively: clearing forest or scrub, cropping, then abandoning the area to return to its original cover. Usually clearing is by the "slash and burn" method. Undergrowth and trees are cut and left to dry, then burned. Crops, usually a mixture, are planted through the ashes, after light tillage. The ashes are a source of nutrients and reduce soil acidity. Yields are generally good the first year, but they ordinarily decline the next year. That, and invading weeds, may prompt abandonment, often after one to three years; longer cropping delays the regrowth of woody vegetation unless some care is taken. Occasional variations include leaving the felled vegetation unburned, and *chitemene* cultivation of the Congo-Zambesi watershed in Africa, in which felled scrub is concentrated in small circles before being burned.

A planted tree crop is an occasional alternative to a forest fallow. This is an old technique used in Hokkaido, Japan, southern China, Burma, Malaysia, Papua New Guinea, several parts of West Africa, and Java. If cropping is lengthened or fallows shortened, grasses tend to replace woody growth in the fallows. "Permanent cultivation" results from the elimination of fallows. Grass fallow and permanent cultivation systems, unlike forest fallow systems, are either horticultural or agricultural. Whereas plows are very difficult to use in recently cleared forests, they readily break ground that has been in grass or under cultivation, as do hand tools. Heavy hoes are the tools of choice in Africa; spades in Europe. Wooden digging sticks are used in the Pacific islands, though spades have replaced them in most places.

More frequent cropping makes horticulture more intensive, first because work goes into a given area of land in more years, and second because inputs usually increase. Grass, no matter how well tilled, grows back, requiring more frequent weeding, though ingenuity helps; for example, the Sudanese *hariq*, a burn of cut grass timed to catch emerging growth, suppresses regrowth for weeks. Harvesting removes plant nutrients, and few soils have reserves to support frequent cropping. Some techniques may improve the utilization of nutrients, such as digging in crop residues, but in the long run cultivators must import nutrients, enhance biological processes that "fix" atmospheric nitrogen (that is, put it into forms that plants can take up), or both.

One solution is to gather dead leaves, grass, and other vegetation from surrounding areas and work it into garden soils. The practice mines the surrounding soils of nutrients but may be sustainable if enough uncultivated land is at hand. Kitchen wastes, animal manures, and human feces are often recycled, usually onto "home gardens," permanently cultivated sites near habitations. Deliberate application of human feces is common in East and South Asia; it is rare in sub-Saharan Africa and scattered elsewhere. Legumes fix nitrogen and can thereby aid intensive horticulture.

"Wet" systems—that is, those in natural wetlands or irrigated areas—are often readily sustainable. Irrigation water brings in variable amounts of nutrients. Rice and taro, a tropical root crop, thrive in shallow, flooded fields; nitrogen-fixing microorganisms are often active in the water, contributing to sustained yields. One way to exploit lands that are permanently or seasonally flooded is to move soil from ditches onto planting surfaces. Such surfaces are known as "island beds" in the Pacific, where they are often low and are used for crops that tolerate waterlogged soils, and as "drained fields" in tropical America, where they are higher and used for diverse crops. The Mexican *chinampas*, or "floating gardens," are an example. Muck and vegetation from the ditches fertilize crops. Another usually sustainable system is "decrue cultivation," on fresh soil left behind by receding floodwaters. On the whole, the settlement patterns of horticulturalists are more like those of agriculturalists than unlike them. One exception is the frequent association of long fallow horticulture with "shifting cultivation," in which the settlement is regularly moved. In some societies it is moved with each clearance of new gardens.

One distinctive social feature of horticulture is a greater role of women in food production (as opposed to food processing) than in plow agriculture. Anthropologists M. Kay Martin and Barbara Voorhies found that women contribute more labor than men in 50 percent of horticultural societies but only 15 percent of agricultural societies. Men contribute the most in 17 percent and 81 percent, respectively. In the remainder the work is equally divided.

Applications

Study of the variety of horticultural systems that exist furnishes knowledge with which to dispel Eurocentric judgments of their "primitiveness." Europeans, when they embarked on colonial expansion, were mainly plow-using agriculturalists and had a developing love of mechanical solutions to practical problems. In the slash-and-burn and other fallow systems of their colonies they saw few implements, and they tended to overlook the environmental knowledge necessary for success. Plants were usually not grown in rows, but in complex, irregular patterns. A system that many colonial observers saw as disorder actually takes advantage of complementary habits of the plants and diverse microenvironments in the clearing.

Contemporary thinking regards horticulture as a viable system in its own right. As economist Ester Boserup has demonstrated, intensive forms of horticulture (or agriculture) readily develop when demand increases, principally because of mounting population pressure. In preindustrial cultivation the use of draft animals for tillage saves labor, but forest fallow systems do not require tillage, and their yields compare quite favorably with those of preindustrial agriculture per unit of labor spent. Horticulture that supports dense populations often, but not always, requires more labor than agriculture to produce the same amount of food. In the right circumstances preindustrial horticulture offers good returns on labor.

Horticulture predominated in the precolonial Americas and the Pacific islands, not out of primitiveness, but because there were no domesticated animals suitable for draft purposes. In most of sub-Saharan Africa, horses do not thrive, and pasture, not generally of good quality, is more in demand for dairy and beef cattle than for draft oxen. Colonial-era depopulation accounts for some of the predominance of long fallow systems in parts of Africa, the Pacific islands, and the Americas; archeology reveals large areas with abandoned intensive systems.

Postwar population growth has strained the capacities of many horticultural systems in developing countries, in many places causing a shift from sustainable to nonsustainable land use. This, plus demand from growing urban markets and pressures to commercialize production, has created a changing social and economic environment, to which many horticulturalists are having trouble adapting.

Agricultural development programs now often build on existing horticultural knowledge, particularly in the tropics. One important example is row intercropping, in which traditional crop mixtures are planted, but in rows. This gives most of the yield advantage gained by the old complex intercropping methods, and it allows tillers, power hoes, and other machinery to pass between rows. Many horticulturalists stand to gain by adopting plows and either draft animals or tractors. Not all horticulturalists are able to become plow agriculturalists, however; many lack capital or enough land of the right kind to repay the investment.

Consequently, much research on horticulture is on sustainable methods to raise yields. Much of the needed agronomic knowledge (for example, concerning the use of chemical fertilizers to maintain soil fertility or the breeding of new crop varieties for higher yields and disease resistance) builds on previous research on larger-scale agricultural operations. Other issues may be peculiar to horticultural operations or—as most workers in the fields describe them—small, "low resource" operations.

One specific agronomic strategy for the development of horticulture, one with great promise for sustainable development in tropical countries, is agroforestry, variously the alternation of tree crops with gardens or the permanent cultivation of mixed gardens of trees and annuals. Both are new versions of old strategies. Trees, because their roots bring up nutrients from lower soil layers that most crop plants cannot reach, can be valuable adjuncts to crops. Harvesting wood for timber, fuel, and other purposes removes nutrients that would be recycled in a forest fallow system, but some is left behind in debris and leaves; in addition, several of the tree species involved fix nitrogen. Mixed gardens of trees and annuals replicate and extend an old strategy mostly used in home gardens in the past. Continuing research focuses on selection and breeding of trees, interrelations with annual crops, and uses for tree products. Despite the antiquity of the basic methods, they are unfamiliar to many potential producers and consumers in target populations, and in many places social and economic research is needed.

"Farming systems research" has grown as an interdisciplinary approach to understanding the diverse agronomic, ecological, and social issues confronting farmers in developing countries, and much of the effort has targeted horticulture. Research teams, which generally include sociologists and other social scientists, explore links among such diverse variables as investment, the division of labor and profits between men and women, market demands, expectations of rewards from proposed changes, and farm ecology, often with the aim of evaluating specific innovations.

Context

The distinction between horticulture and agriculture originated with the Romans, but it was nineteenth century anthropologist Lewis Henry Morgan who made it part of a general model of social evolution. Horticulture, Morgan wrote, originates in the

"Upper Status of Savagery"; agriculture comes two stages later, in the "Middle Status of Barbarism."

Friedrich Engels adopted Morgan's scheme of social evolution, which became a part of orthodox Marxist theories of history. A Marxist and feminist writer, Evelyn Reed, in a 1974 book, cited the role that women play in horticulture and revived Morgan's scheme, including the idea that matriarchy preceded patriarchy.

In the 1940's and 1950's, some anthropologists revived social evolutionism, trying to remove such value-laden baggage as labeling cultures "savage." Leslie White proposed that cultural evolution is essentially a process of increasing energy capture, a proposition that has since echoed in some human ecological writing. White did not distinguish between horticulture and agriculture but argued that a system that combines plant and animal husbandry is "superior" to one based on plants alone. Like Morgan, he argued that the transition to plow agriculture would have important societal consequences, though his model is more flexible than Morgan's.

Morgan's premise that horticulture preceded agriculture has some archeological support from regions where both plants and animals were domesticated early, and White's generalizations that keeping animals for draft and other purposes adds to energy capture can hardly be faulted. The case for consistent societal associations, however, is weak. Horticulture has, like agriculture, supported dense populations, including urban concentrations and elites. For example, states and urban civilizations arose in the precolonial Americas and sub-Saharan Africa. The best case for White's energy theory is perhaps early modern England. There, during the "agricultural revolution," both the numbers of livestock and their contribution to agriculture increased in conjunction with increased use of water and power and the burning of coal, processes that led to the industrial revolution.

The most important trait of horticulture to remember is its variety. The absence of plows and animal or tractor power imposes some limits, but those limits are not as great as has often been maintained. Many sociology and anthropology texts still identify horticulture with only its extensive forms, such as slash-and-burn cultivation. To gardeners and agricultural scientists in developed countries, horticulture is something utterly different: ornamental gardens and small vegetable gardens, sometimes orchards and vineyards. In these, the use of small power implements, such as rototillers, may obscure the original distinction between agriculture and horticulture.

Bibliography

Allan, William. *The African Husbandman*. New York: Barnes & Noble Books, 1965. A classic survey of sub-Saharan horticulture, mostly as it was years before population growth strained these systems. Attention is also paid to pastoralism, and a few examples of plow cultivation are included. A geographic perspective, with good information of patterns of settlement and their relation to food production. Good bibliography on colonial era sources.

Denevan, William, and Christine Padoch, eds. *Swidden-Fallow Agroforestry in the Peruvian Amazon*. Bronx, N.Y.: New York Botanical Garden, 1988. A good survey in a fairly representative part of the Amazon basin of traditional fallow horticulture and the response to pressures for development. Several contributions exhibit both social and ecological insights. Contrasts sustainable and nonsustainable land use in a fragile environment. The bibliography reflects the interdisciplinary interests of the contributors.

Kidd, Charles V., and David Pimentel, eds. *Integrated Resource Management: Agroforestry for Development*. San Diego: Academic Press, 1992. Probably a better introduction or sampling than some previously published proceedings of agroforestry conferences. An interdisciplinary work with an ecological focus.

Landauer, Kathleen, and Mark Brazil, eds. *Tropical Home Gardens*. Tokyo, Japan: United Nations University Press, 1990. Proceedings of a conference held in 1985 on gardens of mixed annuals and perennial. Includes reviews of the literature, both global and regional. The dominant perspective is ecological, complemented by the perspectives of economists, sociologists, anthropologists, agronomists, foresters, and others. Broad geographical coverage, with emphasis on Indonesia, the host country.

Office of Technology Assessment. *Enhancing Agriculture in Africa: A Role for U.S. Development Assistance*. Washington, D.C.: Government Printing Office, 1988. Besides discussing the U.S. role, this volume surveys the present status of horticulture ("low resource agriculture") among rapidly growing populations. Attention is given to land degradation and conservation measures, and to yield-raising techniques, including crop and livestock improvement intercropping, agroforestry, aquaculture, transitions to agriculture using draft animals, and sociological issues of tenure and labor. Reportorial writing. Includes a limited bibliography.

Poats, Susan V., Marianne Schmink, and Anita Spring, eds. *Gender Issues in Farming Systems Research and Extension*. Boulder, Colo.: Westview Press, 1988. About gender, mostly women's roles in farming systems, but also one of the best introductions to the philosophy and methodology of farming systems research, particularly in the introductory part. Multiple selections on Latin America and the Caribbean, Asia and the Middle East, and Africa, but not on the Pacific nor developed countries. Papers unfortunately tend to be heavy on specialist jargon, much of it gratuitous.

Ruthenberg, Hans. *Farming Systems in the Tropics*. Oxford, England: Clarendon Press, 1971. Mostly about horticulture, this book is strongest on Africa and weakest on the American tropics. Mostly agronomic and ecological, only occasionally sociological, but offers excellent descriptions and illustrations.

Daniel E. Vasey

Cross-References

HUNTING AND GATHERING ECONOMIC SYSTEMS

Type of sociology: Major social institutions
Field of study: The economy

A hunting and gathering economy is a mode of subsistence that relies on collecting wild plants and hunting game. Early sociologists used food foraging societies to develop progressive theories of social evolution and social change.

Principal terms

BAND: a grouping of thirty to one hundred individuals who identify with a particular home range and share resources

DIVISION OF LABOR: the allocation of economic tasks

DOMESTICATION: a process whereby wild plants and animals are genetically altered by human intervention in order to foster desirable traits

ETHNOGRAPHY: the detailed study of a particular society and its culture

FISSION-FUSION SOCIETY: a system of flux in which band members fragment into household units when resources are scarce and reunite when resources are plentiful

HORTICULTURE: the cultivation of domesticated seeds that are grown on small plots of land without the use of draft animals or irrigation

HOUSEHOLD: a domestic group that cooperates as an economic unit on a daily basis

SEASONAL ROUND: the seasonal movement within a ranging area as resources become available

SOCIAL INSTITUTION: a pervasive pattern of social relationships with recognized positions or statuses and roles with appropriate social behaviors attached to statuses and roles

Overview

A hunting and gathering economy is a subsistence strategy that depends on the collection of wild plants and animals. As the oldest of human economic institutions, it originated with the beginnings of humankind. Until the domestication of plants and animals, it was the only economic pattern for a period of time that included about 99 percent of human existence. Although a society that "lives off the land" may be distinguished in many ways from one that "cultivates the land," a hunting and gathering economy is still organized around universal economic processes that are involved in the gathering, producing, and distribution of goods and services among individuals. In this endeavor, food-foraging economies also vary among themselves in the resources that are available for consumption, the level of technical skills necessary for individuals to participate in economic processes, the kinds of tools used in conjunction with labor, and the technological complexity that is required for a society to exploit a specific ecological zone.

Until horticulture, or simple farming, was first adopted in the Near East about ten thousand years ago, hunters and gatherers occupied climatic regions around the globe, from the tropical rainforests and coastal areas to the near-deserts and frozen Arctic zones. Yet during this time the human population numbered less than ten million persons, with a population density of one or two individuals per square mile. In certain respects, contemporary hunters and gatherers parallel the lifeways of prehistoric foraging societies, in part because foraging for food requires individuals to live in small groups and to follow a nomadic and flexible lifestyle. Consequently, individuals in food-collecting societies will disperse, or "fission," when resources are scarce and congregate, or "fuse," when resources are plentiful and concentrated.

Contemporary hunter-gatherers are arranged into loosely organized bands of thirty to one hundred individuals who embody what is called a "band-level" society. A band is an autonomous political unit of self-sufficient families or households that share a common foraging range and move about this region in a "seasonal round." Since each family is a well-defined economic unit, households are free to join or leave a band depending on individual preference and procurable resources. In every domestic household, economic labor is strictly divided according to age and sex: Men hunt and women gather, while the old and young are exempt from subsistence activities. Among all contemporary hunting and gathering societies there is little formal leadership beyond the domestic household, little stratification, and an egalitarian decision-making process; above all, there is an abiding "principle of reciprocity," a form of economic exchange that advocates the sharing of foods, goods, and services.

The Andamanese are hunter-gatherers who once inhabited tropical islands on the eastern edge of the Bay of Bengal in Southern Asia. Favored with a moist and warm coastal climate, the Andaman possessed a bounty of natural resources that included wild honey, roots, fruits, seeds, civet cats, wild pigs, large lizards, snakes, and abundant marine animals.

In his ethnography *The Andaman Islanders* (1922), A. R. Radcliffe-Brown describes Andamanese bands as having a production strategy that is associated with a definite ranging area, economic units that are composed of domestic households, and a sexual division of labor that is fairly clearly marked. Adult females in the Andamanese economy are responsible for the gathering of fruits, plants, prawns, and crabs, while adult males are involved in fishing and hunting enterprises. In turn, economic activities are linked with technological skills and tools. Males make and use bows and arrows, adzes, knives, ropes for harpoon lines, and seaworthy dugout canoes, while females make and use digging sticks for harvesting wild plants and fishnets for catching prawns, crabs, and other small fish. On a daily basis, Andaman women also gather firewood, carry water, and prepare the family meal.

While these coastal dwellers practiced no horticulture, the easily obtainable and concentrated coastal resources enabled them to congregate frequently and to spend part of the year in semipermanent settlements. This more sedentary lifestyle is reflected in Andamanese manufactured goods, which are a noticeable departure from those of most hunter-gatherers. For traveling on the water, the Andaman built canoes from hollowed-out logs. They built sturdy settlement huts and produced a variety of durable, bulky goods that included wooden buckets, cups and plates made of sea-shells, heavy clay cooking pots, and sleeping mats with wooden pillows.

In comparison, the Dobe !Kung are hunter-gatherers who inhabit a hot, semiarid savanna on the edge of the Kalahari Desert in southern Africa. In this harsh climactic zone, the !Kung are always on the move, and their economic institution is adapted to exploit an enormous variety of widely dispersed resources. In this pursuit of food procuring, the !Kung sexual division of labor recruits males for the hunting of game and females for the gathering of plants.

Richard Lee's ethnography *The Dobe !Kung* (1984) describing !Kung life in the 1960's, depicts !Kung males as highly skilled hunters who will pursue almost any-thing—from warthogs, porcupines, guinea fowl, antelopes, and leopard tortoise to pythons. Male weaponry includes bows and arrows, spears, knives, hooks, ropes, and occasional use of well-trained dogs for capturing small game that are then speared. While fresh meat is always the prized food, vegetables, fruits, and nuts are the abundant and predictable foods that make up the bulk of the !Kung diet. According to Lee, "the !Kung have an astonishing inventory of over 100 edible plants: 14 fruits and nuts, 15 berries, 18 species of edible gum, 41 edible roots and bulbs, and 17 leafy greens, beans, melons, and other foods: 105 species in all." In the gathering process, Lee reports, !Kung females have exceptional technical knowledge about the growing conditions of wild plants, which they collect by either picking or digging into the soil with a sharpened wooden stick.

In contrast to the Adamanese, the !Kung production strategy depends upon a highly mobile and fluid population with frequent "fission" of the band. This flexible lifestyle is reflected in their provisional dwellings and in the nature of !Kung manufactured goods, which are mostly light, portable items such as sewing materials or fire-making kits that are easily stored and transported.

Applications

Information on the economic systems of hunting and gathering societies is mostly drawn from ethnographic accounts of aboriginal populations such as the Andaman and !Kung who survived into the nineteenth century. During this era, hunter-gatherers still lived in most parts of the globe, although aggressive farmers had already pushed most food foragers into marginal ecological zones where climatic soil conditions made cultivation impractical. Yet even under these limited environmental conditions, hunt-ers and gatherers still managed to assemble successful economic systems that afforded an adequate and reliable food base with only a few cases of hardship documented. The realization that contemporary hunter-gatherers did not fit the stereotype of starving peoples living "nasty, brutish, and short" lives was documented in the classic volume *Man the Hunter* (1968, edited by Richard B. Lee and Irven DeVore), the proceedings of a symposium that brought together seventy-five distinguished scholars in the field.

Since the 1970's, long-term field studies of the adaptive responses of modest, food-collecting peoples living under diverse environmental circumstances have been especially important in providing practical information on how economic systems operate in particular ecological settings. Equally important, extended research has revealed that, despite the variety in adaptive conditions, all food-collecting societies share a core of economic patterns that can serve as an economic baseline by which to compare them with industrialized economies. First, by and large, hunter-gatherers meet their dietary needs with a minimal energy budget, while foods grown in industrial societies are far more costly in energy terms. Second, hunter-gatherers normally preserve their resource base, while industrialized societies normally deplete theirs, suggesting the possibility that demands may soon exceed resources. Third, hunter-gatherers eat well, although they expend minimal labor, have considerable leisure time, and often live long lives with minimum stress and anxiety. Marshall Sahlins, in *Stone Age Economies* (1972), called them "the original affluent society," and Elman Service wrote in "The Hunters" (1966) that "many hunting-gathering peoples are quite literally the most leisured peoples in the world." In comparison, the economic forces in industrialized societies compel individuals to work longer and harder than workers in any past societies, and often create considerable stress and anxiety in the process.

Thus, while industrialization has led to a substantial increase in material benefits, as a practical matter, foraging economies can serve as a corrective yardstick by which to assess potential problems of energy flow, environmental abuse, and the social and emotional consequences of modern subsistence modes. In this regard, Gerhard Lenski, Jean Lenski, and Patrick Nolan considered modes of production from simple hunting and gathering to industrialized societies and concluded in their book *Human Societies* (1991) that "there is no simple one-to-one correspondence between technological advance and progress in terms of freedom, justice, and happiness."

Studying economic systems cross-culturally has also helped sociologists appreciate how social relationships differ among individuals in market economies (in which individuals offer goods for sale to others) and marketless economies (in which goods are not for sale but are exchanged through social mechanisms). In market-dominant economies, gathering, production, and distribution are governed by "market principle" of supply and demand, and economic life is primarily based on private profits. In foraging (marketless) economies, resources are pooled according to a "principle of reciprocity," and economic life is governed by an egalitarian ethic of sharing. In turn, the way goods are exchanged seems to influence other social institutions in a society. For example, societies that have economic institutions in which members have equal rights to resources also have political institutions that uphold what is perhaps the most cherished of Western democratic ideals: the belief that all members of a society are social equals.

Finally, inquiry into a food-foraging lifestyle in which individuals interact with their physical environment on a daily basis is a useful way to assess the potency of economic forces. According to Lenski, Lenski, and Nolan, most variations in human societies can be understood in terms of the differences in habitats and subsistence technologies.

Context

Interest in hunter-gatherers is a longstanding sociological tradition that goes back to the formative years of sociology when nineteenth century evolutionary notions of order, progress, and continuity were used to understand the development of societal types. In England, Herbert Spencer, in his *Descriptive Sociology* (1873-1881), made extensive use of information collected on foraging societies in an attempt to understand social progress and social change from simple societies to the modern political state. By using standard categories to examine variations in the features of human societies, Spencer attempted to document how social phenomena are interrelated in an effort to develop generalizations about the operation of human societies.

In France, Émile Durkheim focused on change in economic systems in his *De la Division du travail social* (1893; *The Division of Labor in Society*, 1933). In this classic monograph, Durkheim attempted to show how units of a social system are coordinated and how the basis of social solidarity changes as individuals move from simple food-foraging economies to complex state societies. In *Les Formes élémentaires de la vie religieuse: Le Système totémique en Australie* (1912; *The Elementary Forms of the Religious Life: A Study in Religious Sociology*, 1915), Durkheim continued his analysis of progressive social evolution by using data drawn from Australian food foragers to try to uncover the origins of society. While the evolutionary schemes of both Spencer and Durkheim were tainted by a belief that primitive societies, and hunter-gatherers in particular, were savages at the most elementary stages of humanity, both scholars were major figures in helping to legitimate sociology as the discipline concerned with the workings of human societies.

In contemporary sociology, there has been a renewed emphasis on hunting and gathering societies, partly because of a rekindling of interest in evolutionary concepts and a realization that humans evolved in a food-foraging context. For example, many of the physical attributes of human beings, such as upright walking, a large brain relative to body size, language, and a sexual division of labor were all acquired when humans lived solely by food collecting. Additionally, human nutritional requirements, social needs, and even emotional responses to stress and aggression are now being viewed as adaptive responses acquired when humans foraged for food. Thus, despite the fact that the food collectors of the world are rapidly disappearing and this societal type will probably soon vanish, this lifestyle is still an important meeting ground for current economic issues and for its potential importance in providing insights into "human nature" and other legacies acquired during that long historical phase when all humans were nomadic food collectors.

Bibliography

Bettinger, Robert. *Hunter-Gatherers: Archaeological and Evolutionary Theory*. New York: Plenum Press, 1991. This book is a comprehensive overview of the history of research and theory in relation to hunter-gatherers and an overview of contemporary evolutionary and materialist perspectives. For readers who want a greater understanding of the background and conceptual frameworks in hunter-gatherer research.
Bicchieri, M. G., ed. *Hunters and Gatherers Today*. New York: Holt, Rinehart and

Winston, 1972. This edited book provides a general perspective on hunting and gathering with a collection of eleven contemporary food-collecting societies. These descriptive ethnographies are drawn from all parts of the world and paint a general picture of hunter-gatherer lifeways.

Johnson, Allen, and Timothy Earle. *The Evolution of Human Societies: From Foraging Group to Agrarian State*. Stanford, Calif.: Stanford University Press, 1987. This book uses an evolutionary framework to focus on the developmental sequence of human societies, beginning with food foragers. It also summarizes the evolution of economic behavior in a broad environmental and cultural context.

Lee, Richard. *The Dobe !Kung*. New York: Holt, Rinehart and Winston, 1984. This is an excellent case study of the !Kung foragers of the Dobe area of northwestern Botswana. This ethnography is particularly rich in detail and offers the reader a realistic picture of this foraging culture as they were living as food collectors in the early 1960's when Lee did his field research.

Lenski, Gerhard, Jean Lenski, and Patrick Nolan. *Human Societies*. 6th ed. New York: McGraw-Hill, 1991. This book takes an evolutionary-ecological approach to understanding the social evolution of human societies. Essentially, these sociologists argue that a society's economic institution usually sets the limits of what is possible for a society and its institutions. It also serves as the prime mover in social change.

Maryanski, Alexandra, and Jonathan Turner. *The Social Cage: Human Nature and the Evolution of Society*. Stanford, Calif.: Stanford University Press, 1992. This book looks at "human nature" and the biological foundations of human societies. Essentially, these sociologists argue that when humans abandoned a foraging lifestyle, they began to construct sociocultural cages that infringe on human needs for parity, freedom, mobility, and individualism. This work is one example of the revival of evolutionary thinking in sociology, using food-foraging societies as a baseline for understanding the legacy of humankind.

Radcliffe-Brown, A. R. *The Andaman Islanders*. Cambridge, England: Cambridge University Press, 1922. This book is the result of fieldwork by the author in the Andaman islands begun in 1906. Radcliffe-Brown is one of the founders of a theoretical approach known as structural-functionalism (or simply functionalism).

Symposium on Man the Hunter (1966, University of Chicago). *Man the Hunter*. Edited by Richard B. Lee and Irven DeVore. Chicago: Aldine, 1968. This classic volume was the result of a conference that brought together seventy-five international hunter-gatherer scholars to discuss the current status of food collectors throughout the world. It resulted in reappraisal of some basic theories of hunting and gathering people.

A. R. Maryanski

Cross-References

Agrarian Economic Systems, 60; The Agricultural Revolution, 67; Communal Societies, 297; Horticultural Economic Systems, 903; Population Size and Human Ecology, 1428; Types of Societies, 1906.

HYPOTHESES AND HYPOTHESIS TESTING

Type of sociology: Sociological research
Field of study: Basic concepts

Hypotheses are clear and precise statements that provide tentative answers to research questions. Hypotheses make predictions about the relationship between variables. The predictions are found to be supported or unsupported by empirical testing.

Principal terms

DIRECTIONAL HYPOTHESIS: a hypothesis that makes a specific prediction regarding the variables being studied—for example, that television violence increases aggressive behavior in children

EMPIRICAL TEST: defining and measuring variables that can be observed; often includes statistical analysis of the data

NONDIRECTIONAL HYPOTHESIS: a hypothesis that does not make a specific prediction regarding the variables being studied, for example, television violence affects aggressive behavior in children

OPERATIONAL DEFINITION: the defining of a variable or construct in a specific and concrete way, describing the operations of how it will be observed and measured

PROBABALISTIC CONFIRMATION: confirming or disconfirming a hypothesis using the principles of probability theory

QUANTITATIVE ANALYSIS: analysis performed by obtaining measures that attempt to categorize and summarize observations through the assignment of numbers, then statistically analyzing these numbers

SCIENTIFIC METHOD: a method for acquiring knowledge that is characterized by systematic observation, experimentation, experimental control, and the ability to repeat the study

Overview

For any discipline to thrive and grow as a science, it is imperative that good research questions be formulated and answered. The development and testing of hypotheses plays an essential role in the quest for new knowledge. All research questions at some point must be framed as clear and precise statements that can be empirically tested; these statements are referred to as hypotheses.

According to social scientists Chava Frankfort-Nachmias and David Nachmias in their book *Research Methods in the Social Sciences* (1992), a hypothesis possesses four characteristics. First, it is derived from a research question and must be written using clear and precise language. For example, a frequently asked research question is: "Does violence on television cause children to behave aggressively?" For this question to be answered, it first must be framed as a hypothesis. Clear and precise language must be used and definitions must be assigned to a number of conceptual terms such as "violence," "children," and "aggressively." One must specify, for example, whether "violence" refers only to acts of physical aggression directed at others or whether verbal threats and acts such as spitting at another person should be included. Similar problems can be found with the label "children." Specifically, the age group to be included must be decided; it must be clarified, for example, whether a twelve-year-old is a child or an adolescent.

To arrive at a clear hypothesis, terms must be operationally defined so that they can be observed. For example, "violence" could be operationally defined as the number of times a female child hits, kicks, punches, or throws a doll. It would then be possible to categorize how violently a child behaves after viewing a series of violent television programs. An operational definition is established by the researcher not only for the purpose of clarifying what is being measured but also to allow other scientists to repeat the study using the same methods of measuring the variables.

A second characteristic of a hypothesis is that it is value-free. In other words, it should be written as an objective statement that does not reflect the researcher's own personal values and biases. (When a personal belief or preference is inserted, it should be made clear to the reader.) A third characteristic of a hypothesis is that it is specific. Using the example given previously, a hypothesis would need to express the nature of the relationship between watching television and aggressive behavior. Whether viewing violent television increases, decreases, or has no impact on aggressive behavior would need to be spelled out clearly. Most hypotheses are framed in terms of a specific prediction. In this way, a hypothesis can be seen as a tentative answer to a research question that needs verification. The literature frequently refers to this kind of a hypothesis as a directional hypothesis. On the other hand, some hypotheses are specific yet do not predict a particular direction of the relationship between the variables. This type of hypothesis is referred to as a nondirectional hypothesis.

The fourth and last characteristic of a hypothesis is that it must be testable. Once data have been collected, it must be possible to organize or manipulate the data in such a way as to confirm or disconfirm the research hypothesis. In other words, evidence should suggest whether it is probably true or false. The testable nature of the hypothesis is what challenges the researcher to improve methods or find new methods to test the veracity of the hypothesis.

Hypothesis testing is not as clear-cut a process as it may first appear. Testing a hypothesis empirically does not lead to a conclusion that absolutely proves that the hypothesis is either true or false. Rather, it leads to a probabalistic confirmation. To test a hypothesis, a researcher must determine how the variables expressed in the hypothesis will be measured, make the necessary observations, collect the data (which is usually in the form of numbers), and then subject the data to quantitative analysis. The quantitative analysis attempts to summarize the vast array of numbers and then to determine whether the results of the study could possibly have occurred by random chance.

Thus, in most instances, quantitative analysis results in a probability statement in which the following rule applies: If the probability of getting the results of the study by mere random chance factors is found to be extremely rare, then one concludes the results are attributable to the variables of the study and not to chance. The hypothesis would receive either confirmation or falsification in terms of a probabalistic statement.

Applications

One of the benefits of hypothesis testing is that it makes possible the testing of, and therefore the reevaluation of, existing theories. Theories provide the framework within which hypotheses are formulated and tested; their overall organization of ideas makes possible the questions, thoughts, and predictions that go into the creation of hypotheses. In turn, the outcome of experiments that test the hypotheses formulated under these larger theories reflects back on the validity of the theories themselves. Therese L. Baker, a social scientist, in her book *Doing Social Research* (1988), states that hypothesis testing leads to one of three possible outcomes with regard to testing a theory's ability to explain data: confirmation of a theory, modification of a theory, or the overthrow of a theory. Hypothesis testing is a valuable tool for helping sociologists refine the theories that provide the foundation of the discipline.

Hypothesis development and testing can be best understood through example. Judith M. Siegel, a public health specialist, in her article "Stressful Life Events and Use of Physician Services Among the Elderly: The Moderating Role of Pet Ownership," published in the *Journal of Personality and Social Psychology* (1990), attempts to test the following hypothesis: Pet ownership plays a beneficial role during times of high stress for the elderly. Notice that the hypothesis is clear and value-free. Siegel chose an operational definition of "beneficial" as decreasing the number of doctor visits over a one-year period. She defined "high stress" by using an instrument that measures depressed mood (a common by-product of psychological stress). The hypothesis makes a specific prediction involving the variable pet ownership and the expected beneficial outcome during periods of high stress. It is therefore a directional hypothesis. In addition, the hypothesis is testable. Providing that the two measures for stress are accurate measures and that reliable data can be collected on the number of doctor contacts made by a group of elderly persons, the hypothesis can be confirmed or falsified.

The study involved interviewing and following-up on a group of more than one thousand elderly respondents (sixty-five years of age or older) for a one-year period. The subjects were assessed as to how much psychological stress they were experiencing on multiple occasions. In addition, they were asked if they owned a pet (37 percent responded "yes") and questioned about their affective attachment to the pet. After controlling for differences among subjects on sex, age, race, education, income, employment status, and chronic health problems, Siegel conducted a quantitative analysis that compared the number of physician contacts between subjects who owned pets and those who did not. The results supported her initial hypothesis by showing that elderly subjects who owned pets had significantly fewer physician contacts during the year than those without pets had. Pets appeared to alleviate and buffer some of the stress their owners were experiencing during difficult times.

Another example of hypothesis testing can be seen in a study by Lee A. Rosen, a behavioral science researcher, and his colleagues entitled "Effects of Sugar (Sucrose) on Children's Behavior," published in the *Journal of Consulting and Clinical Psychology* (1988). Rosen attempted to test the veracity of a commonly held belief within American society that sugar produces detrimental effects on children's behavior. He began by pointing out that the few controlled studies conducted in this area so far had produced conflicting results. Some indicate that sugar has a detrimental effect on children's behavior, while others show that it does not. Rosen decided to test the following hypothesis: Sugar can have detrimental effects on children's behavior. Using a controlled experimental design, he studied forty-five children over a fifteen day period. He obtained parental permission, and all the children were instructed that they would be eating breakfast at school. During the first five days, the subjects were randomly assigned into one of three groups. In one group they received a breakfast that contained no sugar (aspartame was used to make the drink sweet)—this was the control condition. A second group received a breakfast that contained 6 grams of sugar (the low-sugar group), and a third group received 50 grams of sugar (the high sugar group). At no time did the children or those involved in collecting the data ever know how much sugar the children in each group were given. During each subsequent five-day period, the children were placed in a different group.

The children were then observed each day on measures such as fidgeting, change in activity level, active movement, vocalization, and aggression. In addition, they were administered various cognitive and performance measures to test their ability to stay on task. Because the outcome variable "children's behavior" is multifaceted, there was a need for many different indicators. Contrary to commonly held social beliefs about the effect of sugar on behavior, no evidence was found to suggest that sugar causes significant changes in children's behavior. The hypothesis was not supported. Rosen and his colleagues believe that the false stigma attached to the ingestion of sugar could be attributable to spurious correlations made through casual observation. For example, eating large amounts of sugar is often associated with certain activities (such as birthday parties) that may contribute to excited or disruptive behavior.

Context

Social scientists Mark Mitchell and Janina Jolley, in their book *Research Design Explained* (1992), suggest that hypotheses may be generated in a number of ways. One source is intuition, in the form of common sense. The hypothesis mentioned earlier regarding the psychological benefits of owning a pet appears to have originated from intuition. The intuition could have easily come about through casual observations of real-life events. The author of the study could have seen that the elderly, particularly those who have recently lost a spouse, develop a close companionship with a pet. This relationship could in turn help moderate psychological distress commonly experienced by the elderly.

Another rich source for hypotheses is existing theory. Theories not only attempt to summarize a large body of data but also attempt to explain the relationships that exist among many different variables. In general, theories allow for a number of predictions (in the form of hypotheses) to be made about future events. Previous research is also a primary source for developing hypotheses. Perusing the sociological literature via books, journals, indexes, and handbooks enables one to see what previous studies have shown. This allows the opportunity for a skilled researcher to pose hypotheses in areas that have not yet been explored.

Hypothesis testing is a critical component in the process of uncovering new knowledge. In any process of critical inquiry, one must keep in mind that the primary objective is to discover the truth about a particular object of study. It was mentioned earlier that a hypothesis can be seen as a tentative answer to a research question. It remains tentative until it has been tested. Even after a hypothesis has been empirically tested and upheld, it is not guaranteed that the scientific community will automatically embrace it. The confidence and credibility that a hypothesis holds in the eyes of the scientific community are dependent on how the data was collected. The particular methods employed to conduct the study are of central importance. If the methods were weak, then credibility is instantly reduced. In addition to the methodology, the ability of others to replicate the findings is critical. In simple terms, a hypothesis that has been repeatedly found to be true through a number of similar experiments is much more likely to be accepted as true than a hypothesis that has not been replicated.

Bibliography

Babbie, Earl. *The Practice of Social Research*. 6th ed. Belmont, Calif.: Wadsworth, 1992. This comprehensive volume is characterized by an informal writing style that explains complex research methods concepts in a way that a novice can understand. A clear description of hypothesis testing can be found.

Baker, Therese L. *Doing Social Research*. New York: McGraw-Hill, 1988. Baker gives the reader a general introduction to the scientific method, including the development and testing of hypotheses. In addition, this book contains some topics that will help the reader evaluate both good and poor field experiments.

Berg, Bruce L. *Qualitative Research Methods for the Social Sciences*. Boston: Allyn & Bacon, 1989. In order better to understand the differences between different types of research strategies used in developing hypotheses, it is necessary to understand the differences between quantitative and qualitative research. This book clarifies that distinction; it also discusses commonly used methods of studying groups of people.

Frankfort-Nachmias, Chava, and David Nachmias. *Research Methods in the Social Sciences*. 4th ed. New York: St. Martin's Press, 1992. This book gives many examples of hypotheses; also explains how hypotheses fit in with the overall picture of social science research. In addition, part 4, "Data Processing and Analysis," highlights quantitative analyses that are available to test hypotheses. Some quantitative methods are also touched on.

Rosen, Lee A., et al. "Effects of Sugar (Sucrose) on Children's Behavior." *Journal of*

Consulting and Clinical Psychology 56 (August, 1988): 583-589. This research performed a much-needed well-controlled study on the effects of sugar on behavior. Although the study has some methodological drawbacks, overall it appears to be one of the best studies done on this topic. This study provides an excellent example of hypothesis testing.

Siegel, Judith M. "Stressful Life Events and Use of Physician Services Among the Elderly: The Moderating Role of Pet Ownership." *Journal of Personality and Social Psychology* 58 (June, 1990): 1081-1086. This article provides an interesting and surprisingly nontechnical example of the process of hypothesis testing. The introduction and discussion sections provide a rationale for how pets (particularly dogs) could help moderate stress experienced by their owners.

Singleton, Royce, Jr., Bruce Straits, Margaret Straits, and Ronald McAllister. *Approaches to Social Research*. New York: Oxford University Press, 1988. This well-written text discusses various aspects of hypothesis testing in addition to other areas of experimentation such as selecting a research setting, gathering information, how to get into the field, and when a field study should be adopted. The chapter on experimentation can be used to contrast "true" experiments with field studies.

Bryan C. Auday

Cross-References

Causal Relationships, 205; Conceptualization and Operationalization of Variables, 328; Descriptive Statistics, 519; Inferential Statistics, 983; Paradigms and Theories, 1328; Quantitative Research, 1546; Sociological Research: Description, Exploration, and Explanation, 1920; Triangulation, 2071; Validity and Reliability in Measurement, 2136.

IMMIGRATION AND EMIGRATION

Type of sociology: Population studies or demography

Studies of immigration and emigration explore the causes of voluntary population movements and the effects of these movements on immigrants as individuals and society as a whole. The net migration rate is the difference between the number of immigrants and emigrants and refers to whether a society's population is increasing or decreasing through population movements.

Principal terms

ASSIMILATION: becoming a part of, or absorbed into, the dominant culture

CHAIN MIGRATION: the process in which one immigrant enters a new country and then brings other family members, one after the other

EMIGRATION: leaving one's native country in order to settle in a new country

IMMIGRATION: entering a new country or region with the intent to settle there

MELTING POT THEORY: the belief that individuals from various ethnic backgrounds eventually blend into one homogeneous American culture

PUSH/PULL FACTORS: circumstances that force (push) individuals or groups out of their native country or attract (pull) them toward a particular destination

STRUCTURAL FACTORS: economic or political forces that are beyond individual control

Overview

Immigration and emigration are studied by sociologists in a number of different ways; researchers studying demography (population), social stratification, and social mobility are all interested in these phenomena, but they view them from differing perspectives. Demography examines the characteristics of, and changes in, human populations. To demographers, immigration and emigration are two forms of migration.

Migration is one of the primary processes (alongside fertility and mortality) that affect the size, composition, and distribution of a population. Migration simply consists of the movement of people from one place to another. Migration can be internal (within a country) or international, and both types can have significant impacts. Immigration (the movement into a new country) and emigration (movement from a country) are forms of international migration. The term "net migration rate" refers to the difference between the rate of immigration and the rate of emigration. It is expressed as the number of people per 1,000 who enter or leave an area during one year. Migration may have a number of important effects, such as relieving "population pressure" in crowded areas, spreading culture from one area to another, and bringing groups into contact—and possible conflict.

Sociologists also study the experiences of immigrants in relation to prejudice, discrimination, and social stratification and mobility. They explore the differing experiences of immigrants of differing ethnicities and races; such studies have revealed much about the nature of prejudice and about the disparity between the ideology and the reality of American life. A look at various aspects of immigration to the United States allows an examination of these processes at work in the real world. Over the course of immigration to America, beginning in the sixteenth century (if one excludes the first immigration, the prehistoric migration of the ancestors of the American Indians), most immigrants have come for similar reasons: to escape persecution, to find economic opportunities, and to enjoy the freedoms available in the United States. Yet despite the traditional emphasis on the forces that pushed people out of their countries of origin and the separate forces that pulled them toward the United States, a number of studies, such as David M. Reimers' *Still the Golden Door* (1985), emphasize structural forces—economic and political—that have influenced population movements.

Many studies of immigration to the United States identify two massive waves of immigration between 1820 and 1914. The first decades of the nineteenth century brought increasing numbers of immigrants; 151,000 arrived in the 1820's, nearly 600,000 in the 1830's, more than a million in the 1840's, and 2.3 million in the 1850's. Many were Irish Catholics escaping political persecution and famine and Germans fleeing political upheavals. These "old immigrants" came to cities on the East Coast; some moved inland to the farmlands of the Great Plains.

"New immigrants" were those from eastern and southern Europe who arrived between the 1880's and World War I. This second period of immigration far surpassed the earlier waves in numbers, rising from 788,000 in 1872 to 1,285,000 in 1907. By 1914 nearly fifteen million immigrants had arrived in the United States, many from Austria-Hungary, Italy, Russia, Greece, Romania, and Turkey. The federal Dillingham Commission (1907) regarded this group as poor, unskilled, and mostly male, and its report reinforced prejudices about eastern and southern Europeans. It concluded that these immigrants would be more difficult to assimilate into American society. As the children or grandchildren of immigrants became indistinguishable from other Americans, however, the concept of American society as a "melting pot" into which many nationalities merged into one, took hold.

Often invisible in early immigration studies were the numbers of Africans and Latin Americans who had not come voluntarily to the United States. Africans were forcibly brought to the United States as slaves. Many Mexicans did not technically immigrate but were absorbed into the United States when lands from Texas to California were conquered in the Mexican-American War (1846-1848). These groups needed to adapt to a new nation and a new culture, as did European immigrants, but they faced both discrimination and a lack of understanding about their circumstances. Asian immigrants formed another group that was long invisible in immigration histories. Chinese men were imported as cheap labor to build the railroads in the mid-1800's, and they were expected to leave when their job was done. Many Japanese, Filipino, and Korean immigrants came first to Hawaii as agricultural laborers, and some moved on to California.

Some structural reasons for emigration and immigration have not changed greatly over the last three hundred years. Many individuals have come to North America to escape religious or political persecution. Early refugees in this category included the English Pilgrims and French Huguenots. Later religious groups came from Norway, Holland, and Russia, among them Jews and Mennonites. From the early nineteenth century to the present, immigrants have come because of economic changes in their native lands and opportunities in the United States. The enclosure movement in England and Western Europe, which began in the 1700's, forced many peasants off the land. They sought new land in America. Factories brought ruin to skilled artisans, who came to the United States hoping to open workshops. Many Europeans and Asians also came to escape political turmoil. Revolutions in 1830 and 1848 in Europe, and the Taiping Rebellion in China in 1848, led refugees to seek safety in the United States. Twentieth century upheavals such as World War II, the Cuban Revolution, repression in Southeast Asia, and civil wars in Lebanon and El Salvador have continued to bring refugees to the United States.

Immigrants and refugees have not settled equally in all regions of the United States. Large immigrant communities in California, New York, and Florida have led to the need for government services in many languages. Students in schools speak Vietnamese, Spanish, Korean, Ethiopian, Haitian, and a number of Chinese dialects. Many require courses in English as a second language. Courts need to provide translators, and social service agencies struggle to communicate with many immigrant groups.

Some Americans have responded to foreigners with resentment. Some states and localities have passed laws declaring English to be the only official language. Sociologists studying immigration, however, have found that the large number of immigrants has led to a gradual shift in the population of the United States and its culture. Television stations around the country broadcast programs in many languages. Spanish-speaking markets in particular represent many new business opportunities, and large American companies are beginning to offer advertisements in Spanish.

Applications

Americans have been proud of their heritage of immigration yet ambivalent about immigrant groups who have come to the United States. Federal legislation has expressed the varying reactions of Americans toward immigrants and immigration over time. Before 1820 there were no laws requiring lists of passengers arriving in the United States. Immigrants brought skills and talents that were needed by the new country, and they were welcomed. Non-British immigrants in the early nineteenth century, however, did experience discrimination. Irish Catholics and German immigrants, whose religion or language was different from that of the majority, faced ridicule and were stereotyped as drunkards or dullards. Asian immigrants faced racial prejudice, and Chinese people were eventually barred from immigrating to the United States.

Despite mixed reaction to foreigners, the first federal immigration law was not passed until 1875. In that year prostitutes and convicts were prohibited from entering as immigrants. Additional exclusions for lunatics and idiots were added later.

By the 1880's, increasing immigration from areas outside northern Europe, the closing of the frontier, and increasing urbanization led to attempts to control immigration. Some Americans claimed that southern and eastern Europeans were replacing American stock and that immigration produced a declining birthrate among Americans. Others were more worried about Asian immigrants. The Chinese Exclusion Act of 1882 specifically denied entry to Chinese people, while the Foran Act (1885) made it unlawful for employers to import aliens to perform labor in the United States. This law was aimed at large companies who were importing eastern Europeans to fill low-wage jobs instead of hiring American labor, and it reflected suspicion that immigration caused wages to decline. The Immigration Act of 1917 barred Asians not by nationality, but by excluding geographically any immigrants from East or South Asia.

Immigration to the United States was regulated for most of the twentieth century by the Immigration Act of 1924, which reflected the nation's desire to encourage European immigration and discourage non-Western immigrants. This law established a series of quotas for immigrants from all countries except the Western Hemisphere. Larger quotas were assigned to countries whose citizens were more traditionally identified with the American population. The Immigration and Nationality Act of 1952 tightened the quota system.

A significant change in United States policy toward immigration came with the Immigration and Nationality Act of 1965. This law removed strict quotas and Asian exclusion. Instead, it created preferences for persons with certain skills and gave priority to people with immediate family in the United States. The consequences of this legislation led to greater changes in immigration than were anticipated. By 1974, for example, foreign-born physicians made up 20 percent of all medical doctors in the United States. The "brain drain" from developing countries continued, as scientists, engineers, and scholars sought better conditions and higher salaries in the United States. The law also brought increasing non-European immigration, as family members petitioned to bring relatives from Asia, Africa, and Latin America.

The increasing number of undocumented immigrants in the United States has led to calls for policing the U.S. border with Mexico more efficiently and for penalties for employers of illegal immigrants. Illegal immigrants have been accused of stealing jobs from United States citizens, draining social services, and changing the very nature of American society. In 1986 the Immigration and Control Act attempted to resolve these issues for many illegal immigrants. Those who could show permanent residency in the United States since 1982 could become legal residents. Employers who hired illegal immigrants were to be fined, and additional funds were appropriated for stronger immigration enforcement.

Immigration reforms have continued, showing the changing response of American society over time. The Kennedy-Donnelly Act of 1988 permitted a lottery to provide visas for permanent resident status, and the 1990 Immigration Law raised annual immigration ceilings and ended restrictions on homosexuals, communists, and people with acquired immune deficiency syndrome (AIDS); it also granted safe haven status for Salvadorans. This law was not without opposition from those who feared that disease or undesirable ideas would be spread by immigrants.

Refugees have become an increasingly important part of population movements. Emigration from countries experiencing conflict has increased in the twentieth century, and the United States has traditionally thought of itself as a nation receptive to the oppressed. The need to resettle large numbers of eastern European refugees after World War II was recognized by the Refugee Relief Act of 1952. In the 1980's the church-sponsored sanctuary movement broke immigration laws by providing asylum for Salvadorans who feared deportation by immigration authorities enforcing strict refugee policies. The impact of immigration on American society has continued to challenge cherished concepts and ideologies and to highlight prejudices. The idea of the United States as an open door, a place where people from all lands can find a haven, is still shared by many. Since the 1980's, however, this ideal has faced considerable challenges. The large numbers of Central Americans, Asians, and Haitians seeking asylum in the United States has led to tighter controls at borders and interdiction on the high seas.

Context

Immigration studies have focused both on numbers of immigrants and on the circumstances of individual immigrants. Demographers seek to understand the significance of numbers in population movements. Statistics about the net migration rate, for example, indicate the influence of immigration on population growth. For example, during the 1920's, approximately four million immigrants entered the United States, while nearly one million emigrated. The net migration increase was therefore three million. During the Depression years of the 1930's, however, immigration and emigration were nearly equal, and the country experienced no gain in population from immigration.

Immigration studies also seek to understand the changes that occur to individuals and to whole populations. Family ties often become strained when immigrant parents rear children in a strange culture. Some children reject their parents' culture, and many parents cannot understand the pressures their children face in American society. Marriages also undergo stress. Men often come first to the United States, leaving their wives and children behind. While many send money back home, and they often bring their families later, some abandon their families or divorce their wives.

Modern technology has also had an impact on immigration. When the steamship replaced the sailing ship, more immigrants could return home. A percentage of immigrants have always returned to their native lands; some became disillusioned with life in the United States; others returned because they had made enough money to buy land or a shop in their own land. The airplane made international travel faster and cheaper. Modern immigration does not necessarily lead to prolonged separation from one's native land, and this has strengthened ethnic ties.

Nathan Glazer and Daniel Patrick Moynihan, in *Beyond the Melting Pot* (1963), challenged this popularly accepted concept of a melting pot society by focusing on the continuity of ethnic identity. While most immigrants or their families have eventually learned English, become American citizens, and accepted much of the dominant culture, ethnic diversity continues. Many immigrants rely on ethnic assistance. Chain migration was an important part of immigrant strategies. Early arrivals would often pay for the passage of relatives and then find work for them when they arrived. It was not uncommon for an immigrant to leave Ellis Island with a train ticket for a town in Nebraska or Minnesota, where he or she would be met by relatives.

Sociologists have studied many effects of immigration on American society, especially in the form of ethnic networks and organizations. Churches, both Catholic and Protestant, have reflected the national origins of their parishioners. Many immigrants obtain capital to start businesses from family members or banks run by members of their ethnic group. Ethnic identity has also been influential among voting blocks, especially within the Democratic Party.

While some scholarship, particularly since the 1980's, has stressed structural rather than personal reasons for population movements and has challenged the concept of the melting pot, American society has continued to mold immigrants from many nations. At the same time, American society has changed as a result of this immigration.

Bibliography

Daniels, Roger. *Coming to America: A History of Immigration and Ethnicity in American Life*. New York: HarperCollins, 1990. Begins with prehistoric migrations of American Indians and continues through American history, placing immigration in the context of American society. Provides tables on countries of origin, ethnic enclaves, and net migration rates.

Glazer, Nathan, and Daniel Patrick Moynihan. *Beyond the Melting Pot*. Cambridge, Mass.: MIT Press, 1963. A classic work which explores the experiences of African American, Italian, Irish, and Jewish groups in New York City. Argues against the concept of the melting pot by demonstrating continuing ethnic identity and separate communities of these groups.

Johns, Stephanie Bernardo. *The Ethnic Almanac*. Garden City, N.Y.: Doubleday, 1981. Presents statistics and background on immigration arranged by ethnic group; an easy-to-use reference. Provides good illustrations of ethnic contributions to American society and presents examples of various foods brought by different ethnic groups as well as foreign words added to the English language.

Jones, Maldwyn Allen. *American Immigration*. 2d ed. Chicago: University of Chicago Press, 1992. Offers a clear history of immigration from colonists to modern refugees. Recognizes reasons for emigration and includes immigrants from Asia as well as Europe. Addresses issues surrounding immigration legislation, and the second edition includes a discussion of refugee questions in the early 1990's.

Reimers, David M. *Still the Golden Door: The Third World Comes to America.* 2d ed. New York: Columbia University Press, 1992. The focus on Third World immigration sets this book apart from other immigration studies. While it does refer to Third World immigration in the 1940's, the book's emphasis is on the post-World War II era. Undocumented immigrants and refugees are included, and their impact on immigration policies is discussed.

Thernstrom, Stephan, ed. *Harvard Encyclopedia of American Ethnic Groups.* Cambridge, Mass.: The Belknap Press of Harvard University Press, 1980. An excellent reference work, covering many topics related to immigration and giving information about immigrant and ethnic groups in the United States. Good statistics. Includes essays by Harold Abramson, Michael Novak, and William Bernard.

Yans-McLaughlin, Virginia, ed. *Immigration Reconsidered.* New York: Oxford University Press, 1990. A collection of essays and theories of immigration, approaches to comparative research, and immigrant networks. Includes both sociological and historical perspectives. Raises questions about traditional assumptions regarding immigrant groups, their assimilation, and the relationship between emigration and immigration.

James A. Baer

Cross-References

Annihilation or Expulsion of Racial or Ethnic Groups, 92; Assimilation: The United States, 140; Conquest and Annexation of Racial or Ethnic Groups, 353; Cultural and Structural Assimilation, 405; Ethnic Enclaves, 682; Fertility, Mortality, and the Crude Birthrate, 761; Population Size and Human Ecology, 1428; Population Structure: Age and Sex Ratios, 1434; Racial and Ethnic Stratification, 1579; Xenophobia, Nativism, and Eugenics, 2208.

IMMIGRATION TO THE UNITED STATES

Type of sociology: Racial and ethnic relations
Field of study: Patterns and consequences of contact

Immigration to the North American continent has been occurring since the sixteenth century. Early immigration from the British Isles established the dominant culture of what is now the United States, and immigrants since then have faced conflict and discrimination before being accepted into American society.

Principal terms

ASSIMILATION: the process by which a minority group is absorbed into the dominant culture of a society

COLONIALISM: the purposeful control of a group of native people by another government or a commercial company

IMMIGRATION: the permanent movement of individuals into a country that is not their native country

INDENTURED SERVANT: an immigrant who contracts to work for a certain period of time in exchange for passage

MIGRATION: the movement of peoples within the boundaries of a country or a geographical area

XENOPHOBIA: an irrational fear or hatred of foreigners or others with different appearances or customs

Overview

The movement of people from Europe to the Americas began at the end of the fifteenth century with the urge to explore new lands and to take their riches back to the Old World. The desire to settle permanently in the Americas was caused by upheavals in European society that saw a doubling of the population, battles over agricultural land, and the Industrial Revolution, which threw craftspeople and artisans out of work. While some immigrants came to escape religious persecution, most came with the hope of bettering their economic position. The labor of these immigrants made possible the development of the United States as an industrial nation.

The dominant culture of the early colonies in North America was established by immigrants from the British Isles, and this cultural tradition still prevails in American life. Nevertheless, it was the Spanish who achieved the first permanent settlement, founding St. Augustine (in what is now Florida) in 1565. Other early Spanish settlements included Santa Fe (now New Mexico) and the missions in California founded by Father Junípero Serra. The Spanish political role in early American life ended with the cession of part of Florida to the British in 1763, the return of Louisiana to the French in 1800, a treaty that ceded the remainder of Florida to the United States in 1819, and Mexican independence from Spain in 1821. Yet these early settlements, combined with twentieth century immigration from Mexico, Latin America, and the Caribbean, continue to influence American culture. Spanish is the second most frequently spoken language in the United States.

The Virginia colonies in 1607 were the first British settlement in America. The British immediately saw the need for laborers to develop the new land. They considered American Indians (the Indian population in the seventeenth century has been estimated at from four to eight million) to be an inferior race. Whereas the Spanish colonists had attempted to integrate the American Indians into the life of their settlements (while exploiting their labor), the British colonists first tried, unsuccessfully, to use them as slave labor, then forced them to move off whatever land the colonists wanted for themselves. Through the years, the Indian population was decimated by war and European diseases. A large number of immigrants in the seventeenth century came from the British Isles as indentured servants or convicts. These immigrants usually were assimilated into the general population after their servitude, often prospering in their own enterprises.

Black explorers had accompanied the French and Spanish during early explorations of the North American continent. Landowners in the West Indies had been importing slaves from Africa to work on their plantations for many years before the first Africans were brought to the Virginia colony in 1619. Slavery quickly took hold in America as the solution to the insatiable demand for labor to develop the new land, especially in the South with its economy based on rice, indigo, and tobacco.

Estimates of the numbers of slaves who survived the brutal conditions of the Atlantic passage in the seventeenth and eighteenth centuries range from hundreds of thousands to millions. This forced migration constituted one of the largest population movements in the history of the world.

Emigration from Europe in the seventeenth and eighteenth centuries was stimulated by political and economic forces that had been building for hundreds of years. Early settlers in addition to the British included significant numbers of Dutch and French people. The voyage by sailing ship, which could take from one to three months, was fraught with hardship—disease, overcrowding, and deprivation of food and water. Nevertheless, the population of the colonies was approximately 2.5 million by the beginning of the revolutionary war. By the early eighteenth century, most Americans were native born.

The greatest wave of immigrants, an estimated thirty million, came from Europe between 1815 and World War I. In the mid-nineteenth century, the Irish, victims of British land laws and several years' failure of the potato crop, became the largest group of immigrants. The second-largest group, German middle-class artisans and landless peasants, came as a result of an increase in population and the upheaval of the Industrial Revolution. Others emigrated from Belgium, Denmark, France, the Netherlands, and the Scandinavian countries. Ellis Island in New York was the port of entry for most immigrants from 1890 until 1954.

On the West Coast, an estimated 100,000 Chinese laborers were imported. These immigrants, considered a threat by native workers, were often treated like slaves. Between 1890 and 1924, a wave of immigrants began coming from Italy, eastern and central Europe, and Russia. A number of European Jews also came to escape religious persecution. Smaller groups came from the Balkan countries and the Middle East. These people, with different appearances and customs, were not as easily assimilated as had been the people of western or northern Europe.

Until the early twentieth century, the United States government welcomed newcomers. While some local and state laws restricted the entry of lunatics, the illiterate, anarchists, or people with communicable diseases, there was little regulation of immigration. The late nineteenth century, however, saw an upsurge of demands for restrictive legislation born of the fear that the quality of American life was being eroded by the newcomers. In the early 1920's, in response to this fear, the federal government began to regulate immigration.

There was little immigration during the Great Depression of the 1930's. Following World War II, however, and in the years since, a new wave of immigrants has come to the United States, many of them from Asia, Mexico, the Caribbean, and South America. According to one estimate, by 1990, 6 percent of the population of the United States had been born in a foreign country. The increasing entrance of unknown numbers of undocumented immigrants since the 1970's had, by the late 1980's, created a sentiment for new restrictive legislation.

Applications

The history of immigration to the United States is, in many ways, a record of ethnic and racial conflict. Almost all new immigrant groups have faced a degree of resistance, ranging from quiet disapproval to blatant discrimination and violence, before being accepted as part of the American population. History books have traditionally romanticized the idea of the American "melting pot" in which the cultures of all ethnic groups combine into a new, unique American culture. More recently, however, many scholars have argued that becoming an American essentially entails adopting the ways of a dominant culture that is strongly based on Anglo-Saxon traditions and ideals; this phenomenon of adaptation has been termed "Anglo-conformity." Nevertheless, immigrant groups have affected the culture of the United States in many ways, great and small.

As for the immigrants themselves, far from being the poor and oppressed people celebrated in myth and poetry, most were healthy, ambitious young men and women. The weak and hopeless did not have the necessary energy to pull up stakes and take the risks required to start again in a new land. Identifying with their national origins and seeking to protect their own traditions, these immigrant groups often struggled against one another and against the larger society to find a place in American society.

Immigrants during the colonial period, faced with immediate threats to their survival on the frontier and the backbreaking labor needed to develop the land, apparently gave little heed to ethnic identification or cultural difference. These early settlers (disregarding the fact that people were already living there) believed that Divine Providence had given them this new land, and they achieved a political unity that welcomed newcomers. In the late eighteenth century, however, Congress, fearing foreign-born political dissidents, passed the short-lived Alien Acts in 1798 to expel suspected foreign spies. Although local and state controls on immigration had attempted to prohibit "undesirables" from entering, the first major federal immigration legislation excluded prostitutes and convicts in 1875.

Nativism, a political and social movement that pits native-born Americans (themselves descendants of earlier immigrants) against newer arrivals, has been a persistent theme in American history. The movement was particularly strong in the mid-nineteenth century during the massive influx of Irish Catholics escaping famine in Europe. These Irish immigrants were persecuted by native Protestants fearing political domination by the Roman Pope.

These religious quarrels often ended in violence. In Charlestown, Massachusetts, in 1834, a mob burned the Ursuline convent in the belief that the nuns had kidnapped young women and were forcing them into the Catholic sisterhood. In 1844 a series of riots in Philadelphia between Catholic and Protestant workers left many dead and injured and resulted in extensive destruction of property. This xenophobia, directed against the Germans and other "foreigners" as well as the Irish, culminated in the Know-Nothing Party, a political organization that attempted to influence the elections of 1854 and 1855 but ultimately declined as the nation headed toward Civil War.

On the West Coast, a similar pattern of persecution was directed against Asians. Chinese immigrants began coming during the Gold Rush of 1848. Unlike the Irish, who immigrated in family groups, most Chinese were men who did not plan to stay; they intended to make money and return to their homeland. Chinese workers were employed by the thousands in building the railroads, as well as on farms and in many menial occupations. Bigotry against the Chinese took many forms, including broad accusations of vice and idolatry. Considered inferior and a threat to native-born Americans, Asians became the target of increasing resentment and violence. In 1882 the Chinese Exclusion Act was passed by Congress; it remained in force until 1943.

Japanese immigrants began to enter the United States in the early twentieth century and were blamed for taking away jobs by providing cheap labor. A "gentlemen's agreement" between the governments of Japan and the United States in 1907 limited the number of Japanese immigrants. By 1924 all Asians were excluded from entering the United States. Discrimination against Asians after the Japanese attack on Pearl Harbor in 1941 resulted in the unconstitutional internment of more than 100,000 Japanese Americans, most of them citizens, and the confiscation of their property. In 1988 Congress offered an apology and partial financial restitution to the families of these Japanese Americans.

A new form of nativism intensified in the 1980's and 1990's, based on the realization that there was a large and increasing population of undocumented immigrants, most of whom had entered or were remaining in the United States illegally. The majority of these undocumented immigrants were from Mexico, but there were also many from Asia, Latin America, and the Caribbean. The problem, many people began to believe, was that these workers and their families were taking jobs away from American citizens and were placing a financial strain on government educational and welfare programs. The economic downturn of the late 1980's deepened such concerns. Considerable debate occurred concerning the reality or fantasy of this "threat" and concerning the actual costs versus benefits of the undocumented population; it was noted, for example, that many do pay taxes and that many perform jobs that most native-born Americans do not want.

Context

Immigrants to the United States, despite their many cultural differences, have shared the common experience of being uprooted from their familiar ways of life and of having to adjust to the lifeways of a new culture. As these immigrants become assimilated, they begin to think of themselves as Americans; ironically, members of assimilated groups may then begin to distrust more recent immigrant groups as being threats to the "American way of life" to which the older immigrants feel they belong. The traditional pattern of assimilation is for first-generation immigrants to begin at the bottom of the economic ladder and work their way upward. They often settle in ethnic neighborhoods and continue to speak their native language. The second generation, having been educated in the public schools, tends to reject the "foreign" language and customs of their parents. Members of the third generation often return to their heritage, seeking both to be acculturated Americans and to recover their roots.

The most glaring exception to this pattern has been the lack of true assimilation of African Americans. Because they were brought involuntarily to the United States and because the vast majority lived in slavery for more than three hundred years, they have faced unique handicaps. Following the Civil War, blacks in the South experienced a brief period of political power during Reconstruction, but the backlash of the white supremacy movement put an end to this hope. The rise of the terrorist Ku Klux Klan, voting restrictions that kept African Americans from voting, Jim Crow segregation laws, and a Supreme Court decision that gave approval to segregated facilities (*Plessy v. Ferguson*, 1896) were among the factors that stood in the way of assimilation following slavery. Slavery has left a legacy that still haunts the social, political, and cultural life of the United States.

Several social and political movements in the late nineteenth century created a national demand to restrict immigration. Nativism was strong; the Ku Klux Klan's activities were directed against "foreigners" as well as against African Americans. The fact that the appearance and customs of eastern and southern Europeans were different from other European Americans made them easy to identify, and this made them easy targets for discrimination. So-called scientific theories about race were prevalent among white Europeans and Americans at the time, and these theories assumed the superiority of Anglo-Saxon and Nordic peoples. This belief led to the eugenics movement. Racial purity was believed to be desirable, and there was a fear that "inferior" races would breed with the native-born European Americans and would lead to a morally debased American population.

In the Immigration Act of 1924, Congress established quotas for immigrants based on a complex set of rules about national origin, favoring northern Europeans. The first significant deviation from this policy came when President Harry S Truman used his executive powers to grant asylum to European refugees fleeing World War II. The McCarran-Walter Act (the Immigration and Nationality Act of 1952) revised the quota system used to determine immigration; it maintained the exclusion of immigration from Asia. The Immigration Act of 1965 finally ended the system of quotas based on national origin.

Bibliography

Borjas, George J. *Friends or Strangers: The Impact of Immigrants on the U.S. Economy*. New York: Basic Books, 1990. Discusses the effects of immigration objectively, using the methodology of an economist.

Coppa, Frank J., and Thomas J. Curran, eds. *The Immigrant Experience in America*. Boston: Twayne, 1976. A collection of essays from a television series, *The Immigrant in American Life*, produced in 1973. An in-depth account of eight major immigrant groups.

Dinnerstein, Leonard, Roger L. Nichols, and David M. Reimers. *Natives and Strangers: Blacks, Indians, and Immigrants in America*. 2d ed. New York: Oxford University Press, 1990. Emphasizes the idea that while British colonists dominated the early development of the United States, other immigrant minorities, including black slaves, contributed to the building of the nation.

Jones, Maldwyn Allen. *American Immigration*. Chicago: University of Chicago Press, 1960. Emphasizes the ways that immigrants have defined the growth of the United States and the role of immigration in American history. Synthesizes the work of historians and social scientists.

Morganthau, Tom. "The Cover: Is America Still a Melting Pot?" *Newsweek* 122 (August 9, 1993): 16-23. A cover story on the contemporary issue of the perceived threat of the newer immigrants, legal and illegal, and their effect on the quality of American life.

Novotny, Ann. *Strangers at the Door: Ellis Island, Castle Garden, and the Great Migration to America*. Riverside, Conn.: Chatham Press, 1971. An anecdotal account of the experiences of immigrants at Ellis Island. Offers a wealth of drawings and photographs that bring immediacy to the experience.

Simcox, David E., ed. *U.S. Immigration in the 1980's: Reappraisal and Reform*. Washington, D.C.: Center for Immigration Studies, 1988. Essays and statistical surveys on demographics and the forces that have caused immigration into the United States.

Marjorie J. Podolsky

Cross-References

THE INCEST TABOO

Type of sociology: Major social institutions
Field of study: The family

The incest taboo is the term traditionally used for the social prohibition of sexual relations between members of the nuclear family other than relations between the husband and wife; in some societies the prohibition extends to specific groups of other relatives. There has been some sociological debate as to whether "taboo" is too strong a word for societal rules or prohibitions against such practices.

Principal terms
> ENDOGAMY: a requirement that society members seek marriage partners within a socially defined group (such as a clan or tribe)
> EXOGAMY: a requirement that society members seek marriage partners outside a socially defined group (such as the nuclear family)
> HOMOGAMY: the tendency of individuals to marry people with similar social backgrounds
> PROGENY: children; the common descendants of a progenitor
> PROPINQUITY: the tendency of individuals to mate with or marry others who live nearby
> SOCIALIZATION: the process wherein people learn and internalize the norms, values, and role of their society
> TABOO: an absolute ban against the performance of a particular behavior; stronger in its meaning than "rule" or "prohibition"

Overview

Incest has occurred throughout history and, it may be assumed, prehistory. Anthropologists have noted that two of the most common themes reflected in artifacts across cultures are immortality and incest. Some types of rules and prohibitions regarding incest exist in all societies. The parameters of the incest prohibition vary, however, as, to some degree, does the severity of the proscription against it. The term "incest taboo" came to be used for this prohibition early in the twentieth century to emphasize the apparent universality of the rules against incest and the strong abhorrence with which it is held in most societies. There has since been debate, however, over the appropriateness of the term "taboo" as applied to these rules against incest. Since the early twentieth century, some sociologists and anthropologists have pointed to a number of societal exceptions to the prohibition and argued that taboo is too strong a term.

Sigmund Freud stated in his writings that he believed that human cultures began with the acceptance of the incest taboo; if it did not exist, sons in the primal family would fight to eliminate their fathers and brothers in order to mate with their mothers and sisters. Brenda Seligman later put forth a similar theory. She held that destructive jealousies arose when people had intrafamilial sex; therefore, the father protected his sexual "rights" to the mother by banning sexual relations between mother and sons. In turn, the mother denied the husband access to the daughters.

Through most of European history, discussions of incest were largely relegated to descriptions of the practices of out-groups and, primarily, of exotic, distant cultures. Travelers, for example, would return with tales of incest and cannibalism among other tribes or civilizations. Such reports of incest—as a part of the general sexual "ease" of barbarian cultures—were eventually discredited by twentieth century ethnographers, who found no societies in which indiscriminate sexual practices existed. The focus on incest as a foreign abomination certainly was related to the fact that incest occurred (in fantasy and in fact) but was considered too terrible a subject to discuss without it being removed to a safe distance. One well-known incident of incest in England occurred in the early nineteenth century, when the poet Lord Byron was involved in an incestuous (and scandalous) relationship with his half sister. Outside such rare publicized incidents, incest was not generally open to public discussion until the 1970's, when the problem began to be examined more openly; its incidence was studied by social scientists and found to be greater than many had anticipated.

Researcher Linda Tschirhart Sanford has demonstrated that statistical data on incest in the United States are unreliable, in part because different states have different legal definitions of incest and in part because many cases of incest go unreported. Incest frequently remains a family secret. Nevertheless, a number of attempts to quantify the data have been made. Blair Justice and Rita Justice found that (as of 1979) confirmed cases of incest were growing significantly, at rates between 50 and 500 percent, depending on the location; their data took into account reports at both metropolitan and state levels. Another researcher reported that from 4 to 5 percent of the American population was involved in breaking the incest taboo; another scholar argued with that figure, holding that the incidence rate might be as high as 15 percent. Yet another researcher showed that the reported incidence of incest had increased from one person in a million in 1940 to one person in a hundred in 1950 to one in twenty in 1970. Writing in 1987, James B. Twitchell held that approximately 10 percent of the American population had engaged in intrafamilial sex.

Approximately 90 percent of cases involve father-daughter incest. Some sociologists have identified several characteristics typical of perpetrators. Their backgrounds, for example, often include sexual abuse, physical abuse, or both, desertion of a father figure, broken homes, and a general lack of warmth and understanding while growing up. Other studies have found that the typical perpetrator is in his mid- to late thirties, that the average age of the incest victim is eleven, and that the average incestuous relationship lasts between three and five years.

The psychological effects of incest, as of all forms of child abuse, are profound. For adult perpetrators, the psychological effects may be mitigated by how the individual defines incest. Fathers may stop short of actual sexual penetration, for example, allowing them to believe that nothing is wrong if they define incest only as an act involving full sexual penetration. Most victims of incest pay a heavy price. Many become convinced that their family is about to fall apart in the near future. They sense the unhappiness and tensions that exist between their parents, even if they do not understand how or why, and many believe that they are responsible for that unhappiness. Many complications can result from incest, and the results can be unpredictable. When a father is incestuously involved with a daughter, she may submit quietly because she believes that submission is a way to hold the family together. It has been reported that some daughters seem to gain a sense of power through keeping incest secret, feeling that they are, perhaps single-handedly, preserving the family. Yet many more victims suffer from keeping the secret.

Incest disrupts the emotional maturation and the normal socialization of the young victim. Often, for example, victims are observed to be incapable of engaging in age-appropriate activity and believe that they do not fit in with others in their age group. Some withdraw and are labeled shy or timid. Other victims go to the opposite extreme, "acting up" to get attention or becoming involved in delinquent behavior; they may become involved with drugs, truancy, or sexual promiscuity. Finally, the incest victim eventually develops a sense of having been betrayed: Once a victim is old enough to learn that incest is forbidden in the eyes of society, she feels betrayed by someone whom she had earlier respected, trusted, and loved.

Although the vast majority of reported parent-child incest involves father-daughter incest, young sons are sometimes also victims. Mother-son incest is rare; some researchers have concluded that only 3 percent of incest cases involve mother-son or mother-daughter incidents. Thus, 97 percent of the time, regardless of whether a daughter or son is the victim, the father is the perpetrator. The effects of incest on boys are as severe as on girls, with the boys facing an additional trauma; they must struggle to come to terms with the homosexual aspects of their father's actions (and their own actions, regardless of the fact that they had no choice in the matter).

There is considerable disagreement about the prevalence of brother-sister incest. Some experts have argued that it may be even more prevalent than parent-child incest; others have said that the evidence does not support that conclusion. The problem of definition is very difficult regarding this type of incest, at least partly because the boundaries of what constitutes normal behavior vary widely. Some analysts, for example, believe that sex-play between siblings—either opposite-sex or same-sex siblings—should be considered normal until the age of seven or so.

Applications
The major purpose of the incest taboo is to prohibit, within the family, sexual acts that cut across generational boundaries. Most authorities hold that violations of such boundaries disrupt and weaken the family and may destroy the unit. A prime reason for the taboo (and its probable origin) is the widespread belief that such sexual activities stir passions and jealousies. Incest also confuses family members about their proper roles within the unit. The taboo especially protects young children, who need both a nurturing environment and a chance to become independent and to fulfill roles outside the family. Psychologist Carl Jung held that the taboo also serves an important psychological function, that of fostering separation and individuation. Further, until

modern geneticists challenged "folk" wisdom, it was widely believed that family "inbreeding" would cause mental and/or physical deformation among progeny.

Among early peoples, another function of the incest taboo was to help provide for the security and defense of the band or tribe by forcing the young of one family to mate with members of another; thus members of a society augmented their strength by creating a network of alliances based on kinship. Thus the principle of exogamy dominated that of endogamy among many peoples. The practice of endogamy did not die, however, mainly because of propinquity—the fact that individuals have more contact with others living nearby—and homogamy, the tendency to marry within one's own social group.

In the early Christian era, a person was considered guilty of incest if that person had sexual relations with any relative closer than his or her thirty-second cousin. Later, the Church of England specifically listed thirty relatives that a woman was prohibited from marrying. In non-Western culture, it is notable that the Chinese once forbade marriage between individuals who had the same surname.

Even as incest was classified as a crime by many historic societies, the practice never disappeared. It was also not viewed equally negatively by all societies. For example, in ancient Egypt, there were many cases of brother-sister and father-daughter marriage and incest within the royal family for the purpose of concentrating rather than diffusing royal power and wealth. The historic Cleopatra was probably the most famous result and practitioner of incest. She married a sibling and was both her husband's niece and his sister. As in the Egyptian dynasties, incest was practiced among the ruling families of ancient Hawaii and among the rulers of the Inca Empire in Peru. In both empires, inbreeding assured a "pure blood line" for the throne. There was also incest among powerful and wealthy families in ancient Persia and in several of the historic Greek city-states. In most cases when incest has been approved, it has been allowed for some higher purpose. Some nineteenth century Mormons in Utah, for example, practiced incest so that daughters and sisters would not have to marry outside the church. In India the Hindu-Sakta sect believed that incestuous sex represented a higher level of intercourse and an advanced step toward religious perfection.

In modern American society, there are some people who violate or ignore the incest taboo. In the 1980's, for example, one scholar investigated at least twenty cases of brother-sister incest and marriage in white middle-class suburban America in which the taboo violators were happily rearing families. Another researcher reported a case of a married middle-class woman in her late twenties who regularly visited her father and served as his maid and cook; she also regularly had sex with him. (The woman said that she was honoring the promise she had given her mother when the mother was on her deathbed: The daughter had promised to "take care of Dad.") Such behavior and the apparent lack of dire consequences have led some researchers to question the incest taboo altogether. They speak instead of "transactional patterns" that enable a family to continue to function in a nontraditional way. As one scholar noted, incest can be seen as a way of "reprogramming" a dysfunctional family and thus allowing the family to continue as a unit. Another researcher noted that in one incestuous family that he observed, intervention by outside authorities—seeking to rectify what they considered to be a pathological wrong—was strongly resisted by all family members, who seemed satisfied with their familial roles and relationships.

Context

In the 1920's, Edward Westermark asserted that humans had an "instinctive" aversion to incest. Later researchers, however, fully discredited the concept of such human instincts, so Westermark's thesis was also discredited. Martin E. P. Seligman believed that jealousies between husband and wife led both to deny the other sexual access to the couple's progeny. Many sociologists and psychologists do not accept Seligman's view, however; they argue that men have had so much authority over women that the wife could never have denied the husband sexual access to his children if he strongly desired such access.

Bronislaw Malinowski offered a different view. He held that incest is organizationally dysfunctional in that it prevents the socialization of the child. Thus the incest taboo, the health of the family, and the existence of society itself are coterminous. Without the taboo, neither human culture nor society as we know it could exist, because culture and society depend on familial organization. In other words, to Malinowski, the incest taboo represents a functional prerequisite of society. Talcott Parsons advanced a compatible view. He held that the taboo literally forces people out of their immediate family into marriages of their own—to the benefit of society—where the taboo continues to operate, thereby assuring the constant creation of new families and assuring that they will be held together by the common enforcement of the taboo. Further, for all families, the taboo continues to define roles within the unit and to define what is allowed and not allowed. According to Parsons, failure to heed the incest taboo would create "self-liquidating" families and would ultimately destroy society. Yet another entrant into the debate was Claude Lévi-Strauss; writing in the 1960's, he returned the stress to the idea of alliances and to the concept that exogamy and the incest taboo operate hand-in-hand, forcing individuals in society always to increase their parameters and form new alliances.

Despite the continuing belief that incest is a moral wrong and is rightly forbidden by the incest taboo, evidence continues to mount that in modern society, as throughout history, there are many exceptions to the rule. Christopher Bagley, for example, studied 425 incest cases and labeled many intrafamily unions as "functional incest" that represented responses to changing events and that allowed the family to stay together and continue functioning as a unit.

Bibliography

Arens, W. *The Original Sin: Incest and Its Meaning*. New York: Oxford University Press, 1986. Arens' fairly brief volume analyzes the problem of incest itself. The book has a good summary of modern sociological thought on the breaking of the taboo and its consequences.

Brownmiller, Susan. *Against Our Will: Men, Women, and Rape*. New York: Simon &

Schuster, 1975. Brownmiller looks at incest within the framework of a discussion of the prevalence of rape in Western societies. Her book was influential in focusing new attention on rape, incest, and violence against women.

Justice, Blair, and Rita Justice. *The Broken Taboo: Sex in the Family.* New York: Human Sciences Press, 1979. This effort, an in-depth study of incest, tries to be all-inclusive on the subject. It includes discussion of the origin and function of the taboo. Sixteen chapters cover everything from the definition of incest to the consequences and human costs of the practice.

Sanford, Linda Tschirhart. *The Silent Children.* Garden City, N.Y.: Anchor Press, 1980. This work, one that should appeal to lay audiences as well as college audiences, deals broadly with the problem of child molestation; approximately one-third of the work deals directly with incest and its consequences on the entire family as well as on the young victim.

Twitchell, James B. *Forbidden Partners: The Incest Taboo in Modern Culture.* New York: Columbia University Press, 1987. After chapters discussing the "enigma" and horror of incest, Twitchell's work focuses on incest and how it is depicted in modern popular culture. Includes three appendices useful to both sociologists and psychologists.

James Smallwood

Cross-References

Child Abuse and Neglect, 218; The Family: Functionalist versus Conflict Theory Views, 739; Rape, 1592; Sociobiology and the Nature-Nurture Debate, 1913; Spouse Battering and Violence Against Women, 1959; Violence in the Family, 2157.

INDUSTRIAL AND POSTINDUSTRIAL ECONOMIES

Type of sociology: Major social institutions
Field of study: The economy

In the opinion of many social scientists, industry-based economies in the United States and other countries will be replaced by postindustrial economies in which central importance is assigned to the generation of new knowledge and the storage and transfer of information.

Principal terms

CAPITAL: money or wealth that has been invested in the means of production, including land, factories, and machinery

DEINDUSTRIALIZATION: the closing of industrial facilities in one country or region as a result of the movement of capital to other countries or regions or to nonindustrial investments

ECONOMIZING MODE: the traditional mode of operation of a corporation in which it seeks to maximize its profit by means of the careful allocation of scarce resources

SOCIAL CLASS: a group within society with a specific social status and problems which is recognized as such by members of other classes

SOCIOLOGIZING MODE: the effort on the part of a corporation to identify the true needs of society and to derive income from meeting them in a rational way

STRUCTURAL DIFFERENTIATION: the notion that as institutions increase in size and in the complexity of the functions that they perform, they necessarily form specialized subsystems with distinct responsibilities

Overview

Industrial societies are a relatively recent development in the history of civilization. Prior to the eighteenth century, the vast majority of human activity in any part of the world was devoted to extracting the necessities of life from nature, at first by hunting and gathering, then by agriculture, mining, and fishing. In preindustrial society, the highest status and political power were associated with the ownership of land. Between the aristocracy of landowners and a lower class of agricultural workers and domestic servants, a rudimentary middle class of merchants and skilled tradesmen existed.

The beginning of industrial society is generally associated with the Industrial Revolution, which is sometimes taken to have begun with the invention of the steam engine at the beginning of the eighteenth century. The steam engine offered an almost limitless source of energy, far in excess of that available from human or animal muscle. Readily available energy made possible the concentration of production in factories and the specialization of labor, which made possible increased productivity. New occupations developed: semiskilled workers who were needed to tend the new machines took their place at the top of the working class, and engineers, the designers and refiners of the means of production, became new members of the middle class. Financing the growth of industry required the development of capitalists, wealthy individuals who could provide the initial funds needed for production machinery. Capitalists could accumulate wealth more quickly than could landowners, who relied on agriculture and thus formed a wealthy upper middle class that was excluded from the aristocracy more by tradition and style of life than by lack of wealth.

In the United States, the principal economic trends between the end of the Civil War and the end of the twentieth century caused a shift of the working population first from agriculture to manufacturing and then from manufacturing to the service sector. The departure of workers from agriculture was a consequence of improved agricultural productivity, resulting from the development of farm machinery, chemical fertilizers, and crop-management techniques. Growth in manufacturing resulted from an influx of workers into urban areas and the exploitation of coal energy and petroleum and hydroelectric power. At the outset of the twentieth century, industrialization received additional stimulus from the development of electric power transmission technology, which allowed energy to be transmitted over long distances, and of the assembly line, a production strategy introduced by Henry Ford, which allowed workers to increase their output by several times.

The demands of military production during World War II brought about the increasing automation of factories, eliminating jobs for many semiskilled workers. As other nations recovered from the war, their production capabilities became comparable with those of the United States, luring investment away from American plants. With improved communication and transportation, resulting in part from computer technology, increasing numbers of corporations turned to globally integrated manufacturing, in which as much of the factory work as possible was done in countries with much lower wages than the United States. The growth of the industrial sector slowed to a point at which economists began to speak of the deindustrialization of the United States. At the same time, the service sector grew quickly enough to absorb most of the increase in the working population. By 1960, more Americans worked in the service sector than in industry and agriculture combined.

For many social analysts, the growth in the service sector, and particularly in the number of teachers, professors, scientists, social scientists, and technical specialists, marked the transition to a postindustrial economy based on the growth of knowledge and new technologies for the storage and transmission of information. In contrast to industrial society, in which trial and error was the principal means of innovation and engineers played a key role in industrial development, in the postindustrial society primacy is given to theoretical knowledge and the elucidation of basic scientific principles as providing the major source of innovation. In the postindustrial society, the key individuals in the production of goods are no longer the capitalists who control the flow of investment, but the expert managers needed to coordinate global production and sales. These experts view themselves as practitioners of a learned profession rather than as competing businessmen, and they exchange information freely with each other and with university scholars and government specialists. They are less driven by the profit motive and more concerned with making a positive contribution to society. The government comes to play an increased role as a stabilizer of the economy, patron of research, and stimulator of innovation.

It is noteworthy that the shifts from an agrarian economy to an industrial economy and from an industrial economy to a postindustrial economy both involved the principal technology of the emerging sector reducing labor requirements. Thus, the farm machinery produced in the early stages of the industrial period and the synthetic fertilizers produced during the latter stages did much to increase the productivity of agriculture, making it possible for an ample food supply to be produced by a very small fraction—less than one twentieth—of the working population. Likewise, the development of the science of self-regulating systems and electronic computer technology made possible the automation of factories and the globalization of production, which reduced the need for American industrial workers.

Applications

The concept of an emerging postindustrial society is most often associated with Harvard University professor Daniel Bell, who, in a series of essays and in the widely noted *The Coming of the Postindustrial Society* (1973), traced the demographic evidence for the change in American society and examined in some detail the sociology of the growing class of knowledge workers.

The early years of the Industrial Revolution were harsh indeed from the standpoint of the workers. Pay was low, the hours were long, and child labor was common. The German economist and historian Karl Marx, author with Friedrich Engels of *Manifest du Kommunistischen Partei* (1848; *The Communist Manifesto*, 1850), predicted increased class conflict between the proletariat, or industrial working class, and the capitalist class until, by force, the basis for a new and more just society was established. According to Marx, all other social classes would be absorbed into the proletariat as the relentless drive to accumulate capital drove wages even lower. According to Bell, the goal of a more just society will be achieved in the postindustrial society through the activity of a distinct social class—that of scientists and social scientists in government, industry, and the educational establishment.

As late as 1900, farmworkers outnumbered factory workers, and white-collar service occupations accounted for less than one-fifth of the work force. By 1940, there were twice as many farmworkers as factory workers and more than a third of the work force was in white-collar occupations. By 1968, white collar and other service workers approached 60 percent of the work force. In that year there were 2,800,000 teachers in the United States, about a million professional engineers, and nearly 500,000 scientists. By 1980, more than 45 percent of the work force in the United States was directly concerned with the generation and transmission of information.

In a sense, the origin of the present-day knowledge industry can be traced to the founding of the first scientific societies and the first published scientific journals in the sixteenth century. As measured by the number of journals, the growth of this social group has been phenomenal throughout the Industrial Revolution and to the present day. By 1800, some one hundred scientific journals had been established; by 1850, one thousand; and by 1900, ten thousand. By 1950, some three hundred periodicals were devoted to the publishing of brief abstracts of the scientific papers to be found in tens of thousands of journals. The astonishing growth of the scientific literature reflects a remarkable process of specialization, itself an excellent illustration of the sociological principle of structural differentiation, which states that as a social institution becomes larger and confronts a more complex task, a specialization of function develops within the institution. As scientific knowledge has grown, the subject matter has been organized into a vast array of specialties and subspecialties so that individual scientists remain able to identify and follow developments that are pertinent to their own work. The integration of scientific and, more generally, academic specialists into government and industry has grown steadily since World War II.

Bell asserts that the increasing importance of knowledge workers—that is, scientists and others who are concerned with basic or theoretical knowledge in the postindustrial economy—implies an expanded role for government in assuring the smooth functioning of society. By the middle of the twentieth century, the U.S. government had already accepted a regulatory role in the economy in the interests of preventing the more extreme effects of the business cycle. The increased role of the government also results from the centrality of theoretical knowledge in the postindustrial society. Because the advances in production and the stable operation of business are tied to the application of fundamental scientific and economic principles, all industries have a stake in the advancement of fundamental knowledge. Corporations will not, however, be willing to invest a substantial amount of resources in the development of new knowledge that will benefit themselves and competitors equally, so they prefer to see public funds devoted to this purpose. The government thus must become the principal patron of research and postgraduate education. Bell further predicted a transition in corporate behavior from an economizing mode, in which the corporation tries to maximize its income, regardless of the consequences, to a sociologizing mode, in which corporations value their contribution to the well-being of society as well as their ability to increase profits, since the scientific and technical workers would have less concern with personal wealth and more concern with seeking to see their knowledge applied to benefit society.

The notion of a postindustrial society has its critics. Many writers have preferred to use the term "information society" instead of the term "postindustrial society" to indicate the importance of the growing group of occupations, from librarian to computer scientist, concerned with the storage and use of information, without implying a deemphasis on manufacturing. Others question that a healthy information society can exist apart from the control of production facilities. The intense global economic competition of the 1980's and 1990's has engendered a new emphasis on production and a concern about the cost-to-benefit ratio of pure scientific research but has not slowed the development of new information technologies.

Context

Colleges were established in colonial America primarily to prepare the sons of landowners to take their places as leaders of society and to guarantee a supply of clergymen adequate to meet the needs of a growing population. The role of education as a potentially productive force in the U.S. economy began to be recognized at the time of the Civil War. In 1861, the Massachusetts Institute of Technology opened; it was the nation's first engineering school. In 1862, Congress passed the Morill Act, granting the income from the sale of a substantial portion of land in each state to create a college for "agriculture and the mechanical arts." The Johns Hopkins University, founded in 1876, was the first institution to emphasize the generation of new fundamental knowledge through research and the first to establish graduate programs in individual academic disciplines for scientists and other scholars. The first university-level business school, the Wharton School, opened in 1881.

Before World War II, universities and industry coexisted with relatively little interaction except for the hiring of university graduates by corporations. Those who completed advanced academic work generally became professors or teachers. Industries depended on engineers and individual inventors for innovation, which was often the result of a tedious process of trial and error, as was the case in the invention of the electric light, the telephone, and the phonograph. The war, however, placed demands on industry which led to new modes of interaction between industries, universities, and government. War plants demanded new levels of production that made it necessary to recruit scientists and mathematicians from university faculties as expert consultants. The Manhattan Project, which developed the first atomic bombs, demonstrated the value of theoretical knowledge in a unique way. The government committed vast resources to the project based on the calculations of physicists that such a weapon could be constructed. So little of the actual explosive material required was available that there was no question of developing bombs by trial and error. Instead, the results of a very limited number of experiments had to be combined with fundamental scientific principles to design a bomb that would work the first time. Among subsequent inventions based on advances in scientific theory are those of the transistor, the laser, and the integrated circuit.

At the close of the war, Vannevar Bush, who had been director of the wartime Office of Scientific Research and Development, led a campaign to establish a government agency, the National Science Foundation, to continue government support of basic scientific research. In the influential essay "Science: The Endless Frontier," Bush set forth the rationale for continued support of basic scientific research by the United States government as a source of continuing innovation for industry.

The foundation, established in 1950, quickly established a program of federal grants to universities to support basic research and also provided direct financial support to students doing advanced work in science. The government also established a number of national laboratories, to be operated by universities and industrial firms, intended to support the development of nuclear energy for military and peaceful purposes, while the armed forces developed their own programs of grants to universities to fund basic and applied research with potential military applications. Thus began a pattern of interdependence of industry, government, and universities which vastly increased the number of scientists and engineers who were available to participate in a postindustrial economy.

Bibliography

Bell, Daniel. *The Coming of the Post-Industrial Society*. New York: Basic Books, 1973. This influential book documents the shift of American workers from the agricultural and industrial sectors to the service sector, and argues that economic activity in the resulting postindustrial society will be more consciously directed toward the benefit of society as a whole.

Cohen, Stephen S., and John Zysman. *Manufacturing Matters: The Myth of the Post-Industrial Economy*. New York: Basic Books, 1987. Despite the subtitle, the authors have little disagreement with Bell about the demographic and economic trends. They do disagree with him, however, about the role of scientists and other knowledge specialists in the economy, and they believe that a stronger manufacturing sector is needed for economic health.

Dordick, Herbert S., and Georgette Wang. *The Information Society: A Retrospective View*. Newbury Park, Calif.: Sage Publications, 1993. This work updates the demographic information cited by Bell and attempts to show that progress toward an information-based postindustrial society is occurring on a worldwide basis.

Feigenbaum, Edward, Pamela McCorduck, and H. Penny Nii. *The Rise of the Expert Company*. New York: Vintage Books, 1988. This book describes how one aspect of information technology, the "expert system program," is changing the decision making process in many companies. It provides an interesting illustration of how knowledge can be preserved and marketed as a commodity.

Donald R. Franceschetti

Cross-References

THE INDUSTRIAL REVOLUTION AND MASS PRODUCTION

Type of sociology: Social change
Fields of study: The economy; Sources of social change

Beginning in the late eighteenth century, the Industrial Revolution centered on the production of goods by machine power rather than by muscle, wind, or water power, ushering in the age of mass production.

Principal terms
ALIENATION: a feeling of being cut off from the mainstream of society or from the goods one produces
FACTORY SYSTEM: a system of economic production that brings many workers together to produce a finished product
LUDDISM: violent resistance to industrialization; it takes its name from groups in early nineteenth century Europe who destroyed mechanical devices
PROLETARIAT: a term coined by Karl Marx to identify those people who had no capital other than their own labor and thus had to work in the factories of Europe during the early stages of industrialization
URBANIZATION: the rapid population growth of cities

Overview

Prior to the mid-eighteenth century, all of humanity lived in what sociologists call preindustrial societies. Although the basic institutions of these societies differed greatly in the various regions of the world, most of them shared a number of characteristics. The overwhelming majority of the people in preindustrial societies were engaged in subsistence farming. Most preindustrial societies had privileged ruling classes whose wealth and political power were based on land ownership. Established religious bodies upheld the landed aristocracies through teaching that the existing political and economic order represented the will of God, and the aristocrats in turn perpetuated the religious bodies by persecuting any rival religious movements. Both the landed aristocracies and the established religious bodies had vested interests in maintaining the status quo. Both were resistant to any sort of change, had no interest in or concept of "progress," and were mistrustful of new ideas or nonconformity in thought or deed. Social mobility in preindustrial societies was (and is) extremely limited. Formal education for the great majority of the people of such societies is nonexistent.

During the late seventeenth and early eighteenth centuries, an intellectual revolution called the Enlightenment occurred in western Europe that challenged the basic assumptions of preindustrial societies and helped lay the groundwork for the Industrial Revolution that followed. In England, Isaac Newton taught that the universe operates, not according to the whims of God, but according to natural laws that are knowable and usable by humanity through observation and the scientific method. Philosopher John Locke wrote that at birth all people are "blank slates"; what they become depends on their environment. Taken together, the premises of Locke and Newton fatally weakened the foundations of preindustrial society: If the members of the landed aristocracies were not fitted by birth to rule—if its members were not morally, physically, or intellectually superior to the other members of society—then on what grounds could they claim justification for monopolizing political and economic power? If the earth and the rest of the universe (and by implication human society) operate according to natural laws which are knowable by individual human beings through the exercise of their intellects, then how could the existence of a privileged clergy that claimed to be the only agency capable of intervening for humanity with an all-powerful God and a mysterious and unknowable universe be justified? Most important, if humanity can discover the natural laws governing human societies, would it not be possible to create an abundance of material goods for all and a political system that would assure justice for all?

Throughout the first half of the eighteenth century, the ideas of the Enlightenment, which questioned virtually all the aspects of preindustrial society, circulated throughout western Europe and North America. This intellectual ferment, critical of the status quo, played a major role in the onset of the Industrial Revolution and in the great political revolutions of the eighteenth century in France and America. Equally important in the coming of the Industrial Revolution was the new spirit of scientific investigation and innovation, also an outgrowth of the Enlightenment. Yet the Industrial Revolution would not have occurred had it not been for several other prerequisites present in western Europe, especially in England.

Most economists agree that industrialization in a given area will occur only when several vital ingredients are present in that area: markets for the increased production of goods; a source of power to replace muscle power in the production of goods; raw materials to fuel increased production; a cheap and mobile source of labor; a reliable transportation system to bring the raw materials to the place of production and transport the manufactured goods to the markets; an entrepreneurial class with sufficient capital to make and market the goods and a willingness to risk their capital, and a government favorably disposed toward trade and commerce.

By the middle of the eighteenth century, all the prerequisites for what economist Walt Rostow terms the "take off" into sustained industrial growth were present in England. From England, the Industrial Revolution spread relatively rapidly, first to Holland and Belgium and down the Rhine River in continental Europe, then to the United States, and then to France and northern Italy. By 1830, all those areas had entered into the "take off" phase of industrial growth. By the middle of the nineteenth century, electricity and petroleum began to replace steam and coal as the power sources of the revolution as it expanded into central Europe. As the demand for raw materials and new markets grew in the industrialized areas, the entrepreneurs of the European nations and the United States pushed their governments into imperialistic foreign policies. The governments and entrepreneurs of the industrialized nations established colonies in Africa, Asia, and Latin America and on the islands of the Pacific. From their colonies the imperialists took raw materials; to the colonized peoples they sold their manufactured products. Among the populations of the industrialized nations, racism became institutionalized as contact with the colonized peoples seemed to prove the "superiority" of white people. Contact with industrial societies usually resulted in the total breakdown of preindustrial societies. The natural resources of the colonized areas were plundered by the colonizers.

Colonial rivalries and economic competition between the entrepreneurs of the industrialized nations were major factors in the two world wars of the twentieth century. Those wars so weakened the economies of the European states that they could no longer dominate the people of their empires. After World War II, the great empires began to undergo a process sometimes called decolonization. As anticolonial movements succeeded in overthrowing foreign domination, their new governments introduced programs to "modernize" their areas—in other words, to industrialize. With "help" from multinational corporations and financial and technological aid from their former colonizers, most areas of the world have experienced or will soon experience the Industrial Revolution.

Applications

For all the human societies it has affected, the Industrial Revolution has been a two-edged sword. On the one hand, it has brought enormous benefits to hundreds of millions of people. On the other hand, it has created most of the social problems that threaten to overwhelm modern society. Whether the positive features (and the enormous profits) of the revolution outweigh its negative aspects remains a matter of intense debate.

The majority of people in preindustrial societies live in conditions that could, from a modern, Western perspective, be called abject poverty—although it should be noted that the conditions of people in preindustrial societies today differ from those that existed before industrialization and colonial expansion in the West impinged upon their lands and lives. In contemporary preindustrial societies, people seldom have more than the bare necessities of life. Life expectancy is low because health care and medical technology are rudimentary or nonexistent and nutrition is inadequate. Epidemic disease and chronic malnutrition are commonplace; housing is often scarce and modern sanitation facilities nonexistent. Education is rare for anyone outside the elite.

Members of mature industrial societies enjoy widely accessible medical care based on scientific technology. Coupled with adequate nutrition for most people, this has led to a steadily increasing life expectancy for members of industrialized societies. Elementary education is universal in industrialized societies. Sanitary facilities and housing are usually adequate. Entertainment and cultural opportunities, and even higher education, are available to most people. All these developments are the result of the massive production of goods and services made possible by industrialization.

Nevertheless, industrialization has not been an unmixed blessing. Modern society appears to be in imminent danger of choking on its own wastes, of exhausting the raw materials which sustain it, of tearing itself apart through internal feuds between factions trying to control it, and even of destroying the ecosystem of our planet. These conditions, too, are direct outgrowths of the Industrial Revolution. In every area where it has occurred, industrialization has destroyed traditional social relationships and institutions. Former subsistence agriculturalists and artisans have had to become factory laborers, with resultant alienation and anomie. In every such society, resistance to economic and social change has brought violence (as in the Luddite movement in Europe). Political change rapidly follows economic change, sometimes leading to revolutions that cause widespread death and suffering (as epitomized by the Russian Revolution of 1917). Most of the "-isms" of the modern world—including Marxism, fascism, and totalitarianism, which caused much of the destruction of human life that occurred in the twentieth century—are essentially attempts to deal politically with the most important question raised by the Industrial Revolution: how to distribute equitably the abundance of goods and services it made possible.

Industrialization has also contributed to (or caused, depending on which authority one consults) the population explosion of the past three centuries and its companion, urbanization. The great increase in the world's food supply and the strides in medical technology made possible by industrialization have led to a world population problem that will soon reach crisis proportions. Urbanization has been a feature of industrialization in every area where it has occurred. According to several forecasts, at the early 1990's rate of population growth, there would be one human being for every square foot of land area on the earth by the year 2200. At 1990's rates of urban and suburban sprawl, most of that land area would be paved.

According to other projections, however, humanity will not survive to overpopulate or pave over the earth's surface because of other problems associated with industrialization and urbanization. People living in cities produce an ever-growing amount of garbage, the disposal of which pollutes groundwater and the atmosphere. There is also an increasing problem regarding the disposal of toxic and radioactive wastes. The demand for more paper and more farmland has led to the destruction of rain forests, with ecologically disastrous results. Many of the raw materials on which industrial technology are based will be exhausted within, at most, a few centuries.

Context

Most historians and economists agree that the Industrial Revolution began in England around 1760. From England it spread first to western Europe, then to the United States, then to southern and central Europe by 1830. Through imperialism and cultural diffusion, industrialization had spread to most areas of the world by the late twentieth century. During those two-plus centuries, the Industrial Revolution arguably became the most powerful agent for social change in the history of the human race. The people of every area that has experienced industrialization have witnessed the destruction of their traditional institutions and social relationships. Yet although the social destruction and turmoil accompanying industrialization have often traumatized the people experiencing it, those same people and their descendants generally experienced steadily rising real wages, an improving standard of living, and an increased average life span. What the future holds for humanity, given the seemingly unstoppable process of industrialization, depends on which authorities one consults. The range of opinions regarding the future can be appreciated by a look at viewpoints representing opposite ends of the spectrum: the neo-Malthusians and the cornucopians.

The so-called neo-Malthusians are named for Thomas Malthus, the late eighteenth and early nineteenth century political economist. Malthus argued that human food supplies can only increase arithmetically, while human populations increase geometrically, thereby guaranteeing that populations will always outstrip available food supplies. When the population of an area outgrows its ability to feed itself, it will face automatic reduction through pestilence, famine, and war. Malthus' students warned that humanity has in the past undergone and will in the future undergo an endless cycle consisting of periods of plenty, peace, and prosperity; periods of increasing scarcity and turmoil; and periods of want and social catastrophe.

The neo-Malthusians point out that the resources of the earth are limited. There is not enough coal or petroleum, enough arable land, enough fresh water, enough metal ores, and so on, to supply the needs of an infinite number of people. Eventually, they agree, the human population of the earth will reach Malthus' critical number. When that point is reached, industrial society will inevitably collapse. Related to the neo-Malthusians are those economists and ecologists who say that modern industrial society will never reach the point of having consumed all the world's natural resources because it will destroy itself first. Agents for this destruction, they argue, include industrialization's wastes and pollution, destruction of the ecosystem (of which humanity is a part), and destruction of the ozone layer which protects the earth from ultraviolet radiation.

Conversely, the cornucopians maintain that technology will overcome all the problems identified by the neo-Malthusians and many others the neo-Malthusians cannot even imagine. According to the cornucopians, the technology made possible by the Industrial Revolution will eventually not only provide an abundance of everything for all members of the human race but also conquer all disease, lead humankind to the stars, and usher in a golden age the features of which are presently unimaginable.

Bibliography

Ashton, T. S. *The Economic History of England: The Eighteenth Century*. London: Methuen, 1955. An exhaustive account of the progress of industrialization in England by that country's leading mid-twentieth century authority. Statistics, charts, and graphs abound. Written in a ponderous and forbidding style, but invaluable for the insights it provides. Extensive bibliography and thorough index.

Braudel, Fernand. *Capitalism and Material Life, 1400-1800*. Translated by Miriam Kochan. New York: Harper & Row, 1974. A sweeping account of the forces that produced the Industrial Revolution. Contains an excellent exposition of preindustrial society and a valuable discussion of the role of capitalism in industrialization. Extensive bibliography and adequate index.

Eisenstadt, S. N. *Modernization: Protest and Change*. Englewood Cliffs, N.J.: Prentice-Hall, 1966. An excellent introduction to modernization theory, an understanding of which is a useful tool in studying the Industrial Revolution. Especially helpful in understanding the social consequences of industrialization. Good bibliography and index.

Habakkuk, H. J. *Population Growth and Economic Development Since 1750*. Leicester, England: Leicester University Press, 1971. One of the few book-length treatments of the relationship between population growth and industrialization. Contains many charts, graphs, and maps detailing population growth and industrialization throughout the world since 1850. Large bibliography and thorough index.

Hartwell, R. M., ed. *The Causes of the Industrial Revolution in England*. London: Methuen, 1967. An excellent exploration of the main prerequisites necessary to produce the "take off" into sustained industrial growth. Hartwell argues that several areas of western European and North America were in an economic stage called "incipient industrialism" in the middle of the eighteenth century but that only England possessed all the necessary ingredients to initiate the Industrial Revolution. Maps, tables, graphs, bibliography, and index.

Henderson, W. O. *The Industrialization of Europe, 1780-1914*. London: Thames & Hudson, 1969. Vividly illustrated with many rare photographs and prints, this book concentrates on the human dimension of the Industrial Revolution. Shows the entrepreneurs and the workers as people rather than statistics. Concerned only with the process of industrialization in Europe before World War I. Short bibliography and good index.

Hobsbawm, E. J. *Industry and Empire*. Baltimore: Penguin, 1969. Clearly defines the relationship between industrialization and imperialism. Suggests that imperialism was beneficial to colonized areas because it brought the benefits of industrialization to distant areas of the world. Maps, charts, tables, index, and bibliography.

Landes, David S. *The Unbound Prometheus: Technological Change and Industrial Development in Western Europe from 1750 to the Present*. London: Cambridge University Press, 1969. An exhaustive chronicle of the evolution of the European Industrial Revolution. Shows the positive and negative effects on the institutions of areas undergoing industrialization and on their populations. Many graphs, tables, and maps. Good bibliography and adequate index.

Lane, Peter. *The Industrial Revolution: The Birth of the Modern Age*. London: Weidenfeld & Nicolson, 1978. Persuasively argues that the Industrial Revolution created the institutions of most areas of the contemporary world. Draws heavily on previous scholarship, but good writing helps the student to gain insight more easily than do many of the works based on original sources. Excellent bibliography, good index.

Paul Madden

Cross-References

INDUSTRIAL SOCIETIES

Type of sociology: Social structure
Field of study: Types of societies

Industrial societies, while they exist in various stages of development, all have common features related to the manufacture, transportation, and marketing of goods. Features include urban-centered populations, private or public means of mass production, an advanced technology, and complex transportation and communication infrastructures.

Principal terms
> CAPITALISM: an economic system based on the private or corporate ownership of goods and the means of producing them in a free, competitive market
> DIALECTICAL MATERIALISM: the Marxian theory of change based on a process of synthesizing opposing forces, such as labor and capital
> INDUSTRIAL REVOLUTION: the rapid socioeconomic change brought about by the invention and use of machines to produce durable goods, originating in eighteenth century England
> LAISSEZ-FAIRE: a doctrine opposing government interference in industry and trade
> SOCIALISM: an economic system based on the public ownership of goods and the means of producing them in a market controlled by the state
> URBANIZATION: the process of shifting from a rural to a city population base

Overview

Industrial societies emerged during the Industrial Revolution, beginning in the late eighteenth century. The Industrial Revolution started in England, preceded by the rise of a business-minded middle class and the advent of key inventions essential to a factory-based economy. The first of these was the steam engine. Burning Great Britain's abundant coal, it provided an efficient source of power, freeing people from the hardest kinds of toil. It was used to drive other, more complex machines, such as power looms and spinners in textile factories, and its use soon spread as technology found new ways to use raw materials, particularly iron and coal. Equally important, the steam engine revolutionized transportation, leading to vast railroad networks and great fleets of merchant steamers, providing England with vital trade links to the distant corners of the globe.

Inevitably, the revolution led to considerable social upheaval, including a major demographic shift from a rural to an urban population base. Promised work drew throngs of people from country hamlets to new factories in cities which, like Birmingham and Leeds, seemed to spring up overnight. There, in large, centrally powered plants, where the process could be easily supervised, workers and machines efficiently fabricated goods at remarkably low cost and unprecedented speed.

The change also brought much human misery. Skilled artisans could not compete with the machines and often had to take demeaning, unskilled jobs to survive. Workers, including women and children, frequently worked long hours in factories that were at best dreary and at worst filthy and unsafe. Their tasks, like their very lives, were routine and repetitive. They also lived in crowded, unhealthy conditions, in many cases close to abject poverty. Even when work conditions were not deplorable, industrialization seemed based on a new kind of enslavement. In the older farm and cottage economy of the preindustrial era, many craftspeople, their own masters, had been free to work when they pleased, usually in more pleasant surroundings than the urban tenement districts afforded. Under the new system, with factory hours set and working conditions and pace determined by machines, work became mechanical and monotonous, inspiring no pride in the task.

In the face of humanitarian objections to the exploitation of labor, particularly of children, factory owners cited the economic theories of Adam Smith. Smith, in *The Wealth of Nations* (1776), reasoned that capitalism was both a natural and rational laissez-faire system governing the supply and demand of human goods and services and argued that it should not be tampered with by governments. They would later add justification based on the social and economic implications of the nineteenth century scientific theories of Charles Darwin. Darwin's theory of evolution through natural selection was misapplied in ways he never intended by social thinkers who decided that Herbert Spencer's concept of the "survival of the fittest" could be applied to humans in society as well as to species of animals.

The Industrial Revolution spread throughout Europe, quickly sweeping to the east and south, and England soon found that it had strong industrial rivals, especially Germany. It was also transported to the United States, first to the eastern seaboard states, then westerly, as the frontier continued to push toward the Pacific. As it expanded, industrialization was continuously revitalized by technological advances, particularly in the waning years of the nineteenth century and the first two decades of the twentieth, when, some suggest, a second industrial revolution occurred, made possible by the harnessing of electrical power, the invention of such devices as the petroleum-fueled engine, the telephone and wireless, and the adoption of new distribution and production techniques such as mail-order marketing, the assembly line, and interchangeable parts. At the same time, the revolution spread yet further—to Russia and then Japan, countries that in only a few decades would emerge as great world powers, then to less developed countries with large populations, such as India and China.

Wherever it occurred, the Industrial Revolution significantly transformed society, often in troubling ways. In many countries, children were worked up to fourteen hours a day and were required to live as apprentices, poorly housed and fed in company-owned buildings. Such practices outraged many humanitarians and encouraged social protest, as in the fiction of Charles Dickens. In England, the scandalous excesses finally forced a reluctant Parliament to pass child labor laws that halted the worst practices. British laborers also organized, mostly in preunion groups known as "friendly societies" that sought the political power to redress their grievances. Eventually, often in defiance of law, some workers resorted to walkouts, protest marches, and strikes to force owners to improve their wages and working conditions. Their progress was slow, their rights hard-won, and their triumphs few.

Karl Marx conceived of the management-labor fight as a class struggle and argued that it would not end until the workers organized and formed socialistic states, wresting the means of production from private hands. After World War I, his philosophy had a profound influence on the economies and sociopolitical reorganization of some European nations, especially the Soviet Union, which comprised Russia and allied countries.

In the United States, the growth of industry led to a standard of living that became the envy of the world. Until the Great Depression began in 1929, the American economy flourished as it exploited its great industrial capacity through its tremendous growth in population and the country's expanding frontier. The nation seemed to have an inexhaustible ability to use its own products, partly because manufacturers quickly learned a simple lesson—that workers were also consumers—and generally treated them better than their counterparts elsewhere. Furthermore, American democracy has always allowed some fine tuning of capitalism. In the great slump of the 1930's, under President Franklin D. Roosevelt, the government took some drastic measures to prime the economy's pump, create jobs, and assure a more equitable distribution of the nation's wealth. Although conservatives protested these "socialistic" measures, the changes helped the nation's economic recovery.

During World War II, the United States, through its impressive industrial production, became "the arsenal of democracy" and established itself as the most powerful country in the world. In the war's aftermath, under Cold War conditions, it continued to manufacture arms, constantly adjusting to innovations in such fields as nuclear physics, jet propulsion, microelectronics, robotics, and plastics. It was also slowly evolving into a postindustrial society, one in which the shift was away from manufacturing to services relating to the exchange and retrieval of information made possible by a new, computer-age technology and global economy.

Applications

Throughout much of its two-hundred-year history, the industrial movement has been under the scrutiny of social commentators. Some credit Dickens with being the godfather of industrial sociology, a discipline which for years has studied industry-related issues ranging from management-labor problems to the social impact of factory-based economies. It has been largely concerned with the consequences of industrialization itself, particularly its impact on the individual, the family, and the community and the alienating effects of urban life. One topic of study, for example, has been the decline of the extended family that had been the principal social unit in rural, preindustrial communities.

Industrial sociology has addressed both the work and nonwork roles of the individual—how, for example, the worker might best use the leisure time afforded by automation or how he or she might cope with such job-related problems as fatigue. It has also been concerned with society as a whole; for example, sociologists have studied society's ability to modify its structures in the face of a greatly accelerated rate of technological change. Although industrial sociologists share a concern about changing conditions and the numerous controversies arising from them, there is no dominant theory governing either the method of their inquiries or their interpretation of data. In *Sociology, Work, and Industry* (1980), Tony J. Watson identified "five theoretical strands of the sociology of work," these being "the managerial-psychologistic," "the Durkheim-systems," "the American interactionist," the "Weber-social action," and the "Marxian." All have claims to being scientific in approach.

The first strand, the managerial-psychologistic approach, evolved from the work of F. W. Taylor, who advanced the notion that industrial sociology should address itself to humans' instinctive needs. He believed that management, to be successful, must understand human nature. Only then can it gain the full cooperation of the worker, by overcoming, in particular, "soldiering," or an innate human tendency to loaf. Taylor's influence, manifest in the human relations school of thinkers, is seen in sociological paradigms dependent on psychological explanations of work behavior.

The seminal figure in the next strand, Émile Durkheim, argued against the reductionism of psychological explanations and advanced a holistic concept of society as a composite organism, to be approached pathologically. His stress on the community, its diseases and cures, also influenced the human relations school, notably Elton Mayo, its chief proponent. At the core of its concern was the creation of a managerial class scientifically trained to foster productive management-labor relations through improvements in the working environment, new work incentives, and good communications. The second major thinker in the Durkheim-systems strand was Vilfredo Pareto. He introduced the "system" concept, which stressed the need to integrate the individual into the factory community. Only then, he said, could the system avoid the troubling diseases of the industrial society.

The third strand, the interactionist group of industrial sociologists, originated at the University of Chicago. Their principal concern has been with "symbolic interactionism," stressing the ways in which individuals view themselves within a "mutually interdependent relationship" with society rather than in a "one-sided, deterministic one." This group has maintained a tradition of empirical investigation begun by Robert Park, and it lays great stress on the symbols of interaction—words, gestures, and clothes, for example. Work is perceived by them as a social drama, with the worker playing a social role.

The fourth strand, Weber-social action, has its origins in the theories of German sociologist Max Weber. His followers stress the need to reconcile micro concerns (focusing on individual workers and their tasks) with macro concerns (the much larger patterns of culture and history). In *Die Protestantische Ethik und der Geist des Kapitalismus* (1904; *The Protestant Ethic and the Spirit of Capitalism*, 1930), Weber perceived a "process of rationalization" in history in which social life is "demystified" as the rational criteria of science and technology supplant magic and tradition. Two important notions in Weber's theory are "legitimate order" and the "paradox of consequences." The first refers to any of an infinite variety of potential social patterns that inspire belief in its actors; the second refers to the fact that human actions often have consequences that, contrary to intentions, prove harmful rather than beneficial. Weber has been credited with prompting a shift in industrial sociology from a principal concern with managerial problems to larger issues—how, for example, work relates to political systems. The last strand, the Marxian, evinces a similar concern.

The writings of Karl Marx and Friedrich Engels have had a profound influence on modern industrial sociology. Their notion of economic determinism, based on dialectical materialism, has inspired much commentary, both pro and con. Their theories have also provided an analytical method emulated by many sociologists, even those who reject Marx's conclusions, especially the inevitable collapse of capitalism. Marx and Engels believed that work is a social process and that under capitalism, workers are "alienated" because they do not own their tools or have control over the products of their labor. They are thereby denied a personal sense of human fulfillment, only attainable when the class struggle between the proletariat (working class), bourgeoisie (middle class), and capitalists (owning class) ends with the triumph of socialism. These two concepts—worker alienation and class struggle—have had a major impact on much sociological inquiry.

Context

From a great variety of perspectives, contemporary industrial sociologists have addressed several issues relating to industrial growth, retrenchment, and postindustrial change. Their focal concerns differ in accordance with the stage of industrial development under study—whether, for example, they are studying an emerging industrial nation, such as Mexico, or one in which the Industrial Revolution has largely ended, such as the United States.

Studies undertaken by industrial sociologists, increasingly comparative in nature, have helped elucidate options for political leaders and governmental agencies. Less attention is being paid to urbanization, labor-management relations, and other persistent issues of the past. There is a pronounced tendency to focus on large organizations, such as mammoth cooperative structures and huge and intricate bureaucracies. Of principal concern in the United States is the growing role that education must take in adapting workers to the changes transforming the nation into a postindustrial society. The need to retrain skilled and semiskilled workers is a familiar theme, increasingly placed on political agendas at both state and national levels.

Another concern is the negative impact of megalithic national and international corporations on small businesses, which, lacking the capital, infrastructure, and technology of giant corporations, are threatened with extinction because they are unable to compete. Also studied has been the part played by government-mandated welfare entitlements on small businesses. American industrial sociologists have also addressed the results of major sociopolitical change, such as that brought about by the Civil Rights movement. Prime issues through the 1970's and 1980's were job discrimination against women and racial minorities and the problems of the growing "underclass," that segment of the population said to be lacking the motivation or skills, including functional literacy, to find full-time work paying a living wage. Perhaps the greatest sociological problem under scrutiny is what many perceive as a general deterioration in the quality of life in the United States, manifest in a soaring crime rate, breakdown of the family, loss of traditional values, and declining personal income. The United States, like any other industrial society, continues to pose provocative problems for sociologists of all theoretical casts.

Bibliography

Blumer, Herbert. *Industrialization as an Agent of Social Change: A Critical Analysis.* Edited by David R. Maines and Thomas J. Morrione. New York: Aldine de Gruyter, 1990. Blumer, who coined the term "symbolic interaction," suggests in this study that industrialization, although it is an agent of social change, is neutral and affects the social order only at specific "entry points" at which change can occur. His work is a useful if demanding introduction to the interactionist approach in industrial sociology. The book includes a very helpful introduction to Blumer's views by Maines and Morrione.

Dicken, Peter. *Global Shift: Industrial Change in a Turbulent World.* New York: Harper & Row, 1986. Dicken studies the "deindustrialization" process in contemporary industrial societies and the adjustment problems confronting older industrial nations. A helpful study of industrial societies with thorough coverage of specific industries and useful aids for further study.

Ghosh, Pradip K., ed. *Industrialization and Development: A Third World Perspective.* Westport, Conn.: Greenwood Press, 1984. This is a significant source for the study of emerging industrial societies in Third World nations between 1960 and 1984. Contains a richly annotated bibliography and listing of other important aids, including research institutions and United Nations information sources.

Kemp, Tom. *Historical Patterns of Industrialization.* London: Longman, 1978. This cogent survey covers the broad sweep of industrialization and offers an excellent introductory chapter on the Industrial Revolution, "Industrialization in Historical Perspective." Chapters on three countries—Canada, Japan, and India—are useful illustrations of the patterns of Kemp's focus. Includes an annotated guide to further study.

Mayo, Elton. *The Human Problems of an Industrial Civilization.* New York: Viking, 1960. This classic study by a leading figure in the human relations school of industrial sociology addresses problems (such as fatigue, low morale, and boredom) faced by industrial workers. It reviews the famous experiment conducted at the Hawthorne Works by Western Electric Company and the impact it had on worker productivity. Mandatory reading for students seriously interested in industrial sociology.

Spaulding, Charles B. *An Introduction to Industrial Sociology*. San Francisco: Chandler, 1961. This work was designed as an academic text for undergraduate students. It has an exclusive focus on American industry and society. It is richly endowed with statistics, case examples, tables, graphs, and other study aids. Coverage of industrial relations, business, and unions is admirably clear and direct.

Watson, Tony J. *Sociology, Work, and Industry*. London: Routledge & Kegan Paul, 1980. Watson attempts to integrate the "strands" of the sociology of work that he identifies in chapter 2 of his study, providing a useful survey of the theoretical approaches making up both the larger field of general sociology and the specialization within it. Watson's discussion is often difficult, however, being both abstract and complex, and not recommended for the novice. The work includes an extensive bibliography.

John W. Fiero

Cross-References

Alienation and Work, 80; Capitalism, 191; Cities: Preindustrial, Industrial, and Postindustrial, 253; Class Consciousness and Class Conflict, 271; Industrial and Postindustrial Economies, 940; The Industrial Revolution and Mass Production, 946; Industrial Sociology, 960; Marxism, 1127; Unionization and Industrial Labor Relations, 2096; Urbanization, 2129.

INDUSTRIAL SOCIOLOGY

Type of sociology: Major social institutions
Field of study: The economy

Industrial sociology focuses on the study of people in relation to work—how their viewpoints and actions are shaped by different forms of work organization and cultural patterns. Answers to these questions help to explain the conditions that affect job satisfaction, workplace relationships, and organizational efficiency.

Principal terms
ACTIONS: actual, visible behavior, as distinct from attitudes or feelings
HIERARCHY: an organizational system of graded positions, from high to low, that considers such factors as authority, prestige, and income
INCENTIVES: the material (such as pay and benefits) and nonmaterial (such as interesting work) rewards for staying with an employer, working harder, or taking more training
MOTIVATION: the desire to strive for available incentives; motivation can range from very high to very low
PRODUCTIVITY: the amount of goods produced, or services provided, in relation to the work hours used; fewer hours and more production equals higher productivity
RELATIONSHIPS: the nature of the ties (which may be trusting or wary, cooperative or hostile) among persons in the same hierarchical level and across levels
WORK ORGANIZATION: an organization whose members earn a living by their actions in it, in contrast to voluntary organizations such as social clubs
WORK SATISFACTION: a person's overall positive or negative outlook on a specific job and work setting

Overview

The roots of industrial sociology lie in the writings of economist Adam Smith, philosopher Karl Marx, efficiency expert Frederick Taylor, and the industrial researchers Fritz Roethlisberger and William Dickson. Though these analysts' views sometimes clashed, their concerns became the central theme of industrial sociology. Smith's *The Wealth of Nations* (1776) explained that specialized, repetitive tasks in a division of labor sharply increase productivity but that workers' mental health suffers. In *Das Kapital* (1867; *Capital: A Critique of Political Economy*, 1886), Marx noted that people's natural inclination to enjoy work and to do it voluntarily is stifled by the economic necessity of working for others' profits while following others' orders. Taylor's *Scientific Management* (1911) emphasized that economic incentives overcome humans' normal preference for working less. In *Management and the Worker*

(1939), Roethlisberger and Dickson proposed that employees' attitudes and actions are mainly influenced by the social setting of the workplace; satisfied, productive workers are the result of membership in friendly work groups and managers who listen to personal and work problems.

A wide range of topics are now found in industrial sociology—for example, occupational mobility, income distribution, gender and race discrimination in workplaces, how people get jobs, the meaning of work, labor unions and labor relations, work and family, work organization in other countries, and historical study of work. While this list offers some idea of breadth of industrial sociology, there are core issues which persistently hold attention. Repetitive work, for example, may damage psychological well-being, including self-esteem. If this is true, can work be organized differently without causing productivity losses? Perhaps by stimulating a "natural" inclination to work—if indeed there is such a predisposition—work could be structured so that motivation is not tied to material incentives. How important are economic incentives in the motivational picture? How do employees assess their present jobs, and what is meant by a "good" job?

These are questions which much of the research in industrial society investigates. In one form or another, these issues reflect the important puzzles of work life raised by the earlier analysts. Definitive conclusions have eluded researchers.

While all industrial sociologists might not agree, most think that lifelong repetitive work does affect self-esteem in a negative way. The sense of self among workers with repetitive jobs is less favorable than among persons with more challenging tasks. An industrial hierarchy allocates many rewards at various levels, among which are judgments of worth that affect workers' own beliefs. Unskilled or semiskilled workers can be trained to do enriched (more complicated) tasks, but—especially for small firms—training costs often look very high to employers, and the productivity gains may not seem sufficient to be worth the investment. The issue of incentives is closely linked to what most people mean by a "good" job. Generally, good jobs provide more advantages by offering larger amounts of a variety of rewards (ranging from pay and vacations to interesting work). Put another way, higher positions in the hierarchies of the work world are attractive for three reasons: They confer a measure of social importance, offer less routinized work, and provide financial rewards (and therefore, security). Sociologists debate what would happen if work were voluntary and not required for survival, but most doubt that humans are born with an urge to work.

Closely related to these questions is the issue of job satisfaction, the single most researched topic by industrial sociologists. Thousands of studies have been devoted to it. A large share (two-thirds or so) of employed men and women, it turns out, are either very satisfied or somewhat satisfied by their jobs. In *The State of the Masses* (1986), sociologists Richard Hamilton and James Wright reviewed numerous surveys conducted over many years. They point out that when respondents do register their dissatisfaction, most frequently it involves economic factors such as fears of unemployment or losing income to inflation. Moreover, while high overall, satisfaction is lower among younger (under thirty years old) workers and among black employees.

Researchers have also examined the association between work attitudes and actions. A persistent and important finding is that job satisfaction and job behavior are only weakly related or even not related at all. Nevertheless, two behaviors—being absent from one's job or looking for another—are consistently associated with dissatisfaction.

Because of the increased entry of other nations' goods into the United States market and the importance of exports for the U.S. economy, in the 1980's industrial sociologists began to take a closer look at foreign companies' practices. They wondered whether there were methods that Americans could learn in order to improve quality and productivity. Japanese firms gained attention for their widespread and successful use of quality circles (QCs), small groups of production workers that meet for about an hour weekly. On the basis of their hands-on experience and investigation of a problem, detailed suggestions are offered by QCs for improving quality and productivity in their own work area. As noted by sociologist Robert Cole in *Strategies for Learning* (1989), Japanese companies formed QCs in the mid-1950's and greatly benefited. This inspired a growing number of U.S. companies to install similar groups, sometimes called "workers' participation" programs or "employee involvement groups." Other industrial sociologists compared Japanese and U.S. employees. In *Culture, Control, and Commitment* (1990), James Lincoln and Arne Kalleberg found that work satisfaction was higher among U.S. workers, as was commitment to the organization. Yet Japan's high product quality and productivity is impressive, so Lincoln and Kalleberg concluded that attitudes and actions are separate facets of work life. These sorts of studies examine the basic questions of work, though from a global perspective in keeping with the contemporary economic interdependence of the United States with other nations' economies.

Applications

The research findings of industrial sociology have various applications. They are used in the education of managers, for example, especially in gaining the MBA (master of business administration) degree, in on-site research or consulting focused on business problems, and in the education of sociology and other undergraduate and graduate students regarding work matters.

Industrial sociology has made a major contribution to the education of MBA students. As future managers, their understanding of the human dimension in the workplace is an important educational matter. This has been aided by integrating industrial sociologists' research and ideas into business education. To illustrate, Rosabeth Kanter's *Men and Women of the Corporation* (1977) is a widely read analysis of women's difficulties in gaining acceptance and advancement in the male-dominated business world. Kanter argues that without government intervention, neither women nor other minorities will make much headway in increasing their proportions of executive posts beyond a token representation. Robert Jackall's *Moral Mazes* (1988) is often assigned reading. His study of managers reveals in detail how the pressures of daily business decisions can lead to expedient solutions while deflecting moral judgments. An employee's goal of trying to please the boss, Jackall reports, has the potential to stimulate ethically dubious actions. David Halle, in *America's Working Man* (1984), demonstrates in his case study of a chemical plant that workers may keep cost-cutting and time-saving steps in the production process a secret. This gives them extra time to relax and prevents others, above them in the hierarchy, from using that information to demand more production. These are only a few examples of the types of sociological research that contribute to MBA programs and thus challenge future managers to consider solutions to these serious issues.

Researching and consulting are closely allied, since many problems require close analysis before advice can be offered. Kanter illustrates this role of industrial sociology. Kanter's *The Change Masters* (1983) explains why firms have difficulties in changing their ways of doing things and offers ways to overcome the difficulties. The cases explored in this book were researched by Kanter, and the firms discussed in it sought her counsel. Her advice revolves around the idea that rigid hierarchies obstruct problem solving by delaying decisions, inhibiting information about problems from reaching top levels of the hierarchy, and not tapping information that is available at lower levels of the organization. Both the pace and quality of decisions can be improved by, as much as possible, sending decisions to be made down to those persons most directly involved with a problem—in short, by integrating employees into decision-making processes. William Ouchi studied Japanese companies and then wrote *Theory Z* (1981). It summarizes the core of his advice as a highly respected consultant to U.S. companies. Japanese companies, he comments, create a climate in which everyone has a sense of belonging. Members trust the company to look out for its employees' interests, and the company trusts the employees to do their best for the firm. While mutual trust and loyalty take time to develop, they pay off for companies as well as employees. Ouchi recommends that U.S. firms also take this road.

Most industrial sociologists are employed by universities and colleges as teachers of undergraduate or graduate students. The theories and findings of this area of sociology are thus passed on to students who will have the opportunity to apply in their jobs what was learned in the classroom. Here, too, an internationalist, as well as historical, outlook is encouraged. For example, a portion of a course in industrial sociology might examine a number of large-scale comparative work organization issues. Topics could include discussing the types of economic systems that are most productive and provide the most job security. When and why labor unions were formed, and the conditions that strengthen and weaken unions, could also be examined. Knowledge of these sorts of materials provides a larger context for understanding current work issues. Sensitizing students to workplace issues, providing new perspectives from which to view problems, offering methods of empirical investigation, and indicating findings to date are major tasks for industrial sociologists.

Context

Industrial sociology began to emerge as a distinct subfield of sociology in the late 1930's. For a decade, economic depression had hit the United States, pushing unemployment up and pulling companies' earnings down. Not surprisingly, productivity was a concern. Roethlisberger and Dickson's research, published in *Management and the Worker*, was aimed at ways to increase productivity. Others had attempted this earlier, with emphasis on the economic factors of base pay, piece rates, and job security. The data reported by Roethlisberger and Dickson, however, created new possibilities. They placed the social elements of work organization at the center of attention: norms, values, sentiments, listening, talking, groups, and methods of supervision all became important. This fresh approach attracted sociologists, stimulating them to extend industrial research and theory. The subfield of industrial sociology was beginning to surface.

By the 1950's there were university courses called "industrial sociology." Industrial sociology was also sharing parts of its focus on work with several other academic specialties: another subfield of sociology that studies complex organizations, industrial psychology, an area termed "organizational behavior" in business schools, and "labor studies" courses in industrial relations departments. Industrial sociologists themselves held opposing views of such work issues as the conditions that lead to higher productivity. The target of industrial sociology has expanded, from concern with production industries to any sort of work, including service providers and government organizations. Industrial sociology had become comprehensive, with ample room for diverse research and many different perspectives.

Bibliography

Applebaum, Herbert. *The Concept of Work: Ancient, Medieval, and Modern*. Albany: State University of New York Press, 1992. In this clearly written book, Applebaum describes what people at various points in time thought about work and what they actually did. Applebaum takes the reader from Greece and ancient Rome to the Middle Ages and then into modern times, in each instance providing historical background. Looks at Europe and the United States but not at Asia.

Erikson, Kai, and Steven Vallas, eds. *The Nature of Work: Sociological Perspectives*. New Haven, Conn.: Yale University Press, 1990. This anthology presents the research and views of leading analysts of work. The essays deal with such topics as alienation from work, labor in concentration camps, how work affects personality, and the size and uses of the "irregular economy" (cash transactions for legal or illegal services or products to avoid taxes or arrest). A broad-ranging, very readable collection.

Gillespie, Richard. *Manufacturing Knowledge: A History of the Hawthorne Experiments*. New York: Cambridge University Press, 1991. An account of what are probably the most famous social science experiments ever conducted. They were intended to answer the question, What motivates employees to work harder? Though the findings were long accepted in sociology, their validity has become controversial; Gillespie describes the debates. This is an absorbing and thought-provoking book and is exceptionally well written.

Halle, David. *America's Working Man*. Chicago: University of Chicago Press, 1984. Halle's study of chemical plant workers describes how they protected their jobs by letting management know that only experienced workers could actually keep the plant running, since the formal written procedures were incomplete. Halle reports what really goes on, and why, when labor and management are suspicious of each other.

Hodson, Randy, and Teresa A. Sullivan. *The Social Organization of Work*. Belmont, Calif.: Wadsworth, 1990. This text is a good introduction to industrial sociology. Topics covered include methods of analysis, work and family, job satisfaction, labor unions, work in manufacturing and in services, work at different levels of hierarchies, and consequences of the global economy.

Juravich, Tom. *Chaos on the Shop Floor*. Philadelphia: Temple University Press, 1985. The data for this study of a factory are Juravich's experiences while working there. Through his observations, one learns of the rigid hierarchy that governs production. Even when equipment or materials are faulty, a situation which is quickly obvious to the workers, no one higher up listens. This nicely crafted book indicates that production would benefit from listening to workers.

Womack, James P., Daniel T. Jones, and Daniel Roos. *The Machine That Changed the World*. New York: Rawson Associates, 1990. This major worldwide study of the automobile industry explains how faster methods for designing cars, fewer workers needed to build them, and speedier and more quality-driven production have changed the nature of this industry, which serves as a model for other sectors of the U.S. and other economies. The authors present their findings and projections in clear language.

Curt Tausky

Cross-References

Alienation and Work, 80; Computers, Automation, and the Economy, 316; Industrial and Postindustrial Economies, 940; The Industrial Revolution and Mass Production, 946; Industrial Societies, 953; Leisure, 1075; Primary, Secondary, and Tertiary Sectors of the Economy, 1512; Unionization and Industrial Labor Relations, 2096; Women in the Labor Force, 2185; Workplace Socialization, 2202.

INEQUALITIES IN HEALTH

Type of sociology: Social stratification
Field of study: Dimensions of inequality

Inequality in health and in access to health care is readily apparent between the sexes, among racial and ethnic groups, across income levels, and across age groups. Public policy attempted to address this problem through such programs as Medicaid and Medicare, established in the 1960's.

Principal terms
ACCESS: the dimensions that describe a population group's entry and passage through the health care delivery system
EQUITABLE ACCESS: the condition that exists when the ability to use health services is based solely on need and not on individual characteristics or ability to pay
MEDICAID: a state-operated medical insurance program for low-income patients
MEDICARE: a federal health insurance program targeted primarily at people over sixty-five
MORBIDITY: the rates of illness in a population
MORTALITY: the rates of death in a population
TOTAL ACCESS: the condition that exists when services are available wherever and whenever a patient needs them and the entry point to the system is well defined

Overview

Although American society is based on a philosophy of freedom and equality, when it comes to levels of health and health care, a number of inequalities are readily apparent. There are many ways to measure the health levels of a population. Three of the most often used measures are mortality, morbidity, and health care utilization. These measure, respectively, the rates of death in a population, the rates of illness, and how health services are used.

The inequalities in levels of health and illness are visible between the sexes, across racial and ethnic groups, across social class, and by age. Each of these demographic characteristics represents a source of inequality in health. Females, for example, tend to live longer than males but tend to be sicker. Also, women tend to use more health care services than men. Women average about 1.5 more visits to a physician per year than men. Overall, women account for nearly 60 percent of all physician visits each year. Part of this difference may be attributed to the fact that men are more likely to lack health insurance than women. Medical sociologist Fredric Wolinsky notes in his book *The Sociology of Health* (1988) that differences in morbidity rates between males and females are attributable to social differences in the "perception, evaluation, and treatment of mild chronic conditions."

Racial and ethnic inequities also exist. Whites account for nearly 90 percent of all physician visits each year. Blacks are more likely than whites to lack health insurance, and the percentage of blacks covered by Medicaid insurance is three times the percentage of whites. Thirty-one percent of Hispanics are not covered by any health insurance, and an additional 16 percent are covered by Medicaid. Poorer people, those from the lower socioeconomic classes, tend to be sicker than their middle- and upper-class counterparts. Although they tend to be sicker, they use fewer health services in general. Poorer patients are less likely than affluent patients to have a regular source of medical care and are less likely to have contact with a physician during the year. Thanks to government intervention, lower-income patients are able to utilize hospital services to a somewhat greater degree than they once were.

In terms of age, the group with the most visits per year are the elderly, age sixty-five and older. The elderly average more than six visits per person per year. Those over sixty-five also account for 25 percent of the total annual health care expenditures in the United States. In other words, the elderly use more services and spend disproportionately more money on health care than any other age group. They also tend to be sicker, have more chronic illnesses, and have higher mortality rates than younger age groups.

One of the main reasons for these inequities is the lack of access to health care for some segments of the population. Considerable research has gone into the study of the inequalities in access to health care in the United States. In the early 1990's, the United States was the only Western industrialized nation without some form of national health insurance. National health insurance typically assures all members of society equitable access to health and medical care. That is, the receipt of medical care is based on the individual patient's level of need. Additionally, as a means of maintaining reasonable levels of cost and quality, nationalized systems tend to offer total access. Total access implies that services are available wherever and whenever a patient needs them and that the entry point to the system is well defined. This entry point tends to be a primary care physician who also serves as a guide to the patient's journey through the health care system.

The inequalities in health in the United States continued without raising much concern until the early 1960's. The significantly poorer health of the old, the poor, and minorities prompted a major change in national health policy. In an attempt to close the gap between the haves and the have-nots regarding health care, Congress amended the Social Security Act of 1935. These amendments were passed in 1965 as Title XVIII, *Health Insurance for the Aged* (or Medicare), and Title XIX, *Grants to States for Medical Assistance Programs* (or Medicaid). The passage of these two amendments partially narrowed the gap between the poor and elderly (who were until that time uninsured) and those who could afford health insurance. Medicare and Medicaid paid providers a fair and reasonable cost for their services.

The major problem with Medicare and Medicaid, however, was an increasingly heavy financial burden on state and federal governments. Costs continued to grow unabated into the 1980's. In 1982, Congress passed the *Tax Equity and Fiscal*

Responsibility Act, which was designed to control Medicare and Medicaid costs by limiting payments to physicians and hospitals. Perhaps the most memorable component of the act was the implementation of Diagnosis Related Groups (DRGs). DRGs, developed at Yale University, grouped together similar medical diagnoses. Based on national information concerning the length of hospital stays, the government set a payment schedule. Therefore, providers were no longer reimbursed according to their costs but were reimbursed according to a relatively strict set of guidelines. There was an attempt to entice providers to be more cost effective in the care they provide by setting DRG payments. If the hospital could treat the patient for less than the prescribed amount, the hospital could keep the difference as profit. If they could not, the hospital was responsible for making up the difference.

The DRG reimbursement system has been analyzed and criticized on a number of grounds. Some researchers have noted that the incentive to provide less costly care has really resulted in poor and elderly patients being released before being completely cured. Such problems led many experts to concur, by the late 1980's, that the only way to eradicate the inequalities in health and health care was to redesign and restructure the American health care system.

Applications

Improving access to health care in the United States has long been a focus of sociologists and health policy makers. In their book *Health Care in the U.S.: Equitable for Whom?* (1980), sociologists Lu Ann Aday, Ronald Andersen, and Gretchen Fleming presented a theoretical framework designed to explain the inequality of access to health care as it existed in the 1970's. They argued that by better understanding the nature of unequal access, policy makers could begin the undertaking of instituting policy change aimed at making access equitable. Equitable access implies that people will receive medical care based on their need for that care rather than their demographic characteristics (such as gender, race, ethnicity, or age).

The theoretical framework developed by Aday, Andersen, and Fleming includes health policy as an integral component of the access problem. In fact, they view policy formulation as their starting point. Changes in health policy theoretically have an impact on the characteristics of the delivery system and potential access indicators. Characteristics of the delivery system include the availability and the distribution of health care services. Potential access indicators include patients' personal characteristics, their ability to pay for health services, and the need for those services. Changes in the delivery system are also hypothesized to affect potential access indicators. Changes in the characteristics of the delivery system and in access characteristics both, in turn, affect the use of health services and the level of satisfaction patients have with the medical care they receive. These changes may lead to alterations in health policy, beginning the cycle once more.

For example, some subgroups of the population, most notably the elderly and those with low incomes, were seen as having severe access problems during the early 1960's. Over time, these inequalities appeared to be increasing. Therefore, as a form of public health policy, the federal government instituted two new programs designed to provide publicly financed health insurance: Medicare and Medicaid. Both programs became law in 1965, and they had immediate impacts on the access problems of the elderly and the poor. These policy changes revised the characteristics of the delivery system by making health care more widely available. They also improved the potential access of these two groups dramatically. In turn, the use of health services by the elderly and the poor increased.

By utilizing this framework and comparing data over time, Aday, Andersen, and Fleming concluded that major governmental policy changes such as the Medicare and Medicaid programs helped in some ways to promote more equitable access to health care over time. Providing insurance coverage to the elderly and to low-income populations brought health and medical care to millions of Americans who otherwise would not have received adequate treatment. As they state,

> Our data suggest that previous health care financing efforts—Medicare and Medicaid—have been quite successful in reducing access inequities for the aged and the poor, respectively. Financial barriers still exist, however, but primarily for particular groups, e.g., the elderly with serious illness, the uninsured who fall in between the economic statuses of the publicly and privately insured, individuals of Spanish heritage, and people with needs not generally covered by existing financing schemes (e.g., dental care, outpatient drugs).

One additional outcome of these programs was a spiraling increase in the health care costs paid by the federal and state governments. As a result, policy adjustments were made. Most of the adjustments took the form of restricting eligibility for enrollment to Medicare and Medicaid. These changes in turn affected changes throughout the rest of the framework in a cyclical fashion.

Context

Inequality in health and health care has always existed in the United States. Prior to the twentieth century, health care in the United States was neither very effective nor very popular. The level of physician knowledge and skill was extremely low, especially compared to today's standards. Although the first American hospital was opened in Philadelphia in 1713, it was nothing like its modern counterpart. Eighteenth century hospitals were primarily a place where people went to die rather than institutions developed to cure disease.

As medical knowledge advanced, physicians became marginally better at providing care, and by the mid-nineteenth century hospitals began providing state-of-the-art technical care and undertaking medical research. By the early twentieth century, however, major changes were underway. In 1910, the famous Flexner Report was published. This report uncovered the poor state of American medical schools and stated that physicians were inadequately trained to practice "modern" medicine. As a result, major attempts to standardize medical education and practice were implemented.

Just as physicians were better trained after the Flexner Report, hospitals began providing better care. This was caused, in large part, by the movement of physicians into all areas of the hospital. One side effect of these improvements was an increase in the cost of medical care. Cost became a primary factor in determining whether an individual received care. Once cost became a primary factor in the provision of care, inequalities grew.

Medical sociologist Paul Starr, in his Pulitzer Prize-winning book *The Social Transformation of American Medicine* (1982), notes that a major health policy decision took place in the 1920's. That decision was to develop an insurance industry aimed at providing coverage for the middle class rather than to focus on public health improvements. The spiraling cost of health care and the lack of a national health care plan made insurance a necessity. By focusing on the middle class, insurance further increased the disparity in health levels and access to health care between the poor and minorities and the middle and upper classes.

Bibliography

Aday, Lu Ann. *At Risk in America: The Health and Health Care Needs of Vulnerable Populations in the United States*. San Francisco, Calif.: Jossey-Bass, 1993. This large volume addresses the health care requirements of disadvantaged, low-access population groups. The resource section provides a good listing of the information available from various government agencies and data sources, and the bibliography is thorough and exhaustive.

Aday, Lu Ann, Ronald Andersen, and Gretchen V. Fleming. *Health Care in the U.S.: Equitable for Whom?* Beverly Hills, Calif.: Sage Publications, 1980. This book is rather technical in its presentation of data from three national surveys of access to health care. It provides a sound theoretical framework for analyzing the various facets of inequitable access to health care in the United States.

Armstrong, David. *An Outline of Society as Applied to Medicine*. 3d ed. London: Wright, 1989. A short, easy-to-read book designed to outline various topics within the field of medical sociology. The two chapters on the social patterns of illness are pertinent for better understanding the topic of inequalities in health.

Jonas, Steven. *An Introduction to the U.S. Health Care System*. 3d ed. New York: Springer, 1992. A useful introduction to the way health care is delivered in the United States. Each chapter ends with two to three pages of relevant references. This book is well indexed and is useful for gaining a better understanding of how the health care system works.

Raffel, Marshall W., and Norma K. Raffel. *The U.S. Health System: Origins and Functions*. 3d ed. New York: John Wiley & Sons, 1989. This book provides a concise history of the development of health care in the U.S. It has no bibliography, but there is a useful appendix which lists the acronyms commonly used in the health care field.

Starr, Paul. *The Social Transformation of American Medicine*. New York: Basic Books, 1982. Starr's book won the Pulitzer Prize and the C. Wright Mills award for the best book in the field of sociology. It presents a detailed and exhaustive effort to analyze the historical development of medicine in the United States. It is long and is sometimes a bit difficult to read, but it is an interesting account of the rise of physicians and hospitals in our society.

Wolinsky, Fredric D. *The Sociology of Health: Principles, Practitioners, and Issues.* 2d ed. Belmont, Calif.: Wadsworth, 1988. This book provides an excellent overview of the field of medical sociology. It is recommended for those with little or no background in the field. It is easy to read, is well indexed, and has a complete bibliography.

Ralph Bell

Cross-References

Acquired Immune Deficiency Syndrome, 8; Health and Society, 852; Health Care and Gender, 858; Inequalities in Political Power, 972; The Medical Profession and the Medicalization of Society, 1159; Medical Sociology, 1166; The Institution of Medicine, 1185; Social Epidemiology, 1793.

INEQUALITIES IN POLITICAL POWER

Type of sociology: Social stratification
Fields of study: Basic concepts of social stratification; Dimensions of inequality

Inequalities in political power exist in all societies and states, although in democratic states there is a stated desire and concerted attempt to provide the same political rights and responsibilities to all citizens. Inequalities in political power may serve as the impetus to rebellion by suppressed groups; they also may indicate overt or unintentional attempts by those in power to keep certain groups unequal.

Principal terms
AUTHORITY: legitimate or rightful power that is generally acknowledged
CONVENTIONAL POLITICAL PARTICIPATION: participation that is ordinary in a democratic system, such as voting and writing to legislators
EQUALITY OF OPPORTUNITY: the situation that exists when everyone in a society has the same economic, political, and social rights
EQUALITY OF OUTCOME: the situation that exists when everyone in a society has the same rights and rewards as everyone else, regardless of talent, skill, or work
FRANCHISE: the right to vote
INEQUALITY: the existence of unequal rights, rewards, or responsibilities among different groups in a society
POWER: the ability of one person to get another person to do what the first person wants him or her to do; power may be coercive or persuasive
SOCIAL STRATIFICATION: a relatively permanent ranking of statuses and roles within a group or society; it necessarily involves inequality among groups, most often based on control of power and resources
UNCONVENTIONAL POLITICAL PARTICIPATION: various types of participation that may be either lawful, such as marches and demonstrations, or unlawful; unlawful participation may be nonviolent (civil disobedience) or violent (rebellion)

Overview

Political inequality is present in all societies and in all states at all times. Sometimes it is the result of intentional action to keep a group or groups from exercising political power; examples include the long suppression of the black majority in South Africa or the denial in parts of the southern United States of the right to vote to African Americans prior to the Civil Rights movement. Other times, political inequality is the result of economic or social inequalities that exist between classes or other groups of individuals in a particular society.

Power generally refers to the ability of one person to make another person do what the first person wants him or her to do. This may be done by means of persuasion or coercion. Legitimate power exists when authority is accepted by those over whom it is exercised; coercive power, on the other hand, is enforced by punishment and reward. Political power refers to a more specific form of power relations in which a person has the ability to exercise some control over the institutions and mechanisms of the state that control his or her life.

Political equality exists when all individuals in a given society or state are given the same political rights and responsibilities or the same opportunities to exercise political rights and responsibilities. Inequalities of political power most obviously refer to the lack, by certain persons or groups, of the ability to exercise power over the political institutions and mechanisms of the state in which they live.

Inequalities in political power differ dramatically from state to state and from group to group within each state. What is accepted as a political right or power may also differ within and between states. For example, totalitarian or authoritarian states, by definition, provide little in the way of political equality; rather, they provide for the total or near-total control of most groups and individuals by one all-powerful group or individual. In this situation, inequalities of political power are at their most stark. Yet in democratic or republican states, in which political power is shared by the citizenry and in which political equality is at its greatest, widespread inequalities in economic or social concerns still exist. These inequalities contribute to or exacerbate political inequality. For example, in the United States, whose extremes of wealth and poverty are relatively stark, it is the poorest individuals who most often choose not to vote or to engage in other forms of legitimate political participation. The concerns and needs of these individuals, therefore, are not usually of primary concern to policy makers. This is one manner in which existing social and economic inequalities exacerbate political inequality.

Various types of inequality—economic, social, and political—are interrelated; they influence and reinforce one another in a variety of ways. The consequences of political inequality are linked with other valued resources, for example, in that the lack of political equality may cause a lack of economic power or social status. Likewise, people with little economic power or social status may, even in a state that legally provides equality of opportunity, find themselves unequal to others in terms of power to influence policy choices in the political system.

There are other consequences of political inequality that may be more damaging to the state. Individuals denied the right to express their political views equally with other citizens may choose to express their political desires via extralegal means, such as through civil disobedience or even through violent rebellion or revolution. Although it may be in the interests of a society's dominant group to restrict access to the political system, it is against their interests to provoke subordinate groups to the extent that political instability results.

Applications
Inequality in political power must be seen as an element of inequality in general,

such that some people have and others do not have certain prized qualities, rights, or duties. Political power, in its essence, is the ability to govern or to share in governing the state in which one resides. In a democratic or republican political system, political powers include all those things that enable a citizen to go about governing or expressing his or her desires to the chosen representatives of the governed.

These activities may be undertaken in a number of ways, but the process usually involves the exercise of the right to political participation in its myriad forms. Political participation may be either conventional or unconventional. Conventional political participation includes activities such as communicating views to one's elected representatives, usually through letters or telephone calls. It also entails voting for those representatives in regularly scheduled elections. Other facets of conventional participation include working on campaigns in a voluntary capacity, contributing money to a candidate's campaign for office, wearing a political button or displaying a political poster or bumper sticker, and otherwise expressing one's views to or about the political system and its representatives in an accepted, legitimate, and lawful manner.

Unconventional political participation in a democratic political system may be either legitimate or illegitimate. Legitimate but unconventional political participation includes activities which are not illegal but which are more or less uncommon means of expressing one's views toward policy or decision makers. Examples of unconventional political participation that is legitimate and lawful are organized marches, pickets, and protests that express to elected officials one's views regarding specific policy concerns and governmental decisions.

Unconventional political participation can also be illegitimate, or unlawful. This form of political expression may be further subdivided into violent and nonviolent activities. Illegitimate participation that is nonviolent includes civil disobedience and similar acts of intentionally breaking a law to make a point or serve a political purpose. This type of lawbreaking, it is assumed, causes no harm to any person or property. Unconventional political participation that is illegitimate and violent includes riots, rebellions, and revolution. Only those actions that are chiefly instigated for political purposes or that express a political aim are acknowledged as political participation.

Thus, for an individual in a democratic political system, political participation may take many different forms. Individuals may choose to participate extensively or not at all; they may choose to express their political opinions and desires through freedom of speech, freedom of assembly, or merely as the right to exercise the franchise. An individual in a democratic political system thus would seem to have political equality with all other citizens. Yet regardless of the type of government involved, all industrialized nations and modern societies are stratified societies, and this stratification affects various groups' political power. Running for office and lobbying for a cause both cost money, and running for high national office requires considerable amounts of money. Subordinate or minority groups, because of economic stratification, are less able to be involved in the highest levels of politics than society's dominant group. In addition, long-standing inequalities in wealth or income may make some individuals less likely to recognize whatever opportunities do exist and to take advantage of them.

In the United States, political power is primarily exercised by the most vocal classes and groups in the society. Thus, the poor, those without equal access to basic necessities, wealth, income, or education, rarely exercise much political leverage. Elected representatives listen and respond to those who let their views be known, be they wealthy oil lobbyists or loud and insistent interest groups. They listen most attentively to those who have contributed financially to the success of the representative or the representative's party. Welfare mothers and homeless men rarely have an advocate in the halls of government, since they themselves are not there either as representatives or as voices participating in the political process.

As noted, to argue that this results in inequalities in political power is both true and untrue. Strictly speaking, it is untrue in the sense that all individuals have been granted the exact same rights to be able to affect the political system. In practice, however, it is true that many economically disadvantaged and less educated groups do not participate in the political process and do not have the financing necessary to influence the political process at high levels. Thus, they are to varying degrees overlooked in the policies and actions of government. The political process often involves passionate competition among groups vying among themselves to effect change that will suit their needs. Unorganized groups or individuals unrepresented by groups are left out of this system and thus have little political power.

In the United States, members of the economic elite—those who occupy the highest 10 to 20 percent of income and net wealth—are often the same individuals who run for and are elected to public office, especially at the national level. Thus, holders of economic power and prestige often also become the holders of political power and prestige. This fact is largely attributable to the process by which national political leaders are chosen. In contests for the presidency, for example, viable candidates must achieve the nomination of the Democratic or Republican Party. They must then endure a lengthy and tortuous process of primaries, caucuses, and media assaults. Competing in the preliminary contests, be they small state caucuses or large state primaries, and effectively answering the media's exposés of one's past life require extraordinarily large sums of money. This money may (rarely) come from the candidate's own pockets, but it usually consists of a combination of small donations, large donations, and federal matching funds. Since the 1974 Federal Election Campaign Act reforms of the presidential campaign-financing process, the presidential race has become less beholden to very large givers, although this has not much affected the available pool of presidential hopefuls.

Those beginning the long path to the nomination must be wealthy enough to forgo most or all income for the twelve, eighteen, or often twenty-four months of the campaign ordeal in order to travel from state to state stumping for support. Once the nomination is secured, they must continue, even increase, the grueling pace in their final race for the office. Most Americans, beholden to mortgage payments and other monthly bills, cannot afford those financial sacrifices. Frequently, therefore, presidential nomination seekers come from either the near-rich classes or from current congressional or gubernatorial officeholders. These officeholders run for president while drawing their paychecks as a U.S. senator or a state governor, even though they are incapable of carrying out all the duties of their office while on the campaign trail. Most occupations (and employers) are not so forgiving.

Context

Inequality is a frequently discussed topic within the field of sociology. Sociologists have struggled to understand and to explain the interrelated notions of power, rewards, and inequality. Much of this discussion has taken place within the area of social stratification. Those social scientists studying social stratification seek to understand the relatively permanent rankings, statuses, and roles within groups and societies, and therefore they study the many dimensions of inequality, including inequalities of basic necessities and inequalities of political power.

Perhaps the original theorist of social stratification was Karl Marx, who argued in the nineteenth century that societies evolve through a series of stages, each characterized by a dominant exploitive class. The last exploitive stage, he believed, is capitalism, which will be succeeded by socialism and later by a classless communist society. To Marx, then, political inequality is inherent in all precommunist political systems and will end only when these systems are replaced by communism.

The next major thinker and writer to discuss political inequality was Max Weber. Weber saw three forces at work in determining political inequality, rather than the single force of economic inequality seen by Marx. According to Weber, class, status, and party all play a role. Thus, one of the major differences between Weber and Marx is that Weber acknowledged the importance of status groups such as the peasantry and the aristocracy. According to Weber, any one of these three factors could affect any other, and any one of them could be exchanged for any other.

Later thinkers on power, particularly sociologist Talcott Parsons, introduced the concept that within any society there is a limited amount of power available. If one group increases its power, then there is less power available to other groups in the society. Parsons called this idea the zero-sum concept of power, borrowing the notion from game theory, in which any increase of power for one person results in a corresponding decrease in power for some other person or group.

Other discussions on power centered on community power. Writers such as Helen and Robert Lynd in the late 1920's studied "Middletown" (Muncie, Indiana) and concluded that one family was the dominant economic power there and that this family successfully controlled all aspects of community decision making. Another major study in community power was done by Floyd Hunter in the late 1940's and early 1950's. He studied "Regional City" (Atlanta, Georgia) and concluded that a small economic elite dominated the city in its own self-interest. In the late 1950's, Robert Dahl conducted a study of New Haven, Connecticut, and concluded that no identifiable elite dominated the economic, political, and social arenas there. He concluded that there was a high degree of public control over decision makers. Dahl's study, then, presents a more benign view of power in American communities, seeing a far greater degree of political equality than did the earlier writers.

Bibliography

Bachrach, Peter, and Morton Baratz. "Two Faces of Power." *American Political Science Review* 56 (December, 1962): 947-952. This article was a major criticism of Dahl's study of power in New Haven, Connecticut. It argued that Dahl's methodology and findings were suspect.

Dahl, Robert. *Who Governs? Democracy and Power in an American City.* New Haven, Conn.: Yale University Press, 1963. The classic community power study of New Haven in which Dahl concluded that there was no ruling elite.

Domhoff, G. William. *The Powers That Be.* New York: Random House, 1978. Domhoff argues that the owners and managers of large banks and corporations dominate the United States. He documents their overrepresentation in economic and governmental posts, as well as their great wealth and income, as evidence of ruling-class power.

Lasswell, Harold D. *Politics: Who Gets What, When, and How?* New York: McGraw-Hill, 1936. This is one of the earlier sociological examinations of political power. It defines politics in terms of power relationships.

Lipset, Seymour M. *Political Man: The Social Bases of Politics.* Garden City, N.Y.: Doubleday, 1960. An influential and now classic examination of mass culture, society, politics, and power relationships.

Michels, Robert. *Political Parties: A Sociological Study of the Oligarchical Tendencies of Modern Democracy.* Translated by Eden Paul and Cedar Paul. New York: Dover, 1959. A classic study, originally published in 1911, of democratic states. Michels concludes that a few individuals will always rise to the top and come to dominate a society and argues that political equality cannot be legislated because oligarchical tendencies are inherent in humankind.

Mills, C. Wright. *The Power Elite.* New York: Oxford University Press. 1956. An important study that demonstrates that an elite composed of the wealthy and powerful will always dominate society. Mills's book is often cited and has been very influential.

Parsons, Talcott. "The Distribution of Power in American Society." In *Structure and Process in Modern Societies.* Glencoe, Ill.: Free Press, 1960. This is Parsons' influential work on political power relationships and inequality in the United States.

Lisa Langenbach

Cross-References

INFANT MORTALITY

Type of sociology: Population studies or demography

The infant mortality rate is one of the most widely used general indices of health care in the United States and other countries. It is measured as the annual number of deaths among infants under one year of age per thousand live births.

Principal terms
CAUSE OF DEATH: the disease or injury that initiates a train of morbid events leading directly to death
GESTATION: the period in which young are carried in the uterus, from conception to birth
NEONATAL INFANT: an infant less than 28 days old
POSTNEONATAL INFANT: an infant aged 28 to 364 days
PRENATAL: taking place before birth
SUDDEN INFANT DEATH SYNDROME (SIDS): the cause ascribed to the sudden, inexplicable death of an infant of less than one year of age

Overview

In 1991, more than 36,000 of the 4 million babies born in the United States never survived to their first birthday. This equaled an infant mortality rate of 8.9 infant deaths per 1,000 live births within the first year of life. In 1990, the infant mortality rate for the United States was 9.2 infant deaths per 1,000 live births. At the time, this was the lowest infant mortality rate ever recorded, down 6 percent from 1989. In raw numbers, 38,351 infants died in 1990, and 39,655 infants died in 1989 in the United States. These statistics, compiled annually, are from the Centers for Disease Control's Health Statistics Vital Statistics System. In 1989 the morality rate for infants of white mothers and black mothers (including Hispanic and non-Hispanic) was 8.1 and 18.6 infant deaths per 1,000 live births, respectively. From 1988 to 1989, the neonatal mortality rate—the death rate for infants under 28 days old—declined from 6.3 to 6.2 deaths per 1,000 live births. In 1989, the overall postneonatal mortality rate—the death rate for infants age 28 days to one year—was unchanged for the fourth consecutive year.

Between races, there has been a consistent discrepancy of infant mortality rates in the United States. In 1990, the mortality rate of black (including Hispanic and non-Hispanic) infants was 18.0 infant deaths per 1,000 live births. This was a decrease of 3 percent from the 1989 infant mortality rate of 18.6 infant deaths per 1,000 live births among blacks. For white (including Hispanic and non-Hispanic) infants, the death rate decreased 6 percent, from 8.1 infant deaths per 1,000 live births in 1989 to 7.6 infant deaths per 1,000 live births in 1990. In 1989, a child's risk of dying within the first year was 2.3 times greater for black infants than for white infants. In 1990, this discrepancy increased; black infants were 2.4 times as likely to die within the first year as white infants.

From 1989 through 1990, the infant mortality rate decreased from eight of the ten leading causes of infant death. Leading decreases were for respiratory distress syndrome, accidents, and sudden infant death syndrome (SIDS). Increases were for newborns affected by maternal complications of pregnancy and intrauterine hypoxia. In 1989, the largest increase occurred in disorders relating to short gestation and unspecified low birth weight. By race, there is a difference in causes of death for infants. For white infants, the leading cause of death was birth defects; for black infants, the leading cause of death was disorders relating to short gestation periods and low birth weights.

Infants with birth weights of under 5.5 pounds are forty times more likely to die as infants than normal weight babies are. Though low birth weight infants make up only 7 percent of all newborns in the United States, they account for approximately 60 percent of infant deaths. The national rate of low birth weight remained unchanged in the 1980's, although the infant mortality rate declined from the use of high-technology medicine. Little progress was made in the 1980's in getting women into prenatal care in the earliest stages of pregnancy, an approach that can reduce the incidence of low birth weight.

The second leading cause of infant mortality in the United States is sudden infant death syndrome, the abrupt and unexplained death of an apparently healthy infant. From 1980 until 1988, 47,932 infants born to U.S. residents died from SIDS. During that time, overall SIDS rates declined 3.5 percent for white infants and 19.2 percent for black infants, although the SIDS rate during the 1980's was higher for black than white infants. This decline was mostly in postneonatal infants; neonatal SIDS cases represented a relatively small proportion of the total SIDS cases.

The phenomenon of SIDS appears to have a geographical link. For white infants, overall SIDS rates for 1980 through 1988 were highest in the West, followed by the Midwest, South, and Northeast. For black infants, in 1980 SIDS rates were highest in the Midwest, followed by the West, Northeast, and South. In 1988, the Northeast had the lowest overall SIDS rates. These consistent regional variations in SIDS rates during the study period are unexplained.

In 1985, the average infant mortality rate in developed countries was 18 infant deaths per 1,000 live births. In less developed nations, particularly in Africa, the infant mortality rate approaches 200 infant deaths per 1,000 live births in some nations. The average infant mortality rate in these countries is approximately 90 infant deaths per 1,000 live births.

During the 1970's, the infant mortality rate decreased 5 percent per year in the United States. In the 1980's, this rate decreased 3 percent per year. With an infant mortality of 8.9 infant deaths per 1,000 live births, the United States had the twenty-third-lowest infant mortality rate in the world, down from twentieth place in 1980.

Japan's infant mortality rate is the lowest in the world and is half that of the United States. Other nations with low infant morality rates include Finland, Denmark, Canada, Hong Kong, Norway, Iceland, France, and Sweden. These countries have infant mortality rates of 7 to 10 infant deaths per 1,000 live births.

Applications

The problem of infant mortality has plagued civilization throughout the ages. In the eighteenth century, for example, the numbers of infants put into foundling hospitals always increased during times of near famine, because there was no possibility of any expansion of already meager food supplies; when institutions were not available, infants were sometimes abandoned to die. In modern times, similar reactions to infant mortality have been observed in poverty-stricken countries; parents have been observed to withdraw love from already weak infants to leave more resources for other infants with better chances of survival. Such behavior is not always seen, however; in other poor communities, especially where the birth rate is low, love is still expressed for weak infants, and grief reactions are observed when they die.

In the United States, there is a discrepancy in infant mortality rates by race. While total infant mortality declined in the 1970's, the gap in infant mortality between black and white infants increased. Differences in socioeconomic status and access to care do not entirely explain the disparity, suggesting that other factors not available in routinely collected data may need to be examined.

Though factors other than socioeconomic ones appear to exist, the differences in infant mortality rate by race may largely reflect factors such as socioeconomic status and access to medical care. In 1990, nearly three times as many black and white infants were members of families with incomes below the poverty level. Because of income differentials, black women are less likely to have health insurance that covers the costs of care for pregnancy and childbirth.

In the United States, an extreme example of this is observed in the Mississippi Delta. In this area, teenage pregnancy, poverty, and infant mortality may be linked, as Mississippi ranks near the bottom of United States statistics for health care for poor children. In 1989, one-third of the state's children lived in poverty, defined as annual family income of $12,675 for a family of four.

One of the main reasons for high infant mortality in the United States is that many infants are born with low birth weights. This is largely the result of a lack of prenatal care by mothers who either cannot afford to go to a doctor or who do not know how to nurture a developing fetus. Other causes of low birth weights include smoking and drug abuse by mothers. When pregnancies are unintended, which is the case with the majority of teen mothers, the survival chances of the infant decreased, resulting in high costs to society. It costs hospitals nearly eight times as much to care for low-birth-weight infants as it does to handle a normal delivery. African American infants are as likely to be born underweight as are babies born in less-developed countries such as Cameroon and Zaire.

To increase birth weights and lower infant mortality rates in the United States, greater prenatal care must be given to expectant mothers. Up to 40 percent of African American women do not receive prenatal care for the first trimester of pregnancy. During the 1980's, the percentage of women receiving early and regular prenatal care did not improve. One-third of pregnant women, 1.3 million each year, did not receive adequate prenatal care. In 1988, 73,000 pregnant women in the United States had no

prenatal care, a 50 percent increase over the 1980 rate. Without health insurance, many pregnant women cannot receive early and regular medical attention throughout pregnancy. Infants born to women who did not receive care before delivery are three times as likely to be born with low birth weight and four times more likely to die than those whose mothers began to receive care during the first trimester.

Efforts to reduce the infant mortality rate include expanding access to prenatal care for low-income families through changes in Medicare eligibility. Increased use of prenatal care is likely to have the greatest impact on neonatal deaths resulting from causes other than birth defects. It has been estimated that for every dollar spent on pregnancy, three dollars are saved in after-delivery hospital costs.

The countries with lower infant mortality rates than the United States generally provide a wider range of publicly financed health and social services than the United States does. In these other developed nations, public health insurance accounts for most outlay for health care. In less developed nations, decreases in infant mortality can be made by the provision of better nutrition and health care for pregnant women, family planning, and improved child care.

Context

Throughout history, the belief in the value of childhood has changed along with economic conditions. When economic conditions are good, childhood is treated as of greater importance, and greater love and care are lavished on children. Conversely, when economic conditions are less favorable, children are not cared for as well. A common belief of medieval parents was that childhood was an unimportant phase of life, and parents typically had several children in order that a few would survive.

Although such views were prevalent in medieval times, it was known that human infants are the most vulnerable of mammal offspring and the most dependent on outside help and protection for the longest time. In the prosperous thirteenth century, for example, French communities seemed to love babies as much as more modern communities have. Before the eighteenth century, however, the high incidence of infant mortality generally made it difficult, if not impossible, for mothers to love their babies with full commitment.

In medieval times, general methods of caring for infants contributed to the high infant mortality. Until the mid-eighteenth century, infants were not suckled. These infants thus often had poor nourishment and missed the social contact and heat provided by a nursing mother. Babies were swaddled to keep them warm. When swaddled, they were not always cleaned, a neglect that often led to infection. The poor hygiene and the lack of social contact often was fatal; for example, in one Dublin foundling hospital at the end of the eighteenth century, the mortality rate was 99.6 percent.

In the twentieth century, a worldwide effort was made to lower infant mortality rates. The infant mortality rate is often used to reflect the general welfare of a country—that is, the degree to which adequate medical care, food, and other necessities are available to the entire population.

982   *Sociology*

Bibliography

Broek, Jan O. M., and John W. Webb. *A Geography of Mankind.* 3d ed. New York: McGraw-Hill, 1978. In this text, many demographic features are discussed. Parts of chapters and several graphs discuss the infant mortality rate. Broek and Webb use the infant mortality rate to discuss overall health in several countries.

"Infant Mortality—United States 1990." *Journal of the American Medical Association* 269 (April 7, 1993): 1616-1618. Reports the infant mortality statistics compiled by the Centers for Disease Control. The article also states goals for reducing this rate.

Miller, G. Tyler, Jr. *Environmental Science: An Introduction.* Belmont, Calif.: Wadsworth, 1986. Miller discusses many environmental problems and points toward what undeveloped countries must do to lower their infant mortality rates. Miller also uses several chapters and graphs to discuss many factors of population dynamics.

National Commission to Prevent Infant Mortality. "One-Stop Shopping for Infants and Pregnant Women: Improving Access Means More than Locating Services Under One Roof." *Public Welfare* 50 (Winter, 1992): 26-34. Explores many means by which poor women can receive prenatal care. Emphasizes the need to coordinate services so that care may be swiftly given.

"Sudden Infant Death Syndrome—United States, 1980-1988." *Journal of the American Medical Association* 268 (August 19, 1992): 856-858. Statistics for sudden infant death syndrome are reported; a discussion of the geographical dispersion of SIDS is included.

Tucker, Nicholas. "Boon or Burden." *History Today* 43 (September, 1993): 28-35. Tucker explores child rearing in medieval times. He finds that children's health was directly tied to the economics of the time. In prosperous times, children were well cared for; in times of famine, children may have been abandoned, as they were such trouble to feed. Tucker suggests that many practices led to infant mortality, including unclean conditions.

David R. Teske

Cross-References

Demographic Transition Theory of Population Growth, 499; Fertility, Mortality, and the Crude Birthrate, 761; Life Expectancy, 1087; Malthusian Theory of Population Growth, 1113; Population Growth and Population Control, 1421; Population Size and Human Ecology, 1428.

INFERENTIAL STATISTICS

Type of sociology: Sociological research
Field of study: Data collection and analysis

Inferential statistics involve a set of procedures that use sample data to make inferences about characteristics of a population. Sociologists use inferential techniques to test hypotheses about a variety of social phenomena.

   Principal terms
   DESCRIPTIVE STATISTICS: a branch of statistics that involves the use of numerical indices to summarize basic characteristics of a distribution of scores
   ESTIMATION: the use of a numerical characteristic of a sample to infer a population characteristic
   HYPOTHESIS TESTING: a decision-making process that considers whether assumptions made about a population are true given what is known to be true about a sample
   NORMAL DISTRIBUTION: a continuous distribution of a random variable in which the mean, median, and mode are equal; sometimes called a "bell-shaped" curve
   PARAMETER: a measure of a variable taken from a population
   POPULATION: the entire aggregate of individuals, items, scores, or observations from which random samples are drawn
   RANDOM SAMPLING: a method of sampling in which all items in the population have an equal probability of being selected
   SAMPLE: a set of items, scores, or observations selected from a population
   STATISTIC: a measure of a variable based on a sample of scores or observations
   STATISTICAL HYPOTHESIS: a numerical statement making a prediction regarding the potential outcomes of a study

Overview

Inferential statistics involve techniques that researchers use when they want to draw conclusions about specific aspects of a large group of individuals based on data collected from a smaller group. A population is defined as a collection of individuals, scores, or objects that represent the entire universe of observations of interest. A sample is defined as a limited number of individuals, scores, or objects that are drawn from the population. The sample, or subset of observations, is presumed to be representative of the population. In any research situation, the specific population to which generalizations are made needs to be defined. The population in one study, for example, could be defined as all the registered voters in the state of Washington. Since it would be too difficult to collect data from all the voters of the state, a sample of voters could be used to represent all the voters of the state. In inferential statistics, there is an assumption that any information obtained from the sample will probably hold true for the population.

There are two related branches in the field of inferential statistics: estimation and hypothesis testing. A parameter is a numerical characteristic of a population (such as the "average"). A statistic is a numerical characteristic of a sample. Estimation uses sample statistics to infer population parameters.

In hypothesis testing, researchers begin by making provisional statements about the characteristics of a population. Data are obtained from a sample and used to test the credibility of these statements. Thus, hypothesis testing is a decision-making process, one that considers if the original assumptions regarding the population are true given what is known to be true about the sample. A sociologist might want to test the hypothesis that attitudes toward foreign aid are associated with political party affiliation. A sample of Republicans and Democrats is used to obtain answers to questions about foreign aid. Inferential statistical procedures are then used with the sample data to decide whether there is an association between party affiliation and attitudes in the population of all Republicans and Democrats.

Statisticians make a distinction between descriptive and inferential statistics. Inferential techniques are grounded in probability theory and use samples to make inferences about populations. Descriptive statistics are numerical indices that describe important characteristics of an obtained set of data. Here the investigator is not concerned with estimating population parameters or in testing hypotheses about a population. Two examples of important characteristics of a set of observations are measures of central tendency and measures of variability. Measures of central tendency reflect the middle of the distribution, or where in the distribution scores tend to cluster. The mean (average of all the scores), the median (the point in the distribution below which lie half of the scores), and the mode (the score that occurs most often) are common measures of central tendency. Measures of variability are numerical indices that reflect how spread out the scores are in a distribution. One measure of variability is the range, which is the highest score minus the lowest score in the distribution. Another measure of the degree to which scores are spread out is the standard deviation—roughly speaking, the average distance all the scores are from the mean of the distribution.

If the researcher is interested in the above indices only as clues to the characteristics of the unknown population from which the sample is taken, then the focus shifts from describing the sample to using the sample values to infer population parameters. This change in perspective introduces an important concept involved in inferential statistics: random sampling. A random sample is a sample of scores taken from a population in such a way that each score of the population has an equal chance of being included in the sample. Random sampling is important in inferential statistics because it increases the likelihood that the sample will be representative of the population. In descriptive statistics, random sampling is irrelevant since the researcher is only interested in the obtained set of scores.

Applications

A research hypothesis is a statement about the expected outcome of a study. Examples of research hypotheses are, "There is a greater prevalence of mental illness among an urban population compared with a rural population"; "The number of homicides increases during economic recessions"; and "There is a relation between the amount of education of parents and the number of children they have." In conducting a study to answer a research hypothesis, the use of inferential statistics requires the hypothesis to be stated in a specific numerical form called a statistical hypothesis. Statistical hypotheses always come in pairs—null and alternative hypotheses. Following is an example of how null and alternative hypotheses are stated in a research method commonly used in sociology, the correlational design.

When two variables are correlated, such as educational level of parents and number of children, it means that the variables are associated, or occur together. The statistical index of a correlation is called a correlation coefficient, a number that can range from -1 to +1. The higher the absolute value of the coefficient, the stronger the association between the variables. A positive correlation means that higher values of one variable occur with higher values of the other variable. For example, the more violence children watch on television, the more aggressive they are with peers. A negative correlation means that higher values of one variable are associated with lower values of the other variable. For example, among parents, higher levels of education are associated with fewer offspring. If two variables are unrelated, the correlation coefficient is zero.

In the context of a correlational design, the null hypothesis is a numerical statement that there is no relation between two variables. The symbol for a population correlation is the Greek letter ρ ("rho"). The null hypothesis is denoted as H_0. Thus, the null hypothesis is expressed as $H_0: \rho = 0$. The researcher typically wants to reject the null hypothesis, that is, to disprove the statement that $H_0: \rho = 0$. As stated previously, statistical hypotheses appear in pairs. The second statistical hypothesis is called the alternative hypothesis, denoted H_1. In this example, the alternative hypothesis is stated, $H_1: \rho \neq 0$. Note that the null and alternative hypotheses are mutually exclusive (they both cannot be true) and collectively exhaustive (no other outcomes are possible).

Statistical hypotheses are always statements about populations, not samples. Data from a sample are used to decide if the null hypothesis is probably false. As an example, a sociologist randomly selects fifty married couples. Information about the educational level of the parents and their number of children is obtained. A correlation coefficient is computed based on this sample. Hypothesis testing involves making a decision. The decision here is whether the sample correlation is large enough to reject the null hypothesis that states there is no correlation between educational level and number of offspring, in the population. Stated differently, can the researcher conclude that the population correlation coefficient is not 0? If the sample correlation is "large enough," the researcher will reject the null hypothesis and accept the validity of the alternative hypothesis; that is, the researcher will favor the statement, $H_1: \rho \neq 0$. Accordingly, the researcher will feel confident that the research hypothesis is supported—that there is a relation between parents' educational level and their number of children. Statisticians have established guidelines for when the null hypothesis should be rejected. If there is sufficient evidence to reject the null hypothesis, the researcher will say that the finding is statistically significant. Note, however, that the term "statistically significant" does not necessarily mean the finding is important. It is a statistical concept that refers only to the likelihood that the null hypothesis is false. Whether the finding is important has nothing to do with statistics. The importance of a statistically significant finding is subjectively determined by the scientific community.

It is important to understand that hypothesis testing is probabilistic. To say that the outcome of a study is statistically significant means that the null hypothesis is *probably* false. There is uncertainty in hypothesis testing because one is using a sample to represent a population. It is possible that the sample is not a perfect representation of the population. When the sample does not perfectly reflect the population, there is sampling error. The more the characteristics of the sample deviate from the characteristics of the population, the greater the sampling error. What if, for example, simply by bad luck, the fifty married couples in the study were not a true reflection of the population of married couples? The investigator might be making a mistake in rejecting the null hypothesis. One way to reduce the likelihood of making such a mistake is to use large samples (collect many observations). Large sample sizes tend to provide a more accurate picture of the population. No matter how large the size of the sample, however, there will always be some uncertainty in hypothesis testing, and there will always be the possibility that the null hypothesis has been mistakenly rejected. It is also possible to err in the direction of not rejecting the null hypothesis when one should.

Statisticians have developed numerous hypothesis-testing procedures that apply to many different study designs. Consequently, the field of inferential statistics has broad applicability, ranging from the behavioral sciences to biology, agriculture, and industry.

Context

The development of inferential and descriptive statistical techniques evolved from an ancient process of tabulating numerical information about nations known as "state arithmetic." The word "statistics" itself originated from the German *Statistik*, coined by Gottfried Achenwall, a German political geographer around 1748. Achenwall engaged in the collection of information regarding the strengths and weaknesses of the nation in order to make predictions about the future of certain economic, social and political resources.

The roots of formal inferential statistical methods began in the 1600's in Europe during a time of great scientific awakening. Tremendous advances in mathematics and physics were being made by such people as Galileo, Johannes Kepler, Isaac Newton, and Blaise Pascal, among others. In 1662, the Englishman John Graunt published a comprehensive study using statistics to detail the weekly mortality rate of Londoners. Included in the twenty-year study were descriptive measures of death and disease as well as one of the first examples of inferential estimation. Using a crude table of mortality rates, Graunt could estimate the average life expectancy of individuals based on their current age, economic status, and family history. This mortality table became quite popular with insurance companies operating in London during that time. Graunt's work of making quantitative comparisons of large groups of people, and then drawing conclusions based on the results, is thought to be one of the earliest examples of sociological research. Similar methods were adopted by later sociologists such as Émile Durkheim, whose seminal work on suicide rates was published in 1897.

The first known example of a statistical test was conducted by John Arbuthnot, an Englishman who wrote a paper in 1710 attempting to prove the existence of God. In that paper, Arbuthnot formed two statistical hypotheses regarding the probability of male and female births in London covering a period of eighty-one years. Using probability theory, he concluded that the higher frequency of male births was not consistent with a random state of affairs. This result lent support to Arbuthnot's notion that some planning was involved in the creation of humankind and that the planning could be attributed to God.

The most important discovery in inferential statistics was that of the normal curve, attributed to the French mathematician Abraham De Moivre in 1733. The concept of the normal (or bell-shaped) curve underlies most modern statistical tests used for hypothesis testing.

An important figure in the development of statistics, and its use in sociology, was Lambert Adolphe Jacques Quételet, a Belgian astronomer who published a major work on human society entitled *Sur l'homme et le développement de ses facultés* (1835; *A Treatise on Man and the Development of His Faculties*, 1842). Using statistical methods and probability theory, Quételet discussed a number of different aspects of society including births, deaths, and criminal behavior as a product of environmental circumstances.

The greatest advances in inferential statistics have occurred in the twentieth century. Mathematicians have developed increasingly sophisticated methods for making inferences. Sociologists now have available numerous statistical tests for testing scientific hypotheses using an array of research designs. The advent of computer technology and availability of statistical software programs allow sociologists to use very large samples and examine relations among many variables.

Bibliography

Blalock, Hubert M. *Social Statistics*. New York: McGraw-Hill, 1960. A comprehensive statistical text written primarily for students of sociology. Most of the book is devoted to methods of inference; the first two sections provide the reader with a good background in statistical theory and descriptive aspects. This is an excellent reference text for those who are not particularly interested in mathematical formulas.

Grimm, Laurence G. *Statistical Applications for the Behavioral Sciences*. New York: John Wiley & Sons, 1993. This textbook devotes a majority of its pages to inferential statistics, including coverage of a variety of specific statistical tests. The reader need not have a strong background in mathematics or prior experience with statistics. An introductory chapter to inferential techniques is provided that covers the basic foundation of hypothesis testing.

Jaccard, James, and Michael Becker. *Statistics for the Behavioral Sciences.* 2d ed. Belmont, Calif.: Wadsworth, 1990. One of the most well-written and organized statistics texts available. Excellent coverage is given to inferential statistics with examples pertaining to the behavioral sciences. The text is written for the introductory student, and each chapter includes instruction in how to present the results of statistical analyses.

Tankard, James W., Jr. *The Statistical Pioneers.* Cambridge, Mass.: Schenkman, 1984. This small paperback book provides a captivating historical background of statistics with detailed examinations of the theorists who contributed to its development. A perfect book for those who are interested in the people behind the theories. This book includes interesting descriptions of statistical theory without the use of mathematics.

Walker, Helen M. *Studies in the History of Statistical Method.* New York: Arno Press, 1975. A standard text of statistical history from the beginning of time. Those more familiar with the basics regarding hypothesis testing and methodology will gain a new perspective of statistics not usually covered in beginning texts. Although complex proofs are discussed throughout the book, their understanding is not necessary in order to gain an appreciation of the history of statistics.

Yule, George Udny, and M. G. Kendall. *An Introduction to the Theory of Statistics.* 14th ed. New York: Hafner, 1950. This large text is considered standard reading for students enrolled in most undergraduate statistics courses in the United Kingdom. Although it is written in a style that is rather unfamiliar to most American students, the text covers all of the basic areas of statistical methods. It is ideally suited for those who possess only a limited knowledge of mathematics.

Laurence G. Grimm
Evelyn Buday

Cross-References

Causal Relationships, 205; Descriptive Statistics, 519; Experimentation in Sociological Research, 721; Hypotheses and Hypothesis Testing, 915; Logical Inference: Deduction and Induction, 1093; Measures of Central Tendency, 1147; Measures of Variability, 1153; Quantitative Research, 1546; Triangulation, 2071; Validity and Reliability in Measurement, 2136.

INHERITANCE SYSTEMS

Type of sociology: Social institutions
Field of study: The family

Inheritance systems are concerned with the succession of the property, authority, names, obligations, and privileges of the dead to the living. The governance of these processes is often determined or strongly influenced by kinship.

Principal terms
BILATERAL DESCENT: the transmission of property rights or descent through both the female and male, in a manner that either is equal or does not emphasize either line
DESCENT: the category of closeness of association with others through kinship
FAMILY: a concept denoting biological relationships involving mating, filiation, and sibship, these explicit and implicit functions of which are found in all known human societies
INHERITANCE: the procedures that apply to the succession of property, privileges, and obligations from the dead to the living
KINSHIP: socially recognized genealogical relationships based on consanguine and/or affinal associations
KINSHIP SYSTEM: a social unit in which all elements are genealogically determined
MATRILINEAL DESCENT: the transmission of authority, name, property, privilege, and obligations primarily through females; also called uterine descent
PATRILINEAL DESCENT: the transmission of authority, name, property, privilege, and obligations primarily through males; also called agnatic descent

Overview
Inheritance is the mechanism regulating the transmission of property, rights, duties, and authority in a society from the dead to the living. It has been a central concern of anthropology and sociology because the rights and obligations set forth by rules of inheritance underlie many social, economic, and political relationships. Generally, inheritance is based on the descent rules practiced by a particular society. There are two types of descent: jural and biological. Jural descent is often based on biological descent and is the mechanism by which rank and property are handed down from one generation to the next.

Biological descent, in colloquial language, means that there is a "relationship by blood" or that people share substance from previous generations. The meaning of "blood relationship" varies from society to society; it is a cultural construct. Some

990 Sociology

peoples behave as if the blood relationship occurs only through a male or female progenitor. Others assume that blood or substance is passed on through both females and males.

Within each descent system there are variations. In unilineal systems, descent is determined through the male ("patrilineal") or the female ("matrilineal"). In the case of bilateral descent systems, an individual belongs to two groups: the mother's and the father's. It must be kept in mind that although the descent system may be patrilineal, matrilineal, or bilateral, that does not mean that the inheritance system is uniform. In one patrilineal society, an offspring may inherit only the name of the father, while in another, all the children inherit the father's name but only the eldest son inherits the family property.

Inheritance and descent are not always traceable. People can claim common origins, as is the case of people with a common clan membership. They claim a common ancestor but cannot actually trace all the connections. Some societies allow for adoption, while others can claim descendance or inheritance on a spiritual basis; in Christianity, for example, the Apostle Paul teaches that Christians are spiritual descendants of Abraham and inherit the covenant relationship claimed by Abraham's descendants. Descent groups exist in horticultural communities because they provide the basis for the structural framework of the society.

Applications

In inheritance systems, four principles are usually followed. First, men generally control property. Even if resources are owned by a female, they are usually under her brother's control. Second, inheritance rules are based on the descent system: it is the system of descent that determines group membership and position, and this fact influences inheritance practices. Third, inheritance in all systems occurs through both the male and female line; however, the importance and determination of what is inherited differs from group to group. Fourth, primary kin do not mate. The definition of primary kin varies according to different cultures. In some groups, primary kin may be those with a common father; in others, they may be those with a common father's father.

Patrilineal (also called male or agnatic) inheritance and descent are most common. The patrilineal system dominates where the male is the breadwinner or where the resources acquired by the male have greater symbolic significance. For example, in some societies both males and females bring in food, but that hunted by men is considered more important and prestigious than that gathered by females.

In patrilineal systems, members of the lineage trace their descent through males to a common ancestor. Thus, male and female siblings belong to the same group as their father, father's father, father's siblings, and father's brother's children. Although a woman belongs to the descent group of her father, her children do not belong to the same group.

In a patrilineal system, women are of little importance. They neither control nor bring resources to the descent group. Property and children belong to the males. There is, however, variation. Often, women control matters within the house and can gain prominence by bringing a good dowry. In the patrilineal system, the son inherits the family name; thus, the father-son-brother tie dominates and residence is patrilocal—that is, with the male—and often includes the male's descent group.

An example of a patrilineal society is China before World War II, where a family consisted of aged parents, their sons and their sons' wives, their grandsons and their grandsons' wives, and so on. Residence was patrilocal, with the father and male relatives dominating. The primary social unit was the *tsu*, which consisted of males who traced their descent back about five generations to a common ancestor.

Women were passed on to other families in marriage and had no claim to property or offspring. Dowry was practiced, and the bride's family sent gifts and resources to the groom's family. Often, the bride maintained control of that dowry and used it to provide loans, on which she might collect interest. Also, she had control of the domestic realm. She retained membership in her father's descent group. This did not mean that she was powerless. Depending on her family of descent, her mother would assist her at birth, and her brothers would help her if she was mistreated by the family into which she married.

Chinese families preferred to obtain women from families of lower status than their own; such women made more submissive wives because they did not have strong backing from their own families. Such a woman's dowry would also be greater, since a lower-status family would pay more to have a daughter marry into a higher-status kin group, giving the female's kin group access to a more powerful lineage. In essence, the power that a woman held in her new household depended on the strength and willingness of her lineage to support her. Unfortunately, in most cases, such support was not forthcoming.

Matrilineal systems are different from patrilineal societies in that descent occurs through the female line. Such systems are found where women are the primary breadwinners in a horticultural economy. Although descent occurs through the female line and women may have considerable authority, their authority is not exclusive—they share it with men. The position of women is, however, higher than it is in patrilineal communities.

In a matrilineal system, children belong to the descent group of the mother. This group includes the mother, the mother's mother, the mother's siblings, and the mother's sister's children.

In matrilineal societies, the marriage tie is usually weak because the future of the male lies with his sister. His children do not belong to him. Authority rests in the sister's family. It is the wife's brother who distributes family resources, organizes work, settles disputes, distributes inheritance, and supervises rituals and work. The male's future lies with his sister's son. The crucial relationships are mother-daughter-brother.

An example of a matrilineal society is that of the Hopi of northeastern Arizona. The Hopi are an agricultural people who have lived in the region for more than two thousand years. The society is divided into clans that are based on matrilineal descent. At birth, each individual is assigned to the clan of the mother. In fact, for the Hopi, the sense of self is tied to the clan, not the individual. Marriage is clan exogamous. Each clan is divided into a subclan, or lineage, that is headed by a woman—usually, the eldest female. It is this woman's brother or maternal uncle, however, who manages lineage affairs, although she is not a mere figurehead. She solves disputes and has other areas of authority. Decisions at all levels are made by a consensus of the men, but women have considerable influence behind the scenes.

Residence is matrilocal, and the married couple live with a maternal relative, often in a separate house but on family land. Husbands farm their wives' land, and the harvests belong to their wives. For the man's labor, his wife gives him food and shelter. The father has no real authority over his son. The children are disciplined by the mother's brother. A man's loyalty is divided between his wife and sister, but if his wife believes that he is not providing adequately, all she has to do is place his belongings outside the door and he must leave—the divorce has taken place.

Double descent, which also influences inheritance, comes in two forms; double descent and ambilineal descent. In double descent, matrilineal descent serves some purposes and patrilineal descent serves others. In ambilineal descent, the individual can belong to either the male or the female line, but not to both.

Bilateral descent and inheritance are transmitted through both the male and the female line, and they do not favor either one. As a result, the organization and determination of membership are very different from those of the descent systems described previously. In the previously described systems, membership is determined by having a common ancestor. In a bilateral system, group membership is determined by others' relationship to an individual. Thus, the unit is neither corporate nor permanent but continually changing, because the individual's parents die, children are born, and the unit ceases to exist when the individual dies. In this system, there are no permanent leaders and no set rules for inheritance.

An example of the bilateral system is found in Western industrial societies such as the United States. In this system, there is an emphasis on mobility and individuality. Groups, which are called "kindred," are centered on an individual. They initially consist of the individual's parents, siblings, and relatives on both the father's and the mother's side. The membership of the individual's kindred varies from culture to culture, but it usually consists of people who share a common great-grandparent.

Kindred come together for specific occasions, such as baptisms, school graduations, and funerals. Marriage is kindred exogamous, but inheritance is usually by will, not by custom; and, although a system of rights and duties exists, many of its functions have been usurped by the state, and dependence on kindred is not generally considered essential for survival.

Context

The study of inheritance led to a focus on kinship as an aspect of social structure. The inquiry began with lawyers and the legal profession, the influence of which is seen in the legal terminology of concepts such as rights, claims, and *patriae*. This is because of the importance of inheritance, succession, and marriage. All societies pass on social position and property at death, and these are usually passed on to kinsmen. For the sake of orderly succession, societies have rules regarding which kinsmen inherit what. Marriage also influences legitimacy, inheritance, and succession.

Lawyers generally referred to Roman law for ideas concerning rules to determine marriage, inheritance, and succession. During the nineteenth century, lawyers were strongly influenced by evolutionary concepts in their attempts to explain social institutions. Sir Henry Maine, a student of comparative jurisprudence, argued in his *Ancient Law* (1861) that the "patriarchal joint family" was the original form of the Indo-European family. J. L. McLennan, an ethnologist, argued against Maine's thesis and posited in *Primitive Marriage* (1865) that the original form of kinship was through females.

Lewis Henry Morgan, an anthropologist, spent his life studying the Iroquois. His *Systems of Consanguinity and Affinity of the Human Family* (1871) was also influenced by the concept of evolution, but it established kinship as a central focus of study.

As psychoanalysis became popular, American anthropologists such as Franz Boas and Robert Lowie and the Polish anthropologist Bronislaw Malinowski challenged evolutionary explanations and attempted to explain kinship in terms of a people's culture, focusing on feelings and sentiments among kinsmen. The prominent change in kinship studies came when the English social anthropologist A. R. Radcliffe-Brown, by using the comparative approach, sought to find generalizations along the lines of the "laws" in the natural sciences. Although the search for laws has now been abandoned, the comparative method is still prominent.

Building on the work of Radcliffe-Brown, British social anthropologists such as Edward Evans-Pritchard and Meyer Fortes set forth the functions of descent units. As a result, kinship was perceived in two ways: looking at a whole society to determine how kinship groups are formed and function, and deciphering the network of relationships that bind individuals. Later, Claude Lévi-Strauss's *Les Structures élémentaries de la parenté* (1949; *The Elementary Structures of Kinship*, 1969) refocused kinship studies on terminology and the formation of alliances.

Kinship was the foundation on which much of the structural-functional anthropology was based. The study of kinship was considered important because all societies had kin relationships in one form or another. Kinship was also the basis of establishing relationships, which determined the rights and duties of members in a society. It was also a means of establishing a relationship with the external world. In addition, it was posited that certain kinship systems were related to adaptation technologies or environments. For these reasons, kinship was crucial to the structural-functional theoretical orientation.

Although kinship once was the major focus of social anthropology and was prominent in the disciplines of sociology and anthropology in general, it has not been emphasized in recent years. Theoretical concerns began to focus on symbols, economic and political development, and other issues. Kinship analysis, with the emphasis on descent, related individuals to bounded groups. There was a contradiction: How can people belong to groups that are seemingly unbounded by descent? Also, with the

994   *Sociology*

emphasis on alliance, the value of differentiating between politico-jural and domestic domains within groups was challenged.

Marilyn Strathern (1988) argued that it was a defect of Western thinking to make the person the center of social relations. She held that the emphasis should be on differentiating relationships.

During the 1960's and 1970's, the core concepts of kinship had been challenged as faith in the structural-functional model eroded. Researchers began to realize that one could not assume kinship systems provided a system of rights and duties for orderly reproduction and inheritance in all societies.

With the rise of the feminist movement in the 1960's, feminist anthropologists focused on kinship theory to determine the female place and potential. In past literature, women were associated with the "domestic" realm, not the politico-jural realm, which made them universally less valuable. Anthropologists such as David Schneider and feminists challenged this assumption, successfully arguing that concepts such as "patrilineal descent" and "patrilineal inheritance" disguise complexities and distinctions.

Also, the assumption that the fundamental units of kinship are genealogical was challenged. In the past, researchers had assumed that

> creating human offspring—through heterosexual intercourse, pregnancy, and parturition—constitutes the biological process on which we presume culture builds such social relationships as marriage, filiation, and co-parenthood.
> Although it is apparent that heterosexual intercourse, pregnancy, and parturition are involved in human reproduction, it is also apparent that producing humans entails more than this. (Yanagisako and Collier, 1994).

Given the current state of knowledge concerning kinship, inheritance, and descent, the focus in the future will be on the symbolic meaning of relationships. There will be a stronger emphasis on the meaning set forth in the specific culture being studied rather than on looking for general laws or classifications. This change will have ramifications in that the researcher will start with a different set of assumptions. For example, Yanagisako and Collier (1994) state:

> Rather than assume that the fundamental units of gender and kinship in every society are defined by the difference between males and females in sexual reproduction, we ask what are the socially meaningful categories people imply and encounter in specific social contexts and what symbols and meanings underlie them.

Bibliography

Borofsky, Robert. *Assessing Cultural Anthropology*. New York: McGraw-Hill, 1993. A superb collection of articles setting forth a critique of different fields of anthropology and new directions of research.

Fox, Robin. *Kinship and Marriage*. Baltimore: Penguin Books, 1967. The best total treatment of kinship and inheritance systems. Sets forth the guiding principles of kinship and the variations and rationale for each system from a structural-functional perspective.

Schneider, David. *American Kinship: A Cultural Account.* Englewood Cliffs, N.J.: Prentice-Hall, 1968. A crucial work that set new directions in the study of kinship, emphasizing values, meanings, and interpretations.

Strathern, Marilyn. *The Gender of the Gift: Problems with Women and Problems with Society in Melanesia.* Berkeley: University of California Press, 1988. A critique of traditional kinship studies from a feminist perspective. It is one of the key works that changed the direction and focus of the field of kinship. It is, however, a difficult book to follow.

Yanagisako, Sylvia, and Jane Collier. "Gender and Kinship Reconsidered: Toward a Unified Analysis." In *Assessing Cultural Anthropology*, edited by Robert Borofsky. New York: McGraw-Hill, 1994. A superb review article critiquing the field of kinship and setting forth a proposal for new directions in research concerning family and kinship.

Arthur W. Helweg

Cross-References

Arranged Marriages, 134; The Family: Functionalist versus Conflict Theory Views, 739; The Family: Nontraditional Families, 746; Nuclear and Extended Families, 1303; Patriarchy versus Matriarchy, 1349; Residence Patterns, 1635.

INSTITUTIONAL RACISM

Type of sociology: Racial and ethnic relations
Field of study: Theories of prejudice and discrimination

Institutional racism refers to the manner in which a society's institutions operate systematically—directly and indirectly—to favor some groups over others regarding access to opportunities and valued resources. This concept helps explain how a society can discriminate unintentionally against particular groups.

Principal terms
DISCRIMINATION: the denial of opportunities and rights to certain groups on the basis of race or ethnicity
ETHNIC GROUP: a group distinguished principally by its distinctive cultural heritage
IDEOLOGY: a system of belief about reality that usually reflects and supports the interests of one segment of society over those of others
INSTITUTIONS: stable social arrangements that perform basic activities in society; legal institutions such as courts, for example, enforce laws made by political institutions
MINORITY GROUP: any group that, on the basis of physical or cultural characteristics, receives fewer of society's rewards; a "minority" group, therefore, can be in the majority numerically, such as blacks in South Africa
PREJUDICE: arbitrary beliefs or feelings about an individual of a certain ethnic or racial group or toward the group as a whole
SEGREGATION: the physical separation of groups, usually imposed by one group on another
SOCIAL STRATIFICATION: a system in which groups are ranked hierarchically; ethnic or racial stratification is one type of stratification

Overview

Racial discrimination, in the most general sense, is the denial of equal opportunities and rights to groups on the basis of race or ethnicity. The study of institutional racism (sometimes called institutional discrimination), rather than looking at individual attitudes as an explanation for racial inequality, focuses on the way society itself is structured or organized. Sociologist Joe R. Feagin distinguishes among four types of discrimination, and he includes two types of institutional racism in his typology: "direct institutionalized [institutional] discrimination" and "indirect institutionalized discrimination." An example of the former, which was documented by Diana Pearce in a 1976 study in Detroit, is the practice by real estate companies of "steering" African Americans away from homes in white areas. This direct form of institutional discrimination is the easiest to identify, understand, and (given the will) eradicate. Most sociologists, however, use the term "institutional racism" to refer to the second type noted by Feagin, indirect discrimination.

The term was coined in 1967 by African American civil rights activist Stokely Carmichael (Kwame Toure) and Charles V. Hamilton. Toure and Hamilton were attempting to shift attention away from individual, overt, and direct forms of racial discrimination as the principal explanation for the persistence of racial inequality. To distinguish between individual and institutional racism, they offered the following example in their influential book *Black Power: The Politics of Liberation in America* (1967):

> When white terrorists bomb a black church and kill five black children, that is an act of individual racism, widely deplored by most segments of the society. But when in the same city—Birmingham, Alabama—five hundred black babies die each year because of the lack of proper food, shelter and medical facilities, and thousands more are destroyed and maimed physically, emotionally and intellectually because of conditions of poverty and discrimination in the black community, that is a function of institutional racism.

From the perspective of sociologists studying unintentional and indirect forms of institutional racism, consequences are the most important indicator of discrimination. If the results or consequences of a policy or practice are unequal along racial lines, then indirect institutional racism is thought to exist. As sociologist Jerome Skolnick avers, "a society in which most of the good jobs are held by one race, and the dirty jobs are held by people of another color, is a society in which racism is institutionalized no matter what the beliefs of its members are."

In the 1980's, statistical evidence of racism could be found in every institutional area. In 1980, African Americans, for example, constituted nearly 12 percent of the population of the United States but only 1.5 percent of the country's elected officials. Almost 50 percent of all prison inmates in the U.S. are black. The dropout rate for blacks in education is twice that of whites. The infant mortality rate for whites in 1985 was 9.3 per 1,000 live births, but for blacks it was 18.2 per 1,000. The maternal mortality rate in 1984 for whites was 5.4 per 100,000 lives births; for black women it was 19.7. Forty-three percent of black children and 16 percent of white children under the age of eighteen lived in poverty in 1986, and the median per capita wealth for blacks in 1984 was $6,837, compared to $32,667 for whites. These inequities strongly suggest the existence of institutional racism.

In their book *Institutional Racism in America* (1969), Louis Knowles and Kenneth Prewitt provide examples of the consequences of racist practices, irrespective of intent, in the United States' economic, educational, political, legal, and medical institutions. Knowles and Prewitt noted, for example, that in the 1960's blacks owned no more than 50,000 businesses. If black ownership were proportional to the black percentage of the U.S. population, then blacks should have owned closer to 500,000 businesses. As long as minority groups are receiving less than their proportional share of society's rewards, institutional racism is said to be operating.

The fact that blacks do not own businesses proportional to their percentage of the population alludes to another important element of institutional racism: the interrelatedness of institutions. A society's institutions are interrelated in ways such that exclusion from one frequently means exclusion from all. Harold M. Baron has called this phenomenon the "web" of urban racism. Black enterprise in the United States has been stifled by discrimination in education and the job market and by discriminatory banking practices that make it difficult for African Americans to secure loans to start businesses.

An example of what sociologist Martin Marger calls the "spillover" effect of discrimination from one institutional area into another concerns the fact that, in the past few decades, new industrial jobs have been created in the suburbs and not in urban areas. Often factories are built in these outlying areas for economic rather than racial reasons, but because of real estate practices (among other factors) such as those documented by Pearce in Detroit, African Americans are highly concentrated in urban areas where there are few well-paying and secure jobs. In effect, therefore, decisions to establish new firms in, or to relocate old ones disproportionately to, the suburbs discriminate institutionally against African Americans.

The study of institutional racism also places considerable importance on the deep historical roots and lasting effects of direct racial discrimination. The effects of earlier practices, policies, and laws that were designed purposely to exclude and harm particular groups have continued to be felt even after most of them were eliminated by legislative and other measures. The cumulative effect of this discrimination left African Americans and other racial and ethnic minorities—notably Mexican Americans/Chicanos, Native Americans, and Puerto Ricans—at a competitive disadvantage with majority group members in virtually every institutional area.

Applications

Knowledge gained from the study of institutional racism is applied in a number of ways in attempts to counter institutional racism. Among the many approaches are civil rights legislation; executive orders, such as those for affirmative action; and changes in the criteria used by admissions offices in higher education.

Historically, college admissions officers have relied on so-called objective criteria in their decisions. The most important of these criteria have been class rank, grade point average, scores on the Scholastic Aptitude Test (SAT), participation in extracurricular activities, and the quality of the high school attended by applicants. While it was not necessarily the intent of colleges to discriminate against members of minority groups, reliance on these criteria, in effect, did so. Minority-group applicants, for example, are disproportionately poorer than majority-group applicants. As a consequence, they are more likely to have attended poorly funded schools that offer fewer extracurricular activities and that generally provide a lower-quality education. Minority students also are more likely to have to work and to care for siblings, which in turn affects their academic performance and participation in extracurricular activities.

Because of studies of institutional racism, universities and colleges were able to see how their admissions policies were discriminating against members of certain groups. In the 1960's, most of these institutions adjusted their admissions processes, including the criteria used to determine admissibility and predict academic potential, to take into account the disadvantaged positions in which members of minority groups find themselves. Instead of automatically penalizing students for not participating in extracurricular activities, for example, admissions officers obtained information from applicants and high school guidance counselors on the activities available in the school and on applicants' responsibilities, including work, which may have made it difficult for them to participate in school-sponsored programs. Admissions officers also began to consider possible biases in standardized tests and accorded test scores less weight in their decision to admit or not to admit a student.

Affirmative action programs are principally intended to be remedies for institutional discrimination. Affirmative action requires race consciousness rather than "color blindness," because (as studies of institutional racism have shown) society is structured in such a way that race-neutral or color-blind policies exclude members of minority groups. In the area of employment, for example, affirmative action programs were created to increase the pool of qualified minority candidates and to eliminate discriminatory practices from the selection process. Approaches include advertising positions in places where potential candidates from minority groups can be reached more effectively.

A long-standing and common recruitment practice has been to hire new workers through personal connections. Because of prior racial discrimination, however, the people doing the hiring were disproportionately white, and their connections tended to be white as well. Hence, African Americans and members of other minority groups often were excluded. Affirmative action programs have sought to eliminate this practice, which, even if its practitioners did not intend it to be, is discriminatory. Advertising positions widely, even nationally when possible, has been one remedy prescribed.

A seemingly innocuous practice used by some police agencies provides another example of institutional racism. Many police forces maintained a minimum height requirement, which placed Latinos, Asians, and women at a disadvantage. Because members of these groups generally tend to be shorter than white or black males, this requirement reduced significantly the pool of qualified applicants from these groups. Although the height requirement seemed to be neutral, or nondiscriminatory, it in fact discriminated against particular groups; intent is not necessary for a requirement to be discriminatory. In many instances, such discriminatory job requirements have been eliminated or modified.

In yet another example, seniority systems, established to provide job security for longtime employees, discriminate against minority group members. Blacks are adversely affected in disproportionate numbers by this practice because, as a group, they were denied job opportunities on the basis of race until court decisions and legislative initiatives made it illegal to discriminate on this basis. Being the most recently hired employees, they would be the first fired when layoffs became necessary. While seniority systems may not have been established to discriminate intentionally against members of certain groups, they did so nevertheless. As a consequence, the courts in a number of instances have ordered employers to cease the practice.

The Civil Rights Act of 1991, signed into law by President George Bush, was drafted partly in response to a number of Supreme Court decisions that, in effect, required plaintiffs in discrimination suits to prove intent on the part of the defendant, usually an employer. The bill stipulates that once the plaintiff is able to show that an employer's practice adversely affects a particular group, then the burden falls on the employer to "demonstrate that the challenged practice is job related for the position in question and consistent with business necessity." The bill is consistent with an approach designed to counter institutional discrimination. A practice is deemed discriminatory if it has a disparate impact on any group, irrespective of intent.

Between the election of President Ronald Reagan in 1980 and the passage of this bill, the tendency had been to place the burden of proof increasingly on plaintiffs in discrimination cases. In other words, plaintiffs had to prove that an employer intended to discriminate against them—a very difficult, often impossible, task. This approach of the 1980's was a departure from the approach that began in the 1960's, based on countering institutional discrimination. The Civil Rights Bill of 1991 returned, although in a somewhat weakened fashion, to the earlier approach intended to counter institutional racism.

Context

Prior to the 1920's, few sociologists studied race relations. When they did, beginning with the work of such sociologists as Edward Ross, Lester Ward, and William Sumner, the tendency was to view discrimination as conscious acts performed by prejudiced individuals; this view continued to dominate until the 1960's. The assumption inherent in this "prejudice causes discrimination" model, as noted by Joe Feagin and Clairece Feagin, is that the way to eradicate racial discrimination is to eliminate racial prejudice. It was believed that, with time, this would happen. Racial discrimination was seen as an aberration, inconsistent with American ideals of equality and justice. Swedish sociologist Gunnar Myrdal captured this belief well in the title of his classic and influential work on discrimination in the United States, *An American Dilemma: The Negro Problem and Modern Democracy* (1944).

Beginning with the pioneering work on immigration by American sociologist Robert Park in the first half of the twentieth century, immigration scholars as a rule predicted the eventual assimilation of various ethnic groups. While most conceded that the situation of African Americans was unique in some respects, their assimilation into American society was also predicted. Along with this, it was thought, would come the diminution and eventual elimination of racial prejudice. Milton Gordon, in the 1960's, developed a more sophisticated theory of assimilation, in which he distinguished between cultural and structural assimilation. Structural assimilation refers to the ability of members of a minority group to participate in such societal groups and institutions as businesses, government, and private clubs; Gordon pointed out that cultural assimilation does not assure equal opportunities in these areas.

In the 1950's and 1960's, the Civil Rights movement made great strides in attaining legal equality for African Americans and other minorities. Robert Blauner observed that initially the Civil Rights movement adopted the view that blacks, if guaranteed legal equality, would be able to assimilate into American society. In time, however, it became increasingly apparent to civil rights activists as well as to many scholars that racist ideologies and prejudiced attitudes were not the "essence" of racism. Rather, racism was inherent in society's institutions. Blauner wrote in *Racial Oppression in America* (1972) that "the processes that maintain domination—control of whites over nonwhites—are built into the major social institutions." Because these institutions "either exclude or restrict the participation of racial groups by procedures that have become conventional," Blauner stated, prejudice is not needed as a motivating force.

This realization quickly led to a fundamental change in the study of race relations, a change spurred by the cultural climate of social unrest and protest during the 1960's. The Black Power movement of the 1960's called attention to how little the status of blacks had changed or promised to change despite progressive civil rights legislation and a reduction in racial prejudice. This relatively new way of analyzing racial stratification shifted the focus from individual expressions of racism to the manner in which society itself was structured and operated to favor some groups over others.

Bibliography

Baldwin, James. *The Fire Next Time*. New York: Dell, 1963. Although Baldwin's book predates the concept of institutional racism, it presents a beautifully written analysis of racism and an unrivaled statement on being black in the United States. The book also predicted the Watts riot and the civil unrest in many cities in the mid- to late 1960's.

Blauner, Robert. *Racial Oppression in America*. New York: Harper & Row, 1972. In this series of essays, Blauner's central thesis is that racial minorities in the United States are internal colonies created by the capitalist system. Includes case studies in institutional racism. Particularly well suited to a college audience. Contains a good index but no bibliography.

Carmichael, Stokely, and Charles V. Hamilton. *Black Power: The Politics of Liberation in America*. New York: Vintage Books, 1967. Writing in the aftermath of the urban unrest of the 1960's, the authors, both civil rights activists (Hamilton is a political scientist as well), exhort African Americans to seize the initiative in effecting social change. Labeled by some as an unbalanced critique, the book nevertheless is valuable to students of race relations. Especially recommended for students with a knowledge of African American history.

Feagin, Joe R. *Racial and Ethnic Relations*. Englewood Cliffs, N.J.: Prentice-Hall, 1989. This popular introductory text focuses on theories and research current at the time of its publication and discusses racial and ethnic minorities in their broader social contexts. Well documented; both the index and notes at the end of each chapter are very useful. Two other good introductory texts that provide excellent bibliographies should also be noted: Richard T. Schaefer's *Racial and Ethnic Groups* (HarperCollins, 1990) and Martin N. Marger's *Race and Ethnic Relations: American and Global Perspectives* (Wadsworth, 1991).

Feagin, Joe R., and Clairece Booher Feagin. *Discrimination American Style: Institutional Racism and Sexism.* Englewood Cliffs, N.J.: Prentice-Hall, 1978. This remains one of the best and most accessible discussions of institutional racism and sexism. By comparing institutional racism and sexism, the authors enhance understanding of each and illuminate the nature of institutions. Contains footnotes and a very good index but no separate bibliography.

Jones, James M. *Prejudice and Racism.* Reading, Mass.: Addison-Wesley, 1972. A concise and well-written discussion of prejudice and discrimination, drawing on work from several disciplines. The sections on institutional and cultural racism are especially good. Both high school and college audiences will find this source accessible and beneficial. Includes a good bibliography as well as separate name and subject indexes.

Knowles, Louis L., and Kenneth Prewitt, eds. *Institutional Racism in America.* Englewood Cliffs, N.J.: Prentice-Hall, 1969. A collection of essays that analyze institutional racism in various institutional areas, such as the economy and education. While dated in some respects, it remains a good introduction to the subject for a general audience. The chapter by Harold M. Baron on the interrelatedness of institutions is particularly instructive.

Héctor L. Delgado

Cross-References

Affirmative Action, 21; Apartheid, 127; Assimilation: The United States, 140; Caste Systems, 198; Internal Colonialism, 1015; Racial and Ethnic Stratification, 1579; Segregation versus Integration, 1707; Sexism and Institutional Sexism, 1728; Social Stratification: Analysis and Overview, 1839.

INSTITUTIONS AND TOTAL INSTITUTIONS

Type of sociology: Social structure
Field of study: Key social structures

Social institutions are the organizational systems a society uses to address one or more of its basic needs. Human socialization occurs within social institutions such as the family and schools, as society shapes the ways in which people think, feel, and act. Total institutions impose regimented routines with the goal of resocializing people by depriving them of any other source of social experience.

Principal terms
   INSTITUTIONS: stable social arrangements that perform basic activities in society; major spheres of social life that are organized to meet basic human needs
   RESOCIALIZATION: in the context of total institutions, the deliberate control of a social environment to alter a subject's personality radically
   ROLE: a pattern of expected behavior that is attached to a particular status
   SOCIALIZATION: the lifelong social process in which individuals develop their human potential and learn the patterns of their culture
   STATUS: a recognized social position that an individual occupies
   TOTAL INSTITUTION: a setting in which people are isolated from the rest of society and are manipulated by an administrative staff

Overview

In *Die Protestantische Ethik und der Geist des Kapitalismus* (1904; *The Protestant Ethic and the Spirit of Capitalism*, 1930 [Talcott Parsons, trans.]), Max Weber, a founding father in the field of sociology, used the phrase "rationalization of society" to denote the historical change from tradition to rationality as the dominant mode of human thought. He noted that, while members of preindustrial societies embrace tradition, industrial capitalism fosters rationality. Rationality, in turn, promotes the emergence of distinctive social institutions. In hunter-gatherer societies, the family was the center of virtually all activities. Gradually, the social institutions, including religious, educational, political, and economic systems, became separate from the family. These social institutions are rational strategies for more efficiently meeting pervasive human needs. For example, the transmission of a technologically developed and literate culture from one generation to the next requires formal schooling, and with continuing technological and scientific development, as the web of rationality becomes more complex, educational systems must expand. Socialization of the modern individual is accomplished in countless familiar settings, related to social institutions that foster the development of those qualities that people associate with being fully human. In spite of, and sometimes because of, the socializing influences of these varied settings, deviant individuals emerge whom society frequently thrusts into highly controlled, rationally designed settings that encompass the special world of the total institution. This type of socialization, which often takes place where people are confined against their will in prisons or mental hospitals, typifies the total institution. According to the social psychologist Erving Goffman, in *Asylums* (1961), total institutions have three distinctive characteristics. First, staff members supervise all spheres of daily life, including where residents (who may be called "inmates," "prisoners," or "enlisted personnel") eat, sleep, and work. Second, a rigid routine subjects inmates to standardized food, sleeping quarters, and activities. Third, formal rules govern how inmates behave in every setting, severely limiting their freedom of choice.

Total institutions impose such regimented routines with the goal of resocialization. The total institution is, in effect, a change agent, designed to control the social environment in order to radically alter the resident inmate's, prisoner's, or soldier's personality. The power of the total institution to work as a change agent lies in depriving people of any other source of social experience. An inmate's isolation, for example, is achieved through physical barriers such as walls and fences (usually with barbed wire and guard towers), barred windows, and locked doors. Once the inmate is cut off in this way, his or her entire world can be manipulated by the administrative staff to produce lasting change in him or her. Short of this, the total institution at least elicits immediate compliance from its subjects.

Resocialization is a two-part process. First, the staff attempts to erode the new subject's established identity. This involves a series of experiences that Goffman describes as abasements, degradations, humiliations, and profanations of self. The boot camp sergeant is particularly adept at imposing this social environment. Typically, subjects are required to surrender personal possessions, including clothing and grooming articles normally used to maintain a person's distinctive appearance. In their place, subjects receive standard-issue items that make everyone alike. In addition, subjects are given standard haircuts so that, again, what once was personalized becomes uniform. For example, new prisoners are searched, weighed, fingerprinted, photographed, and issued a serial number. Once inside the walls, individuals surrender the right to privacy. Guards often demand that inmates undress publicly as part of the admission procedure, and guards routinely conduct surveillance and searches of prisoners' living quarters. These "mortifications of self" undermine the identity and autonomy that inmates bring to the total institution from the outside world.

The second part of the resocialization process relates to efforts to build systematically a different self. The staff manipulates the subject's behavior through a system of rewards and punishments. The privileges of obtaining a magazine or a few cigarettes may seem trivial to someone on the "outside," but in the rigid, controlled environment of the total institution, they can become powerful motivations toward conformity. Noncompliance carries the threat that privileges will be withdrawn. In more serious cases, the inmate may suffer physical pain or isolation from other inmates. The duration of confinement in a prison or mental hospital also relates to administrative policy, since the confinement term is generally dependent upon the degree of cooperation with the staff that an inmate displays. Goffman emphasized that conformity in a total institution must reflect both inward motivation and outward behavior. Even a person who does not outwardly violate the rules may still be punished for having an "attitude problem." The total institution may be an old-age home, a boarding school, a military academy, a naval ship, or a psychiatric hospital, but all of these organizations have in common the assumption of total responsibility for every facet of the lives of the people who reside within them.

The common goal of the resocialization process in total institutions is to socialize the inmates to behave in ways that suit the organization's needs. In most of these organizations, however, there is also a strong inmate culture. This culture consists of norms that specify ways of resisting the officials' control in favor of such values as mutual aid and loyalty among the inmates. Thus, in Bruce Jackson's *Outside the Law: A Thief's Primer* (1972), one seasoned convict graphically compared the penitentiary to a prisoner of war camp, in which the officials are the enemy and the inmates are the captured. A state of mutual distrust and antagonism is built into the system. Yet the same prisoner also described another aspect of life in total institutions. Often, inmates develop "institutionalized personalities." As they try to conform to the norms of the organizations, they become increasingly dependent on the routines and constraints of minimal freedom and, hence, minimal responsibility. This provides the inmate with a deep sense of security and a fear of even attempting to cope with the responsibilities of the "outside world" after a long period of incarceration. In fact, many released prisoners have intentionally committed crimes in order to return to prison, to again find security, an easy, routinized lifestyle, and perhaps the opportunity to engage in the activities of prison life, from baseball to homosexual liaisons.

Applications

Considerable change in a human being's thought processes, personality, and emotional state can be effected by resocialization in a total institution. The rebuilding of the self is extremely difficult, however, and as John Irwin notes in his book *Prisons in Turmoil* (1980), no two people are likely to respond to the program of a total institution in precisely the same way. Some inmates may experience "rehabilitation" or "recovery," signifying change that is officially approved, while others become embittered because of the perceived injustice of their incarceration. Those who spend a considerable period of time in a total institution, with its rigidly controlled environment, may become completely institutionalized. They may then be incapable of fostering the independence required for living in the outside world. For this reason, halfway house programs have been instituted by prisons and mental hospitals to ease the transition of their subjects into the outside world following a prolonged period of incarceration.

Only relatively recently, for the most part in the second half of this century, has the goal of rehabilitation been taken seriously as a function of prisons. Rehabilitation may be viewed as an effort to return the reformed criminal to society as a productive, law-abiding citizen. Critics of the prison system, many of whom argue from a social conflict perspective, often claim that far from rehabilitating their inmates, prisons in fact function as "schools for crime." As early as 1864, the great English philosopher and economist Jeremy Bentham described prisons as schools for wickedness. After all, when one is constantly in close contact with only hardened criminals, one can hardly expect to learn the higher virtues of life. Only in more recent years have a variety of studies in the field of criminology attempted to discern what can be done to increase the deterrent effects of prison and prevent it from becoming a community that socializes people into hardened criminals as the true end product of the so-called "resocialization process."

Yet there is an alternate body of sociological research that defends prisons as a means of deterrence and a necessary form of retribution. James Q. Wilson (1977) presents the functionalist position, arguing that societies need the firm moral authority they gain from stigmatizing and punishing crime. He believes that prisoners should receive better forms of rehabilitation in prison and be guaranteed their rights as citizens once they are released from prison. He also argues, however, that to destigmatize crime would be to lift from it the weight of moral judgment and to make crime simply a particular occupation or avocation that society has chosen to reward somewhat less, or perhaps more than other pursuits.

No matter what their sociological perspective may be, serious students of the American prison system generally agree that by far the least successful aspect of prison life is rehabilitation. In Jackson's extensive interviews with prison inmates, he found that few people within the walls of the prison take seriously the notion of rehabilitation. For most, prisons exist to punish, restrain, and scare. Most other efforts are likely to be regarded as distant ideals, out of touch with reality. Research conducted in the 1970's consistently found that the only effective rehabilitation programs in prisons, measured by lower rates of recidivism, involve job training. Indeed, during the 1980's, as the recession deepened and prison populations more than doubled, sociologists and criminologists found that men from very poor and minority backgrounds were beginning to regard prison as the only way they could obtain job training, health care, and other social services. At the very least, prisons provided "three hots and a cot," in prisoner parlance, or food and shelter. Prisons, after all, provide more adequate housing than the large urban shelters for the homeless do, and in addition to food and shelter, one gets a chance to improve one's skills and self-confidence. As Frank Butterfield (1992) noted, in Western society there is an exaggerated belief in the efficacy of imprisonment. The warehousing of people in prisons is predicated on the false assumption that if society makes life really terrible for some people, it can reform them. Actually, such treatment only serves to make them more dangerous.

In summary, prisons and other total institutions will continue, in some form, to fill important functions in the system of social control, but they cannot substitute for voluntarily shared norms and values and the will to adhere to them in daily life.

Context

The work of Erving Goffman grows out of the still-developing field of social psychology, which resulted from the nexus of the disciplines of psychology and sociology. Goffman's research is grounded in earlier, trailblazing work in the field of social psychology by men such as George Herbert Mead and Charles Horton Cooley. Mead's approach has often been described as social behaviorism, emphasizing the importance of mental process in the development of the "self," through the interpretation of social experiences. Cooley suggested that others represent a mirror, or looking-glass, in which one perceives oneself as others see one. Thus, Cooley used the phrase "looking-glass self" to capture the idea that the self is based on how others respond to us. Goffman, and others who have concentrated on the significance of total institutions, take the theories of Mead and Cooley a step further, revealing the impact of the total institution in the resocialization of the "self." For example, the sociologist Philip G. Zimbardo, in the classic article "Pathology of Imprisonment" (1972), reported on his investigation of prison violence in an artificial "laboratory," or mock prison. Briefly, his research gives strong credence to the hypothesis that the character of prison itself, as a total institution, and not the personalities of prisoners and guards, causes prison violence. A growing body of research reveals the necessity for further studies into the dehumanizing effects of the social character of total institutions.

Bibliography

Bentham, Jeremy. *Theory of Legislation*. London: Trubner, 1864. Bentham's philosophical writings remain an inspiration for a critical and enlightening evaluation of law and jurisprudence more than a century after their original publication.

Butterfield, Frank. "Are American Jails Becoming Shelters from the Storm?" *The New York Times*, July 19, 1992, p. E4. Butterfield develops an incisive commentary on the emerging functions of prisons in the absence of needed support systems in the larger society.

Goffman, Erving. *Asylums*. Garden City, N.Y.: Anchor, 1961. This classic work includes a compendium of highly readable essays on the social position of mental patients and other inmates of mental hospitals. This book, more than any other, established the significance of the study of total institutions.

Irwin, John. *Prisons in Turmoil*. Boston: Little, Brown, 1980. Irwin provides a relatively recent analysis of problems deriving from prisons as total institutions. Prison riots can be better understood in the light of Irwin's work. The book prods the social conscience of the nation to consider the true social ramifications of these "human warehouses."

Martindale, Don. *Institutions, Organizations, and Mass Society*. Boston: Houghton Mifflin, 1966. Martindale provides a comprehensive analysis of total institutions in the context of a full understanding of the theory of complex organizations in modern society. Although it is heavy with theory, the book serves to provide a comprehensive theoretical understanding of the place of total institutions in modern society.

Mennell, Stephen, et al. "Food in Total Institutions." *Current Sociology* 40, no. 2

(Autumn, 1992): 112-115. This article provides a current critique of food as a representation of the nature of the total institution. Hospitals, prisons, the military, and many other institutional settings bear a much-deserved reputation for serving unpalatable food. The rationale for this practice within the context of the total institution is particularly revealing.

Weber, Max. *The Protestant Ethic and the Spirit of Capitalism.* Translated by Talcott Parsons. New York: Charles Scribner's Sons, 1958. This classic work has had a profound influence on the development of sociology as a social science. Weber's analysis of the rationalization of society, as noted above, is given a complete analysis in this book. It is fascinating to discover how predictive Weber has been on so many social fronts.

Wilson, James Q. *Thinking About Crime.* New York: Vintage, 1977. Wilson provides a perceptive analysis of crime and penology that is balanced, thoughtful, and fully cognizant of the latest criminological and sociological theory and practice, while critiquing the pervasive role of the prison as a total institution in western culture.

Zimbardo, Philip G. "Pathology of Imprisonment." *Society* 9 (April, 1972): 4-8. This article has been widely cited in sociology, psychology, and social psychology textbooks as a classic study of the nature of the prison as a total institution. More recent replications of this study have only served to reinforce its veracity. It is deserving of careful analysis by anyone interested in pursuing a study of total institutions.

Robert D. Bryant

Cross-References

Authoritarian and Totalitarian Governments, 153; The Criminal Justice System, 380; Labeling and Deviance, 1049; Prison and Recidivism, 1519; Socialization: Religion, 1894; Workplace Socialization, 2202.

INTERACTIONISM

Type of sociology: Origins and definitions of sociology
Field of study: Sociological perspectives and principles

Interactionism is a methodological approach and a set of philosophical tenets in sociology and related disciplines of the social sciences. Interactionism views social phenomena as cases of interaction between human agents; in the interactionist view, humans—rather than institutions or impersonal forces—are seen as the primary actors in social phenomena.

Principal terms
ACTION PROCESS: a process composed of two phases—what happens within a unit ("decision") and what happens between units ("communication")
ACTOR: an individual interacting with other persons or with objects as a thinking organism, as opposed to interacting as a purely physical being
DRAMATISM: a method of analysis of interaction which emphasizes the role of the person as agent in social action
MICROSOCIOLOGY: the sociological approach that emphasizes the study of small groups rather than entire institutions or societies
SYMBOLIC INTERACTION: interaction in which emphasis is on the symbolic value of objects, actions, or language

Overview

Interactionism is a major theoretical perspective from which sociologists view human societies and groups. It is often considered, along with functionalism and conflict theory, one of the three central approaches to sociological theory and research. As the term itself suggests, interactionism focuses on how individuals interact—how people direct their relationships and their behaviors regarding one another. Interactionist approaches are less frequently applied to large-scale sociological studies (macrosociology) than to the study of how people act and react in small groups; it may be considered the central approach of microsociology. Interactionism has been used extensively in studies of socialization—how people, from infancy on, learn the knowledge and appropriate behaviors of their society—and in examinations of how people interact in any small-group setting. It has been used widely, for example, in the study of marital and family relationships. It has also been used in studies of education that involve small-scale interactions, such as those in the classroom between teachers and students and among students themselves. More than any other major sociological perspective, interactionism represents the coming together of sociology and social psychology.

The study of symbolic interaction is one sociological approach to interactionism. It recognizes that crucial importance of symbols in people's lives and interactions. A symbol, in the simplest definition, is anything that stands for something else or carries a meaning beyond that which is readily visible on the surface. People in a group share a belief in the meanings of certain symbols, and, according to symbolic interactionism, their interactions are largely based on these beliefs and understandings. Clothing is one example of a symbol; certain uniforms (as a police uniform or sports uniform) or modes of dress (conservative business attire) symbolize aspects of the wearer's status in ways that are immediately apparent to members of a certain group but may be unknown to outsiders. Language can be considered a set of symbols that make communication possible; other symbols make possible nonverbal interaction and communication.

The theories of American scholars Charles Horton Cooley and George Herbert Mead radically advanced the theory of interactionism. Cooley theorized that the self develops in the process of interacting with others and that the self and the other are in the same field and of the same immediacy. Mead took the further theoretical step of envisioning the individual as both the subject and object simultaneously in the same system of interpersonal interaction. Mead also saw socialization as arising from the interplay of the subjective and objective aspects of the self and the other. Indeed, Mead's social psychology went even further, denying that personality can be interpreted apart from its articulation through social interaction. Even the genetic inheritance of humans could and must be understood in this way, he maintained. Mead's system combined the mental and physical aspects of humankind in a continuity related to the evolutionary process from primitive life forms to humans; it also combined the symbolic and the behaviorist approaches in a unified synthesis.

Dramatism, or dramaturgy, represents a mid-twentieth century social sciences approach to interactionism that may be seen as a reaction against social science attempts to reduce humans and their actions to the level of the physical objects and actions observed in the physical sciences. Dramatism also recognizes the philosophical problem of "other minds": One never has access to anyone else's mind, but only to physical manifestations of imputed thought and reflection. Sociologist Erving Goffman was instrumental in developing the dramaturgical approach; he emphasized that people choose to present certain aspects of themselves to others, and he noted that the social context is important in how an individual decides to present himself or herself at any given moment.

Central to the dramaturgical approach is the examination of real-life human behavior and interaction as one would view the behavior of characters in a play. Characters in a play have no true interior dispositions, being fictional creations, but human emotions and motives are ascribable to these characters by virtue of what they say and do. This is equivalent to a perspective on the actions and interactions of real human actors because, although they, unlike dramatic characters, have interior dispositions and reflections, nobody can have direct access to the interior dispositions of other minds.

Sociologist Talcott Parsons was an early pioneer of the use of dramatistic terminology, and there is a clear humanistic tendency in dramatism; it avoids the physical or behavioristic reductionism that lurks in some modern sociology. Making a vital distinction between "action" and "mere motion," advocates of dramatism approach the dichotomy of man's speechless nature and his articulable interactivity: "Motion" is necessary for "action"; "motion" can exist without "action"; and "action" is not reducible to "motion." Through the approach and terminology of dramatism or dramaturgy, some modern sociologists have sought to avoid the reified abstractions that have at times threatened to engulf sociological writing. Ironically, although dramatism has been perceived as hostile to a mechanistic view of humans and society and as friendly to symbolic action, the view of dramatism is as reconcilable to mechanism as to most other views, for the "play" may be viewed as an enormous clockwork mechanism with every point functioning in harmony and mutual adjustment.

Interactionist theory had become quite sophisticated by the late twentieth century. The proposition of the double contingency of interactions, for example, emphasizes that the achievement of a goal depends not only on the actor's successful manipulation of the physical environment but also on the successful manipulation of other humans who are themselves actors. Parsons, among others, has employed games theory in interactionist analysis, which seems a perfect analogy, since in the typical game or sport one must contend both with physical objects—for example, a ball and a field—and with other actors—the other players, some of whom are one's teammates and some of whom are opponents.

Complex societies with significant division of labor contain interaction subgroups that interact with one another as organizations as well as with the individual human entities in the society. The primary condition necessary for the integration of interactive subgroups into a common culture is a "shared basis of normative order." Religion, ethical philosophy, and the like often contribute to the normative order, but language seems to be the most basic conveyer of value. Religion and philosophies within a society often vary, as may the degree of adherence to them. Language, however, tends to be the universal component of culture, and language's value-bearing function carries its own sanction; one who alters the value meaning of a language risks incomprehensibility in one's speech and writing.

Interactionist theoreticians have also come to speak of generalized media of interaction that control behavior by symbolic means—they represent to human actors the symbolic meanings of important objects. Money is perhaps the most obvious example of a mechanism of interaction. Economists would say that money has no "use value" but only "exchange value," whereas a commodity such as food would have value both in use and in exchange. Money stands for objects such as food.

Applications

In the social sciences, the nature of human interaction is never a peripheral question but is always an essential issue at the core of every inquiry. One area in which interactionist approaches have been widely employed is in the study of the family.

Sociologists have studied how the subgroups within the family—such as husband and wife, siblings, and parents and children—communicate. They might note, for example, who begins conversations, who is allowed to interrupt conversations, and who speaks the most. Such patterns can indicate differences in power and prestige within the family. Nonverbal patterns (such as seating patterns at mealtimes) also give indications of power differences.

Another notable application of interactionism (and one that overlaps with studies of the family) has been in the study of socialization. Interactionist sociologists study the concept of the self and how it emerges and develops. One's sense of identity, they believe, emerges from one's interactions with others. Socialization, they stress, is not a one-way process; people are not socialized passively into their culture. Rather, people throughout the life cycle take an active part in their own socialization. Young children (such as those in their "terrible twos"), for example, test the boundaries of acceptable behavior. There is an interplay between parent and child as each reacts to the other. Similarly, there is interaction between children and teachers—and among students—when children go to school. During adolescence, interaction with peers becomes the major influence on socialization. In adulthood, socialization continues through interactions with employers, coworkers, and romantic or marital partners.

Another way to look at the applications of interactionism is to note some of those who have been influential in the development of interactionist ideas (Charles Horton Cooley and George Herbert Mead, whose work was central to the sociological concept of interactionism, have already been noted). Sigmund Freud, the founder of psychoanalysis in the early twentieth century, contributed enormously to the development of interactionist theory. Freud looked to mental states as causes of behavior; in particular, he looked at the complex interrelationships among parts of the mind.

In his famous triadic model of the human mind, Freud postulated an id—a subconscious mental level that combines primitive instinctual drives with repressed desires and reactions from the conscious mind—and a superego, a kind of culturally generated conscience mechanism in which the demands of religion, society, and other authority structures are internalized. The id and the superego interact with the ego, which is the conscious personality of the individual and which contains its own hierarchy of motivations. These motivations are formed in part by the internal interaction of id and superego and in part by the interaction with other egos, which may act as agents of socialization.

After Freud, the next pioneer of interactionist theory was the French sociologist Émile Durkheim. Durkheim believed that it was both necessary and desirable to distinguish between the social environment and the individual to a degree beyond Freud's conceptualization. Durkheim's greatest contribution was to envision the world of social objects apart from their internalization in the subject. He saw that the social environment could establish normative standards for the individual and could sanction compliance or noncompliance. In Durkheim's theory, the normative element transcended the individual, and objectification of normative values in the form of social institutions was vital. Durkheim's other great contribution to the theory of interactionism was the recognition of the role of symbolism in the "collective representations" of the normative values of society.

Max Weber, the German sociologist, succeeded in bridging the idealist and the materialist systems for understanding human interaction and human motivation. To Weber, one could explain courses of action only by understanding the meaning of the motives of actual individuals. Weber saw that within social systems there are unit-by-unit interchanges (whether performances, sanctions, or exchanges) in which there is a constant "sending" and "receiving" of positive and negative reinforcements.

New philosophical outlooks were introduced into the modern analysis of interactionism in the forms of existentialism, phenomenology, and radical empiricism. Thinkers such as Søren Kierkegaard, the Danish philosopher and theologian, and Friedrich Nietzsche, the German linguist and philosopher, developed the existentialist perspective. Existential thinkers, with their strong emphasis on human will, have been unprepared to see human organisms as purely manipulated objects, and this concept has influenced the social sciences. The phenomenological tradition, with deep roots in continental philosophy, became identified in the twentieth century with German philosophers such as Edmund Husserl and Martin Heidegger. The phenomenological approach in the social sciences involved relating the structures of society and culture to the immanent feelings and experiences of individuals, which then could be used to critique social institutions.

Following World War II, there were greater attempts to employ a primarily empirical approach to interactionism in the social sciences. The social psychologist Kurt Lewin emphasized an environmentalism which stressed altering human behavior through group participatory experiences. Robert F. Bales and his followers utilized technical observation and analytical methodology of small-group interactions and applied the results to larger structures. Finally, American sociologist George C. Homans used a mixture of the behaviorist experimental psychology of B. F. Skinner, economic theory, and industrial organizational theory to advance general interactionist theory.

Context

In sociology, as in all the social sciences, one of the most difficult of theoretical problems is to schematize the interaction of human entities with one another and with their social environment. When systematic, empirical science developed in the sixteenth and seventeenth centuries, scientists such as Galileo and philosophers such as the French thinker Rene Descartes created the complex methodologies of the experimental, observational sciences. They operated with a simple dichotomy of the human as subject/knower and the phenomena of the physical universe as the objects—the things known.

Even in regard to the study of the behavior of physical objects, such a simple dichotomy is not truly adequate, but when the objects of study are human persons and their social constructs, the schema collapses entirely. When the human entity is both subject and object, or observer and observed—as in all the social sciences—the nature of social interaction becomes crucial to the understanding of all else. When human entities and their social constructs are the objects of knowledge, a dangerous circularity of reason threatens, because human knowledge and the means of its acquisition and validation are themselves the products of human interaction, are themselves social constructs, and are themselves the objects of social scientific investigation.

Bibliography

Durkheim, Émile. *The Division of Labor in Society*. Translated by George Simpson. Glencoe, Ill.: Free Press, 1960.

_____ . *The Elementary Forms of the Religious Life*. Translated by Joseph W. Swain. New York: Macmillan, 1954.

_____ . *The Rules of Sociological Method*. 8th ed. Edited by George Catlin. Translated by Sarah A. Solovay and John H. Mueller. Glencoe, Ill.: Free Press, 1958. These three books (first published in 1893, 1912, and 1895, respectively) present interactionist theory both in terms of methodological theory and in terms of practical application to specific sociological projects.

Mead, George H. *Mind, Self, and Society: From the Standpoint of a Social Behaviorist*. Edited by Charles Morris. Chicago: University of Chicago Press, 1963. Mead's work, first published in 1934, combines discussion of advances in psychology and related fields with Mead's interactionist theory.

Parsons, Talcott. *Social Structure and Personality*. New York: Free Press, 1964. Especially useful in this work by Parsons is the chapter "Social Structure and the Development of Personality: Freud's Contribution to the Integration of Psychology and Sociology."

Tiryakian, Edward A. *Sociologism and Existentialism: Two Perspectives on the Individual and Society*. Englewood Cliffs, N.J.: Prentice-Hall, 1962. This volume struggles with the philosophical and methodological problems of reconciling social scientific analysis with the humanistic view of human as free agent.

Weber, Max. *The Theory of Social and Economic Organization*. 1922. Translation by A. M. Henderson and Talcott Parsons. Glencoe, Ill.: Free Press, 1947. The Weberian perspective on interactionism is well presented in this study.

Patrick M. O'Neil

Cross-References

Conflict Theory, 340; Dramaturgy, 566; Exchange in Social Interaction, 715; Functionalism, 786; Microsociology, 1192; Social Groups, 1806; The History of Sociology, 1926; Sociology Defined, 1932; Symbolic Interaction, 2036.

INTERNAL COLONIALISM

Type of sociology: Racial and ethnic relations
Fields of study: Maintaining inequality; Policy issues and debates; Theories of prejudice and discrimination

Internal colonialism refers to the structured relations of oppression that affect a given community that is usually defined by racial or ethnic differences. The internal colony is geographically submerged within the colonizer's territory and is forced to coexist unequally within the larger society. This concept is useful as a critique of alternative theories of racial and/or regional discrimination which fail to capture the ongoing severity of exploitative relations.

Principal terms
COLONIALISM: the process by which one nation conquers and subsequently establishes state domination through direct, formal means over a culturally distinct people who inhabit a geographically distinct territory
DE FACTO SEGREGATION: racial and other forms of social separation that result from informal social mechanisms of discrimination
DE JURE SEGREGATION: racial and other forms of social separation that are produced by formal, legal mechanisms
EXPLOITATION: an institutionalized practice of unequal exchange relations, based on an imbalance of social power, in which one party benefits at the expense of another
INTERNAL COLONY: a community that is subjected to colonial control and that is located within the national borders of the colonizer
NATIONALISM: the ideological and political expression of social groupings that seek to advance the interests of their established, suppressed, or emerging nations
UNEQUAL EXCHANGE: institutionalized economic relations between industrialized countries and their Third World trading partners, in which the former continually benefit at the expense of the latter

Overview

Colonialism is essentially a process of state conquest and a form of domination in which a nation exercises formal means of control over foreign territories. European colonialism spanned centuries of time and included, for example, the Spanish conquest of the New World, which began in the late fifteenth century, and the English, Dutch, Portuguese, and Italian colonization of the African continent. The systematic economic exploitation that accompanied European colonialism helped to fuel Europe's accumulation of wealth and to supply raw materials for the great industrial revolutions of that region. Throughout the entire twentieth century, European and U.S. colonialism in the Caribbean has persisted because of a variety of strategic military, economic, and geopolitical interests.

Internal colonialism differs from colonialism proper in that it refers specifically to the domination of a community that lies within the colonizer's effective national borders. The inhabitants of internal colonies therefore live in extremely close proximity to the colonizer and are typically subjected to intense pressures to conform to the cultural norms of the larger society. At the same time, however, they are deprived of the possibility of equal participation in the larger society's social institutions.

As in the conventional colonial context, the colonizer systematically enforces a regime that denies the rights of the colonized to equal political and economic participation. This denial frequently involves using ideological mechanisms and repressive institutions to contain any resistance that arises within the internal colony. Although both forms of colonialism involve the systematic oppression of an identifiable people, internal colonialism can often be characterized by its reliance upon semiformal and informal means of separation in maintaining the effective boundaries of the colony.

The key elements to identifying the formation of an internal colony are a historical dimension based on the development of coercive processes that led to the geographical concentration and/or confinement of a community within the larger context of the colonial power; the pervasive and ongoing practice of institutionalized discrimination against the colonized population; the widespread prevalence of racist ideologies through which the colonized population becomes denigrated by others in the larger society, while the colonized themselves experience self-denigration and feelings of inferiority; and the comprehensive denial of self-determination for the colonized population, including formal and informal means of denying full political participation and the freedom to organize independent and legitimate representative bodies.

Internal colonialism becomes deeply intertwined with all the basic institutions of any society in which it is found. Educational structures are designed for the colonized and attempt to deny them knowledge of their own history and cultural roots. Political structures designed to represent the colonized formally are recognized on terms set by the colonizer, often including the incorporation of individuals from the oppressed community who, to some extent, accept the status quo of domination and agree to collaborate with it.

Economic relations between an internal colony and the larger society invariably revolve around the superexploitation of labor. Religious institutions, to the extent that they are successfully imposed upon the colonized, often play an important role in managing the tensions between the dominant and subordinated populations. The legal order likewise becomes involved by exposing the colonized to police and/or military forces outside their control, often leading to a variety of forms of repressive treatment, including the criminalization of anticolonial resistance.

In response to the pervasive exercise of social control, internal colonialism invariably generates popular protest, and the outcome is a struggle that is intended to liberate an oppressed community from the exploitative dynamics of the system. One common expression of this resistance is the development of nationalist forms of struggle whereby the colonized community explicitly seeks liberation from colonial control over the geographical space where it is situated. Another form of struggle, also nationalist, primarily advocates active participation in solidarity with the anticolonial struggle of foreign lands that they view as their own. A third important form of anticolonial struggle takes the form of accommodation in which protest is aimed at ending the discriminatory practices of the larger society and achieving social reforms that can make possible the full participation of the colonized as citizens of the larger society.

Wherever internal colonialism is practiced, the tendency for growing social inequalities to fuel social conflict forces the colonizer to evaluate continually the relative benefits of perpetuating the internal colonial system. Because conventional colonialism is disappearing in the modern world, it is likely that internal colonial struggles will become increasingly prominent as flash points of international tension.

Applications

Internal colonies exist throughout the world. Some of the most spectacular cases have been the "Bantustans" of southern Africa, the Israeli-occupied territories of Palestine, the Basque region of Spain, and the Baltic Republics during the Soviet era. The populations of internal colonies are regarded variously as "national minorities," "refugee communities," "indigenous peoples," or as "undefined" or "native" species of people who are not generally entitled to share in full citizenship and the exercise of political power. All such cases imply a historical confrontation in which a colonial power successfully annexed or displaced whole communities to the extent that they became geographically subsumed into the larger society of the colonizer.

An analysis of national minorities within the United States could potentially apply the concept of internal colonialism to at least the following communities: Puerto Rican communities, African American communities, various Native American reservations, the Chicano communities of the southwestern United States, Alaskan Eskimo (Inuit) communities, and indigenous Hawaiian peoples. The industrialization and national expansion of the United States were carried out at the expense of these colonized communities, which have remained to some degree subordinated ever since.

In the case of Native Americans, internal colonialism was created from the systematic forcible displacement of native peoples from their lands and their involuntary resettlement elsewhere on the North American continent. Although treaties were initially signed with various native nations which ceded new territorial rights, the United States eventually decided in 1871 that it would no longer recognize the existence of "Indian Nations" and henceforth considered tribal authorities as representatives of "unconditionally surrendered nations." Land reservations that were set up by the federal government became formally placed under the complete control of the colonizer, and various coercive policies were henceforth practiced that manipulated the educational, political, economic, and religious activities of native peoples. Resistance on the part of these colonized communities has erupted periodically, and

1018 *Sociology*

many native peoples have continued to practice nationalist struggle in search of cultural sovereignty and self-determination.

The African American community was initially formed out of conventional colonial means of subjugation but subsequently developed along the lines of internal colonialism. The entry of African Americans into North American society has its roots in the European colonization of the African continent and the subsequent rise of the slave trade. Because of the supply of slave labor that was available to the West, the institutionalization of plantation slavery emerged in the southern United States, as it did in many Caribbean and Latin American countries. The ruthless exploitation of Africans of various cultural origins led to the creation of a "slave culture" in which previous linguistic and religious practices were almost entirely eradicated, with the imposition of English and the Christian religion.

The systematic discrimination that followed the abolition of slavery served to maintain a high level of racial segregation, preserving dense concentrations of African Americans in the southern regions of the former plantation states, known as the Black Belt. During the early part of the twentieth century, the demand for labor created by U.S. industrialization led to a massive migration of African Americans to urban centers, including most principal northern cities. De jure segregation remained strong throughout the United States, however, and formal legal mechanisms were used to keep blacks separated from whites in a variety of institutional settings, such as educational, transportation, and even military institutions. Even more pronounced was the widespread practice of de facto segregation, which reinforced internal colonialism through strong residential segregation and informal barriers to the participation of blacks in sports, the mass media, and virtually every other social institution.

Years of struggle have failed to eradicate the exploitative dynamics experienced by African Americans, leading to periodic shifts between nationalist and more accommodationist forms of struggles for equality. Various "return to Africa" movements that developed throughout African American history, such as the movement founded by the great Caribbean leader Marcus Garvey, are one manifestation of black resistance to internal colonialism. During the Black Power movement of the 1960's, organizations such as the militant Black Panther Party arose in response to widespread police repression and openly struggled for the liberation of "the Black colony of North America." A more contemporary organization, the New Afrikan People's Organization (NAPO), advocates independence of the southern five-state region that composes the Black Belt. Accommodationist black movements, however, have rejected the nationalist struggle against "internal colonialism," instead favoring demands for full social equality for African Americans as United States citizens.

In the case of Puerto Rico, an actual colonial relationship with the island led to the displacement of Puerto Ricans to the U.S. mainland, where large, racially segregated communities formed in cities such as New York City and Chicago. The widespread migration of Puerto Ricans is more recent than that of African Americans, but many similar characteristics of internal colonialism have been used to oppress Puerto Ricans. The process of "ghettoization," fueled by internal colonial dynamics, has resulted in

Puerto Ricans becoming the poorest Latino minority group in the United States, second in poverty only to Native Americans. Puerto Ricans have resisted their exploitation with a strong sense of nationalism, retaining their national identity as defined by their attachment to their island homeland, and many have actively participated in the nationalist struggle for Puerto Rican independence.

In the case of the Chicano population, the nineteenth century U.S. annexation of the northern half of Mexico was part of the general expansionist logic that led to the internal colonialism of many Native American nations. Those Mexicans who remained in what became U.S. territory formed the initial part of the Chicano population. Since that time, Chicanos have experienced a variety of exploitative dynamics similar to those that contemporary Puerto Rican communities have experienced. This has, in turn, resulted in the creation of a variety of Chicano rights movements, including some nationalist organizations that advocate Chicano self-determination and even reunification with Mexico for Chicano communities located in the American Southwest.

Context

The concept of internal colonialism has been used in a variety of ways, both in an analytical manner by scholars and in an ideological manner by political movements. In its scholarly form, it is most readily associated with the critique of capitalism, and it was implicit in many of the classic works of Marxism and neo-Marxism. Vladimir Ilich Lenin suggested that advanced capitalist exploitation included the use of internal colonialism as a means of extracting higher profits from national minority communities created out of territorial expansionism. The Italian leftist politician Antonio Gramsci likewise employed the concept, describing the underdeveloped, agrarian south of Italy as an internal colony of the industrial north.

The common thread of early and more contemporary usages of internal colonialism rests in exploitative practices that are typically glossed over or diminished by official political jargon or alternative scholarly concepts. Sociologists have employed the term "internal colonialism" in order to analyze more precisely the means of exploitation that characterize racial or ethnic relations in specific settings. For example, a view of Native Americans as a racial "minority" does not sufficiently communicate the special context in which their systematic oppression is experienced. Likewise, the view of Puerto Rican experience as that of just another migrant community fails to capture the colonial mechanisms that led to the displacement of Puerto Ricans to the United States and their subsequent exploitation as "U.S. citizens."

In North American sociology, Robert Blauner popularized the use of the term "internal colonialism" in his *Racial Oppression in America* (1972), where he argued that it best captured the essence of racial oppression as experienced by black America. Although the term was utilized at least a decade earlier by C. Wright Mills, Blauner more explicitly advocated it as an explanatory concept.

An even more systematic utilization of the term was employed by Michael Hechter in his *Internal Colonialism: The Celtic Fringe in British National Development, 1536-1966* (1975). Hechter's work explored the multidimensional system of political, economic, and cultural discrimination practiced by the British against Irish, Scottish, and Welsh peoples. His use of the concept stresses the important role played by the cultural devaluation of an internal colony by its colonizer. This practice helps facilitate a division of labor in which individual prospects for social mobility are systematically linked to specific cultural backgrounds.

The ability of internal colonialism as a concept to characterize the institutional source of oppression tends to make it quite popular with political resistance movements. For example, when the Black Power movement of the 1960's referred to black ghettoes as internal colonies, it helped to provide ideological ammunition for more radical forms of struggle for "national liberation." It is precisely this political usage of the term that leaves many sociologists reluctant to deploy it in their work, viewing its ideological connotation as too strong and too judgmental.

This reluctance notwithstanding, many social scientists continue to see the concept as analytically useful. For example, internal colonialism helps explain, where conventional theories have failed, why steady economic growth fails to diminish and eventually eradicate regional or interethnic inequalities in various areas. Indeed, when internal colonial relations are in place, economic growth tends to intensify the inequality between the two counterparts rather than to address that inequality. In spite of these facts, however, theorists of internal colonialism will need to refine the concept further if it is to enter the social scientific mainstream.

Bibliography

Blauner, Robert. *Racial Oppression in America*. New York: Harper & Row, 1972. This book departed from conventional sociological approaches to race and ethnicity by applying the notion of internal colonialism to the African American struggle. Blauner, a noted sociologist, argues that internal colonialism helps to supplement more conventional analyses of advanced capitalism and more adequately explains the complexity of racism in the United States.

Blaut, James M. *The National Question: Decolonizing the Theory of Nationalism*. London: Zed Books, 1987. A highly theoretical treatise that surveys the various theories of nationalism and colonialism. The author is particularly critical of Joseph Stalin's theory of internal colonies as "national minorities" and argues that Marxist theorists must decisively reject Stalinist conceptions. Throughout the work, he makes empirical references to Puerto Rico and argues that Puerto Rican communities within the United States are engaged in an anticolonial struggle.

Hechter, Michael. *Internal Colonialism: The Celtic Fringe in British National Development, 1536-1966*. Berkeley: University of California Press, 1975. A detailed historical application of internal colonialism as an analytical concept, based upon a European case study. The author shows that the diminished social status of peoples subjected to internal colonialism is the product of a "cultural division of labor" that serves the interests of the colonizer.

Hind, Robert J. "The Internal Colonial Concept." *Comparative Studies in Society and History* 26 (July, 1984): 543-568. This very useful review for the beginning student of the concept of internal colonialism takes a critical view of the lack of scholarly consensus on the scientific value of the concept.

Locke, Richard, and Antony Stewart. *Bantustan Gaza*. London: Zed Books, 1985. An illustrated case study of a persistently volatile region characterized by a ruthless internal colonialism. Likening Gaza to the "Bantustans" of apartheid South Africa, the British authors describe how Arabs are exploited for their cheap labor while they are denied self-determination in their own homeland by Israeli settlers and occupation forces.

Love, Joseph L. "Modeling Internal Colonialism: History and Prospect." *World Development* 17 (June, 1989): 905-922. This article offers the advanced student an in-depth scholarly treatment of internal colonialism, starting with the various ideological traditions associated with the concept and suggesting that it can be transformed into a very precise analytical tool. The author prefers to define internal colonialism as an economic concept, one useful in the Third World context where it can be related to existing theories of economic development.

Richard A. Dello Buono

Cross-References

Annihilation or Expulsion of Racial or Ethnic Groups, 92; Conquest and Annexation of Racial or Ethnic Groups, 353; Ethnic Enclaves, 682; Industrial and Postindustrial Economies, 940; Pluralism versus Assimilation, 1374; Racial and Ethnic Stratification, 1579; Segregation versus Integration, 1707; Social Stratification: Analysis and Overview, 1839.

ISLAM AND ISLAMIC FUNDAMENTALISM

Type of sociology: Major social institutions
Field of study: Religion

The second largest religion in the world, Islam is one of the primary sources of social change in the contemporary world. Islamic fundamentalism refers to the beliefs and behaviors of those who regard Islamic laws and values as the only legitimate principles for organizing Islamic societies and are willing to use any means, including violence, to achieve this goal.

Principal terms
FUNDAMENTALISM: a belief in the timeless and universal nature and application of religious commandments
IDEOLOGY: ideas produced for justifying or maintaining the political, economic, cultural, and social interests of a society or a specific group
MODERNIZATION: the gradual change in the social, economic, and political institutions of a society as a result of increasing industrialization, urbanization, and literacy and education, as well as changes in traditional values and beliefs
SECULARIZATION: the process whereby the influence of religious values and beliefs over various aspects of life is reduced
SOCIAL MOVEMENT: a prolonged collective effort for either preventing or promoting social change

Overview

The term "fundamentalism," which has a Christian origin, refers to views advocating complete and universal application of religious commandments. Popular media have used "Islamic fundamentalism" as a catchphrase for the ideology and practices of contemporary militant Islamic movements that desire complete implementation of Islamic laws in their respective countries. Used as such, the term has essentially become synonymous with terrorism and fanaticism. Muslims generally are unhappy with the term "Islamic fundamentalism" because strict implementation of Islamic laws is a necessary aspect of their religion, because militancy is not a universal feature of Islam, and because militant Muslims represent only a small fraction of the Muslim population.

The Islamic world is vast and varied. The Islamic politic is so diverse and complicated that it does not lend itself to simple categorization. Even Islamic fundamentalism is not a monolithic phenomenon. Within Islamic movements there are numerous differences of opinion about proper interpretation of the Quran (Koran), the form and structure of Islamic government, the role of women and their proper dress code, the strategies for implementing Islamic laws, and the quality of leadership needed for the

Islamic community. Many of these differences are based on the differences in political power, class background, gender affiliation, and ethnic status of individuals involved in these movements.

Many have viewed Islamic fundamentalism as a purely religious movement. Given the political objectives of those who use fundamentalism as a religious ideology, however, it is misleading to characterize Islamic fundamentalism as a purely religious phenomenon. Fundamentalism has been used by Islamic activists as a political tool to attain secular objectives. In the nineteenth century, Muslim Turkish rulers used Islam as a political ideology for expansion of Ottoman rule. Islam was also used as a political weapon against European colonial expansion in Africa and the Middle East. In the late 1970's, Ayatollah Khomeini effectively used religious symbolism for political mass mobilization that resulted in the overthrow of the shah of Iran in 1979.

Islamic fundamentalism shares many features of fundamentalist movements around the world. As described by Lionel Caplan in the introduction to *Studies in Religious Fundamentalism* (1987), these features include belief in the authority, infallibility, and universal application of religious books; viewing history as a "process of decline from an original ideal state"; rejection of a separation of the sacred and the profane; group formation as a reaction to a perceived or real threat or crisis; and viewing gender equality as a sign of moral decay.

These characteristics are all applicable to Islamic fundamentalism. Islamic fundamentalists believe that society should be organized on the basis of Quranic commandments and Islamic traditions that apply to all aspects of human life and are seen as the only legitimate source of prosperity for humanity. Islamic countries should rid themselves of all foreign influences, especially Western secular values, because these secular values replace the authority of religion with human reason. While important in human affairs, reason is believed to operate effectively only if it works within the contours determined by God.

Islamic fundamentalists reject the idea of the separation of the sacred and profane and separation of the church and the state. The Quran proposes a society in which all individual and social aspects of life are subject to religious laws. The rule of the Prophet Muhammad and the kind of community he built in the seventh century provide good examples for a "good society." After the Prophet, the temptations of materialism and power corrupted Islamic leaders. It is therefore seen as the responsibility of Muslims to regenerate Islam in their countries by overthrowing corrupted leaders.

Believing strongly in a "Western conspiracy against Islam," Islamic fundamentalists view the West as the source of many problems in their nations. The West, they believe, is determined to humiliate and destroy Islamic identity and community. An Egyptian fundamentalist thinker, Seyyid Qutb, once argued that the West had waged an all-out war against Islam. Examples of such intentions include colonial manipulation of Islamic nations, the indifference to genocide of Bosnian Muslims in the former Yugoslavia, the destruction of the Iraqi military infrastructure during and after the liberation of Kuwait, and the support for Salman Rushdie's book *The Satanic Verses* (1989), in which he allegedly defames the Prophet and his family.

Consequently, to a fundamentalist, the spread of Western cultural products (especially such items as motion pictures and pornographic videos) is a deliberate ploy to debase the Islamic community by propagating sexual laxity under the guise of women's freedom. Freedom as advocated by Western liberalism is viewed as giving the individual a "license" to do what he or she wishes without any consideration of moral values. Real freedom, according to fundamentalists, is a freedom to be able to exercise God's commands. To counter this Western ploy, Muslims should abandon Western values and move their politics toward the realization of an independent and powerful family of sovereign Muslim nations.

Adhering to these general goals, Islamic fundamentalists often customize their objectives to various stages of Islamic movements and political conditions. Before maturity, many of these movements are issue-oriented and make specific demands. Like other social movements, they use various dissatisfactions in the society as a means of mobilization, while their goal is total assumption of power. For example, in Egypt, Kuwait, Turkey, and Saudi Arabia, they have used agitational tactics to demoralize existing governments. In Iran, prior to the revolution, Ayatollah Khomeini used mass mobilization as a tactic to neutralize the army, demoralize the bureaucracy, and overthrow the shah's regime. In Pakistan and Sudan, fundamentalists have used factional politics by allying themselves with various factions in government or the military. In Jordan and Algeria, they used the existing parliamentary system as a means of obtaining power. As a minority in India, Kashmiri Muslims have been asking for more social justice and political autonomy. When confronted with suppressive governmental actions, many of these fundamentalists have resorted to violence by adopting terrorist acts and guerrilla tactics.

The Islamization efforts by the Islamic fundamentalists are often hampered by the two major social forces. First are the strong nationalist feelings of various Muslim countries, with their diverse linguistic, cultural, ethnic, and social traditions. Historically, these unique features of Islamic societies have stood in the way of Pan-Islamic movements seeking to unite all Muslims around the world. The second problem is the substantial size of secularly oriented middle classes in these countries; they have received modern Western education and have no desire to give up their lifestyles.

Applications

The Islamic revolution in Iran has clearly served Muslims all around the world as an example of the potential power of Islam. Since the mid-1970's, there has been an increase in the number of Islamic movements with a fundamentalist ideology. Muslim societies have experienced an increase in mosque attendance, adoption of Islamic dress code among women, political participation of fundamentalists in national politics, and political and agitational challenges to secular governments by fundamentalists. In Syria, the Muslim Brotherhood has been violently challenging the government of President Hafez al Assad. In Egypt, the Muslim Brotherhood has challenged three successive presidents, Gamal Abdel Nasser, Anwar el-Sadat, and Hosni Mubarak. Prior to its invasion by Iraq in 1990, Kuwait experienced numerous violent antigovernment activities by fundamentalist groups. The monarchy in Morocco has been challenged by Islamic fundamentalists. In Algeria, after the success of Islamic groups in gaining a majority in 1992 elections, the government launched a massive crackdown on Islamic forces.

In dealing with the fundamentalist challenge, rulers of many Muslim countries have employed a two-pronged approach: On the one hand they have called for stricter implementation of Islamic law (Sharia), and on the other hand they have launched a virulent attack against militant Islamic groups. In 1992, the Algerian army nullified the results of elections and declared the Islamic Salvation Front, which had won an electoral majority, to be illegal. In Egypt, followers of Muslim fundamentalists are routinely searched, arrested, and jailed. In the meantime, the secular governments in these countries have increased their allegiance to Islam by giving more visibility to Islamic symbolism and traditions.

This regeneration of the Islamic ethos caught Western politicians and social scientists by surprise. To a Western world preoccupied with the growing economic problems of recession, environmental challenges, and the aftershocks of the disappearance of the Soviet Union, the challenge of Islamic fundamentalism is disconcerting. Like the Arab nationalist movements in the 1950's and 1960's, Islamic fundamentalism is both radical and anti-Western.

A number of reasons have been given for the rise of Islamic fundamentalism since the 1970's. The explanations are varied and even, at times, contradictory. Some observers view the new assertiveness of Islamic forces as a result of increased Muslim confidence in themselves and their culture. This confidence is attributed to the increase in economic power of the oil-producing Muslim countries in the 1970's. There are flaws in this attribution. While such an economic power was present in oil-producing countries, the Islamic activists and their constituencies were not among those reaping the benefits of such prosperity. Furthermore, the emergence of fundamentalist activism has not been limited to oil-producing countries.

The most popular explanation is the "psychocultural" explanation. According to this view, the rise of Islamic fundamentalism is related to a mood of despair and humiliation among Muslims as a result of continued failure to achieve success in their confrontation with the West. One version of this theory focuses on the Western military challenges to the Muslim countries. Since the nineteenth century, Islamic countries have had no success against Western violations of Muslim sovereignty. The military defeat of the Ottoman Empire and the subsequent division of Muslim lands into client states by the European countries, the establishment of the state of Israel, several Arab military defeats by Israel, numerous coups d'état supported by the Western countries, and, finally, the defeat of Iraq by the allied forces in 1991 have resulted in a deep sense of humiliation and defeat. These defeats did not result in a fascination with the Western military power, as had happened previously in some countries. On the contrary, Muslim activists argued that the real cause of these failures was lack of reliance on Islam. To be successful, Islam should be used as the sole source of legitimation and mobilization against Western power.

A third set of theories emphasizes the failure of Western-originated economic, political, and ideological systems in the Muslim countries. After liberation from Western colonial control, Muslim countries began to adopt variant forms of socialism and liberal capitalism. The new states established in Muslim lands raised the people's expectations for economic growth, a better standard of living, political independence, national pride, and democratic rights.

These expectations, however, remained largely unfulfilled. During the postindependence period, political corruption continued, and civil liberties continued to be suppressed. Economic policies initiated by the ruling elite widened the gap between the rich and the poor. The introduction of Western values weakened the traditional value system and resulted in social and religious alienation. Indirect foreign interference in national life continued. Therefore, modernization programs adopted after World War II have contributed to the emergence of Islamic fundamentalism as an alternative to these failed models.

A fourth explanation views fundamentalism as a defensive posture against Western secularism, which has undermined traditional values. Since Napoleon's expedition to Egypt in 1798, the Muslim cultures in the Middle East and in south and central Asia have been experiencing a secularization process. Returning to tradition, fundamentalism defends Islamic heritage against encroachments by Western social values, cultural norms, and political and economic patterns.

The process of modernization in Muslim societies was initiated by the modernizing elite, who were often educated in secular Western educational institutions. Rarely did these leaders draw their ideas of social, political, and cultural change from the traditional culture of their own societies. The imported Western ideas of nationalism, liberal democracy, socialism, and women's liberation wrenched the social fabric of these societies. Since they were not rooted in the cultural context of these societies and were imposed by powerful elites without the participation of the masses, they resulted in polarization of the Muslim community and culture by pitting forces of religion against modernity, native against foreign, modern against traditional, and secular against sacred. While the upper and middle classes adopted Western secular culture, the religious forces and masses remained loyal to traditional ideas and practices. With the failure of modernization to transform these societies successfully, a backlash set in: Western ideologies, values, and norms were to be rejected. "Western" came to represent all things alien, ungodly, colonial, and "wrong." Islamic tradition was considered original, native, and "right."

Context

As a sociological phenomenon, fundamentalism is certainly not unique to the Muslim world. Some sociologists have argued that the political, cultural, social, and religious conditions of the post-Cold War era are ripe for the development of global fundamentalism. According to these social scientists, the interaction between contradictory trends toward secularism and religiosity calls for generically fundamentalist religious responses to the moral crises of the modern world. The increasing presence of political and religious forces such as militant Sikhs and Hindus in India, antiabortion Roman Catholics in the United States, the ultraorthodox Haredim and Gush Emunin in Israel, new Christian rightists and charismatic Protestants in North and Central America, neo-Shinto nationalists in Japan, Muslim Brotherhoods in Arab countries, and Shi'a radicalism in Iran, Lebanon, and other parts of the world are all cited as examples of this kind of fundamentalist response to changes brought about by secular forces of modernity.

For more than four decades, sociologists subscribed to the view that traditional societies are bound to adopt the characteristics of modern industrialized societies. Once on the road toward industrialization and modernization, the religious values and beliefs in these societies become less significant and are inevitably replaced by secular beliefs and attitudes.

The global resurgence of religious activism in the past decade, especially in the Islamic countries, testifies to the inaccuracy of such a view. To the surprise of many politicians and policy makers, both developed and less-developed societies have been experiencing a surge in religious fervor. At first, Western politicians viewed Islamic fundamentalism as an irrational phenomenon not worthy of serious attention. This general dismissal contributed to negative journalistic accounts of these movements as subversive, reactionary, and obscurantist.

The resilience of Islamic fundamentalists in pursuing their goals and their bold and violent actions against Western political interests has forced Western political leaders to take this movement more seriously. The simultaneous growth of fundamentalist movements around the world has increased social scientists' interest in this phenomenon. Earlier biased, superficial, and nonscientific approaches have been replaced by more serious, academic, and balanced approaches.

The rise of Islamic fundamentalism tends to be viewed in two opposite fashions. The first perspective, represented by sociologists of religion, views this revival of religious activism both as showing the continued significance of religion in political life and as providing evidence against the secularization thesis. The second perspective, mainly held by Marxists and secular advocates of modernization theory, views such revivalism as a transitional, defensive, and reactionary effort on the part of traditional forces and groups whose positions are threatened by the forces of modernization. According to the latter view, the increasing rationalization of the world, the increasing advancement of science and technology and demand for their by-products, the globalization of forms of social life, and the decreasing significance of the supernatural in controlling forces of nature will eventually either make fundamentalist ideologies obsolete or force their advocates to adjust their views and practices to modern life.

Bibliography

Butterworth, Charles E., and I. William Zartman, eds. *Political Islam*. Newbury Park, Calif.: Sage Publications, 1992. This is a good collection of essays about various aspects of politicization of Islam in Iran, Egypt, the new Muslim republics in central

Asia, Nigeria, and Morocco. A good source for identifying various voices in Islamic fundamentalism. College-level reading.

Esposito, John L. *The Islamic Threat: Myth or Reality?*. New York: Oxford University Press, 1992. A very important book in dealing with the founded and unfounded fears of Islamic fundamentalism in Western countries. Includes a balanced analysis of stereotypes and exaggerated images of both the West and Islam. A must for anyone interested in a clear understanding of Islamic politics in the modern world.

Jansen, G. H. *Militant Islam*. New York: Harper & Row, 1979. A clear account of the development of Islamic militancy during the 1970's. Although a bit outdated, it still represents a clear statement of the Islamization movement. Appropriate for both college and high school levels.

Marty, Martin E., and R. Scott Appleby, eds. *Fundamentalisms Observed*. Chicago: University of Chicago Press, 1991. The first of three major books on the nature, history, types, and influence of fundamentalist movements on society. Though a bit specialized, the articles in these collections are seminal to understanding this phenomenon from a cross-cultural and comparative perspective. The other two volumes, also edited by Marty and Appleby, are entitled *Fundamentalisms and the State: Remaking Polities, Economies, and Militance* (1993) and *Fundamentalisms and Society: Reclaiming the Sciences, the Family, and Education* (1993).

Piscatori, James P., ed. *Islam in the Political Process*. New York: Cambridge University Press, 1983. This collection contains several readings about the nature of Islamic politics and the politics of Islamization in Pakistan, Iran, Turkey, Algeria, Senegal, Syria, Iraq, Saudi Arabia, and Sudan.

Ali Akbar Mahdi

Cross-References

Buddhism, 165; Christianity, 231; Churches, Denominations, and Sects, 246; Judaism, 1029; Religion: Beliefs, Symbols, and Rituals, 1598; Religion: Functionalist Analyses, 1603; Religion: Marxist and Conflict Theory Views, 1610; Religious Miracles and Visions, 1623.

JUDAISM

Type of sociology: Major social institutions
Field of study: Religion

Judaism is one of the world's major religions, with origins deeply rooted in antiquity. Its chief features are monotheism, historical ethnocentrism, and a strong moral foundation.

Principal terms

ASHKENAZI: Diaspora Jews who migrated to the Franco-German area of Europe during the medieval period

DIASPORA: the territory of Jewish settlement outside the Holy Land (Palestine)

ETHNOCENTRISM: a belief in the superiority of one's own religion or culture

GHETTO: an urban ethnic enclave, originally designating Jewish quarters in European cities

HOLOCAUST: the Nazi death camp program of extermination carried out against Jews

MONOTHEISM: a belief in a single, supreme deity

POGROM: a systematic persecution and massacre

SEPHARDI: Diaspora Jews who migrated to the Andalusian-Spanish area of Europe during the medieval period

ZIONISM: the movement to establish a Jewish state in Palestine

Overview

Judaism has a complex history of development that has been traced as far back as the twentieth century B.C.E. Most scholars agree, however, that modern Judaism is rooted either in the Haskala (the Enlightenment) of the Ashkenazic Jews of eastern and central Europe in the eighteenth century C.E. or, somewhat earlier, in the acculturation of the Sephardic Jews in Italy and western Europe. These two branches of Diaspora Jews, with some minor doctrinal differences, held firmly to the traditional beliefs of Judaism and the basic authority of the Talmud, the collection of rabbinical writings making up the religious and civil codes of Jewry.

While monotheism, messianism, and other fundamental tenets of their faith remained intact, adherents of Judaism gradually broke with the passivity that had marked Jewry throughout the Middle Ages, rejecting its self-perception as a people patiently awaiting redemption from their suffering in exile among the gentiles, infidels who persecuted them for their beliefs or, worse, expelled or destroyed them in pogroms.

While the insularity that marked Jewish communities in the Diaspora never completely vanished, from the end of the eighteenth century on there was a greater trend toward cultural assimilation, especially in North America and industrialized Europe.

A principal figure in encouraging Jews to adapt to their host nation's culture was Moses Mendelssohn (1729-1786), a German philosopher whose defense of Judaism, *Jerusalem: oder über religiöse Macht und Judentum* (1783; *Jerusalem: A Treatise on Ecclesiastical Authority and Judaism*, 1838), while proclaiming that faith to be divinely ordained, accepted the notion of a universal religion, based in reason, of which Judaism was but one part. An important biblical commentator, Mendelssohn helped translate Jewish scripture (the Torah) into German and worked assiduously to convince other Jews that in their cultural assimilation they need not sacrifice their religious orthodoxy.

Acculturation was furthered by what has been called the Emancipation, brought about through the repeal of discriminatory laws. By the nineteenth century, in most European nations emancipated Jews could study at universities and enter such professions as medicine and law, long prohibited to them. It was a considerable step forward: Through much of their history, in their dealings with Christians, European Jews had been limited to such activities as itinerant trading and usury (money lending). The risk for Jewry was that in adopting the culture of their host nations, Jews would abandon their faith, as did happen in some families. While most did not go to that extreme, many did begin to think of themselves as citizens of their adopted country first and as Jews only by religious conviction.

This new spirit of cultural assimilation inevitably led to religious reform, particularly in the first decades of the nineteenth century. Reformists held that many traditional beliefs and religious observances of Judaism were simply incompatible with the exigencies of modern life. In France, under Napoleon, a Sanhedrin (Jewish council or tribunal) was convened in 1807 to formulate a new definition of Judaism that would reflect modern realities. It rejected the ancient concept of Jewish nationhood and limited rabbinical authority to spiritual matters alone, accepting civil jurisdiction over all secular concerns, including marriage. In Germany, in mid-century synods, reformers proclaimed that Jews were bound only by the moral law of Judaism, not by its specific forms and rituals. Their ideas led to the use of the vernacular in religious services and the abandonment of such time-honored practices as the observance of the ancient dietary laws.

The reform movement proved most durable in the United States, brought in by German Jews who, in the 1840's and succeeding decades, migrated to North America in great numbers. Before the end of the century, most synagogues in the United States had become Reform temples, with membership in the Union of American Hebrew Congregations, formed in 1873. In 1885, a conference of Reform rabbis drafted the Pittsburgh Platform, proclaiming that Judaism was no longer a national faith and that the Talmud was to be interpreted not as canon law but as religious literature. In Europe the movement fared less well, particularly in eastern Europe, where persecution rebuffed efforts of Haskala reformers to establish their identity as loyal nationalists. In Russia, a reaction to Jewish assimilation set in with the terrible pogroms of 1881 and 1905, which foreshadowed the Holocaust in Nazi Germany.

An entrenched distrust of gentiles, warranted by continued persecution, convinced most European Jews to maintain both their religious orthodoxy and their distinct folkways. They often remained insular by choice, even when no longer obliged to do so. In Germany, to counteract the influence of the Reform synagogues, which were eroding the unique religio-ethnic identity of the Jews, Samson Raphael Hirsch (1808-1888) and his followers promoted Neo-Orthodoxy, whose adherents argued that traditional rituals and observances should not be sacrificed to cultural assimilation. Their teaching served as the basis for the Western Orthodoxy that would eventually rival the Reform movement in the United States as fresh waves of European immigrants reached New World shores.

A third movement, Conservative Judaism, trod the line between Reform and Orthodox Judaism. It, too, emerged in Germany, when, in 1845, a group led by Zacharias Frankel (1801-1875) broke ranks with a Reform synod held in Frankfurt. The Conservatives were unwilling to limit the use of Hebrew in services, insisting that, historically, the language was too intricately bound to the expression of the faith to allow its discontinuance in worship. They did, however, accept the central reform concept of Judaism as a developmental or accretionary religion.

Conservatism also flourished in the United States and in the twentieth century became the third member of the sectarian triad that now accounts for the religious preference of most American Jews.

Applications

Discrimination against Jews in the Diaspora has continued despite the fact that in most industrialized nations its legal sanctions have been removed for almost two centuries. It partly results from the fact that residual discrimination against ethnic minorities tends to outlive legalized or institutionalized discrimination, even when there are statutory safeguards against it. Anti-Jewish discrimination is compounded by the fact that it has evolved from both anti-Judaism and anti-Semitism, which are not precisely the same thing, though the distinction between them is largely moot.

Anti-Judaism first arose in antiquity, in both polytheistic paganism and Pauline Christology. According to many scholars, the earliest Christians, themselves Semites, had to compete with Jews in efforts to win new converts to their separatist faith. At the time, the Hebrews were militant and zealous proselytizers who dared to defy even the Romans, as their unyielding mass suicide at Masada in 73 C.E. testifies.

In the Diaspora, at least in the medieval Christian world, the Jews carried the stigma of being "Christ killers" and a reputation for theological intractability for not accepting Jesus as the true messiah. Their ethnocentrism led to terrible suspicions—that, for example, they desecrated the host, sacrificed Christian children (the notorious "blood libel"), and brought on the Black Death (1348-1350) by poisoning wells—but the persecutions largely remained religiously based. Some Jews, notably moneylenders, were despised for other reasons, but the official sanctions against them were usually imposed more on theological than ethnic grounds. Ironically, given contemporary events in the Middle and Near East, in some Islamic areas, notably in Spain, the Sephardic Jews, considered "people of the book," were often treated much better,

Sociology

and some even rose to great political prominence. It was there, under the Arab sponsorship of arts and letters, that they produced the Golden Age of Hebrew Literature (c. 1000-1150 C.E.).

The persecution of Jews until the time of the Enlightenment was partly prompted by their self-imposed insularity, their insistence that they were in exile from their Promised Land. For their distinct self-identity they were forced to pay a terrible price. For example, by the end of the sixteenth century, in most European cities they were required to live in their own quarter, or ghetto, under all sorts of legal restrictions and prohibitions. They were at times expelled from some countries, including England.

Jews who later gave up the self-concept of belonging to a nation in exile had a right to press for an end to sanctioned discrimination and expect it, finally, to end in practice. Even in the United States, however, with its fundamental doctrine of religious freedom, Jews did not escape a more insidious sort of persecution based on ethnic prejudices rather than strong religious convictions. Jews were often accused of being clannish, secretive, miserly, aggressive, and, at times, un-American. Among other important Americans, industrialist Henry Ford was rabidly anti-Semitic. He used the newspaper he controlled, *The Dearborn Independent*, to spread the totally unfounded but widely believed idea that there was an international Jewish conspiracy dedicated to overthrowing legitimate governments by fostering atheism and anarchy. It was to counter such errant libel that the ecumenical National Conference of Christians and Jews was founded in 1928.

In Europe, particularly in post-World War I Germany, the Jews were subjected to an increasingly virulent persecution that would reach its full horror under the regime of Adolf Hitler. Many disillusioned Jews had already turned to Zionism, believing that their only hope lay in the creation of a nation of their own in Palestine, their ancestral home. Some Jews did place their hopes on radical sociopolitical change, including socialism and communism, but most rejected the atheism at the core of Marxism. Modern Zionism was actually a rekindling of beliefs that had been suppressed in the Enlightenment and Emancipation, centering on the idea that someday, under the providential guidance of Jehovah, the Jews would return from exile, restored to their rightful nation-home. It would take its vigorous secular and militant "back to Jerusalem" form after the Holocaust, resulting in the creation of the state of Israel, but it was advocated decades earlier, even in the United States, where the new Zionism was espoused by the Reconstructionist followers of Mordecai Menahem Kaplan (1881-1983) as early as the 1920's.

Zionism in Europe was even more trenchant. By the end of the nineteenth century, liberal Jews who had sought an end to Jewish-Christian conflict had had their hopes dashed in eastern Europe, especially Russia, where the Orthodox church aided and abetted the pogroms and disseminated the spurious *Protocols of the Elders of Zion*, one source of the Jewish conspiracy theory that poisoned the minds of many non-Jews. Despairing of ever reconciling their Jewish culture to the non-Jewish religions and cultures of their host nations, Jews in eastern Europe either hunkered down in their segregated tradition, emigrated, or sought solutions in Zionism. Zionism also attracted radical antireligious Jews and socialistic Jews whose Zionism was purely secular in vision.

The plight of nonemigrating European Jews was gravely intensified with the rise of Hitler's Fascism and his racist theories of Aryan supremacy. While most European Christians stood by silently and watched without protest, Hitler vilified the Jews. They were an easy scapegoat, especially in the romantic anti-intellectualism that characterized the Nazi vision of the world. When he came to power, Hitler began a systematic campaign of persecution that, during World War II, culminated in the "final solution"—the genocidal extermination of Jews. Jews were rounded up throughout the conquered nations of Europe and North Africa and sent to extermination camps, where more than six million were put to death.

The Holocaust severely reduced the number of Jews in Europe, which, until the war, had been the center of Jewish culture and tradition in the Diaspora. In effect, it severed the ties of many emigrant Jews to their past, totally obliterating such important Jewish cultural enclaves as the Warsaw ghetto. It also resulted in a major demographic shift, moving the centers of contemporary Judaism away from Europe to the United States and Israel.

Context

It was in the Holocaust that the Jews experienced the greatest single calamity in their history, surpassing even their loss of sovereignty over Palestine with the Roman destruction of Jerusalem in 70 C.E. The Nazi efforts to exterminate the Jews resulted in three major changes: the destruction of whole communities of Diaspora Jews in Europe and North Africa, the disappearance of millennial Jewish settlements in Islamic countries in the Middle East, and the "ingathering" of exiled Jews in the nation-state of Israel.

Although Israel was created in 1948 as a secular democracy, it fostered pride in Jews throughout the world, particularly in its succession of victories over the Islamic nations that had vowed to drive the Jews out of the Holy Land. Many liberal Jews who had neglected or even rejected their heritage before the Holocaust, made a new commitment to it in the post-World War II years. They also won the sympathy of many Christians, shocked by the great horror and dehumanizing impact of the Nazi policy. As Stephen Sharot notes in *Judaism: A Sociology* (1976), in the postwar "Western Diaspora there was a sharp decline of overt anti-semitism and all forms of discrimination." Cultural and religious insularity, where it persists in the West, reflects choice rather than compulsion.

Using familiar sociological terms, Sharot makes a distinction between "instrumental" and "expressive" associations in society. The former is used to refer to groups established primarily for socializing, the latter to groups formed to achieve some desired goal. The vestiges of anti-Semitism in the West are largely found in expressive associations, as, for example, in private clubs, where membership may exclude religious, ethnic, or racial minorities. Discrimination of that sort is culturally endemic, and as history repeatedly confirms, virtually impossible to eradicate.

The Holocaust taught Western Jews to be vigilant. They remain acutely aware that it was in pre-Nazi Germany that Jews had made the greatest intellectual, artistic, and socioeconomic post-Enlightenment advances and that within a generation under Nazi persecution they were deprived of everything: their citizenship, livelihood, possessions, freedom, and, finally, even their lives. Still, as Sharot argues, "the constraints on Western Jews to make a choice between two identities and cultures are not so great as they were in many countries in the nineteenth century." Some post-Holocaust "Jew baiting" has occurred in the West. In the United States, for example, Jews have been subject to vicious diatribes by members of the Nation of Islam and by some right-wing extremists, but these have become an embarrassing anomaly that has found no popular appeal. In the West, as Sharot maintains, "religio-cultural pluralism and the social acceptability of Jews are now the norm rather than the exception."

Bibliography

Hexter, J. H. *The Judaeo-Christian Tradition*. New York: Harper & Row, 1966. An excellent, concise overview of the evolution of ancient Judaism and the Hebraic foundations of early Christianity in the Roman era. Recommended for the lay reader interested in comparative religion from a historical rather than a theological approach. Includes a select bibliography current through 1963.

Katz, Steven T. *Post-Holocaust Dialogues: Critical Studies in Modern Jewish Thought*. New York: New York University Press, 1983. In this survey of major contemporary Jewish philosophers and theologians, Katz critically analyzes the thinking of Martin Buber, Eliezer Berkovits, Richard Rubenstein, Emil Fackenheim, and Ignaz Maybaum. His final chapter, "The 'Unique' Intentionality of the Holocaust," offers an important assessment of Hitler's genocidal intent. Katz's notes are extensive, but he appends no bibliography.

Parkes, James. *End of an Exile: Israel, the Jews, and the Gentile World*. Marblehead, Mass.: Micah Publications, 1982. This book reprints an earlier text by Parkes, a Christian Zionist, and adds an appendix dealing with American Zionism, including essays by Reinhold Niebuhr and Carl Voss. Deals with Judaism and the creation of Israel from a sympathetic Christian perspective.

Patai, Raphael. *The Vanished Worlds of Jewry*. New York: Macmillan, 1980. Patai offers a fine survey of Jewry in Europe, North Africa, India, and the Near East, showing how its rich tradition was severely damaged by the Holocaust and the expulsion of "millenial" Jews from Muslim countries in Asia Minor. Includes a gallery of compelling photographs.

Sharot, Stephen. *Judaism: A Sociology*. New York: Holmes & Meier, 1976. This text reviews and interprets modern Judaism in the light of quantitative data gathered in demographic studies of Jewish communities, principally in the United States. It is a solid introduction to a comparative analysis based on the concepts of acculturation and deacculturation in both pre- and post-Holocaust Judaism.

Steinberg, Milton. *Basic Judaism*. New York: Harcourt, Brace, 1947. A brief, lucid survey of the "beliefs, ideals, and practices which make up the historic Jewish faith."

It explains the fundamentals of Judaism in simple terms unencumbered by excessive historical detail. It is a good introduction for non-Jews, but it is not a scholarly source.

Wigoder, Geoffrey. *The Encyclopedia of Judaism*. New York: Macmillan, 1989. This text is a great companion work for further study on Judaism. It is rich with illustrations from world art and architecture, and the coverage of key terms is excellent. Its index and cross-referencing are both extensive, but it is somewhat flawed as a research tool by the lack of a bibliography.

John W. Fiero

Cross-References

Annihilation or Expulsion of Racial or Ethnic Groups, 92; Anti-Semitism, 114; Christianity, 231; Ethnic Enclaves, 682; Ethnicity and Ethnic Groups, 689; Islam and Islamic Fundamentalism, 1022; Religion: Beliefs, Symbols, and Rituals, 1598; Religion: Functionalist Analyses, 1603; Religion: Marxist and Conflict Theory Views, 1610; Socialization: Religion, 1894; The Sociology of Religion, 1952.

JUVENILE DELINQUENCY: ANALYSIS AND OVERVIEW

Type of sociology: Deviance and social control
Fields of study: Controlling deviance; Forms of deviance

Juvenile delinquency consists of acts committed by minors that violate the law of the jurisdiction in which the act occurred. Juvenile delinquency is a major concern because it involves harm both to victims and to the offenders themselves, sometimes portends involvement in adult crime, and reveals the failure of conventional institutions to socialize children adequately.

Principal terms
  BIRTH COHORT: a group of people whose membership is defined by being born within the same period
  CONFLICT THEORIES OF DELINQUENCY: theories that emphasize the political and economic interests served by creating laws and selecting particular groups of offenders for punishment
  CONTROL THEORIES OF DELINQUENCY: theories that emphasize the multiple social and psychological factors that encourage or discourage involvement in delinquency
  DELINQUENT OFFENSE: a violation of the criminal law committed by a minor that would be a crime if committed by an adult
  JUVENILE COURT: a county-level court with jurisdiction over minors charged with delinquent and status offenses as well as over minors who are dependent and neglected
  LABELING PERSPECTIVE: an orientation for studying social deviance that emphasizes the social response to offending behavior and offenders
  PARENS PATRIAE: literally "parent of the country"; the principle under which the state protects minor children seen at risk of being harmed
  SOCIAL DISORGANIZATION: the failure of conventional social institutions, such as family and school, to socialize children and constrain behavior
  STATUS OFFENSE: a violation of the law that is only a violation when committed by a minor
  STRAIN THEORIES OF DELINQUENCY: theories that explain the cause of delinquency by emphasizing the frustration experienced by youths who do not have access to legal methods to achieve success

Overview

It was only at the end of the nineteenth century that crimes committed by children were given the distinctive label "juvenile delinquency." Before then, children charged with crimes were prosecuted in criminal courts, though their youth might cause judges to impose less severe punishments if they were convicted. Children sentenced to incarceration were sent to adult prisons in the sixteenth and seventeenth centuries, though sometimes they were separated from adults.

Under English common law, which emerged during the eleventh and twelfth centuries, children under the age of seven who committed crimes were not subject to the criminal law. Between the ages of seven and thirteen, children could be held responsible for their crimes, depending on their individual capacities.

In the fifteenth century, specialized chancery courts were created in England. These courts operated under the principles of *parens patriae*, the right and obligation of the sovereign to look after those subjects who could not take care of themselves. *Parens patriae* provided the philosophical inspiration and the public rhetoric of the first American juvenile court, established in Cook County, Illinois, in 1899. Under this philosophy all children who are at risk of harm, arising either from their own delinquent behavior or from parental neglect or abuse, come under the jurisdiction of the juvenile court.

In the 1960's a distinction was drawn between acts that are crimes if committed by adults, called "delinquent offenses," and acts that are illegal only when committed by children. The second category, called "status offenses," typically includes running away, being truant from school, and being disobedient to parents.

The major source of official data on juvenile delinquency in the United States is the Federal Bureau of Investigation's (FBI's) annual Uniform Crime Reports, compiled from reports of local police departments. In 1992, there were 1.6 million arrests of youths (under age eighteen) in the United States. These arrests of youths constituted 16 percent of all arrests. Youths were involved in 112,000 (18 percent of all) arrests for serious violent offenses and 608,000 (33 percent of all) arrests for serious property offenses. The offense for which youths are most commonly arrested is known as larceny-theft (402,000 arrests in 1992). The Uniform Crime Reports does not provide arrest data for most status offenses, though it did report in 1992 that 146,000 youths were arrested for running away. There are more than three times as many arrests of boys as of girls, though in the early 1990's arrests of girls were increasing faster than arrests of boys. Blacks are over-represented among arrested youths: In 1992, 27 percent of juveniles arrested were black, while blacks represented 16 percent of youths in the general population.

The pattern of officially recorded offenses over the entire childhood and adolescence of a group of people has been studied to reveal the concentration of delinquency. In the first large U.S. "birth cohort" study, conducted by sociologists Marvin E. Wolfgang, Robert Figlio, and Thorstin Sellin (*Delinquency in a Birth Cohort*, 1972), the police contacts of 9,945 boys who were born in 1945 and grew up in Philadelphia were analyzed. Thirty-five percent of the boys had at least one police contact while growing up. Among the many variables examined, race and socioeconomic status were found to distinguish most strongly between boys who had a police contact and those who had none. Most striking among the findings was the high concentration of arrests among a small proportion of boys: Only 6 percent of the boys were arrested five or more times, but that small group of "chronic recidivists" was responsible for 52 percent of all the arrests. Subsequent cohort studies done in Philadelphia and elsewhere have confirmed this finding of a high concentration of offenses among a small proportion of youths.

Another way delinquency has been studied is through "self-reports." This method involves surveying a large group of youths about their own delinquent behavior. Typically, they complete questionnaires anonymously to ensure confidentiality and encourage honesty in reporting. Annually, since 1975, sociologists Lloyd Johnston, Patrick O'Malley, and Jerald Bachman have surveyed a nationally representative group of U.S. high school students using the self-report method. The results appear annually in "Monitoring the Future," summarized in the *Sourcebook of Criminal Justice Statistics*, edited by Timothy Flanagan and Kathleen Maguire. These surveys have shown low, stable rates of involvement in minor theft, damage, and injury offenses since the beginning of the series in 1975. The use of most recreational drugs—marijuana, cocaine, stimulants, sedatives, tranquilizers, and alcohol—peaked in the late 1970's and has slowly declined since then. These self-reports have clearly established that alcohol has always been the most popular recreational drug, with 51 percent of high school seniors in 1992 reporting that they had used alcohol within thirty days preceding the survey, and 77 percent reporting that they had used alcohol within the preceding year.

Self-report surveys confirm the finding, based on arrest reports, that boys are more delinquent than girls. Self-report studies do not consistently confirm that blacks are generally more delinquent than whites. For many types of offenses—including status offenses, drug use, and public order offenses—there is little if any difference in involvement by race. The best available self-report evidence does indicate, however, that lower-class black youths do commit more serious, violent offenses than do members of other population groups.

Applications

During various periods government efforts to reduce delinquency have clearly been shaped by theories and empirical evidence developed by sociologists. In the 1930's, for example, sociologist Clifford R. Shaw conducted studies of slum neighborhoods in Chicago. From his observations, Shaw concluded that these neighborhoods, though poor, had informal social structures, including indigenous leaders. Shaw led the creation of the Chicago Area Project, consisting of more than a dozen separate neighborhood organizations established to solve a wide range of local social problems. Unlike nearly all prior and subsequent government-sponsored efforts to help poor people, the Chicago Area Project sought to empower people to help themselves. Indigenous leaders were identified by neighbors and employed by the project as salaried workers. They were trained in community organization by sociologists. Although an agency of the state of Illinois paid the salaries of all project employees, the state did not choose the leaders or dictate project activities.

The leaders first brought their neighbors together to identify local problems, which included street litter, insufficient recreation, poor-quality schools, hazardous traffic conditions, and widespread delinquency. Then they found ways to solve these problems. Some community improvement was accomplished solely through the organizations' own efforts—for example, supervising recreation programs and removing trash from city streets. Other activities involved working with political officials in activities such as volunteering to supervise juvenile offenders on probation.

Many of the neighborhood organizations established under the Chicago Area Project lasted for decades and were successful in improving residents' quality of life on many dimensions. The effects of the project on reducing delinquency were never rigorously documented, but the Chicago Area Project did provide successful models both for organizing communities and for reaching delinquents through direct, personal intervention. (Solomon Kobrin presented an analysis of the project in "The Chicago Area Project: A Twenty-five Year Assessment," in the *Annals of the Academy of Political and Social Sciences*, vol. 322, 1959, edited by Helen L. Witmer.)

In more recent years, the response to delinquency has stressed retribution and incapacitation, because a substantial proportion of serious, violent crimes are committed by juveniles and because less-punitive responses seem to have been ineffective. The central problem facing juvenile justice officials is how best to allocate scarce resources among the many offenders who come to their attention. Beginning in the 1970's, the cohort studies previously cited provided the empirical basis for a rational system of resource allocation.

Incarcerating all juvenile offenders is both impractical and unnecessary, according to these studies. Though about a third of boys have some contact with police during their adolescence, nearly half of them have only one contact, usually for a minor offense. Although precisely what motivates these children to end their delinquent careers is uncertain, one police contact seems to be sufficient to persuade them to stay out of trouble in the future. At the other end of the continuum are the chronic recidivists, those juveniles who are arrested at least five times. Though making up only 6 to 8 percent of all youths, they are responsible for 50 to 60 percent of all arrests.

This high concentration of delinquency among a relatively small proportion of youths fits well with a delinquency reduction strategy focused on chronic offenders. The results of cohort studies have been widely cited in support of a range of proposals to improve the effectiveness of both the juvenile system and the criminal justice system. Longer periods of incarceration, for example, have been adopted as a strategy to restrain the repeat juvenile offenders responsible for most delinquency. Many of the one-time offenders, shown in the cohort studies to be unlikely to commit another offense, are now diverted from the juvenile justice system to child welfare or counseling organizations.

Recognizing that criminal careers are continuous (that is, they are only artificially divided into "juvenile" and "adult" segments), some states have lowered the age when juveniles may be transferred to the criminal court for prosecution for serious offenses. For the same reason, some states have made juvenile arrest records available to criminal courts, because the "first-time" offender in court for sentencing may actually have a long record of juvenile offenses.

The cohort studies reveal that those juveniles who start their offense careers while they are very young have an especially high risk of continuing their offenses through adolescence and into adulthood. Early intervention to prevent continued offending has, therefore, been proposed, though the form this intervention should take is unclear. All these changes in the response to juvenile delinquency have been informed by cohort studies conducted by sociologists.

Another of the controversies that sociologists have participated in has been the contribution of the women's movement and feminist ideology to female delinquency. In the 1970's, female sociologists, critical of the traditional exclusion of girls from studies of delinquency, urged greater attention to girls as both offenders and victims. The pattern of arrests of females has changed over time; there have been increasing numbers of arrests for violent offenses. Female delinquency itself seems unaffected by the women's movement; girls are typically arrested for traditional property crimes, motivated by personal needs or desires unrelated to any ideology.

Girls have often been treated more harshly than boys by the juvenile justice system, though that pattern is changing. In an effort to punish girls for, and "protect" them from, premarital sexual activity, girls have been institutionalized for minor offenses such as running away, while boys who commit the same offenses receive less severe punishment.

Context

The first sociologists to study delinquency were associated with the University of Chicago early in the twentieth century. They saw delinquency as an urban problem, largely caused by the corrupting influences of city life and poverty. Sociologists Clifford R. Shaw and Henry D. McKay, in *Juvenile Delinquency and Urban Areas* (1942), found delinquency rates were highest close to the center city, where there were high rates of other social problems: illness, alcoholism, unemployment, adult crime, and poverty. They concluded that these problems were produced by "social disorganization," the breakdown of conventional social institutions.

Shaw and McKay observed that successive generations of juveniles trained their younger friends and siblings in delinquency. Sociologist Edwin Sutherland developed this theme further in his theory of differential association (*Principles of Criminology*, 4th ed., 1947), the best-known theory of delinquency. Sutherland argued that delinquency is learned, just as any other form of behavior is learned. This learning, which includes both techniques of delinquency and attitudes supporting delinquency, occurs within intimate primary groups.

In the most frequently cited article in all sociology ("Social Structure and Anomie," in *American Sociological Review* 3, October, 1938), sociologist Robert K. Merton extended the concept of anomie, or normlessness, coined by the nineteenth century French social philosopher Émile Durkheim. Merton focused on the mismatch between the social pressure to succeed and the absence of legitimate opportunities to do so, a condition producing "strain." Some people adapt to this strain by substituting alternative (often illegal) means of achieving the goal of financial success.

The structural-strain theory of delinquency, as articulated by sociologists Richard A. Cloward and Lloyd E. Ohlin (*Delinquency and Opportunity: A Theory of Delinquent Gangs*, 1960) was used in the development of a national social policy initiative by President Lyndon Johnson's administration. Cloward and Ohlin proposed that the problem of delinquency was rooted in the absence of legitimate job opportunities for poor people. The Johnson Administration's War on Poverty program was designed to provide skill training and jobs for poor people, with delinquency reduction as one goal.

The juvenile court was one among many developments of the Progressive Era (roughly from 1900 to 1920) of American history, a period characterized by increased government attempts to solve widespread problems created by industrialization and urbanization. Sociologist Anthony Platt, writing from the conflict theory perspective, has noted that *parens patriae* was used by the juvenile court to extend its control over more children, primarily to maintain order within the existing social class structure. Writing from the labeling perspective, sociologist Howard S. Becker (*Outsiders: Studies in the Sociology of Deviance*, 1963), claimed that delinquency is not a quality inherent in a child's behavior but is the product of rule-making and enforcement by politically powerful groups.

Control theorists emphasize the social and psychological factors in each child's world that either draw the child into delinquency or insulate the child from delinquency. Sociologist Travis Hirschi sees delinquency as a natural phenomenon, inherently attractive to most children. For Hirschi, it is the rejection of delinquency by most youths that needs to be explained. Hirschi's own "social bonding" theory (*Causes of Delinquency*, 1969) asserts that delinquency occurs when the emotional ties between children and their parents and friends are weakened. This theory has received the strongest empirical support among all the sociological theories of delinquency.

These theories of delinquency were developed almost entirely within the context of male delinquency. Some evidence suggests that female delinquency may be influenced by many of the same processes, but the operation of these processes in the lives of girls has not been well studied. In addition, strong evidence of a hereditary component in delinquency has emerged. Sociologists will have to reconcile this new evidence with traditional social structural and social psychological explanations.

Bibliography

Bartollas, Clemens. *Juvenile Delinquency*. 3d ed. New York: Macmillan, 1992. A solid, clearly written overview of the broad range of issues included in the study of delinquency: its nature and extent, theories of causation, family and school influences, the juvenile justice system, and prevention efforts. Intended for an undergraduate audience.

Gaines, Donna. *Teenage Wasteland: Suburbia's Dead End Kids*. New York: Pantheon Books, 1991. Describes the anomic condition of working class youths whose employment prospects are undercut by economic changes. Analyzes the context of the suicide of four suburban teenagers. Examines the history and significance of rock and heavy metal music and others aspects of youth culture in the 1970's and 1980's. Written in a passionate, journalistic style.

Gottfredson, Michael R., and Travis Hirschi. *A General Theory of Crime.* Stanford, Calif.: Stanford University Press, 1990. Describes predominant characteristics of criminal and delinquent acts and concludes that low self-control produces most crime and delinquency. Critically evaluates all major theories of crime and delinquency. An argumentative, lively style holds readers' attention.

Hirschi, Travis. *Causes of Delinquency.* Berkeley: University of California Press, 1969. The first statement of social control theory. Though this book describes in detail an empirical test of that theory, the clear writing style and low level of statistical analysis make it accessible for most readers.

Platt, Anthony M. *The Child Savers: The Invention of Delinquency.* 2d ed. Chicago: University of Chicago Press, 1977. Critically analyzes the late nineteenth century social context in which youth crime was redefined as delinquency and the juvenile court was established. Examines closely the elitist social agenda advanced by the predominantly upper-class women who advocated establishment of a separate juvenile court.

Wolfgang, Marvin E., Robert M. Figlio, and Thorstin Sellin. *Delinquency in a Birth Cohort.* Chicago: University of Chicago Press, 1972. Describes the first large-scale study of the officially recorded delinquency of a birth cohort of urban males in the United States. The finding that a small proportion of boys was responsible for most delinquency was widely influential in the passage of laws providing more punitive responses to repeat offenders.

Joseph E. Jacoby

Cross-References

FEMALE JUVENILE DELINQUENCY

Type of sociology: Deviance and social control
Field of study: Forms of deviance

Delinquency refers to conduct by juveniles that violates the criminal law. It also refers to the violation of laws pertaining solely to juveniles, which is called a status offense. Female juveniles, according to official statistics, more frequently violate status laws and are incarcerated for longer periods of time than delinquent males. There is some evidence that female delinquency is becoming more serious in nature.

Principal terms
FEMINISM: the doctrine advocating social and political rights for women equal to those of men
INDEX OFFENSES: the list of eight serious offenses compiled by the Federal Bureau of Investigation in the Uniform Crime Reports, the primary source of official crime data in the United States
JUVENILE DELINQUENCY: the violation of criminal or status laws by an individual under the age of majority (usually eighteen)
JUVENILE JUSTICE SYSTEM: the legal rules, agencies, and organizations responsible for the administration of juvenile justice and the control of delinquency
NON-INDEX OFFENSES: less serious offenses listed in the Uniform Crime Reports published by the FBI; they include status offenses for juveniles
PATERNALISM: the practice by which governing individuals, businesses, or nations act in the manner of a father dealing with his children
STATUS OFFENSE: an act that violates the laws governing appropriate behavior for children and that is illegal only for them

Overview

Information is needed before behavior can be studied. There are three major methods of collecting data about crime and delinquency in the United States. They are the Uniform Crime Reports (UCR), compiled annually by the Federal Bureau of Investigation (FBI) from arrest data submitted by police; the National Crime Survey, which surveys victims of crime; and self-report studies, which ask juveniles about their involvement in criminal or delinquent activity. Victim surveys and self reports have helped illuminate what the National Commission on the Causes and Prevention of Violence (1969) called the "dark side of crime." These measures supplement the FBI's official statistics, partially filling the gap between the amount of crime actually committed and that recorded by police.

Official statistics show that females are arrested at a higher rate than males for status offenses, but self-report studies indicate that males commit as many, if not more, status offenses than females. Criminologist Rachelle Canter reports no evidence of more female involvement in status offenses than males. Nevertheless, females have traditionally been overarrested for status offenses such as truancy, running away, incorrigibility, and sexual misbehavior.

Sociologist LaMar Empey suggests in his book *American Delinquency: Its Meaning and Construction* (rev. ed., 1982) that police use a double standard when dealing with male and female delinquents. Empey states that although females steal, burglarize, drink, and skip school just as boys do, they are more likely to be taken into custody when they run away from home, disobey their parents, and are sexually active. Criminologist Christy Visher notes that younger females receive harsher treatment because police officers probably adopt a more paternalistic attitude toward them to deter any further deviation from socially approved sex role behavior. Criminal justice officials see girls as needing protection from the immoral influences in society or from their own sexuality—hence the greater tendency to incarcerate girls for either status offenses or sexual misbehavior.

In their book *Girls, Delinquency, and Juvenile Justice* (1992), Meda Chesney-Lind and Randall Sheldon confirm that the juvenile justice system has a sexual double standard that views females as commodities who must have their sexuality controlled. They say parents and police respond differently to the same behavior in boys and girls. Parents of girls are more likely to call the police than are parents of boys, and the police are more likely to arrest girls than boys for running away or sexually "acting out." The juvenile justice system appears to be committed to parental authority and control over girls even when it is arguably not in the best interest of the girl.

Chesney-Lind notes that girls have frequently been returned to abusive parents after running away, only to run away again. Each brush with police increases the impression that the juvenile is incorrigible or unruly, when in fact she may simply be trying to survive by escaping an abusive environment. Many young women who run away from abusive homes are forced to beg, steal, or turn to prostitution in order to survive on the streets. Sociologist Mary Odem states that the juvenile court has been an important tool in the control of female juveniles, especially those living in single-mother homes.

Sociologist Ronald J. Berger notes that official statistics show that, after prostitution and running away, young females are most frequently arrested for property crimes such as larceny-theft (a charge stemming primarily from shoplifting), forgery, counterfeiting, fraud, embezzlement, and liquor law violations. Sociologist Rosemary Sarri studied 1,735 midwestern youths and found that while male-to-female ratios were similar for minor offenses such as truancy, a significant number of males admitted to committing more serious crimes than females. This information parallels the Uniform Crime Reports, which shows that males are arrested for about 80 percent of the serious offenses, nationwide, while females are arrested more frequently for status offenses. Sarri's study revealed, however, that some female juveniles were involved in more serious offenses such as gang fighting and hitting teachers.

For most offenders, commitment to an institution usually comes after conviction of a serious crime. For female juveniles, however, incarceration is a common result of being adjudicated delinquent. This determination comes most often after the commission of a status offense. Coramae Richey Mann, in her book *Female Crime and Delinquency* (1984), cites a New York study which found that most of the female juveniles recommended for incarceration were black girls who had violated sexual norms or disregarded their parents' authority. Their behavior consisted of choosing undesirable boyfriends, staying out too late, or being sexually promiscuous.

A Washington state study reported by the United States Department of Justice revealed that girls were committed to institutions twice as often as boys. The girls were likely to be nonwhite, from broken homes, and having trouble in school. Ruth Glick and Virginia Neto, in their *National Study of Women's Correctional Programs* (1977), found that girls who committed felonies and misdemeanors were treated more leniently than girls involved in status or noncriminal behavior. Girls who were charged with offenses such as ungovernability or curfew violation were treated more harshly than boys charged with similar conduct; moreover, girls were treated more harshly even for first offenses.

Applications

Knowledge gained from the study of female juvenile delinquency has led to the realization that females are treated differently by criminal justice authorities because they are female, regardless of their behavior. Because of the system's paternalistic view of females, many girls' lives have been altered irrevocably by institutionalization. Chesney-Lind argues that the juvenile justice system has played an important role in the criminalization of girls' survival techniques and has been used by those in power to reinforce sex roles demanding the obedience and subservience of females in a patriarchal society.

Research studies have been designed to examine stereotyping of females by police and prosecutors. Candace Kruttschnitt studied the offenses with which women are charged and the offenses of which women are convicted and found a substantial degree of discrepancy between those categories. She notes that women are most frequently arrested for theft, drunkenness, disorderly conduct, drug law violations, and assaults. They are most frequently convicted of forgery, fraud, and drunken driving. Kruttschnitt believes that regardless of a woman's actual conduct, what she is ultimately arrested for and adjudicated for may depend more upon her race, income, and who her victim is than upon any specific legal violation. Decisions made by the police and prosecutors early in the process shape official statistics as well as the image of the female offender and her offenses. Kruttschnitt's research shows that females are stereotyped by criminal justice officials and lumped into categories even before formal charges are decided.

The increasing awareness of the kind of treatment females have received in the past and their increasing numbers in correctional facilities has prompted the American Correctional Association (ACA) to study the situation of the female offender in the United States. Their book *The Female Offender: What Does the Future Hold?* (1990) profiles the juvenile female offender.

The ACA reports that the average juvenile female offender is between the ages of fourteen and seventeen and is a member of a minority group. She has never been married. She comes from a single-parent home or a broken home. The average girl has run away from home between ten and twenty times because she was insecure about parental love. She is easily influenced by her peers and uses drugs to feel better. She has attempted suicide between one and four times because she believed that no one cared about her and life was too painful to continue. She has been a victim of sexual abuse, most likely by a male member of her family. She has used alcohol, cocaine, speed, and marijuana. The average female juvenile offender has been arrested between two and nine times, beginning when she was twelve years old, and she is a high school dropout.

Although most female juveniles are incarcerated for property offenses and running away, an increasing number are being punished for committing violent offenses. The ACA reports that 22 percent of incarcerated female juveniles in the United States were arrested for more serious crimes including assault, arson, burglary, robbery, and murder. Freda Adler, in her book *Sisters in Crime* (1975), commented that because of the women's liberation movement, women are taking their place next to men in all aspects of life, including criminality. She predicted an equalizing trend in which female crime statistics would parallel men's in both the amount of crime committed and the type of offenses.

Although there has been some increase in female crime in official statistics, the explosion of serious offending predicted by Adler in 1975 has not occurred. LaMar Empey states that while overall, girls are still not as delinquent as boys, many girls report committing illegal acts traditionally considered to be "male" offenses.

Some criminologists explain the increase in female delinquency as simply a change in the way the criminal justice system reacts to females. Concern about the "new kind of female offender" as well as increasing sensitivity toward sexual discrimination has led some to surmise that female behavior has not actually changed; rather, they say, the system's response to it has. Berger states that evidence is mixed but does not support the idea that society's reaction is solely responsible for the increasing rates in female juvenile delinquency. He cites changing gender roles and role strain stemming from a more complex society with conflicting expectations about acceptable female conduct. It is conceivable that as women are more fully accepted in traditionally male professions and endeavors, their behavior will more fully resemble male behavior. One likely ramification of the increased social awareness of female delinquency is that females will no longer be relegated to a footnote or considered unworthy of study. In that sense, women will have achieved equality.

Context

Criminal behavior has traditionally been considered a male phenomenon. Early criminologists saw female criminality as an aberration rooted in sexual activity. Female juveniles were not considered worthy of study; their characters and their actions were stereotyped. Both social scientists and criminal justice practitioners believed that they already knew the kinds of behavior in which girls participated and why. Female juveniles were arrested and incarcerated for incorrigibility or sexual acting out because the male-dominated society wanted to protect them from their own sexuality. Girls who were considered too "free and easy" were locked up "for their own good."

With the advent of the women's liberation movement in the 1960's, female offending was almost glorified by some writers as an example of women's ascendence to equality. A new breed of more violent female offender was described. Female gang members were interviewed and observed, their fighting and looting described in detail. Social scientists took note, immediately debating whether there really was a change in female offending and, if so, what the cause might be. Changing social roles and expanding life possibilities were discussed as possible contributors to the increase in female delinquency. Author Susan Faludi points out that those who opposed the women's liberation movement have claimed that radical feminism is the cause of society's increasing disruption, including more criminal behavior by females. Ilene R. Bergsman has called for specific research and programming for juvenile female offenders, claiming they have been ignored for a century and hence are in desperate need of correctional attention.

Criminologists most frequently look at delinquency in gender terms, trying to explain each type separately. Coramae Richey Mann cautions, however, that looking at criminality as a male or female phenomenon, rather than as a human phenomenon, is to make the mistake of looking at only one side of the issue. She claims that "any effort to understand the causes of crime must include both sexes, all ages, all classes, and all ethnic groups in the model." She recommends a unisex theory of crime and delinquency, saying that the traditional approach of studying male versus female behavior has failed to explain the origins of crime and delinquency.

Bibliography

Adler, Freda. *Sisters in Crime*. New York: McGraw-Hill, 1975. A provocative and well-written thesis that discusses the women's liberation movement and its impact on female criminality. Adler created controversy and prompted hundreds of books and articles in response to her claims that a new kind of female criminal was emerging.

American Correctional Association. *The Female Offender: What Does the Future Hold?* Laurel, Md.: Author, 1990. A clearly written study of the policy implications of the rapid growth in the number of females being incarcerated. Recommends specific strategies to address major issues such as facility design, programs, security, classification, and visitation.

Berger, Ronald J. "Contemporary Trends in Female Delinquency: Stability or Change?" In *The Sociology of Juvenile Delinquency*, edited by Ronald J. Berger. Chicago: Nelson-Hall, 1991. This is a collection of essays designed to provide a sociological perspective on delinquency. The book is divided into six sections that examine all aspects of the phenomenon, from the social construction of deviance to the experience of being a delinquent to the function of the juvenile justice system. Entries range from scholarly essays to magazine articles, keeping the reading lively.

Chesney-Lind, Meda. "Girl's Crime and Woman's Place: Toward a Feminist Model of Female Delinquency." *Crime and Delinquency* 35 (January, 1989): 5-29. Chesney-Lind argues that traditional theories of delinquency are inappropriate and inadequate to explain female delinquency and official reactions to it. She discusses how the circumstances surrounding girls' crime have been ignored, thus blaming the victim. A thoughtful piece, well documented and persuasively written. Includes an extensive bibliography.

Empey, LaMar T. *American Delinquency: Its Meaning and Construction.* Rev. ed. Homewood, Ill.: Dorsey Press, 1982. This introductory text discusses methods of data collection and theories of delinquency, and it places modern issues into a historical context. It is well written and fully documented. Includes a glossary of important terms and subject and author indexes.

Mann, Coramae Richey. *Female Crime and Delinquency.* Tuscaloosa: University of Alabama Press, 1984. Examines the problem of crime and delinquency from a female perspective in an attempt to balance the traditional male discussion of these issues. The author claims to write for people specializing in criminology, law, sociology, and psychology, and for the public at large. She has succeeded in her task of creating a scholarly work that is also quite readable. The book includes vivid descriptions of custodial facilities for women and girls in the United States.

Kate Parks

Cross-References

Child Abuse and Neglect, 218; Conflict Perspectives on Deviance, 334; Crime: Analysis and Overview, 373; The Criminal Justice System, 380; Juvenile Delinquency: Analysis and Overview, 1036; Prostitution, 1526; Role Conflict and Role Strain, 1655; The Women's Movement, 2196.

LABELING AND DEVIANCE

Type of sociology: Deviance and social control
Field of study: Theories of deviance

According to labeling theory, deviance is defined by society when a generally accepted rule or custom is violated. Thus, the term "deviance" represents a value judgment that is applied to individuals who do not conform to a social norm. Such labels generally carry negative and lasting connotations that may profoundly influence persons to whom they are applied.

Principal terms
DEVIANCE: in labeling theory, this term refers to a value judgment by society for behavior that violates social rules or expectations
RULE-BREAKING: the violation of a social rule, whether it is an explicit or implicit rule
SOCIAL CONTROL: all practices and forces that are designed to maintain social order and conformity within society
SOCIAL NORMS: rules and expectations for acceptable behavior within society
SOCIAL REACTION: another term for labeling; it stresses the view that deviance is more of an "audience effect" than a characteristic of the offender
STIGMA: the intense social disapproval and alienation that follow the assignment of deviant status

Overview

Labeling theory explains deviance in terms of a violation of social norms or rules that is followed by social disapproval and sanctions. In this view, particular acts themselves are not deviant; rather, acts become deviant when society declares them unacceptable. Thus, deviance is in the eyes of the beholder. Deviance is a social value judgment that is passed upon those individuals who do not conform to social norms.

The labeling theory of deviance is based on two assumptions. First, for someone to be called "deviant," that person must have broken a rule. Rules generally refer to the social norms and expectations for acceptable behavior. These rules, or norms, may be explicitly formulated, as in the case of laws and regulations. Many social rules, however, are implicit, since they are not clearly articulated. Norms about interpersonal behavior, such as facing a person to whom one is speaking and maintaining fairly consistent eye contact, are examples of implicit rules in society. Rule-breaking per se is not sufficient for defining deviance according to the theory. If the rule violation is undetected, then no label will be assigned to the violator, and therefore he or she will not qualify as deviant. For example, an individual who cheats on income taxes will not be declared a criminal if the fraud is not detected. The second component of the labeling theory of deviance focuses on the reaction of society to the rule-breaking. If a social norm violation is noticed, it becomes defined as deviance (the perpetrator is labeled "deviant"), and this label leads to social disapproval and a host of other negative consequences. This emphasis on the negative social reactions to norm violations is reflected in the other term used in reference to the labeling theory of deviance: social reaction theory.

The basic premises of labeling theory were clearly articulated by sociologist Howard S. Becker in his influential book *Outsiders: Studies in the Sociology of Deviance* (1963):

> Social groups create deviance by making the rules whose infraction constitutes deviance, and by applying those rules to particular people and labeling them as outsiders . . . deviance is not a quality of the act the person commits, but rather a consequence of the application by others of rules and sanctions to an "offender." The deviant is one to whom that label has successfully been applied; deviant behavior is behavior that people so label.

In their original formulations, labeling theorists stressed that deviants do not form an identifiable homogeneous group; instead, deviants are simply individuals who have been publicly labeled as having violated social conventions and subjected to various forms of reprimand. A multitude of labels exist in society to categorize specific types of norm violations: "Criminality" is used for behavior that violates laws, "perversion" is assigned to behavior that does not conform to norms for sexual behavior, and "drunkenness" applies to alcohol usage that society considers excessive. Labels also exist for violations of minor social norms, such as "obnoxious," "crude," and "ignorant."

The ultimate purpose of labeling individuals as deviant is social control or pressure to conform to the norm (pressure to become "normal"). The social control function begins with the assignment of an undesirable label which is associated with social disapproval and stigma. For some forms of deviance, more intrusive social interventions are employed, such as incarceration or hospitalization. Sociologist Thomas J. Scheff provides illustrations of these ideas in his book *Being Mentally Ill: A Sociological Theory* (1984). According to Scheff, a minor norm violation may result in the person being labeled "odd," but more serious violations or a recurrent pattern may lead to a diagnosis of "mental illness." Once this label is used, society reacts to the "deviant" based on traditional stereotypes of mental illness or insanity. As Scheff notes, a label and its associated stigma are very resistant to change; the terms "mental patient" and "former mental patient" both carry negative and lasting connotations in society.

Labels may exert effects on those to whom they are assigned. A person assigned a particular label may accept and enact the assigned role. A person declared "crazy" may ultimately act crazy because it is expected; the label becomes a self-fulfilling prophecy. The initial rule violation has been called primary deviance; secondary deviance occurs when the deviant label is accepted by the "offender" and becomes incorporated into the individual's self-concept and social identity. In this view, secondary deviance represents the deviant accepting, enacting, and fulfilling the assigned label.

In sum, a person who violates social norms tends to be viewed as "deviant" and is subjected to subtle or overt pressure to conform. If the person resists the pressure and demands of society, stigmatization and social alienation generally follow. Finally, some of the labeled individuals enact a deviant role, leading to a deviant career and to more long-term social condemnation and stereotyping.

Applications

Labeling theory has been applied to a variety of social problems, including crime, mental illness, physical disabilities, drug abuse, and racial prejudice. The theory has been particularly influential in challenging many accepted views of mental illness. Scheff noted that classifying behavior as abnormal can only occur within the context of the standards of a particular society. In his view, cultural relativism applies to mental illness: What is normal in one culture may be abnormal in another. Presumed signs or symptoms of mental illness are just as easily described as normal behavior depending on the setting, persistence of the behavior, existing stereotypes, and—most important—the presence of observers. An individual's behavior is more likely to be explained as mental illness if it violates some norm, is persistent, matches existing cultural stereotypes of insanity, and is observed by others. This is particularly true if the audience is composed of persons who accept the concept of mental illness. Scheff sought to develop, in his own words, "a theory of mental disorder in which psychiatric symptoms are considered to be labeled violations of social norms and stable 'mental illness' to be a social role."

A dramatic illustration of these principles was provided by psychologist David Rosenhan. Rosenhan and several colleagues presented themselves for admission at different psychiatric hospitals in the United States. All participants masked their true identities and initially complained of hearing voices, but otherwise they exhibited no signs of distress. Once hospitalized, the "pseudopatients" behaved cooperatively and normally, never referring again to the voices. In every instance, the pseudopatients were labeled mentally ill, typically schizophrenic. The deception was never discovered by the mental health professionals or staff. (Ironically, the only people who expressed suspicion were the "real" patients.) Rosenhan and colleagues were kept in hospitals for an average of nineteen days before being discharged. During their hospital stays, even the most innocuous behavior displayed by the participants was commonly interpreted as pathological by hospital staff (boredom, for example, was reported by staff as "anxiety"). When finally discharged, the pseudopatients were usually described as "improved," with the implication that they still suffered from mental illness.

Labels are very resistant to change. Once a person has been diagnosed as mentally ill, he or she will frequently be subjected to a lifetime of social alienation. The stigma of mental illness is powerful and lasting, as evidenced by associated prejudice and discrimination in employment, social status, and general relationships. Aspiring politicians have lost or had to withdraw from elections when it was discovered that they had previously received treatment for psychiatric problems. Once a person has been labeled mentally ill, he or she may be subtly rewarded for playing the part and punished for attempting to return to a conventional role in society.

Results such as those of Rosenhan and others have been used to criticize accepted concepts of mental illness. The antipsychiatry movement was born because of opposition to the negative consequences of psychiatric labels. Even prominent psychiatrists, such as Thomas Szasz, have ardently criticized existing views of mental illness. According to Szasz, what is referred to as mental illness could more accurately be called "problems in living." According to him, the notion of mental illness should be abandoned, since it is a myth. The term "mental illness" is simply used to describe the behavior of those considered to be different. Consistent with basic principles of labeling theory, Szasz argued that the concept of mental illness is merely an effort to persuade nonconforming individuals to modify their behavior and beliefs in a socially desirable direction, another illustration of social control.

Although these criticisms have influenced terminology and practices in psychiatry, they have not revolutionized the field. Positive influences have included the abandonment of some stigmatizing terms (such as "moron" and "idiot," which were formerly official terms to describe mental retardation), systematic efforts to increase the reliability of psychiatric diagnoses, and legislation to prevent discrimination against individuals purely on the basis of their having received a label of mental illness. Proponents of psychiatric diagnoses have also pointed to possible flaws in Rosenhan's study. One criticism is that psychiatrists would naturally assume that someone seeking admission to a psychiatric hospital suffers from mental illness. After all, with the exception of Rosenhan and colleagues, well-adjusted individuals do not seek psychiatric treatment or complain of hearing voices.

Critics of the labeling perspective on mental illness also note that some behaviors, such as murder and suicide, are virtually universally recognized as deviant or abnormal. Proponents of the psychiatric model have argued that psychiatric problems exist independently of labels and cultural definitions. For example, a person could be instructed to fake a medical illness, such as migraine headache, and could ultimately receive a diagnosis of and treatment for the condition. This does not prove, however, that migraine headaches do not actually exist and that physicians fabricate stigmatizing labels. Finally, being labeled mentally ill does not inevitably lead to negative consequences. Some patients benefit from treatment and lead productive lives in spite of having previously received a particular psychiatric label.

Context

Labeling theory represents one of the major theories of deviance in sociology. One of the original theories of deviance was offered by Émile Durkheim, who was concerned with the function that deviance serves in a society. According to Durkheim, deviance occurs in all societies and serves several positive purposes. Deviance helps consolidate cultural values and social norms. Identifying and punishing violations of laws and social norms emphasizes what is acceptable and "normal." In this way, violations increase solidarity and cohesion in society by drawing attention to deviant behavior and its consequences. Societal responses to deviance foster unity and conformity. Deviance may also serve as a catalyst for social change; when a large number of people violate a particular norm, society at large may be forced to reconsider and modify that norm.

Another major theory of deviance is the conflict perspective. Two basic components of this theory are social inequality and relative power. Social norms and laws are formulated by the powerful elements of society, generally the wealthy upper socioeconomic class. These norms and laws are designed to maintain the status quo, and anyone who challenges or violates the norms will be branded a "deviant." Social inequality is manifested in the fact that powerless groups, the lower socioeconomic class and minorities, are more likely to be classified as "deviant." For the same violation, a powerless person is more likely to be considered deviant than a powerful person. Therefore, according to conflict theory, the inequality in wealth and power in society shapes norms and laws to maintain the power structure. The powerless and those who threaten the system are stigmatized to maintain this uneven balance.

Labeling theory was a leading influence in the study of deviance in the 1970's and remained the conventional wisdom for nearly a decade. Although it has lost much of its preeminent status in sociology, few other theories have received the wide acceptance labeling theory once had. It is widely recognized that definitions of abnormality or deviance vary considerably across cultures. Further, the potentially damaging nature of labels is better understood. The study of mental illness has greatly benefited from labeling theory. Most comprehensive discussions of diagnosis and psychiatric labels include cautionary discussions about the dangers of labeling.

It seems unlikely that any single sociological theory of deviance will explain the diversity of phenomena that "deviance" comprises. The theories are complementary, however, in that they account for different aspects of the phenomena in question. The unique contribution of labeling theory is its focus on social value judgements and on how these may exacerbate existing problems.

Bibliography

Becker, Howard S. *Outsiders: Studies in the Sociology of Deviance*. London: Free Press, 1963. Becker's book is considered the classic presentation of the labeling theory of deviance. In the book, Becker applies labeling theory to several nonconforming practices, including marijuana smoking.

Goode, Erich. *Deviant Behavior*. 3d ed. Englewood Cliffs, N.J.: Prentice-Hall, 1990. An introductory text on the sociology of deviance. The general theories of deviance are summarized and applied to drug use, sexual deviations and variations, criminal behavior, and mental illness.

Macionis, John J. *Sociology*. 3d ed. Englewood Cliffs, N.J.: Prentice-Hall, 1991. A popular introductory text that offers an overview of the foundations of sociology, deviance, social life, social inequality, social institutions, and social change.

Robertson, Ian. *Sociology*. 3d ed. New York: Worth, 1987. Another popular introduction to the field of sociology. Theories of deviance and applications are summarized in several contexts.

Scheff, Thomas J. *Being Mentally Ill: A Sociological Theory*. 2d ed. New York: Aldine, 1984. A standard labeling theory text in which the principles are applied to mental illness. Scheff presents the theory in nine propositions and reviews relevant research findings.

Schur, Edwin M. *Labeling Women Deviant: Gender, Stigma, and Social Control*. Philadelphia: Temple University Press, 1983. Gender issues are discussed in the context of labeling theory. The author notes cultural stereotypes and their detrimental effects on women in a male-dominated culture.

Szasz, Thomas. *The Myth of Mental Illness*. Rev. ed. New York: Harper & Row, 1974. A psychiatrist's controversial but influential book on the use of mental illness labels to promote conformity in society. The author also applies his views to the practice of psychotherapy, which he describes as a secular religion.

Richard D. McAnulty

Cross-References

Crime: Analysis and Overview, 373; Cultural Norms and Sanctions, 411; Cultural Transmission Theory of Deviance, 424; Deviance: Analysis and Overview, 525; Deviance: Functions and Dysfunctions, 540; Interactionism, 1009; Juvenile Delinquency: Analysis and Overview, 1036; The Medicalization of Deviance, 1178; Stereotyping and the Self-fulfilling Prophecy, 1984; The Structural-Strain Theory of Deviance, 1990.

LEGITIMACY AND AUTHORITY

Type of sociology: Major social institutions
Field of study: Politics and the state

Authority is the legitimate use of power. Authority and legitimacy depend on societal norms, values, and beliefs. For this reason, ruling elites always try to influence mass beliefs and values in order to maintain the legitimacy of the institutions they control and thus reinforce their authority.

Principal terms
AUTHORITY: power that is exercised legitimately
BELIEFS: shared ideas about what is true
LEGITIMACY: the belief that some particular use of power is right or proper
NORMS: shared rules and expectations about behavior
POWER: the ability to control or influence the acts of others
SANCTIONS: rewards and punishments for conforming to or violating norms
VALUES: shared ideas about what is good and desirable

Overview

Although scholars frequently relate the concept of authority to the phenomenon of government, the concept appears in all associations and not merely in governmental circles. Every association in a society has its own structure of authority. Organization creates authority. Where there is no organization, there is usually no authority, and vice versa. Similarly, the idea of legitimacy has always had a particular association with the state. In this case too, however, the notion has been extended to the study of leadership, hierarchy, and management in social units of all kinds, especially organizations. Sentiments of legitimacy arise even in social situations in which ties are intimately affective and dependency is great (as in the relationships of children and parents).

According to the renowned sociologist Max Weber, authority originates from one of three forms of legitimacy: traditional, rational-legal, and charismatic. Traditional legitimacy is based on established beliefs in the sanctity of family rights, which are passed down from one generation to another, and the moral need to obey leaders. In the case of rational legitimacy, which is usually based on laws and on recognized legal regulations, authority is formally conferred by general designation of the interested group on a given person. In modern societies, this is the most common form of authority, and its source is the rule of law. Modern governments, industrial societies, and bureaucratic structures all derive their authority from rational legitimacy. Charismatic legitimacy is based on the voluntary and spontaneous submission of the masses to the rule of persons who are endowed with extraordinary personal heroic qualities.

By virtue of these qualities, such persons are deemed capable of accomplishing great, and even miraculous, things. For that reason, they are sometimes perceived as having been appointed by God. They operate beyond the boundaries of legitimacy.

Usually, there is a shared conception of a legitimate order arising from a network of social relationships, which, in turn, guarantees the legitimacy of the persons in formal organizations who help to maintain that order through the exercise of authority. To help the designated persons accomplish their tasks, their positions are backed by power, including the threat of, or the actual use of, physical force. Not all power, however, is legitimate: A carjacker who forces one to turn over his or her car at gun point is exercising power, not authority. The representative of a financial institution who repossesses a car because the owner failed to pay, however, is exercising authority. Thus, what clearly distinguishes authority from power, coercion, and force is legitimacy. In this respect, legitimacy is a sentiment whereby people feel morally obligated to submit to power that is perceived to be valuable and conforms to the general will of the society.

The right to exercise authority—that is, the right to make decisions and enforce them—is attached to offices, and this right receives the support of all those who belong to the organization and who conform to its norms. The person who is subjected to an order by a competent authority has no alternative but to obey. Through a system of procedures, roles, and relationships defined by coercive social rules, a society's system of government becomes a means of controlling behavior. Coercive social rules (norms, beliefs, values, laws, and conventions) have the following two features: First, they are prescriptive—that is, they require people to behave in a particular way; second, they are backed or enforced by an effective form of social sanction or pressure. Social norms legitimate the use of force by defining it as correct, appropriate, or permissible although, inasmuch as people believe the institutions in which power is vested to be legitimate, the use of force will hardly be required. If people begin to question the legitimacy of the institutions, however, and perceive their laws, rules, and decisions to be unjust and improper, then they may no longer feel morally obligated to abide by them. Institutional power will then rest not on constituted authority but on sheer force alone. In such cases, governments rely on repression by police or military forces to exercise power over their populations.

Applications

No government can survive for long without authority. This much celebrated concept, many people believe, is threatened in modern society. Over the years, it has become fashionable to say that authority is in difficulty, in crisis, and in decline. The arguments and reasons given for this analysis vary. In *Authority Revisited* (1984), Roland J. Pennock quotes Hannah Arendt as saying that authority has vanished from the modern world. In Samuel Huntington's view, the problem stems from an overemphasis on egalitarianism. The fabrics of social institutions (family, school, state, and church) are all said to have been affected by this decline of authority. Authoritative offices are increasingly challenged by those who are subject to them and increasingly burdensome to those who occupy them. Others have traced this decline to times past, putting the blame on Martin Luther, who they claim destroyed the power of religion by means of his attack on the Church, and Thomas Hobbes, who attacked tradition in his writings. According to Max Weber, religion and tradition are the two most ancient sources of legitimate authority. Nevertheless, in spite of this pessimism, the general consensus is that authority is still very much alive.

In its application, the concept of authority (and hence that of legitimacy), may sometimes be confusing. In his book *The Social Order* (1970), Robert Bierstedt contends that authority is sometimes confused with two other phenomena; namely, "competence" and "leadership." In the first case, a person may be described as "an authority" on a given subject, such as baseball, classical music, radioactivity, or Shakespeare. In this sense, authority is related to influence rather than power. This kind of authority has nothing to do with legitimacy or obligation. It is a recognition of competence that induces people voluntarily to accept the opinions of those who have excelled in their specialized fields of endeavor. According to Bierstedt, people voluntarily respect the competence of others, whereas authority requires submission. Authority requires an office or a status, whereas leadership does not. The police officer, the judge, and the monarch represent authority because they are all backed by legitimate power, but all three may lack leadership qualities. Paradoxically, when an order or a command is said to be issued by a "competent authority," in the etymological sense, it does not imply that the authority is competent, but that it is legitimate. Thus, people will obey the (unreasonable) command of a superior whose authority they recognize and disobey the (reasonable) command of one whose authority they question. In other words, superior knowledge, superior skill, or superior competence may sometimes be irrelevant in the exercise of competent authority. One who commands may be no wiser than those who obey.

The second phenomenon with which authority is sometimes confused is leadership. Ironically, Bierstedt singles out Max Weber, one of the greatest and most influential of all sociologists, as being largely responsible for this confusion. This confusion derives from Weber's classification of charisma as a source of legitimate authority. It is the view of many others, however, that charisma is a form not of authority but of leadership (although leadership qualities more often than not allow an individual to rise to a position of authority). Leadership depends on the personal qualities of the leader. Authority, however, need not involve a personal relationship of any kind. In a military establishment, for example, thousands of men are sent on a mission even though they may not know the officer who is responsible for the orders. Thus, in a leadership relationship, the person is basic; in an authority relationship, personal identity is irrelevant. An authority relationship is one of superordination and subordination; the leadership relationship is one of dominance and submission. No one is required to follow a leader. An organization whose members wish it to survive must create authority where initially there was leadership. The leader who has been instrumental in establishing the organization may eventually be indisposed or may quit. Unless his or her role has been institutionalized, such a contingency might

jeopardize the health of the organization. After his or her status as been institutionalized, the leader may even be deposed from his or her position of authority and a
successor named without damage to the organization.

What, then, sustains the authority that is exercised by the military officer over his
troops? Why does a subordinate obey a superordinate when he disapproves of the
command? Why does an inferior obey a superior whom he or she may dislike or may
never have met? Technically, both the superordinate and the subordinate recognize
that they are operating in a status relationship and that personal sentiments have no
relevance to the exercise of authority. Thus, ideally, the army officer or foreperson or
judge is required to exercise the same kind of authority over a sibling that he or she
does over an enemy. In the ideal case, the exercise of authority is supposed to be wholly
impartial, objective, impersonal, and disinterested. Any exercise of authority, however, depends upon the willingness of officials and the public to respond positively to
commands or rules. In other words, ultimately, the official relies on the existence of
good will. The single policeman exercising his authority in a crowd is assuming,
especially under normal circumstances, that, with due respect for his badge, the crowd
will allow him to exercise that authority. Effective authority thus depends on cumulative, individual acts of compliance or confidence, with those in positions of authority
acting on the assumption that the requisite compliance will be forthcoming. The
ultimate reason that people submit to authority is that it is supported, sanctioned, and
sustained by the group it serves.

Context

The concepts of authority and legitimacy existed long before the birth of nation-
states. Eminent philosophers dating back to the times of Plato, Aristotle, and Socrates
attempted to conceptualize them. Even so, placing these two concepts in their right
context has been a strenuous and an ongoing process. They have both generated
controversies, partly as a result of their theoretical foundations. It is assumed, for
example, that force that is not consented to or perceived as being right cannot constitute
a legitimate form of authority. In practice, however, conventional wisdom has increasingly demonstrated that only a very thin line separates "force" from "legitimate
authority." Initially, Max Weber presented the two concepts in a very antithetical way;
that is, he proposed that both concepts are opposites in every sense except that
legitimate authorities can use coercive force. It has been proved by tradition on
numerous occasions, however, that coercive force can and does play a part in helping
to create legitimacy, especially the rational-legal form of legitimacy. It often happens
that structures of authority that we subsequently legitimated originate in force. On
several occasions, following a coup or revolution (sometimes bloody), the successful
government has been tolerated and, eventually, if not immediately, accepted as
legitimate. In other words, force itself may well be a value that governs perceptions
of legitimacy.

How, then, does a government become legitimate? Civil legitimacy can be obtained
through the expression of the general will. The concept of the general will describes

the moral values and political aspirations that are shared by the members of a community and to which the policies of its government must broadly conform if that government is to be considered legitimate. Bases of legitimacy are thus values within a particular society that govern perceptions that authority patterns are rightly consti- tuted and therefore are worthy of support. People may accept a government as legitimate because they believe that it is well grounded and justifiable, when in fact it is not. Sometimes it happens that what people believe to be a sound foundation may turn out to be unacceptable at a later date. When that happens, new criteria of legitimacy are applied. At one time, the American colonists considered British rule to be legitimate and acceptable. After a period of grievances without redress, however, they came to believe that the government was no longer legitimate, so they disregarded its authority, revolted, and established their own government. Modern constitutional government makes one characteristic of civil legitimacy clear: Governmental offices are ordered by trust rather than exercised by dominion. This characteristic is expressed in the institution of periodic elections. In a democracy, more often than not, elections are expressions of the general will of the majority. There is, in fact, an analogy between legitimacy and voting. One presumably votes for a party (or a candidate) because one considers it (or him or her) worthy of support, and people accord legitimacy to an authority pattern for the same reason. Thus, the electoral procedure serves as a means of legitimizing the assignment of a person to an office of authority. In recent times, however, popular elections have become so predominant a criterion of legitimacy that almost every nation (including totalitarian ones) feels obligated to pay lip service to the institution of elections.

Bibliography

Bierstedt, Robert. *The Social Order*. 3d ed. New York: McGraw-Hill, 1970. Even after twenty years, this book still serves relatively well the needs of the social science student. The topics are treated in a logical rather than a random order. The book simplifies the study of the concepts of legitimacy and authority and is highly recommended.
De George, Richard T. *The Nature and Limits of Authority*. Lawrence: University Press of Kansas, 1985. This is an attempt to put into perspective what authority is, what its forms are, which of its functions can be justified, and when it should be challenged or resisted. It also deals extensively with the issue of legitimacy. Very easy to comprehend and thus appropriate for beginners.
Eckstein, Harry, and Ted Robert Gurr. *Patterns of Authority: A Structural Basis for Political Inquiry*. New York: John Wiley & Sons, 1975. Proposes a relatively dif- ferent approach by equating political analysis with the study of authority patterns in any and all social units. Provides a rationale, concepts, methods, illustrative data, and theoretical justifications for further systematic research into the subject.
Pennock, Roland J., and John W. Chapman, eds. *Authority Revisited*. New York: New York University Press, 1984. This volume in the NOMOS series (29) is more or less an update of Carl J. Friedrich's *Authority* (1958). It addresses a wide variety of

issues, including the concepts, perspectives, and contexts of authority. Suitable for the advanced reader.

Raz, Joseph. *The Authority of Law*. Oxford, England: Oxford University Press, 1979. This book deals extensively with the concept of legitimacy. It provides the reader with a comprehensive analysis of the justification of authority.

Olusoji A. Akomolafe

Cross-References

Authoritarian and Totalitarian Governments, 153; Bureaucracies, 172; Cultural Norms and Sanctions, 411; Democracy and Democratic Governments, 483; Power: The Pluralistic Model, 1484; The Power Elite, 1491; Traditional, Charismatic, and Rational-Legal Authority, 2064.

LEGITIMATION OF INEQUALITY: THE MASS MEDIA

Type of sociology: Social stratification
Field of study: Maintaining inequality

The legitimation of inequality by the mass media refers to the manner in which society's mass media institutions, such as radio, television, film, magazines, and newspapers, foster perceptions of class, race, gender, and ethnicity that reinforce cultural stereotypes and make "commonsensical" and legitimate the unequal status of various groups.

Principal terms
DISCRIMINATION: the denial of opportunities and rights to a certain group on the basis of such attributes as race, ethnicity, class, religion, or gender
FALSE CONSCIOUSNESS: a Marxist term referring to beliefs held by the working class which run counter to, or do not further, their best interests
HEGEMONY: the process by which an ideology is created and maintained in society
IDEOLOGICAL STATE APPARATUS (ISA): one of the social systems, such as education, religion, or the mass media, that make up the super-structure of, and are the primary reinforcers of, ideology in culture
IDEOLOGY: a system of beliefs about reality that usually reflects and supports the interests of one segment of society over those of another
INEQUALITY: a disparity in distribution or opportunity, usually as a result of discrimination
LEGITIMATION: the process by which a belief, practice, or value is justified or naturalized in a society, specifically with reference to an ideology or ideological system
SOCIAL STRATIFICATION: a system in which groups are ranked hierarchically
STEREOTYPE: a standardized mental picture held by members of a group that represents an oversimplified, critical, or prejudicial judgment about members of another group; stereotypes are often used to legitimize discrimination

Overview

The legitimation of inequality in the mass media involves the extent to which the mass media, like other sociocultural institutions such as government and education, make social inequalities based on class, ethnicity, and gender seem legitimate and normal. Numerous sociologists and media critics have explored mass media discourse,

asking how the mass media articulate the dominant ideology in society in order to
engineer the acquiescence of the working class and thus legitimize their unequal status.
Theorists have also extended the exploration of class-based inequalities to include
inequalities based on gender, race, and ethnicity.

The mass media, significant creators and transmitters of cultural ideas, values, and
norms, have come under increasing scrutiny as a transmitter of ideology. Beginning
in the mid-1970's, sociologists and communication theorists began to reconceptualize
the mass media's role in society. There has been considerable discussion of how the
mass media, no longer viewed as a neutral instrument of information transmission,
create "reality" and legitimize inequality in their presentation of news and entertainment.

Sociologists and media critics have identified a number of ways by which the
mass media legitimize inequality, such as reinforcing prejudicial stereotypes, de-
emphasizing class inequalities, promoting the mythologies of social mobility and
equality of opportunity, celebrating consumerism rather than political involvement,
and making status quo visions of social stratification commonsensical.

One of the more obvious ways the media legitimize inequality is through their
promotion and reinforcement of stereotypes that make "natural" and acceptable the
inferior status of women and minorities. Communication theorist Douglas Kellner
noted in 1987 that ethnic stereotypes in early films, for example, rationalized the
unequal status of blacks and whites in society: "In the first decades of film . . . blacks
were stereotyped as comical—eye-rolling, foot-shuffling, drawling, usually in the role
of servant or clown—precisely the image fitting the white power structure's fantasy
of keeping blacks in their place." Numerous content analyses of print and electronic
media have pointed out the inequalities between men and women and between whites
and minorities when it comes to such things as potential for career advancement, social
prestige, power, and authority. These stereotypes, critics argue, promote discrimination against women and various ethnic groups rationalized on the basis of the
portrayals of these groups in the mass media.

Other media critics argue that the mass media's reliance on stereotypes to portray
gender, race, and ethnicity in both news and entertainment programming may have
the added effect of concealing inequalities based on class. Emphasizing social divisions such as age, sex, and ethnicity masks audiences' awareness of their membership
in a particular class and of the unequal treatment they may receive as members of that
class. It is also argued that to the extent social inequalities are acknowledged by
audiences, the mass media may act as a pacifier to soothe the pains of such inequalities.
According to media critic Susan Sontag in her book *On Photography* (1977), "a
capitalist society requires a culture based on images. It needs to furnish vast amounts
of entertainment in order to stimulate buying and anaesthetize the injuries of class,
race, and sex." Mass media entertainment fare, in other words, provides daily distrac-
tions from the harsh realities of people's social situations and keeps them passively
accepting those situations.

Other critics claim that the mass media legitimize inequality by promoting the ideologies of social mobility and equality of opportunity. Both of these ideologies are central to the mythology of the American Dream—the prevalent myth in American culture that all citizens have equal opportunity to gain wealth, status, and happiness and that the United States has a classless society of potential entrepreneurs poised to climb the ladder of social and financial success. Media critics argue that because the American Dream mythology is so prominent in the mass media, citizens do not feel the need to rebel against political systems and programs which, in reality, do not benefit them. These programs and political systems are perceived as *potentially* benefiting them in the future. For example, television game shows promote the idea that everyone has an equal chance to win large sums of money. Therefore, even if one is a blue-collar worker who currently has no investments, one should vote against capital gains taxes because someday one might be the beneficiary of such a policy. Karl Marx, in the nineteenth century, labeled this perspective "false consciousness," or beliefs held by the working class which run counter to, or do not further, their best interests. These beliefs, fostered by the mass media and other social institutions, instead support the interests of the ruling class and legitimize the unequal status of various groups in society.

According to some critics, another way the mass media legitimize inequalities is by making the current social order seem natural or commonsensical. Media critics argue that television news, for example, promotes the status quo. Groups that engage in behavior that challenges the current social or political system through demonstrations or protests are portrayed by the media as deviant or dangerous. This slant promotes the idea that political change is destabilizing, threatening to social harmony, and thus wrong.

A number of critics maintain that the mass media legitimize inequality by replacing political choice with consumer choice. Mass media audiences, it is argued, are invited to define themselves in terms of lifestyle choices rather than class membership. Mass media fare, by portraying and rewarding consumerism and conspicuous consumption, obscures and compensates for radical inequalities in income, opportunity, and social influence. Todd Gitlin, for example, argues that the mass media, particularly television, depoliticize the public by encouraging viewers to experience themselves as antipolitical, private individuals. Television, according to Gitlin, accustoms people to think of themselves as, and behave as, "a *market* rather than a *public*, as consumers rather than citizens" (Gitlin's essay appears in *Television: The Critical View*, 1987, edited by Horace Newcomb). Sontag agrees, claiming that in a "mass mediated society," a change in images replaces true social change. When consumer choice replaces political choice, class consciousness disappears; individuals no longer identify themselves as members of a class with common political interests such as national health care or union-scale wages. As a result, citizens "buy happiness" rather than vote for significant political changes that might benefit their status in society.

Applications

Marxist critics of the mass media often call for what Douglas Kellner labels "emancipatory" popular culture as a way to challenge the mass media's legitimation of inequality. "Emancipatory" culture, according to Kellner:

> challenges the institutions and way of life and advanced capitalist society. It generally has the quality of shock, forcing people to see aspects of the society that they had previously overlooked, or it focuses attention on the need for change. It rejects idealizations and rationalizations that apologize for the suffering in the present social system, and, at its best, suggests that another way of life is possible.

Kellner, for example, argues that the popularity of the television miniseries "Roots" attested American audiences' receptiveness to a historical drama that dealt with oppression, racism, and struggle: "*Roots* offered a vivid picture of the effects of slavery and racism. . . . [It] took the point of view of the oppressed and for almost the first time in television history attempted in a dramatic forum to present blacks as complex human beings." Just as *Roots* challenged racial stereotypes and inequalities, he says, the 1970's Norman Lear television show *Mary Hartman, Mary Hartman* dramatized and criticized both gender roles in relationships and consumerism. According to Kellner, "*Mary Hartman* used formal-generic subversions and surrealism to convey a critical picture of the life of the 'typical American housewife and consumer.'" In another essay in *Television: The Critical View* (1987), edited by Horace Newcomb, Farrell Corcoran agrees with Kellner's assessment of *Mary Hartman* as emancipatory television, saying that television shows such as *Mary Hartman* "become interventions into the process of naturalizing the world of representations, interrupting imaginary involvement, and evoking the active, critical, distanced viewing recommended by Brechtian aesthetics." Both Kellner and Corcoran concede, however, that very little television programming qualifies as emancipatory culture.

Although no single television show or mass media portrayal can radically alter social consciousness regarding class, ethnicity, or gender, emancipatory mass media fare may cause audiences to question stereotypes, prejudicial attitudes, and actions. Yet even those advocating such programming concede that it is unlikely that much of it will reach the American airwaves. As Kellner notes, there would have to be a "radical transformation" of existing entertainment and broadcasting industries for this to occur, and such a transformation is not likely to occur in the foreseeable future.

Context

Since the mid-1970's, as a result of both the cross-fertilization of American media studies and sociology and the influence of European media studies on American studies, there has been a significant change in how sociologists interpret the mass media's impact on social stratification. Prior to the influence of European-based Marxist studies, functionalism was the major theoretical perspective from which the media were viewed. Functionalist theory saw the mass media as essentially neutral instruments for disseminating ideas, information, and cultural trends. By the 1950's, although researchers began asking questions about media persuasion and audience behavior (in what has come to be known as the media "effects" tradition), there was still no exploration of the media's role in transmitting the dominant ideology.

During the same period of time, although some sociologists had adopted a Marxist perspective in order to study, for example, the impact of education and government on social stratification, they had yet to extend their inquiry to include the mass media. Graham Murdock and Peter Golding, in a 1977 essay, commented, "Given the central role of mass communications in relaying social knowledge and social imagery, this collective silence on the part of sociologists concerned with stratification 'represents an extraordinary ommission.'" Although sociologists had documented the ownership and control in media industries, very few researchers had demonstrated how this ownership and control resulted in media fare that supported the dominant ideology. Sociological theorists seemed to take for granted that mass media form and content would support the ruling class ideology, although few attempts had been made to describe how the media legitimized inequality.

In the mid-1970's, American media studies began to be influenced by Marxist-based European studies, most notably the French school led by Louis Althussar and the British school led by Stuart Hall (from the Birmingham Centre for the Study of Culture). These two traditions, in turn, drew on the work of the Frankfurt school, particularly the work of Theodore Adorno and Max Horkheimer, and the writings of Italian theorist Antonio Gramsci.

Althussar used Marx's base/superstructure model to explore how components of the superstructure—what he called ideological state apparatuses (ISAs)—reinforced ideology to engineer the consent of the masses. Although he did not focus on the mass media, he argued that the church, schools, and the family acted as ideological state apparatuses whose function is to reinforce and recycle the dominant repressive ideology in society.

The work of Stuart Hall, David Morley, John Hartley, and John Fiske has been central to contemporary exploration of how ISAs, particularly the mass media, legitimize inequality. Theorists in the British cultural studies tradition, like their American counterparts (such as William Carey and Lawrence Grossberg) have explored the ideological work of mass media institutions as well as the processes by which audiences interpret or make sense of mass media messages in the light of their material conditions. Unlike earlier theorists such as Adorno and Horkheimer, who had tended to see the mass media as monolithic and the audience as an undifferentiated and passive mass, contemporary theorists prefer to talk about heterogeneous audiences actively negotiating meaning with mass media discourses to interpret media content in diverse ways.

Stuart Hall, for example, refers to "Marxism without guarantees" to describe the process by which ideological messages are negotiated by audiences. Mass media discourse, according to Hall, is a "site of struggle," and ideology, rather than being monolithic, is shot through with contradictions. In the United States, for example, the privately owned and operated mass media, rather than being the propaganda arm of the government, are driven by the profit motive. Ideological messages, although they may be the by-product of mass media programming, are not the central intent. Mass media institutions may therefore present material that challenges the dominant ideology if they believe such content would garner higher ratings, greater circulation, or increased advertising dollars.

Bibliography

Barthes, Roland. *Mythologies*. Translated by Annette Levers. New York: Hill and Wang, 1972. A seminal work in the analysis of culture, myth, language, and the mass media. Barthes provides an ideological critique of the "sign-systems" of mass culture (semiotics).

Berger, John. *Ways of Seeing*. New York: Penguin Press, 1977. Demonstrates how European oil painting from 1500 to 1900 and the modern mass media make the ideology of conspicuous consumption commonsensical and reinforce the idea of women as objects of that consumption.

Fiske, John. "British Cultural Studies and Television." In *Channels of Discourse*, edited by Robert C. Allen. Chapel Hill: University of North Carolina Press, 1987. Provides a good summary of the British cultural studies tradition. Details contemporary neo-Marxist critics' exploration of the mass media as a "site of struggle" over meaning, where ideological messages are complex and filled with contradictions, and where active and diverse audiences construct meaning from their own experiences.

Hall, Stuart. "Culture, Media, and the Ideological Effect." In *Mass Communication and Society*, edited by James Curran, Michael Gurevitch and Janet Woollacott. Beverly Hills, Calif.: Sage Publications, 1979. Hall is a significant figure in the British cultural studies tradition, and this essay explores his idea of "Marxism without guarantees" to describe the process by which ideological messages are negotiated by audiences.

Kellner, Douglas. "TV, Ideology, and Emancipatory Popular Culture." In *Television: The Critical View*, edited by Horace Newcomb. 4th ed. New York: Oxford University Press, 1987. An important and readable exploration of changes in ideology under the impact of the communications revolution. Synthesizes various theories of ideology to explore the mass media's transmission and transformation of mythology and hegemonic ideology in American society. Offers the idea of "emancipatory culture" as a solution to the ideological domination of the mass media.

Murdock, Graham, and Peter Golding. "Capitalism, Communication, and Class Relations." In *Mass Communication and Society*, edited by James Curran, Michael Gurevitch, and Janet Woollacott. Beverly Hills, Calif.: Sage Publications, 1979. The authors argue that the ideological domination of the capitalist owners of the means of production plays a central role in maintaining class inequalities. Their essay documents the concentration of media industries into the hands of a few corporate entities and the increasing diversification of media conglomerates into related sectors of communication and leisure industries. Both of these trends, they claim, provide the means through which symbolic domination is maintained and the inequality of the classes is legitimized.

Rowland, Willard, and Bruce Watkins, eds. *Interpreting Television: Current Research Perspectives*. Beverly Hills, Calif.: Sage Publications, 1984. In their introduction to this edited anthology, the authors provide an overview of the major Marxist-based approaches to interpreting television that emerged in the 1970's and 1980's. Articles by some of the major figures in contemporary media criticism, such as Horace Newcomb, Paul Hirsch, Joli Jensen, John Hartley, and John Fiske, are included.

Tuchman, Gay. "Mass Media Institutions." In *Handbook of Sociology*, edited by Neil Smelser. Newbury Park, Calif.: Sage Publications, 1988. The author provides an extensive critique of the functionalist approach to media analysis.

Susan Mackey-Kallis

Cross-References

Conflict Theory, 340; Gender Inequality: Analysis and Overview, 820; Gender Socialization, 833; Inequalities in Health, 966; Inequalities in Political Power, 972; Legitimation of Inequality: Religion, 1068; Social Stratification: Analysis and Overview, 1839; Social Stratification: Marxist Perspectives, 1852; Social Stratification: Modern Theories, 1859; Socialization: The Mass Media, 1887.

LEGITIMATION OF INEQUALITY: RELIGION

Type of sociology: Social stratification
Fields of study: Maintaining inequality; Religion

Religion traditionally provides one of society's greatest forces for cohesion, but religion also serves to divide people. Religion constructs and expresses a wordview, and often religious systems support the status quo. This constitutes an implicit endorsement of the society's inequities as well as its strengths.

Principal terms
INEQUALITY: a condition in which some groups possess limited amounts of one or more resources, in a comparison to a dominant ("majority") group, which blocks the upward mobility of other groups
LEGITIMATION: the process by which a social reality receives approval by a dominant group, involving the propagation of an ideology justifying the system
RACISM: the systematic denial of rights, privileges, status, or access to resources on the basis of one's physical characteristics (such as skin color) or genetic heritage
RELIGION: personal beliefs dealing with issues of ultimate reality and the nature of the relationships between humanity and one or more deities; also, the communal expression of those beliefs
SOCIAL CONFORMITY: the tendency of persons to behave similarly to the actions of a reference group, creating social groups with enforceable expectations about members' behavior
THEODICY: a religious legitimation of injustice, often arguing that human perceptions of inequality are wrong because they do not adequately appropriate the deity's absolute information and moral virtue

Overview

Throughout the world, societies distribute resources differentially. Not all persons possess the same amount of goods or the same amount of rights, privileges, and status. This unequal distribution of resources falls into patterns that point to social practices of inequality. Inequality is more than a differential of resources, however; inequality also systematically diminishes a group on the basis of some other factor, such as race, ethnicity, gender, sexuality, religion, or some other variable.

Since most societies believe that goods should be distributed according to some sort of ideal system—an ideal that does not reflect the actual distribution of resources—these societies develop ideological explanations of the inequalities. Perhaps a particular society's justification suggests that all persons should have prosperity but that some people are lazy and do not receive a full share for that reason. Alternately, such ideologies can claim that a specific group does not deserve an equal share because of their natural lack of certain virtues or abilities. Such assertions may claim that a certain ethnic group lacks an intellectual ability for higher-paying jobs or that women should be paid less because they naturally have a lower level of endurance for physical work. Regardless of any scientific basis for such claims of variance, these claims function as social ideologies that "explain" the observed inequalities. These sorts of ideologies legitimate the inequality and encourage the society to continue the systematic discrimination.

Religion has often functioned as a legitimating ideology. Throughout his writings, Karl Marx developed a thorough condemnation of religion's ability to legitimate inequality. Marx's critiques focused especially upon European forms of Christianity. Along with Friedrich Engels, he argued extensively that Christianity's social principles and historical modes of organization necessitated the existence of a ruling class that would oppress others. The notion of charity, central to both Judaism and Christianity as well as other religions, received specific defamation: Charity, Marx argued, was nothing more than a value for wealthy elites who could thus conceal some of the inequities of their social system without actually redressing the problems. By supporting the status quo as the system designed and favored by God, religion (in Marx's view) taught the masses to be submissive while teaching the ruling class to treat them with contempt and humiliation. Religion, Marx said, functioned as "the opiate of the people." (Opiates were popular mild analgesics in Marx's time, similar to aspirin today.) Marx regarded religion as a type of painkiller. The masses would lose their sense of their actual pain in the midst of religious promises of idealized futures and the religious valuation of the status quo; religion would thus desensitize the masses and convince them to ignore their true problems. In this fashion, religion worked to perpetuate the inequalities plaguing society.

Peter L. Berger, a contemporary sociologist, focuses on the ways people construct notions about how the world really is and how society should be. He argues that there is a strong social component in this construction of ideas about the world that influences even the perceptions of supposedly "objective" facts. Religion operates as a legitimating force in Berger's sense: Religion presents a statement of what is true about God and humanity. On the basis of this religious assertion, people make assumptions about reality and act to organize society in ways consonant with such views. In religious terms, human perception of injustice denies God's sovereignty and thus calls forth theodicy, the defense of God against accusations of injustice in the world.

Beyond theodicy, religion involves itself in establishing pervasive worldviews that justify the status quo by teaching values that should be rewarded. Thus, those who do not possess resources are "sinners" who do not respect the right values; they therefore deserve their unequal access to goods and their lower status in society. This common religious attitude blames the victim of inequality. There are other factors at work within religion as well. Religions often emphasize the benefits of moral virtue in some form of afterlife, which may encourage apathy about present worldly conditions. In general, religion tends to justify the current patterns of the world order and to legitimate the inequalities present within it, often claiming that the present state of the world is the will of God, even though many religions' theology opposes such injustice.

Applications

Sociologist M. Wesley Perkins argued in 1983 that religion provides a source of contentment that sedates social conscience. Many people who identify strongly with a religious group believe that equality already dominates in the world and thus believe that there is little need to act concerning inequalities. Perkins suggests that religions produce a social conformity that changes perceptions; that is, religious people not only conform to expectations but also perceive that there is less difference between themselves and others. Many religions espouse an equality of personhood, however, and people who hold firmly to these religions tend to desire equality more actively.

Perkins finds evidence for the most often identified pattern of religion and attitudes about equality—that moderately religious people are more prejudiced than society as a whole, but that devoutly religious people are much less prejudiced than other believers and than society as a whole. Thus, religion legitimates the world in its current organization, blinding some of its adherents to the injustices present within the world. Persons of strong religious faith, on the other hand, more religious than conventionality allows, extend this countercultural self-identification to a deep commitment to fighting inequalities.

A clear example of religion's divided response to inequality occurred during the United States' internal debates about slavery during the nineteenth century. In many cases, churches kept slavery alive and functioning through an ideological justification of slavery's correctness. Many contemporary sources reflect on the evils of the church for supporting slavery. Differing views on slavery divided many churches. Abolitionists as well as proslavery forces understood religion, especially Christianity, to support their own positions. The debates on both sides were heavily flavored with biblical language, as each side sought biblical prooftexts. Those favoring slavery showed how Jesus never condemned slavery, how the apostle Paul ordered slaves to be submissive, and how the Old Testament records Israel's history both as slaves and as slave owners. On the other hand, antislavery forces emphasized not only Christianity's religious-cultural values of freedom and respect for humanity but also its equal access to God and salvation; they quoted Paul's release of a slave in the New Testament book of Philemon and the Old Testament story of God's rescue of the Jews from slavery in the Exodus from Egypt. Each side used religion to legitimate its own positions about the inequality of slavery.

Likewise, Christianity's record of treatment of women is mixed. Feminists often charge the church with perpetuating sexism in society, and the church's traditional exclusion of women from positions of authority underscores their point. Many of the

United States' largest Christian denominations, as well as large groups within Judaism and many other religions, forbid women to achieve the highest status within their religion. The Roman Catholic church and the Southern Baptist Convention, the two most numerous American Christian denominations, do not recognize the ordination of women. Both of these organizations, as well as other Christian groups, have experienced this as a point of fierce contention, and neither has been entirely successful at squelching dissent. Many other Christian groups, as well as the more liberal Jewish synagogues, accept women in roles of official religious leadership.

Once more, both sides of the debate cite scripture as an authority. Some Christians argue that the Old Testament's view of Eve as succumbing to temptation and Paul's statements about the roles for women in the New Testament book of 1 Corinthians forbid contemporary women to take positions of leadership such as the pastorate or the priesthood, lay roles such as teaching, or even roles in the larger society such as political leadership or responsibility in domestic life. Other Christians, however, focus on Jesus' inclusion of women in his entourage, the feminine images for God in the Bible (such as Isaiah 42:14 and Matthew 23:37), and general religious principles of love, responsibility, and acceptance as warrants for the full inclusion of women in religion and in society.

It is difficult if not impossible to characterize adequately the variety of religious thought in the United States. Though many sociologists have suggested a correlation between the strength of religious commitment and the acceptance of various races as full members of society, there are people of strong religious commitment who believe in exclusion and in inclusion of women and various racial groups. There do not seem to be any easy answers regarding the problems of racism and sexism in religious communities themselves or regarding the influence of religion on society as a whole.

Other examples could be used to illustrate the mixed record of religion's legitimation of inequality in the United States. Though religion as a whole has played a significant role in encouraging oppression and inequality throughout the history of the world, many strong adherents of religion have fought inequality through progressive social programs for the poor and for others devalued by society. Persons of faith are on both sides of most controversial social issues, such as abortion and homosexuality. Religion as a whole has contributed to vast inequalities in society, but religion has also worked against such injustice.

Context

Religions have always provided a means to rationalize the world, including the status quo of any inequalities. Furthermore, religions are systems that make claims of truth, and thus they provide a rationale for the devaluation of people who hold opposite claims to truth. Since the Enlightenment, Western thinkers have recognized religion's ability to legitimate inequality.

The future of research into religion's legitimation of inequality must expand the boundaries of inquiry. Religion is one variable in attitudes toward racial, ethnic, and gender discrimination, as well as economic exploitation, but it is not the only significant factor. There is insufficient statistical evidence to demonstrate adequately how religion interacts with other variables in attitudes about inequality. Religion needs to be analyzed along with other ideologies, such as political attitudes and social philosophy, to determine the specific role that religion plays in legitimating inequality. Some forms of religion may advocate and foster racial equality, for example, while continuing sexual domination. The correlations between these different types of inequality deserve much further investigation by sociologists of religion.

One of the chief problems with any study of religious attitudes toward inequality is the variation within religious groups themselves. Many religions, such as Judaism and Christianity, as well as many of the other prominent religions within the United States, have a strong ideological commitment to equality and to the social welfare of all humanity. These values are present within the religious groups themselves to varying degrees. Yet inequality is also a cultural value in the United States, and the difference between cultural legitimation of inequality among people of religious belief and religious legitimation of the same inequality among the same people is exceedingly difficult to detect and analyze. One individual might accept inequality on the basis of culture, while another might accept it on the basis of religion, while yet a third might reject the same inequality on the basis of religious belief against pervasive cultural attitudes.

Sociologists need to focus more attention on the growing pluralism of religions. Christianity has lost some of its dominance within American religion. Eastern religions and New Age religions are rapidly growing, and these newer forms of American religion may have distinctively different attitudes and cultural influences than the types of religious adherence typically studied. The notion of American civil religion needs radical reconsideration in the light of such diversity. Furthermore, the larger religions of Christianity and Judaism have experienced an increasing fragmentation of their own attitudes. Interreligious differences need further attention, especially considering the strong influence of Fundamentalists and the growing tension between Fundamentalists and liberals. Also important to consider is the growth of sectarian groups with widely divergent practices and ideologies in comparison with "mainstream" religion.

Bibliography

Berger, Peter L. *The Sacred Canopy: Elements of a Sociological Theory of Religion.* Garden City, N.Y.: Doubleday, 1967. Berger's theories have significantly influenced the sociology of religion. This book states his positions on the social functions of religious belief, including legitimation, building upon the sociology of knowledge developed by Berger and Thomas Luckmann in *The Social Construction of Reality* (1966).

Brown, Joanne Carlson, and Carole R. Bohn, eds. *Christianity, Patriarchy, and Abuse: A Feminist Critique.* New York: Pilgrim Press, 1989. These essays address Christianity's implicit assumptions that legitimate misogyny and justify abuse and violence against women and others who are devalued by the religion. This controversial and excellent book contains a range of approaches, from the theological to the sociological to the practical.

Cone, James H. *Black Theology and Black Power*. Reprint. San Francisco: Harper & Row, 1989. Cone analyzes the white oppression of African Americans and reworks theological symbols to create a theology of liberation for other races. The preface of the 1989 reprint (the work was first published in 1969) adds Cone's perspective that questions of race must be embedded within a discussion of economics and class in the United States.

Daly, Mary. *Beyond God the Father: Toward a Philosophy of Women's Liberation*. Boston: Beacon Press, 1973. Daly critiques Christian misogyny, demonstrating how the church has promoted inequality. See also Daly's other books, such as *The Church and the Second Sex* (1968) and *Gyn/Ecology* (1978).

Davis, David Brion. *Slavery and Human Progress*. New York: Oxford University Press, 1984. Davis analyzes how ideologies of "progress" supported the enslavement of Africans in western Europe and the United States. Religion offered the notion of "Christianizing the pagans" by enslaving them, claiming slavery as a discipline that could teach both culture and religion, leading to salvation—an end that justified any means.

Feagin, Joe R., and Clairece Booher Feagin. *Racial and Ethnic Relations*. 4th ed. Englewood Cliffs, N.J.: Prentice-Hall, 1993. This textbook views many aspects of race relations, including some causes of racial tension in many different racial and ethnic groups prominent in the United States. Offers a helpful context for the understanding of religious factors in racial inequality.

Lincoln, C. Eric. *Race, Religion, and the Continuing American Dilemma*. New York: Hill & Wang, 1984. Lincoln explains the interrelationships of race and religion as they developed in the United States. This is perhaps the single most significant book for comprehending the religious legitimation of the oppression of African Americans and for understanding the intertwined growth of distinctive African American religion.

Roberts, Keith A. *Religion in Sociological Perspective*. 2d ed. Belmont, Calif.: Wadsworth, 1990. Roberts presents an even-handed overview of issues in the sociology of religion, with special attention to religion in the contemporary United States. His comparison of functionalist and conflict approaches is very helpful, and the book provides a good context for the issues of religion, race, and gender.

Ruether, Rosemary, and Eleanor McLaughlin, eds. *Women of Spirit: Female Leadership in the Jewish and Christian Traditions*. New York: Simon & Schuster, 1979. This book provides fifteen essays about the history of women's leadership in various Jewish and Christian communities. This enjoyable historical reading possesses good social insight, offering case studies in the religious legitimation of oppression against women as well as religious argumentation for the full inclusion of women.

Wood, Forrest G. *The Arrogance of Faith: Christianity and Race in America from the Colonial Era to the Twentieth Century*. New York: Alfred A. Knopf, 1990. This survey of Christianity's influence on the history of racism (especially against

African Americans) in the United States provides stinging indictments of the role of religion in legitimating inequality. Specifically noteworthy is the study's amount of detail in the exact denominational responses to issues such as slavery.

Jon L. Berquist

Cross-References

Caste Systems, 198; Gender and Religion, 813; Legitimation of Inequality: The Mass Media, 1061; Political Influence by Religious Groups, 1394; Socialization: Religion, 1894; The Sociology of Religion, 1952.

LEISURE

Type of sociology: Major social institutions
Field of study: The economy

Leisure simply refers to the ways people spend their free time when they are not working. Sociologists have examined how changes in society affect leisure-time pursuits as well as how leisure affects social relations.

Principal terms
CULTURAL ELITES: small groups in society who are seen as highly educated and culturally sophisticated in their leisure activities
GAME: an aspect of leisure that is oriented toward fun and is not considered a serious activity
HIGH CULTURE: a form of leisure pursuit often chosen by cultural elites
LEISURE: an activity that is freely chosen and intrinsically rewarding; often characterized as a state of relaxation or inactivity
MASS CULTURE: a term initially used to characterize the culture of a modern mass society with its mass media; now often used to mean popular culture
POPULAR CULTURE: the cultural forms enjoyed by the populace, including the leisure and recreational activities of typical segments of a society
RECREATION: active forms of leisure, also freely chosen and intrinsically rewarding

Overview

Leisure is generally considered as free time—time not spent doing something for utilitarian purposes, such as working. In Western preindustrial society, there were some one hundred holidays a year, but much of this time free from work was anything but leisurely. These "free" days were often set aside for civil or religious events that required individuals to perform certain duties or services. Because they entailed a set of obligations, such days cannot be construed as leisure days. The definition of leisure must therefore include more than simply freedom from work. It must also include freedom from other social forms of obligations, such as visiting relatives or traveling back and forth to work. Leisure should be freely chosen so that the activities involved are intrinsically rewarding and satisfying (cleaning out the attic or washing the car would not be considered a leisure activity).

Leisure might best be thought of as "empty" time: time not required to be devoted to something, time which can be spent doing what one wants. This form of leisure has typically been associated with social elites, because these individuals do not have to work, as Thorstein Veblen pointed out in his classic study, *The Theory of the Leisure Class* (1899). The historical association of leisure with this social class resulted in what is termed "high culture," in which leisure is a form of cultivation resulting from preoccupation with the higher values of life—hence the derivation of the reference to a person who has "class" or is "cultured."

Elite culture persists, but industrialization gave rise to another form of culture; it is known as popular or mass culture, since the majority of the populace can participate in it. Popular culture in turn gave birth to another form of leisure, recreational leisure.

Recreational leisure abides by the basic distinction of time free from work, but the concept does not qualitatively assume that certain forms of leisure are inherently better or higher than others. It is leisure for the populace; as such it involves material consumption in the same sense that the leisure activity usually requires product purchases: televisions, radios, film tickets, stereos, appropriate attire, tools or utensils, and so on. The Marxian view sees such leisure as another industry, necessary to keep the wheels of production greased.

Mass leisure has its roots in the mass production of goods that began in the 1920's in the United States. Industrialization allowed more goods to be produced than were absolutely necessary; with this situation, advertising rose concurrently with the new industries to direct people's activities and get them to consume products they might not otherwise want or need. Stuart Ewen calls these industrialists "captains of consciousness" in a 1976 book of the same name because their agreement to provide workers with better pay for fewer hours (the eight-hour day and the 40-hour week) was simply to give them more money and more time to pursue activities in which they would spend their newfound "wealth," which would flow back into the industrialists' coffers.

Seeing leisure strictly as a billion-dollar industry is sometimes referred to as the societal view of leisure. This view suggests that society needs leisure to sustain it; the view tends to ignore the individual's desire for leisure activity when not working. People in modern societies do fill their time between work, especially between Friday and Monday, by seeking some form of leisure. It is not surprising that a key function of this leisure for many individuals is to renew themselves for the workplace. Indeed, the Latin root of the word recreation (*recreatio*) means "restoration" or "recovery." People in industrialized societies, while they may purchase products, look to leisure for its restorative value. Their time is filled with activity, both passive (watching television, listening to the radio) and active (hiking, jogging, barbecuing). A central purpose of the "free time" activity for the individual is to shake off the fatigue of work and be rejuvenated to face the renewed demands of the workplace.

This repetitive cycle of work-leisure may make it seem that one's primary purpose in life is to work and that leisure has no other purpose than to restore one's energy. This is not a new concept. As social historian Witold Rybczynski points out in his provocative book *Waiting for the Weekend* (1991), the modern repetitive cycle of week and weekend is not unlike premodern societies' two discontinuous modes of being: the sacred and the profane. In this parallel, in the profane mode, where life is fixed (although it is chaotic and full of the mundane), existence is linear. Like the work week, it is a progression of days, weeks, months, and years. The weekend, however, is sacred; it is a Platonic time out; a time apart from mundane problems and mundane concerns. It is in this space that leisure is largely pursued in industrial societies. Instead of the handful of people who once participated, it is now available to all society's members.

Applications

Leisure has been tremendously influenced throughout the industrial age by changes in technology. The first such change was the invention of the printing press using movable type by Johann Gutenberg around 1450. Early printing was largely confined to political and religious tracts, and Gutenberg's invention did not substantially affect leisure pursuits until the birth of the novel some 250 years later. Daniel Defoe's adventure story *Robinson Crusoe* (1719) and Samuel Richardson's romance novel *Pamela* (1740), set the standards for popular reading. These early novels were enthusiastically received by men and women of the eighteenth century because they were relatively cheap (because of printing technology) and were simple stories simply told: Appreciating stories of ordinary people such as Tom Jones did not require a deep and extensive classical education rooted in symbols and mythology. People would gather in groups—family groups, groups of friends, or even a group of servants in the kitchen—at the end of the day, and those few who were literate would read aloud to the others. Reading, then, in addition to being a solitary activity, was a group leisure activity. The popularity of reading increased in the nineteenth century as education of the masses became more widespread and eventually compulsory. More people learned to read, and the reading of choice had high entertainment value, primarily consisting of lighthearted tales of romance and intrigue.

Electrical wonders began to proliferate as industrialism increased in the twentieth century. In particular, radio directly affected how Americans spent their leisure time. The low cost of a radio contributed to its widespread appearance in households across the country, and people gathered around the radio in the evening hours to listen to live comedies, dramas, and musical performances.

Since leisure time is finite, it is axiomatic that the growth of one leisure form must displace previous forms of leisure. During the first half of the twentieth century, radio partly replaced reading, and radio would soon find itself replaced during the second half of the century by television. Invented in the early 1920's, television did not become widely available and economically accessible to the public in the United States until the affluent post-World War II period.

Radio and then television qualify as leisure activities because people engage in them after working hours of their own volition, and many find the experience to be intrinsically rewarding. Despite the elitist condemnation of television as a "vast wasteland," Americans watch an average of forty-five hours of television a week. (Statistically, African Americans watch nearly twice that amount, and women over fifty-five watch more than any other group.) Television is not necessarily passive; it is often used as a catalyst for social interaction. Many sporting events, for example, are not watched in isolation but are a part of a social gathering. The social aspect of television has not been lost on entrepreneurs—sports bars have increased markedly and feature special pay-per-view events for their customers as well as in-house games. Leisure has been shaped throughout the twentieth century by electrical and electronic developments, and they continue to influence and change leisure activities. Successive generations are introduced to new electronic gadgetry that helps them adapt to the electronic world. One generation grew up on pinball; the next was trained on video games.

Reading, radio, motion pictures, and television are not the sole leisure-time activities of Americans. Reading and radio, even the cinema early in the twentieth century, might have been restorative after a strenuous day of hard physical labor; television, while relaxing, seems to be less restorative. A new form of exhaustion began to replace physically exhausting work on the job in the second half of the twentieth century. Work is often tedious and less physically draining; jobs requiring exertion are far less common than they once were. This explains the growth of exercise (aerobics, athletic clubs, martial arts lessons) as a major leisure activity. It also helps explain the need for packing the weekend with activity, since this is the time that is largely set aside for leisure. The weekend, as Rybczynski points out, is filled with activity; it is a time to *do* things. People rush around frantically to cram in as much activity as possible during this short period and do indeed seem to be restored by it.

American leisure contains an active-passive relationship. People go somewhere to do something, but what they do is most often somewhat passive. People go boating, then ride around for hours on the lake; they go to the beach, then lie down; they go to theme parks, such as Disneyland or Six Flags, and then stand in long lines. People can feel like they are "doing something"—and they are active to an extent—but they also enjoy such activities because they are not straining them too much. By the time the weekend ends, people may feel exhausted, but this is a qualitatively different feeling from the exhaustion encountered in the workplace. Therefore, such leisure activities have a rejuvenating and restorative effect.

Context

No one disputes the importance of leisure. The perennial focus of leisure studies has been on the quality of leisure life. The debate has typically been split between advocates of high culture and popular or mass culture. High culturalists see culture as having a specific educational function: The purpose of culture is to stimulate, to inform. In this tradition, high culture is a repository of society's great cultural traditions. Another group of high culturalists assumes that culture is supposed to be exploratory, creative, and revolutionary. Both groups see popular culture as a diluted form of culture. Marxist sociologists, who believe that culture should stimulate awareness, would rephrase Karl Marx's original dictum and say that popular culture has replaced religion as the opiate of the masses. High culturalists would agree.

Because elitists have cast a historically pejorative shadow over anything lower than high culture, the study of the more pervasive cultural forms did not begin until the 1950's and 1960's. Even then much scholarly effort was less research-oriented than it was interested in justifying the study of people's leisure activities. Initially this was accomplished by distinguishing between popular culture and mass culture. In this early tradition, popular culture was posited as qualitatively better than mass culture; popular culture was defined as culture with an artistic commitment which mass culture lacked. This hazy distinction was an attempt to justify the study of the recreational activities of the middle class. The distinction no longer is widely employed, and the term "popular culture" is most often used interchangeably with "mass culture" for any form of leisure activity.

Once a theoretical justification was laid for the study of popular leisure as a legitimate form of scientific inquiry, studies of leisure activities began in earnest, a major step in the advancement of leisure studies. Implicitly it acknowledges the importance of leisure in people's lives and allows sharper, more definitive research to be conducted about how leisure shapes life, an area which was long neglected and only began to emerge as a major focal point during the 1980's and after.

Bibliography

Ewen, Stuart. *Captains of Consciousness: Advertising and the Social Roots of Consumer Culture*. New York: McGraw-Hill, 1976. A history of the emergence and importance of advertising in shaping leisure desires. The author's thesis is extended in a related work, *Channels of Desire: Mass Images and the Shaping of American Consciousness* (McGraw-Hill, 1982).

Huizinga, Johan. *Homo Ludens: A Study of the Play Element in Culture*. Boston: Beacon Press, 1962. Huizinga suggests, half humorously and half seriously, that our species should be renamed from *Homo sapiens* to *Homo ludens*, which means "man at play," since this, not work, is our primary function.

Kando, Thomas. *Leisure and Popular Culture in Transition*. St. Louis: C. V. Mosby, 1975. An excellent detailed overview of the major issues and arguments surrounding high and popular culture and the purpose of leisure. Kando clearly sides with the popular culturalists.

Lynes, Russell. *The Tastemakers*. New York: Grosset & Dunlap, 1954. This witty critique discusses some of the people and pressures that shaped American taste in the mid-twentieth century. Included in this series of essays is Lynes's landmark "Highbrow, Lowbrow, Middlebrow."

Pieper, Josef. *Leisure: The Basis of Culture*. Translated by Alexander Dru. New York: New American Library, 1963. Here leisure is defined as empty time, time spent in contemplation. The author argues that it is this form of leisure which is largely responsible for the advancement of civilization.

Rybczynski, Witold. *Waiting for the Weekend*. New York: Viking, 1991. A thumbnail history of leisure, with special focus on the increased place of the weekend in shaping leisure time in contemporary society. A highly provocative analysis of how people spend their time between Friday and Monday. A related analysis by the same author is *Home: A Short History of an Idea* (Penguin, 1987).

Veblen, Thorstein. *The Theory of the Leisure Class*. New York: New American Library,

1953. An early landmark first published in 1899, of how elites misuse their wealth in their pursuit of leisure. Veblen developed the idea of conspicuous consumption in this work: Elites ostentatiously display their wealth, thereby setting standards which ultimately trickle down in diluted form to the populace who desire to imitate the leisure habits of the upper class.

John Markert

Cross-References

Aging and Retirement, 47; High Culture versus Popular Culture, 870; Industrial Sociology, 960; Socialization: The Mass Media, 1887; Technology and Social Change, 2043; Values and Value Systems, 2143; Workplace Socialization, 2202.

LIBERATION THEOLOGY

Type of sociology: Major social institutions
Field of study: Religion

Liberation theology refers to a radical study and interpretation of Christian religious doctrines and the Bible in the light of human social life.

Principal terms
DOCTRINE: any idea that is taught or advocated by a religious or ideological body and presented for group or public acceptance
LIBERATION: the act of freeing a person or a group from a repressive or oppressive situation
OPPRESSION: any unjust act or situation that prevents a person or group from full self-actualization or self-realization; oppression may be mental or physical
POVERTY: a condition in which people find themselves lacking the means for providing basic material needs
PRAXIS: practice as distinguished from theory; in liberation theology, praxis is the practical application of church teachings and theology
THEOLOGY: a rational, systematic study of religious and scriptural truths, of the way God reveals himself, and of the relationship between God and humanity
VATICAN II: also called the Second Vatican Council; a meeting of Catholic bishops in Rome from 1962 to 1965 that produced a major rethinking of doctrines and how to relate the church to a changing world

Overview

Liberation theology is a religious social movement that began in the Roman Catholic church in Latin America. It uses religious faith and the Christian gospel to demand that the church, to be the true light of Christ on earth, concentrate its energy on freeing people from oppression and poverty. Liberation theology seeks to aid the poor and the oppressed by directly involving them in social, political, religious, and civic affairs. It draws attention to the sociopolitical and economic structures that maintain injustice and inequality and endeavors to change the unjust structures.

Though the term, loosely used, also refers to various theologies that focus on liberating a people from the confines of racial (black theology), gender (feminist theology), and colonialist (Asian or African theologies) prejudices, liberation theology is the child of Latin American Catholicism. The term was coined in July, 1968, and first used in Chimbote, Peru, as *teología de la liberación* (theology of liberation) by Gustavo Gutiérrez, a Peruvian Catholic priest and theologian and one of the advisers to the second Consejo Episcopal Latinoamericano (CELAM, or Latin American Bishops' Conference) held in Medellín, Colombia, in August, 1968. The bishops met there to discuss how to apply the liberalizing tone of Vatican II (1962-1965) to Latin America. It was for this conference that Gutiérrez first outlined liberation theology. The Medellín conference allowed liberation theology to inspire its pronouncements and documents on peace and justice.

In many ways, the roots of liberation theology go far back in history, to the era of the Spanish conquest of the New World and the destruction of the Aztec, Incan, and Mayan civilizations. The Catholic church came to the Americas with the Spanish, and many in the church simply watched as the native peoples were subjected to a smallpox epidemic, oppression, enslavement, and death. The church was divided over this oppression even then, however; some bishops and priests fiercely protested and resisted such treatment of the natives. They wrote letters of protest to Spain and Rome, arranged legal defenses for the natives, and encouraged disobedience of government policies. In 1511, for example, Antonio de Montesinos sermonized against the cruel servitude under which the natives were being held.

In the nineteenth century, Latin America broke away from the colonial domination of Spain and Portugal. Latin American independence was strongly opposed by the Catholic church but was supported by a number of radical clergymen and theologians. The church's conservative stance put it at odds with the new independent governments, and the church faced a crisis of relevance and identity.

In the 1930's, the Latin American church began to build what was termed a "New Christendom," a concept that placed the church on the side of development and progress and therefore on the side of liberal Latin American governments. By the 1960's, however, the projects of New Christendom had failed, and military coups had occurred first in Cuba and then in Brazil. Again the church's effectiveness and relevance were being questioned. Many young people found Marxism attractive. Within the church itself, the voices of critical theologians were heard. Bishop Dom Hélder Camera denounced capitalist violence and poverty. He tried to raise the consciousness of the poor through literacy, and he organized bishops from Latin America, Africa, and Asia to write and publicize a document that called for wealth to be shared by all and to liberate the Third World.

Camilo Torres, a priest, theologian, and sociologist, organized a "United Front" to combat poverty in Colombia by bringing together professionals, workers, peasants, and ghetto inhabitants to work for social change. Facing hostility from church and university authorities, Torres left the priesthood and joined a guerrilla movement (the Army of National Liberation), convinced that an armed confrontation had become inevitable to bring social change. He taught that it was the duty of every true Catholic to bring a revolutionary change and that the Catholic who did not lead a revolutionary life lived in "mortal sin." Torres was killed in an ambush in 1966; to many young Latin Americans, Torres' death elevated him to martyrdom, even sainthood. His writings and speeches were widely published, inspiring many followers to form "camilista groups" in Colombia, Bolivia, Ecuador, Peru, and Venezuela.

It was during this period that Vatican II tried to rejuvenate the Catholic church. Following it, the church in Latin America sought answers concerning church involvement in politics, Marxist ideology, socioeconomic development, and the role the clergy should play in the life of Latin Americans. The CELAM meeting of 1968 in Medellín authoritatively supported controversial programs for social change in Latin America, including the active pastoral and theological support for the elimination of poverty, central to liberation theology.

Applications

The CELAM conference of 1968 gave liberation theology a degree of official recognition. The conference agreed that Latin American bishops could not remain indifferent to the social injustices that kept the majority of Latin Americans poor and oppressed. Among other things, the documents of CELAM II pointed out that the exploitive structures of dominance constitute "serious sins" and that such a situation of injustice was equivalent to "institutionalized violence." It put the blame for provoking revolutions on those who possess and control the greater share of power, culture, and wealth. The conference committed the Latin American church to radical social change, arguing that the creation of a just social order is a Christian task and that the church must show "solidarity with the poor." Toward this end, a global organization to educate the people about social and economic issues was to be integrated into pastoral work. Small communities, grass-roots organizations, and collaborative work with non-Catholic institutions and churches were encouraged.

Liberation theology applied these and other ideas in Latin American countries. One such application of liberation theology was found in the formation of *communidades eclesiales de base* (church base communities, or simply base communities). Ranging in size from ten to seventy members, base communities are small groups of local Christians led by catechists (lay people versed in basic Catholic doctrines). The groups meet regularly at churches, study the Bible, and commit themselves to working together to establish a more just society and to improve their communities by cooperatively attempting to meet their needs for sewage disposal, electricity, water, food, and roads. The groups arose from the liberation theologians' interpretation of Jesus' statement, "Where two or three are gathered in my name, there am I in their midst" (Matthew 18:20), as a call for people to see themselves—rather than the priest, the building, or the church authorities—as the church.

In contrast to traditional churches, base communities emphasize equality, small-group Bible study, lay leadership, raising the consciousness of members, and socio-economic and political activism. Begun in Panama and Brazil when liberation theology had not yet received active church recognition, base communities later drove home the importance of Vatican II's demand for the "common priesthood of the laity." By the 1970's, base communities had spread in Bolivia, Chile, Colombia, the Dominican Republic, Ecuador, El Salvador, Honduras, Nicaragua, and Paraguay. They offered to liberation theology a means of educating the people at the grass roots about critical social awareness and conscientization. In areas where church and liberation theology headquarters could not reach base communities physically, they used radio broadcasts to disseminate messages.

Christian Smith, author of *The Emergence of Liberation Theology* (1991), points out that liberation theology has applied various tactics, including organizing and participating in strikes, protests, rallies, and marches; organizing consciousness-raising programs for the poor; working for socialist political candidates; issuing official church pastoral letters and documents that oppose poverty, repression, and injustice and that call for liberating structural changes; diffusing liberation theology to pastoral workers who in turn diffuse it to Catholic laity; offering the church as a sanctuary for repressed progressive and leftist political militants; organizing peasant occupations of land owned by speculators; collecting and publicizing information about abuses of human rights in order to damage oppressive military and governmental powers; and agitation for improved neighborhood services. In a few cases, mostly limited to Central America, tactics have also included aiding guerrilla insurgents; participating in popular, armed insurrections and revolutions; and advising or serving in revolutionary government administration. Former priest Phillip Berryman points out that liberation theology has opened church facilities for refugees fleeing violence from the countryside. Liberation theology has also manifested itself physically in "priest groups"—organizations of priests who take progressive, vocal, and radical positions on political, social, economic, and church affairs. Research centers to help plan strategies relevant to Latin American realities have also been formed in many Latin American countries through the efforts of liberation theology.

Perhaps the ultimate example of the application of liberation theology in a real-life situation is that of Archbishop Oscar Romero of San Salvador. Noting the widespread unjust arrest and killing of people, the harassment of the clergy and university students, the displacement of the poor in rural areas, and the brutal activities of government and right-wing forces, Romero made a passionate plea in a broadcast sermon to the army not to kill innocent people, urging them to disobey an immoral human law to uphold divine law:

> My brothers, they are part of our very own people. You are killing your own fellow peasants. God's law, "Thou shalt not kill!" takes precedence over a human being's order to kill. No soldier is obliged to obey an order that is against God's law. No one has to obey an immoral law.

Berryman notes that Archbishop Romero even took the bolder, more dangerous step of "ordering" the soldiers to stop the repression. A few days after that sermon, he was shot dead while saying Mass in March, 1980. His funeral was disrupted by a bomb and gun attack.

Context

Sociologists have long been interested in the study of religion, dating back to such social science pioneers as Karl Marx and Max Weber. Religion is viewed as one of society's major social institutions, and different sociological perspectives have emphasized different aspects of this institution. Conflict theorists have noted the use of religion by ruling classes in maintaining the status quo and continuing to subjugate lower classes, whereas functionalist theorists emphasize the role of religion in helping to bring people together and form a societal consensus regarding values.

Certainly in the history of Christianity—the Catholic church of the Middle Ages in particular—one can find many examples of ways the church sought to maintain the status quo and, in fact, to maintain its own power and wealth. Liberation theology, in its emphasis (even insistence) on social action and on bringing its consciousness-raising message directly to poor and oppressed people, represents a dramatic break from this history. With its determination to disrupt and reform the status quo, liberation theology was guaranteed to create controversy and division within the church, and indeed it did. Liberation theology stands as an example of religion as social movement.

Studies of theology have traditionally focused on European-style systematic theology, which has always used conceptual instruments such as Platonism and Aristotelianism in its reflection. Liberation theology, on the other hand, is based on socioanalytical mediation rather than abstract metaphysical philosophy. It begins from, and aims at, praxis, and it uses the social sciences. It is an interpretation of Christianity that comes from the experiences of the poor and is an attempt to help the poor interpret their own faith in a new way.

Though it began in Latin America, liberation theology is not uniquely Latin American; it has become a world theology that emphasizes practical concerns. It has been associated with black theology and feminist theology, particularly since theological conferences in Detroit in 1975 and 1980, and has been associated with the theological expressions of Third World countries in Asia and Africa since the Dar-es-Salaam (Tanzania) Conference in 1976. It can therefore be seen as a general Christian movement for human liberation. Berryman has noted that some of the social positions taken by liberation theologians seem irreversible, since they are essentially identical to official Catholic teachings since Vatican II. (Particularly crucial are the ideas that no defense of freedom or of a "Christian" civilization can legitimize the murder of those who stand up to defend their rights and that full respect for human rights will demand a new kind of society.) Gutiérrez has explicitly noted the movement's concern with the "non-person"—the person not recognized as human by an existing social order. The ultimate question for liberation theology, he says, is how to "proclaim the Father in an inhuman world, the implications of what it means to tell the non-person that he or she is a child of God."

Bibliography

Berryman, Phillip. *Liberation Theology*. Philadelphia: Temple University Press, 1987. Written by a former Catholic priest from his own experience and the experiences of liberation theologians, Berryman's book is most informative and is one of the best on this movement. Its language is clear and unencumbered by theological and sociological technicalities. It situates liberation theology within church and biblical doctrines; while making Latin America its main focus, it shows how liberation theology has become a universal phenomenon.

Gibellini, Rosino. *The Liberation Theology Debate*. Maryknoll, N.Y.: Orbis Books,

1988. This book makes good use of theological, philosophical, and sociological terminologies. It has an appendix containing interviews with Gustavo Gutiérrez and Clodovis Boff, two leading liberation theologians. Includes a list of publications on liberation theology from Orbis Books, publications covering Asian, African, Jewish, Latin American, and general Third World liberation theologies.

Pottenger, John R. *The Political Theory of Liberation Theology: Toward a Reconvergence of Social Values and Social Science.* Albany: State University of New York Press, 1989. Pottenger's book is a good academic book that discusses not only the methodology but also the religious, political, ethical, economic, and ideological contexts of liberation theology. It has impressive biographical sketches of thirteen liberation theologians and includes a detailed bibliography.

Schall, James V. *Liberation Theology in Latin America.* San Francisco: Ignatius Press, 1982. A 402-page book of selected essays and documents related to liberation theology in general and the manner in which it is practiced in Latin America in particular. Various views and stands are considered, ranging from a secular position by Jeanne Kirkpatrick, former U.S. ambassador to the United Nations, to church pronouncements by Pope John Paul II.

Smith, Christian. *The Emergence of Liberation Theology.* Chicago: University of Chicago Press, 1991. Using graphs and numerous tables of statistical data, the book looks in detail at liberation theology in Latin America as a radical religious and social movement. Sociological theories and analytical tools are used. Includes an impressive bibliography, detailed notes, and an index. Its scholarly approach does not hinder its accessibility.

I. Peter Ukpokodu

Cross-References

Christianity, 231; The Church and African American Life, 239; Class Consciousness and Class Conflict, 271; Political Influence by Religious Groups, 1394; Religion: Functionalist Analyses, 1603; Social Movements, 1826; Socialization: Religion, 1894.

LIFE EXPECTANCY

Type of sociology: Population studies or demography

Life expectancy is the average time a cohort of people of a given age would be expected to live under the assumption of fixed, age-specific death rates. Life expectancy at birth is a widely used summary measure for comparing mortality levels between different populations or subpopulations. Life expectancy is also the basis for important business decisions such as the funding of pension and insurance plans.

Principal terms
AGE-SPECIFIC DEATH RATE (ASDR): the percentage of persons in an age interval who die in one year divided by the mid-year population in that age interval
COHORT: any group that shares a common experience at the same time, such as being born in the same year or being graduated from high school in the same class
CRUDE DEATH RATE (CDR): the total number of deaths in a population in one year divided by the mid-year population
DEMOGRAPHY: the study of the size, composition, and change of human population in relation to birth, death, and migration as well as to social, biological, and ecological determinants and consequences of population change
LIFE EXPECTANCY: the number of years a cohort of people is expected to live on average, given current age and assuming that mortality levels remain constant
LIFE TABLE: a basic demographic model for studying the history of a hypothetical population; from a life table, life expectancy at various ages and values of other life table functions can be calculated
PERSON-YEAR: a unit representing one person having lived one year; two persons living one year would equal two person-years

Overview

At its simplest, life expectancy is the amount of time an individual at a given age can be expected to survive. The concept has also been applied to calculations of how long inanimate objects, such as machines, can be expected to operate without failing. Similar approaches are also used to estimate the time that a person will remain at a particular location or social status. Calculation of life expectancy is most often based on historical patterns of mortality.

Mortality in a population, in its simplest form, can be represented as a crude death rate. The crude death rate, or the number of deaths in a population in a given year divided by the mid-year population, however, often conveys an inaccurate impression of a population's health. A population dominated by young persons, for example, may have a low crude death rate even though few survive past the age of fifty.

Consideration of survival and death for particular age groups is more useful for assessing the status of a population. Age-specific death rates are comparable across populations and over time, permitting better evaluation of programs for health and security; however, age-specific rates can be overwhelming in their detail. A summary measure that collects age-specific death rates into one number is also helpful in describing the status of a population. Life expectancy is one such measure. In most instances, life expectancy at birth or at any other age is estimated using a "life table," often calibrated for a specific country or region, or for specific subpopulations, such as gender and ethnic groups. Complete life tables present information for all single year ages, while abridged life tables present data for age groups, such as five-year or ten-year intervals.

Life tables are based on the probability of dying during an age interval, which is calculated as the number of deaths between the beginning age of the interval and the beginning age of the next interval, divided by the total number of persons at the beginning of the age interval. The probability of dying can also be calculated from age-specific death rates that are available in published vital statistics.

Beginning with a hypothetical number of births, called a radix (l_0), life tables "die-off" persons as they age according to estimated mortality probabilities (q_x). The hypothetical population is eventually reduced to a small number who survive to the upper age limit, or life span, or to an open-ended interval such as "90 and above." Averaging the various amounts of time that persons in the population will survive from a given age (x) gives the life expectancy (e_x). In other words, life expectancy for a given age is calculated as the total person-years (T_x) that members of an age cohort would live after that age divided by the number of persons in the cohort at the initial time.

For example, there might be 100 persons of exactly 18 years of age ($l_{18} = 100$) in a given year, and the probability of dying before reaching their nineteenth birthday might be 4 percent ($q_{18} = .04$). During the year, 4 persons would be expected to die, with 96 persons reaching age 19 ($l_{19} = 96$). During the interval, 96 persons each lived one person-year, and the four who died averaged one-half person-year each, equalling two additional person-years and totalling 98 person-years ($L_{18} = 98$). As this cohort of persons experiences each additional year, some survive and some do not. The percentage that dies increases with age as health problems associated with aging take their toll. Each year the total number of person-years is accumulated as total person-years ($T_{18} = L_{18} + L_{19} + L_{20} + \dots$). Life expectancy is calculated as the total future person-years (Tx) to be lived by the cohort divided by the number of persons at age X (l_x). If one has calculated that the 100 persons age 18 will produce a total of 5,000 future person-years before they have all died ($T_{18} = 5,000$), then life expectancy at age 18 is 50 years ($T_{18} / l_{18} = e_{18}$, or $5,000 / 100 = 50$). The expected age at death for these persons age 18, therefore, will be 68 years on average (18 + 50). Some persons will die this year, whereas others will live into their nineties. Given no additional information, one cannot predict who will live and who will die, but one can speak to the average expectancy of life. Given additional information, such as smoking behavior or individual preference for high-speed motorcycle rides, adjustments to the model can be made.

In 1990, the world's highest life expectancy at birth was 79 years and existed in Japan. The lowest was 42 years, and it existed in West African countries. Life expectancy at birth in the United States was 47 years in 1900; it increased to 75 years in 1990. Life expectancy in the United States has been increasing very slowly since the 1960's, with some disadvantaged subpopulations actually experiencing declines resulting from teen violence, substance abuse, and inadequate health care.

Patterns of mortality and, therefore, life expectancy are affected by both individual and environmental factors. Individual factors include age, gender, race, and health-related behavior such as smoking, drinking, and diet. Genetic factors, such as a family history of circulatory, respiratory, or digestive disorders, can reduce life expectancy, as can employment in risky occupations, such as machine operations, transportation, and agricultural labor.

Applications

Demographers and public health officials engaged in measuring the health of large populations frequently cite life expectancy, particularly life expectancy at birth. The United Nations and other international organizations often employ life expectancy as an index of health conditions. Within a nation, differences in life expectancy provide potent evidence of the impact of economic and social stratification. Historical studies document that at least since the twelfth century, the life expectancy of lower social classes has been consistently less than that for upper classes. In the United States, comparisons of life expectancy between subpopulations show severe disadvantages associated with poverty and location in areas with high levels of disease or violence. In some urban centers in the United States, for example, one quarter or more of all deaths to persons in their later teen years are attributable to guns.

A range of business and health professionals depend on reasonable estimates of life expectancy in order to meet future obligations, including employee pension funds, health and life insurance policies, and capital replacement. The field of actuarial science has expanded dramatically since the 1970's with increasing demand for cost projections and long-range planning in both the public and private sectors. Life table methods have gained widespread application in other fields, such as industrial planning, where machine failure time is modeled using the same techniques used to predict human life expectancy. Two types of applications will be examined here. The first is a classic example of planning employee pensions, and the second is an application to planning equipment purchases.

An actuarial specialist in a large corporation has been asked to estimate how much money needs to be set aside each year in order to fund an employee pension plan. The problem is complex; there are numerous employees at different ages and skill and pay levels. They have spent varying amounts of time with the corporation. Realizing that she does not have much time, the specialist chooses to map out an estimate for one employee and then replicate the procedure for the others.

Given a retirement age of 65 and a commitment to pay some fixed income, such as $3,000 per month, to the employee from retirement until she or he dies, the actuarial specialist needs to know how long the employee is expected to survive. An average life expectancy of 15 years beyond retirement, given that the employee reaches age 65, would require an average total pension payment of $540,000. In the United States and other developed countries, female life expectancy is considerably longer than male life expectancy. As a result, for a given retirement income, larger employee pension contributions are required for female employees. If pension benefits accrue to surviving spouses, then estimates must incorporate more complicated joint probabilities of survival for either spouse.

In the above analysis, employees enter the life table by being born (a single increment) and leave the table by dying (a single decrement). A more sophisticated multiple-decrement analysis could include probabilities of employees leaving the pension scheme in ways other than dying, such as through changing employers, taking early retirement, or being fired and losing retirement benefits. Multiple-decrement analysis is very powerful and is now widely applied. N. Krishnan Namboodiri and C. M. Suchindran's book *Life Table Techniques and Their Applications* (1987) details how tables are assembled and interpreted.

In a second application of life table analysis, a consultant has been asked to budget future purchases of replacement equipment for a large apparels mill. The mill uses several hundred sewing machines of varying ages. One simple strategy would be to purchase equipment on the assumption that failure rates are constant over time. This approach, however, may increasingly underestimate actual machine failure rate as the stock of machines ages. Alternatively, historical data on machine failure time can be assembled to construct a life table indicating the average expectancy of future operation, given that a machine has worked a specific number of years. An inventory of the current ages of sewing machines combined with expectancy of future operation can then inform the budgetary process. Regular analysis of capital stock can help a business to avoid uneven replacement costs and depletion of capital.

In addition to forecasting failure times for the machines, life tables include estimates of the probability that machines will fail within a specific time period (say, in the fourth year of operation), the total production time that can be expected for all machines of a specific age during a given time period, and so on. Given adequate maintenance records, specific explanatory variables, such as frequency of lubricating sewing machine parts, can be related to failure time. Thus, a business can weigh the costs of servicing machinery against the benefits of increased machine longevity. This form of information is of clear benefit to businesses.

Life expectancy and life table methods are applicable to a wide variety of situations in which the incidence of an event (such as birth, contraceptive use, migration, unemployment, incarceration, or mechanical failure) is involved. Whenever survival rates or failure rates are different over the life course of a person, animal, or machine, life expectancy and life table methods can be applied.

Context

Englishman John Graunt, sometimes called the father of demography, prepared among the earliest documented work on survival patterns in 1662. This work led directly to the creation of life tables. British astronomer Edmund Halley's life table on the city of Breslau, published in 1693, is the first documented attempt to analyze mortality systematically using the life table methodology. Halley is noted as the inventor of the term "expectation of life."

As vital statistics such as births, marriages, and deaths became more systematic and reliable in European countries during the 1800's, the possibilities for compiling realistic life expectancies grew. Life tables became a standard feature in U.S. government population reports in the 1900's. Throughout the twentieth century, life table publications have become more frequent (they are now published annually) and have been assembled for larger numbers of subpopulations. Differential expectations of life by race, occupation, socioeconomic status, and place of residence have fueled debates about social inequities. Publication of life tables for developing countries has been hampered by the same lack of accurate vital statistics that affected more developed countries in the 1800's. Since the 1960's, the United Nations has been publishing collections of life tables for developing countries in their annual *Demographic Year Book*.

A number of significant trends in the analysis of life expectancy are certain to continue. Countries lacking sufficient vital information will work to improve registration of births and deaths as well as to prepare more reliable population estimates. The number of developing countries producing life tables and estimates of life expectancy will continue to increase. Countries that already have aggregate tables will endeavor to produce more precise tables of subpopulations. The demand for better information on life expectancy will continue to be dominated by those enterprises most involved in the financial implications of survival, in particular insurance and pension funding. National governments, being the largest-single providers of both, will continue their involvement in expanding knowledge of life expectancy.

In social science and business, research using the life expectancy framework is placing increasing emphasis on determining the impacts of individual and environmental factors that can affect individual variation. The impacts of smoking cessation programs on mortality rates, of workplace regulations regarding employee safety, and of coastal development on wildlife populations are examples of analyses that can be pursued within the life expectancy framework.

Improvements in the analysis of survival are presenting new ways to inform government and business. Multi-increment and multidecrement life tables open up the possibility of analyzing situations in which people can join or leave a population in different ways. Multidimensional tables, which simultaneously consider more than one population, permit better analysis of variables that may influence outcomes such as machine failure or death. Sophisticated forms of survival analysis are now employed to analyze the effects of factors such as gender, race, or other individual characteristics rather than simply preparing separate tables. The future holds considerable promise for the evolution of life expectancy analysis.

Bibliography

Namboodiri, N. Krishnan, and C. M. Suchindran. *Life Table Techniques and Their Applications*. Orlando, Fla.: Academic Press, 1987. This book begins with the fundamentals of constructing and interpreting life tables and steps through a variety of advanced applications. The emphasis is on survival or event analysis techniques. Most accessible to readers with a moderate background in statistics.

Palmore, James A., and Robert W. Gardner. *Measuring Mortality, Fertility, and Natural Increase: A Self-Teaching Guide to Elementary Measures*. Honolulu, Hawaii: East-West Center, 1983. This is an introductory-level book on the basic demographic measures. It is a well-organized book with explicit definitions, examples, and thoughtful exercises and questions. Discussions of life table construction and calculation of life expectancy are very readable.

Schoen, Robert. *Modeling Multigroup Populations*. New York: Plenum Press, 1988. This is an advanced book divided into three parts: the basic life table model, multistate models, and two-sex models. Basic knowledge of calculus is helpful in interpreting the models.

Shryock, Henry S., Jacob S. Siegel, et al. *The Methods and Materials of Demography*. Edited by Edward G. Stockwell. New York: Academic Press, 1976. Often referred to as the demographer's bible, this book covers a wide range of demographic techniques, including background, methods, and examples from numerous contexts. Though somewhat dated, this book continues to be a basic text for students of demography.

Sinquefield, Jeanne Cairns. *Single and Multiple Decrement Life Table Procedures for the Analysis of the Use-Effectiveness of Contraception*. Chicago: University of Chicago Press, 1973. This book discusses the application of single and multiple decrement life table procedures to contraceptive studies. It also outlines alternative methods of collecting data for life table analysis of use-effectiveness of contraception. Sample computer programs are included.

James H. Fisher
Jichuan Wang
Jiajian Chen

Cross-References

The Aging Process, 53; Demography, 506; Fertility, Mortality, and the Crude Birthrate, 761; Infant Mortality, 978; Population Growth and Population Control, 1421; Population Size and Human Ecology, 1428; Population Structure: Age and Sex Ratios, 1434.

LOGICAL INFERENCE: DEDUCTION AND INDUCTION

Type of sociology: Sociological research
Fields of study: Basic research concepts; Data collection and analysis

Research is like any other learning or decision-making process: It involves collecting information on a topic and then using logic, along with some basic assumptions, to draw conclusions (or inferences) about that topic. Deduction and induction are the two most basic types of logic utilized in the scientific search for knowledge.

Principal terms

DEDUCTION: the process of arriving at a specific conclusion or prediction by applying a premise (a general law, hypothesis, or assumption) to a particular case

EMPIRICAL: based on direct observation and measurement using the physical senses

FACT: a proposition or piece of information upon which people can agree; generally based on direct (empirical) observation rather than feelings or opinions

FALSIFICATION: disproving a proposition or hypothesis by testing a prediction derived from it

HYPOTHESIS: a model or educated guess about the status or cause of some phenomenon, usually arrived at via induction and stated as a proposition

INDUCTION: the process of arriving at a general law, premise, or hypothesis by discovering some similarity across a set of related facts

INFERENCE: the process of making an educated guess about something using either induction or deduction; alternatively, the outcome or conclusion resulting from that process

PREMISE: a general law or hypothesis that is assumed to be true and from which an inference or prediction can be deduced

PROPOSITION: a statement, educated guess, or hypothesis about the state or condition of something; it may or may not be factual

STATISTICAL INFERENCE: an inference made by applying some basic assumptions and/or laws of statistics to a set of observations

Overview

Research is like any other learning or decision-making process; it involves collecting information on a topic and then using logic, along with some basic assumptions, to draw conclusions (or inferences) about that topic. There are several steps involved in this process.

The first step is defining the topic. This is not as easy as it may sound. Many of the topics sociologists study involve terms that different people define differently, such as religion, family values, and social deviance. None of these topics or terms has a one-to-one correspondence with a directly observable behavior. Yet in order to collect information, or data, the topic and terms must be defined in a way that can somehow be counted or otherwise measured in the same way by each person involved. Such definitions, called "operational definitions," are often very limited, but without them, research could not proceed.

The second step is collecting information. If a clear operational definition has been created, then the data collected will be "empirical"—that is, they will be based on a measuring technique that involves the physical senses, and anyone who examines the data will be able to agree on what was observed. (This does not mean that everyone will agree on an interpretation of what was observed.) Empirical information is more reliable than information based on intuition or "gut feelings" about a topic; thus the former is referred to as fact, the latter as opinion.

The third step is to look for patterns in the data. This is the process of "induction"—discovering a pattern or drawing a conclusion based on a large set of individual facts. Everyone uses induction in everyday life when they make generalizations based on their experience. If every time a woman encounters a particular neighbor, the neighbor yells at her, she may conclude that this neighbor is a grumpy person. Her conclusion is a "hypothesis" or "inference"—she is making an educated guess about the world based on discovering a pattern in a set of observations. Such conclusions are stated as "propositions"; one proposes that a certain conclusion is true, but one does not know for sure.

In fact, it could well be that the woman's proposition is wrong. Maybe her neighbor is generally very nice but she only sees him when he is doing yard work, and the pain from his arthritis puts him in a bad mood; maybe he is partially deaf and the woman is misinterpreting her observations. In the first case, her conclusion is wrong because her observations are not random and are not representative of all possible observations of her neighbor. In the second case, her conclusion is wrong because her operational definition of grumpiness (yelling) is also an operational definition of deafness. Induction is not a foolproof process; conclusions or inferences derived through induction are logical, educated guesses, but one can never "prove" anything through induction.

It is possible, however, to *disprove* an inductive inference. Once an inference or hypothesis is derived, it can be stated as a proposition or assumption about the world. The proposition can then be used as a "premise" (a supposition) in a deductive argument, and its predictions can be tested.

Deductive arguments are usually phrased as "if/then" statements, followed by a fact and a conclusion: *If* a certain premise or proposition is true, *then* a certain prediction must be true. Thus, if the prediction has been tested and documented to be fact, then the premise must be true. A hypothesis derived via induction can be tested by making it a premise in a deductive argument and then collecting empirical data to observe whether the facts match the prediction. Deductive inferences are always true if the premise is true and the deduction is valid; thus, if a deductive prediction is tested and the facts do not match the prediction, one knows that either the deduction is invalid or the premise (the hypothesis) is false. If the facts do match the prediction, then the premise (hypothesis) may be true but is not *necessarily* true: Although the premise can be disproved, it can never be proved.

In a way, deduction is the opposite of induction. With induction, a single, generalized conclusion, hypothesis, or inference is drawn from a large set of facts; with deduction, a large set of specific predictions (one could say "hypothesized facts") can be inferred from a single, general law, supposition, or premise. Hypotheses that have many of their predictions tested without ever being falsified are those that survive to become scientific theories.

In summary, induction is used to make educated guesses about the world by drawing generalizations from empirical observations. While these educated guesses can never be proved, deduction can be used to make and test predictions derived from them. This method of making educated guesses about the world and then testing them by testing their predictions is called the "hypothetico-deductive method"; it is the major process of truth-testing utilized in scientific inquiry.

Applications

In the social sciences, applying the hypothetico-deductive model is trickier than it is in the physical sciences, because the phenomena being studied usually have many simultaneously contributing causes. This means that for any particular instance of a phenomenon, there are a number of possible explanations—any of which may be correct, either singly or in combination. Many factors, for example, contribute to the phenomenon of childhood delinquency.

In situations such as this, it is impossible to make straightforward deductions (and, therefore, to test inductively derived hypotheses), because there are no simple, valid "if/then" arguments. For example, if one were to hypothesize that poverty is one of many factors contributing to juvenile delinquency, one could not simply argue that "If poverty contributes to juvenile delinquency, then poor children will be juvenile delinquents" and then test one's prediction. If poverty is only one of many causes of juvenile delinquency, then some impoverished children will become delinquents, but not all will. Likewise, some nonimpoverished children will become delinquent for other reasons. Therefore, it is not only impossible to prove the hypothesis (because one can never truly prove a hypothesis) but also impossible to disprove it: It may happen that the facts do not confirm one's prediction but that the premise is still true.

In any field of study, if the phenomenon being studied has multiple, perhaps simultaneous, interacting causes, hypothesis testing must rely on the use of "statistical inference." A statistical inference is a deductive conclusion that is stated in terms of probability rather than certainty. Thus, a hypothesis or other conjecture may be rejected with a certain degree of confidence rather than being disproved.

Using known laws of probability, it is possible to make some valid deductive arguments of a statistical nature, stated as: If a certain premise is true, then the probability of a certain outcome is 95 percent (or 90 percent, 99 percent, and so on). One can then test the prediction, and if it is not confirmed, one can conclude "with 95 percent confidence" (or 90 percent, or 99 percent, and so on) that the premise is not true.

If one has made a statistical inference with 95 percent confidence (the most commonly used confidence level in the social sciences), there remains a 5 percent probability of being mistaken. This a called making an "alpha error." When using statistical inference then, one cannot claim to disprove a hypothesis but, rather, to "reject" it with a certain level of confidence.

Thus, to go step-by-step through the logical processes involved in determining the factors that contribute to delinquency, one would first specify exactly what is meant by "juvenile delinquent" by defining it in a way that is observable and measurable and ensures that everyone can (at least temporarily) agree on the definition. A possible operational definition might be "all individuals under age eighteen who have been arrested two or more times." Second, one would collect as much data on delinquency as possible, by making empirical observations and measurements. For the definition just given, one would need to look at police records to find a group of "delinquents" and then collect information about them from as many sources as possible. Third, one would look for patterns in the observations and, using induction, generate several hypotheses about the possible causes of delinquency. One might, for example, find that a large percentage of the delinquents came from poor neighborhoods, came from single-parent households, had been involved in alcohol-related crimes, showed poor school performance, and had low expectations for their future. Thus, one might hypothesize that each of these factors is one of many factors that contribute to delinquency. Fourth, one would state each hypothesis as a proposition that could be used as the premise of a deductive argument. (For example, "Poverty is one cause of delinquency.") Fifth, using the rules of deduction (and some knowledge of probability), one would generate several statistical predictions to test each premise (hypothesis)—for example, "*If* poverty is one contributing cause of delinquency, *then* we will find greater rates of delinquency (at a level that is 'statistically significant') in poor neighborhoods than in rich neighborhoods." Sixth, one would collect new empirical data and observe whether those data support or refute each hypothesis. That is, one would go to different areas, without reanalyzing one's original observations, and see whether one finds the same patterns associated with delinquency as one had found previously. Finally, one would use deduction to arrive at a conclusion, or inference, about the truth or untruth of each hypothesis. That is, utilizing statistical analyses of the new data, one would make a decision about whether to reject or temporarily accept each hypothesized cause of delinquency.

When a hypothesis is supported, the best thing to do is to repeat the entire testing process again—there is, after all, a 5 percent chance that one has made a mistake. If the process is repeated and the hypothesis is supported again, then the probability of having made a mistake is only 5 percent × 5 percent, or 0.25 percent. Thus, even though one can never prove one's hypothesis, each time the testing process is repeated, one's confidence level in the results increases. It is also important to test the hypothesis using a new operational definition, since, generally, each operational definition is fairly narrow.

Context

Induction and deduction are not exclusively the tools of researchers; they are natural processes that people use every day. Logical inference happens so automatically that people do not even realize when it is occurring. In the middle of winter, for example, people may put on their coats before leaving the house—without even checking the temperature—because they "know" that it will be cold outside: Since they have observed that it has always been cold on winter days in the past, they induce that it always will be cold on winter days in the future. Then they deduce that because all winter days are cold, and because today is a winter day, it must be cold outside today.

In general, it is a good thing that people do not have to make every inference consciously; most human behavior is based on what has been learned about the world through making and applying inferences, and it would simply take too long if one had to check the facts of every instance without being able to assume that the future will, in many ways, be similar to the past. This assumption—that the laws of the universe do not change unpredictably—is called the assumption of "uniformitarianism." It is a basic assumption of all science and of most nonscientific thinking as well. On the other hand, although we rely on logical inference for most of our daily decisions, sometimes we make mistakes. Because inductive inferences can never be proved, we assume that they are correct until they are disproved; in the meantime, we act on them—sometimes in error.

Stereotypes, for example, are a kind of generalization based on induction. Even though a stereotype may be true in some (or even in many) instances, people make a fundamental error if they therefore assume that all specific instances will fit the stereotype. If one makes a decision based on a stereotype without actually checking whether it holds true in a particular instance, one is acting with prejudice—that is, acting according to a pre-judgment. If the decision is an important one with lasting consequences for someone's well-being (for example, whether someone goes to jail, gets custody of his or her children, or is fired from a job), then any prejudice that affected the decision can be harmful.

Since logical inference is a fallible process, one should test one's assumptions before acting whenever circumstances suggest that a decision is important. Since the consequences of decisions based on sociological research can be great, researchers generally will not make claims without first testing them many times. "Replication," the act of repeating research studies to double-check the results, is a necessary part of scientific inquiry.

Bibliography

Capaldi, Nicholas. *The Art of Deception: An Introduction to Critical Thinking*. Buffalo, N.Y.: Prometheus Books, 1987. Chapters 1-3 introduce the logic of deduction; chapters 5 and 6 discuss attacking someone else's argument and defending one's own (respectively); chapter 7 is on cause and effect. This is an easy-to-read layperson's guide to not being fooled by someone else's logical trickery. Examples are drawn from many interesting areas, such as law and advertising.

Kornblith, Hilary. *Inductive Inference and Its Natural Ground.* Cambridge, Mass.: Cambridge University Press, 1993. This philosophical essay addresses the questions "Why do people naturally use induction?" and "What is it about the world and about the human mind that leads us to automatically generalize from our experience?" Addresses the philosophy of "natural kinds" and the kinds of reasoning humans do well and do poorly. Includes a good reference section.

Manicas, Peter T., and Arthur N. Kruger. *Logic: The Essentials.* New York: McGraw-Hill, 1976. An excellent source, this college-level textbook is much more accessible than most: There is minimal use of symbolism and extensive use of easy, verbal examples. Among other topics, it covers definitions, "truth" and "proof," syllogisms, induction, deduction, probability, statistical inference, "laws," and the scientific method.

Medawar, Peter B. *Induction and Intuition in Scientific Thought.* London: Methuen, 1969. Medawar is a Nobel laureate as famous for his popular essays as for his research. This brief book (only 59 pages) is a must-read for anyone interested in the role of induction in science. Unlike most philosophical treatments, this is very user-friendly (despite its British style). Also available (perhaps more readily) as volume 75 of the Memoirs of the American Philosophical Society.

Platt, John R. "Strong Inference." *Science* 146 (October, 1964): 347-353. This classic article presents the philosophy of scientific falsification, whereby scientists rule out different hypotheses one by one, leaving the strongest and presumably correct hypothesis as the sole survivor of rigorous attempts at disproof. Platt argues that the social sciences will remain "soft" until this approach is utilized on a more regular basis.

Singleton, Royce, Jr., Bruce C. Straits, Margaret M. Straits, and R. J. McAllister. *Approaches to Social Research.* New York: Oxford University Press, 1988. This upper-level college research methods textbook may be the only one to include an extensive discussion of logical inference (chapter 3). Recommended for those who want more technical information than is included in this entry but who do not want to read an entire logic text.

Linda Mealey

Cross-References

Causal Relationships, 205; Conceptualization and Operationalization of Variables, 328; Experimentation in Sociological Research, 721; Hypotheses and Hypothesis Testing, 915; Interential Statistics, 983; Quantitative Research, 1546; Samples and Sampling Techniques, 1680; Triangulation, 2071; Validity and Reliability in Measurement, 2136.

THE LOOKING-GLASS SELF

Type of sociology: Socialization and social interaction
Field of study: Interactionist approach to social interaction

Self-identity can be significantly shaped by an individual's perceptions of the views that others have of him or her. To this extent, individuals conceive of themselves in terms of how they think they are "mirrored" in others' minds. In turn, people's personalities mirror the evaluations that they imagine are occurring in the minds of others. The "looking-glass self" is a metaphor for this phenomenon.

Principal terms
CONJUNCTIVE SENTIMENTS: feelings that create bonds and connectedness, as opposed to disjunctive sentiments
HUMAN NATURE: the features, characteristics, and tendencies of people, especially as they are considered as a whole species
INTERNALIZE: to make something (as a belief) a part of oneself and of one's mental makeup and nature
OBJECTIVITY: seeing things as they are; evaluating things accurately and fairly rather than subjectively
ROLE: a part played in society; a social function
SELF-CONCEPT: personal identity; the collection of ideas that one has about oneself and one's nature
SOCIAL INTERACTION: mutual involvements of people in society
SOCIALIZATION: the process of learning and internalizing appropriate attitudes, behaviors, and values so that one has an identity and can function in society and perform various social roles
SUBJECTIVITY: having to do with opinion; a mental or personal reality that is biased or otherwise lacking in objectivity
SYMBOLIC INTERACTIONISM: a school of thought in sociology that stresses the importance of interpersonal social experiences in shaping one's personal identity

Overview

In his book *Human Nature and the Social Order* (1902), the pioneering American sociologist Charles Horton Cooley introduced, somewhat incidentally, the term "looking-glass self." This metaphor has since become a standard concept in American sociology—with a larger meaning than Cooley himself first implied or envisioned, and with important implications in psychology, ethical studies, theories of child-rearing, and other fields. Cooley meant by this term that to some degree individuals develop their identities or self-concepts, and come to understand and define themselves, by considering the ideas and reactions that they think others have about them—especially others who seem significant in their lives. Thus, in the process of socialization, which is especially critical at the earlier stages of life but is always occurring, people mold their natures and personalities and assume their roles in response to their reactions to the other people in their social contexts. In that sense, according to Cooley, one's "self" may be said to "mirror" social aspects that are outside oneself; it reflects society itself in many individualized ways. The concept actually implies an interacting pair of mirrors. First one imagines oneself pictured (and judged) in the mind of another; then one mirrors in one's mind those judgments that one imagines, thus regulating one's behavior and partially defining oneself.

What is "reflected" in the mirror of one's own mind includes the value systems, self-definitions, and judgments of others in the surrounding society. In this view, one's self-development does not necessarily depend upon objective social realities; rather, it comes about because one perceives or conceives of others' responses in certain ways. Thus the feedback that one *thinks* one is getting from society may actually be more important than any objective reality outside oneself. As sociologist George J. McCall and J. L. Simmons summarized Cooley's theory in 1966, "our imaginations of self reflect our interpersonal concerns." Patricia R. Jette, writing in *The Encyclopedic Dictionary of Sociology* (1986), says that the "looking-glass self" theory distinguishes three separate components that contribute to the development of self: the responses of others to the individual; the individual's perception of what these responses are, were, or might be (which may differ from the actual responses); and the individual's patterned internalizing of these perceived responses so that they become parts of his or her self-concept and behavioral makeup. In this latter stage, the individual molds a self that reflects the social surroundings and people in it—as she or he has subjectively perceived them.

Noting the precise way in which Cooley first used his term can help one to apply it with its original subtleties. In *Human Nature and the Social Order*, the term occurs in the chapter entitled "The Meaning of 'I,'" one of two chapters about "the social self." Cooley makes clear, in proposing the term "looking-glass self," that it is not intended as an absolute definition of the nature of the self but is merely one "very large and interesting" category in which the self (or the "I") is defined by its social surroundings. According to Cooley's original language, one imagines oneself appearing in some other mind, and then "the kind of self-feeling one has is determined by the attitude . . . attributed to that other mind. A social self of this sort might be called the reflected or looking-glass self."

Cooley goes on to quote an anonymous verse couplet: "Each to each a looking-glass/ Reflects the other that doth pass." Thus Cooley's first use of the term suggests that, in any social interaction, each of two minds is a mirror: that of a self-conscious person, and that of another person who is a reacting "mirror." In real life, one can imagine some interchanges, especially among social peers, as working both ways, in a balanced fashion—with each person simultaneously being both a self-conscious actor and an evaluating judge. Young people in the earlier stages of socialization, however, or people lacking in social power, would be most likely to function in the self-conscious roles, while those who are older, more powerful, or more authoritative would be most likely to be the self-assured "judges" whose opinions matter enough for the other person to take them into account and allow them (perhaps unconsciously) to govern behavior.

Social psychologists such as Tamotsu Shibutani emphasize the importance of Cooley's ideas in the socialization process. In Shibutani's view, the "looking-glass self" means simply that "each person's orientation toward himself is a reflection of the manner in which he is treated." Cooley noted what Read Bain confirmed in the 1930's—that children know other people as objects, and call others by name, before they sense themselves as separate entities. Many experts agree that children see themselves as recipients of action before perceiving themselves as actors. Therefore, their evolving natures as active selves acquiring personalities will be likely to mirror the way they have been treated by others; they first gain self-identity from social interaction.

Cooley's metaphor, like any analogy, embeds both the merit of vividness and the danger of distortion. Though McCall and Simmons call Cooley's looking glass a "somewhat clouded" concept, the term is commonly used by sociologists to help explain certain aspects of the process by which all people achieve their identities, regulating and in effect fine-tuning and modulating them as they go. Most sociologists grant that Cooley's idea contains an important truth.

Applications

The generalized examples that Cooley used when he first mentioned the looking-glass self in 1902 are good beginning points for illustrating how the concept works in real life. Cooley suggests, first, that as we pass a real mirror and "see our face, figure, and dress" reflected, we are naturally interested, and we are either pleased or not, depending on whether what we see measures up to what we would like to see. Similarly, when we meet another person, we readily imagine ourselves as mirrored in that person's mind—"our appearance, manners, aims, deeds, character, friends, and so on." In the next step, we find ourselves imagining what that other person's judgment of our "reflected" selves may be. The third stage triggered by this sequence is a reflective feeling in ourselves "such as pride or mortification" when we conceive of this judgment.

Cooley himself admits that the metaphor of the looking glass is not adequate to explain the second of these three components—that is, the subjective evaluation of the onlooker. The nature and role of the onlooker is strategic in any such hypothetical situation, because one will be concerned about the onlooker's evaluation only if that person seems somehow significant. Assuming the onlooker's importance in one's life, Cooley says, one will be ashamed to seem reticent if one knows the onlooker is straightforward; one will not want to seem cowardly if one knows the onlooker is brave; and one will hesitate to appear gross if one knows the onlooker is refined. One may, in a certain social situation, boast to one onlooker about how one made a sharp business deal, but with some other person whom one perceives as having different social values one might try to hide the very same fact. In these senses, then, the outside mirror of the onlooker's mind actually determines the nature of one's social self, generating one's behavior and role in a given setting.

Though Cooley's examples do not imply that the whole of anyone's self is determined by the process of such interactions, one can see how—generally speaking, from earliest childhood onward—one is likely to shape oneself to fit what one anticipates to be the expected judgments of those with whom one is dealing. In individual situations throughout life, even after one's identity is rather fully formed, one tends to adopt the contextual roles that one thinks of as suitable when mirrored in the minds of others. Thus in one's grandmother's living room or at a church service, one may in effect be one person, while at a basketball game one may reveal an entirely different self; this is role-playing behavior. Proud parents may discuss their children freely with other parents, but, with some degree of consciousness, they may refrain from mentioning their children when talking to someone who is childless—or who has recently lost a child in a car accident. In these cases, the looking glass of social surroundings and audience shapes one's perceived identity.

Although Cooley illustrated only interchanges between two adults and did not specifically explore the implications that his concept has for childhood socialization, the looking-glass self helps to explain early identity development: A young child tends to become a combination of the features that are approved and desired in society. Society always puts pressure on individuals to conform to its values and judgments in order to receive approval; thus humans—who generally seek acceptance and want to be well thought of—shape their social actions according to the signals they get from the social mirror into which they are always looking. Since children tend to internalize what they encounter outside themselves and to act as if it were valid and true, it is clear that those who are treated as worthwhile entities have a better chance of becoming socially productive than those who are treated with abuse or disregard. The development of negative self-concepts as children discourages individuals from acting later as if they have positive contributions to make to society.

Context

Sociology, which studies patterns of human behavior in social contexts, became a recognizable discipline in the nineteenth century, although many predecessors—writers and theorists in various fields—anticipated its main concerns. As a general social science it is less specialized than, say, economics or law. In some of its focuses it parallels the interests of psychology; this is true of its interest in the nature of the self—personal identity, the self-concept, the nature of the "I" in society. Cooley was addressing this subject when he first mentioned the looking-glass self.

Cooley's idea, in fact, seems to be as much a psychological concept as a sociological term, since it comments on the workings of an individual mind. It has particular implications for studies of such psychological phenomena as repression (the exclusion from consciousness of socially unacceptable desires or impulses) and sublimation (the redirection of primitive urges, such as sex, toward goals that are "higher" or socially favored). These terms, however, seem more compatible with Freudian psychoanalytic theory than with Cooley's sociology. As Shibutani points out, Cooley tended to be mainly interested in "conjunctive sentiments," whereas Austrian doctor and psychiatrist Sigmund Freud often focused on "disjunctive sentiments" in the childhood years that had negative effects on personality. Still, both Freud and Cooley "in their theories of the formation of personal idiom . . . stressed the importance of adjusting to particular people" and especially to a "significant other."

Psychological behaviorists, who focus on the reality of external actions and who stress stimulus-response interactions, might adapt Cooley's concept, but Cooley was not a behaviorist, and he thought that behaviorism omitted much of the "mystical" nature of human beings. Cooley's original explanation of the looking-glass self notably includes the workings of a mind and implies some degree of consciousness, choice, and social control—aspects that behaviorists deemphasize or deny.

Theoretical sociology in the twentieth century has tended in three major directions: conflict theory, structural-functional theory, and symbolic interaction theory. Cooley's ideas, including the looking-glass self concept, fit best into the last of these categories. Conflict theory, influenced by Karl Marx, interprets social change in terms of underlying conflict (such as economic inequities); structural-functional theory emphasizes the balancing process by which major social institutions interact; and symbolic interaction theory stresses various patterns of social communication and their meanings and values. While Cooley is an important early figure in the interactionist movement, the major figure is George Herbert Mead, who incorporated various ideas put forward not only by Cooley but also by the progressive educational philosopher John Dewey and the pragmatic philosopher William James. Symbolic interactionism not only entered mainstream sociology but also has influenced areas of psychology, psychiatry, and cultural anthropology. Ideas about the self, role-playing, and the social grounding of self-evaluation are central to symbolic interactionism, which emphasizes that individual identity develops and has meaning only in the contexts of a social environment and human interconnectedness.

Throughout most of Western history, the idea of human nature was discussed separately from the idea of social order, and often human nature was viewed as a theological topic. The position of such sixteenth century Protestant thinkers as John Calvin, for example, was that human nature was basically evil and needed salvation to reform it before society could ever be improved. The eighteenth century Swiss-French theorist Jean-Jacques Rousseau, by contrast, tended to see human nature as innately good and suggested that humans are corrupted by their social contacts and institutions. Cooley's theories were generally important because they linked ideas about human nature and about society inextricably together. Cooley's famous phrase on this point is, "Self and society are twin-born." The discipline of sociology generally assumes this idea to be true.

Like other sociologists of his era, Cooley spoke of the human species collectively but seldom examined varieties of social organization other than his own. Thus critics note that his ideas have an American bias, presuming white, Anglo-Saxon, Protestant (WASP) values. Cooley believed in social progress, and he had faith that change was directional—evolutionary or progressive—rather than cyclical. He hoped that sociology, including his own research and study, could contribute to social progress, and he listed methods for social reform. Because Cooley took an idealistic, humanistic, and liberal stance, he opposed those who wanted sociology to be more scientific. Sociologist Roscoe Hinkle has called his position "sociological romanticism." In general, Cooley's statement that "the imaginations [that] people have of one another are the solid facts of society" not only summarizes the central idea of his looking-glass self theory but also epitomizes many of his other notions about social interaction.

Bibliography

Cooley, Charles Horton. *Human Nature and the Social Order*. New York: Charles Scribner's Sons, 1902. Reprint. New York: Schocken Books, 1964. This basic work by Cooley introduces the term "looking-glass self." Arguing that what is called "human nature" has no reality independent of the social order that an individual human identity mirrors, Cooley assumes an American, democratic context and supports a value system that in retrospect appears to be white, Anglo-Saxon, Protestant, and liberal. A preface (1930) by the social psychologist George Herbert Mead evaluates Cooley's "contributions to American social thought."

_____ . *Social Organization: A Study of the Larger Mind*. New York: Charles Scribner's Sons, 1909. Reprint. Schocken Books, 1967. Here Cooley shows himself the moralist, discussing the false conflict (as he sees it) between selfish individuals and the larger society. Cooley argues that each self exists only as a member of all and that, as he says, "We must improve as a whole." Philip Rieff's introduction provides a helpful context and background.

_____ . *Social Process*. Carbondale: Southern Illinois University Press, 1966. In this work, first published in 1918, Cooley develops his theories of social change, ideas which have been given less attention than his interactionist ideas about the development of personality. The helpful introduction by Roscoe C. Hinkle gives an overview of Cooley's ideas and evaluates Cooley's importance as a sociologist.

Healy, Mary Edward. *Society and Social Change in the Writings of St. Thomas, Ward, Sumner, and Cooley*. Westport, Conn.: Greenwood Press, 1972. A Catholic scholar discusses Cooley's ideas about the self and socialization in the context of the larger topic of social change and in relation to other theorists. Healy emphasizes Cooley's philosophical aspects and notes that he acknowledged himself to be more philosopher than scientist. Well indexed, with a useful bibliography. First published in 1948.

McCall, George J., and J. L. Simmons. *Identities and Interactions*. New York: Free Press, 1966. In incidental ways these sociologists incorporate Cooley's ideas into their own generalized views. They underplay the concept of the looking-glass self, however, by calling Cooley's mirror "somewhat clouded." Indexed.

Shibutani, Tamotsu. *Society and Personality: An Interactionist Approach to Social Psychology*. Englewood Cliffs, N.J.: Prentice-Hall, 1961. In this study of how personalities develop from interactions between people and their social contexts, Cooley's name and theories recur more frequently than any others except those of Sigmund Freud and George H. Mead. This well-indexed book integrates Cooley's ideas with those of many theorists.

Roy Neil Graves

Cross-References

Dramaturgy, 566; Exchange in Social Interaction, 715; Interactionism, 1009; Microsociology, 1192; Significant and Generalized Others, 1748; Statuses and Roles, 1978; Symbolic Interaction, 2036.

MAGNET SCHOOLS

Type of sociology: Major social institutions
Field of study: Education

Magnet schools are public educational institutions in United States cities—including elementary, middle, and high schools—that attract students by offering various kinds of enticing educational options. Many magnets have been instituted since the mid-1970's to promote voluntary racial integration in public education while meeting students' individual needs and interests.

Principal terms

AFFIRMATIVE ACTION: efforts by government or other institutions to correct past wrongs toward a racial or ethnic minority group

CREAMING: the "skimming off" of the most gifted students as they are attracted by magnet schools with high academic standards

CURRICULUM (*pl.* CURRICULA): a set of courses offered by an educational institution

DUMPING: parents' sending disgruntled or troublemaking students to an academic magnet school

INTEGRATION: the mixing of the races in a social institution

MANDATE: an authoritative order, such as one from a school board or court; a mandatory reassignment is an official directive that a student change schools

MULTICULTURALISM: the maintenance of the separate cultural patterns of minority groups, as opposed to submerging them into the dominant culture

SEGREGATED SCHOOL: an educational institution at which students are mainly or solely of one racial or ethnic background

TRACKING: putting students into certain curricula (such as technical, academic, or remedial) that control their later options in life

WHITE FLIGHT: the movement of white families from ethnic neighborhoods, and white students' abandonment of urban schools for private or suburban schools

Overview

The first International Conference on Magnet Schools—held March 9-12, 1977, in Dallas, Texas—brought together educators and political and legal experts to discuss the implications of the magnet school movement, a growing trend in American education since the mid-1970's. The movement's purposes were to give students and their parents choices about education and to promote racial integration in urban schools. Though the conference was termed "international," magnet schools are mainly a United States phenomenon, having arisen in response to the need to find voluntary ways to integrate urban schools. Rural school systems have often included the option of a centrally located "technical" high school, but systems of multiple magnet schools are neither necessary nor feasible in areas with scattered population. In small towns, racial integration has usually been accomplished by the much simpler means of consolidating two existing segregated systems into one.

The term "magnet school" is a metaphor based on the concept that a magnet is a mechanism that attracts. Mary Haywood Metz, an expert in the sociology of education, says in her book *Different by Design: The Context and Character of Three Magnet Schools* (1986) that such schools "accomplish racial desegregation on a voluntary basis; they attract volunteers by offering innovative education." Robert Thornbury, in *The Changing Urban School* (1978) defines "magnet school" in a way that emphasizes parental choice: "A city school in the U.S. where the curriculum or catchment [enticement or "bait"] is designed to attract parents and therefore pupils." The challenge of a magnet school is to offer an attractive alternative; if located in a minority or marginal neighborhood, its program must be doubly appealing to counteract white fears and prejudices. Such terms as "optional," "alternative," and "neutral site" schools have also been used to designate what are, in essence, magnets.

The practical and sociological implications of magnet schools are complex. First, the magnet approach goes against the long-cherished "neighborhood school" concept. Magnets to some extent uproot both teachers and students. Transportation of students to magnets can be complicated, usually being accomplished by having them meet at central points—often the local schools they formerly might have attended—for busing to the magnet site.

Metz points out that the two main goals of magnets—desegregation and educational innovation—are not closely related, and efforts to advance one may work against the other. Though partly bound by common interests, students at a magnet school have widely varying social, economic, and ethnic backgrounds, and these disparities may cause tensions. Other constituency problems may arise. Metz notes that both "creaming" and "dumping" are predictable outcomes of instituting magnet schools, especially "academic" magnets that offer superior preparation for college and "gifted and talented" magnets that by definition are selective rather than democratic. Creaming occurs partly because better-educated and affluent parents, ambitious for their children, push them into demanding programs; students from such backgrounds have enjoyed many initial advantages before arriving at the magnet school. Thornbury, taking an international perspective, notes the irony that Americans in the late 1970's responded to an "educational crisis" by reinventing the very kind of elitist school that the British were trying to abolish. E. C. Royster and others, however, in their *Study of the Emergency School Aid Act Magnet School Program* (1979), describe the obverse pattern of "dumping," whereby disruptive or poor students may be pushed by their parents, teachers, or counselors into the academic magnets. A mix of the "best" and "worst" students in a school makes it hard for that institution to keep a single focus. Metz concludes, however, that the patterns of creaming and dumping tend to balance each other out democratically.

One danger, especially with elementary and middle magnet schools, is that "tracking" occurs before students have the independent capabilities to choose their own life courses. Yet despite such concerns and various practical problems, magnets offer the attractive option of a public educational system based on choice, student interest, and institutions with a clear sense of their mission. Mario D. Fantini, an authority on alternative education, says that the magnet schools shift their interest from the traditional three R's (reading, 'riting, and 'rithmetic) to a focus on the "learner's quest for developing a talent" and notes that citizens whose talents are undergirded with suitable training have better chances for financial and emotional satisfaction. Fantini proposes that schools make better use of professional experts as teachers and role models and exploit centers of expertise such as the World Trade Center that already exist outside the framework of education.

Applications

The magnet system in Dallas, Texas, helps exemplify how such schools work. A precedent existed in one technical trade school that had been established in 1929, but the real beginnings came in 1970 when the Metropolitan Alternative School was established for students who were not functioning well in regular school contexts; by 1977 this program had grown to include five schools in different areas of Dallas. Some working students elected this alternative part-time. A third high school alternative, opened in 1971, was a large complex called Skyline Career Development Center, which attracted students from all over metropolitan Dallas. The twenty-eight career fields that students can pursue there range from architecture to advanced science; half of each school day focuses on such specialties, with the rest centering on basics. Some Skyline students go into the work force upon graduation; others go on to college.

In 1976, under a federal court mandate, four new magnet schools were established in Dallas, with curricula in arts, the health professions, transportation, and business and management. Two other magnets were opened during 1977-1978, offering high-school programs in human services and in law and public administration. Each of these six magnets was administered by an outstanding professional in the curricular field, with trained educators in the roles of assistant principals or directors. Some of the magnets were called "centers" and "institutes." The Dallas business community was actively involved, and the magnets offered experiences usually reserved for college— training in business and observation in hospitals, for example.

Dallas also established elementary and middle school magnets. Any student in grades four through six can seek admission to any of five "Vanguard" schools, which focus on fundamentals, Montessori training, expressive arts, individual guidance, and education for the academically gifted and talented. Five academies similarly attract qualified seventh and eighth graders for study in career exploration, in-depth studies of the "classical" academic disciplines, environmental science, and (in two separate magnets) gifted/talented education. A certain amount of continuity exists between some of the elementary and middle school options, while other junior high magnets allow students new starts and focuses.

Metz's sociological study of schools in a real midwestern city that she calls "Heartland" shows further how magnets operate. This city had somewhat fewer than 100,000 students; black enrollment in public schools was almost 50 percent. Responding to a desegregation court order in the mid-1970's, the city school board established a plan that included two sets of magnets, one set drawing from the whole city, the other from smaller "attendance areas" (with children of a different race being drawn from larger "zones" around those areas). This plan shows the complexity of magnet programs. Locating magnets in black neighborhoods and closing some mainly black schools were parts of the effort in Heartland to meet the court's expectation that 25 to 50 (later 25 to 60) percent of the city's black students would attend desegregated schools.

The citywide magnet schools in Metz's field study were three middle schools serving sixth through eighth graders; each had a distinctive, attractive program. One offered individually guided education, another "open education" of a sort devised by the faculty, and another an "enriched traditional curriculum" for selectively admitted gifted/talented students. In practical experience, the three schools developed very different natures; often their successes and failures were attributable less to their ideologies than to politics, personalities, and the institutional histories of the schools themselves. The "open" school, for example, in an old building on the edge of a black neighborhood, offered the most distinctive program; its history predated the "magnet" movement, and its philosophy was to encourage students to take responsibility for their own learning. This school saw itself as an underfunded underdog with unconventional methods.

One negative effect of the magnet program in Heartland was that 90 percent of the students bused to magnets were blacks, generating complaints from the African American community of a "black burden." (As Christine H. Rossell noted in 1990, minority groups have typically felt themselves to be carrying the main burden of school integration.) Another social outcome in Heartland was that the magnets enrolled more middle-class than working-class students and developed the reputation of being elite enclaves. Some contention over the allocation of resources to magnet and nonmagnet schools developed. Teachers' unions opposed staffing the magnets selectively, even though their curricula called for specialists; a program of placing teachers by seniority, with some special assignments, was eventually worked out. One general effect in Heartland was to increase parental involvement in schools; this was deemed sometimes supportive, sometimes intrusive.

A 1990 report by Rossell on school integration in Buffalo, New York, offers a third example of citywide magnets in operation. In 1976, the year Buffalo began a desegregation plan based on magnets and voluntary choice, the city had 57,000 students in its public schools. Overall, half of the students were white—a decline from about 64 percent from ten years earlier. A balanced fifty-fifty racial mix, however, did not occur at most schools, because "white flight" had left many city schools mostly black. In fact, the average black child in Buffalo in 1976 attended classes in which fewer than 30 percent of the students were white.

The Buffalo magnet program did not bring about full integration, but it did produce a better racial balance. By 1980, the white enrollment in a typical classroom had increased from almost 30 percent to about 40 percent. That year, however, the courts decided that progress was too slow and imposed mandatory reassignments of some students in order to speed integration.

Rossell compares the progress toward integration in Buffalo between 1976 and 1980 with an analogous situation in Dayton, Ohio, where a mandatory reassignment plan was instituted in 1976. Though school integration in Dayton jumped in 1976, by 1980 it had declined. Rossell's conclusion is that over several years, magnet schools worked at least as well in Buffalo as forced reassignment worked in Dayton to bring about integration. The advantage in Buffalo's magnet approach was that it preserved individual choice. In both Buffalo and Dayton, declines (of about 20 to 25 percent) in white enrollment during the period from 1967 to 1985 worked against statistical improvements in integration levels in the city school systems.

Context

Though "alternative" schools offering special programs have long existed in the United States, most of them historically were private, not public. After the United States Supreme Court ruled in 1954 that segregated schools were inherently unequal and thus unlawful, the process of dismantling segregated school systems began. In large cities, the racial and ethnic makeup of schools' student populations reflected segregated housing patterns. While "freedom of choice" sounded good, it generally resulted in only token desegregation in the 1960's. Few whites chose to attend mostly black schools, often located in poorer neighborhoods. Black and other minority students technically had the choice of attending formerly all-white schools, but the schools were inconveniently located and promised both a hostile environment and strong academic competition. Forced busing of students to achieve artificial racial balance, an approach to integration often mandated by the courts in the 1970's and 1980's after voluntary methods failed, was generally unpopular among students and parents of all races.

The "alternative" schools of the liberal 1960's, unofficial features of the counter-culture, offered new social models based on parental and student initiative. In this idealistic context sprang up the idea of "magnet" programs to attract student bodies with common interests but diverse economic and racial backgrounds, thereby creating student cohesion that transcended ethnic barriers. Little discussion of "alternative" schools occurred before the 1970's in the sociological and educational literature, but a 1973 Gallup Poll showed that 62 percent of parents and 80 percent of educators favored more educational options for students. By 1976, about one-fourth of the nation's school boards were offering "alternative" schools, and after that the trend grew. Rossell compares magnet schools to the "carrot," and forced busing to the "stick," as methods of getting the donkey of segregated schools to move in the right direction. The location of magnet schools has proved strategic to achieving racial balance; if the schools with attractive programs and superior resources are put into minority communities, effective integration may occur voluntarily.

Magnet schools became popular at a time when many American cities sensed their own decline. Middle-class whites were fleeing to the suburbs or putting their children in private academies to avoid overcrowded, underfunded, and sometimes dangerous city schools. One part of the early mission of magnets was to consolidate economically diverse student populations. A magnet school might even help rejuvenate a declining neighborhood by giving it new respectability. Many magnets were established in the context of pressure by courts to do something to foster desegregation, and most have been carefully monitored not only by educational boards but also through judicial review to see if they meet the tests of fairness and social utility.

Nolan Estes, superintendent of the Dallas Independent School District, offers the optimistic view that "the Magnet School is the wave of the future, both in terms of its academic excellence, and of the hope it offers youngsters of every race and background." Estes sees magnets as "a solid educational concept that will serve students well today and will also prepare them for the diverse choices that await them in the twenty-first century." By the early 1990's, many school districts were asking courts to reverse mandatory student-assignment plans put into place in the early 1970's, attempting to return to programs based on freedom of choice. The countermovement of ethnicity, however, began to work against magnet programs; some minority communities wanted local schools where their culture could be maintained and actively promoted. By 1990 many on both sides of the color line were disillusioned with the ideals of integration and cultural assimilation.

It seems likely that the magnet pattern is not a fad and will survive in American public education as one means of effecting social equity and excellence in teaching and learning. Rossell, who summarizes research findings showing that "magnet schools have a positive effect on student achievement," believes that voluntary plans, including magnet schools, should fully replace mandatory reassignment. Her conclusion is that, because "deliberation and the exercise of choice are the essence of what it means to be human, a policy that allows choice and also achieves a socially desirable goal is the morally superior alternative."

Bibliography

Borman, Kathryn M., and Joel H. Spring. *Schools in Central Cities: Structure and Process.* New York: Longman, 1984. Discusses curricula in magnet schools—including art, college preparatory, and career education—and examines programs in Philadelphia, Houston, and Cincinnati as tools for desegregation.

Estes, Nolan, and Donald R. Waldrip, eds. *Magnet Schools: Legal and Practical Implications.* Piscataway, N.J.: New Century Education, 1978. This report on the first annual International Conference on Magnet Schools (held in Dallas, Texas, in 1977) contains nine separate papers by eminent educators, government leaders (including Senator John Glenn), and jurists. An editorial introduction and epilogue as well as two bibliographies, frame discussions of the magnet school movement through the middle 1970's.

Metz, Mary Haywood. *Different by Design: The Context and Character of Three Magnet Schools.* New York: Routledge & Kegan Paul, 1986. This data-based study examines and evaluates social outcomes during the 1970's in three middle schools in a large Midwestern city. The schools offered individual guidance, open education, and a gifted/talented program. Race, class, and politics figured heavily in the magnets' successes and failures.

Rossell, Christine H. *The Carrot or the Stick for School Desegregation Policy: Magnet Schools or Forced Busing.* Philadelphia: Temple University Press, 1990. Explores successes and failures of magnet programs. Rossell concludes that, despite the administrative complexities created by voluntary choice, magnets have been socially successful and have shown whites to be capable of rising above prejudice. Also concludes that more magnets should be located in minority neighborhoods.

Thornbury, Robert. *The Changing Urban School.* London: Methuen, 1978. Discusses magnets as a social phenomenon unique to the United States. Provides examples of how such schools worked in the 1970's to encourage integration, but expresses concern about "creaming."

Roy Neil Graves

Cross-References

Alternatives to Traditional Schooling, 86; Compulsory and Mass Education, 309; Education: Conflict Theory Views, 579; Education: Functionalist Perspectives, 586; Education: Manifest and Latent Functions, 593; Educational Vouchers and Tax Credits, 614; The Sociology of Education, 1939; Tracking and Inequality in Education, 2057.

MALTHUSIAN THEORY OF POPULATION GROWTH

Type of sociology: Population studies or demography

English political economist Thomas R. Malthus theorized that the human population tends to increase much more rapidly than the food supply can increase to support it but that various "checks" help to slow the population increase. Malthus' theory has been both controversial and influential.

Principal terms
ABSTINENCE: not participating in something, such as sexual activity
CAPITALISM: an economic system based on private or corporate ownership of capital goods and on a free market system, with no central government control of production and distribution
DEMOGRAPHY: the study of population, including population size, makeup, and processes of change through time
DEVELOPING COUNTRY: a nation that is poor and not highly industrialized
EMPIRICISM: the practice of relying on experience, observation, and experiment to determine what is true
FERTILITY: the ability to bear or father children
HOMEOSTASIS: a relatively stable relationship or equilibrium between the components of a situation, as between population and food supply in a society
LAISSEZ-FAIRE: a "hands off" or "let it alone" policy in government
MIGRATION: movement from country to country or place to place
PRAGMATISM: a practical philosophy that judges the value of things by how well they work
SUBSISTENCE: the minimum requirement, as of food and shelter, necessary to support life

Overview

More than any other single writer and thinker, English political economist Thomas R. Malthus (1766-1834) influenced the way population patterns and population growth are viewed. In the late eighteenth century, Malthus came to believe that a generally held optimistic view of human progress was based on false assumptions. He published his famous work *An Essay on the Principle of Population* (1798) to voice his concerns and explain his own theory about the ultimately harmful effects of population growth. Five years later, he published an expanded edition of his essay, in which he added empirical data on population collected during European travels and expanded his thesis with recommendations on how to hold down population increase. The essay was instantly met with outrage, debate, and controversy, which has never entirely subsided.

Malthus argued that human population tends to increase in a geometric progression, while the resources necessary to sustain human population—especially food supplies—increase only in arithmetic progression. Though hypothetically this imbalance would generate an inadequate food supply to maintain life, Malthus argued that certain "checks" on population growth occur, either automatically or as a result of individual and social planning.

A geometric progression is a pattern such as 2, 4, 8, 16, 32, 64 . . . in which the ratio of any number to the one just before it remains the same; if such a progression is charted on a left-to-right line graph, the line will soon curve sharply upward. An arithmetic progression of numbers, by contrast, is a sequence such as 2, 4, 6, 8, 10 . . . in which the difference between any term and the one just before it remains constant; a left-to-right graph of such a progression shows a straight line tilting upward toward the right. The essential point is that a geometric progression increases much more rapidly than an arithmetic progression does.

Despite the theoretical differences in the rates of increase of population and of resources, Malthus believed that, in practice, some kind of homeostasis or equilibrium tends to develop between population and food supply—that is, population numbers tend to remain proportional to the means of subsistence rather than increasing rapidly and divergently from them. This happens, Malthus argued, because various controls on overpopulation growth will (or may) operate in real-life situations, including what he called "positive checks" (such as disease) and "preventive checks" (such as sexual abstinence and delayed marriages). Positive checks happen automatically, while preventive checks require overt initiatives. Malthus also thought that prosperity tends to encourage higher birthrates—leading an affluent society, in cyclical fashion, to produce more people than can be fed adequately.

Though the general tendency in Europe before 1800 had always been for countries to interpret population growth as a sign of progress and national strength, Malthus saw unregulated growth as adding to social problems and increasing poverty, pushing more people in a society downward toward a miserable subsistence level of survival. While the first edition of his essay stressed the occurrence of such "natural" controls on overpopulation as famine, pestilence, war, and starvation, the second edition argues that these are not inevitable if the institutions and customs of human society show adequate foresight and provide rational alternatives.

Though Malthus did not advocate contraception as an artificial method of birth control, he did see "moral restraint" as the least painful approach to solving the population dilemma that his theory asserted. Such restraint included sexual abstinence, delayed marriages, and decisions not to marry at all. Malthus also proposed some institutional changes in society, including repeal of the Poor Laws in England (which he thought encouraged people to stay poor), government efforts to raise wages and increase production of resources, and general education to help people behave with enlightened self-interest. In further revisions to the essay after 1803, Malthus proposed certain public works projects that would not compete with private industry as means of social improvement.

Applications

Numerous writers since Malthus have debated whether his theories accurately reflect the real relationship between population and life-supporting resources. During productive eras and in certain parts of the industrialized world it has seemed to many that observable facts disprove his theories, while in other times and situations Malthusian predictions have seemed grimly realistic. Among the problems in determining the truth of Malthus' theory—which is complex and contains many alternative scenarios—are that patterns of migration and immigration come into play; that resources in addition to food (such as fuel sources), which Malthus did not directly consider, also have major effects on life in developed societies; and that, in addition to the kinds of "checks" on population that Malthus discussed, artificial methods of birth control such as contraception and abortion have, in later eras than his own, played major roles in slowing population growth.

It is generally accepted that Malthus' theory was flawed; the most obvious weakness is that the world's food supply has increased more dramatically than he imagined. Malthus could not have foreseen the profound effects that technology, beginning with the Industrial Revolution, would have on agricultural production. New technology, ranging from equipment to new strains of plants to the widespread use of fertilizer and pesticides all helped to increase food production in the so-called green revolution. Yet regardless of the fact that his contrasting of geometric population increase with arithmetic food supply increase has been shown to be inaccurate, the underlying principle—that the increasing human population can have disastrous regional effects—has been shown, in the twentieth century, to be true. Moreover, it remains to be seen how severe the detrimental effects of high technology agriculture will be in the long run—for example, as the use of harsh chemical fertilizers exhausts soils.

To illustrate how the Malthusian theory applies, it is important to envision the relationship between population and food supply that Malthus described in his hypothetical model. Malthus' own example, as summarized by his biographer Donald Winch, develops the basic argument: Assuming a population in Britain in 1798 of seven million (the actual population, according to Winch, was around ten million), then the country's

population had the power to double every twenty-five years (from 7 to 14 to 28 to 56 million by 1883), but food production could only increase by a constant factor (from 7 to 14 to 21 to 28, half the amount that would be needed to support the population in 1883).

In such a situation, with inadequate food to go around, the basic struggle for mere survival would fall mainly on the poorest citizens, those—in Winch's words—"at the bottom of society's pyramid." On these people, in particular, the "positive" checks (such as disease and starvation) and perhaps the "preventive" checks (such as delayed marriage and sexual abstinence) would gradually begin to operate. More generally, preventive checks would work throughout all levels of society as resources became scarcer and citizens' perceptions of hard times made them less optimistic about bearing and rearing children. Meanwhile much suffering would have occurred.

Malthus' own examples of late marriages illustrate how he thought preventive checks might help to ward off the worst kinds of social disasters through voluntary individual action. English women in Malthus' day often married in their mid-teens, and their years of fertility might typically last thirty years—through their mid-forties. Malthus thought that females have a greater capacity for virtue and "moral restraint" than males, and thus he thought that they might take the lead in instigating late marriages. The average marriage age for a woman might then rise to twenty-eight or thirty, effectively cutting in half a typical married woman's child-bearing years and thereby reducing the sizes of typical families.

Though Malthus' gloomy predictions did not come true in 1883 England, population has been shown to be affected in devastating ways any time human numbers in a region outstrip its capacity to support human life. The "positive" checks that overpopulation sets in motion are in fact such destructive negative forces as famine and disease. In one example from the early 1990's, the television images of starving people in Somalia—infants and adults reduced to skin and bones, ill and barely able to move—seared the consciences of more affluent Western countries and eventually prompted the collective intervention of the United Nations, including the United States, in an effort to disrupt the "natural" Malthusian pattern and save the lives of hundreds of thousands. Other mass starvations in the twentieth century in various underdeveloped countries have reminded the world recurringly that what Malthus predicted can happen naturally if social controls and governmental planning are not in place or are unable to prevent the pattern.

The tendency of human populations to outrun their resources to the point of widespread misery seems demonstrably real. In *Homage to Malthus* (1975), Jane Soames Nickerson asserts that the bleak predictions of Malthus have proved to be social realities in the twentieth century; she noted a Rockefeller Foundation report stating that in the 1970's,

> of the 2.5 billion people living in the world's less developed countries, 1.5 billion are malnourished, and 500 million are starving. The magnitude of the problem baffles the imagination. It would seem that vast populations have come into being far exceeding their own resources.

Nickerson cites statistics from the United Nations Demographic Yearbook for 1972 showing a total increase in world population from 1950 to 1972—that is, during a single generation—of more than 50 percent. The highest rates of increase occurred in the poorest areas (Latin America, Africa, and Asia). Mexico's population in the mid-1970's was increasing at a rate of 3.5 percent annually and was, according to Nickerson, "a good illustration of what Malthus foresaw, since nearly half the population of Mexico is illiterate and very poor."

Context

In his writings Malthus follows the calm logic of a reasonable late eighteenth century man concerned with two highly complex topics: political economics and morality. His thinking interweaves ideas in complex ways, incorporating deductive logic with considerations of the limited empirical data available in his day. Though the discipline of sociology was not clearly defined in the 1790's, Malthus in retrospect seems a thinker with significant implications for later sociologists who have sought to understand the economic and demographic patterns that shape society, control quality of life, produce poverty, and influence social change.

Malthus, who thought of his concerns as "moral and political," was a sincere Christian minister with a noble purpose—to improve society. He disagreed with the views of the political philosopher William Godwin—in particular with Godwin's optimistic argument in *Enquiry Concerning Political Justice* (1793) that humans are basically rational beings who might live harmoniously, in utopian fashion, without institutions or laws. Malthus' first essay was partly an attempt to argue for a more practical view of human nature. As has often been noted, Malthus was not entirely original and was especially indebted to the precepts of the Scottish economist Adam Smith, a pragmatist with real ethical concerns who has had wide influence in the field of economics.

In the early decades of the nineteenth century, Malthus' chief rival in the arena of economic theory was David Ricardo, a rigid British utilitarian economist who thought, among other things, that trying to raise wages would only increase population so that wages would always tend to stay at subsistence levels, whatever society tried to do to erase poverty. The laissez-faire theories of Ricardo tended to dominate nineteenth century discussion. John Maynard Keynes, a leading Western economist of the twentieth century, agreed with Malthus that, through planned, collective action, societies can substitute rational options for naturally "inevitable" social and economic forces.

Since the bearer of gloomy tidings is seldom welcome, it is not surprising that during the nineteenth century, "Malthusian" became a mostly negative word: Many did not want to accept Malthus' theory because it seemed to describe a problem with no good solutions and because it questioned the common notion that a nation's prosperity depended on an ever-growing population. Too, throughout the nineteenth century, when the British Empire was prospering as a dominant force in world trade and when colonial lands and resources seemed unlimited, the dismal patterns that Malthus described did not seem to many English people to be apparent in their own society. Somewhat later, twentieth century Marxist economics rejected Malthusian theory, blaming the capitalistic system rather than demographic forces for such widespread social problems as poverty, disease, hunger, and class conflict.

In the years following World War II, awareness of the world's population increase gradually began to receive attention once again. The late 1960's and early 1970's, in particular, saw a reawakening of concern about the future. It was realized that the earth's resources are finite and were being consumed at a rapid rate. As ecology began to be an area of widespread study, population theory was debated within the context of the earth's carrying capacity—that is, the size of the human population that the earth can support. Typifying the concerns, even fears, voiced at the time was Paul Ehrlich's widely influential book *The Population Bomb* (1968). An international movement advocating zero population growth (ZPG) was influential in framing late twentieth century social policies, particularly in industrialized nations. Though many reformers and social planners have used Malthus' predictions to support more aggressive programs of birth control, including contraception, than Malthus himself proposed, the Catholic church, with its worldwide influence, continued to oppose using artificial methods of controlling population, urging "moral restraint," as Malthus did, to curb overpopulation and its attendant problems.

Bibliography

Malthus, Thomas Robert. *An Essay on the Principle of Population: Or, A View of Its Past and Present Effects on Human Happiness*. Reprint. New York: Augustus M. Kelly, 1971. One of many available versions of the enlarged, second essay (the 1803 edition, somewhat changed in successive editions). Adds evidence to support the original argument of the first essay and shifts it focus from arguing against human perfectibility to supporting the larger Malthusian theory. Includes Malthus' various prefaces.

_____. *First Essay on Population, 1798*. London: Macmillan, 1926. Reprint. New York: St. Martin's Press, 1966. The historical starting point for understanding Malthus' theory. A preface by Austin Robinson and notes by James Bonar set the work in its first context. Malthus' rationality and plain style make the work surprisingly understandable. The first essay is widely available in various formats.

Nickerson, Jane Soames. *Homage to Malthus*. Port Washington, N.Y.: Kennikat Press, 1975. A study of the relevance of Malthus to modern world problems. The author is in sympathy with Malthusian principles and represents him—against such criticisms as those of Marxists and "Tory Romantics"—as a benevolent clergyman with useful insights, a kind of prophet speaking to the late-twentieth century world. A scholarly but personable book.

Petersen, William. *Malthus*. Cambridge, Mass.: Harvard University Press, 1979. This work by an academician focuses on Malthus' theories and ideas; includes a useful chapter called "The Malthusian Heritage." Extensive notes, a bibliography, and full indexing.

Place, Francis. *Illustrations and Proofs of the Principle of Population*. Reprint. New York: Augustus M. Kelly, 1967. Place founded the modern birth control movement. This book, first published in 1822, tries to show that "moral restraint," which Malthus had urged to control overpopulation, is inadequate to accomplish this end. The editor's introduction (1967) is useful for its historical perspective on Malthus and his contemporaries and the ideas over which they argued.

Smith, Kenneth. *The Malthusian Controversy*. London: Routledge & Kegan Paul, 1951. Well-organized, well-indexed, and rich with facts and scholarly analysis. Traces the historical origins of Malthus' theory and the controversy that surrounded it. Includes critical analysis and evaluation of the theory's applicability to such

topics as perfectibility, wages, emigration policies, and birth control.
Winch, Donald. *Malthus*. Oxford: Oxford University Press, 1987. This short, readable work introduces Malthus' career and discusses his ideas and influence. A good starting place for nonexperts. Indexed, with suggestions for further reading.

Roy Neil Graves

Cross-References
Demographic Transition Theory of Population Growth, 499; Fertility, Mortality, and the Crude Birthrate, 761; Life Expectancy, 1087; Population Growth and Population Control, 1421; Population Size and Human Ecology, 1428; Zero Population Growth, 2215.

TYPES OF MARRIAGE

Type of sociology: Major social institutions
Field of study: The family

Marriage in its various forms is an important sociological topic because what a society thinks about marriage influences what it thinks about sex roles, gender, the family, and happiness. To understand a culture, it is important to understand its preferences regarding marriage.

Principal terms
ENDOGAMY: the practice of marrying within a particular group to which one belongs
EXOGAMY: the practice of marrying outside a particular group to which one belongs
GROUP MARRIAGE: a marital relationship in which two or more individuals share two or more spouses
MARRIAGE: a union between two or more individuals that is usually meant to be permanent, is recognized legally or socially, and is aimed at founding a family
MONOGAMY: a marital relationship in which an individual has only one spouse at a time
POLYANDRY: a marital relationship in which an individual has more than one husband at a time
POLYGAMY: a marital relationship in which an individual has more than one spouse at a time; sometimes used to mean "polygyny"
POLYGYNY: a marital relationship in which an individual has more than one wife at a time

Overview

Marriage is an extremely widespread institution that occurs in virtually every known culture. Marriage, unlike cohabitation, usually involves a commitment to a permanent union. This commitment is recognized by law or custom. Marriage generally occurs between individuals of opposite sexes, but some cultures recognize same-sex marriage. For example, Cheyenne Indians could take a same-sex partner as a "second wife."

By marrying, one assumes certain rights and duties, which vary from culture to culture. In the Nayar culture of India, the husbands of a marriage do not have any obligations toward the children of the marriage; the wife's family provides for the children. In Western culture, however, the husband is expected to provide for the offspring of his marriage. Different kinship systems may result in different sets of marital rights and duties, but one marital right that is almost universally recognized is the right to have sexual relations with one's spouse or spouses.

Marriage is a means to legitimize both sexual relations and the children who result from them. Sociologist William Graham Sumner noted in *Folkways* (1960) that marriage, as an ongoing relationship, is important as a means of taking care of children and educating them.

Some cultures regard marriage as necessary to fulfill a duty to family or tribe. Many African societies believe that dead ancestors are reincarnated in new children. Having children is thus regarded as necessary for letting the ancestors live and even for one's own rebirth.

In a variety of cultures, some people marry for economic or political reasons. Small clans, for example, may need to "trade brides" in order to increase the labor pool available during seasonal harvests, and marriages to form political alliances between European countries are well documented. At the same time, in many cultures people marry because they love other people and want to spend their lives with them in a socially recognized and respected manner.

According to ethnographer George Murdock's *Atlas of World Cultures* (1981), the preferred form of marriage differs widely from culture to culture. Monogamy, in which an individual is married to only one other individual at a time, is the preferred form in Europe and in the areas of the world settled by Europeans. In these areas, other forms of marriage have been regarded as less civilized, but monogamous marriages in which the partners set up a separate household from their relatives are the preferred form of marriage in only about 12 percent of the 563 cultures studied by Murdock. Polygamy, in which an individual has more than one spouse at the same time, is a popular marital arrangement in Africa, East Asia, and the Pacific Ocean region. Polygamous marriages in which partners reside apart from their other relatives are preferred in about 36 percent of the cultures studied by Murdock. Murdock classifies as extended families 44 percent of the cultures studied. Since extended families are groups of related families that are living together, this category leaves it unclear whether the members of these families are practicing monogamy, polygamy, or both.

Polygamy has two forms: polygyny and polyandry. In polygyny, an individual has two or more female spouses at the same time. In cultures where the women are laborers, it may be economically beneficial for a man to have more than one wife. In other cultures, having many wives may be a status symbol, a means of showing off one's wealth. In polyandry, an individual has two or more male spouses at the same time. Polyandry is rare, appearing in no more than 1 percent of the cultures studied by Murdock. Poverty is one motivation for polyandry. If there is a tax on houses in which married women reside, poverty-stricken brothers may share a wife.

Different cultures have different practices concerning the selection of mates. In India, many marriages are arranged by parents, and the parents are likely to consult an astrologer about whether a prospective match will be auspicious. In contrast, in the United States, individuals generally select their own mates. Selection is not based on astrology, but on love, physical attraction, and compatibility, among other things.

Both the Indian system of marriage and the American system of marriage have traditionally been endogamous. Endogamy is the practice of marrying within one's own group. Traditionally, in India's caste system, one is born into a caste and is expected to marry within that caste. To marry someone from a lower caste is regarded as polluting the higher caste member and may cause that person to be ostracized. Beyond the middle of the twentieth century in the southern United States, there were laws against marriage between partners of different races.

Generally, the custom of marriage within one's own group does not allow marriage within one's own immediate family. The incest taboo against marriage between parents and their children and marriage between siblings is fairly universal. The Ptolemaic dynasty in Egypt provides an exception. Regarding themselves as gods, the Ptolemies could not marry non-gods, so they married each other. Cleopatra was the product of twelve generations of marriages between siblings.

The incest taboo is one basis for the practice of marrying outside a particular group to which one belongs. The particular kinship system in place in a culture determines who is covered by the incest taboo. Some traditional Africans regard cousin marriage as incestuous, but Arabic Muslims do not.

Applications

The only legal form of marriage in the United States is monogamy. In the nineteenth century, Mormons practiced polygyny and defended their practice as a matter of religious freedom. In *Solemn Covenant: The Mormon Polygamous Passage* (1992), historian C. Carmon Hardy documents the national outcry that arose against the Mormons. Polygamy was castigated as a barbarous threat to Western civilization. Americans who believed in the superiority of Western culture regarded polygamy as a throwback to the instability and disorder of non-Western cultures. Mormon polygyny would not be tolerated, and in 1890 the United States Supreme Court upheld the decision to outlaw polygamy in the United States.

Traditionally, American marriages have been patriarchal. In the twentieth century, however, American marriages have become more egalitarian. More American women are playing an active role in family decision making. In addition, traditional gender roles for women have shifted from homemaking to both homemaking and working outside the home. Between 1977 and 1988, the number of American children with working mothers increased from 48 percent to 60 percent. Many working mothers experience conflict between their work roles and their family roles, and as a result have no children or fewer children.

American divorce rates are among the highest in the Western world. The expectation is that at least half of all first marriages will end in divorce. Major reasons for divorce include alcohol or drug abuse, conflicts over gender roles, value differences, sexual incompatibility, and marital infidelity. Most divorced people remarry; second marriages, like first marriages, end in divorce more than 50 percent of the time.

In the latter third of the twentieth century, the old idea of monogamy as having one mate for life is no longer the norm in the United States. Many Americans seem to be practicing serial monogamy, in which one has one mate at a time but one mate after another. Some people regard this system of marriage as a modified form of polygamy, since it involves having more than one spouse during a lifetime.

Unlike American culture, many other cultures approve of having more than one mate at a time. In *Facing Mount Kenya* (1965), anthropologist Jomo Kenyatta described the practice of polygyny among the Gikuyu. According to Gikuyu custom, the larger the family, the better it is for the man and the tribe. With more wives, a man can have more children. A man is expected to provide male children to help with the defense of the tribe and female children to have and to rear further children. Upon marrying, one's primary duty is to reproduce. A key Gikuyu belief is the larger the family, the happier the family.

There is no limit on the number of wives a Gikuyu may have. In the early twentieth century, Gikuyu men averaged two wives, but some men, because of poverty, had only one wife. A wealthy man might have as many as fifty wives.

Each wife has her own hut in the husband's compound, and each wife is assigned a plot of land to cultivate. The husband provides labor for all and allocates collectively owned resources. The wives take turns cleaning the husband's hut, cooking for him, and doing other chores around the compound.

According to Kenyatta, the wives do not resent sharing a husband with one or more other women. In fact, once the first wife becomes pregnant, she may actually encourage her husband to marry again so that there will be someone to do the chores after she has given birth.

In preparation for a polygynous way of living, the Gikuyu learn from an early age to share. Males are taught early that they should be able to love many women, and females are taught to share, too. To avoid jealousy among wives, a husband sets up a schedule of love-making visits to their huts.

In the evenings, when the husband has male visitors from his age group, the wives are expected to visit with them in the husband's hut as a sign of group solidarity. If a visitor has traveled far and will spend the night, a wife may openly invite him to stay in her hut. Because sharing is emphasized, the husband is not supposed to object. The unity of the age group is partly the result of a mutual concern for collective enjoyment.

At the same time, a woman caught receiving a male visitor secretly in her hut is subject to harsh penalties. This kind of adultery is rare, however, since there are socially acceptable means of accomplishing the same end. Repeated adultery, barrenness, and impotence are grounds for divorce among the Gikuyu.

Another kind of multiple-mate marriage is polyandry, in which a woman has more than one husband at a time. According to anthropologist Peter, prince of Greece and Denmark, polyandry may be rare worldwide, but it was the predominant form of marriage in Tibet prior to the Chinese Communist occupation in 1950.

Fraternal polyandry, in which brothers marry one wife and live together, was the preferred form of polyandry. Tibet's harsh natural environment made survival difficult, and polyandry was one way to keep the population down. Another reason for polyandry was the desire to avoid dividing family property. A Tibetan custom was that when children married, they would take over the parents' property. If the children took different wives, the parents' property would have to be divided—something that could have made survival more difficult.

The Tibetan family was patriarchal. It was expected that the wife would be subject to her husbands. The head of the family was not the eldest man, but the most influential man or the first-wed man in case the men did not all marry the woman at the same time. The men made some agreement about when they could have intercourse with their wife. The wife appeared to have little, if any, say in the matter.

Jealousy was not something that men in such marriages could afford. Preserving family unity was more important because it seemed necessary for survival in Tibet's difficult natural environment. The emphasis on family unity helped the men suppress jealousy and also made divorce rare.

Context

As early as the eighteenth century European Enlightenment, French philosophers dreamed of discovering laws of society that were similar to the laws of physics. Aware that different societies had different forms of marriage, Charles-Louis Secondat, baron de La Brède et de Montesquieu, was still confident that there were social laws that could explain the differences. He, along with Jacques Turgot, postulated evolutionary stages through which societies travel. While European society was regarded as the most evolved, there was great interest in finding out more about the other stages on the evolutionary ladder. This led nineteenth century researchers to theorize about the nature of the first social arrangements. Were they loosely organized groups of individuals or families? What was their political structure? What form of marriage came first on the evolutionary ladder?

In the late nineteenth century, in *The Origin of the Family, Private Property, and the State* (1985), Friedrich Engels claimed that group marriage came first and gradually developed into monogamous marriage. Engel's evidence for his claim was primarily linguistic; he noted that among the Iroquois Indians, one's father's brother was also called "father." He believed that the only way to explain this linguistic usage was to regard it as reflecting an earlier form of marriage—group marriage. Many scholars have criticized this reliance on language, however, noting that the language used by the Iroquois might just have been a polite form of address rather than a residual trace of group marriages.

If group marriage did come first, however, what eventually led to monogamy? In group marriages, paternity could be difficult to determine, so descent would have been traced through the women. In these circumstances, women also would tend to have more political power. All this would have changed when men, as owners of cattle, became more wealthy and more powerful than women. Men would have wanted to leave their property to children who were indisputably their own. Thus, according to Engels, the accumulation of property and the concern over its inheritance led to monogamy. Many scholars have pointed out, however, that monogamy might have arisen from changes in sexuality or ideology instead of changes in economics.

However monogamy came to be, Engels claimed that it was designed to establish the man's supremacy in the family. The woman became the man's subject—his servant and sexual property. While her sexual freedom was abolished, the man's was only lessened. In effect, there was monogamy *only for women*. The resulting tension between husband and wife was similar to that found between classes in society, and liberation was called for in both situations. Engels questioned whether monogamy was the best form of marriage, especially for women. His work has influenced many feminists, but he painted monogamy at its worst; it is possible for monogamous unions to be based on fairness, love, and mutual respect. Critics of monogamy may insist that it does not lead to personal fulfillment for either women or men. While this may be true for some, 90 percent of Americans believe that a monogamous marriage is an important part of a good life. Predictions of the demise of monogamy seem premature.

Twentieth century social scientists have continued their interest in cross-cultural studies of marriage, but they have been less concerned with how marriage began and evolved than with how marriage is related to socioeconomic conditions, ethnicity, individual personality, place of residence, the status of women, gender-role expectations, and ideas of gender and family.

Bibliography

Engels, Friedrich. *The Origin of the Family, Private Property, and the State*. New York: Viking Penguin, 1985. Originally published in 1884, this work is a good example of Marxist attempts to explain social changes in terms of economic changes.

Hardy, B. Carmon. *Solemn Covenant: The Mormon Polygamous Passage*. Urbana: University of Illinois Press, 1992. Chapter 2 of Hardy's work is entitled "Civilization Threatened: Mormon Polygamy Under Siege." It gives an interesting blow-by-blow account of the national campaign against Mormon polygamy.

Kenyatta, Jomo. *Facing Mount Kenya*. New York: Vintage Books, 1965. Himself a Gikuyu, Kenyatta gives an insider's view of most aspects of Gikuyu culture. He shows how easy it can be for an outsider to misinterpret a culture.

Murdock, George Peter. *Atlas of World Culture*. Pittsburgh: University of Pittsburgh Press, 1981. This work compares 563 cultures in terms of twenty-seven categories, including family organization. A concluding chapter summarizes findings in tables. This source is extremely valuable for anyone interested in cross-cultural comparisons.

Peter, prince of Greece and Denmark. "The Tibetan Family System." In *Comparative Family Systems*, edited by M. F. Nimkoff. Boston: Houghton Mifflin, 1965. Prince Peter's article on Tibetan polyandry is thorough and interesting. His dissertation, *A Study of Polyandry* (Mouton, 1963), is an extended, detailed study of various systems of polyandry.

Strong, Bryan, and Christine DeVault. *The Marriage and Family Experience*. 5th ed. St. Paul, Minn.: West, 1992. This popular introductory text takes an interdisciplinary approach to the study of marriage. Its 600 pages include chapters on sexuality, gender roles, parenting, and the meaning of marriage.

Sumner, William Graham. *Folkways*. New York: New American Library, 1960. Originally published in 1906, Sumner's important cross-cultural study includes separate chapters on sex mores, the marriage institution, and incest.

Vander Zanden, James W. *The Social Experience*. 2d ed. New York: McGraw-Hill, 1990. Vander Zanden's 662-page introductory sociology text covers the basic topics of sociology in clear, lively, and focused prose.

Westermarck, Edward. *A Short History of Marriage*. New York: Humanities Press, 1968. Although Westermarck sometimes seems to have an ethnic bias, his book is an important resource, containing separate chapters on endogamy, exogamy, monogamy and polygamy, and polyandry and group marriage.

Gregory P. Rich
Lanzhen Q. Rich

Cross-References

Arranged Marriages, 134; The Family: Functionalist versus Conflict Theory Views, 739; The Family: Nontraditional Families, 746; Inheritance Systems, 989; Nuclear and Extended Families, 1303; Patriarchy versus Matriarchy, 1349; Residence Patterns, 1635; Romantic Love, 1661.

MARXISM

Type of sociology: Social change
Field of study: Theories of social change

Marxism is a system of inquiry that focuses on the different types of societies associated with different modes of production. Marxist analysis examines the structural inequality that limits every historical society, particularly capitalist society; it explores the prospects for attaining a form of society that would restore creativity and freedom to all human beings.

Principal terms
ALIENATION: the loss of human beings' creative powers when these are controlled and exploited by others
CAPITALISM: a mode of production and associated form of society based on the market and private ownership of the means of production
CLASS: a group formed by unequal social relations of production and distinguished by differences in property ownership and control of the labor process
HEGEMONY: the process by which an economically dominant class establishes political and cultural control of a society
HISTORICAL MATERIALISM: a precise term for "Marxism," a system of thought that emphasizes change in modes of production and the societies associated with them
LABOR: the essential human capacity for creative, purposive, and cooperative action to satisfy needs and form societies
MODE OF PRODUCTION: the patterning of the activities and relationships of human beings as they engage in labor to satisfy their needs and wants
REVOLUTION: a transformation of political, economic, and social structures in which a dominant class loses power

Overview

Marxism is a system of thought and inquiry based on the work of Karl Marx (1818-1883), a social theorist and revolutionary, and his coauthor, Friedrich Engels (1820-1895). Marx's central premise is that human nature is characterized by the capacity for creative and purposive action—"labor"—that has effects in the establishment of institutions and the accumulation of material culture. When agriculture enabled human beings to produce a surplus of food, conflicts arose in society over these products and over control of the labor process, initiating a process of social differentiation and growing inequality.

Human societies thus moved from a stage of equality ("primitive communism") to a succession of historical societies characterized by structures of inequality and exploitation. In the Mediterranean region and Europe, this sequence includes the slavery-based societies of the ancient world, feudalism, and capitalism. Each social formation (or type of society) is structured by its specific relations of production as well as by its specific form of the "forces of production": the way human beings organize activities, knowledge, and material objects to confront the problems of survival. These two elements—the forces and relations of production—are together called the "mode of production." In turn, the mode of production gives shape to the political and cultural institutions of each type of society. This conception has led to the erroneous view that Marx was an "economic determinist"; Marx, however, emphasized that the mode of production in all social formations is not a self-regulating mechanism external to society but a set of relationships between human beings, a social institution.

Marx focused his analysis on capitalism, the mode of production and type of society that rose to global dominance by the middle of the nineteenth century. Capitalism is a mode of production in which the means of production are owned privately and economic decisions are made by private firms in response to the market mechanism; the capitalist's motivation for production is realizing a profit from exchange value, and not the criterion of use value. To Marx the structure of capitalism was based on the relationship between capitalists (owners of the means of production and buyers of labor power) and wage laborers (who do not own the means of production and are therefore constrained to sell their labor power in order to make a living). In precapitalist modes of production, the subordinate classes were coerced into producing a surplus for the dominant classes, but in capitalism this unequal and exploitive relationship is masked by the fact that workers freely consent to sell their labor power to capitalists at prevailing wage rates. Workers produce goods whose exchange value is greater than workers' wages, so when the goods are sold at their exchange value, capitalists realize "surplus value." Surplus value is the form in which capitalists appropriate a surplus from workers without resorting to the coercion typical of slavery and serfdom.

On the one hand, capitalism is a system of inequality and exploitation; on the other hand, it contains a promise of freedom from scarcity and exploitation because of the enormous potential of the forces of production it generates. Under the pressure of relentless competition among capitalists, technological innovation soars and thus makes conceivable a future without scarcity and exploitation. In this future, each individual would be able to recognize his or her unique talents and potentials. All would cooperate in sustaining life, a task made easy by the intelligent use of machinery, and the division of labor would disappear, eliminating the narrow specialization that reduces labor under capitalism to a monotonous routine. Marx's vision of the future is one of freedom. As he wrote in *Manifest du Kommunistischen Partei* (1848; *The Communist Manifesto*, 1850), the future could consist of "an association, in which the free development of each is the condition for the free development of all." This future cannot be realized within the framework of capitalist institutions of private ownership, production for profit, and wage labor. For example, automation in the capitalist economy eliminates jobs and thus has a disastrous effect.

Capitalism, according to Marxist views, continues to consign most people to alienated conditions of labor and condemns a majority of the globe's population to poverty, despite its enormous technological dynamism. The potential locked within capitalism can only be realized when the system is replaced by socialism and ultimately by communism—that is, when institutions of ownership and political power are brought into line with the possibilities inherent in the forces of production. To Marx, in sharp contrast to utopian socialists, this transformation cannot come about by an act of will and imagination; it can only begin to take place in the most developed capitalist countries and only through the action of the working class organized as conscious agent of such a transformation. Marx commented that human beings make history, but not in circumstances of their own choosing. In other words, the future is formed in the dialectic of acting Subject (the working class as agent) and determined Structure (the most advanced forms of capitalism).

Marx's writing spanned four decades and produced fifty volumes of published works; as he matured as a theorist, he moved from philosophical concepts to analysis of economic structures. He responded to historical changes and events of the nineteenth century—the revolutions of 1848, European colonial expansion, the U.S. Civil War, the Paris Commune, and the spread of industrialization. Friedrich Engels published theoretical writings that have also become part of the essential outline of Marxism. Thus, they left a huge and complex legacy of social theory that has been divided, added to, and debated by generations of theorists and revolutionaries.

Applications

Applications of Marxist theory to revolutionary practice are distinct from applications of Marxist inquiry to questions in the social sciences; only the latter will be reviewed here. Since the end of the nineteenth century, many sociologists who are not Marxists have tried to answer the questions Marxists raise. Since the 1960's, the influence of Marxism on sociology has expanded; Marxist views of capitalism and class structure have influenced many subfields of sociology, especially "macrosociology"—the study of whole societies and global processes.

One subfield that has been deeply influenced by Marxism is the study of class structure and stratification. Beginning with German sociologist Max Weber, many non-Marxist sociologists have engaged in "a debate with Marx's ghost," offering a looser definition of class and paying more attention to status and political power as independent dimensions of inequality. Marxist sociologists continue to emphasize ownership of enterprises, purchase of labor power, and control of production processes as hallmarks of class dominance. They have carried out studies of capitalist class structure with attention to new strata and contradictory class positions. Closely related inquiries examine the way in which class inequality is reproduced from generation to generation; Marxist theory has become a major explanatory perspective in the sociology of education, through studies of schools and the interaction of school culture with working class cultures of students.

A second major area of application is the study of work under capitalism. A number of scholars, both Marxist and non-Marxist, have observed workplaces, labor markets, and the effects of technology on work. Much of this research has been guided by the notion of "alienation" as a characteristic of work under capitalism, in which neither the labor process nor the product is controlled by workers.

A third application of Marxist theory appears in studies of the relationship between the state and society. In most capitalist societies, the state is not the "night watchman" posited by laissez-faire ideology but takes an active part in economic regulation, social services, and infrastructure development. Both Marxist and non-Marxist scholars explore conditions under which the state expanded its functions to intervene in the capitalist economy. Another area of political sociology informed by Marxism is analysis of the form of states in terms of class structure. Marxist theory has also influenced the study of revolutions and types of societies that emerge after revolutions. Barrington Moore and Theda Skocpol are two social theorists whose work has been influenced by Marxist inquiries into the relationship of state and society. A fourth area of sociology in which Marxist theory is influential is in the analysis of global inequalities. Dependence theory and world systems theory look at the global capitalist economy as an integrated and uneven whole and analyze processes within it, especially international flows of capital and labor, the social impact of economic cycles, and unequal relationships between developed core countries and the weaker periphery.

Marxism has an impact on culture theory, the analysis of cultural representations. In this field, which spans sociology and the humanities, Marxism is in a dialogue with feminist, psychoanalytic, and linguistic theories. One of the most influential concepts is Marx's "commodity fetishism." A fetish is an idol made by human beings who then worship their own creation as a divine force. Marx uses the term "fetishism" to refer to an analogous process of mystification in capitalist society: The capitalist economy is formed by relationships between human beings, who then misconstrue and misrepresent their own creation as an omnipotent, compelling, external, alien "thing" that has power over them. Ongoing social relations between living people are misexperienced as relationships between dead objects, between prices of commodities following supposedly immutable "laws of supply and demand." The concept of fetishism guides culture theorists who document how social relations are represented as fixed and natural things rather than as products of interaction and discourse.

Context

Marxism as a theory in the social sciences has changed in response to global economic, political, and social change. It began as an effort to understand capitalism, and its concepts are continually developing to account for changes in capitalism itself. After Marx's death, Marxists in Europe and North America formed a network of socialist parties called the Second International. Its theorists tended to emphasize the structural side of the transition to socialism, the increasing instability of the capitalist economy. Vladimir Ilich Lenin, Russian revolutionary, offered an alternative model: In his theory of imperialism, he pointed to the global nature of capitalism and posited that socialist revolution could begin in the periphery rather than in the developed center of the capitalist system. He emphasized the shift from industrial to finance capitalism and proposed a new role for the party, as a vanguard organization that must take initiative in capturing and transforming the state. With the Bolshevik Revolution in Russia (1917), Western socialist parties split into socialist and communist parties, with the latter committed to the Leninist model. The revolution touched off a major split in Marxist theory. In the Soviet Union, Marxist thought had to legitimate state practice and leaned heavily toward emphasizing the role of the party and the subjective or "voluntarist" side of historical transformations. In the West, Marxist theory engaged in dialogues with varieties of non-Marxist thought and shifted back and forth between emphasis on consciousness and emphasis on structure.

Two major currents of Marxism that developed before World War II continue to influence both Marxist and non-Marxist sociology. Antonio Gramsci (a theoretician of the Italian Communist Party) has had a lasting impact on sociology by introducing the concept of "hegemony"—the process whereby the economically dominant class translates economic power into political and cultural dominance. He analyzed the role of intellectuals in supporting or challenging hegemony. His work is particularly relevant to developed capitalist societies in which the system appears to hold the allegiance of large parts of the working class. Before it was dispersed by the onset of Nazism in Germany, the Frankfurt Institute explored theoretical connections between Hegelian Marxism and the growing body of psychoanalytic thought. A lasting influence of this milieu is the writing of Walter Benjamin, whose analysis of cultural production underlies most work—non-Marxist as well as Marxist—in the culture theory that emerged in the 1980's and 1990's.

One can trace a shift away from issues of consciousness back to issues of structure beginning with the work of Leo Huberman, Paul Baran, and Paul Sweezy in the United States in the late 1950's and 1960's. Baran and Sweezy analyzed the emergence of monopoly capitalism—capitalism associated with giant corporations, an interconnection of capital and government, and a reduction of free market competition. Ernst Mandel's work also explores the capitalist economy in the later twentieth century. At a more philosophical level, French structural Marxists (most notably, Louis Althusser) tried to remove the Hegelian influence in Marxism and to replace it with a model of societies as determined structures that owed much to Émile Durkheim in sociology, to Ferdinand de Saussure in linguistics, and to Jacques Lacan in psychoanalysis. Althusser's theory of social formations even converged with contemporary functionalist sociological theory. Meanwhile, more concrete studies were done by Serge Mallet and Andre Gorz on new technical and managerial strata and by Harry Braverman on capitalist management practices that deskill workers. Braverman has had a strong influence on sociological studies of the impact of computerization and technology on the labor force. In the postcolonial era, Marxists returned with renewed energy to issues of imperialism; they updated this concept with the analysis of dependency in "underdeveloped nations," showing how these regions were caught up in an unequal global capitalist system. These trends coincided with the upsurge of the New Left, with hopes for a worker-intellectual alliance in France and Italy in the late 1960's, and with the accession to power of revolutionary forces in Vietnam and elsewhere.

As prospects for these movements faded and European communism as well receded after electoral victories in the 1970's, Marxism found itself increasingly in a dialogue with non-Marxist culture theory, feminism, and post-structuralist and postmodernist thought. Some Marxists repudiate the notion of the "postmodern," emphasizing the continuity of capitalism; others (such as Frederic Jameson) theorize that new "postmodern" forms of culture do indeed accompany advanced capitalism. This dialogue was accelerated by the collapse of socialist systems in Eastern Europe and the Soviet Union; the evident difficulties in creating viable socialist societies have forced Marxist thought back into a reflection on agency and discourse.

Marxism is above all a challenge to capitalist hegemony in the economy, in politics, and in social theory. As long as capitalism remains the prevailing form of society, Marxism exists as the expression of an alternative vision of the human future as well as an ongoing mode of inquiry into the structure of capitalist society.

Bibliography

Burawoy, Michael, and Theda Skocpol, eds. *Marxist Inquiries: Studies of Labor, Class, and States.* Chicago: University of Chicago Press, 1982. A collection of research articles that address questions raised by Marxism, this volume illustrates the impact that Marxist thought has on contemporary sociology. Some essays are technical, but Burawoy's introduction is a good overview.

Engels, Friedrich. *The Origin of the Family, Private Property, and the State.* New York: Viking Penguin, 1985. Engels' classic exposition of the history of these institutions, first published in the nineteenth century. His discussion of the family is of continuing interest to feminists.

Howard, Dick, and Karl Klare, eds. *The Unknown Dimension.* New York: Basic Books, 1972. The essays in this book review European Marxist social thought of the twentieth century, with clear expositions of the ideas of major theorists.

McLellan, David. *The Thought of Karl Marx.* London: Macmillan, 1971. Explains the basic ideas of Marx; the material is treated in chronological order and in terms of major concepts. The exposition is accompanied by excerpts from Marx's writings. Excellent organization.

Marx, Karl. *Selected Writings.* Edited by David McLellan. Oxford, England: Oxford University Press, 1977. The definitive one-volume collection of Marx's writings, exemplary for comprehensiveness, chronological order, and the length and representativeness of the selections.

Zeitlin, Irving. *Ideology and the Development of Sociological Theory.* 4th ed. Englewood Cliffs, N.J.: Prentice-Hall, 1990. Places Marx and Engels within the history of sociology, showing how sociological theory developed in the "debate with Marx's ghost."

Roberta T. Garner

Cross-References

MASS HYSTERIA

Type of sociology: Collective behavior and social movements

Mass hysteria refers to a collective attack of panic or psychosomatic illness that occurs in a tension-filled environment and is based in an unfounded interpretation of events as being direly threatening. Such experiences are short-lived and are usually triggered by a small number of initial cases from which similar reactions spread quickly through a population.

Principal terms

CONTAGION: the coursing of an affect or symptom through a population by means of transmission from one individual to another

CONVERGENCE: the sudden appearance of an affect or symptom at all points in a large group of people, who react equivalently to the same stresses

INDEX CASES: people who are the first to exhibit the effects that will rapidly spread to others during an outbreak of mass hysteria

MASS PSYCHOGENIC ILLNESS: a form of mass hysteria in which there is a group attack of psychosomatic sickness, moving by way of spontaneous imitation of index cases

REBOUND OUTBREAK: an episode of mass hysteria that involves a small original occurrence that dies down but is then followed by a larger recurrence

RUMOR: false information that moves by word of mouth or, occasionally, through the mass media, providing the framework for an explosion of mass hysteria

Overview

In March, 1954, in Seattle, Washington, the papers began reporting that, in a nearby small town, residents had found their car windshields scratched and pitted. Police suspected vandalism. Rumors flew that this damage was linked to the radioactive fallout from recent nuclear bomb detonations in the Pacific. On April 15 and 16, nearly 250 Seattle residents called the police to report that their windshields had been affected. The people in the city and even the local government began panicking. Residents were covering their autos with tarpaulins, and the mayor appealed to the president for emergency aid. In a few days, however, the fear was gone. The rumors ceased and the hubbub subsided. Experts who studied the situation discovered that the windshield pitting was caused by average wear and tear, but that this deterioration was something, like slight scratches on an individual's eyeglasses, that a person would not notice unless his or her attention was drawn to it.

This episode represents a classic example of mass hysteria, which can be defined as a sudden, irrational spreading of fear or fear-induced illness through a large group of people.

A close analysis of the events in Seattle would indicate such important features of mass hysteria as a background of environmental tension and hearsay, a triggering event, a number of early model cases, a particular way of spreading from person to person, and a typical speed and duration of eruption.

The Seattle panic occurred in the generalized atmosphere of apprehension that ushered in the nuclear age. Nuclear explosions were unimaginably destructive and, because of radioactive fallout, uncertain in consequence. Who knew whether nuclear tests hundreds of miles away could damage car windshields? Incidents of hysteria that have occurred in smaller and hence more easily studied groups have provided sociologists with more details about the kind of charged environment that fosters these outbreaks. In examining workplace incidents, Michael Colligan and Lawrence Murphy (1982) point to "the presence of physical stressors . . . strained labor-management relations, and . . . lack of interpersonal communication between workers" as being among the factors that are supportive preconditions for an outbreak of mass hysteria.

Anxiety about the dangers of nuclear fission was widespread in the United States in the 1950's, yet only Seattle experienced a time of public hysteria. Clearly, to pinpoint the reason for this or similar episodes it is necessary to go beyond the tense atmosphere and look at the network of interrelated factors that would include a triggering change in the wider situation, a number of initial cases (called indexes) of the panic or illness, and a rumor linking the index cases to the triggering event.

The incident of the "mystery gas," analyzed by Sidney Stahl, can be used to illustrate these interlinked causes. A data processing center at a Midwestern university had come under unusual stress when noisy building construction had begun nearby. The triggering event was the placement of a diesel engine next to one of the open windows of the center. A number of workers—index cases—began coming down with something: tearing, vomiting, and fainting. Concurrently, the rumor was spreading that a mystery gas was escaping from the diesel, and this rumor helped bring on mass effects whereby the whole office of thirty-five women got sick.

Whereas, in this case, trigger, index, and rumor were bunched together in time and space, the preceding factors in the Seattle incident were more distinguishable because of their separation in geography and time. The nuclear test that presumably triggered the hysteria took place some time before and at a great distance from the place of outbreak. The index cases were in another town, and the associated rumor spread for two weeks before the occurrences took place.

The Seattle chronology represents a good example of a rebound outbreak, which is a case of mass hysteria in which a small onset is followed by a lull and then by a second, more full-blown eruption.

The window-pitting story also illustrates the idea of convergence. This takes place when a large number of people, affected by the same stressors, begin to panic or get sick simultaneously. An even more sensational panic outbreak of this type was started by the radio, which could reach into the homes of the whole nation at one time. On Halloween night in 1938, the Mercury Theater, directed by Orson Welles, broadcast an updated, documentary-style presentation of H. G. Wells's *The War of the Worlds*

(1898), which described a Martian takeover of the earth. Although the show was preceded by an explanation that the program was fictional, many listeners tuned in late, missed the disclaimer, and reacted as if the United States were under attack from space. In this case, the sheer reach of the transmitting medium ensured a convergent outbreak.

More modest eruptions of mass hysteria, though, tend to spread through contagion; that is, they move from one person to another. One of the most elaborately studied occurrences of contagion was examined in *The June Bug* (1968) by Alan Kerckhoff and Kurt Back. In a textile mill, a few people became sick, and rumor ascribed their illnesses to bugs that had arrived in a shipment of cloth. More and more workers came down with the disease. The authors see the illness as first spreading from outsiders (people with few social contacts), then moving into and among circles of friends, and then, near its peak, jumping from clique to clique, affecting and infecting everyone.

Finally, both the rapidity of the spread of the hysteria and the shortness of its tenure—these outbreaks rarely outlast a week—indicate both the hysteria's precariousness, for it is based on dispellable rumors, and its temporary significance, since, for one moment, it perfectly jells a population's inarticulate, inner turbulence.

Applications

Mass hysteria is not a thing of the past. It is true, however, that more careful control of broadcasting and publishing in the United States, spurred by Welles's startling program, has ensured that panics will not again be spread by the mass media. The very outrageousness of such events as the Martian scare, when a potentially traumatizing rumor was beamed into millions of homes, prompted all mass media programmers to scrutinize carefully what effects unusual material might have and keep potentially dangerous programs from being presented. Although hysteria on a large scale, fostered by the media, has disappeared, however, smaller outbreaks, in places such as factories and schools, have continued to occur.

Institutional outbreaks are short-lived, but they do disrupt the functioning of the beset organizations and leave permanent scars on those affected. Therefore, sociologists, especially those working with industry, have sought ways to head off the outbreaks of mass hysterical episodes or to defuse them if they do occur. Yet, as social scientists have sought to investigate cases of mass hysteria, they have found themselves confronted with difficult ethical questions.

The biggest methodological question facing someone studying, in an industrial setting, an incident of mass psychogenic illness (MPI), which is mass hysteria that has resulted in an outbreak of psychosomatic sickness, is this: How can a sociologist maintain objectivity when he or she obviously favors the interpretation of the events given by a firm's management rather than by the involved workers? Joseph McGrath explains what is involved:

> The affected have a stake in maintaining their definition of the causal agent [whether they believe it is a June bug, mystery gas, or some other provocateur]; otherwise . . . they

are deluded, gullible, or malingering. Setting managers . . . have a stake in redefining the problem as a case of "mass psychogenic illness" [or else] they are likely to have some degree of responsibility for the triggering event . . . [and] researchers . . . certainly have a stake in maintaining that MPI definition . . . otherwise, there would be nothing for them to investigate!

Since the analyzing sociologists' preconceived point of departure clashes with the viewpoint of the affected, when social scientists question workers about the cause and progress of an outbreak, the workers will tend to be less than forthcoming and cooperative. Because of this discord, sociologists have often resorted to subterfuges in collecting data. In preparing *The June Bug*, for example, which was researched two months after the mass eruption, the questioners posed as scholars making a survey of workers' attitudes in general. They only asked a small fraction of their questions, as if incidentally, about the outbreak, thus seeming not particularly concerned or prejudiced about it.

Even though they have worked against formidable obstacles, sociologists have been able to point to a number of ways to handle or forestall mass hysterical outbreaks. The most obvious, if not always feasible, method of preventing mass hysteria in industrial settings is to reduce stress. Workplaces where such outbursts occur are tense ones, often overcrowded, with tedious work and antagonistic labor/management relations. In fact, one population in which mass hysteria has been very common in the later twentieth century has been among women in mass-production facilities in the Third World, where labor conditions are far from optimal.

It has been noted that in these and most other hysterical eruptions in workplaces, the affected are predominantly women. This, it is said, is because, especially in the Third World, women are clustered in the more boring and coercively disciplined jobs. Further, it has been proposed that women are most often affected in these episodes because they are taught not to question male managerial authority. Therefore, W. H. Phoon argues that Malay females become involved in mass psychogenic illnesses because they are angered by their working conditions yet do not dare voice their protests for fear of social disapproval in their milieu; instead, they bottle up their frustration until it explodes.

Short of restructuring the labor situation to establish more harmonious relations of production, James Pennebaker suggests that workers who are at risk be taught to recognize the typical ailments associated with stress so that they can distinguish physical maladies produced by psychological difficulties from those that are externally caused. This will help them to guard against mistaking symptoms of stress and overwork for the products of mysterious toxins.

Scientists have cautioned against trying to meet a mass hysterical outbreak head on. Instead, indirect methods, such as the ones used to control the mystery gas incident, should be adopted. In the case of the mystery gas, managers did not pooh-pooh the affected workers' ideas and tell them there was no such gas, but told them that they had discovered the source of the gas and eliminated it.

It is also important to keep in mind, sociologists add, that, illusionary as the rumored cause may be for an outbreak of mass illness, those who fall victim to it are genuinely sick and should be treated as patients. Those who get sick at work should be given sedatives, when advisable, allowed to rest, and then sent home out of the heady atmosphere of the mass hysterical chain reaction.

Context

The first stirrings of sociology as a science in Europe, though not in America, centered on crowd behavior. Fear of the unleashed fury of rioting mobs was great at the end of the nineteenth century, and to prevent social upheavals, sociologists tried to understand the motivations that would cause a crowd to collect and act in different types of situations, including ones that led to mass hysteria.

The pioneering work in the field was the French sociologist Gustave Le Bon's *Psychologie des foules* (1895; *The Crowd: A Study of the Popular Mind*, 1896). Le Bon argues that an individual degenerates in a crowd, giving in to atavistic urges. According to this conception, mass hysteria breaks out in a group because, once people are gathered in a collectivity, even if they are college professors (he notes), they will give way to rumors and superstitions that they would scoff at if they were isolated from the group and therefore were in their right minds.

Citing Le Bon as his main authority and reacting to Austria's defeat in World War I, Sigmund Freud, the founder of modern psychology, linked crowd psychology to libidinal energy. For Freud, a smoothly functioning organization, such as an army, will handle stress well, even if it has to give up civilization's normal prohibitions (as army members have to give up taboos against killing), as long as each group member is imaginatively linked through libidinal bonds to an exalted leader, such as a general or a pope. If these bonds are disturbed and there is no erotic cohesion in the organization, then people will be prone to hysterical reactions, such as battlefield panic.

In the second half of the twentieth century, with the specter of mob violence receding in the West, the understanding of mass hysteria, within the broader field of crowd behavior, became less ethically oriented. (Freud and Le Bon seemed as much concerned with condemning as fathoming what they studied.) Elias Canetti, Nobel Prize-winning novelist, in his *Crowds and Power* (1978), took a phenomenological and multicultural approach. He tried to see what basic characteristics, such as the human predisposition to form herds, inspired crowd reactions the world over. Thus, he looked at a panic at a mosque in the Middle East to identify universal traits discoverable in the melee.

American sociologists have focused on small-scale institutional outbreaks of hysteria. *The June Bug* (1968), by Alan Kerckhoff and Kurt Back, is one of the best of these studies. Its investigation sheds light on what types of people are most often drawn into hysterical outbreaks, what conditions nurture these eruptions, and through what channels they spread.

Other American scholarly works have paid attention to cases of mass psychogenic illness in mass-production sites in Third World countries. Such studies became prominent in the 1970's and 1980's as U.S. corporations became closely tied to factories in developing countries that were either their suppliers or subsidiaries. Sociologists' concerns reflected those of American businessmen who were interested in smooth production.

Bibliography

Canetti, Elias. *Crowds and Power*. Translated by Carol Stewart. New York: Seabury Press, 1978. The author is a true original in both style and content. His exposition concentrates on carefully registering examples and allowing theories to arise from these illustrations. The heart of his argument is the distinction between packs; small, purposeful groups; and larger crowds. He illuminates mass hysteria in terms of this difference.

Colligan, Michael J., James W. Pennebaker, and Lawrence R. Murphy, eds. *Mass Psychogenic Illness: A Social Psychological Analysis*. Hillsdale, N.J.: Lawrence Erlbaum, 1982. This book is a treasure trove of fourteen essays on different aspects of mass psychosomatic sickness. Of special interest are such essays as one that examines the obstacles to objective studies of mass outbreaks, ones that apply different theoretical frameworks (such as that of perception theory) to explain the deep structures of outbreaks, and ones that relate mass illness to other forms of collective behavior. Each essay has a good accompanying bibliography.

Freud, Sigmund. "Group Psychology and the Analysis of the Ego." In *Beyond the Pleasure Principle, Group Psychology, and Other Works*. Vol. 18 in *The Standard Edition of the Complete Psychological Works of Sigmund Freud*. 24 vols. Translated by James Strachey. London: Hogarth Press, 1953-1974. This work is perhaps less valuable for its insights into mass hysteria than for its allowing the reader to see one of the key thinkers of the twentieth century—Freud created a whole system of psychology—grapple with the problems of crowd behavior. Freud's chief point is that crowd relations are determined by the same sorts of forces that govern families. Distorted, displaced erotic bonds rule both.

Kerckhoff, Alan C., and Kurt W. Back. *The June Bug: A Study of Hysterical Contagion*. New York: Appleton-Century-Crofts, 1968. Through the close study of one textile mill, the authors attempt to understand how a mass psychosomatic illness arises and spreads. They divide the affected into two categories: believers and adopters. The believers are people who are easily swayed by rumors, and the adopters are those who readily imitate others. The two character types act to generate mass hysteria under proper conditions. The book contains appendices in which the research methods are discussed and the questions asked the affected are provided.

Sartre, Jean-Paul. *Theory of Practical Ensembles*. Vol. 1 in *Critique of Dialectical Reason*. Translated by Alan Sheridan-Smith. Edited by Jonathan Ree. London: NLB, 1976. This book, written by one of the major philosophers of the twentieth century, analyzes crowd behavior by way of a basic distinction between the purposeless, anomic crowd (the series) and the active, motivated crowd (the fused group). Though the book is difficult and makes no concessions to the reader, it does represent a consistent attempt to relate all types of collective behavior to primal categories of group life.

James Feast

Cross-References

Collective Behavior, 291; Crowds and Crowd Dynamics, 393; Mass Psychogenic Illness, 1141; Mobs, Riots, and Panics, 1226; Rumors and Urban Legends, 1667.

MASS PSYCHOGENIC ILLNESS

Type of sociology: Collective behavior and social movements
Fields of study: Forms of deviance; Patterns of social interaction

Mass psychogenic illness (MPI) refers to the collective occurrence of physical symptoms and related beliefs among two or more persons in the absence of any identifiable or demonstrable physical causes for the symptoms and beliefs. It is a disorder stemming from psychological causes. Mass psychogenic illness helps to explain certain fairly frequent and often unusual patterns of collective behavior.

Principal terms
> COLLECTIVE BEHAVIOR: behavior exhibited by groups; usually considered to be spontaneous and unstructured action by fairly large numbers of people
> CONTAGION: the spontaneous outbreak of illness among a group of people, regardless of whether it is attributable to physical causes
> EPIDEMIC: a rapidly spreading attack of disease that affects large numbers of people at the same time
> HYSTERIA: in psychology, the manifestation of symptoms of a disease or disorder for which no physical cause exists
> INFECTIOUSNESS: the ability of contamination or illness to be passed from one person to another

Overview

Manifestation or outbreaks of mass psychogenic illness (MPI) have been recorded since antiquity and continue through the present. An early example is the dancing manias of the fifteenth and sixteenth centuries in Europe. The dancing manias arose in Aachen in 1374 sometime after the Black Plague epidemic of the fourteenth century. They spread rapidly in the Rhine basin and along pilgrimage routes. It usually affected groups of a few hundred people; they often shed their clothes and then danced, made chopping movements, held or clapped hands, threw themselves to the ground, and convulsed and jerked uncontrollably. These behaviors continued for hours or days until the participants became exhausted.

Another instance of MPI occurred in an industrial setting in the late 1700's. A female worker in a cotton factory put a mouse on the breast of another woman who had a phobia of mice. This woman immediately fell into violent convulsive fits that continued for a day. The next day, three women fell into similar violent convulsions; six more did on the next day. It was believed that a contaminated bag of cotton was causing a disease. Upon arrival of a doctor, fourteen more people were seized, for a total of twenty-four, only one of whom was a man. When all were finally convinced that there was no disease coming from the cotton, no other people were affected.

Mass psychogenic illness is considered an illness or disorder because those affected present symptoms of a physical sickness. The illness or sickness is labeled "psychogenic" to denote that there are no demonstrable physical or organic causes for the behaviors. Thus it is presumed that such behaviors arise from psychological causes. "Mass" refers to the fact that MPI by definition affects and involves many people. Thus it is an example of collective behavior. As noted, the dancing manias involved large groups of people simultaneously infected. That is, they could be said to have reached epidemic proportions. Additionally, dancing manias spread rapidly over large geographical areas. It can be said that MPI is an example of a contagion (outbreak of an illness) that is infectious in that symptoms are passed from one person to another.

Since 1800, outbreaks of mass psychogenic illness have been frequently reported in the scientific literature. In 1982, François Sirois conducted a comprehensive survey of the literature between 1870 and 1980 on eighty-eight reports of MPI. Sirois found seven variables that identify the various aspects of MPI. The first concerns persons, place, and time. Half of the occurrences of MPI occurred in schools, a quarter in towns and villages, 17 percent in factories, and the rest in various locations such as hospitals. Women were almost exclusively involved in 80 percent of the cases, primarily in closed settings (such as a hospital or factory) but less so in open towns. These women were mostly adolescents (60 percent). The number of persons affected varied from a few to several hundred in rare cases. Outbreaks were either short-lived (one day) or could last a few months; typically they ranged between three and fourteen days.

The second variable is symptoms. The pattern of symptoms depended on when the MPI occurred. Prior to 1914 they were mainly movements, as in the dancing manias. After 1914 MPI was more commonly expressed in fainting, nausea, abdominal problems, headaches, or dizziness. These symptoms were expressed suddenly and abruptly. The third variable is the characteristics of MPI individuals. It has been suggested that MPI occurs in a group composed primarily of normal persons who are highly suggestible; in this concept, it occurs because of the regressive effect of crowd behavior on intellect and emotions. Additionally, the group contains a small number of emotionally unstable persons. Variable four concerns group characteristics, but no clear patterns emerge here. Some reports found social isolates, less subject to pressures to conform and more prone to contagious behaviors, to be the catalysts for MPI. Other reports, however, suggested the initiation of MPI among strong interpersonal networks. It has also been suggested that those who stand out in a group—isolates, leaders, new members—are the probable catalysts. Additionally, the degree of isolation and cohesion in the group is believed to be an important condition for an outbreak. If a group is isolated it is less able to verify perceived threats from the outside and so becomes vulnerable to MPI. If the group is cohesive, spread of MPI among group members is facilitated.

Variable five is the analysis of outbreaks by setting. In schools, four times as many women as men exhibited mass psychogenic illness. The women were less than twenty years old. The duration of MPI was either short or long, and the incident involved large numbers. About 30 percent of the group was affected. Occurrence in factories affected women only, in the twenty to forty age range, with a duration up to two weeks.

Occurrences affected large numbers of people. Occurrences in towns involved both men and women of all ages. MPI in institutions usually occurred in postadolescent segregated women. About 15 percent of the group was affected.

Variable six concerns aspects of MPI in occupational settings. The outbreak of MPI in a cotton factory described previously provides an accurate picture of the typical outbreak in an industrial setting. It was found to be sudden and explosive, to last about a week, and to affect about 10 percent of the workforce; rumor played a central role. Subsequent industrial reports suggest that the symptoms change according to the particular type of work and belief system. Attack rate is inversely related to group size, about 8 to 10 percent in large groups and 30 to 50 percent in small groups. Finally, variable seven is course and occurrence. Factors which facilitate the spread of MPI can promote its duration or rebounding. These factors include mass media, physical and visual proximity, excitement, reuniting of the group, and the persistence of rumors.

Applications

The sudden and spontaneous outbreak of an illness among a group of people is a distressing and disruptive event. It is made even more so when a physical cause for the illness is not obvious or cannot be identified. Outbreaks of the illness may recur over time, or symptoms may be too vague and nonspecific to permit accurate diagnosis and treatment. If it occurs in an occupational setting, the workplace may become an occasion for anxiety, fear, rumor, and confusion. There is usually lost productivity and disruption of the work routine.

Mass psychogenic illness has occurred throughout history and across cultures. That MPI is a widespread and fairly common phenomenon with potentially disruptive effects suggests that it is worthy of study and understanding. Light can be shed on MPI through examination of two particular instances, one from the 1970's (mystery gas) and one from the late seventeenth century (the Salem witch trials).

According to researcher Sidney M. Stahl, in the early spring in the early 1970's, on a midweek day, a majority of the thirty-five keypunch workers of the data processing center of a midwestern university became ill, exhibiting symptoms of headaches, smelling a strange and burning odor, hyperventilation, nausea, vomiting, burning and teary eyes, and fainting.

When the workers returned to work the next day the symptoms recurred within an hour. Prior to the commencement of work the third day, an emergency room physician and a professor of environmental studies met with the workers and suggested that an inversion of the atmosphere had caused smoke from a nearby building to accumulate in the data center. The workers were not told that tests found no evidence whatsoever of smoke accumulation. They accepted this explanation. Only one worker experienced symptoms that day. The worker was quickly sent home before others could react to her symptoms, and the contagion was over.

The mystery gas incident is typical of instances of MPI occurring in the workplace. These incidents can be viewed as a warning sign to employers that certain conditions in the workplace need to be changed. For example, several studies indicate that MPI is the result of stressful events. In the mystery gas episode, an addition to a building adjacent the data center was under construction. This entailed continual use of heavy machinery and unanticipated dynamite blasts of bedrock. Also, workers in the data center labored under rather unpleasant, stringent, and rigid working conditions. Those workers who were most dissatisfied with their jobs were the ones most likely to exhibit MPI. Immediately preceding the outbreak, a large diesel engine was operated under one of the open windows of the data center. The majority of the workers who exhibited MPI worked by this window. Management subsequently reevaluated its policies and instituted positive changes concerning the organization of the work performed and the supervision of that work. A less sympathetic management might have interpreted the MPI as insubordinate and disruptive behavior and fired the workers.

The most famous and notorious instance of mass psychogenic illness was the occurrence of seizures among girls that led to the witch hunts and executions in Salem, Massachusetts, in 1692. This event was initiated when a number of young girls, one after the other, were seized with fits. They raved and fell into convulsions and violent contortions; they experienced vocal outbursts, feelings of being pinched and bitten, and flailing and kicking. Such fits among adolescent girls had occurred earlier in New England and had been attributed to Satanic possession and witchcraft. When the girls were pressed to identify who was tormenting them, they named three people. Even when these three were arrested and jailed, however, the MPI did not cease. It became a contagion, spreading to dozens more girls and young women who showed the same physical symptoms and also named names. As a result, between June and September, 1692, fourteen women and six men, from age five to seventy-one, were put to death. Scores more were imprisoned as witches.

Finally, in October, 1692, as a result of dismay by more enlightened citizens and intervention by the state government, the rules of evidence were changed so as to make it essentially impossible to obtain a conviction. The witch craze was effectively ended.

The circumstances associated with this occurrence of mass psychogenic illness are instructive. Salem Village was a Puritan community that was torn and under siege as it attempted to free itself from Salem Town and its taxes. The village's first three ministers had caused bitter dispute and controversy. The fourth minister and his West Indian slave regaled some adolescent girls in his kitchen with stories of fancy, possibly involving voodoo, and told their fortunes. These girls had been reared as Puritans, and Puritanism demanded strict adherence to austere rules, discipline, and self-control. The kitchen sessions, with their risky indulgence in fantasy and magic, when combined with the stress in Salem Village, may have precipitated the onset of MPI. In any event, the outbreak of MPI that culminated in the witch trials happened among these teenage girls shortly after the kitchen sessions.

It also appears that the witch trials were used as an excuse to settle local feuds and property disputes. Salem Village land owners, whose wealth and power had eroded, pursued witches as a means to reacquire former wealth and power. The fact that almost all of the victims were women is also instructive. These women tended to be unusual—some owned property, some did not go to church—and it has been suggested that these women were the victims of persecution by a fearful and threatened male power structure.

Context

Behavior that could be called hysteria has been described since antiquity. In general, hysteria refers to the occurrence of symptoms of disease for which no physical cause can be found. It can occur in individuals, where it is known as conversion disorder and is studied by psychology. It can also occur among a group of individuals, where it is known as mass psychogenic illness (MPI) and becomes a concern of sociology. Throughout history, hysteria has been attributed to various causes, from the ancient Greek explanation of a sexually unsatisfied womb wandering through the body in search of satisfaction to possession by Satan. The modern study of hysteria, however, commenced with Sigmund Freud's work in the late nineteenth century. Much of Freud's work on hysteria centered on unexplainable (and sometimes neurologically impossible) cases of paralysis. Hysteria was seen as pent-up emotional energy that disrupted normal functioning and could be converted into physical symptoms. The whole process took place without the person's awareness in the unconscious part of the mind.

Hysteria is an important behavior to study for a number of reasons. Since hysteria can mimic virtually all physical diseases, it is important to be able to distinguish those instances of illness that are attributable to psychological causes from those that result from physical causes. Unfortunately, especially at the group level, the study of mass hysteria has often been relegated to a residual category of research. That is, only if standard medical technology fails to explain behavior are sociologists and psychologists called upon. This is probably attributable to the medical orientation of those initially on the scene; also, the need to find immediate answers to what may be a vexing and disruptive problem will suggest looking for physical causes. To establish the event as an occurrence of MPI requires a more complicated and time-consuming process. Since MPI does occur fairly often, however, ideally it should be considered a coequal with hypothesis of physical causation.

It is also important to study mass psychogenic illness because it helps to better understand how a number of sociological phenomena affect group behavior. A number of variables have been demonstrated to be important in influencing the nature and course of MPI—for example, gender, socioeconomic status, stress, and social support systems. Understanding how these variables influence MPI will increase sociology's knowledge of the relevance of these variables in social situations in general.

In the overall history of sociology, mass psychogenic illness provides a window into understanding how society explains strange and unusual behaviors and how these explanations change as social science and society evolves. MPI can serve as a clue to understanding, uncovering, and correcting tensions and stresses in social situations that seem always to precede and facilitate outbreaks of MPI.

Bibliography

Colligan, Michael J., James W. Pennebaker, and Lawrence R. Murphy, eds. *Mass Psychogenic Illness: A Social Psychological Analysis*. Hillsdale, N.J.: Lawrence Erlbaum, 1982. A thorough treatment of mass psychogenic illness. The book consists of fourteen articles grouped into three categories: overview, research methods, and theories. The book is oriented primarily toward MPI in the workplace but is indispensable for anyone interested in a comprehensive treatment of MPI.

Freud, Sigmund. *Group Psychology and the Analysis of the Ego*. London: International Psycho-Analytical Press, 1922. Freud's analysis of hysteria and its role in collective behavior is presented. Freud's work on hysteria marks the beginning of scientific study of this behavior. Freud stressed the breakdown of the superego (conscience) in controlling the primitive impulses of the id.

Holmes, David. *Abnormal Psychology*. New York: HarperCollins, 1991. This popular introductory textbook focuses primarily on discussion of hysteria in the individual (conversion disorder). Holmes also discusses mass psychogenic illness and provides a good understanding of the place of hysteria within somatoform disorders, a group of psychological disorders that express themselves in symptoms of physical illness.

Karlsen, Carol F. *The Devil in the Shape of a Woman*. New York: W. W. Norton, 1987. An interesting and perceptive treatment of the Salem witch trials.

Kerckhoff, Alan C., and Kurt W. Back. *The June Bug: A Study of Hysterical Contagion*. New York: Appleton-Century-Crofts, 1968. The authors present a thorough and detailed examination of an instance of mass psychogenic illness which occurred in a large factory in 1962. About two hundred employees were stricken by a mysterious illness, which was attributed to an insect bite. The book is similar in form to the Colligan volume cited above.

Lazarus, Richard S. *Psychological Stress and the Coping Process*. New York: McGraw-Hill, 1966. Lazarus is a noted authority on how people cope with stress. Mass psychogenic illness can be viewed as a coping response by a group to stress. Inevitably, some sort of social stress or pressure precedes and facilitates outbreaks of mass psychogenic illness.

Laurence Miller

Cross-References

Alienation and Work, 80; Collective Behavior, 291; Crowds and Crowd Dynamics, 393; The Environment and Health, 647; Health and Society, 852; Mass Hysteria, 1134.

MEASURES OF CENTRAL TENDENCY

Type of sociology: Sociological research
Field of study: Data collection and analysis

Measures of central tendency are numerical indices that indicate the "middle" of a distribution of scores. The most frequently used measures of centrality are the mean, median, and mode. Sociologists use these measures as a way to summarize important characteristics of quantitative data.

Principal terms

INTERVAL SCALE: a scale of measurement in which equal differences between numbers correspond to equal differences in that which is being measured

MEAN: a measure of central tendency that is often referred to as "the average"

MEASUREMENT: the assignment of numbers to observations according to a predetermined rule

MEDIAN: the point in a distribution below which fall half the scores

MODE: the score in a distribution that occurs most frequently; when using a nominal measure, the category that contains the greatest number of observations

NOMINAL SCALE: a measurement scale in which data are in the form of names, labels, or categories

NORMAL DISTRIBUTION: a symmetrical, bell-shaped curve

ORDINAL SCALE: a scale of measurement in which data are ordered by rank

RATIO SCALE: a scale of measurement that has the characteristics of an interval scale and has a meaningful zero point

SKEWED DISTRIBUTION: an asymmetrical distribution in which scores tend to bunch at either the left or right end of the curve

Overview

Sociologists gather information, or data, to gain knowledge about the behavior of groups of people. The field of sociology is very broad, and sociologists' research interests range from the individual in the context of groups to the "behavior" of societies. Sociologists, indeed all scientists, have numerous research methods available for the collection of data. One method of collecting data is to observe or interview a number of people and report findings in the form of a narrative. This is an example of qualitative research. Qualitative research is in contrast to quantitative research; the latter approach is characterized by the assignment of numbers to observations. Measures of central tendency are numerical values that reflect the "middle" of an arranged list of numbers (called a distribution of scores). Not all quantitative research, however, uses data that can be described by the three most common measures of central tendency—mean, median, and mode. It is the scale of measurement that determines which measure(s) of central tendency can be meaningfully used.

Measurement is the assignment of numbers to objects or events according to predetermined rules. Since a sociologist can use different rules for assigning numbers, the same number can have different meanings, depending on the assignment rule. Moreover, it is not the actual numbers that are of interest; it is what the numbers represent that is the focus of study. There are three different ways in which numbers are used in sociology.

First, numbers are used to name things, in what is called a nominal scale of measurement. The numbers on football jerseys, social security numbers, and designating females as "1" and males as "2" in a data set are examples of the use of a nominal scale. When using a nominal scale, one cannot interpret the numbers as meaning anything beyond the labels themselves. There is no quantity implied by the numbers, so a higher number does not represent "more of something" than a lower number does. Variables that are measured on a nominal scale are qualitative variables, and they represent one example in which numbers are used in qualitative research. Sociologists often use nominal scales and summarize their findings in a cross-tabulation table. A cross-tabulation table indicates the number of observations in various categories. For example, a sociologist might be interested in the relation between gender and political party affiliations. Several categories are established: male/Democrat, female/Democrat, male/Republican, and female/Republican. The data are presented in the form of a frequency count (the number of people in each category). The use of a nominal scale of measurement precludes the use of certain measures of central tendency.

Second, numbers are used to rank things, in what is called an ordinal scale. An ordinal scale is used to identify the relative position of an observation in relation to another observation. Ranking individuals in terms of leadership ability, ordering cultures in terms of the freedoms accorded women, and ranking twentieth century presidents of the United States according to their popularity are all examples of the application of an ordinal scale to some variable of interest. Even though ordinal scales are quantitative, there is only a limited sense in which quantity is implied. Rankings reflect more or less of something but not how much more or less. That is, the difference between observations ranked first and second may not correspond to the amount of difference between the observations that are rank ordered fourth and fifth.

Third, numbers are used to represent quantity. An interval scale of measurement is similar to an ordinal scale in that different numbers represent more or less of the variable being measured. The critical distinction between an ordinal and interval scale is that the interval scale assumes that numerically equal distances on the scale represent equal distances on the dimension underlying the scale. For example, intelligence quotient (IQ) scores are assumed to lie on an interval scale such that the difference in the amount of intelligence between a score of 95 and 100 is the same as the difference in the amount of intelligence between scores of 110 and 115. A ratio scale has all the properties of an interval scale in addition to possessing a meaningful zero point.

Height, weight, time duration, and annual income are examples of variables that lend themselves to being scored on a ratio scale. With ratio scales, a number that is twice as large as another number represents twice as much of the thing being measured. It is important to understand the differences and similarities between scales of measurement, because some measures of central tendency can only be used with certain scales.

Applications

The arithmetic mean is the most common measure of where in a distribution scores tend to "bunch." The mean is not only useful when describing a central characteristic of a distribution but is also often used in formulas for evaluating the plausibility of a research hypothesis. The arithmetic mean is obtained by summing all the numbers of a distribution and dividing by the number of scores in the distribution. The term "average" is often used to refer to the mean. (Technically, however, the term "average" can denote any of the three measures of central tendency.)

In what way does the mean reflect the center of a distribution of scores? If the mean of a distribution is subtracted from every score in the distribution, some of the resulting numbers will be positive in sign and some will be negative. These numbers are called deviation scores. The sum of all the positive and negative deviation scores will always equal zero. In other words, the magnitude of the negative deviation scores perfectly balances the magnitude of the positive deviation scores. If another number, different from the mean, is added to the distribution, the mean will shift so that the sum of all the deviation scores still equals zero. The mean defines the "middle" or center of the distribution in that the mean is the numerical value that perfectly balances the positive and negative deviation scores.

There is a very important consequence attached to the way the mean is computed. For example, if ten scores have values close together and an eleventh score that is much higher than the other ten scores is included, a shift occurs. The mean will shift toward the eleventh score so as to satisfy the arithmetic rule discussed previously. When there is a small number of scores in a distribution, one extreme score can have a dramatic effect on the mean. The mean will then not convey an accurate picture of where in the distribution the scores tend to center.

A second measure of central tendency is the median. The median is the point in the distribution below which lie 50 percent of the scores. The median divides the distribution based on the frequency or number of scores above and below the median. Unlike the mean, the actual values of the scores in the distribution do not influence the median. If a researcher has recorded the annual income of one hundred families, the median is the annual income above which lie the highest fifty annual incomes and below which lie the lowest fifty annual incomes. The third measure of central tendency is the mode. The mode is the score that occurs most frequently in a distribution. If two scores share this distinction, then the distribution has two modes. (A distribution cannot have more than one mean or median.)

Using the mean as an index of central tendency has several advantages. First, the mean takes into account all the scores in a distribution. For this reason, the mean usually offers a good representation of the central tendency of a distribution. Second, the mean is a stable measure of central tendency when a researcher is repeatedly sampling from the same population. This feature of the mean is important when one wants to use the mean of a sample to infer the mean of a population. Third, because of the first two reasons, the mean is used in many statistical formulas. Nevertheless, when deciding which measure of central tendency to use to describe the center of a distribution, there are certain circumstances in which the mean is not the most desirable measure of central tendency.

The point was made earlier that an extreme score can have an undue influence on the mean, thus creating a misleading impression of the center of a distribution. If there is a large number of scores in a distribution, one extreme score might not have much of an influence on the value of the mean. Some distributions, however, have a relatively large number of high or low scores; such situations are called skewed distributions. Even if there is a large number of scores in the distribution, one will not have a particularly good measure of central tendency when the distribution is skewed.

Some variables of interest to sociologists are usually skewed, such as the annual incomes of families. The lowest possible annual income is zero; however, there is no limit to the highest annual income. Consequently, the values of annual income tend toward the higher end of the distribution. In this case, the median is the measure of choice. Since the median is not influenced by the value of extreme scores, it provides a more accurate description of the middle of a skewed distribution than does the mean.

The mode is used when one wants to convey the most typical score. Students at a university might be asked to name their favorite leisure activity. A researcher might report that 12 percent state "dancing," 50 percent report "television," and 38 percent say "sports" is their favorite pastime. These three activities are categories on a nominal scale. In this instance, there is no way to compute a mean or median, but the mode can be declared as "television." Whenever the data are in the form of "how many" (a nominal scale) rather than "how much" (an interval or ratio scale), the mode is the only appropriate measure of central tendency. Sociologists often report the most typical response to an item on a survey. In doing so, investigators are reporting the modal response to that survey item. Moreover, when sociologists use cross-tabulation tables, the data are in the form of a frequency count; here the only meaningful measure of central tendency is the mode.

Each measure of central tendency has its own advantages and disadvantages. When one is using descriptive statistics, the goal is simply to communicate the features of a distribution in as accurate a manner as possible. Further, there is no rule that says one cannot report two, or even all three, measures of central tendency, depending on the scale of measurement.

Context

It is impossible to identify the first use of any of the measures of central tendency. The use of the mean appears to be older than the use of the mode or median. The earliest writings of Pythagoras offer three formulas for the mean, each one capturing a different aspect of central tendency. The arithmetic mean was included as one of the formulas. The significance of the mean is intimately tied to the discovery of the normal distribution. A normal distribution is depicted by the symmetrical bell-shaped curve so often displayed in textbooks. Before sociologists began to use the mean as a measure of central tendency, mathematicians were applying the concept of the normal curve to games of chance and, later, to astronomical observations. One of the problems confronting early astronomers was the unreliability of measuring the distance between objects in the universe. It was often noted that the distribution of measurement errors followed the shape of the normal curve, but astronomers were undecided about which of several measurements to use. In 1755, Thomas Simpson suggested that taking the mean of all the observations is the best measure of the "true" distance between objects. Since measurement is an essential aspect of all science, including sociology, Simpson's recommendation has become an integral part of analyzing any variable measured with an interval or ratio scale.

One of the first uses of the normal curve, as it applies to social phenomena, appears in the work of Lambert Adolphe Quételet (1796-1874). Quételet's contributions to the social sciences are among the most extensive in the history of statistics. He was the first scientist to quantify the occurrence of various crimes by age, climate, sex, and education. Since he concluded that the causes of crimes do not lie within the individual but are products of society, Quételet could be called the first sociologist. Although many of his studies used the method of frequency counts and cross-tabulation tables, data for which the mode is the only appropriate measure of central tendency, he influenced an entire generation of researchers interested in quantifying human behavior by using interval and ratio scales. Quételet maintained that the measurement of "mental and moral traits" would form a normal distribution and that the mean was a measure of the "average man." He postulated that the "average man" is nature's ideal and that deviations from the mean represent the influence of interfering factors. Quételet's belief that the "average man" is nature's ideal never received many adherents. It is certainly easy to name certain traits for which the average would not be the most desirable "score"—intelligence, kindness, productivity and so on. Nevertheless, Quételet's work has had a profound influence in the fields of psychology, sociology, and anthropology.

Measures of central tendency have become a cornerstone of quantitative research in sociology. Theories of social phenomena may come and go, but measures of central tendency will continue as essential indices for communicating one aspect of the pattern of data collected in sociological studies.

Bibliography

Brown, Foster L., Jimmy R. Amos, and Oscar G. Mink. *Statistical Concepts: A Basic Program*. 2d ed. New York: Harper & Row, 1975. This is an excellent paperback book that presents many topics in statistics in the form of "learning modules." The module that covers measures of central tendency is presented as a series of "frames." Each frame has three parts: a brief explanation of a concept, a question about the concept, and the correct answer. This "programmed instruction" approach to teaching has been shown to enhance learning. The reader will be able to master the basic concepts of central tendency in approximately thirty minutes.

Grimm, Laurence G. *Statistical Applications for the Behavioral Sciences*. New York: John Wiley & Sons, 1993. Chapter 3 provides an in-depth introductory discussion of the mean, median, and mode. The author provides formulas for computing the mean and median when data are presented as a list of numbers as well as when data are presented in summary tables. Grimm also provides a discussion of the advantages and disadvantages of each measure of central tendency and offers tips on when to use each measure. Assumes no prior knowledge of statistics.

Phillips, John L., Jr. *How to Think About Statistics*. Rev. ed. New York: W. H. Freeman, 1992. The author presents numerous introductory topics in the field of statistics. Emphasis is on the conceptual basis of statistics rather than on calculation. Each measure of central tendency is first discussed and then applied. The content is very easy to understand.

Walker, Helen M. *Studies in the History of Statistical Method*. Baltimore: Williams & Wilkins, 1929. This book is a classic. Published in 1929, it remains the best treatment of the history of statistics. Many sections of the book will be difficult for the beginning student; however, the interested reader can skip those sections with formulas and concentrate on the historical development of basic concepts in statistics. The authors provides many interesting stories about the lives and times of major figures in the development of statistics.

Weisberg, Herbert F. *Central Tendency and Variability*. Newbury Park, Calif.: Sage Publications, 1992. The first half of this eighty-seven page monograph provides a thorough discussion of measures of central tendency. Useful for an advanced understanding of the statistical basis of measures of central tendency. For the student who has already taken a course in statistics, this is a good source for gaining a deeper understanding of measures of central tendency.

Laurence G. Grimm

Cross-References

Descriptive Statistics, 519; Experimentation in Sociological Research, 721; Inferential Statistics, 983; Measures of Variability, 1153; Quantitative Research, 1546; Surveys, 2030; Validity and Reliability in Measurement, 2136.

MEASURES OF VARIABILITY

Type of sociology: Sociological research
Field of study: Data collection and analysis

Measuring variability involves determining the difference that exists among members of a group or between different groups. Variability is a fundamental concern in the social sciences; measures of variability include range, average deviation, and standard deviation. Research not only describes the amount of variability in data but also attempts to identify the source of that variability.

Principal terms

DISTRIBUTION: specifies how frequently a variable takes each of its possible values, from the lowest to the highest

INFERENCE: the drawing of a conclusion based on a sample concerning the facts of the population from which the sample was selected

MEAN: the average value of a variable

OUTLIER: a value that lies outside the normal range of responses for a particular variable

QUALITATIVE VARIABLE: variables, such as sex, race, language, or political party, that classify observations according to nonquantitative attributes

QUANTITATIVE VARIABLES: variables, such as age, income, IQ, height, or weight that are measured in magnitude

SIGNIFICANCE TEST: a statistical test for determining whether the conclusion based on a sample holds true for the population from which the sample was drawn

STATISTIC: a value calculated from a sample with a view to the characteristics of the population from which the sample was drawn

VARIABILITY: the dispersion or spread of the values of a variable

VARIABLE: any variable quantity used to measure a certain characteristic or attribute of individual objects

Overview

If one were asked to describe a group of people, one would be most likely to do so first by stating things the people have in common. These similarities, such as being "young" or "rich," may be called the group's modal characteristics. Modal characteristics are those that occur most often. One might then, however, note ways in which individual members differ. Variation (variability) within a group can be as significant as a group's modal tendencies. In fact, the measurement of variability—the degree of variation or difference—is fundamental to all statistical description and analysis.

Both qualitative and quantitative variables are used to measure the characteristics of a sample or population. Methods of measuring the variability of qualitative variables are generally limited; methods of measuring quantitative variables will be emphasized here. The simplest measure of variability for quantitative variables is the range. If data can be ranked or sorted from the lowest to the highest value, the range is simply the difference between the two extremes. The range does not tell much about the data set as a whole, however, because it considers only the two extreme values. Changing one of the extremes gives the false impression of a shift in all the data.

A modification of the range is the interquartile range (IQR). Quartiles are constructed by ranking observations by a particular variable, then dividing the data distribution into four equal-sized parts. An example would be ranking or sorting 100 people by age. If 25 people (25 percent of the sample) are below 20 years of age, 25 people are between 20 and 29, 25 people are 30 to 44, and 25 people are 45 or older, then age 20 is called the first quartile, or 25th percentile. Age 30 is the second quartile, also called the 50th percentile, or median. Age 45 is the third quartile, or the 75th percentile. The IQR is the range that covers the "middle half" of the data. In this example, the IQR ranges from 20 to 45 and equals 25 years. If a value falls more than 1.5 times the IQR below the 25th percentile, or more than 1.5 times the IQR above the 75th percentile, it is considered a potential mild outlier. If it falls more than 3 times the IQR below the 25th percentile, or more than 3 times the IQR above the 75th percentile, it is considered a serious outlier.

Often a researcher is interested in observing how a data set clusters near the average, or "mean." If x is the value for one of n observations and $\bar{x}$ is the mean for all observations, then $x - \bar{x}$ is the distance of the observation from the mean, or the deviation from the mean. The sum of the deviations for all members of the data set is always 0, because the positive and negative deviations exactly cancel out. Mean deviation (MD) overcomes the cancellation problem by calculating the average of all deviations in terms of absolute values; counting only the distance from the mean and not its direction, positive or negative. MD is an intuitive measure of variability, but it is inconvenient for mathematical derivation because of the absolute values.

The most widely used and important measure of variability is standard deviation, which is also based on the deviation of each observation about the mean. There are three steps to calculating standard deviation. First, calculate the total sum of squares (TSS), which is the summation of all the squared deviations: TSS = $(x_1 - x)^2 + (x_2 - \bar{x})^2 + \ldots + (x_n - \bar{x})^2$. Second, divide TSS by $(n - 1)$, where n is the sample size. The result is the sample variance: $s^2 = $ TSS $/ (n - 1)$. The symbol s^2 indicates the sample variance. Third, calculate the square root of the sample variance; this is the sample standard deviation. The letter s is used to indicate standard deviation.

For the larger population from which the sample was drawn, the standard deviation is indicated by the Greek letter sigma, σ. The steps for calculating σ are the same as those for calculating s, except that the TSS should be divided by N, the total number of observations in the population, instead of $n - 1$. The sample standard deviation, s, is an unbiased estimate of the population standard deviation, σ. As sample size increases, the value of s becomes closer to the value of σ. When no information other than the range is available, the standard deviation can be approximately calculated as one-fourth of the range, assuming that data are distributed normally.

The "empirical rule" aids in interpreting the numerical value of the standard deviation. If a bar chart, or histogram, of the variable is symmetric and approximately bell-shaped (thus showing what is referred to as a normal distribution), then about 68 percent of all values should fall within plus or minus one standard deviation of the mean. About 95 percent of all values fall within two standard deviations of the mean, and about 99.7 percent of all values fall within three standard deviations of the mean. Values that are more than two standard deviations different from the mean are often termed "outliers" and should be inspected for possible errors. Alternatively, the Chebyshev inequality may be used for the same purpose. The inequality states that regardless of the data distribution, at least 75 percent of the data fall within one standard deviation of the mean and at least 88.9 percent of the data fall within three standard deviations of the mean.

These measures of variability (range, average deviation, and standard deviation) are all absolute measures. When the scales of measurement are different for different variables, the absolute measures of variability are incomparable. The relative measure of variability, coefficient of variation (CV), is recommended for comparison of variability between variables with different measurement scales. CV is the standard deviation divided by the mean.

Applications

An anecdote about a man crossing a river illustrates the importance of variability. The man was told that the river was an average of 2 feet deep, so he began to wade across. He drowned, however, because the fact that the river averaged 2 feet in depth hid the fact that, in places, it was very deep. In other words, the variability of the river's depth was not taken into account.

Measures of variability are important summary tools for data description. For example, researchers might want to compare the high school grade point averages (GPAs) and scores on the Scholastic Aptitude Test (SAT) of two groups of students, each of which has five members. The following table shows the two groups' GPA and SAT scores.

	Group 1						Group 2			
	1	2	3	4	5	1	2	3	4	5
GPA:	3.0	3.8	3.2	3.6	3.4	3.4	3.2	3.6	3.3	3.5
Mean	3.40					3.40				
Range	0.80					0.40				
SD	0.32					0.16				
CV	0.09					0.05				
SAT:	600	900	800	850	850	800	700	900	760	840
Mean	800					800				
Range	300					200				
SD	117					76				
CV		0.15					0.10			

The average GPA and SAT scores are all equal for the two groups. Yet one cannot say that the students in the two groups have the same GPA and SAT scores. Clearly they are not the same, as the measures of variability differ significantly. First, the GPA and SAT scores of group 1 are more dispersed than those of group 2. The range, standard deviation, and coefficient of variation of group 1 are all larger. Further, the coefficients of variation are larger for SATs than for GPAs, particularly in group 1. This indicates that individual variability is actually greater in SAT scores.

When a measure (such as pounds) cannot be compared directly to another measure (such as inches), standard deviation needs to be used for comparing an individual in a group with the group as a whole. For example, a student is 5 feet 8 inches tall and weighs 120 pounds. If the average height and weight among his classmates are 5 feet 6 inches and 115 pounds, respectively, can one say that the student is relatively taller than he is heavier when compared with his classmates as a whole? Suppose that the standard deviation is 15 pounds for weight and 3 inches for height in the student's class. The student's weight would then be about 0.33 standard deviations above the mean weight (the student's weight minus the average weight, divided by the standard deviation of weight: 120 pounds − 115 pounds / 15 pounds). His height would be about 0.67 standard deviations above the mean height (the student's height minus the average height, divided by the standard deviation of the height: 5 feet 8 inches − 5 feet 6 inches / 3 inches). Therefore, one can conclude that the student is in fact relatively taller than he is heavier compared with his classmates. The values of 0.33 and 0.67 are called standardized scores.

The measure of variability is important in evaluating samples for precision. The variability of a sample statistic (such as the sample mean) is called sampling error. If one takes numerous samples under similar conditions from the same population, it is possible to compare directly each sample mean with an average for all sample means, thus creating a standard deviation of the sample means or sampling error. The sampling error or standard deviation of the sample mean, however, is usually estimated based on one sample. For example, the standard deviation and mean of a sample are s and $\bar{x}$. The sampling error is estimated as the sample standard deviation divided by the square root of the sample size.

Political polls often estimate the proportion of respondents who would vote for a particular candidate. When a political poll indicates that the potential sampling error for the proportion voting for a candidate is 3 points, it means that the standard deviation for the proportion is estimated to be about 3 percent. This indicates that the actual proportion voting for the candidate is probably within a range of 6 points above or below the number given by the poll. For a normal distribution, 95 percent of cases fall within two standard deviations of the mean; thus, a range of 6 points (twice the sampling error) will include 95 percent of all the potential poll results. The smaller the standard deviation of the sample mean or the larger the sample size, the smaller the sampling error and the more precise the sample.

Measurement of variability is crucial in statistical inference. When one makes conclusions based on sample observations, one has to conduct a significance test to determine whether the conclusion holds true for the population from which the sample was drawn. Standard deviation and sampling error are required in many statistical formulas for tests of significance.

The total variability observed in data, measured as the total sum of squares (TSS), is not a meaningful summary measure of variability. TSS is crucial, however, for variability analysis in the social sciences. TSS is often separated into two parts: variation that can, to some extent, be predicted, given other related information, and variation that appears random and unexplainable given the available information. For example, through more advanced statistical analysis, it may be found that some variation of SAT scores in an area may be attributable to differences in the quality of schools or to the economic background of the student's family. The remaining variation remains unexplained. No matter which part is larger, some social or policy implications may be drawn from the analysis. As other information becomes available, additional unexplained variation may be accounted for. If a significant part of variation in SAT scores is explained by a variable, say the student/teacher ratio, it implies that the school district should consider increasing the teaching staff in order to improve student performance.

Context

Variety, diversity, and change are universal in any society. The development of a society is characterized by increasing specialization, greater complexity, and a more pronounced degree of social differentiation. There is a long history of using statistical measures of variability for summary reports in government and private agencies. For the social sciences, however, the task is, to a certain extent, not only to describe diversity and differentiation but also to explain the reasons for the differences. For example, how and why do economic situations vary over time? To what extent are students' educational achievements attributable to family background? How can one evaluate public opinion toward policies or political candidates? What accounts for failures of manufactured products? Variability measures and analyses have been extensively used in these kinds of studies.

Since the late 1960's, when computer statistics packages became available, empirical studies in the social sciences have relied heavily on statistical analysis. As it is almost impossible for social studies to generate the type of experimental data used in the natural sciences, social studies are most often based on data collected from survey samples. Inferences about population characteristics are made on the basis of statistical analysis of the sample data. Measures of variability are essential for describing the sample data as well as for testing the significance of the inferences. The business world increasingly employs measure of product variation in order to optimize production inputs and processes. Statistically sound quality control can make the difference between profitability and bankruptcy.

In his book *Statistical Methods for Research Workers* (1925), Ronald A. Fisher, one of the founders of modern statistics, said: "Statistics may be regarded as (i) the study of population, (ii) the study of variation, (iii) the study of methods of the reduction of data." Although statistical techniques have improved remarkably in the ensuing decades, the basic principle of statistical analysis continues to be the understanding, explaining, and predicting of variability, based on representative samples. Studies of social differences, variety, diversity, and change can provide more accurate and reliable results if variability analysis is conducted with advanced statistical techniques.

Bibliography

Bohrnstedt, George W., and David Knoke. *Statistics for Social Data Analysis*. 2d ed. Itasca, Ill.: F. E. Peacock, 1988. In chapter 3, Bohrnstedt and Knoke introduce and discuss a number of alternative measures of variability for qualitative variables.

Darlington, Richard B., and Patricia M. Carlson. *Behavioral Statistics: Logic and Methods*. New York: Free Press, 1987. This book discusses some basic statistical concepts, data description techniques, and widely used inferential techniques with rich examples from social science. A useful feature of this book is that it includes some instruction for the use of major statistical packages.

Edwards, Allen L. *Expected Values of Discrete Random Variables and Elementary Statistics*. New York: John Wiley & Sons, 1964. This book emphasizes measures of variance and standard deviation for variables that can take only the value of 1 or 0 (standing for "yes/no," or "happened/not happened," and so on) and variables measured in the form of ranks.

Hartwig, Frederick, and Brian E. Dearing. *Exploratory Data Analysis*. Beverly Hills, Calif.: Sage Publications, 1979. This is a good book for people with no mathematics or statistics background to use to start learning about data description and analysis. Readers can obtain a basic knowledge of variability.

Hildebrand, David K. *Statistical Thinking for Behavioral Scientists*. Boston: Duxbury Press, 1986. Hildebrand's book is written in conventional language. It is accessible to students with only a high school mathematics background. Basic concepts of measures of variability are discussed in chapter 1.

Jichuan Wang
James H. Fisher
Jiajian Chen

Cross-References

Experimentation in Sociological Research, 721; Inferential Statistics, 983; Measures of Central Tendency, 1147; Quantitative Research, 1546; Samples and Sampling Techniques, 1680; Surveys, 2030.

THE MEDICAL PROFESSION AND THE MEDICALIZATION OF SOCIETY

Type of sociology: Major social institutions
Fields of study: Medicine; Theories of deviance

Medicalization occurs when nonmedical problems or events—social problems and natural life processes—are labeled and treated as medical problems. Although not solely responsible, the medical profession, by virtue of its status in society, plays an important role in determining which social problems and events will be handled as medical problems by providing medical labels, diagnoses, and treatment plans.

Principal terms

DECONTEXTUALIZATION: taking something out of context; for example, if homelessness is defined as mental illness, homelessness' social context of unemployment and lack of affordable housing can be ignored

DEVIANCE: action or behavior that is inconsistent with what a particular society defines as normal and acceptable

LABELING THEORY: states that once an individual's behavior has been classified, society will see and treat the individual with respect to that definition, which in turn will cause the individual to conform to the definition; for example, individuals labeled as schizophrenics will be treated by others as mentally ill and will learn to act like schizophrenics

MEDICAL MODEL: a procedural structure that consists of defining a problem in scientific, technological, medical jargon; adopting a biological and/or chemical explanation of the problem that is consistent with current knowledge in medicine; and using medical intervention to "treat" the problem

NATURAL LIFE PROCESSES: states of being, changes, or events that occur throughout the life cycle; for example, sexuality, childbirth, child development, adolescence, menstruation, menopause, aging, and death

PROFESSION: an organization that has political control and a monopoly over its activity through formal education, licensing, regulations, and symbols

SOCIAL CONTROL: the use of formal and informal mechanisms by society to enforce dominant beliefs, values, and behavior

Overview

Medicalization, in the neutral sense of the word, simply means to define or classify a problem within the medical model. Because of increasing social awareness and critical assessment in the late 1960's and 1970's, medicalization in the social sciences came to mean a critique of the ever-increasing power and authority of the medical profession to define not only social problems but also natural life processes as medical episodes. It was argued that medicalization occurred as a direct result of the growth in prestige, dominance, and jurisdiction of the medical community through the process of professionalization.

As outlined by sociologist Eliot Freidson in *Profession of Medicine* (1970), the medical profession, through self-regulation and the ability to regulate the activities of other health care professionals such as nurses, physicians' assistants, and occupational therapists, effectively controls the market for medical expertise, creating a medical monopoly. Concurring with Freidson's observation and his call for the deprofessionalization of medicine, political activist Ivan Illich, in his controversial book *Medical Nemesis* (1976), criticizes the medical establishment for the creation of iatrogenesis (illness caused by medical practice). He accuses the medical profession of extending its jurisdiction beyond biological illnesses and diseases to the sociocultural realm. The result is the "medicalization of life," ranging from needing a doctor's permission to miss school to medical judgments regarding eligibility for disability benefits and the right to die.

Defining social and cultural events as medical problems causes them to become decontextualized and individualized. For example, the diagnosis of chronic fatigue syndrome (an illness that primarily affects white-collar professionals) or carpal tunnel syndrome (which is the result of repetitious movement and is common among employees who use computer terminals) ignores the technological changes and working environments in which the symptoms occur. Instead of addressing the sociocultural causes of illness, such diagnoses cause individuals to be treated or medicated to help them cope, reinforcing the status quo.

Freidson and Illich do not point out that medical systems and practitioners are part of the larger society. Arguing against medical imperialism or conspiracy, sociologists Barbara Ehrenreich, Renee Fox, and Irving Zola suggest that medicalization is the result of the institutional structure, organization, and economics of health care as well as public acceptance. In a study of the development of obstetrics as a specialty, social historians Richard Wertz and Dorothy Wertz present several reasons for the decline in midwifery during the nineteenth century. As male physicians struggled to control the childbirth market in order to secure a steady income by endorsing extensive interventions, middle- and upper-class women's attitudes changed as well. It was considered more respectable and fashionable to rely on male physicians from the upper and middle class than to rely on midwives. During the twentieth century, technological advancements in medical procedures have facilitated the expansion of medicalization to include prenatal lifestyles and postnatal interaction. Women's inexperience in breast feeding has been labeled "insufficient milk syndrome," and breasts that do not conform to the Western ideal have been seen as the cause of "nipple problems"; both "conditions" require medical interventions. As cultural anthropologists Brigitte Jordan in *Birth in Four Cultures: A Crosscultural Investigation of Childbirth in Yucatan,*

Holland, Sweden, and the United States (1993) and Robbie Davis-Floyd in *Birth as an American Rite of Passage* (1992) document, childbirth has come to be viewed to varying degrees as a medical condition (in some cases, even as an illness) that can only be treated by a qualified medical professional, in spite of the natural childbirth movement.

Another example of the development and expansion of medical authority in conjunction with changing sociocultural attitudes and support is provided by sociologist Sydney Halpern's *American Pediatrics: The Social Dynamics of Professionalism, 1880-1980* (1988). Noting the importance of intraprofessional segments, interest groups, and society's emphasis on specialization, Halpern documents the rise of psychosocial pediatrics in the mid-1950's. During the 1920's and 1930's, pediatrics was responsible for the supervision of healthy children. Because the general practice of pediatrics was perceived by practitioners as tedious, dull, and routine, and was equated with low professional status, academic pediatricians promoted the necessity of a subspecialty in the 1950's and 1960's to attract students. Deviant behaviors—temper tantrums, bed-wetting, sleep disturbance, and discipline problems—became redefined as medical problems. Founded in the 1970's, psychosocial pediatrics was recognized as a separate subspecialty by the American Academy of Pediatrics in the 1980's, and federal and state governments began to provide medical reimbursements for psychosocial services, acknowledging society's acceptance of the redefinition of children's deviant behavior as an illness.

Without society's structural support, medical professionals could not be as influential in defining social problems as they are within their own domain. Western society, in particular the United States, values scientific knowledge, medical expertise, and technological skill, and Westerners often turn to medical experts to solve social, religious, and jural problems ranging from violence to unemployment. Faith in the scientific method and the medical model also makes possible medicalization by other interest groups. For example, a small group of Vietnam veterans was responsible for the diagnosis of post-traumatic stress disorder (PTSD) and its inclusion in 1980 in the third edition of the *Diagnostic and Statistical Manual of Mental Disorders* (DSM-III, the official diagnostic catalog of psychiatric illnesses). Similarly, lawyers, in an effort to reduce murder charges for their clients, were influential in the recognition of premenstrual syndrome (PMS) as a treatable illness.

According to Karen Pugliesi, the diagnosis of PMS sanctions women's feelings and expressions of anger in a socially acceptable way for both society at large and individual women. Because the PMS diagnosis provides a biological etiology (cause)—hormones—for the expression of feelings, such expression does not threaten valued images of the role of women as family harmonizers. Thus, women and other family members do not have to address issues of inequality, conflict, or chronic role strain. The advantage of medicalization in some cases is increased compassion for individuals exhibiting unacceptable or deviant social behavior, as is evident in the insanity defense.

Medicalization can also occur in opposition to the medical profession. For example, several consumer groups and patient rights advocates have called for euthanasia—medically assisted death—in some cases of terminal illness. The medical profession is opposing the medicalization of dying on ethical grounds, claiming that to do so would violate its life-saving oath.

It is also important to note that medicalization is bidirectional. Demedicalization can occur when society or an influential interest group no longer finds medical definitions or treatments to be appropriate. As a result of protest from the gay liberation movement, for example, homosexuality was removed from the DSM in 1973 by the American Psychiatric Association. The independent living movement is advocating a redefinition of people with disabilities (beginning with terminology—"physically challenged" is preferred to "disabled") in order to minimize their contact with medical care. And women who successfully inseminate with "turkey basters" or other devices challenge the necessity of medical intervention. Besides organized groups, other factors may lead to demedicalization in varying degrees, including technological advances such as home blood pressure kits, blood sugar kits, and home pregnancy tests as well as cost-containment policies encouraging self-care.

Applications

The process of medicalization uses the medical model, which focuses on individual pathology, physiological etiologies, and biomedical interventions to address deviant behavior and monitor normal behavior. Invoking the medical model causes the power to define, label, and intervene to shift from laypersons or nonhealth professionals to health professionals. For example, by medicalizing childbirth, physicians have come to control childbirth by means of constant monitoring, regulation of medications, induction of labor, and assisted delivery; in the past, women delivered by themselves or with the help of midwives. In cases of violent crime, psychiatrists and psychologists now determine whether the offenders are mentally ill. Members of the clergy or jurors might view behavior judged by health care professionals to be indicative of mental illness as a sin or a crime.

Once medically labeled and seen as falling within the domain of medical professionals, the problem or event is subjected to medical management. Treatment occurs in doctors' offices, community clinics, hospitals, and institutions. The final step in medicalization occurs when medical jargon becomes popular rhetoric. For example, defining children who are misbehaving as hyperactive or as suffering from a learning disorder has become commonplace.

In the last twenty years, there have been a number of case studies depicting medicalization to various degrees. Studies focusing on social deviance have examined such areas as madness, alcoholism, homosexuality, addiction, hyperactivity, learning disabilities, eating disorders (bulimia and anorexia), obesity, child abuse, and infertility. As has been noted above, the modern approach to childbirth is an example of the medicalization of a natural life process. Among other areas that have been medicalized are those of sexuality, child development, adolescence, menopause, aging, and death.

Thomas Cole, in his book *The Journey of Life: A Cultural History of Aging in*

America (1992), traces the change in definitions of old age between the Reformation and World War I, demonstrating the redefinition of aging as a disease. By the early twentieth century, aging was viewed as a biological process that was open to scientific inquiry. Focusing on the consequences of the medicalization of aging, Carol Estes and Elizabeth Binney contend that the medical model dominates aging research and funding. It also dictates access to services for the elderly through Medicare and Medicaid policies that require a physician's signature.

As indicated previously, medicalization need not be introduced or consciously supported by the medical profession. In her study on homelessness in New York City during the 1980's, anthropologist Arline Mathieu demonstrated the conscious use of medical labeling by politicians in conjunction with the media to divert attention from the immediate social causes of poverty: unemployment and the lack of adequate, affordable housing. By linking homelessness with mental illness, the city government was able to enforce social control and justify the removal of the homeless from public places by emphasizing the need for medical treatment. In 1987, the mayor of New York City declared that any homeless person could be taken to a psychiatric hospital for fifteen days of observation. Because of the growing number of homeless people and legal challenges to the constitutionality of forced institutionalization, policies designed to medicalize the homeless were replaced with policies designed to criminalize the homeless in 1989.

Because they are part of a major social institution, medical systems support dominant cultural beliefs and values, including racial bias, stereotypes, and Western ideals of physical and mental attractiveness. In her article "Medicalization of Racial Features: Asian American Women and Cosmetic Surgery" (*Medical Anthropology Quarterly* 7, March, 1993: 74-90), medical anthropologist Eugenia Kaw shows how plastic surgeons use medical jargon to describe the Asian American eye and nose as medical conditions to be treated. For example, the eyelid is characterized as having "excess fat" or "an absent or poorly defined superior palpebral fold," which is said to give the patient/client a sleepy or dull look. The small flattened nose is considered to exhibit "poor lobular definition," which is held to be associated with passivity. In both cases, racial prejudice associated with genetic physical features is present. Because of facial appearance, Asians in general and Asian women in particular have been stereotyped as being passive and dull. In order to escape racial prejudice and because Asian American women have internalized Western values to some degree, they seek "double-eyelid" surgery, nasal implants, and nasal tip refinement.

As the foregoing examples indicate, the consequences of medicalization can be far-reaching. It is clear that the role of medical professionals in the process of medicalization can take various forms, depending upon the organization and status of medical systems in different societies. As the organization of medicine continues to change in the United States, shifting from private practice and fee-for-service systems to corporate structures in which physicians are employees, instituted in an effort to reform health care and control costs, the role and status of the medical profession are sure to change, as is the extent of medicalization.

Context

Sociologists have always been concerned with issues of social control, power and authority, and inequality as well as with social institutions. Émile Durkheim (1858-1917), the father of sociology, believed that all societies exercise social control through laws and customs. Whereas some societies used repressive controls, complex societies integrated individuals through common values reinforced by means of social interaction. Drawing upon the work of Durkheim, the German sociologist Max Weber, and the psychoanalyst Sigmund Freud, sociologist Talcott Parsons demonstrated the controlling function of medicine in complex societies in his book *The Social System* (1951). When deviance (inappropriate behavior) is equated with illness, medicine and the acceptance of the "sick role" become the appropriate controlling devices for deviance. According to Parsons, the "sick role" requires that individuals follow a set pattern of norms and expectations controlled by doctors.

Although some early medical sociologists were concerned that medical social control would replace all other forms of social control, this has not occurred. What has occurred is an ever-increasing expansion of medical definitions and treatments for social problems and events in correlation with the rise of professionalization. Because of the authority to diagnose and treat that is vested in physicians, labeling theorists such as psychiatrist Thomas Szasz and sociologist David Rosanhan argue that illness is a consequence of the definition applied to certain behaviors by specific groups. Unfortunately, once the label is applied, both society and the labeled individual tend to act in accordance with the characteristics of the label.

Medicalization is an outgrowth of research interests in social control, professionalization, and labeling theory. Because medicalization is dependent on institutional structure, social organization, and the role and status of medicine within society, changes in sociopolitical and economic environments will influence the process of medicalization in the future.

Bibliography

Cole, Thomas R. *The Journey of Life: A Cultural History of Aging in America.* Cambridge, England: Cambridge University Press, 1992. By tracing popular images of old age throughout history, Cole demonstrates the medicalization of aging and the rise of gerontology and geriatrics.

Conrad, Peter, and Rochelle Kern. *The Sociology of Health and Illness: Critical Perspectives.* New York: St. Martin's Press, 1981. This collection of essays focuses on the social production of disease and illness, the social organization of medical care, critical debates, and alternative health care systems. Of particular interest are the chapters on professionalization, racism and sexism, and medical industries.

Conrad, Peter, and Joseph W. Schneider. *Deviance and Medicalization: From Badness to Sickness.* St. Louis: Mosby, 1980. Through an excellent literature review, the authors trace the increase in the use of the medical model, which replaced earlier religious and moral models in the definition of deviance. Especially useful as a reference tool.

Freidson, Eliot. *Profession of Medicine.* New York: Dodd, 1970. This is an excellent book on professionalization in general as well as on medicine in particular. Freidson effectively argues in favor of limiting both the extension of professional knowledge and professional autonomy.

Halpern, Sydney A. *American Pediatrics: The Social Dynamics of Professionalism: 1880-1980.* Berkeley: University of California Press, 1988. This is a case study of the development of pediatrics as a specialty. Using a historical analysis, the author contends that career enhancement, social status, and income were motivating forces in the development of pediatrics.

Illich, Ivan. *Medical Nemesis.* New York: Pantheon, 1976. This often-quoted, controversial book calls for the deprofessionalization of medicine. Illich argues that medical interventions and health policies can cause iatrogenesis—pain, sickness, and death—directly or indirectly by supporting industries and social institutions that generate ill-health.

Jordon, Brigitte. *Birth in Four Cultures: A Crosscultural Investigation of Childbirth in Yucatan, Holland, Sweden, and the United States.* 4th ed. Prospect Heights, Ill.: Waveland Press, 1993. This book demonstrates the degree of variation in the medicalization of childbirth within and between cultures. Even though Jordan's book stresses ideological alternatives to defining childbirth as an "illness" to be "treated"—notably, as a natural life event—all her examples show increasing medicalization.

Van Esterik, Penny. *Beyond the Breast-Bottle Controversy.* New Brunswick, N.J.: Rutgers University Press, 1989. For those interested in a global perspective, Van Esterik focuses on the role of medical knowledge, institutions, and practitioners in promoting the use of infant formula instead of breast-feeding in Third World countries. Students familiar with the Nestlè controversy in Latin America will find this book very interesting.

Waitzkin, Howard. *The Politics of Medical Encounters.* New Haven, Conn.: Yale University Press, 1991. Through case studies, Waitzkin explores how doctor-patient interactions minimize the social context of patient complaints and contribute to social control. For example, women who complain about the drudgery and demands of housework are medicated to conform to the social structure. This action serves to reinforce the existing social condition.

Joann Kovacich

Cross-References

The Aging Process, 53; Deviance: Biological and Psychological Explanations, 532; Health and Society, 852; Labeling and Deviance, 1049; Medical Sociology, 1166; Medical versus Social Models of Illness, 1172; The Medicalization of Deviance, 1178; The Institution of Medicine, 1185.

MEDICAL SOCIOLOGY

Type of sociology: Major social institutions
Field of study: Medicine

Medical sociology is an area of study that focuses on the social aspects of the causes and effects of health and illness within society. In doing so, medical sociologists attempt to explain the complex relationships between social characteristics and the development, treatment, and curing of illness; they also analyze the organization of health care.

Principal terms

DEVIANCE: behavior that violates social norms
FUNCTIONALISM: the view that society is composed of a set of interrelated parts that must maintain a balance to work together
PRESTIGE: social honor given to a person based on the social role the person occupies
SOCIAL NORMS: rules of acceptable social behavior defined by a social group
SOCIAL ROLE: a pattern of behavior defined by the expectations of the ways individuals behave in particular social situations

Overview

Medical sociology is the study of the social facets of health and illness. It applies sociological principles to the study of topics such as the organization of health care, the socialization of health professionals, sociocultural responses to illness, the nature of the patient-practitioner relationship, and virtually every other health-related subject. Sociologist Robert Straus suggested in 1957 that medical sociology could be divided into two subcategories representing two different approaches to studying similar phenomena. The first he called the sociology of medicine. This category comprises the application of basic sociological theories and principles to the study of medical issues. The sociology of medicine represents an academic pursuit indicative of a basic research approach designed to gain better understanding and insight as to how the health care system operates. The second category is sociology *in* medicine, which includes those who work in medical environments attempting to use sociological principles to help solve medical or patient care problems and represents an applied research approach.

For example, one medical sociologist examining the patient-practitioner relationship might view the interaction between the patient and the physician as an example of the ways people of different status behave in a particular situation. Understanding how patients and physicians deal with one another should provide greater insight into, and understanding of, the ways in which members of society interact in general. This approach is indicative of the orientation of the sociology of medicine. Another medical sociologist may study the relationship between a patient and a physician to understand better what methods of communication work well and which ones result in a breakdown in communication. By better understanding the nature of the interaction in this manner, the sociologist hopes to improve the level of communication between the patient and the practitioner. This approach exemplifies the orientation of sociology in medicine.

Medical sociologists traditionally have been employed primarily in sociology departments in universities. They can also be found in schools of public health, medical schools, health administration programs, and allied health profession programs. Nonacademic medical sociologists are employed by federal, state, and local agencies as well as by health care consulting organizations. In either case, they may adhere to either or both of the approaches to medical sociology, although academic medical sociologists tend to adhere to the sociology of medicine approach, whereas medical sociologists in nonacademic positions tend to subscribe to the sociology in medicine approach.

What adherents to both approaches have in common is their search for the causes and consequences of health and illness. As the field of medicine continues to advance at a staggering rate, medical sociologists are confronted by a widening array of outcomes of progress. Each new technological innovation has ramifications for people involved in the health care system, both as patients and as providers of care. Medical sociology strives to provide coherent analyses and explanations of these effects.

Applications

The medical sociological perspective has been applied to every aspect of health, illness, and the delivery of health care. Perhaps the most important application is in analyzing and assessing the nature of the patient-practitioner relationship.

The results of research conducted by medical sociologists are used to gain a keener understanding of how the health care system works and how social factors affect the ways in which individuals interact with different components of the system. Sociologist Talcott Parsons, in his book *The Social System* (1951), developed and presented his view of the social nature of the relationship that develops between a patient and a doctor. As a functionalist, Parsons conceived of society as consisting of interrelated parts. Every member of society occupies multiple social statuses, each with sets of expected behaviors known as roles. For society to continue running smoothly, every member must fulfill his or her role obligations. Those failing to fulfill their roles are considered deviant by society. Deviant behavior is potentially disruptive to the social system and must therefore be controlled.

Illness temporarily prevents people from fulfilling the tasks and obligations associated with their roles. To maintain social order, Parsons maintains, the sick individual must assume a new role, which he termed the sick role. The sick role, like every other social role, comes complete with a set of tasks and obligations that the individual is expected to fulfill. First, the sick individual must recognize that being ill is undesirable and must try to get well. Second, the individual is obligated to seek technically competent help. (To Parsons, technically competent help takes the form of a physician.) The third obligation is that the sick individual must comply with the treatment prescribed by the physician. In return for meeting these obligations, the individual occupying the sick role is granted two exemptions. First, the individual is exempted from responsibility for his or her own illness. Second, the individual is temporarily exempted from performing his or her normal roles. The collective goal of this process is to return the sick individual to his normal roles as quickly as possible.

At the same time, physicians occupy a professional status which also has a set of role expectations. First, the physician is expected to act in the patient's best interests rather than in his or her own interests. Second, he or she must be guided by established rules of professional behavior. These rules represent ethical guidelines that the physician is expected to follow during the course of treatment. Third, the physician is expected to apply a high degree of skill and knowledge to solve the patient's health problems. Finally, the physician must be objective and emotionally detached when dealing with the patient. In return for fulfilling these role expectations, the physician is accorded the following three privileges. First, the physician is granted access to personal and emotional intimacy with the patient. Second, the physician is granted "practice autonomy," or the freedom to practice competent medicine in the way the physician sees fit. Third, physicians are granted professional dominance; that is, only licensed physicians can practice medicine in American society.

When the people occupying these roles interact, the outcome is, according to Parsons, predictable. Because Parsons views illness as a subset of deviant behavior, it is logical that the physician must, as part of the professional role, assume the responsibility for controlling the patient's behavior. This aspect of the patient-practitioner relationship mandates that the physician be in control. That is, the physician has the power in the relationship and the patient, by the definition of the sick role, must obey. Parsons argues that the power in the relationship shifts from the patient to the physician for three reasons. First, physicians have a high level of prestige in Western society. Second, the physician is assumed to have the expertise that the patient needs and wants in order to regain health. Finally, the patient is dependent on the physician because he or she lacks the knowledge that a competent physician possesses. The combination of the second and third reasons results in a "competence gap": a wide gap between what the patient and the physician know about medicine and between their respective levels of expertise.

The Parsonian view of the patient-practitioner relationship is considered to be the traditional sociological perspective. More recently, however, medical sociologists Marie R. Haug and Bebe Lavin, in their book *Consumerism in Medicine: Challenging Physician Authority* (1983) and in other research on the topic, present a different view of the patient-practitioner relationship. Haug and Lavin view the patient as a consumer of health care rather than as a deviant. Given this consumerist perspective, the patient is seen to have every right to question the physician and challenge physician authority when necessary, and the patient need not blindly obey the physician's directives. Therefore, the consumerist model is in direct opposition to the traditional Parsonian view of the patient-practitioner relationship.

One assumption of this perspective is that patients have become more intelligent about their own health and about health care in general. The proliferation of medical self-help books and magazines, the coverage of medical advances in newspapers, and television coverage of a wide range of health care issues have all served to educate patients. This increased level of education, in turn, has made the patient less dependent on the physician. In other words, the wide competence gap that Parsons believed is the basis for the shift of power to the physician has narrowed considerably. This narrowing of the competence gap, according to Haug and Lavin, has shifted the power back to the patient (or consumer).

The emergence of the patient as consumer is part of the more general societal consumerist movement. Since the 1960's, consumers have achieved greater power. Proponents of the consumerist approach in health care believe that the patient, like any other customer, is entitled to the type and quality of service he or she wishes. Therefore, rather than blindly accepting the physician's authority, the consumerist patient wants and deserves an equal voice in the development of a treatment plan.

The consumerist approach to the patient-practitioner relationship continues to grow among patients. In general, older patients still consider the physician to be the sole power broker in the relationship; younger patients are demanding and receiving greater input regarding how the relationship will operate. The results of sociological research on the nature of the patient-practitioner relationship have helped social scientists to understand better the nature of social interaction and have provided guidance in building better relationships between patients and their doctors.

Context

In his book *Medical Sociology* (1980), medical sociologist Minako K. Maykovich describes the development of the field of medical sociology as an evolutionary process involving the merging of medicine and sociology. This process can be viewed as flowing through three distinct stages. The first, known as the embryonic stage, covers the historical period through the Renaissance. During this stage, both medicine and sociology were indistinguishable from religion, which formed the basis of human attempts to explain daily occurrences. During the divergent stage (the seventeenth through the twentieth centuries), medicine and sociology began developing as separate disciplines. (Medicine began developing much earlier than sociology, which did not appear until the late nineteenth century.) It was not until the mid-twentieth century, during the convergent stage of development, that the melding of medicine and sociology occurred. Most of the converging process occurred in the United States. Thus, historically speaking, medical sociology is a relatively recent phenomenon. As medical sociologist William C. Cockerham notes in his book *Medical Sociology* (1989), medicine was not the sole factor in the development of medical sociology:

What prompted sociologists to organize medical sociology as an area of sociological inquiry in its own right was neither medicine nor biology, but the realization that medical practice represented a distinct segment of society with its own unique social institutions, social processes, occupations, problems, and behavioral settings.

Although some work in the area appeared during the first half of the twentieth century, medical sociology was viewed as more of an interest than a discipline. In 1955, however, the Committee of Medical Sociology was formed by the American Sociological Association (ASA). This served as the first step toward legitimizing medical sociology as a separate and distinct field of study. The ASA formally recognized and added the Section of Medical Sociology to its complement of specialty sections in 1959. The following year, a separate ASA-sponsored quarterly publication, the *Journal of Health and Social Behavior*, became the official journal of the section and still serves as a primary source of the most recent research in the field.

The Section on Medical Sociology has grown steadily since its inception. In the early 1990's it had more than 1100 members, and, as Cockerham pointed out, "one out of every ten American sociologists is a medical sociologist." Research on every aspect of the field increases daily. As Cockerham has declared, "the position of medical sociology itself is very healthy."

Bibliography

Armstrong, David. *An Outline of Sociology as Applied to Medicine*. 3d ed. London: Wright, 1989. This short, easy-to-read book highlights several of the key topics covered by medical sociologists. The bibliography is also short and basic and is not very thorough.

Brown, Phil, ed. *Perspectives in Medical Sociology*. Belmont, Calif.: Wadsworth, 1989. Brown presents forty-five articles on a variety of topics central to the field of medical sociology. These articles are broken into five parts and thirteen sections. Most of the traditional aspects of the field are covered, and several newer areas of interest are highlighted.

Cockerham, William C. *Medical Sociology*. 4th ed. Englewood Cliffs, N.J.: Prentice-Hall, 1989. A good introductory text overviewing the field of medical sociology. What differentiates this book from other generic medical sociology texts is its public health approach. This book has an extensive bibliography.

Haug, Marie R., and Bebe Lavin. *Consumerism in Medicine: Challenging Physician Authority*. Beverly Hills, Calif.: Sage Publications, 1983. A thorough analysis of the role of consumerism in the American public health care system. The topic is reviewed from both the patient and physician perspectives.

Jonas, Steven. *An Introduction to the U.S. Health Care System*. 3d. ed. New York: Springer, 1992. A useful introduction to the way health care is delivered in the United States. Each chapter ends with two to three pages of relevant references. This book is well indexed and is useful for gaining a better understanding of how the health care system works.

Maykovich, Minako K. *Medical Sociology*. Sherman Oaks, Calif.: Alfred, 1980. An introductory text to the field of medical sociology. Its unique feature is the application of general theoretical orientations to research in health care. The book is somewhat dated, but it does provide an excellent analysis of the historical development of medical sociology as a field.

Parsons, Talcott. *The Social System.* Glencoe, Ill.: Free Press, 1951. Outlines Parsons' functionalist perspective on the nature of social order and disorder. Recommended primarily for those with advanced knowledge of sociology, as the book is often difficult.

Raffel, Marshall W., and Norma K. Raffel. *The U.S. Health System: Origins and Functions.* 3d ed. New York: Wiley, 1989. This book provides a concise history of the development of health care in the United States. It has no bibliography, but there is a useful appendix which lists the acronyms commonly used in the field.

Straus, Robert. "The Nature and Status of Medical Sociology." *American Sociological Review* 22 (April, 1957): 200-204. This article outlines the differences between sociology in medicine and the sociology of medicine.

Wolinsky, Fredric D. *The Sociology of Health: Principles, Practitioners, and Issues.* 2d ed. Belmont, Calif.: Wadsworth, 1988. This book provides an excellent overview of the field of medical sociology. It is recommended for those with little or no background in the field. It is easy to read and well indexed, and it has a complete bibliography.

Ralph Bell

Cross-References

The Germ Theory of Medicine, 839; Health and Society, 852; Health Care and Gender, 858; Inequalities in Health, 966; The Medical Profession and the Medicalization of Society, 1159; Medical versus Social Models of Illness, 1172; The Medicalization of Deviance, 1178; The Institution of Medicine, 1185; Social Epidemiology, 1793.

MEDICAL VERSUS SOCIAL MODELS OF ILLNESS

Type of sociology: Major social institutions
Fields of study: Key social structures; Medicine

The accepted models of illness and disease delineate the role of the health care system and its professionals in Western society. In order to foster clear expectations and assign responsibilities, definitions of health and disease are needed. Without agreement on what constitutes illness, the medical profession faces increasing demands for intervention in a variety of physical, mental, emotional, and social problems.

Principal terms
DISEASE: a theoretically unhealthy condition; an impairment of normal functioning
EMPIRICISM: the belief that theoretical constructs, such as those of health, illness, and disease, can be defined without reference to value judgments or cultural norms
HEALTH: freedom from disease or illness
HEALTH CARE SYSTEM: the broad spectrum of service providers intended to have a positive effect on the health of individuals in society
ILLNESS: an unhealthy condition; an undesirable condition that confers upon its bearer the sick role
MALADY: a condition that involves suffering or the increased risk of suffering death, pain, or disability
NORMATIVISM: the belief that theoretical constructs, such as those of health, illness, and disease, cannot be defined without reference to value judgments or cultural norms
SICK ROLE: a social structure conferred upon the bearer of an illness which brings with it elements of diminished responsibility and obligation to strive for health

Overview
During the twentieth century, the abilities of the medical profession to cure disease, alleviate pain, and improve health grew tremendously. The expectations of these abilities have grown even more. Medical professionals are now often cast in the role of gate-keepers, able to control access to an enormous variety of services by their diagnoses of what constitutes eligibility through medical need. More and more conditions are being defined as diseases, from social ills, such as poverty, to addictions of all sorts, to predilections for certain lifestyles. The classification of a condition as a disease establishes the authority and obligation of the medical profession to attempt to cure it, as well as the expectation that the bearer of the disease will wish to be cured.

The classic, empirical, medical model of disease is the most time-honored, at least in the stated belief of what constitutes disease, if not the common use of the term. This model holds that disease is present when an organism or one of its parts is not functioning as it was designed to do by nature. Health, then, is the efficient functioning of an organism as it has evolved genetically. An advantage of this view is that it is applicable to all living organisms: humans, animals, and plants. An organism can be determined to be healthy or diseased without reference to symptoms that are subject to interpretation by either their bearer or their evaluator. This model does not address, however, the question of exactly what nature intended for a specific organism. Because a few members of a species can do something, does that mean that nature intended for the whole group to be able to do it?

Another model of disease is based on statistical evidence of what is normal. Disease is that which is statistically deviant. Again, this model is attractive in that it is not based on value judgments, but it ends up classifying many things that society sees as positive traits, such as extreme intelligence or strength, as disease. Its supporters argue that the determination of what is normal is often based on statistical evidence. If 98 percent of an adult population can talk, then it is abnormal not to be able to talk.

Both of these medical models of illness leave something to be desired. Neither is satisfactory in answering the question of whether an organism is diseased when a malfunction or nonfunction is present but does not cause impairment to the organism as a whole. The sickle-cell trait, for example, is an adaptation that is designed to protect the bearer from malaria, but it makes the organism more likely to contract certain blood disorders. According to medical models, this is a disease, but under ordinary circumstances a person with this trait would be considered completely healthy.

These models also do not address the other extreme, when nothing in an organism seems to be malfunctioning yet symptoms of ill health are present. This is especially common in the area of mental health. Although more and more organic foundations are being established for mental illnesses, such as depression and schizophrenia, other illnesses are still only attributable to nonorganic or unknown causes.

The normative models of health, illness, and disease help to address these issues. Proponents of normativism believe that the concepts of health and its counterparts incorporate societal and cultural values. What is considered illness depends on what a particular culture deems valuable. Dyslexia, for example, would not be considered a disease in a society with no written language. The designation of illness depends on a society's willingness to classify a particular situation as undesirable.

Normative models have traditionally been used in society to determine what constitutes disease, although it is rarely clear that societal values are being incorporated in definitions. Classifications of disease have changed over time, partially because of advances in medical knowledge, but also because of changes in what society sees as desirable. In the seventeenth century United States, it was believed that a disease called drapetomania caused otherwise content and reliable slaves to have the uncontrollable urge to run away from their masters and escape to freedom. Likewise, medical textbooks from previous centuries are full of diseases that were believed to strike at the weaker physiques and sensibilities of upper-class women.

Some writers have proposed a different meaning, for purposes of clarification, for the terms "disease," "illness," and "malady." In 1975, Christopher Boorse presented, in his article "On the Distinction Between Disease and Illness" (in *Philosophy and Public Affairs* 5, no. 1), the argument that the term "disease" should be used to refer to the empirical view of the impairment of normal functioning in an organism. "Illness" then could be used to include normative characteristics of undesirability of the condition to society and to exclude those diseases that do not give the bearer the right to the special treatment that a sick person gets. Charles M. Culver and Bernard Gert, in *Philosophy in Medicine* (1982), suggested using the term "malady" as a more inclusive word to cover any condition that causes the bearer to suffer or be at increased risk of suffering death, pain, or disability. While everyday language does not distinguish between these terms, the consequences of not doing so cause the expectations that the health care system will cure all diseases, illnesses, or maladies to become unrealistically high.

Applications

In Western society, the condition of being ill carries with it certain obligations and expectations. The sick person has diminished responsibilities, often in the form of being excused from work or school, and he or she is not held accountable for his or her actions to as great a degree as usual, especially in cases of mental illness. In return, the ill person is expected to participate in the cure: to follow a doctor's orders, to want to get well. The guidelines of the "sick role" carry with them all sorts of unwritten rules and understandings.

For decades, Western culture has been classifying an ever-increasing variety of behaviors as "sick." Any form of unwelcome behavior, from homicidal mania to the particularly annoying behavior of a child or coworkers, is said to be "sick." This usage implies that the person can and should be cured by a health professional. The health care system has tried to meet this demand, developing techniques and treatments for altering behaviors that had previously been thought merely eccentricities, lack of self-control, or bad luck.

The World Health Organization in 1946 gave the following definition of health: "Health is a state of complete physical, mental and social well-being and not merely the absence of disease or infirmity." This definition has daunting consequences for the health care system. Its extremely broad concept of health forces the system to try to cure such social illnesses as poverty, lack of education, and hunger; undesirable mental states, including discontent and unhappiness; and traditional physical problems.

There are two factors that contribute to the compulsion to label certain conditions illnesses: the sick role and its connotations, and the wish to believe in a cure. These factors have given rise to several controversial classifications.

Alcoholism is now generally accepted as a disease, although in the past it has been variously identified as a crime, a sin, and a moral fault. Advocates for those that suffer from other addictions—drugs, gambling, overeating, and others—continue to lobby to have their particular problems labeled diseases. A label brings with it funding and access to treatment, as well as the excusing of behavior that comes with the sick role. As long as an alcoholic or other addict is doing his or her best to fight the addiction (as perceived by others), then he or she is allowed a fair amount of leeway in behavior, and often is held blameless for past actions.

Homosexuals, however, continue to fight against the label of mental illness that was once conferred on them by the American Psychiatric Association. Although the disease label carries with it the element of diminished responsibility (most Westerners, however, view homosexuality as either not needing an excuse or inexcusable), it also carries the expectation that the disease should be cured. In the case of homosexuals, this implies that, if the classification of disease is accepted, those who "suffer" from this trait must do their best to eradicate this behavior, even through pharmaceutical treatment or surgery. Furthermore, it means that the health care system should devote time, personnel, and money in an attempt to achieve this eradication.

The ramifications of the disease label are perhaps most easily seen in the legal system. A major division in law occurs in determining consequences for the individual who is responsible for deviant actions versus one who is not responsible because of mental illness. Even in a particular case, there are widely varying opinions regarding how culpability should be determined. One of the most recent areas of controversy is the designation of premenstrual syndrome as a valid legal exculpation. Proponents of the disease classification point to the abnormally high hormone levels in those who suffer from the syndrome, thus giving evidence of physical malfunction beyond the control of the sufferer. Others, however, worry that the label and legal use of it will lead to further discrimination against all women, a propagation of the stereotypes of women as slaves to their emotions, irrational, and lacking in self-control. The stigma of the label of disease could, in this case, make the social status of the group worse while benefiting the individual involved.

Context

The controversy over disease classification has arisen along with advances in medical knowledge and the subsequent increased status of the medical profession. The ability to establish physiological bases for conditions previously thought to have been signs of sinful behavior and divine displeasure has allowed many people to seek treatment for conditions that would otherwise have been hidden and ignored as much as possible. This ability has led many to believe, however, that medicine can cure every evil of society. Medicine is called upon to act as a supporter of numerous causes, from the use of physicians as political tools in Nazi Germany, to the day-to-day provision of absence notes from school or work for illness. This medicalization of society continues to expand.

The classification of a particular condition as a disease does not immediately change society's attitudes. Before the introduction of psychotherapy, severely mentally disturbed patients were confined to crude hospitals that were designed not to treat people but to segregate them from the rest of society. With the advent of psychoanalysis, it began to be shown that there were causes for these mental problems and that they were not merely arbitrary signs of God's displeasure. The stigma of mental illness still exists, however, several decades after medicine began to be able to treat many conditions effectively with both drug therapy and psychotherapy.

Other diseases also retain their stigmas, especially those that are considered to be self-caused. Alcoholism may be a disease, but cirrhosis of the liver brought on by drinking does not inspire the same sympathy that, for example, cancer or heart disease does. At the center of society's attitudes toward the victims of AIDS, which is indisputably a disease, lies the belief that sufferers brought it on themselves.

Western culture's perceptions of the duties of the medical profession will continue to expand as long as clear definitions of health, disease, and illness are not established. Unless it can be agreed what constitutes health and the lack of health, the genuine skills of health care professionals will be wasted trying to alleviate suffering outside their own jurisdiction. A brief look at the still burgeoning number of medical malpractice cases illustrates the inflated beliefs in physicians' abilities.

It also must be established whether the role of the health care system is to eliminate disease or to promote health. In the past, people have turned to the medical profession in times of crisis, when illness was obviously present. If health is more than just the absence of disease, a health care system must do more than simply cure people of illnesses. As the concept of health changes, so will the assignment of responsibilities, both to the health-care system, and to those who make use of it.

Bibliography

Beauchamp, Tom L., and LeRoy Walters, eds. *Contemporary Issues in Bioethics*. 3d ed. Belmont, Calif.: Wadsworth, 1989. An anthology of almost one hundred essays on various issues in bioethics, this textbook contains an excellent section on the conceptual foundations of the definitions of health and disease. Included are the World Health Organization's definition of health and commentary on it, as well as the Boorse article "On the Distinction Between Disease and Illness." Each essay has its own bibliography, but no index is included for the collection.

Caplan, Arthur L., H. Tristam Engelhardt, Jr., and James J. McCartney, eds. *Concepts of Health and Disease: Interdisciplinary Perspectives*. Reading, Mass.: Addison-Wesley, 1981. The definitive collection on the topic, this volume contains an impressive array of articles on every aspect of the subject. Written by members of the medical profession, philosophers, ethicists, and others, this work gives a comprehensive overview of the concepts as they existed when it was published. Although it does not discuss some of the more recent controversies, it is an indispensable resource for further study. Essays contain their own notes and bibliographies. Author and subject indexes are provided for the volume as a whole.

Coe, Rodney M. *Sociology of Medicine*. New York: McGraw-Hill, 1970. Dated but easy to understand, this book is good in its assessment of the stigma of illness and in its discussion of other cultures' responses to illness and disease. Includes extensive footnotes, suggested readings, and an index.

Culver, Charles M., and Bernard Gert. *Philosophy in Medicine: Conceptual and Ethical Issues in Medicine and Psychiatry.* New York: Oxford University Press, 1982. This clearly written book is a good place to begin a study of definitions of disease and illness. It includes the discussion of the use of the term "malady" in place of these and examines the consequences of such a change. Includes notes, references, and a limited index.

Eisenberg, Leon, and Arthur Kleinman, eds. *The Relevance of Social Science for Medicine.* Boston: D. Reidel, 1981. A collection of articles meant to demonstrate the relevance of social science to the medical professional, this book is not easy reading, but it contains an excellent section on sickness behavior and the sick role. It also includes an article on the consequences of labeling from biomedical and social perspectives that is extremely thorough in its discussion and documentation. Extensive references plus name and subject indexes.

Freund, Peter E. S., and Meredith B. McGuire. *Health, Illness, and the Social Body.* Englewood Cliffs, N.J.: Prentice-Hall, 1991. A selection of themes in the sociology of medicine, this text sets forth several views on the social context of ideas and experiences of disease. Clearly written and well documented, this is an exceedingly useful book. Appendices include "Literature in the Sociology of Health and Illness" and "Visual Resources" as well as a sixty-three page bibliography and author and subject indexes.

Veatch, Robert M., ed. *Medical Ethics.* Boston: Jones & Bartlett, 1989. The best place to start in a study of concepts of health and disease, this text consists of chapters on various topics written by leading scholars. The chapter "The Concepts of Health and Disease," by Arthur L. Caplan, provides a concise overview of the topic and a good bibliography. An index and a glossary are included for the book as a whole.

Margaret Hawthorne

Cross-References

Alcoholism, 74; Deviance: Biological and Psychological Explanations, 532; Drug Use and Addiction, 572; Health and Society, 852; Labeling and Deviance, 1049; The Medical Profession and the Medicalization of Society, 1159; Medical Sociology, 1166; The Medicalization of Deviance, 1178; The Institution of Medicine, 1185.

THE MEDICALIZATION OF DEVIANCE

Type of sociology: Deviance and social control
Field of study: Theories of deviance

The medicalization of deviance refers to the extent to which medical labels are applied to actions that are considered violations of normative behavior. The sociological conceptualization of medicalization acknowledges the extent to which medicine has become a major institution of social control.

Principal terms

DEVIANCE: the recognized violation of cultural norms

IDEOLOGY: an array of ideas actively expressing the way in which a group views the functioning of society's political, economic, and cultural institutions and activities

INSTITUTIONS: relatively stable arrangements designed to meet societal goals efficiently

MEDICALIZATION: the proliferation of medical explanations for behavior, especially deviant behavior, in various spheres of life

SOCIAL IATROGENESIS: the process whereby the medical profession, in its role as arbiter of illness and disease, defines, and therefore creates, illness

Overview

The medicalization of deviance refers to the practice of defining deviant behavior either as an illness or as a symptom of an illness or disease. Through the application of social iatrogenesis, medical ideology serves as a type of social control that, as sociologists Peter Conrad and Joseph Schneider (1980) contend, "involves defining a behavior or condition as an illness primarily because of the social and ideological benefits accrued by conceptualizing it in medical terms." Conrad and Schneider have proposed the use of a five-stage sequential model in identifying the process of medicalization: defining the behavior as deviant, prospecting, making claims for medical and nonmedical reasons, legitimating (securing the medical turf), and institutionalizing the medical deviance designation.

Acts that have been medicalized during the twentieth century have typically been considered deviant before they have been medicalized. For example, madness, chronic drunkenness, drug addiction, homosexuality, obesity, delinquency, and criminal activities were all considered "deviant" or unacceptable behaviors prior to the publication of medical reports about them. In the second stage, in which the publication of research centering on new diagnoses occurs, the medical etiology and treatment of deviant behavior are used by organizational actors and institutions to facilitate the process of medicalization. During this stage, actors (physicians, investigatory committees, academics, professional and lay organizations, and so forth) begin pushing for medicalized deviance designations, seeking legitimation in the courts. It is at this point that the medical profession may be viewed as an agent of social control. By granting the medical profession partial jurisdiction over criminal behaviors, the state enlists the support of medicine to eliminate potential sources of social instability. The final stage in the medicalization of deviance is institutionalization. Once they are institutionalized, medical definitions of deviance achieve a level of semipermanence in law and medical practice.

Traditional conceptualizations of deviance referred to violations of religious and legal principles, but sociologist Talcott Parsons argued that the American value system—emphasizing activism, worldliness, instrumentalism, and individual achievement—inevitably led to a prioritization of health as a way to attain such achievement. Consequently, in the United States, deviance is more likely to be considered a problem of health than of religion or law. Parsons' most significant contribution to the sociology of medicine was his articulation of the sick role as an integrative or positive application of medicalization. The sick role serves to remove individual responsibility for deviant actions, since illness has hampered clarity of thought, and to exempt the individual from maintaining normal obligations (such as work and family). Although illness allows individuals to deviate legitimately, they must be made to understand that being ill is undesirable, something they are obliged to overcome. In addition, since it is beyond the ability of the individual to overcome his or her illness, he or she is expected to seek competent (professional) assistance and to cooperate with prescribed treatments.

Medical sociologist Eliot Freidson takes issue with Parsons' "value consensus model," contending that the medical profession constructs states of "sickness" and "illness." Since the medical profession possesses absolute jurisdiction over the designation and treatment of illness, it acts as a system of social control by defining roles and regulating entry into them. Medicine may be said to create illness, since the identification and designation of illness and disease imply the creation of a social, not solely biological, experience. The medical profession, then, participates in the creation and sanctioning of the meaning of deviance designations.

In this view, the medical profession is anything but neutral. The ideological assumption of neutrality on the part of the medical profession is significant on at least two levels. First, the active role played by medical practitioners in defining disease and illness must be kept in mind. Second, medical practitioners often collaborate with other authorities by relating medical information to them. For example, industrial and military physicians and physicians in mental health institutions serve as "gatekeepers" who often wield the power to determine fitness for employment, to recommend medical discharges, or to prescribe medicines, thereby enhancing their power as agents of social control.

The medicalization of deviance must also be conceived of as a part of a larger social phenomenon—the individualization of social problems. In 1971, sociologist William Ryan labeled this process "blaming the victim"—in other words, locating the causes of social problems in individuals rather than in societal structures and institutions. The medical profession participates in the individualization of social problems through the exercise of treatment models that are designed to produce physiological and psychological adaptations in individuals rather than to contextualize those individuals' symptoms within an analysis of institutions.

Combining the process of medicalization with the individualization of social problems leads to the depoliticization of deviant behavior, or what sociologists Barbara Ehrenreich and John Ehrenreich have referred to as disciplinary control. If the medical profession can declare a person sick, insane, diseased, or drug addicted, there is no pressing need to view her or his concerns and protestations as potentially legitimate repudiations of existing political, economic, and cultural arrangements. The effect is to delegitimate the person and his or her ideas.

Applications

The conceptualization of deviant activities and behaviors within the context of medicalization has produced two particularly compelling sociological analyses: those of the medicalization of mental illness and the medicalization of the workplace.

While attempting to account for the role played by psychiatry in contemporary society, sociologist David Ingleby suggested that orthodox analyses of mental illness are characterized by three commonly held beliefs: that mental illness is naturally occurring in human beings, that those who offer treatment are driven by the desire to relieve pain and increase happiness, and that the dominating role of the medical profession is rational and justified. Critics of the orthodox view suggest, to the contrary, that mental illness is in large part socially constructed, that treatment is designed to enhance social control, and that the role of the medical profession in administering treatment is neither warranted nor desirable.

Prior to the mid-seventeenth century, the mentally ill were cared for by their families or, often traveling in groups, were free to roam the countryside (they were even floated in large ships known as "ships of fools"). Beginning in the mid-seventeenth century, however, confinement became the preferred means of handling the mentally ill, the unemployed, the disabled, and the poor. Confinement appeared as a Renaissance response to what social theorist Michel Foucault has referred to as the perceived "immorality of unreason" exhibited by the insane. Since those possessing qualities of madness lacked any ability to reason, logic suggested that they were more like animals than like human beings.

The early nineteenth century marks a transition in the ideological rationalization for the treatment of the insane. While the "classical" views held that the insane were incapable of rational thought, reformers such as Jeremy Bentham argued that they lacked self-discipline but were malleable—that is, capable of being "reprogrammed." This was a significant ideological transformation that was concomitant with the rise of capitalist social relations. Reformers championed the construction of multiple public asylums complete with annual inspections. It was the asylum itself, however, characterized by cruel and inhumane practices, that proved to be the greatest obstacle to reform. Recognizing the need to establish more humane treatment practices, nineteenth century reformers refocused their struggle by campaigning for treatment methods based on psychological control, the internalization of norms through behavior modification, and the submission of patients to the "family" of medical practitioners. Patients were promised a cure, and a focus on treatment, not punishment, made asylums more palatable to patients' families.

By 1850, the medical profession had established its place in the treatment of madness by attacking the perceived biological causes of insanity while inflicting extreme physical pain on patients. In addition, seemingly anticipating Parsons' articulation of the sick role, nineteenth century physicians claimed that the incarceration of the insane was a necessary component of treatment, something that served the patients' best interests. In this way, psychiatry assumed a task formerly held by representatives of law—that of acting as an entity of social control.

One may wonder why the medical profession assumed control of the treatment of insanity. Conventional reasoning suggests that physicians assumed prominence when it became apparent that juridical, religious, and familial actions had proved to be incompetent. Therefore, it is most likely, as Ingleby suggests, that "the extension of the doctors' role to the area of social problems was achieved not by the reduction of the latter to malfunctions of the body, but by the creation of a new area of medical expertise, which translated moral problems into technical ones."

The modern era of medical hegemony over deviance designations is characterized by three developments: the primacy of medical expertise; the expansion into new categories of pathology, especially neuroses, which can then be medicalized (for example, in the family, at work, and in schools); and the apparent neutrality of the medical profession at the level of interpretation and intervention. As a result, society is now experiencing what medical sociologist N. Kittrie has referred to as "the therapeutic state," in which a whole host of social problems are subsumed under the category of illness and exposed to treatment. In this way, the medical profession can act as an institution of social control without actually appearing to do so.

The medicalization of the workplace has produced a contemporary form of work-based behavioral control: employee drug testing. The medicalization of the workplace has emerged as a post-World War II phenomenon but has as its historical antecedents two centuries of management-directed efforts to control employees and institutional efforts to curb deviant behavior.

Technologies of surveillance that were initially implemented to effect changes in perceived individual deviance achieved sophistication during the nineteenth century. Jeremy Bentham's conceptualization of the panopticon is a compelling example. The panopticon was an architectural innovation that Bentham proposed as a way to moderate behavior in prison inmates. According to Bentham, if inmates were led to believe that they were continuously under the monitoring eye of prison officials, it would be possible to build a prison without bars. The key was for guards to see without being seen, while prisoners would be seen without being able to see. Components of the concept of the panopticon as a form of social control reappeared with the proliferation of employee drug testing in the 1980's.

The medicalization of the workplace began in the 1920's with the emergence of the initial wave of industrial physicians. Having long recognized the need for a healthy, predictable, sober work force, enlightened employers entered the world of industrial medicine. They were joined by social reformers, professionals, and labor unions. At the same time, industrial physicians initiated their own campaign to attain legitimacy within the medical profession. Because they were hired by firms to act as gatekeepers in determining "fitness for work," however, industrial physicians were often viewed with contempt by the organized medical profession because of their apparent violation of the Hippocratic oath.

Contemporary administration of employee drug testing serves an analogous purpose. Contextualized within the rightward shift of American politics and an associated emphasis on "new sobriety," employee drug testing was viewed as a way to address perceived increases in drug use and abuse, as well as to enhance American economic competitiveness. Drug testing attained political legitimacy in 1986, when President Ronald Reagan issued Executive Order 12564, calling for a "Drug Free Federal Workplace." The "Drug Free Workplace Act" became law in May of 1987. Employers explained their interest in employee drug testing by referring to estimates of lost productivity caused by absenteeism and to increased accident and injury rates, which were ostensibly the results of illicit drug use.

It is in analyzing employee drug testing as a derivative of medicalization that social control becomes apparent. In a society imbued with medicalization, it is possible to separate workers, based on some quality of health, into those who are healthy, and therefore desirable, and those who are sick, and therefore undesirable. Workers who fail drug tests face the stigma of being labeled drug users and are placed (by either choice or force) into "treatment" programs, usually along the lines of employee assistance programs (EAPs). Therefore, they become "wards" of the medical profession and must adopt the behavioral dictates of the sick role. More ominously, perhaps, is the fact that drug tests do not assess levels of productive output or even safety. They cannot even determine current impairment, but they can (when they function properly) identify what workers do in their leisure time. Random drug testing is most indicative of panopticism. Random drug testing is designed as a more efficient way to "select" precisely who will be tested. Since workers are never sure who will be tested, they will change their behavior in the event that they might be tested. The effect is analogous to that of Bentham's panopticon in that workers internalize efforts at workplace control.

The more significant issue for sociologists, however, is that an emphasis on individual qualities of health, as determined by employee drug tests, displaces the locus of attention from the organization of work—its intensity, levels of degradation, alienation, and so forth—and focuses instead on correcting so-called aberrant individual "deviants." If successful, the medicalization of the workplace serves to depoliticize the harmful effects of work as well as those employees who endeavor to change them.

Context

Even though associations between qualities of health and deviance have persisted in nominal references since the time of ancient Greece, it was not until the late nineteenth century that medical definitions of deviance began to achieve cultural hegemony.

Recognition of the increasing dominance of the medical profession as an institution capable of "creating" illness and disease led sociologists to initiate a rigorous analysis of the medicalization of deviance beginning in the 1950's, with the pioneering work of Talcott Parsons, Vilhelm Aubert and Sheldon Messinger, and Thomas Szasz.

The 1960's produced numerous theoretical breakthroughs related to the political, cultural, and economic significance of medicalization in increasing social control over the "different." Perhaps the most influential publication during this decade was Szasz's *The Myth of Mental Illness* (1964), which threw open to debate the social construction of "illness" as a product of the influence of the medical profession's attempts to claim jurisdiction over an ever-widening field of behaviors. In 1964, Thomas Scheff published a similar critique in his *Being Mentally Ill: A Sociological Theory*. On the heels of Szasz and Scheff, Eliot Freidson published his first major work in the area of medical sociology, *The Profession of Medicine* (1970). Freidson's work provided sociologists with the first comprehensive look at the social construction of illness.

Contributions to the literature of the medicalization of deviance continued throughout the 1970's and 1980's with the publication of numerous books and research articles. In addition to Freidson's work, there was Barbara Ehrenreich and Deirdre English's *Complaints and Disorders: The Sexual Politics of Sickness* (1973), followed later in the decade by their important book *For Her Own Good* (1979), which documents the historical encounters of women with the medical profession. French social theorist Michel Foucault added additional theoretical legitimacy to the work of American authors with the publication of numerous treatises on societal control mechanisms. His publication of *Madness and Civilization* (1963), *The Birth of the Clinic* (1973), and *Discipline and Punish* (1979) provide unparalleled theoretical insight into the medicalization of deviance. The publication in 1980 of Peter Conrad and Joseph Schneider's *Deviance and Medicalization: From Badness to Sickness* marked the maturation of a thirty-year-old literature.

Bibliography

Cohen, Stanley, and Andrew Scull, eds. *Social Control and the State*. New York: St. Martin's Press, 1983. This collection of essays addresses issues pertaining to state-sanctioned apparatuses of social control. Includes compelling analyses of the medicalization of the mentally ill, the poor, and the criminal.

Conrad, Peter, and Joseph Schneider. *Deviance and Medicalization: From Badness to Sickness*. St. Louis: Mosby, 1980. This book is essential for anyone who is interested in the study of the medicalization of deviance. Conrad and Schneider provide a thorough theoretical analysis of medicalization that is applicable to many acts previously given deviance designations.

Crawford, Robert. "Healthism and the Medicalization of Everyday Life." *International Journal of Health Services* 10, no. 3 (1980): 365-387. Crawford analyzes contemporary aspects of health and fitness within the context of medicalization. He suggests that the individualization of health problems leaves unaddressed the institutional causes of poor health.

Ehrenreich, Barbara, and Deirdre English. *For Her Own Good: 150 Years of the Experts' Advice to Women.* Garden City, N.Y.: Anchor Press, 1978. Provides in-depth historical and theoretical analysis of the medicalization of women's issues.

Foucault, Michel. *Madness and Civilization.* New York: Pantheon, 1965. This challenging book offers theoretical insight into the social construction of mental illness.

Freidson, Eliot. *The Profession of Medicine.* New York: Dodd, Mead, 1970. Generally considered to be the most significant early contribution to medical sociology and its efforts to assimilate the diverse literature challenging the medical profession's active role in the construction of illness behavior.

Illich, Ivan. *Medical Nemesis.* New York: Pantheon Books, 1976. Provides a critical account of social "iatrogenesis," or doctor-made illness, by providing a thorough analysis of medicalization and the social construction of illness.

Parsons, Talcott. *The Social System.* Glencoe, Ill.: Free Press, 1951. Parsons' extrapolation of the "sick role" formed the foundation for future analyses of the medicalization of deviance. In this volume, he identifies the social ramifications of medicalization in producing systemic stability.

Robert C. Schehr

Cross-References

Conflict Perspectives on Deviance, 334; Crime: Analysis and Overview, 373; Delinquency Prevention and Treatment, 476; Deviance: Analysis and Overview, 525; Deviance: Biological and Psychological Explanations, 532; Deviance: Functions and Dysfunctions, 540; Labeling and Deviance, 1049; The Medical Profession and the Medicalization of Society, 1159; Medical versus Social Models of Illness, 1172.

THE INSTITUTION OF MEDICINE

Type of sociology: Major social institutions
Field of study: Medicine

The institution of medicine is the social institution that deals with the issues that a society defines as medical or as being related to health care. This definition tends to expand as technology increases. Conflict theory, functionalism, and symbolic interactionism are the three most prevalent sociological perspectives used in studying medicine as a social institution.

Principal terms
  CONFLICT THEORY: a theoretical perspective that views social phenomena as being driven by conflict among groups in society that compete for power and economic resources
  FUNCTIONALISM: a theoretical perspective that proposes that society is composed of various social institutions that work together to maintain a stable social environment
  GERM THEORY OF DISEASE: promoted by Louis Pasteur, this theory stated that infectious diseases were caused by bacteria
  MACRO-THEORY: a theoretical perspective (such as conflict theory or functionalism) that examines social phenomena by analyzing societies or large groups within them without focusing on interaction among individuals
  MICRO-THEORY: a theoretical perspective that explains social phenomena in terms of daily interactions among individuals
  SOCIAL EPIDEMIOLOGY: the study of how various diseases are distributed among the population of a society; it makes it possible to determine the likelihood that members of certain social groups will contract various diseases
  SYMBOLIC INTERACTION: a theoretical perspective analyzing day-to-day interactions among individuals; symbolic interaction theory holds that social life is dependent on an individual's ability to interpret social symbols correctly and to perceive correctly his or her own role in relation to the roles of others

Overview

Like many other social institutions, the institution of medicine has not always existed in American society. In early American agrarian culture, many tasks that are now accomplished by other social institutions took place within the family. Education, work, and leisure were primarily the responsibility of one's family. Likewise, medical care was provided at home, usually by the females. A family usually kept a supply of items to be used for medical purposes. In his book *The Social Transformation of American Medicine* (1982), sociologist Paul Starr refers to this as the practice of "domestic medicine," which was part of the woman's role in the home.

American medicine had many difficulties in institutionalizing itself to the extent that physicians were relied upon heavily for the treatment of the sick. Early attempts to charter professional associations (similar to the American Medical Association) to grant licenses to practice were rejected by the rest of society. If physicians were to become the group consulted for the treatment of disease, a medical profession had to be established that would hold the confidence of the rest of American society. Yet prominent physicians envisioned the development of an elitist model for medical practice in which doctors would be viewed as high-status members of society. This type of profession was being developed successfully in Europe, but it was inconsistent with the democratic American temperament. Thus, efforts to elevate physicians to an elite position in American society met with difficulty because to do so was contrary to the prevailing culture. According to Paul Starr, American culture was becoming more egalitarian and democratic, while those in the medical profession sought to elevate themselves to elite positions in society. In addition, the ineffectiveness of many medical treatments was largely responsible for the lack of confidence of the American people in early medicine. People simply did not trust an institution that had not proved that it could deliver services superior to those of other forms of healing.

Several factors played a major role in causing medicine to become an institutionalized profession. First, scientific advances greatly improved medical knowledge and the success of physicians in treating various illnesses. The "germ theory of disease" became more supported as microbiologists found that many infectious diseases were caused by bacteria. As a result of the work of the pioneer chemist and microbiologist Louis Pasteur and others, inoculations and treatments were developed to prevent or treat infection. This success did not go unnoticed by American society. The services that medical professionals offered became viewed as practical, and medicine began to achieve a status higher than that of other forms of treatment.

Another factor affecting the development of medicine as a social institution was its success in establishing the American Medical Association (AMA) in 1847. The AMA was established to exert greater control over the practice of medicine. Its members sought to establish standards that all members were to meet if they desired to practice medicine. It also promoted licensing of those who met those standards and a code of ethics for all physicians. By pursuing these goals, the AMA sought to separate "physicians" from those who practiced alternative healing methods or even "quackery." In 1910, the institutionalization of medicine was furthered by an arrangement between the AMA and the U.S. government. As discussed by medical sociologists Gregory Weiss and Lynne Lonnquist in *The Sociology of Health, Healing, and Illness* (1994), the "Great Trade of 1910" granted governmental blessing to the AMA's power over medical education and licensing. In return, the AMA would provide an organized effort to build an efficient and comprehensive health care system.

After medicine was successfully institutionalized, the role of health care professionals continued to expand. Instead of focusing strictly on the treatment of biological ailments, modern health care providers are involved with evaluating other factors affecting health and illness. Physicians, nurses, and other health care workers are now called upon to evaluate public sanitation, public health policy, diets, lifestyles, stress levels, and exercise. The expansion of the physician's role continues to the present day. Along with many other modern societies, the latter half of the twentieth century found Americans debating the role of physicians in abortion, organ transplantation, fetal tissue research, euthanasia, and many other issues. A focus of future social research will be the extent to which medical professionals allow their role to be expanded into a broader spectrum of social life. The future of these issues rests on how society continues to define the role of the medical institution and whether the medical institution accepts this role.

Applications

The institution of medicine is a popular topic among social researchers. There are few institutions in society which afford a broader range of topics for study than does medicine. In studying social phenomena, most sociologists approach their research using one of three theoretical perspectives: conflict theory, functionalism, or symbolic interactionism. Conflict theory and functionalism view society from a "macro" perspective that analyzes social events by looking at large groups or comparing entire social systems. Unlike conflict theory and functionalism, symbolic interactionism examines society from a "micro" perspective. Microsociology is concerned with the everyday interactions among individuals within a society rather than with the "big picture."

Conflict theory is largely attributable to social theorist Karl Marx. Conflict theorists tend to analyze social phenomena in the context of the inequality among various social groups in society. Their perspective in the study of medicine is no exception. Medicine, like other social institutions, is subject to the same class antagonisms that are present in other areas of society. Because of their model of society, conflict theorists focus their efforts on exploring the inequalities associated with illness, medical practice, and access to health care.

Conflict theorists studying the social demography of health, often referred to as "social epidemiology," examine the reasons why some social groups in society are more likely to contract certain illnesses than are other groups. These researchers are likely to study problems associated with social class, race, gender, and age. These factors are often related to one another, and they often determine one's access to power and resources in a society. People with fewer resources often have less access to health care; the poor, for example, are less able to pay medical bills. Because of their inability to pay, they have fewer choices even when they do have access to physicians. The elderly, racial minorities, and women (especially single mothers) tend to have fewer resources than do other social groups, and they are also more likely to experience difficulties in obtaining medical care. Therefore, they are more likely to suffer from various health-related problems. Complicating matters, social groups with fewer resources are likely to suffer from diseases caused by the work and living conditions of people in various social situations. Conflict theorists assert that the poor are often forced by economic circumstances to work in jobs that jeopardize their health. If they had a choice, they would likely select jobs that offered more personal well-being. The problems faced by these groups virtually always relate to their lack of power, which is caused by a lack of access to economic resources.

Functionalist theory was largely the creation of Talcott Parsons, who also happened to have a profound interest in the medical institution. This theoretical perspective views a society in the same way that medicine views an organism. The human body is an organism composed of various organs that must work in concert in order for the entire body to survive. The functionalist views society in a similar way, asserting that it is made up of interdependent social institutions (the state, religion, family, economy, education, medicine) that function collectively to maintain a stable system. The social institutions are supported by the culture of a society, which maintains the confidence of individuals in those institutions.

Functionalists who study the institution of medicine study how medicine is related to other social institutions to help maintain a stable social environment. In their article "Illness, Therapy, and the Modern American Family," sociologists Talcott Parsons and Renée Fox compared the function of the medical institution with that of the family. They suggested that medicine and the family share similar social functions. They asserted that health care professionals perform the same function within the hospital that parents have traditionally performed in the home. The medical institution has developed in a way that eliminates an additional burden on the already stressed family by making care of the sick its primary function. Family members are able to obtain care from highly trained people using technology that is not available in the home.

In contrast to conflict theory and functionalism, symbolic interactionism is interested in the daily interactions among individuals. Sociologists who use this approach view human interaction as an exchange of symbols. A symbol is an act, gesture, or sign that is used to communicate some type of meaning. According to symbolic interactionists, people can communicate only when these symbols are commonly understood among the people who are trying to interact. In most interactions, language is used to communicate. Interaction between two people is analyzed by examining how each person perceives the other (the sender and receiver of the symbols) and the meaning that each person attaches to the symbols that are being used.

Topics studied by symbolic interactionists include interactions among physicians, nurses, patients, and other health care professionals. For example, in studying the interaction that takes place between doctors and patients, symbolic interactionists assert that what happens in the doctor's office is greatly affected by how the physician and patient perceive each other and the degree to which they both understand the language spoken by the other. If the physician perceives the patient as highly intelligent, the physician may be more likely to expound on diagnoses or allow the patient a greater degree of freedom in choosing the direction of his or her health care. If the physician perceives the patient as unintelligent or uneducated, the physician may take a more paternalistic role, making more decisions for the patients without expounding on all the available options. These types of analysis are common in symbolic interactionist examinations of interactions among physicians, interactions between doctors and nurses, and interactions between patients and their health care providers.

Context

From the time of many preliterate cultures to the present, medicine has been closely connected with magic, superstition, and religion. Historically, disease has often been attributed to problems in the spiritual realm. People suffering from disease were often labeled as "sinners" rather than being viewed as having biological ailments. Thus, most people afflicted with disease sought help from spiritual healers or holy persons of some kind.

The impact of this view began to diminish as germ theory emerged. The germ theory of disease promoted the idea that disease was caused by microorganisms rather than by moral or spiritual deficiencies. Because of Louis Pasteur's success in isolating and treating infectious disease caused by bacteria, the power of the physician in society increased; physicians finally had the means to counteract the effects of many diseases.

The formal subdiscipline of medical sociology emerged during the 1950's and 1960's because of the expansion of the National Institutes of Health in the 1940's, but the study of social factors affecting health and illness is much older. In 1847, the physician Rudolf Virchow was an early proponent of the idea that many social conditions affect the spread of bacteria and the infectious diseases that result from them. For example, the unsanitary conditions in which many poor people lived placed them at greater risk of contracting typhus fever. It is clear that Virchow did not believe that the spread of disease could be explained strictly by biological factors.

Virchow's ideas were proved true during many medical crises, including the American Civil War. In the years between 1861 and 1865, hundreds of thousands of soldiers were crowded together in close living quarters with poor sanitary conditions. Although the number of casualties resulting from Civil War battles was staggering, far more soldiers died of disease than died of wounds received in battle.

Sociologist William Cockerham has noted that the decline in deaths from infectious diseases in the late 1800's was the result of improvements in "diet, housing, public sanitation, and personal hygiene and not medical innovations." Physicians and other medical professionals resisted being connected with these social factors and their effects on disease, but the findings of the social sciences in this area actually served to expand the physician's role even further. In his essay "The Politics of Health in the Twentieth Century," social theorist Michel Foucault predicted that medicine would "assume an increasingly important place . . . in the machinery of power" and that the role of physicians would be "constantly widened and strengthened" when doctors broadened their scope to include social factors related to health.

Foucault was correct in his prediction. In fact, although physicians once preferred to concern themselves with improving their own means of treating infection, they are now charged with evaluating many factors that once were not even considered medical. Modern physicians are now asked to concern themselves with hair loss, the altering of facial features or body shape, and the scrutinizing of lifestyles (diet, stress levels, and exercise). In the early twentieth century, social scientists continued to study the effects of social factors such as class, occupation, and religious beliefs on lifestyles and the ways in which the lifestyles of various groups contributed to health or illness.

In more recent years, medical sociology has expanded to include studies into other areas, including those of medical organizations (hospitals, clinics, health maintenance organizations), doctor-patient interaction, social policy affecting health care, and medical ethics (such as abortion, euthanasia, fetal tissue testing, and genetic testing). If past trends continue, social research involving the institution of medicine will likely have a profound effect on the role of medicine in society.

Bibliography

Conrad, Peter, and Rochelle Kern, eds. *The Sociology of Health and Illness: Critical Perspectives*. 3d ed. New York: St. Martin's Press, 1990. A collection of articles approaching health care from a conflict perspective. It contains many articles on the impact of the social environment on illness, the ways in which medical care is organized, and alternatives to the current system.

Foucault, Michel. "The Politics of Health in the Twentieth Century." In *Power/Knowledge: Selected Interviews and Other Writings*, edited by Colin Gordon. New York: Random House, 1977. Foucault predicts that medicine will become an increasingly powerful institution as it encompasses social aspects of health.

Freidson, Eliot. *Profession of Medicine: A Study of the Sociology of Applied Knowledge*. Chicago: University of Chicago Press, 1988. Freidson provides a useful description of the way in which medicine was (and continues to be) formally organized. In addition, the book includes an excellent discussion of society's definitions of illness.

Galdston, Iago. *Social and Historical Foundations of Modern Medicine*. New York: Brunner/Mazel, 1981. This social history of modern medicine is written from the perspective of a physician rather than that of a sociologist. Galdston follows the development of medicine through a series of episodes of development in the midst of plateau periods.

Jaco, E. Gartly, ed. *Patients, Physicians, and Illness*. Glencoe, Ill.: Free Press, 1958. Although dated, this book is a thorough collection of articles relating the behavioral sciences and medicine. Published in the 1950's, it includes articles from the major functionalist theorists of the period, including Talcott Parsons and Robert Merton.

Parsons, Talcott, and Renée Fox. "Illness, Therapy, and the Modern American Family." *The Journal of Social Issues* 8, no. 4 (1952): 31-44. This early sociological discussion of medicine as an institution compares its functions with those of the family, noting similarities between the roles of parent and health care provider.

Starr, Paul. *The Social Transformation of American Medicine*. New York: Basic Books, 1982. Starr's analysis of the development of American medicine into a strong profession is among the best ever written. Starr examines how medicine evolved out of other social institutions to become a profession whose role has continued to expand.

Weiss, Gregory L., and Lynne E. Lonnquist. *The Sociology of Health, Healing, and Illness*. Englewood Cliffs, N.J.: Prentice-Hall, 1994. This work is a comprehensive overview of how sociology is used to examine health, illness, and medical practice. Includes excellent discussions of the development of medicine, health and the social environment, and doctor-patient interaction.

David P. Caddell

Cross-References

The Germ Theory of Medicine, 839; Health and Society, 852; Health Care and Gender, 858; Health Maintenance Organizations, 864; The Medical Profession and the Medicalization of Society, 1159; Medical Sociology, 1166; Medical versus Social Models of Illness, 1172; The Medicalization of Deviance, 1178; National Health Insurance, 1289; Social Epidemiology, 1793; Women in the Medical Profession, 2191.

MICROSOCIOLOGY

Type of sociology: Origins and definitions of sociology
Field of study: Sociological perspectives and principles

Microsociology involves the study of how people act and react in small-group settings; it may be contrasted with macrosociology, which is concerned with the study of large-scale social processes and institutions. For example, microsociology has examined social interaction in the family and in the classroom.

Principal terms
BEHAVIOR: how individuals overtly act in the presence of others; includes verbal expression
DEVIANCE: the violation of a group norm
GROUP: two or more individuals who are part of a defined membership and who meet regularly to achieve a specific goal
GROUP NORMS: standards of behavior, thought, and values that exist within a particular group
GROUP PROCESSES: the dynamics of interaction, behavior, norms, roles, sanctions, and expression which typify the workings of a group
GROUP VALUES: ideas held by group members about what is most desirable for the group as a whole; ideas may differ, but they involve notions about what the group is and should become
ROLE: the behavior expected of a person with a particular status in a group; identified by a related cluster of behavioral norms
SANCTION: a reward or punishment which shapes behavior and reinforces norms and roles

Overview

The sociology of the late nineteenth and early twentieth centuries focused primarily on the study of large-scale phenomena such as large groups, major social institutions, and even entire societies. Sociologists sought to develop theories that would account for how social institutions—such as the state, the family, religion, and education— function to meet people's needs, how societies change over time, and how conflict within society is created and resolved. This large-scale approach is often termed "macrosociology." Macrosociology might examine, for example, the functions of education in society, the relationship between class and religion, or the causes and effects of social stratification (the domination of some groups by others in a hierarchical arrangement). The two major perspectives that have dominated macrosociological analyses are functionalism and conflict theory.

In the twentieth century, a new approach developed as a number of sociologists became intrigued by the interactions of individuals in small-group settings. This approach became known as "microsociology," which is concerned with studying (often through direct observation) how people act in real-life, face-to-face situations. A considerable amount of microsociological study has centered on educational inter-action, as between teachers and students in the classroom, but microsociology has been applied to the study of small-group processes as they occur within many social frameworks and institutions.

Interest in the study of small groups grew as sociologists came to grasp the workings of societies and to recognize the interrelationship between the individual and the many groups in which he or she participates. Sociologists became interested in identifying and understanding the processes that typified the workings of small groups, including the interconnectedness between the growth of the individual and the growth of the group. This interest involved the work of psychologists, social psychologists, and sociologists; all brought the viewpoints of their respective disciplines to bear on investigation and interpretations of group phenomena.

It was the methodologies of social psychologists, particularly symbolic interaction-ists (who believed that behavior results from interactions constructed by the self) led by George Herbert Mead and Herbert Blumer, that laid the conceptual and methodo-logical foundations for the domain of microsociology. These new methods were important for the development of this new subdiscipline and for the implications it had for sociology in general. The use of experimentation, in which certain variables were controlled among two or more groups and then compared, became a popular method of understanding how change occurs. Borrowed from anthropologists, the use of participant observation, in which the researcher acts as a member of a group and records its rules, norms, and other processes as they are lived, became recognized as a credible means of achieving understanding of group function. The social survey, used in conventional sociology, and the collection of life histories, borrowed from history, were also implemented as means of obtaining knowledge about groups. While seen as controversial by conventional sociologists, these methodologies provided new kinds of data that were rich with possibility. Ensuing research suggested that certain fundamental features exist among all groups. The identification of these features provided an important foundation for guiding subsequent small-group research and analysis.

One of the first features that emerged concerned order. Researchers found that interpersonal behavior among members is ordered and could be detected fairly easily in act-by-act sequences. Further, it was found that phases of disorder are systematically followed by phases of order and that situational factors affect the development and nature of that order. For example, the resignation of a leader might stop all activity and cause confusion (disorder). Almost immediately, however, individuals would act to restore order by appointing a new leader or by distributing tasks among group members.

A second feature essential to interaction systems is the distribution of action among members. Researchers found that patterns tended to develop related to one's rank within the group; with few exceptions, interaction tended to occur toward higher ranks. Although attempts to devise formulas to calculate and predict the direction and frequency of interaction were not particularly successful, the discovery of patterns and of the influences of such factors as members' roles, group goals, and subgroup formations proved invaluable to understanding both the nature and predictability of group phenomena.

The size of the group was found to affect both the nature and quality of interaction within the group. The quality of participation was found to decrease with increased group size. Similarly, increased group size allows for less inhibition among members. Further, regardless of the formal organizational structure of a group, a systematic pattern of interaction among members was always found.

The concept of group emotion emerged as another important feature of group relations. Theodore M. Mills and other sociologists found that, instead of suppressing their individual needs, desires, and feelings, individuals' combined emotional states were affected by the emotional states of others. They also affected the group as a whole. Further, the structures or kinds of group emotions were found to variously affect the function of the group. For example, a group operating from respect and autonomy is more likely to be loyal, creative, and risk-taking, whereas one operating from fear is likely to be more edgy and stagnant. Overall, the growth of the group is either enhanced or inhibited by the structure of group emotion.

The presence and fluidity of norms in groups were identified as another feature central to group process and analysis. In his pioneering work with Edward Shils, *Toward a General Theory of Action* (1951), sociologist Talcott Parsons identified several areas addressed by group norms: the nature and significance of relationships among group members, the kinds of feelings identified with normative roles, and individual significance based upon personal characteristics or role performance. Parsons' work permitted the comparison of groups along these norm domains, thus enriching understanding of how they are learned and maintained, how they evolve, how they influence group interactions, and how they are modified based on group needs.

One of the more prolific and influential of interactionist researchers was Erving Goffman. In the preface to his 1971 text *Relations in Public*, he identified the importance of conducting research on small groups as well as the interrelatedness of these central features. To illustrate, Goffman presented an analysis of games and compared them with social systems in his essay "Fun in Games," included in his 1961 publication *Encounters: Two Studies in the Sociology of Interaction*. As an initial aspect of analysis, Goffman considered what he called "rules of irrelevance." Games involve a focused interaction in which participants effectively agree to establish and submit to rules of recruitment, membership, and play; to limits on overt hostility; and to certain divisions of labor. For the duration of the event, participants adhere to certain rules that are not of the "real" world, while rejecting—or viewing as irrelevant—others under which they might ordinarily serve. Goffman was also intrigued with players' abilities to transform any place or object, of any quality or condition, into a valued and functional field or field piece, again ignoring conventional rules for the duration of the game. Further, roles and norms for games tend to be explicitly defined and strongly enforced. Regardless of the personality of the individual coming to the game, the role and behavioral conventions required to play are readily adopted by participants.

Goffman was also intrigued that these rules about procedures, roles, and norms tell players what to treat as real in a particular game situation. As such, rules represent constructs of expression and interpretation which generate events that are meaningful in the context of the game, and around which entire worlds are built. It is the individual's capacity to engage in this matrix of possible events to create a world different from all others that Goffman found most intriguing. Goffman's work, which spanned two decades, created conceptual frameworks that have continued to contribute to the richness and diversity of small-group research.

Applications
As knowledge from these studies accumulated, sociologists became more involved in researching groups in particular settings. Howard L. Becker's study of deviance, best represented in *Outsiders* (1963) and *The Other Side* (1964), demonstrated that deviance is a social condition that exists only because others value their own norm expectations so much that they are compelled to force others to comply with them.

Similarly, using case studies and autobiographies, Erving Goffman exposed the personal pain and coping strategies of many individuals who found they were unable to conform to standards deemed by society as "normal." In *Asylums: Essays on the Social Situation of Mental Patients and Other Inmates* (1961) and *Stigma: Notes on the Management of Spoiled Identity* (1963), Goffman addressed the life situations of the mentally ill, people with physical disabilities, drug addicts, prostitutes, and the incarcerated. He analyzed the intricate system of communication that leads to stigma and rejection as well as the dynamics that each encounter or interaction brings with it. Those who are able choose to pass as normal as often as possible; the stutterer speaks only when required, for example, and the prostitute lives and shops in neighborhoods apart from her work territory. Goffman's research generated concrete understanding of the nature and impact of these coping strategies, the different sets of rules to which individuals try to conform, and the personal and interpersonal conflict people experience. Further, Goffman provided unparalleled analysis of how primary societal institutions work to establish and maintain roles, norms, and sanctions, as well as how they institutionalize labeling and discrimination. Understanding these dynamics has enabled the human and civil rights movements initiated in the 1960's and regenerated in the 1990's to work effectively toward removing the stigma, and therefore the discrimination, associated with being different.

By the 1970's, microsociological perspectives and research were developed to the extent that they became the preferred method for exploring process and policy. With the racial integration of education in the 1960's and curricular reforms involving women and minorities beginning in the 1970's, schools became primary sites for conducting microsociological explorations. As discrepancies in academic achievement became evident, patterns that related differential achievement to the race, class, and gender of students became established. Researchers were then faced with the challenge of explaining the processes responsible for these outcomes.

One of the most significant findings emanating from this research involved the work of sociologist Ray Rist, who conducted extensive explorations of classroom phenomena. Rist identified a series of processes, beginning with teachers' expectations and differential treatment of certain students, which—when maintained consistently over time—tended to shape students' self-perceptions, achievement motivation, and subsequent academic performance. Various mechanisms, such as tracking, ability grouping, the use of standardized test scores, and counseling, were found to be aiding in the institutionalization of different allocations of educational opportunity. As schools renewed reform efforts in the mid-1980's, the significance of these studies dramatically affected their efforts. As a result, the governors of all fifty states pledged to abolish tracking. Ability grouping has been modified, and awareness courses have been incorporated into the staff development of teachers and counselors.

Context

Claude-Henri de Rouvroy (comte de Saint-Simon) and August Comte are credited with founding sociology as a discipline in the early nineteenth century. Initial sociological explanations of societal formation involved either a functionalist (or structuralist/functionalist) approach or a conflict theory approach. Sociologists Max Weber, Talcott Parsons, and Émile Durkheim were foremost in developing and using functionalist theory. Analysis was based on determining how various institutions meet societal needs. Major premises of this theoretical interpretation included societal balance and consensus.

Karl Marx, Georg Simmel, and Ralf Dahrendorf were among the principal theorists who used a conflict perspective to analyze and explain societal organization and conditions. Central to conflict theory is the idea that different groups in society are in conflict with one another over economic resources and the availability of wealth and power. In this domination-subordination model, the masses are viewed as generally oppressed and exploited by the elite for their own gains.

As sociologists came to understand the nature of social classes, attention was turned to the study of the smaller groups that exist within larger societies. A recognized dichotomy between the individual and smaller groups of membership became recognized as a tension that was connected in intricate ways with the larger institutions or societies to which individuals belong. Sociologists began making connections between the stability or deterioration of societies and the situations, actions, and reactions of individuals within those groups.

One theorist and researcher who was instrumental in facilitating this shift was social psychologist George Herbert Mead, one of the most influential social psychologists of the early twentieth century. Mead worked from the premise that behavior is the result of one's concept of the self, which is constructed through interaction. Mead's work at the University of Chicago, which became known as symbolic interactionism, dominated the thinking and research regarding small-group research for several decades. In the 1930's, after Mead's death, Herbert Blumer, also of the "Chicago school," became the intellectual leader and representative of symbolic interactionism. Blumer was largely responsible for establishing symbolic interaction as a respected, sociologically grounded field in social psychology (as opposed to experimental social psychology). The validity of the methodology used by symbolic interactionists laid a foundation for those sociologists who were interested in further exploration of individuals and the groups to which they belonged.

By the mid-twentieth century, sociologists Kurt Lewin, Talcott Parsons, Edward Shils, Jacob Moreno, Robert Freed Bales, and others had given new direction to the study of groups through their uses of the experimental method in laboratory situations, through applying observation techniques to small groups and communities, and through developing interaction theory. The definition of groups as miniature social systems enabled sociologists to apply conventional sociological concerns and analyses to small groups. They found that, as in large groups, members of small groups needed to find ways to meet the group's goals, to maintain group solidarity, to meet members' needs, and to adapt to the various situations that confronted the group. The discovery that, although each group is unique, all confront these same kinds of problems allowed sociologists to benefit from the rapid development of small-group theory and research.

Between the 1950's and 1970's, training laboratories were established, and training groups were popularized to assist individuals in developing and using their understanding of group process and social change. The conducting of research on small groups expanded from industrial, governmental, and social agencies to families and schools. Major works began bridging the gap between social psychological theory and actual analysis of classrooms.

Much of this new research was influenced by social psychologist Robert Freed Bales. In his book *Personality and Interpersonal Behavior* (1970), Bales provided a shift of focus to more systematic methods of gathering and quantifying information about the interaction that occurs among group members. Bales devised a method of factor analysis that involved statistical calculations that would indicate, among twenty-seven types of group roles and their related value directions, those most typical of each group member. The development of microsociological principles along with systematic and qualitative research established the field as an important contributor to the discipline of sociology.

Bibliography

Bales, Robert Freed. *Personality and Interpersonal Behavior.* New York: Holt, Rinehart and Winston, 1970. This readable, though lengthy, text provides insight into the transition from symbolic interactionist research to the legitimization of observation. Although this system is rarely used, any reader would gain an appreciation for the complexity and significance of Bales's work.
Becker, Howard S. *Outsiders.* New York: Free Press, 1963. Representative of both theory formation and research, this work provides an in-depth presentation and application of deviance theory. While the role of the dance musician of Becker's

1198   *Sociology*

study is dated, the analysis represents a cornerstone of deviance theory, and Becker's discussions of deviance and the moral entrepreneur are enlightening for both the lay and professional reader.

Blumer, Herbert. *Symbolic Interactionism: Perspective and Method.* Englewood Cliffs, N.J.: Prentice-Hall, 1969. A classic for scholars, this clearly written text is essential for the serious student who is interested in knowing one of the most significant early works in microsociological research and theory. Blumer provides a thorough discussion of the essence of symbolic interactionism, its implications for other disciplines, and several applications of the method.

Collins, Randall, ed. *Three Sociological Traditions: Selected Readings.* New York: Oxford University Press, 1985. Part 3 of this book provides an excellent overview of microsociology through representative works of Cooley, Mead, Blumer, Mehan and Wood, and Goffman.

Goffman, Erving. *Stigma: Notes on the Management of Spoiled Identity.* Englewood Cliffs, N.J.: Prentice-Hall, 1963. Demonstrating the early use of ethnomethodology in small-group research, Goffman presents analyses and alternatives for those individuals in society that suffer from being stigmatized. The reader will find Goffman's work enlightening and virtually uncompromised by time; it is particularly relevant in times when tensions between different peoples are unabated.

Knorr-Cetina, K., and A. V. Cicourel. *Advances in Social Theory and Methodology: Toward an Integration of Micro- and Macro-Sociologies.* Boston: Routledge & Kegan Paul, 1981. With compiled contributions, this text provides a variety of perspectives regarding the development of microsociology and its relation to macrosociology. Additionally, topics such as social reconstruction, inherited disorders, law, and space analysis are examined from microsociological perspectives. Suggested for those who have achieved a sound grasp of microsociological method and conceptual treatments.

Mills, Theodore M. *The Sociology of Small Groups.* Englewood Cliffs, N.J.: Prentice-Hall, 1967. This work is particularly useful for providing a survey of thought and research in microsociology. Includes a brief history and detailed descriptions of the various concepts, processes, and research techniques used. The book's strength lies in the many examples used to illustrate small-group research techniques and principles.

Slater, Philip. *Microcosm: Structural, Psychological, and Religious Evolution in Groups.* New York: John Wiley & Sons, 1966. Slater adeptly combines Freudian analysis and microsociological theory to address the concepts of independence, boundary awareness, and leader goals among groups. Chapter 2, "The Attack on the Leader," and chapter 3, "Sexual Liberation Through Revolt," are particularly useful in understanding the application and development of microsociology.

Denise Kaye Davis

Cross-References
Conflict Theory, 340; Dramaturgy, 566; Functionalism, 786; Interactionism, 1009; Social Groups, 1806; The History of Sociology, 1926; Sociology Defined, 1932; Symbolic Interaction, 2036.

"MIDDLEMAN" MINORITIES

Type of sociology: Racial and ethnic relations
Fields of study: Patterns and consequences of contact; Systems of social stratification

Middleman minorities stand, economically and socially, midway between majority groups and other minority groups. They typically engage in brokering occupations; because of their occupations and presumed characteristics (they are often said to be thrifty and clannish), they are often the object of hatred.

Principal terms

CULTURAL FACTORS: the values and norms unique to particular groups that shape their behavior

ETHNIC STRATIFICATION: a situation in which racial and/or ethnic groups are arranged hierarchically such that those nearer the top enjoy greater access to social desirables

MAJORITY GROUP: the group in a society that is socially and politically dominant

MINORITY GROUP: a group that, because of relative powerlessness, experiences discrimination

ROTATING CREDIT ASSOCIATION: a method of raising cash, prevalent in some ethnic groups, that involves the continuous pooling and withdrawal of money

STRUCTURAL FACTORS: factors influencing an individual's behavior that are largely beyond his or her control

Overview

"Middleman" minorities are groups that, in a number of societies around the world, act as intermediaries between producers and consumers. This intermediary position frequently causes conflict with dominant and subordinate groups and includes (primarily) such functions as moneylending, trading, and shopkeeping. Historically, many groups have occupied this niche. They include Jews, the "overseas Chinese," Indians in East Africa, the Lebanese in West Africa, and Armenians in Ethiopia. The fact that such diverse groups, operating in very different societies, exhibit similar traits has led to much theorizing about middleman minorities. According to sociologist Robin Ward, these theories seek to answer three key questions: why particular groups become middleman minorities, why these groups enter into the specific occupations characteristic of middleman minorities, and what causes hostility toward them.

The first question is, in fact, two questions, because social scientists must not only account for why particular groups become middleman minorities but also must explain why others do not. Answers to the first part of this question fall into two broad categories: structural factors and cultural attributes. Structural factors refer to the economic opportunities that unfold before certain groups, thereby enabling them to become traders, moneylenders, or any of the other occupations characteristic of middleman minorities. For example, in "The Koreans: Small Business in an Urban Frontier" (1987), sociologist Ilsoo Kim argues that as Jewish and Italian small business owners have retreated from inner cities, Korean immigrants, using readily available cash, have bought their stores. This option is attractive because, though many are highly educated, their difficulties with English hinder advancement in the professions. Moreover, the Korean community possesses a variety of institutions that facilitate the immigrants' transition into American life. To these structural factors must be added such cultural traits as frugality (which includes hiring relatives at low wages), clannishness, and hard work. Thus, Koreans' success as small-business owners has resulted from a combination of structural and cultural factors. The same is true of other groups, such as the Chinese and Japanese.

In the United States, the success of these groups in small business has been contrasted to the relative lack of it by African Americans. This difference is heightened because African Americans have a much longer history in the United States and because many Asian (especially Korean) small businesses operate in black enclaves of the larger American cities. The answer appears to lie in a combination of structural and cultural barriers. Historically, racial discrimination in obtaining start-up capital has been the chief structural barrier faced by would-be African American businesspeople. Yet, as sociologist Ivan Light argued in *Ethnic Enterprise in America* (1972), this explanation by itself is inadequate, since West Indian immigrants have played the role of middleman minorities in Harlem. He attributes this to West Indians' continuation of the African cultural tradition of rotating credit associations, which allowed them to generate start-up capital within the immigrant community, thereby partially bypassing discriminatory treatment by banks. In contrast, this practice has died out among African Americans; consequently, they have had fewer resources on which to draw to start small businesses.

There are a variety of reasons why middleman minorities enter into particular occupations, some of which have already been discussed. For the sake of convenience, these may be placed into three categories: economic, historical, and sociocultural. Economic factors include situations (as noted for Koreans in the United States) in which groups find that a demand exists in certain areas of society and take advantage of it. This suggests a certain element of chance. As sociologist Donald L. Horowitz has shown in *Ethnic Groups in Conflict* (1985), however, colonial policy in some developing countries steered some groups into particular occupations. Over time, a pattern of ethnic recruitment occurred, and folk beliefs justifying why some groups are more "suitable" to certain occupations arose. Examples include Chinese traders in Malaysia and Sikh artisans in India. These examples illustrate how historical and sociocultural factors overlap to create middleman minorities.

A third key question with respect to middleman minorities is why they are so often the victims of deliberate violence. The reasons for this violence are many, and violence toward middleman minorities originates from both the dominant and subordinated groups in society. Economist Thomas Sowell argues that a general reason for this violence is the view that, despite their usefulness, middleman minority occupations are inherently degraded. Hence, different groups performing the same role in different societies will face similar criticisms. A second reason is that middleman minority occupations become identified with all members of the group regardless of the actual occupations of individual members. This ethnocentric response identifies and inter-twines despised minorities with despised roles. Sowell notes that a third reason for conflict is the ability of middleman minorities to achieve success in the professions. They become seen as formidable competitors and are resented, especially by subor-dinated minorities who view this success as coming at their expense. Political manipulation of latent antimiddleman minority sentiments is yet another reason for violence against middleman minorities. Horowitz shows that this occurs, for example, where subordinated minority groups, seeking to start businesses but finding middle-man minorities as competitors, stir up trouble in an attempt to gain a competitive advantage.

Applications

The middleman minority concept is a useful tool for diagnosing social problems and helping to shape social policy. It helps explain otherwise inexplicable patterns of ethnic stratification and conflict in plural societies, and it highlights some of the mechanisms whereby groups can achieve success.

Most societies with multiple racial and ethnic groups (plural societies) display a pattern whereby these groups are arranged hierarchically in terms of their possession of such social desirables as income, wealth, prestige, and power. This pattern, known as ethnic stratification, interests social scientists because it suggests the existence of underlying social forces common to many societies. One such factor is the tendency for societies to arrange themselves into majority (dominant) and minority (subordi-nated) groups. Because many theories exist as to the cause of this pattern, the effort here will be to describe aspects of the pattern rather than to explain its origin.

The most salient characteristic of the majority/minority group arrangement is that it leads to conflict as majority groups promulgate policies—ranging from assimilation to genocide—and minority groups respond to them. A narrow focus on this major-ity/minority group split, however, fails to describe adequately the full complexity of ethnic stratification and conflict. Measured in terms of income, wealth, prestige, and power, some groups are clearly subordinate to dominant groups yet are superior to minority groups. These intermediate groups are the so-called middleman minorities. Their intermediate status alters the pattern of conflict between dominant and subordi-nated groups, causing it to take unexpected turns. One possibility is that middleman minorities, finding themselves under attack from other minority groups, might attempt to ally themselves with the majority group. Alternatively, the majority group might use middleman minorities as scapegoats. Yet another possibility is that minority groups might ally themselves with middleman minorities because the latter provide useful economic functions.

The 1992 Los Angeles riot illustrates the severity of the conflict that can arise between middleman minorities and other minority groups. In that riot, African Americans, because of perceived inequities in the criminal justice system and resentment of Koreans' relative affluence in economically depressed minority neighborhoods, destroyed many Korean-owned businesses. This type of conflict can result in minority group anger at the majority group becoming diffused: The minority group loses some of its moral authority as its attacks on the middleman minority place it in the role of victimizer. At the same time, the majority group gains allies among the middleman minority in its conflict with the minority group. For example, in the 1993 New York City mayoral election, some observers noted that the white candidate appealed to Korean and Jewish (two middleman minorities) animosity toward African Americans to help unseat the black incumbent mayor. Thus, middleman minorities can be used by the majority group to blunt the demands of another minority group.

Alternatively, the majority group might oppress the middleman minority; historically, such groups have served as scapegoats for various social ills. Nazi Germany's attempted annihilation of Jews is a well-known example of this. Others include the similar policy followed by the Turks against Armenians and the Ugandan expulsion of East Indians. Another possibility is that middleman minorities might ally themselves with other minority groups. Donald L. Horowitz argues that in some societies—for example, in Malaysia—majority group attempts to victimize middleman minorities fail because minority groups regard the majority group as inefficient providers of services compared with middleman minorities.

In the United States, the contrast between the economic success of middleman minorities such as East Indians and Koreans and the relative lack of it by some sections of the African American community and some Hispanics has fueled research into the causes of middleman minority success. Implicit in some of this research is the idea that these principles might, if applied to less well-off minority groups, help them achieve greater levels of economic success. Thomas Sowell, for example, tends to argue that values are the crucial component making for middleman minority success. Specifically, he believes that less-successful minorities should become more frugal and hardworking. A corollary to this belief is that affirmative action is unjustified since it rewards political power rather than the possession of success-oriented values.

On the other hand, writers who view structural factors as having greater impact on ethnic success imply that the experience of middleman minorities cannot be easily duplicated by other groups. For example, sociologist Edna Bonacich argues that these groups owe their economic success to their "sojourner" status. In other words, middleman minorities orient themselves toward their home countries instead of feeling a permanent allegiance to the societies in which they operate. Consequently, they engage in economic behavior and develop values that are compatible with the desire to return to their homelands. For example, they opt for businesses that are easily liquidatable, and they resist assimilation into the host society. Bonacich views indigenous middleman minorities—such as African Americans—as being quite different because their commitment to the host society precludes the development of traits associated with middleman minority success. The debate as to whether values or social structure is more important in determining economic success is ongoing and shaped by historical forces. If a consensus is emerging, it is that some combination of the two factors, rather than either alone, is the key to economic success.

Context

The middleman minority concept has had a long history, rooted in the similar experiences of a number of groups around the world. Particularly important is the experience of Jews in Europe, for as social scientist Walter P. Zenner has pointed out, many of the theories of middleman minorities originated as attempts to explain anti-Semitism. Historically, European Jews have closely matched the profile of the middleman minority. They stood as intermediaries between nobles and serfs, performing such occupations as moneylending and merchandising. They tended to be frugal, hardworking, clannish, and highly educated. The result was economic success but at the cost of great hostility from their non-Jewish neighbors. A variety of negative stereotypes about Jews developed. These included charges of disloyalty (for refusing to assimilate), deviousness, and dishonesty in business. Additionally—and significantly, in societies dominated by Catholicism—they were accused of being anti-Christian. Stereotypes such as these resulted in the ghettoization of Jews and repeated pogroms, culminating in the Holocaust of World War II. Thus, both Jewish economic success and the persecution of Jews in Europe were intimately tied to their peculiar status as middleman minorities.

The historical experiences of Jews closely match those of a number of other such groups, which pointed to the need for a concept to tie a minority group's experiences to its economic function relative to dominant and subjugated groups. For example, sociologist D. Stanley Eitzen has shown the existence of close historical similarities between the Jewish experience and that of the Chinese in the Philippines. As is the case with the Jews in Europe, Chinese contact with the Philippines dates back hundreds of years. By the time the Spanish took control of the Philippines in 1571, the Chinese had already established themselves as craftsmen, merchants, and moneylenders. Initially welcomed by the Spanish for their useful economic function, they soon experienced ghettoization and mass killings (by the Spanish) because of their new economic power. This hostility has lasted through the period of American occupation (from 1898 to 1946) to the present. In the post-1946 independence period, nationalistic fervor combined with anti-Chinese sentiment to limit opportunities for the Chinese in the Philippines. For example, the Filipino government has made it difficult for Chinese to become citizens, limited their ownership of land, and prevented their entrance into certain industries.

The historical similarities between groups are the result of the economic roles they occupy in society rather than of who they are. It seems that a particular combination of brokering occupations and values that enhance economic success in these occupations always leads to hostility. The historical evidence suggests that as long as some groups exist in this mode they will to some degree remain outsiders to the societies in which they live and will suffer success mixed with persecution.

Bibliography

Bonacich, Edna. "A Theory of Middleman Minorities." *American Sociological Review* 38 (October, 1973): 583-594. Bonacich's theory attributes middleman minorities' occupational choices and values (for example, clannishness) to their "sojourner" status—their orientation toward their homelands rather than assimilation into the host society.

Eitzen, D. Stanley. "Two Minorities: The Jews of Poland and the Chinese of the Philippines." *The Jewish Journal of Sociology* 10 (December, 1968): 221-239. In this comparison of two well-known middleman minorities, Eitzen argues that the occupations engaged in by middleman minorities and the values supporting these occupations cause them to be both admired and hated.

Horowitz, Donald L. *Ethnic Groups in Conflict.* Berkeley: University of California Press, 1985. Although his central focus is not middleman minorities, Horowitz critically analyzes the concept in a number of places in the book. He downplays the idea that middleman minority occupations cause conflict.

Kim, Illsoo. "The Koreans: Small Business in an Urban Frontier." In *New Immigrants in New York*, edited by Nancy Foner. New York: Columbia University Press, 1987. Kim argues that a combination of economic opportunity, fiscal preparedness, education, community organization, and values have helped Koreans achieve success in the United States. Unlike writers such as Thomas Sowell, he tends to emphasize the structural factors involved.

Lieberson, Stanley. "A Societal Theory of Race and Ethnic Relations." *American Sociological Review* 26 (December, 1961): 902-910. Lieberson attempts to account for the origin of majority and minority groups. Along the way, he also discusses the origin of middleman minorities. He argues that they result from subordinated indigenous minorities' unwillingness to adopt certain occupations. Consequently, immigrants come in and fill the existing economic vacuum.

Light, Ivan. *Ethnic Enterprise in America.* Berkeley: University of California Press, 1972. This useful book investigates the factors making for success—or the lack of it—among minorities. His comparison of African Americans with West Indian and Asian immigrants focuses on the well-documented role of rotating credit associations in providing start-up capital for small businesses.

Sowell, Thomas. "Middleman Minorities." *The American Enterprise* 4 (May/June, 1993): 30-41. Sowell argues that the possession of certain values is the central characteristic of middleman minorities. These values lead them into brokering occupations and cannot be abandoned without abandoning the middleman minority status itself, but they also inevitably cause conflict with the surrounding society.

Ward, Robin. "Middleman Minorities." In *Dictionary of Race and Ethnic Relations*, edited by E. Ellis Cashmore. London: Routledge, 1988. This article is highly recommended. Ward presents a trenchant discussion of the issues involved in the middleman minority debate.

Zenner, Walter P. "Middleman Minorities: A Critical Review." In *Sourcebook on the New Immigration*, edited by Roy Simon Bryce-Laporte. New Brunswick, N.J.:

Transaction Books, 1980. Zenner's article is a comprehensive overview of the literature on middleman minorities and is worth reading.

Milton D. Vickerman

Cross-References

Conquest and Annexation of Racial or Ethnic Groups, 353; Ethnic Enclaves, 682; Ethnicity and Ethnic Groups, 689; Minority and Majority Groups, 1219; "Model" Minorities, 1233; Prejudice and Stereotyping, 1505; Race and Racial Groups, 1552; Racial and Ethnic Stratification, 1579; Social Stratification: Analysis and Overview, 1839.

THE MILITARY-INDUSTRIAL COMPLEX

Type of sociology: Major social institutions
Field of study: Politics and the state

The military-industrial complex is the web of mutual interests that is believed to tie together high American military officers and executives in defense-dependent American corporations. Sociologists have used the concept to try to understand both the making of American foreign policy and the development of the American economy.

Principal terms

BUREAUCRACY: a type of formal organization that emphasizes the rational and efficient pursuit of goals and that contains a highly structured network of roles and statuses

ELITISM: in political sociology, the notion that major political decisions are made by a tightly knit group with little popular participation

INSTITUTION: a stable social arrangement that performs a basic activity in society; the military institution, for example, wages wars decided on by political institutions

MILITARISM: a societal emphasis on military ideals and virtues and the glorification of war and warriors

MILITARIZATION: the mobilization of an entire society around militaristic goals

PLURALISM: in political sociology, the notion that political decisions are made with the participation of a broad variety of interest groups

POWER ELITE: a close-knit group tied together by the possession of supreme power rather than by shared economic interests

Overview

The term "military-industrial complex" was first uttered in 1961 by President Dwight David Eisenhower, who had been Supreme Commander of Allied Forces in Europe during World War II. In his farewell address, Eisenhower warned his successor to guard against the undue influence that "the military-industrial complex" might wield in national life and in government decision making. Yet even earlier, in *The Power Elite* (1956), sociologist C. Wright Mills had pointed to what he regarded as the increasing influence of military officers in the circles of top government decision makers. Both the general and the scholar saw danger in the new alliance of business and military elites.

Social scientists who use the term do not always agree on either the nature of the military-industrial complex or the groups it comprises. It is seen by many as a tightly knit cabal of powerful men who promote their own interests by exaggerating the foreign threat to American security. Yet some scholars, such as sociologist Stanley Lieberson, regard it as simply a loose coalition of interests, no more powerful than any other Washington lobby. All social scientists who study the topic consider the top military officers and the heads of defense-dependent industries to be part of the military-industrial complex. Many authors also include the civilian bureaucrats in the Defense Department, the members of Congress from districts that are dependent economically on defense spending, the heads of labor unions whose members work in defense industries, and even scientists dependent on military research contracts. The various (and sometimes mutually contradictory) ways in which the term is used lead some scholars, such as the military sociologist Charles Moskos, to doubt whether the term has any analytical utility at all.

Social scientists do not agree on who the senior partner in the military-industrial complex is. Some say that military officers dominate the alliance; others see the business elite as dominant over the military officer class. Social scientists also disagree on the birth date of the military-industrial complex. Some, such as Gregory Hooks, find its origins in World War II; others (such as historian Paul Koistinen) trace its roots back to World War I, or even further back in American history. The majority, however, date the formation of the complex back only as far as the Korean War (1950-1953). All students of the subject agree that the military-industrial complex derived at least some of its strength from the atmosphere of mutual threat and barely contained hostility that prevailed between the Soviet Union and the United States during the Cold War years (1950-1991). Geographer Ann Markusen, for example, shows how the need to build weapons (particularly missiles) for deterrence as well as for use, which arose from prolonged Cold War tensions, affected the location of successful defense firms and what kinds of people they hired.

A topic of particularly heated debate has been the influence of the military-industrial complex on decisions regarding war and peace. Some social scientists, journalists, and other observers ascribe such unfortunate American foreign policy decisions as the unsuccessful military intervention in Vietnam (1964-1973) to the influence of the military-industrial complex. Seymour Melman, an engineer who became an economist, attributes American military intervention in small countries to the existence in the United States of what he calls "military state capitalism," a system in which supreme political, economic, and military power are in the same hands. The question of the influence of top military officers, or of a military-business cabal, on decision-making in questions of war and peace is something that can ultimately be answered only by a historian or a historically trained sociologist, and only years after the event. A comparative study by the historian Richard K. Betts, *Soldiers, Statesmen, and Cold War Crises* (1977), suggests that military officers are no more inclined toward military solutions to problems than are highly placed civilian bureaucrats.

Another important issue in the study of the military-industrial complex is the role played by congressional politics in governmental decisions on what weapons to build and where to build them. Markusen finds that the decisions on the sites of military bases or the awarding of military contracts in the United States of the Cold War era do not seem to have been dictated by vote-hungry politicians. While conceding that members of Congress try to protect defense spending projects that are in their districts already, she also argues that many are not interested in military matters at all. As sociologist Stephen Cobb points out in a 1973 article, members of Congress from districts heavily dependent on defense spending have not been more likely to support a bellicose foreign policy than are members of Congress from districts less favored in this respect.

Scholars also argue about whether the big defense budgets of the Cold War-era United States, often attributed to the influence of the military-industrial complex, hurt or helped the American economy. In *The Permanent War Economy* (1974) and *Profits Without Production* (1983), Melman argues that spending on the military, once regarded by many economists as an economic stimulus, actually acts as a drag on the American economy. Both scholars and journalists have argued that the absence of a heavy defense spending burden helped America's foreign allies, Japan and the German Federal Republic, to devote more effort than the United States did to technological improvements of value to industry. Yet Markusen, a critic of the military-industrial complex, concedes that at least some research done for the military (for example, research on computers in the 1940's and 1950's) had favorable effects on the civilian economy.

Applications

The term "military-industrial complex" has seen much service in political debate. It first became a rallying cry for critics of the status quo during the bloody and unsuccessful Vietnam War. American intervention in that Southeast Asian land aroused widespread concern among the public over the question of how militaristic a society the United States was becoming. As the conflict dragged on and the casualties mounted, people began to question whether there might be some inner dynamic of the American economy that led inevitably to armed intervention abroad, and they asked whether large defense budgets and bigger and better missiles were really necessary for national security.

On college campuses, where such defense-dependent industries as aeronautics firms had traditionally recruited much of their professional labor force, students began to picket and protest against recruiters from companies that produced weapons. In 1969, President Richard M. Nixon's proposals to build the antiballistic missile (ABM) ran into considerable opposition in Congress, the first time since 1950 that weapons spending measures had experienced any difficulty whatsoever in getting passed. A spate of books and articles appeared attacking the military-industrial complex as the source of the nation's foreign policy ills.

By the 1970's, the term had become firmly established in American English, among both scholars and the general public. When the Soviet invasion of Afghanistan and the election of Ronald Reagan to the American presidency in 1980 brought a revival of the arms race between the Soviet Union and the United States, the military-industrial complex was again seen as a villain by those American peace activists who were determined to reverse the arms race. The arms buildup, such activists argued, not only threatened to bring about a nuclear holocaust but also damaged the American economy. The work of the activists was carried out through such organizations as the

Council for Economic Priorities, founded in 1969; the Coalition for a New Foreign and Military Policy, founded in 1976; and the National Commission for Economic Conversion and Disarmament, founded in 1988.

In the 1970's and 1980's, attacks on the allegedly collusive relationship between private defense contractors and top military officers also came from another quarter: It was criticized by advocates of greater economy in government. This camp, consisting of fiscally conservative politicians and disgruntled bureaucrats, wanted to make national defense more efficient rather than to abolish it. One such crusader against alleged Pentagon extravagance, the engineer and maverick Defense Department official A. Ernest Fitzgerald, wrote two books on the subject: *The High Priests of Waste* (1972) and *The Pentagonists: An Insider's View of Waste, Mismanagement, and Fraud in Defense Spending* (1989). In 1985, conservative Republican senator Charles Grassley publicly attacked waste in the Defense Department. The revelation by investigators, in June, 1988, of widespread bribery and other forms of corruption in Pentagon-contractor dealings provided yet more grist for the reformers' mill.

The concept of the military-industrial complex helped reshape Americans' understanding of both international politics and the national economy. For many years after 1950, the main theme of international politics was the Cold War. The average American tended to see this continuing tension between the United States and the Soviet Union as a simple contest between democracy (good) and communism (evil). The theory of the military-industrial complex, by contrast, pointed not to ideology as the main obstacle to Soviet-American amity but to the influence of specific interest groups (the military officer corps and the weapons manufacturers) in both countries. In the 1950's and the 1960's, the average American had viewed the remarkable prosperity of those years as simply the legitimate fruit of Americans' hard work and technical know-how. Students of the military-industrial complex, by contrast, pointed out the key role played by defense spending in the American economy of the Cold War era, detected ways in which such defense spending might ultimately be harming that economy, and predicted how difficult the economic adjustment would be if the Cold War ever ended.

After the Soviet Union collapsed in 1991, cutbacks in the American defense budget followed. Regions that were especially dependent on defense spending, such as Southern California, suffered from sharply rising unemployment. Heads of companies heavily dependent on Defense Department orders strove, not always successfully, to diversify. Conversion to nonmilitary production was difficult, since work done for the Defense Department had not imposed the intense pressure to cut costs found in the civilian marketplace.

Context

The sociologists who were first interested in the military-industrial complex were on the fringes of sociology rather than in the mainstream. When C. Wright Mills published *The Power Elite* in 1956, he was regarded as something of a maverick by his fellow sociologists. The military sociologist Morris Janowitz, who wrote *The*

Professional Soldier in 1960, neither saw the military officers' role in government decision making as inordinately influential nor regarded their relations with defense contractors as especially sinister. Between 1956 and 1965, interest in the topic was largely confined to journalists. The first scholars to pay special attention to the role of defense spending in the American economy were the obscure Marxist economists Paul A. Baran and Paul M. Sweezy, whose *Monopoly Capital: An Essay on the American Economic and Social Order* (1966) came out two years after Baran's death.

As a result of the controversy over American military intervention in Vietnam, the U.S. military's officer corps and its allegedly collusive ties with defense contractors were subjected to a hailstorm of criticism. Economists, political scientists, historians, legislators, journalists, socially conscious members of the clergy, left-wing activists, disgruntled Defense Department bureaucrats, and even a disillusioned former Marine Corps commandant (David Shoup) wrote books and articles or gave speeches denouncing the malign influence of the military-industrial complex. Sociologists Stephen Cobb and Stanley Lieberson tried to test the concept against various data. Although military sociologist Charles Moskos saw the term as more of a slogan than a stimulus for fruitful research, the sociological establishment ultimately made room for it. By the late 1980's, the Sociology of Peace and War was a recognized specialty within the American Sociological Association; the power of the military-industrial complex was one research topic within this specialty.

Although many social scientists and journalists regard the military-industrial complex as dependent on the Cold War for its existence, others, such as Seymour Melman, see it as capable of surviving and of conducting military intervention abroad in any international environment. Economist Bruce Brunton, in a 1991 article, argues that something in the nature of the American polity compels the federal government to keep the military-industrial complex alive. The events of the late 1980's and early 1990's did not definitively resolve this debate.

To be sure, the sudden disappearance of the Soviet threat did cast doubt on the need for a huge military force and a defense industry predicated on the notion of an endless Cold War. The sudden shrinkage in defense spending caused the once-close ties between military officers and private contractors to fray badly, as the military started to manufacture some of its own weapons and as retired officers found that they could no longer count on highly paid jobs with contractors. Yet it was still too soon to bury the military-industrial complex. American military intervention occurred in Panama in 1989, for example, without any Cold War context whatsoever, and by 1993, observers could already detect efforts by the federal government to encourage American arms sales abroad in order to prevent the total extinction of American weapons manufacturers.

Bibliography

Brunton, Bruce. "An Historical Perspective on the Future of the Military-Industrial Complex." In *Social Science Journal* 28 (1991): 45-62. The author, an economist, sees the American military-industrial complex as capable of surviving indefinitely in a post-Cold War future. Brunton traces five elements of the military-industrial complex far back into the pre-Cold War American past, one (the use of private contractors) as far back as the 1880's. Includes endnotes. Suitable for lower-level undergraduates.

Fitzgerald, A. Ernest. *The Pentagonists: An Insider's View of Waste, Mismanagement, and Fraud in Defense Spending.* Boston: Houghton Mifflin, 1989. Fitzgerald's book is part exposé, part autobiography. Its readability is reduced somewhat by the author's repeated attempts to prove that his own actions were always right. Yet Fitzgerald offers a unique perspective on the three-cornered relationship between the military, the contractors, and the Congress during the two final decades of the Cold War. Contains appendices and index.

Markusen, Ann, and Joel Yudkin. *Dismantling the Cold War Economy.* New York: Basic Books, 1992. Discusses both the positive and the negative effects of Cold War-era spending on the American economy. Urges government spending on housing, health, and mass transit to ease the pain of defense spending cutbacks. For the general reader. Tables, maps, endnotes, and index.

Melman, Seymour. *The Permanent War Economy: American Capitalism in Decline.* New York: Simon & Schuster, 1974. The classic exposition of the concept of defense spending as the gravedigger of the American economy. The 300-page text is easy for the general reader to follow. The endnotes are almost as filled with information as the text itself. Tables, graphs, endnotes, appendices, and index.

Moskos, Charles C., Jr. "The Concept of the Military-Industrial Complex: Radical Critique or Liberal Bogey." *Social Problems* 21 (April, 1974): 498-512. A military sociologist traces the historical evolution of the concept, appraises the extensive literature in which it appears, and expresses skepticism about the concept's utility for scholarship. Extensive references and informative footnotes.

Rosen, Steven, ed. *Testing the Theory of the Military-Industrial Complex.* Lexington, Mass.: Lexington Books, 1973. Twelve intellectually stimulating essays by social scientists that critically examine the theory's political and economic ramifications, Especially thought-provoking are the essay by political scientists Jerome Slater and Terry Nardin, attacking the entire concept, and the essays by sociologists Stanley Lieberson and Stephen Cobb. Includes tables, figures, and author information.

Walker, Gregg B., David A. Bella, and Steven J. Sprecher, eds. *The Military-Industrial Complex: Eisenhower's Warning Three Decades Later.* New York: Peter Lang, 1992. Thirteen essays written before the Soviet collapse. Authors include two sociologists, an economist, an engineer, two experts on rhetoric, and Seymour Melman. Hooks's essay, on the Pentagon's relationship with the aeronautics industry in the 1950's and 1960's, stresses the Pentagon's autonomy.

Paul D. Mageli

Cross-References

Capitalism, 191; The Cold War, 284; Industrial and Postindustrial Economies, 940; The Nation-State, 1282; The Power Elite, 1491; War and Revolution, 2164.

MILLENARIAN RELIGIOUS MOVEMENTS

Type of sociology: Major social institutions
Field of study: Religion

Millenarianism is the belief in a thousand-year period of peace and prosperity during which the righteous will enjoy the reign of Jesus on earth. This belief is related to other golden-age myths and can have revolutionary social implications in times of upheaval and anxiety.

Principal terms
APOCALYPSE: a literary genre in which future events are foretold, as a warning or admonition to religious believers; a cataclysm in which God destroys all that is evil and establishes a kingdom of the good
CHILIASM: a set of religious doctrines which includes the doctrine of the millennium; from the Greek *chilioi* ("thousand")
ESCHATOLOGY: the body of doctrines concerning the final state of the world
MILLENNIUM: a period of a thousand years, during which, in Christian belief, the dead will rise and enjoy a period of peace and prosperity during the reign of Jesus
PROPHECY: a form of communication in which current events are used to reveal God's purposes in history or in which future events are revealed to encourage the faithful to maintain their beliefs

Overview

In Christian belief, the doctrine of millenarianism maintains that Christ will return in splendor to rule over his saints (variously interpreted as the martyrs or the whole community of the faithful) in peace and plenty for a period of a thousand years. Satan will be bound for the duration of the thousand years and then will be released for a short period of evil-doing, while the righteous will ascend into heaven with Jesus and the wicked (who have also been revived for the millennium) will be condemned to hell. While there are conflicting features in the various prophecies of the millennium, the key characteristics are the belief in the return of Christ, the resurrection of the dead saints and their joyful participation in Christ's earthly reign, the defeat of the wicked and of the earthly powers hostile to God, and the final judgment of the righteous and the wicked, with their respective rewards and punishments.

Jesus himself, according to recent theological studies, actively built his ministry around the belief in the imminent coming of the kingdom of heaven. In fulfillment of Jewish prophecy, this would be a catastrophic physical event in which history would break off and the world would cease to exist. Yet Jesus, in asserting, "Behold, the kingdom of God is within you" (Luke 17:21, King James Version), also explains that the kingdom in a sense is already here. As the philosopher Karl Jaspers has argued in

Socrates, Buddha, Confucius, Jesus (1962), "the tidings of the kingdom carry a strange ambiguity. The kingdom will come and it is already here." Like other pious Jews, Jesus was reared with the expectation of a golden age still to come, and Christianity took over that confident expectation as it developed out of Judaism.

The millenarian beliefs of the ancient Jews were revealed in the Book of Daniel, which is commonly believed to have been written during the Maccabean revolt, around 165 B.C.E., although it is set in the Babylonian period of Nebuchadnezzar and his Persian successor Darius. It warns of the wickedness of a ten-horned beast, symbolizing an evil world power. The Old Testament prophets had already predicted a Day of Yahweh, in which divine wrath would be meted out to the unfaithful, but they had also promised that a "saving remnant" would survive these terrible punishments. The prime source of Christian millenarian beliefs was the Book of Revelation; chapter 20 envisions an angel who "laid hold on the dragon, that old serpent, which is the Devil, and Satan, and bound him a thousand years" (Rev. 20:2) but also warns that "when the thousand years are expired, Satan shall be loosed out of his prison" and will lead the armies of "Gog and Magog" into battle (Rev. 20:7-8). At the same time, the writer foresees that the martyrs "lived and reigned with Christ a thousand years" (Rev. 20:4). Possibly no biblical text has inspired more urgent commentary, especially from millenarian prophets, than Revelation 20.

Although Christ was ambiguous about the location and duration of the kingdom of heaven, the author of Revelation provided a vivid, specific prophecy of the millennium to come. Cerinthus, a Gnostic who wrote at the end of the first century, imagined a sensual one-thousand-year kingdom of Christ, but Gnostics generally rejected millenarian beliefs. Irenaeus helped to establish millenarian beliefs in the early Church, arguing that it was crucial to believe that Christ's reign will come to pass on this earth. The poet Commodianus and the theologian Lactantius drew on earlier millenarian beliefs to proclaim the splendor of the thousand-year reign. Origen of Alexandria, however, depicted the kingdom of heaven as an internal event in the souls of believers, and Saint Augustine firmly opposed the idea of the millennium. When Christianity exchanged its status as a persecuted sect for that of the official religion of the Roman Empire in the fourth century, the Church quickly set out to suppress millenarian beliefs.

It was previously held by those humanistic scholars who were annoyed by the persistence of millennial beliefs that the Middle Ages were free from millenarian yearnings. Norman Cohn, however, in *The Pursuit of the Millennium* (1957), has shown how medieval theologians reinvigorated the eschatological ideas of the Old Testament prophets. In the Middle Ages, disturbing and frightening events inspired social unrest and violence and led to the formation of salvationist groups. Such causes as excess population on marginal land, outbreaks of plague, changes in authority, and complaints about the corruption of the clergy inspired millenarian beliefs. Local prophets such as John Bull, the priest who helped to organize the Peasants' Revolt of 1381 in England, inspired mass movements by claiming to be ordained to lead the mission of bringing history to a divinely mandated conclusion; in thirteenth century Italy, Joachim of Fiore proclaimed the arrival of the third age of history, the Age of the Spirit. Belief in the millennium increased during the Reformation in the sixteenth century and contributed to the revolutionary fervor of later centuries.

Because of the threat of nuclear war and the rapid rate of social change, millenarian beliefs continued to enjoy wide circulation in the late twentieth century. Despite the constitutional separation of church and state, there is little doubt that many modern American political leaders have been influenced by millenarian ideas. Religious believers to this day find in the set of doctrines concerning the millennium an answer to their urgent questions about the shape of history within the divine plan for humankind.

Applications

Although most mainstream American Christian churches now profess little interest in millenarian beliefs, the biblical promise of the return of Christ still inspires interest in the millennium. Christian fundamentalists regularly continue to debate the possible relationship of events in the Middle East or Russia to the fulfillment of ancient prophecies concerning the imminent return of Christ and his reign among his saints. They debate the timing of the "rapture," in which faithful Christians will be caught up in the air with Jesus, and ponder the nature of the "tribulation," which will follow the freeing of Satan from his shackles.

Historian Norman Cohn sparked controversy by finding "the source of the giant fanaticisms which in our day have convulsed the world" in the "boundless, millennial promise made with boundless, prophet-like conviction to a number of rootless and desperate men"; for Cohn, both Nazi and communist ideology shared the fervent belief in a millennial new age. His effort to link modern totalitarian movements to medieval millenarianism has been hotly debated. It is possible to agree with Cohn that millenarian beliefs underlay many revolutionary political movements since the late Middle Ages, the most conspicuous of which was the notorious Anabaptist uprising at Munster in The Netherlands under John of Leyden (1534-1535). Even Judaism, which had long resisted the political implications of millenarian beliefs, found its millenarian prophet in Sabbatai Sevi, who inspired Jews in the mid-seventeenth century from Holland to Persia with his millenarian fervor.

In England, millenarian ideas can be traced back to the fifteenth century, and by the seventeenth century millenarianism was the norm rather than the exception. Examining English religious beliefs during the seventeenth century, William Lamont, in *Godly Rule* (1969), asked, "What if millenarianism meant not alienation from the spirit of the age but a total involvement with it?" As a member of the first generation of English Puritans, John Foxe wrote his hugely influential *Book of Martyrs* according to the European millenarian ideas he had discovered during his exile under Queen Mary I. Belief in the imminent return of Christ and the inauguration of a golden age became widespread in seventeenth century England. Popular belief in the imminence of unprecedented social upheaval made possible the English Revolution, during which King Charles I was beheaded by a revolutionary tribunal. Millenarian arguments persuaded Oliver Cromwell to readmit the Jews into England, whence they had been

Sociology

banished since the thirteenth century. Such events in so socially stable a country as England never would have occurred without the wide dissemination of millenarian ideas.

Religious sects such as the Diggers and Ranters freely preached the imminent return of King Charles at mid-century. In 1650, the Ranter prophet Abiezer Coppe preached with the urgency of the Old Testament prophets, predicting the Day of Yahweh and the inauguration of a new age: "Thus saith the Lord, I inform you, that I overturn, overturn, overturn. And as the Bishops, Charles, and the Lords, have had their turn, overturn, so your turn shall be next. . . . The Eternall God, the mighty Leveller is comming, yea come, even at the door; and what will you do in that day" (*A Fiery Flying Roll*, 1973). The Fifth Monarchy Men were the most specifically millenarian of the sects of the English Revolution, deriving their name from the prophet Daniel's vision of the four beasts, or empires, who would be destroyed and replaced by the reign of God and his saints.

Although the depth of religious fervor declined with the advent of the Restoration in 1660, when such beliefs came to be dismissed by rationalists as evidence of madness and overheated blood, millenarian beliefs persisted among Quakers and Methodists and resurfaced in the nineteenth century among such Christian sects as the Russellites (now the Jehovah's Witnesses), the Mormons (the Church of Latter-Day Saints), and the Seventh-day Adventists. Christian politicians, from Oliver Cromwell to American presidents at "prayer breakfasts" and election rallies, have often had recourse to the language of the millennium.

Small sects led by charismatic individual prophets, such as Jim Jones in Jonestown, Guyana, in 1978 and David Koresh in Waco, Texas, in 1993, have shown their willingness to commit mass suicide on the basis of millenarian prophecies. In the political arena, president Ronald Reagan once speculated publicly that "we may be the generation that sees Armageddon," the prophesied final battle between Christ and Satan. With the collapse of the Soviet Union and the end of the Cold War, millenarian commentators had to make new political identifications of Gog and Magog and the ten-horned beast of Daniel and Revelation. When federal agents of the American government attacked the stronghold of a millenarian sect (the Branch Davidians) in Waco, Texas, in 1993, they clearly misunderstood the depth and tenacity of millenarian ideas, just as they failed to understand the tradition of believers who are willing to die in order to bring in the millennium.

Context

Beliefs in the millennium, which existed in Old Testament Judaism and were a powerful force in the early Christian church, have a deep-seated psychological appeal and persist among many individual Christians and Christian churches to this day. These beliefs are related to other universal myths of a golden age and the hope of recovering a lost period of peace and prosperity. They imply the belief that lost time is recoverable, as described by the seventeenth century English poet John Milton, who predicted that "time will run back, and fetch the age of gold," and they are related to such secular and nationalistic beliefs as the "sleeping emperor" (such as England's King Arthur or Germany's Frederick Barbarossa), who will someday awaken to lead his country again. In Third World countries in recent centuries they have merged with local myths to form new beliefs, as in the "cargo cults" of Melanesia and elsewhere. There, believers conflated local myths about the "Day of the God" with the beliefs brought by Christian missionaries into the expectation of a period of material ease and prosperity.

Millenarian beliefs have been too easily dismissed as the result of credulous superstition, which would somehow be defeated by the rise of rationalism. They have had potent political implications and often revive during periods of social and political upheaval, as in the late Middle Ages, the revolutions in early modern Europe, and in the twentieth century. As J. F. C. Harrison noted in *The Second Coming* (1979), "millennialism and millenarianism were ways of looking at the world, rather than specific doctrines." At the same time, it has been observed that millenarian beliefs have been paradoxical from the beginning. For one thing, the millennium technically refers to the fixed period of one thousand years prophesied in the Judeo-Christian tradition, but the term can be applied to a perfect age still to come or, as in the golden age myth, used to describe an imagined perfect period in the past. Some sects have argued that the millennium is already here, but that recognition of that reality is only slowly dawning on believers.

Sociologist Bryan Wilson, in *Magic and the Millennium* (1973), has commented on the painful paradox of these beliefs: "Millennialism always promises social transformation, and although always erroneous, it none the less creates a new conscious expectation of social change." For people who are deeply dissatisfied with their material, spiritual, or political conditions, or for whom the concept of an afterlife in "heaven" is too remote, the millennium will always exert a profound appeal. Groups of believers were said to have gathered on mountain tops in expectation of millennial activity in the year 1000 B.C.E., and the advent of the next millennium will doubtless produce comparable expectations.

Always working against millenarian beliefs are commonsense objections; most people simply do not expect divine intervention in their lives or drastic apocalyptic events. Modern Christians frequently view the kingdom of heaven as an internal psychological condition rather than as a dramatic external event, although Jesus himself may have inclined toward the latter position. Also working against millenarian beliefs is the belief that an omnipotent God does not need to work with spectacular dramatic interventions. Millenarianism promises a sudden and climactic reversal of the progress of human history, and it appeals to the persecuted and the paranoid as well as to those hoping for a profound improvement in the human condition. From a sociological perspective, it is its role as a catalyst for the anticipation and inauguration of social change that is millenarianism's most important and enduring characteristic.

Bibliography

Cohn, Norman. *The Pursuit of the Millennium: Revolutionary Messianism in Medieval and Reformation Europe and Its Bearing on Modern Totalitarian Movements.* 2d ed. New York: Harper & Row, 1961. A controversial and wide-ranging pioneering study of the survival of medieval revolutionary millenarianism in twentieth century Nazi and communist ideology.

Coppe, Abiezer. *A Fiery Flying Roll.* Exeter, England: The Rota, 1973 (facsimile of 1650 edition). An outstanding literary example of the revival of leftist millenarian beliefs during the English Revolution (1642-1660), written in a fiery style by a prophet formerly dismissed as "mad."

Harrison, J. F. C. *The Second Coming: Popular Millenarianism, 1780-1850.* New Brunswick, N.J.: Rutgers University Press, 1979. Argues that millenarianism was a way of looking at the world, not a rigid set of doctrines; helpfully studies popular beliefs among people too easily written off as cranks and lunatics.

Jaspers, Karl. *Socrates, Buddha, Confucius, Jesus: The Paradigmatic Individuals.* Edited by Hannah Arendt. Translated by Ralph Manheim. San Diego: Harcourt Brace Jovanovich, 1962. Deftly examines the paradoxical nature of Jesus' recorded utterances about the nature of the Kingdom of Heaven.

Kirsch, J. P. "Millennium and Millenarianism." In *The Catholic Encyclopedia*, edited by Charles G. Herbermann et al. Vol. 10. New York: Encyclopedia Press, 1913. Still useful in its analysis of millenarian beliefs but eager to deny the persistence of these beliefs in the medieval Church.

Lamont, William M. *Godly Rule: Politics and Religion, 1603-60.* London: Macmillan, 1969. Respectfully considers the millenarian thinkers in England in the period leading up to and including the English Revolution.

Thrupp, Sylvia, ed. *Millennial Dreams in Action: Studies in Revolutionary Religious Movements.* New York: Schocken, 1970. A useful symposium on the persistence of millenarian beliefs in Christian and contemporary Third World cultures.

Wilson, Bryan R. *Magic and the Millennium: A Sociological Study of Religious Movements of Protest Among Tribal and Third-World Peoples.* New York: Harper & Row, 1973. Usefully classifies seekers after salvation according to their responses to the world; argues that even if millenarianism is always wrong in promising specific social change, it does create the firm expectation of social transformation among believers.

Byron Nelson

Cross-References

Churches, Denominations, and Sects, 246; Cults, 399; Religious Miracles and Visions, 1623; Social Movements, 1826; Socialization: Religion, 1894; The Sociology of Religion, 1952; Types of Supernaturalism, 2024.

MINORITY AND MAJORITY GROUPS

Type of sociology: Racial and ethnic relations
Fields of study: Patterns and consequences of contact; Systems of social stratification

Minority groups are defined by their powerlessness relative to other groups in a society, and majority groups are the reverse: They dominate other groups. This concept helps explain why and how conflict occurs in ethnically stratified societies.

Principal terms
ANGLO-CONFORMITY: a majority policy which holds that immigrants to the United States must adopt the culture of the dominant group
ASSIMILATION: the process whereby immigrants are absorbed into a society
ETHNIC GROUP: a group that is defined by reference to such cultural characteristics as its religion and language; ethnic groups are self-conscious social units
ETHNIC STRATIFICATION: a situation in which racial and/or ethnic groups are arranged hierarchically such that those nearer the top enjoy greater access to social desirables
HEGEMONY: a situation in which a social class totally dominates a society socially, politically, and culturally
INDIGENOUS POPULATION: a group of people who are long-settled and have claim to a particular territory
PLURALISTIC SOCIETY: a society consisting of large numbers of people from different racial and ethnic backgrounds
POWER: the ability of a social actor (individual or group) to achieve its wishes against the opposition of other social actors
RACIAL GROUP: a group that is defined socially, using physical (biological) features which a particular society deems to be relevant

Overview

"Minority group" and "majority group" are complementary concepts (one implies the other) that denote a hierarchical relationship of dominance and subjugation between groups. The terms carry much emotional and political baggage because of their association with two related concepts, "race" and "ethnicity." To understand minority and majority groups, one needs to distinguish between the sociological viewpoint just outlined and the meanings attributed to the terms by the ordinary person in the street. Sociologists tend to define the concepts strictly, whereas nonacademics define them loosely. This lack of precision lends itself to misconceptions, but it is also true that the sociological viewpoint has inherent problems.

Anthropologists Charles Wagley and Marvin Harris have put forward a widely accepted definition of the term "minority group." In *Minorities in the New World: Six*

Case Studies (1958), they argued that five characteristics identify these groups. First, they are relatively powerless compared with members of the dominant group. Second, they share distinctive cultural and/or physical characteristics that distinguish them from the dominant group. This fact, along with their powerlessness, exposes them to unequal treatment. Third, their distinctive traits cause minority groups to become self-conscious social units. Fourth, an established rule of descent exists for transmitting membership in minority groups across generations. Fifth, members of minority groups tend to marry within their groups.

Most social scientists agree that these criteria are not equally important. They view minority groups' relative powerlessness as the most important criterion distinguishing them from majority groups. For example, in *Majority and Minority: The Dynamics of Race and Ethnicity in American Life* (1991), sociologist Norman Yetman argues that "minority group" is synonymous with the term "subordinate," and "majority group" is synonymous with "dominant." The main implication of this viewpoint is that, contrary to what one might assume, members of minority groups can constitute a numerical majority in their society, and majority group members might be a numerical minority. The classic example of this is South Africa, where blacks, although they constitute approximately 75 percent of the population, were powerless under apartheid, while whites, constituting approximately 14 percent of the population, were dominant.

Sociologists distinguish between racial, ethnic, religious, and gender groups, on the one hand, and minority and majority groups on the other. They view the latter twin concepts as subsuming the others. That is, majority groups and minority groups may consist of distinct races, ethnic groups, religious groups, and gender groups. These various types of majority/minority groups differ from each other symbolically. Thus, racial majority/minority groups are set apart by physical features, ethnic majority/ minority groups by their unique cultural attributes, religious majority/minority groups by unique spiritual beliefs, and gender majority/minority groups by societal expectations of sex-linked characteristics. A minority and majority group might display a number of these characteristics simultaneously. An example of an overdetermined minority group would be black, Haitian, female Catholics.

Nonacademics often adopt a loose definition of minority and majority groups. They tend to completely ignore the latter concept and focus on the former. In this focus, "minority group" becomes synonymous with specific racial and/or ethnic groups, and the term "minority" is often used to refer to individuals belonging to these groups. Thus, in the United States, the term "minorities" is often understood to mean blacks and/or Hispanics. This is controversial, because such usage often occurs in a pejorative context and may be viewed as a way of attacking those two groups. Used in this way, the term "minority" can become a weapon in intergroup conflict.

Adopting the sociological viewpoint on majority/minority groups leaves less room for confusion. Nevertheless, this viewpoint also has problems. To begin with, it seems counterintuitive to suggest that numerical majorities can be, in fact, "minorities." This is not a problem when a group—for example, African Americans—is both numerically smaller and less powerful than the dominant group. As sociologist Pierre L. van den Berghe (*Dictionary of Race and Ethnic Relations*, 1988) has suggested, however, that colonial subjects who vastly outnumber their colonial rulers might take umbrage at the notion that they constitute a "minority." The problem is that the commonsense understanding of "minority" conflicts with sociological usage; therefore, the potential for confusion exists.

Van den Berghe even argues that this confusion is deliberate, since it serves useful political purposes. In pluralistic societies—such as the United States—that have instituted affirmative action programs to aid historically disadvantaged groups, being identified as a "minority group" can prove beneficial in some instances. The problem lies in deciding which groups are minority groups. Blacks and Hispanics are uncontroversial choices, but whether Jews, Japanese Americans, and Chinese Americans should be considered minority groups is more problematic and controversial. These groups, though numerical minorities, enjoy a level of socioeconomic success which far outstrips that of blacks and Hispanics. Thus, the term "minority group," with its connotation of powerlessness and relative deprivation, seems somewhat inappropriate. A fuzzy definition of "minority group," however, would give these economically successful groups a firmer claim to minority status and, with it, even greater access to societal resources. Van den Berghe suggests that similar confusion over the term "majority group" allows the tiny elite who exercise hegemony over the United States to cloud their identity and escape criticism by being lumped into a larger category— white Anglo-Saxon Protestants—who are perceived, mistakenly, as the dominant group.

Applications

The significance of the minority group/majority group concept lies in its ability to explain conflict that occurs between a variety of groups, for a variety of reasons, in different societies. Groups fight with each other because of (among other things) perceived racial differences, cultural dissimilarities, and religion. Despite these apparent differences, the question arises as to whether these conflicts share common features. A key feature is the situation in which a dominant group is imposing its will on a subordinate group. Thus, a common element in group conflict is ethnic stratification.

Ethnic stratification describes a situation in which groups enjoy unequal access to such desirables as wealth, income, privilege, and power. Sociologist Emory Bogardus has demonstrated the existence of such a hierarchy in the United States. In "Racial Distance Changes in the United States During the Past Thirty Years" (1958), he argued that Americans view whites as occupying the topmost rung of the social hierarchy, while blacks, Hispanics, and American Indians fall nearer the bottom. Specific groups may change their relative position because of social and political events; nevertheless, the overall ranking of groups has remained stable for decades. This hierarchical arrangement of racial and ethnic groups is significant because it implies the existence of conflict between them. It must be noted, though, that conflict can also occur in situations in which groups relate to each other on a "parallel" rather than hierarchical basis. Donald Horowitz, in *Ethnic Groups in Conflict* (1985), describes this situation as occurring in plural societies in which groups alternate in dominating specific areas of the society, without establishing a clear-cut overall dominance.

The notion of majority groups and minority groups has been used to help explain the development of ethnic stratification and the patterns of conflict and consensus that develop in plural societies. For example, sociologist Stanley Lieberson has argued that ethnic stratification results from the manner in which plural societies were first settled. He distinguishes between two types: those in which an indigenous population is conquered by an immigrant group and those in which an immigrant group becomes subordinated to an established native population. Both of these situations result in ethnic stratification. In the former, the conquered indigenous population becomes the minority group, and the conquerors form the majority group. In the latter, the immigrant group enters a society on terms laid down by the already established indigenous population. Thus, the immigrants become minority groups and the indigenous population is the majority group.

Sociologists such as Milton Gordon in *Human Nature, Class, and Ethnicity* (1978), George Simpson and J. Milton Yinger in *Racial and Cultural Minorities* (1985), and Peter I. Rose in *They and We* (1990) have shown that a systematic view of the causes of conflict between groups may be obtained by analyzing their relationships in terms of majority policies toward minority groups and the responses of the minority groups. From the viewpoint of the majority group, the following possibilities, ranging from least tolerant to most tolerant, exist: extermination, expulsion, slavery, segregation, and assimilation. In the United States, the policy of assimilation may also be analyzed in terms of the degree of toleration extended by the majority group (in this case, whites). Doing this, according to Gordon, yields—in order from least to most tolerant—Anglo-conformity, the melting pot, and cultural pluralism.

Applying this typology to intergroup relations in the United States helps explain the pattern of conflict that has been observed. Groups have been subjected to different majority policies and have, therefore, responded differently. For example, American Indians have experienced a combination of extermination, expulsion, segregation, and assimilation; African Americans have experienced expulsion, slavery, and segregation; and European immigrants, segregation and assimilation. This typology also jibes with Lieberson's argument that the degree of intergroup conflict depends on whether an immigrant group is subjugating an indigenous population or is being subjugated by that indigenous population. The former situation produces much conflict, since the indigenous population resists domination. The history of white/American Indian contact is an example of this. The latter situation produces less conflict, because immigrants enter a society on terms established by the majority group. If they disagree with these terms, the possibility of returning to their homeland exists (this is not true of subjugated indigenous populations), and, in any case, the majority group can limit the number of immigrants entering their society.

To account fully for intergroup conflict, the viewpoint of minority groups must be taken into account. The crucial question is how they will respond to the majority group's policies. Rose argues that the possibilities include submission, withdrawal, integration, and separation. In submission, members of the minority group internalize the majority group's negative evaluation of them and become self-haters. Those practicing withdrawal take this to the ultimate by attempting physically to become a part of the majority group (by "passing"). Integrationists reject self-hatred and insist on full participation in the society. Separatists reject both self-hatred and the majority group, insisting that self-segregation is the best response to majority group dominance. Of these four responses, submission and withdrawal are the least likely to lead to conflict with the majority group. On the other hand, separation and integration have great potential for conflict, since the majority group might object to members of the minority group either leaving the society or becoming too deeply assimilated.

Context

The concept of minority groups has long been used in Europe to describe national groups who, for whatever reason (for example, through conquest by another group), had come to form small enclaves in societies dominated by other groups. Early in the twentieth century, the concept was adopted by American sociologists seeking a comprehensive term to describe the multifaceted intergroup conflict that has been a recurring theme in American history. With respect to blacks, American Indians, the Chinese, and the Japanese, the conflict seemed to be racial; with respect to groups such as eastern European Jews, the Irish, and Italians, the conflict seemed to revolve around religious and cultural differences. As noted above, the unifying thread was domination by one group (native whites) of these various other groups. This suggested to sociologists such as Donald Young the need for a word to encapsulate all these various conflicts. In *American Minority Peoples* (1932), he suggested that the term "minority groups" be used to describe the distinctive groups who found themselves in conflict with the white majority.

Since the time of Young's proposal, the minority group/majority group concept has gained widespread acceptance because of the universality of intergroup conflict following European decolonialization. This process created new states such as India and Pakistan, but it also led to widespread racial, ethnic, religious, and nationalistic conflicts. Not all of these can be described as minority group/majority group situations, but many are. Examples include the Rodiya and Sinhalese in Sri Lanka, the Hutu and Tutsi in Burundi, and the Osu and Ibo in Nigeria. In *Ethnic Groups in Conflict,* Horowitz gives numerous examples of such conflict occurring in formerly colonized areas.

The more industrially developed areas of the world are also the scene of numerous minority group/majority group conflicts. The conflict between blacks and whites in the United States is perhaps the most well known, but to this could be added French Canadians and English-speaking Canadians, aboriginal Canadians and white Canadians, Australian aborigines and white Australians, white New Zealanders and Maoris, and nonwhite immigrants and whites in the United Kingdom. Even more pressing examples are to be found in eastern Europe, where the breakup of the former Soviet Union has allowed long-standing racial, ethnic, religious, and nationalistic hatreds to flare into open warfare. This breakup has combined with economic recession in western Europe to reawaken antiminority fervor. Thus, in West Germany, eastern European, Turkish, Vietnamese, and African immigrants have been repeatedly attacked by neo-Nazi groups. In France, agitation against Arab and African immigrants led the government to pass laws making it easier to track the movement of these immigrants. Even traditionally tolerant countries such as Denmark have experienced anti-immigrant sentiment. The prevalence of this type of conflict illustrates why the twin minority/majority group concept is likely to retain its utility.

Bibliography

Bogardus, Emory. "Racial Distance Changes in the United States During the Past Thirty Years." *Sociology and Social Research* 43 (November/December, 1958): 127-135. This is one of many works in which Bogardus, using his social distance scale, demonstrates the persistence of ethnic stratification in the United States.

Gordon, Milton. *Human Nature, Class, and Ethnicity*. New York: Oxford University Press, 1978. Gordon's book contains many useful ideas but is not easily accessible.

Horowitz, Donald. *Ethnic Groups in Conflict*. Berkeley: University of California Press, 1985. Horowitz's book is required reading for students of race and ethnicity. Although quite long, it is well written and contains numerous examples of intergroup conflict involving majority/minority situations. One of its few weaknesses is that he focuses mainly on underdeveloped countries.

Lieberson, Stanley. "A Societal Theory of Race and Ethnic Relations." *American Sociological Review* 26 (December, 1961): 902-910. Lieberson's article presents a historically grounded theory that seeks to explain how ethnic stratification arose and influences intergroup conflict. Although the article is short, his argument is plausible.

Rose, Peter I. *They and We*. 4th ed. New York: McGraw-Hill, 1990. This is a well-written and accessible book on racial and ethnic relations in the United States. Much of it focuses on the conflict between African Americans and whites.

Simpson, George, and J. Milton Yinger. *Racial and Cultural Minorities*. 5th ed. New York: Plenum Press, 1985. This textbook presents an encyclopedic discussion of issues related to race and ethnicity. It is well written, accessible, very informative, and required reading for those interested in this field.

Van den Berghe, Pierre L. "Minorities." In *Dictionary of Race and Ethnic Relations*, edited by E. Ellis Cashmore. London: Routledge, 1988. This book is also required reading for students of race and ethnicity. It contains sharp and incisive cross-cultural discussions of topics ranging from affirmative action to Zionism. It is written for nonspecialists and is, therefore, very accessible.

Wagley, Charles, and Marvin Harris. *Minorities in the New World: Six Case Studies*. New York: Columbia University Press, 1958. Wagley and Harris' book has been influential and is well worth reading.

Yetman, Norman, ed. *Majority and Minority: The Dynamics of Race and Ethnicity in American Life*. 5th ed. Boston: Allyn & Bacon, 1991. This collection of twenty-nine articles gives a comprehensive overview of the field of race and ethnicity. Yetman's introductions to the various sections are comprehensive and informative.

Young, Donald. *American Minority Peoples*. New York: Harper & Brothers, 1932. An early book devoted to the subject of minority/majority relations. Young is said to have introduced the concept of minority groups into the sociological literature.

Milton D. Vickerman

Cross-References

Annihilation or Expulsion of Racial or Ethnic Groups, 92; Assimilation: The United States, 140; Conquest and Annexation of Racial or Ethnic Groups, 353; Ethnicity and Ethnic Groups, 689; Pluralism versus Assimilation, 1374; Prejudice and Stereotyping, 1505; Race and Racial Groups, 1552; Racial and Ethnic Stratification, 1579; Slavery, 1754; Social Stratification: Analysis and Overview, 1839.

MOBS, RIOTS, AND PANICS

Type of sociology: Collective behavior and social movements
Field of study: Patterns of social interaction

Mobs, riots, and panics are types of collective behavior that occur on special occasions when the usual laws and norms that regulate behavior fail to do so. Acts of violence and destruction are integral to mobs and riots and usually, but not invariably, to panics. Understanding these phenomena is an essential component of understanding the dynamics of groups.

Principal terms
COLLECTIVE BEHAVIOR: the responses and reactions of groups or assemblies of individuals to various social situations
CROWD: a group of people who interact with one another in a manner consistent with their particular goals, problems, or situational setting
EMERGENT NORMS: the normative guidelines that direct and control the course of action during mob-induced riots and during panics, and which replace the norms and laws of the governing social order
MOB: an aggregate of loosely connected individuals that suddenly fuses into a collective assembly with beliefs and feelings that lead to violent and destructive behavior
PANIC: a strong reaction of fear to a perceived threat which is characterized by a loss of self-control, self-centered behavior, and flight
RIOT: a relatively spontaneous form of collective behavior that is characterized by violent and destructive attacks on people and property

Overview

Mobs, riots, and panics are forms of collective behavior. In these three forms of collective behavior, the behavior is situationally contingent; that is, it occurs on a special occasion rather than on an everyday or routine occasion. The governing social order weakens and loses its capacity to provide direction, form, and an outlet or channel for that behavior. Thus, the norms or general beliefs that order, structure, and guide the group's actions are emergent, situationally derived, or spontaneous. These norms stand in contrast to formalized norms, which are culturally predetermined, established rules that are supported by the force of tradition.

Central to this definition of collective behavior is the concept of the crowd. Sam Wright (1978) defines a crowd as an assembly of interacting individuals that engages in activities that are particular or unique to its goals, its problems, or the occasion. Crowd behavior is inherently neither rational nor irrational. The behavior may be perceived and interpreted as irrational and senseless by individuals who are not part of the crowd. To crowd members, however, their actions are appropriate according to their perception of the situation. The behavior of crowds is guided and constrained by emergent norms. Mobs, riots, and panics can thus be viewed as particular forms of crowd behavior.

Michael Brown and Amy Goldin (1973) characterize a mob as a violative mass of individuals that abruptly coalesces into an assembly with collective beliefs and feelings of anger and frustration for other individuals or institutions. On the basis of these feelings and beliefs, the mob acts illegally in a violent and destructive manner in order to achieve its ends or goals, heedless of the rights of others. From the point of view of outsiders, the behavior of the mob is viewed as irrational, violent, disruptive, and nihilistic. Lynch mobs are a prototypical example. William T. Gossett, former president of the American Bar Association, characterized the forms of protest behavior of the 1960's as mob behavior. Such behavior retarded rather than produced progress, trampled rather than established rights, and impeded rather than enhanced the advancement of civilization. Mobs were the antithesis of the efforts of many generations to produce a civilized society. Mob violence and destruction were not to be tolerated by any society that considered itself to be civilized.

Mobs and riots are indivisible. For example, Rodney F. Allen and Charles H. Adair (1969) defined riots as mob attacks on persons and property. Gary Marx defined a riot as a relatively spontaneous form of illegitimate group violence that contradicted group norms, the same violence that also characterizes the actions of a mob. A riot is thus a type of behavior and a mob is a collective assembly that is characterized by its acting in a riotous manner. Therefore, riots can only be instigated by mobs.

Sam Wright (1978) emphasized that a riot is far different from other collective behaviors, such as the behavior of spectators watching a parade. As distinct from parade behavior, riotous behavior (Wright compares the 1965 riots in Watts with parades) is emergent; that is, not institutional, planned, anticipated, or predictable. The significant behaviors that define the riot are destructive and violent. Several different behaviors may occur simultaneously and independently in the same location, such as looting, assaulting, and throwing rocks. Participants in a riot may alternate among these different behaviors. Behaviors appear and then disappear, to be replaced by yet other behaviors. Whereas a parade requires an audience, many of the behaviors in a riot (for example, looting) do not require an audience.

Panic was defined by Enrico L. Quarantelli in 1964 as a pronounced fear reaction to a perceived threat which is characterized by a loss of self-control that results in nonsocial or nonrational flight behavior. To sociologists, panics are bodily or physical threats, as opposed to nonbodily threats such as going bankrupt (as in financial "panics"). Individuals who panic invariably define a specific situation as highly personally dangerous and immediately threatening to their physical survival if they remain in the situation. An intense fear for personal safety and feelings of impotency, powerlessness, aloneness, and helplessness occur. The individual believes that his or her survival is dependent on a quick reaction. There is a loss of self-control. The person focuses on escaping the threat and becomes highly self-centered. Thus, panic is nonsocial; individuals do not weigh the social consequences of their actions. Escape manifests itself in nonrational flight from the threatening situation. Ordinary social norms, normal patterns of interaction with the group, and possible alternative courses of action are ignored. Panic behavior is not entirely irrational, because the person does not regress to a primitive level of behaving but instead makes use of modes of responding that have been socially learned.

Panics occur in two types of group situations. An unorganized group lacks continuity of existence, awareness on the part of members of being members of the group, and differentiation of function, all of which the organized group possesses. Examples of unorganized groups are passengers on a ship, an audience in a movie theater, patrons in a nightclub or restaurant, and unconnected and unrelated individuals living in different parts of the country but reacting to the same event. A military unit in combat is an example of an organized group.

Applications

In July of 1981, a series of mob-induced riots occurred in Britain's inner cities. The riots began when neo-Nazi white skinheads destroyed several Indian and Pakistani stores and fought with a group of Asians. The Asians also attacked police, whom they believed were only there to protect the whites. In the ensuing mayhem, sixty policemen were injured, twenty-five shops were damaged, seven vehicles were destroyed, and a pub was burned. The next night, in the Toxleth area of Liverpool, police arrested a motorcyclist but were attacked by a gathering crowd, which instigated three nights of riots. A racially mixed mob consisting of hundreds of blacks and whites attacked police, looted, and set fires. In all, more than twenty buildings were gutted, and 225 policemen and thirty-five rioters were injured. Eventually, the riots spread to eleven areas of London and Manchester, as well as to four other cities.

Eleven years later, in May of 1992 in Los Angeles, the most lethal urban riot in U.S. history was precipitated by the acquittal of four white policemen in the beating of Rodney King, an African American man. The rioters were primarily African American and Latino, but some whites were involved. The riot occurred primarily in the African American and Latino South Central area of Los Angeles but did spread to some outlying areas. The riot featured confrontations between mob members and police, racially inspired violence, and widespread looting and vandalism. Fifty-three people died (mostly African Americans and Latinos) and more than 2,300 were injured; more than 600 buildings were completely destroyed by fire; more than 2,200 buildings were damaged by fires, looters, and vandals; and total damages were estimated at $735 million.

These prototypical examples of riots and mob behavior elicited attempts to understand the underlying causes of the riots in the hope that effective steps could be taken to prevent future riots. The forthcoming explanations are illuminating in terms of revealing the complexity and number of causal variables suggested, the difficulties in responding effectively to these variables, and the ways in which the explanations and suggested remedies reflect the political orientations of the analysts. Liberal politicians in America and Britain attributed the riots to a reaction against massive unemployment, particularly among young people, impoverished living conditions, and lack of opportunity caused by the uncaring and insensitive economic policies of Prime Minister Margaret Thatcher's Conservative Party and the Republican Party of presidents Ronald Reagan and George Bush. Desperate people, ignored and unhelped by an insensitive, uncaring, abusive, and often racially biased government bureaucracy and criminal justice system channeled their outrage and frustration into riots. The solutions suggested were to provide the underprivileged with opportunities to become better educated and skilled, to revitalize the economic and social life of the inner city, and to appoint significant numbers of law enforcement officers and judges from all racial backgrounds.

Individuals with a conservative orientation blamed the riots on the mobs. Margaret Thatcher said that the rioters were motivated only by "naked greed." She denied any relationship between poverty and violence, arguing that there were many poor societies in which citizens were scrupulously honorable and would never riot. Articles in the conservative magazine *National Review* blamed the Los Angeles riots variously on a lack of moral courage on the part of the rioters to face up to their problems, a failure of liberal policies, and the failure of the rioters to accept personal responsibility to overcome dependence on government assistance. The black economist Thomas Sowell said that the riots reflected a decline in social standards and institutions and contended that Congress and the president only rewarded the mob for rioting by giving them federal aid and programs.

One of the most famous examples of a panic occurred in 1942 at the Coconut Grove nightclub in Los Angeles. The club was packed; somehow a woman's hair caught fire. She ran across the floor, yelling "Fire!" The eight hundred patrons all tried simultaneously to exit via a single revolving door. The flames and smoke intensified, and the door jammed as patrons pushed it in both directions simultaneously. Patrons were thrown under tables and trampled to death. Those who were left behind swarmed over the fallen people, who piled up in a layer of corpses. In all, some five hundred people were killed. The fire was brought quickly under control; it was the response to the fire that caused most of the deaths.

Another famous panic occurred on Halloween night in 1938, when Orson Welles presented a radio dramatization of H. G. Wells's *War of the Worlds* that was so realistic and effective that millions of Americans thought that the country was being invaded by deadly Martians. The ensuing panic involved at least a million of the six million listeners, which made it the most widespread panic of the twentieth century. People prayed, cried, telephoned farewells, attempted to rescue loved ones or warn neighbors, summoned ambulances and police cars, sought information from newspapers and radios, or fled. Hadley Cantril (1966) attributed the panic behavior to personal susceptibility to suggestion and a failure to analyze the experience critically, which led those who panicked to misinterpret a number of environmental situations. For example, the panic behavior of others was interpreted as corroboratory evidence that the perceived threat was real, which induced further panic.

To the extent that panics are a result of personal susceptibility, there is no remedy for them. All that society can do is to ensure that the environment is as hazard free as possible.

Context

The United States (as well as other countries worldwide) has experienced mob-instigated riots throughout its history. Riots have been linked to several themes. The Stamp Act Riots of 1765 were a violent reaction in the colonies to legislation passed in Britain. The Philadelphia riots in 1844 were anti-Catholic. Some of the most violent riots involved conflicts between labor and management, commencing with the Carnegie Steel conflict in 1892 and continuing into the 1930's. The most frequent and certainly most dramatic and destructive riots, however, have been racial. Riots against Chinese immigrants occurred in Los Angeles in the 1870's. Mexican Americans were viciously attacked by mobs of sailors and civilians in Los Angeles in the zoot suit riots in 1943.

Most of these racially based riots, however, have involved conflicts between African Americans and whites. The first such riot occurred in Rhode Island in 1831. Thirty-three major riots occurred between 1900 and 1949. Between 1915 and 1919 (World War I), there were eighteen major riots. Five major riots occurred between 1940 and 1945 (World War II), the most notable being the Detroit Riot in 1943. The Los Angeles riots of 1965 and 1992 were the two worst in terms of number of participants, amount of destruction, and number of deaths. In addition, lynchings of African Americans by white mobs occurred until relatively recently.

Mobs and riots are thus a core subject area of sociology, touching as they do on collective behavior, group dynamics, race relations, the responses of social institutions and organizations to the needs of various constituencies, the implication of socioeconomic disparities among various racial groups, and the role of violence as a means of attracting attention and resolving problems.

Panics have received much less attention than have mobs and riots. In the 1920's, William McDougall was the first theorist to analyze panics scientifically. Since McDougall's, only a handful of investigations have been conducted. Yet, as Duane P. Schultz (1964) observed, from a theoretical standpoint the cause and conditions of panics need to be studied in order to provide a scientific framework that will allow sociologists to understand and predict crowd or group behavior. The failure to understand the conditions that cause groups to cease functioning adaptively or even exist as groups will be a major obstacle to the attempt to understand collective behavior.

Additionally, the development of nuclear weapons has added a certain urgency to the study of panic behavior. Although the Cold War between the United States and the Soviet Union has ended, nuclear proliferation is widespread, there is an active criminal and black market in nuclear materials, and it is by no means certain that a future nuclear war will never occur. Some researchers have speculated that a nuclear holocaust could unleash mass panic behavior on a nationwide scale that could itself cause chaos, destruction, and social disorder.

Bibliography

Allen, Rodney F., and Charles H. Adair, eds. *Violence and Riots in Urban America.* Worthington, Ohio: Charles A. Jones, 1969. The authors present a detailed and very readable account of major riots from the early 1900's to the 1960's. Included are discussions of the 1919 Chicago Riot and the 1967 riots in Newark and Detroit. Also discussed is the role of violence in American society.

Brown, Michael, and Amy Goldin. *Collective Behavior.* Pacific Palisades, Calif.: Goodyear, 1973. Detailed treatments of mobs, riots, and panics are presented in a single volume. Particularly significant is the discussion of adequately defining these phenomena. The book also contains a useful discussion of the student protest activities of the 1960's in the context of riots.

Button, James W. *Black Violence.* Princeton, N.J.: Princeton University Press, 1978. The author provides a very interesting and detailed analysis of the major urban riots of the 1960's and the ways in which the political system responded to them and dealt with their results.

Cantril, Hadley. *The Invasion from Mars: A Study in the Psychology of Panic.* New York: Harper & Row, 1966. Cantril's work is one of the most detailed scientific treatments of an occurrence of panic. Cantril, a psychologist, analyzed the Orson Welles broadcast of *War of the Worlds* shortly after it happened.

Hartman, Ann. "A Message from Los Angeles." *Social Work* 37, no. 4 (July, 1992): 291-292. Hartman, a social worker, analyzes the 1992 Los Angeles riots from a liberal perspective. She perceives the riots as being caused by "three deep faults in the bedrock of American Society: poverty, lack of opportunity, and racism." For an analysis of this riot from a conservative perspective, consult the June 8, 1992, issue of *National Review* and the July, 1992, issue of *Commentary.*

Jenkins, Philip. *Intimate Enemies: Moral Panics in Contemporary Great Britain.* New York: Aldine de Gruyter, 1992. Almost all the work on panics has focused on disasters such as fires, earthquakes, and wars. Jenkins presents a thorough and informative treatment of how social panics related to perceived threats to children (child abuse, pedophilia, satanism, ritual abuse) developed and occurred in Britain during 1990 and 1991. His treatment is placed in the context of moral panic theory to show how a fertile climate was created by social issues (sexual abuse, gender activism) and institutions (the media).

Schultz, Duane P., ed. *Panic Behavior.* New York: Random House, 1964. This volume contains excellent articles on the characteristics of panic behavior and the conditions that produce panic.

Wieder, Alan. "From Crowds to Mobs." *Equity & Excellence* 24, no. 1 (1988): 4-7. Wieder uses school desegregation in New Orleans in 1960 to show how crowds become mobs and how from their viewpoints they act in a rational manner.

Wright, Sam. *Crowds and Riots.* Beverly Hills, Calif.: Sage Publications, 1978. Wright provides a very well-written, readable, and detailed account of the mechanics of crowd behavior and the ways in which crowds turn into mobs that riot.

Laurence Miller

Cross-References
Collective Behavior, 291; Crowds and Crowd Dynamics, 393; Mass Hysteria, 1134; Mass Psychogenic Illness, 1141; Rumors and Urban Legends, 1667.

"MODEL" MINORITIES

Type of sociology: Racial and ethnic relations
Field of study: Patterns and consequences of contact

The term "model minority" generally refers to a minority group that has attained educational and economic success and has achieved a high degree of assimilation into society. It has most often been applied to Asian Americans, notably Japanese and Chinese Americans. The term has engendered considerable controversy and debate, with many sociologists having come to view it as yet another stereotype that has been used and misused for various purposes.

> *Principal terms*
> ASSIMILATION: the process by which an immigrant or minority group becomes more like the majority or dominant group over time
> DISCRIMINATION: the denial of opportunities and rights to certain groups, most often on the basis of race, ethnicity, or religion
> ETHNIC GROUP: a group distinguished principally by its distinctive cultural heritage
> MINORITY GROUP: any group that, on the basis of physical or cultural characteristics, receives fewer of society's rewards
> PREJUDICE: arbitrary beliefs or feelings about an individual of a certain ethnic group or toward the group as a whole
> STEREOTYPE: an exaggerated generalization about an ethnic or racial group

Overview

The concept of the "model" minority has been studied and debated since the 1960's, when the term first appeared. Its validity has been both defended and attacked, and the possible harmful effects of the concept as an accepted and unquestioned stereotype have been argued. Another particularly contentious issue is that the suggestion that certain minorities are "model" implicitly contains the opposite idea: Other minorities are less than "model" and are perhaps even deficient in some way.

A "model" minority is an American minority group (typically of non-European background) that does well despite having faced discrimination. The criteria by which a minority group is judged as doing well or not doing well vary, but they have included average family income; success in entrepreneurship; children's educational achievement (for recently settled groups); and extent of symptoms of deviance or social pathology. The higher the first three, and the lower the last one, the likelier a group is to be considered a model minority. Since every ethnic or minority group in the United States has produced at least a few high achievers and at least a few failures and criminals, social scientists' judgments of ethnic group success or failure are always statements of averages; they are often based on census data.

The term first appeared in an article in *The New York Times Magazine* of January 9,

1966, entitled "Success Story, Japanese-American Style," by white American sociologist William Petersen. Before World War II, Petersen points out, those Japanese Americans born in Japan could neither own land in California nor become naturalized American citizens; their American-born children (the Nisei) were barred from many types of employment. During World War II, Japanese Americans living in the Pacific Coast states were herded into internment camps. Yet in the two decades after World War II, Japanese Americans achieved a level of education higher than that of white Americans; a level of family income at least equal to that of whites, and a level of social pathology (such as juvenile delinquency) lower than that of whites. Hence, Petersen calls Japanese Americans "our model minority."

In *Japanese Americans: The Evolution of a Subculture* (1969), Harry L. Kitano, a Japanese American sociologist, also uses the term "model minority," acknowledging its origin with Petersen. Kitano expresses ambivalence about the term, which he regards as an ethnocentric white majority's view of a racial minority. Yet, like Petersen, Kitano ascribes the economic success of Japanese Americans after World War II to ethnic Japanese cultural values.

Japanese Americans are not the only Asian American ethnic group that has been noted by social scientists for its level of achievement since the 1960's. Chinese Americans have also been so identified. The business success of both Chinese and Japanese Americans has been attributed by some sociologists and historians to ethnic cultural values, as exemplified by the rotating credit systems that immigrants established to help provide one another with funds to start businesses. Korean business success has been similarly explained. The academic success of Indochinese refugee schoolchildren has been ascribed to the congruence of the refugees' Confucian ethic with the ethic of the American middle class. Louis Winnick, a scholarly expert on urban neighborhoods, went so far as to lump all Asian Americans together as a model minority.

Some non-Asian groups have been viewed as model minorities as well. In the early 1970's, post-1959 Cuban refugees were praised in the mass media for having overcome adversity quickly. Thomas Sowell, a black conservative intellectual, asserts that British West Indian immigrants outperform native-born black Americans economically and educationally. Similarly, Ivan Light argued in 1972 that British West Indian immigrants do better in small business than native-born black Americans; they do so, he said, because of their rotating credit system. Writing in 1993, two journalists (white New Yorker Joe Klein and Haitian émigré Joel Dreyfuss) contended that Haitian immigrants exhibit fewer social pathologies and more signs of economic and educational advance than native-born black Americans. Social scientist Kofi Apraku has described post-1965 African immigrants (such as refugees from Ethiopia) as above average in occupational and entrepreneurial attainment.

Sociologists who employ or support the model minority concept usually adhere to the assimilation model of interethnic relations. According to this theoretical model, the ultimate destiny of any American ethnic or minority group is to climb upward into the broad middle class. Such thinkers tend to see the progress of any ethnic or minority group as a function of its cultural values rather than of the extent of the discrimination it suffers. The relative slowness of any particular group to overcome poverty and win the acceptance of the majority is ascribed, at least in part, to what are viewed as weaknesses in that group's cultural values; hence, one can regard some minorities as "model" and others as less exemplary.

Such structural theorists as sociologist Stephen Steinberg, by contrast, argue that it is not cultural deficiencies that retard minorities' progress but discriminatory barriers erected by the majority. These barriers can be far more widespread and insidious than is first apparent. Such theorists also contend that the seemingly miraculous progress of some model minorities can be explained by the social class background of the immigrants and by the opportunity structure that they found upon arrival rather than by any alleged superiority of those minorities' cultural values.

Applications

The model minority concept has most often been applied in discussions of the relative success of certain Asian ethnic immigrant groups in the United States. The term has engendered much debate because of its implicit criticism of other groups—if these "model" groups could succeed, it suggests, then others should be able to as well. This implication then leads to the question, If certain groups cannot succeed as well as others in American society, where does the problem lie—with discrimination, with the attitudes of the dominant culture, or with the cultural attributes and attitudes of the minority groups themselves?

The model minority concept has surfaced repeatedly in debates over the status of African Americans, the minority group that has been in the United States the longest but that has arguably assimilated least effectively. In the late 1950's and the 1960's, many white Americans felt anxieties about the Civil Rights movement; the urban unrest of the late 1960's exacerbated fears and uncertainties about the future of race relations. Then, in the late 1970's and 1980's, white resentment of affirmative action programs, which primarily benefited African Americans, grew. At the same time, there was some bewilderment that inner-city black poverty persisted despite affirmative action. The model minority concept, with its evidence of Asian American success, seemed to suggest that such programs might not be, or should not be, unnecessary.

Hence, from 1966 onward, the notion of Asian Americans as a model minority found receptive ears among white Americans. By the middle and late 1980's, it was being purveyed in a speech by President Ronald Reagan (in 1984), in magazine articles, and on television news programs (which placed special emphasis on the scholastic achievements of Asian American youth). Although most blacks in the 1980's resented being compared unfavorably with Asian Americans, some conservative black intellectuals, Thomas Sowell, Walter E. Williams, and Shelby Steele among them, defended the concept and pointed to Asian American success as an example for blacks to follow.

Because of its use in arguments over public policy, the model minority thesis is hotly disputed. Thus the laudatory report on Indochinese refugee schoolchildren by

Caplan, Whitmore, and Choy was criticized by sociologist Rubén Rumbaut for having covered only the Vietnamese, Sino-Vietnamese, and Lao, omitting data on the less successful refugees, the Hmong and the Cambodians. The overall high Asian American average in income and education, Asian American scholars Ronald Takaki, Deborah Woo, Peter Kwong, and Arthur Hu point out, hides a bipolar distribution: Chinese immigrants, for example, include both sweatshop laborers and scientists. Many of the Asian American youth who excel in school, it is emphasized, are children of well-educated immigrants who either hold professional jobs in the United States or did so in Asia; Asian immigrant teenagers from poorer, less-educated families are not always high achievers, and they are sometimes members of urban juvenile gangs. Asian American family incomes, it is conceded, may equal or surpass those of whites, but only because of a larger number of earners per family. Per capita income is less than that of whites; moreover, Asian Americans tend to live in areas with a higher than average cost of living, such as Hawaii, New York, and California. Also, Asian Americans statistically must achieve higher education levels than white Americans to equal their incomes.

Sowell's portrait of British West Indian immigrants to the United States as an ethnic success story has also been challenged. These immigrants, economist Thomas Boston argues in *Race, Class, and Conservatism* (1988), exceed both the average British West Indian and the average native-born black American in educational level; hence, the superior West Indian economic performance in the United States is no simple rags to riches story. Sociologist Suzanne Model, using census data, asserts that any West Indian socioeconomic lead over American-born blacks had disappeared by 1990.

If the "model" part of "model minority" has been criticized, so has the "minority" part, at least regarding Asian Americans. Although everyone agrees that certain Asian American groups have been unjustly persecuted, some scholars, such as political scientist Lawrence Fuchs, argue that no Asian American group was ever discriminated against as consistently, or for as long a time, as black Americans were.

Some view the Asian American model minority stereotype as potentially harmful to Asian Americans themselves. Writing in the late 1980's, Ronald Takaki, a historian, and Deborah Woo, a sociologist, warn that widespread acceptance of the stereotype might lead to governmental indifference to the plight of those Asian Americans who are poor and to neglect of programs that would help Asian immigrants learn English and find jobs. Takaki, worried about the loss of legitimate minority status, points to examples of low-income Asian American university students being denied aid under educational opportunity programs. He also thinks that the envy generated among black and white Americans by the model minority stereotype partially explains the violent anti-Asian incidents of the 1980's.

The controversy over the model minority thesis has stimulated scholars to produce more conceptually sophisticated research. In *Immigrant Entrepreneurs: Koreans in Los Angeles, 1965-1982* (1988), for example, authors Ivan Light and Edna Bonacich, going beyond the simple cultural interpretation of Light's 1972 book, distinguish between a group's ethnic resources and its class resources. The Koreans in Los

Angeles, the authors show, differed not only from black Americans but also from Koreans in Korea: They were more likely to be Protestant Christians and to be college educated than Koreans who stayed home. In *Latin Journey: Cuban and Mexican Immigrants to the United States* (1985), sociologists Alejandro Portes and Robert Bach try to explain why Cuban immigrants have prospered as entrepreneurs while Mexican immigrants generally have not. The authors emphasize differences in the structure of opportunities rather than cultural differences between Cubans and Mexicans. Similarly, Roger Waldinger, in *Through the Eye of the Needle: Immigrants and Enterprise in New York's Garment Trades* (1986), argues that the structure of opportunity in New York City, and not immigrant culture, explains the entrepreneurial success of Dominican and Chinese immigrants. John Ogbu, a Nigerian-born anthropologist, distinguishes between castelike minorities (such as American-born blacks and some Hispanics) and immigrant minorities; castelike status, Ogbu contends, leads teenagers to denigrate academic achievement. Another education researcher, Marcelo Suárez-Orozco, uses Ogbu's model to explain differences in academic performance between American-born Mexican American high school students and high school students of Central American refugee background. The debate over structural versus cultural causes of ethnic group success has also led historians to compare past patterns of social mobility of different American racial and ethnic groups.

Context

The early sociological studies of minorities in the United States tended to be divided into studies of ethnicity, focusing on European immigrant groups, and studies of race relations, which concentrated on African Americans and on black-white relations. These overly simple categorizations began to be expanded in the 1950's as social scientists and historians became interested in American minorities that were not European and did not fit into the simple "black and white" dichotomy. Such interest became especially lively when immigration reform in 1965 led to sharply increased immigration from Asia and Latin America. Scholarly pioneers included (besides William Petersen) Alejandro Portes, Harry L. Kitano, Roger Daniels, Betty Lee Sung, Ivan Light, Illsoo Kim, Harold Jacoby, and Sucheta Mazumdar.

White sociologists of a liberal bent, such as Stephen Steinberg, disliked Petersen's model minority concept partly because it was frequently used in polemics against government help for African Americans. The apparent failure of either urban public school systems or the social programs of the 1960's to promote significant social mobility among blacks led such scholars as Steinberg to question the notion of unfettered opportunity implicit in the model minority thesis and to search for structural factors that might differentially affect the mobility of different ethnic groups with identical values.

At first, Petersen's notion that some Asian American ethnic groups could be considered model minorities was accepted not only by white social scientists but also by most second-generation Asian American scholars (and undoubtedly by many other Asian-Americans). The ferment in American universities in the late 1960's and early

1970's, however, produced a wave of ethnic self-assertion not only among black and Hispanic students but also among students of Asian background. According to the radicalized students, people of Japanese, Chinese, Korean, and Filipino origin in the United States suffered a plight analogous to that of blacks and Hispanics; they also shared a common identity as Asian Americans. A number of periodicals were created to express this point of view, including the scholarly *Amerasia Journal* (University of California at Los Angeles, founded 1971). Some of the Asian American students and junior faculty who were most deeply affected by the spirit of the 1960's went on to become professors of sociology and history or to teach in the new departments of ethnic studies that various colleges and universities established (the first was set up at San Francisco State in 1969).

By the mid-1970's, the model minority thesis had become especially unpopular among younger Asian American scholars (many of them third generation), who abhorred the disdain for African Americans and the acceptance of a white worldview that the thesis seemed to them to promote. In the 1970's and the 1980's, historian Ronald Takaki and social scientists Peter Kwong, Deborah Woo, Arthur Hu, Bob Suzuki, Kwang Chung Kim, Won Moo Hurh, and Jayjia Hsia attacked the model minority thesis as a misleading stereotype; other Asian American scholars remained ambivalent about it. By the end of the 1980's, only a few among the younger Asian American scholars (such as historian Reed Ueda) publicly admitted discerning any truth in the Asian American model minority stereotype.

Yet the abuse of the model minority concept for purposes of partisan argument, pointed out by Takaki and others, should not be allowed to obscure the need for historians and sociologists to examine success as well as failure among racial and ethnic minorities that have had to face discrimination. Scholarly explanation of such success or failure in the areas of economics, education, and social pathology should take into account both cultural and structural factors.

Bibliography

Apraku, Kofi Konadu. *African Emigres in the United States: A Missing Link in Africa's Social and Economic Development*. New York: Praeger, 1991. Argues that the United States has been enriched by the flight of highly educated Africans, after 1965, from chaos and tyranny in Africa. Stresses the émigrés' reluctance to return to Africa despite American discrimination and their achievements as professionals and entrepreneurs (successful Ethiopian refugee restaurateurs are mentioned). Bibliographical references; index.

Barringer, Herbert R., Robert W. Gardner, and Michael J. Levin. *Asian and Pacific Islanders in the United States*. New York: Russell Sage, 1993. Mining the 1980 census and some later data sources, the authors compare Asian Americans' income, education, and family structure with those of whites and blacks. They provide little post-1980 information on the Indochinese. Discussion of the scholarly controversy over the model minority thesis is brief but illuminating. Tables; figures; references; indexes.

Gibson, Margaret A. *Accommodation Without Assimilation: Sikh Immigrants in an American High School.* Ithaca, N.Y.: Cornell University Press, 1988. While rejecting oversimplified versions of the model minority thesis, Gibson emphasizes the excellent academic performance of American-born Sikh youth in the face of majority prejudice. Chapters 2 and 9 contain a helpful review of the scholarly debate over immigrant and minority school performance. Photographs; tables; endnotes; references; index.

Kitano, Harry L. *Japanese Americans: The Evolution of a Subculture.* Englewood Cliffs, N.J.: Prentice-Hall, 1969. A second-generation (Nisei) Japanese American sociologist ascribes the economic success of Japanese Americans after World War II to specific cultural traits inherited from Japan. A classic exposition of the model minority thesis (although Kitano is uneasy about the term itself). Footnotes; tables; bibliography; index.

Marger, Martin. "Asian Americans." In *Race and Ethnic Relations: American and Global Perspectives.* 2d ed. Belmont, Calif.: Wadsworth, 1991. Provides historical and sociological information, in succinct form, on Chinese Americans, Japanese Americans, Korean Americans, Filipino Americans, and Vietnamese Americans. An excellent introduction, for lower-level undergraduates, to the model minority controversy and the debate over structural versus cultural causes of Asian American success. Tables; references; index.

Petersen, William. *Japanese Americans: Oppression and Success.* New York: Random House, 1971. This is an elaboration and expansion of the model minority thesis propounded in Petersen's 1966 article in *The New York Times Magazine.* Like the original article, it contains the implicit criticism of black Americans that engendered considerable debate. Includes a historical chapter on the 1942 internment of Japanese Americans. Well organized and easy to follow. Notes; tables; references; index.

Steinberg, Stephen. *The Ethnic Myth: Race, Ethnicity, and Class in America.* New York: Atheneum, 1981. Steinberg, drawing largely on secondary sources, denies that the history of any ethnic group can be seen as a rags to riches story or that culture, rather than Old Country economic backgrounds, made Jews, Chinese, Koreans, Japanese, Cubans, and West Indians successful in the United States. The clearest expression of the structural interpretation. Notes; index.

Takaki, Ronald. "Breaking Silences." In *Strangers from a Different Shore: A History of Asian Americans.* Boston: Little, Brown, 1989. This, one of the most eloquent and easily accessible critiques of the Asian American model minority thesis, is written by a leading Asian American historian. Relies heavily on both mainstream and ethnic periodicals of the 1980's and on the author's own experiences as an Asian American. Endnotes; index.

Waldinger, Roger. *Through the Eye of the Needle: Immigrants and Enterprise in New York's Garment Trades.* New York: New York University Press, 1986. The departure from entrepreneurship of Jews and Italians, the author argues, was crucial in opening business opportunities for Chinese and Dominican immigrants. The introductory chapter contains a helpful summary and critique of the social science literature on cultural versus structural explanations of immigrant entrepreneurship. Index; endnotes; appendices.

Paul D. Mageli

Cross-References

Assimilation: The United States, 140; Cultural and Structural Assimilation, 405; Ethnic Enclaves, 682; Ethnicity and Ethnic Groups, 689; "Middleman" Minorities, 1200; Minority and Majority Groups, 1219; Prejudice and Discrimination: Merton's Paradigm, 1498; Prejudice and Stereotyping, 1505; The Race Relations Cycle Theory of Assimilation, 1572; Values and Value Systems, 2143.

MODERNIZATION AND WORLD-SYSTEM THEORIES

Type of sociology: Social change
Field of study: Theories of social change

Modernization theory postulates that the United States and Western Europe are on the highest level of development and should be emulated by other societies, especially developing and Third World societies. World-system theory, however, argues that European capitalism expanded beyond its borders to establish an international division of labor within a world-economy. This world-economy inhibits developing countries from modernizing.

Principal terms

CORE: in world-system theory, Western European countries, the United States, and Japan, which have specialized in banking, finance, and highly skilled industrial production

DEPENDENCY THEORY: a theory in which underdeveloped regions are considered "internal colonies" that are dependent on, or controlled by, modern industrial states

MODERN SOCIETY: a society that emphasizes professionalism, rationality, planning, and progress; the meaning of this concept varies, but it generally connotes emulating Western European countries or the United States

MODERNIZATION THEORY: a theory according to which the changes that occurred in non-Western societies under colonial rule were necessary to break down indigenous traditions so that higher levels of social development, or "modernity," could be achieved; to become "modern," new nations must emulate the patterns taken by the United States and Western Europe

PERIPHERY: in world-system theory, the exploited former colonies of the core, which supply the core with cheap food and raw materials

POLITICAL ECONOMY: a framework linking material interests (economy) with the use of power (politics) to protect and enhance interests

SEMIPERIPHERY: in world-system theory, the intermediate societies between the core and the periphery

WORLD-SYSTEM THEORY: the theory that European capitalism expanded beyond its borders, beginning in the late fifteenth and early sixteenth centuries, to establish an international division of labor within the framework of a world-economy

Overview

Modernization theory and world-system theory are frameworks within the field of political economy that deal with issues of development and underdevelopment in the

Third World. Modernization theory, which prevailed in the 1950's and 1960's, explained the poverty of underdeveloped countries on the basis of either structural or psychological frameworks. World-system theory became popular as an attack on modernization theory that used a global framework to explain the rise of the West and to analyze the problems of development and underdevelopment within the context of a global economy.

Modernization theory varies in meaning according to who is doing the planning. In general, it means becoming like the United States or a Western European country. The concept generally emphasizes professionalization, rationality, planning, and progress (as defined in the West).

Modernization theory has two frameworks: structural and psychological. Structurally, modernization theorists built on Talcott Parsons' *The Social System* (1951), which held that progressive differentiation was the key to modernizing. It was, however, economist W. W. Rostow, in *The Stages of Economic Growth: A Non-Communist Manifesto* (1960), who argued from an evolutionary position stating that all societies must pass through five fixed stages. All societies, according to Rostow, start as traditional societies in which methods of production are limited, the worldview is "pre-Newtonian," productive resources are largely devoted to agriculture, vertical social mobility is limited, and the value system is fatalistic. During the "period of preconditions," the idea of economic progress is perceived as possible and good, education broadens, enterprising individuals appear, and a suitable infrastructure, especially in the government, develops. In "take-off," the third stage, growth becomes a normal condition. Investment rate increases, one or more manufacturing sectors increase substantially, and a favorable political climate emerges. Finally, technological maturity follows, in which the society has the versatility to produce anything it chooses. Later, social scientists added a sixth stage, Daniel Bell's "post-industrial society" (1973), in which the society shifts from production to service and information processing. Rostow argued that underdeveloped societies have to follow the same process that developed nations have experienced. The problem with his approach was that not all societies pass through the same sequence in the same way.

The foundation of the psychological approach was laid by David McClelland, in *The Achieving Society* (1967), and by Everett Hagen, in *On the Theory of Social Change* (1962). Both argued, in different ways, that a society's development depended on the psychological makeup of its members. They completely neglected the function of social institutions. Alex Inkeles and David H. Smith, in *Becoming Modern: Individual Change in Six Developing Countries* (1974), argued that "modern" people were those who had contact with modern institutions. They did explain, however, why some countries had more modern institutions than others did.

World-system theory attacked modernization theory for its neglect of institutions, the ethnocentric concept that "modern" means being Western, and its erroneous stages of development and psychological postulates. World-system theorists argued that the power of strong manufacturing societies, such as England, resulted from their ability to redirect resources from weaker societies to serve their own ends.

A. G. Frank, in *Latin America: Under-development or Revolution* (1969), was influential in showing how resources were expropriated by the rich. It was Immanuel Wallerstein, however, who made the view prominent. Wallerstein argued that there were historical but not uniform stages of development. He showed that initially every society was a "minisystem"—a community that contained within itself a complete division of labor and cultural framework. Now, however, minisystems no longer exist or are extremely rare. Thus, anthropologists studying "traditional" society miss a major aspect—the community is not isolated.

Historically, what followed, according to Wallerstein, was a world-system in which a single division of labor system developed, cutting across multiple cultural systems. With the advent of capitalism in the 1500's, the state became less central. The state played a minor role in economic transactions, which resulted in the market's creation of incentives to increase productivity. Capitalism succeeded, according to Wallerstein, primarily because of two factors: transportation technology, which enabled long-distance markets to be maintained; and military power, which enabled terms to be enforced.

A world-economy developed that had a core, a semiperiphery, and a periphery. The "core" was made up of societies that developed in manufacturing and specialization but needed a surplus to expand. This they obtained from the "periphery," where resources and labor costs were kept low. The structure developed on both a national and an international level. A core, semiperiphery, and periphery can develop in a country and region as well as internationally.

Applications

World-system theory is important because it explains why some countries are underdeveloped and others are not. If world-system theory is correct in stating that the peripheries are poor and underdeveloped because resources are being siphoned off by the core, there are tremendous ramifications for aid and economic development policies. Unless the cause of the problem is addressed, peripheries will have little or no hope of breaking out of their situation.

World-system theory may not be popular in the United States outside the intellectual community, but it is part of the central thinking of other countries, especially those of the periphery. It is important to understand their perceptions of the world order. The world-system framework is also the result of a long history, and knowledge of what went before will make it possible to avoid needless repetitions in the debate concerning development.

There are many case studies that show how world-system theory works on both the global and the local level. On the global level, Sidney Mintz's classic 1985 study on sugar illustrates how a global system develops. He reveals that before the Crusades, which began in 1096, Europe was dominated by rural people who produced their own goods locally. As a result of the Crusades, Europeans sought to establish and extend trade routes. In 1271, Marco Polo opened trade with China, and by the early 1500's, Europeans were extracting materials from around the world.

Europeans, especially the English, became consumers of these resources, and by 1650, one very popular commodity that was desired by the English nobility was sugar. By 1750, even the poorest English farm laborers used sugar in their tea. The world demand was so great that whole regions adopted plantation and monocrop economy. Their need for labor led to the development of the slave trade and triangle trade systems. In the eighteenth century, the demand for raw cotton by the English led to rapid settlement in the southeastern United States, the development of a plantation and monocrop economy, and the use of slave labor.

As the demand for commodities such as cotton and sugar increased, international trade increased, which led to the rise of the capitalist world economy—a single world system committed to production, sale, and exchange, with the goal of maximizing profits rather than satisfying local or domestic needs. The key attribute of capitalism is the economic orientation to the world market for profit.

What has developed is shown in Fernand Braudel's three-volume work, *Civilization and Capitalism: Fifteenth-Eighteenth Century* (1981, 1982, 1984). He demonstrates that the world is made up of a world-system with numerous subsystems, subsubsystems, and so on, which are all interrelated. Some societies are in the core and are served by those in the periphery. In the heyday of the British empire, India was in the periphery and England was in the core. Currently, Malaysia is in the periphery and the United States is in the core. Even within the United States, however, there are core/periphery relationships; for example, Delta County in Tennessee supplies cheap labor so that products can be sold at a lower price to urbanites or communities in the North.

Malaysia has been colonized and has been on the periphery of the world-system for centuries, but it has now begun to industrialize. Initially, the world demand for Malaysian products resulted in the development of plantation economies and deforestation. By 1970, 10,000 people annually were being displaced from the land. To provide these people with jobs and to stem social discontent, Malaysia encouraged foreign companies to take advantage of Malaysia's cheap labor and build industry there. Western European, U.S., and Japanese companies complied and moved industry in to utilize cheap labor in Malaysia.

Malaysian villagers were hired, and these workers now live different lives. They work for bosses, whereas in the village they worked according to season and need. Schools were altered to teach children to be disciplined and to have values suitable for working in a factory. The work, such as assembling electronics components, is demanding and exhausting. Women are hired over men, and the financial rewards have not met expectations. After she works for a couple of years, the female worker's health typically deteriorates and she has to leave the job. One side-effect has been an increase in mass hysteria. Some women see spirits in the factory; others become possessed by spirits. The reason for the rise of spirit possession is unclear; it may be a means of rebelling so that the women do not have to deal with authorities, or it may be a way of coping with inequality, something alien to the workers' world. Whatever the cause, however, the conditions are a result of the world-system and its influence on Malaysia.

Context

World-system theory has its origins in the seventeenth and eighteenth centuries. In 1817, David Ricardo formulated the classic modern theory of free trade. He argued that unrestricted trade between two countries was always advantageous if they produced mutually desirable goods at different degrees of efficiency. Friedrich List, in *National System of Political Economy* (1841), challenged Ricardo, arguing that in the long term, it might be advantageous to protect or foster industries that cannot compete in the short term. The debate has continued, but world-system theory promoters generally conclude in one way or the other that Ricardo was wrong—they argue that free trade benefits the advanced industrial countries and slows development in the poor countries.

J. A. Hobson's *Imperialism: A Study* (1902) attacked imperialism. Hobson's ideas were built on by Vladimir Ilich Lenin's *Imperialism: The Highest Stage of Capitalism* (1939), which argued that imperialist exploitation prevented the final crisis of capitalism. Lenin neglected to examine the effect of imperialism on peasants in the colonies. Rosa Luxemburg, in *The Accumulation of Capital* (1913), filled that void by examining the spread of capitalism into Egypt and the way in which it deprived peasants of their land and drove them to ruin. Leon Trotsky, in *The Permanent Revolution* (1930), examined the place of semiperipherals in prerevolutionary Russia. It was N. I. Bukharin, however, in *Imperialism and World Economy* (1929), who foreshadowed the work of Wallerstein and other world-system theorists. He wrote about the economic cleavage developing between town and country as well as between industrial and agrarian countries.

Right-wing intellectuals appealed to nationalism by using the world-system approach. Most notable was the Romanian Mihail Manoilescu, who, in *The Theory of Protection and International Trade* (1930), attacked Ricardo's concept of the comparative advantage.

It was in this intellectual climate that Paul Prebisch developed "dependency theory." Prebisch, an Argentinean, headed the United Nations' Economic Commission for Latin America (ECLA). Wallerstein credits him with introducing the concepts of core and periphery. The ECLA report *Relative Prices of Exports and Imports of Under-Developed Countries: A Study of Post-War Terms of Trade between Under-Developed and Industrialized Nations* (1949) showed that terms of trade favored industrial nations and worked against agricultural exporting countries. This report formed the basis of dependency theory, but the concept has since gone beyond economics to include sociological and political theories concerning development. The contribution of dependency theory is that it shows that economic growth has been accompanied by rising inequalities and that rapid urbanization and the spread of literacy have converged with the marginalization of the masses.

Dependency theorists have focused on the inability of Latin American countries to control their own finances. They have also studied the high correlation between repression and the application of capitalist efficiency criteria in Latin America, as well as the phenomena of "bureaucratic-authoritarian" regimes being favored for international finance, poorer countries not having access to current technology, and industrialization based on import substitution creating new forms of dependency.

World-system theory has influenced sociology and anthropology. Wallerstein's 1974 volume was published at a time when modernization theory was being discredited by the Vietnam War, social turmoil in the 1960's wakened social scientists to the inequalities within the United States, and young socialists desired a historical knowledge that was not presented in the functional positivist framework.

Wallerstein's writings countered the antirevolutionary, anticommunist implications of modernization theory. They provided a coherent framework to explain local and international inequalities, and brought a historical perspective to the discipline.

Building on Wallerstein's core-periphery framework, Michael Hechter, in *Internal Colonialism: The Celtic Fringe in British National Development, 1536-1966* (1975), explains ongoing ethnic tensions in core societies. Frances V. Moulder, in *Japan, China, and the Modern World Economy: Toward a Reinterpretation of East Asian Development ca. 1600 to ca. 1918* (1977), shows that Japan developed largely because of its ability to resist economic colonialism.

Although Wallerstein's work was not quantitative, a school of quantitative world-system theorists has developed at Stanford University. It has become popular because it combines the ideological and political emphasis of Marxism and a statistical framework, which seems to bestow legitimacy.

In the field of anthropology, community studies have considered the international influences on behavior—Katherine Verdery's *Transylvanian Villagers: Three Centuries of Political, Economic, and Ethnic Change* (1983) is a good example of such work.

World-system theory is not without its critics and problems. Robert Brenner (1976) shows that Eastern Europe's backwardness caused its dependence, not the other way around. In addition, Wallerstein neglects cultural and social factors and the interplay between class structure and economic growth. Whether dependency is a cause or result still has not been determined. The world-system framework does not explain why different societies in similar context did or did not develop in a similar way. It also ignores the works of scholars such as Max Weber and Robert Merton, who have shown a relationship between religious rationality and the growth of science and development. It assumes that economic growth in the world is a zero-sum game, when in fact the quality of life in the whole world has improved over the last several decades. In spite of these problems, one cannot fault the new way of thinking and insight that Wallerstein and world-system theory have brought to the understanding of human behavior, especially because they have forced sociologists and anthropologists to consider behavior from a global perspective.

Bibliography

Bell, Daniel. *The Coming of Post-Industrial Society: A Venture in Social Forecasting.* New York: Basic Books, 1973. A classic work that argues that modern industrial societies are entering a new phase in which production services and the processing of information are emphasized and in which white collar jobs are most prominent.

Brenner, Robert. "Agrarian Class Structure and Economic Development in Pre-Industrial Europe." *Past and Present*, no. 70 (February, 1976): 30-75. Provides a counter-critique of world-system theory and the ideas of Wallerstein and some of his followers.

Chirot, Daniel, and Thomas D. Hall. "World-System Theory." *Annual Review of Sociology* 8 (1982): 81-106. An outstanding review of the concepts and criticisms of modernization theory and world-system theory.

Mintz, Sidney W. *Sweetness and Power: The Place of Sugar in Modern History*. New York: Penguin Books, 1986. Demonstrates the place of sugar in developing core/periphery relationships in world-system theory.

Wallerstein, Immanuel. *The Capitalist World-Economy*. Cambridge, England: Cambridge University Press, 1979.

_____. *The Modern World-System: Capitalist Agriculture and the Origins of the European World-Economy in the Sixteenth Century*. New York: Academic Press, 1974.

_____. *The Modern World-System II: Mercantilism and the Consolidation of the European World-Economy, 1600-1750*. New York: Academic Press, 1980. These difficult books are the most influential works that explain the world-system approach to understanding and interpreting social change.

Arthur W. Helweg

Cross-References

MONOPOLIES AND OLIGOPOLIES

Type of sociology: Major social institutions
Field of study: The economy

Monopolies and oligopolies have emerged as major social institutions in twentieth century industrial and postindustrial mixed economies. Examining the structure and functions of these institutions, sociologists have concentrated on their effects upon other groups and organizations as well as on their roles in allocating the resources and shaping the welfare of whole societies.

Principal terms

CAPITALISM: an economic system, sanctified by law, in which the ownership of private property and the means of production facilitate the search for profits

CONFLICT THEORY: the perception that society is in a perpetual state of imbalance because of the power struggles of social groups and special interests

GEMEINSCHAFT SOCIETY: any society characterized by the predominance of face-to-face personal relationships—usually a reference to rural or small-town society

GESELLSCHAFT SOCIETY: any society characterized by limited, impersonal, and instrumentalist relationships among its people

MONOPOLY CAPITALISM: a type of capitalism in which major sectors of the economy are dominated by a few capitalists or by managers

OLIGOPOLY: control over similar economic resources by a few producers or sellers

POSTINDUSTRIAL SOCIETY: a formerly industrial society noted for its manufactured goods which subsequently produces fewer goods than it does services and information

PROGRESSIVE RATIONALIZATION: the shift of capitalist producers from competition based on price to competition based on sales, advertising, product differentiation, and goodwill

STRUCTURAL-FUNCTIONALISM: a once-predominant sociological theory that suggests that every social action, positive or negative, makes some contribution to society

Overview

Monopolies and oligopolies have become important, at times central, institutional features of industrial and postindustrial societies. They have solicited intense interest, both theoretical and practical, not only among economists but also among sociologists, other social scientists, and informed publics.

These institutions and their influences are relatively new. They became integral parts of modern social and economic life in the United States and Western Europe only after the last decades of the nineteenth century. For the most part, therefore, they continued to be dynamic and changing institutions at the close of the twentieth century and therefore remained difficult to define precisely or to characterize conclusively. Worldwide, the two predominant modes of organizing economic activities have been capitalism and socialism, and there has been a tendency in the United States and in other developed economies to utilize aspects of both systems. Thus, among experts and nonexperts, monopolies and oligopolies have been subjects of controversy and have been described both admiringly and critically.

From the perspectives of economic determinists, whether followers of Karl Marx or of American reformers and populists protesting economic injustice, the manner in which economic activities are organized determines the structure of social organization. Champions of competitive capitalism (they never describe it as monopoly capitalism) have defended it by arguing that through a "free" market it allocates scarce resources efficiently, converts the self-interest of individuals and groups into widely shared social benefits, and prevents the establishment of rigid social classes by facilitating extensive social mobility.

Critics of competitive capitalism—non-Marxist, Marxist, and neo-Marxist alike—have insisted, on the contrary, that this form of capitalism was never more than a theoretical model, an abstraction that failed to achieve reality anywhere. They have argued that monopoly capitalism rather than competitive capitalism has been the reality. Moreover, monopoly capitalism, as they have seen it, has resulted in profits or economic surpluses being narrowly channeled into the hands of a small class of capitalists, managers, and their hangers-on, creating a growing class of workers and laborers who face impoverishment. In a general sense, these critics, who include European sociologists such as György Lukács, Antonio Gramsci, Louis Althusser, and Maurice Godelier, and Americans such as Harry Braverman, Paul Baran, and Paul Sweezy, have subscribed to conflict theories involving the state, ideology, and economies that explain social organization and social change.

Monopoly capitalism and competitive capitalism seldom have existed in the real world. To be sure, most business people or professionals would like to be monopolists. On a modest scale some are. A small town's only orthodontist, and a neighborhood's sole pharmacist obviously enjoy some measure of monopoly. Economists describe these as actual monopolies. Where large monopolies operate, however, they do so as publicly licensed or franchised utilities: gas and electric companies, and railway, bus, subway, and telecommunications companies. Patents and copyrights are also types of government-enforced, limited monopolies.

None of these examples constitutes a pure monopoly, for what governments give they can also take away. Even actual monopolies—that is, those firms that are the only sellers in their markets—in fact face potential competition as well as competition from sellers in other markets who can offer substitute goods or services. In addition, nearly all businesses fall under some kind of government regulation and therefore are subject to public and political pressures.

What critics of capitalism (however defined) have been fundamentally concerned with have been economic concentration—the control of economic activity in particular industries, economic sectors, or entire economies—and the social consequences that are believed to be attributable to it; for example, managers' technical and bureaucratic controls over workers. In the United States, economic concentration became a major public concern following the nation's dramatic shift during the half-century after the Civil War from an overwhelmingly agricultural society to the world's leading industrial society. This drastic change altered the entire landscape of American life: its values, lifestyles, social organization, and social relationships.

The new business institution symbolizing these changes, and in many ways responsible for them, was the corporation. In every major sector of the new industrial-financial economy—railroads, steel, oil production and refinement, farm machinery, meat packing, banking, insurance, and stock brokering—a handful of corporations dominated in production, in sales, or in shares of the market.

In the United States, many such regnant corporations were legally constituted as "trusts," a term that popularly was synonymous with "monopoly." Between the 1890's and the 1930's, three economists, Britain's Alfred Marshall and Joan Robinson, and Edward Chamberlin in the United States, elaborated a theory about the behavior of such corporations which they dubbed "monopolistic competition," a designation that seems contradictory at first glance. Monopolistic competition, however, describes a market structure in which there are many sellers of differentiated products who make their decisions independently of one another, presuming that these decisions will cause no reaction on the part of their competitors.

As a theory, monopoly competition proved fruitful. Nevertheless, just as was the case with theories of competitive capitalism and monopoly capitalism, the theory of monopoly competition incompletely described the real world of key business activity. Oligopoly seemed more nearly to approximate reality. Oligopoly is the most common type of market organization in the United States. Thus, even though thousands of enterprises may sell identical products, they often resolve themselves into scores of diverse, geographically separate oligopolies.

These oligopolistic industries, moreover, share a number of distinctive characteristics. An oligopoly exists, first of all, when only a few businesses dominate a specific market, such as automobile and steel production, tobacco products, pharmaceuticals, health care management, and aircraft manufacture. Furthermore, because they are few in number in their fields of enterprise, these businesses' decisions are made with an eye to their competitors' reactions. Accordingly, although oligopolies are more responsive to consumer demands than monopolies are, and although they do pass to consumers some portion of the lower prices made possible by their technological advances, they are less consumer oriented than are more independent and more fully competitive businesses.

Applications

Pure or absolute monopolies that are free from some form of competition or from government regulation exist only in economic theory, where they play useful roles in economic modeling. Qualified monopolies (usually public utilities) that operate under franchises or licenses or that control strategic patents have operated in the United States and other developed economies for more than a century. They are often shielded from direct competition on the assumption that throwing local markets open, for example, to the competition of half a dozen private water companies—as was the case until the early twentieth century in London—harms consumers and the general public.

In the United States and Great Britain, there have always been common law strictures against private monopolies. Moreover, in the United States, popular antimonopoly sentiments historically have been part of the ethos of expanding democratic concepts. Thus, the term "monopoly," beginning in the last half of the nineteenth century, was loosely and generally applied in the United States to the largest and most dominant businesses in key sectors of the economy. The major railroads, along with Standard Oil, Carnegie Steel (later United States Steel), the Armour Meatpacking Company, and major firms in distilling, building construction materials, pipe manufactures, banking, and warehousing, were all denounced by the press and the public alike as monopolies and trusts that were controlled by robber barons.

These antimonopoly outcries did not diminish with time. By the 1960's, for example, they were aimed at powerful trade unions such as the International Brotherhood of Teamsters, the United Mine Workers, and the United Automobile Workers. One result of these antimonopoly sentiments was the enactment of America's distinctive federal antitrust legislation, beginning in 1890 with the Sherman Antitrust Act, which was followed in 1914 by the Clayton Act and still later by additional legislative extensions and refinements.

Antimonopoly campaigns involved more than debates over the economics of efficient resource allocation and efficient production, important as they were. Concentrations of economic power also raised profound questions concerning the structure of American society and the functions of key social institutions. Like the public, social scientists have long argued about the maldistribution of wealth attributed in part to aggregate concentrations of wealth and economic power. For example, federal estimates of income distribution in 1986 revealed that 50.4 percent of family income went to the top two-fifths of the nation's families, while 4.6 percent went to the lowest fifth. Is such a distribution conducive to raising necessary investment capital and stimulating economic growth or is it simply the result of nonproductive exploitation of wage earners and a detriment to growth? Behind this and similar questions lay attempts to assess the impacts of the competitiveness of real-world monopolies and oligopolies.

Excluding publicly regulated monopolies and competitive monopolies, monopoly competition has become a familiar feature of the economic landscape. Where there are many sellers selling products that are differentiated by advertising, brand names, packaging, location, service, or goodwill, monopoly competition may exist. Characteristically, most monopolies make their decisions independently of what they believe the others will do. The fast food industry, which was made prominent in the last decades of the twentieth century by dominant chains such as McDonald's, Wendy's,

Hardee's, and Taco Bell, each operating hundreds of geographically scattered stores, advertising intensively, and changing menu specialties frequently provides a good example of private monopolies in competition.

Oligopolies have played an even more familiar role in American life. The mention of Ford, General Motors, and Chrysler commonly sums up the manufacture of American automotive vehicles. Wal-Mart, Sears, Kroger, and Kmart are names that have readily identified the nation's dominant retailers. McDonnell Douglas, Northrup, Grumman, and Boeing were for decades the principal aircraft designers and manufacturers, while the leaders of the banking sector for many years could be substantially accounted for by listing Citicorp, Chase Manhattan, J. P. Morgan, Security Pacific, and BankAmerica.

Attempts to determine whether the social and economic effects of oligopolies have been more beneficial than harmful have produced inconclusive results. Certainly, oligopolies mesh their decision making in regard to prices, products, and technologies. Their consumer prices likewise have not been the lowest that technological progress would allow, yet they have been set below monopoly price levels. In addition, while some oligopolies gained power by adding to their original productive capacities, others have done so by means of various types of mergers. Merger movements, too, have been subject to controversies about their social impacts. Clearly, the dominance of certain areas of the economy by oligopolies in some cases virtually precludes opportunities for potential competitors to enter the industry: Witness the difficulties of gaining entry into the automotive, aircraft, and communications industries. In other industries, however, such as electronics and fast foods, entry has been relatively easy.

Context

Because the structure of economic institutions affects—some argue that it determines—the structure of the rest of society, sociologists often have concentrated their research on the economies of various societies. Karl Marx (1818-1883) remains the most famous of all theorists on economics and society. The publication of Marx's major works closely coincided with the rapid expansion and maturation of industrial capitalism. His passionate analysis of its organization and function were responsible for shifting the interest of subsequent generations of scholars away from political and intellectual forces as the critical factors behind social organization and toward economic activities as the major determinant of social structure.

While Marx recognized the achievements of capitalism and believed that they had prepared the way for humankind's movement toward communism and the dictatorship of the proletariat, he focused his critique on capitalism's exploitative features: its tendencies at all levels toward monopoly, the capitalist's skimming of the fruits of the worker's toil, and the worker's subsequent degradation and impoverishment. In so doing, he unknowingly created an intellectual industry of Marxists and non-Marxists alike that would focus its investigations of key social institutions on every major society's economy.

Throughout the twentieth century, capitalism has undergone dynamic changes, so much so that even where capitalist ideologies persist, they do so in the midst of what are really mixed economies. Accordingly, many of Marx's descriptions have become obsolete and many of his predictions have failed. Nearly everyone, however, continued to assign a vital role to economic activity as a major influence on the organization of the entire structure of contemporary society.

Neo-Marxian sociologists thus have reinterpreted and readapted Marx's basic themes and beliefs, rather than his examples or predictions, to fit twentieth century economic realities. Problems posed by concentrations of wealth and economic power, by monopolistic behavior in the marketplace, and by the manipulation, control, and exploitation of workers retained command of these sociologists' interest. Harry Braverman, for example, writing in the 1970's, pointed to the ongoing exploitation of labor, including new generations of white-collar workers, by a new generation of monopoly capitalism's managers. Similarly, Paul Baran and Paul Sweezy described and deplored the spiraling cycles of waste that characterized societies dominated by monopoly capital.

Many Neo-Marxians, however, shifted their empirical emphases away from these problems to overall critiques of American society and other Western societies. In Marxian terms, they attacked the cultural superstructure built upon capitalist economies, stressing the repressiveness and irrationality of rational-technical society. In the 1960's, for example, Herbert Marcuse declared that modern technology, as its use became more perverted, would lead to the development of new forms of totalitarianism, degrading human beings and suppressing their individuality "pleasantly" by means of external controls such as television and packaged ideas. In the 1970's, sociologists such as Zoltan Tar and Martin Jay criticized the West's "mass," "administered," or "one-dimensional" culture. Still critical of the kinds of societies that the economies of developed (including socialist) countries had thrown up, Henry Jacoby, Trent Schroyer, and Jürgen Habermas, among others, decried the bureaucratization of modern life, which placed humankind in an "iron cage." They were likewise disturbed by the progressive rationalization of and disenchantment with science and technology, which were being employed to control masses of people and which denied them effective interpersonal relationships. Thus, into the 1990's, sociologists were refining their research to account for the sweeping changes that had affected economies characterized by new concentrations of wealth and power, by monopoly competition, and by oligopolies.

Bibliography

Baran, Paul, and Paul M. Sweezy. *Monopoly Capital*. New York: Monthly Review Press, 1966. An informative and engaging neo-Marxian interpretation of the subject. Stresses the impacts of surpluses and waste generated by the American economy on other social institutions. Includes notes, a bibliography, and an index.
Braverman, Harry. *Labor and Monopoly Capital*. New York: Monthly Review Press, 1974. Concentrates on the degradation of work in the twentieth century, updating a central theme in the work of Marx by treating white-collar and service workers

and management's impersonal control techniques. Makes interesting reading. Notes, a bibliography, and an index are included.

Bronfenbrenner, Martin, Werner Sichel, and Wayland Gardner. *Macroeconomics*. 3d ed. Boston: Houghton Mifflin, 1990. Chapters 27, 28, and 29 are fine explanations of monopolies and oligopolies for nonexperts. Ample illustrations, tables, and charts enhance the reader's understanding. A superb introduction to the subject. There is no bibliography, but many reader aids, useful glossaries, and an index are included.

Edwards, Richard. *Contested Terrain*. New York: Basic Books, 1979. Concentrates on the transformation of work in an economic world of monopolies and oligopolies by means of new managerial controls that convert the workplace into a contested terrain. Emphasizes the replacement of personal controls by impersonal technical and bureaucratic controls. Contains notes, a bibliography, and an index.

Habermas, Jürgen. *Toward a Rational Society*. Translated by Jeremy J. Shapiro. Boston: Beacon Press, 1970. A German sociologist critiques the use of science and technology as instruments of control in modern economies, including socialist economies. Notes, a bibliography, and an index are included in this interesting, important work.

Marcuse, Herbert. *One Dimensional Man*. Boston: Beacon Press, 1964. A German sociologist and a folk-hero of the 1960's, Marcuse attacks the irrationality of rational societies that are outgrowths of modern consumer economies. Marcuse denounces the subtle, often pleasant, means of control exerted over the masses by managerial elites. A still interesting but somewhat polemical analysis.

Ritzer, George. *Sociological Theory*. New York: Alfred A. Knopf, 1983. Excellent in its sociological analyses (Chapters 9 and 10), both non-Marxian and Marxian, of the effects of modern capitalism, monopoly, and oligopoly on social structure. The presentation is clear, interesting, and orderly. Biographical sketches, notes, an outstanding bibliography, and a useful index are included.

Clifton K. Yearley

Cross-References

Alienation and Work, 80; Bureaucracies, 172; Capitalism, 191; Corporations and Economic Concentration, 360; Industrial and Postindustrial Economies, 940; The Industrial Revolution and Mass Production, 946; Industrial Societies, 953; The Power Elite, 1491; Social Stratification: Marxist Perspectives, 1852.

MORAL DEVELOPMENT: KOHLBERG

Type of sociology: Socialization and social interaction
Field of study: Development, personality, and socialization

Lawrence Kohlberg hypothesized that a child's understanding of the basis for moral rules typically changes with his or her maturing ability to reason and to reflect on social relationships. The rules are seen first as authority-given absolutes, then as requirements for enduring social relationships, and finally as principles necessary for justice.

Principal terms

CONFORMITY STAGE: Kohlberg's stage three; moral rules are understood as based on their necessity for maintaining close relationships

CONVENTIONAL LEVEL: includes Kohlberg's stages three and four of moral reasoning based on maintenance of social relationships; stages before are preconventional, and stages after are postconventional

INSTRUMENTAL RELATIVISTIC STAGE: Kohlberg's stage two, in which moral rules can be adjusted to the mutual satisfaction of the interacting parties

LEVEL OF MORAL REASONING: the principle for classifying stages, based on the individual's understanding of conventions for maintaining social relationships as the reason for rules; levels are preconventional, conventional, and postconventional

POSTCONVENTIONAL LEVEL: includes the highest stages, five and six; moral rules are themselves adjusted based upon their usefulness (stage five) and principles of justice (stage six)

PUNISHMENT AND OBEDIENCE ORIENTATION: Kohlberg's first and most basic stage; moral rules are seen as absolute edicts of authorities

SOCIAL SYSTEM ORIENTATION: Kohlberg's stage four; moral rules are judged by their impact upon remote and complex social relationships such as social institutions or national interest

STAGE OF MORAL REASONING: a developmental period in Kohlberg's sequence based on the individual's understanding of the reasons for moral behavior

Overview

Psychologist, educator, and philosopher Lawrence Kohlberg (1927-1987) outlined in the 1960's a sequence of changes that occur in the logic that maturing children, adolescents, and young adults employ as they reason about the basis of right and wrong. In their studies, Kohlberg and his associates typically presented the respondent with a moral dilemma that involved a conflict between two moral rules. To cite Kohlberg's own most famous example, a young man, Heinz, can only save his wife from dying of cancer by stealing a drug which the local druggist refuses to sell to him. Moral prescriptions to obey the law, to honor and protect one's family, and to preserve a human life at all costs cannot all be observed simultaneously. Whether the respondent thinks that Heinz should steal the drug is of less interest than the logic and reasons for the person's decision. Kohlberg maintained that the logic used by children in solving such dilemmas progresses through an invariant series of stages. Based upon the maturation of the child's reasoning capacity, the sequence of changes is found in all cultures. The logic at each successive stage is more comprehensive in scope and therefore more adequate than the logic of the preceding stage. In every culture, however, some people remain arrested at the earlier, less adequate stages, even in adulthood.

The evolution occurs through six stages of reasoning. The first two are considered "preconventional"; they occur before the child can understand and articulate considerations such as loyalty, love, and responsibility (social conventions) as relevant to questions of right and wrong. The first and earliest stage is summarized as the "punishment and obedience orientation." The preschool and early school-age child accepts the rules of authorities as absolute and self-evident. The rightness of such rules is established by the very fact that violations of these rules lead to punishment. Situations are dealt with in terms of slogans: "It's wrong to steal." One should do what one's parent, a police officer, or God says. Appreciation of a social context that might make telling such truths as "You're too fat" as less than a totally virtuous act is absent. Some very concrete-minded adults continue to reason at a stage one level.

Kohlberg called the second stage "instrumental relativism." It begins when the child's simple allegiance to the commandments of authority is disrupted, usually in the middle school-age years, by a growing capacity to understand the concerns of others immediately present. This maturation leads to an understanding that rules are only agreements to achieve mutual satisfaction; they are "instrumental." If the players in a game are not satisfied, they can change the rules. Thus, a certain flexibility is introduced into moral decision making. This is an improvement over stage one absolutisms. Considerations of loyalty to parties not present (social conventions) are not yet important. Therefore, if two individuals decide to break the rules—to cheat, for example—and no one else discovers it, the two people involved may see nothing wrong with their action. To the stage two reasoner, this may be acceptable behavior. It is no accident that many juvenile delinquents remain arrested at level two.

Stages three and four constitute the conventional level. Stage three, called the "conformity" stage, typically begins to emerge in late childhood or early adolescence. This is a time when children have developed the cognitive ability to see and evaluate their behavior from the perspective of third parties who are not present at the time of a moral decision. At this time the approval of peers and models typically becomes important. "Right" is living up to what is expected of one by those close to one—being trustworthy and loyal, and being a good person worthy of being loved. At this stage it might be argued that Heinz should steal the drug to save his dying wife because he loves her, or it might be argued that Heinz should not steal the drug because "other people have the right to expect that others will not take what belongs to them." The stage three appeal is to motives that spring from empathetic involvement with others. Stage three reasoning is the basis for such folk wisdom as the "golden rule." Many "nice" people who have had no special concern with social or administrative problems remain on level three.

Stage four, still at the conventional level of moral reasoning, has been described as the "social system" or "law and order" orientation. At some point, middle to late adolescents begin to confront circumstances, either directly or vicariously, in which duty to the organization or society in general is a primary consideration. There is a concern for the social order and an awareness that even silly rules have some validity because if all individuals selectively violated rules they considered silly, society would break down. The sort of actions that may be required to uphold the social system may contradict those based on empathetic considerations alone: The manager who must fire the inefficient worker whom she likes or the judge who must sentence his friend to prison are cases in point. Living up to those duties to the social system except when they conflict with other such duties is considered right. Such reasoning, which requires a comprehension of the functional requirements of social systems, is more adequate than stage three reasoning. It permits the expansion of moral rules to cover an additional class of problem. A majority of mature, well-educated adults probably reason on stage four.

The postconventional stages are considered higher stages in that they are more adequate and comprehensive in coping with the most puzzling dilemma of all: Cannot society's rules and laws be morally wrong? What does it mean, for example, to be a good guard in a concentration camp? Such dilemmas can only be dealt with by positing some values or principles that are fundamental to any just society. Stage five reasoning involves an appreciation that society's rules must be useful in serving to promote the life, liberty, and happiness of the greatest number. This is called, therefore, the "utilitarian" stage. Stage six, the final stage of "principled moral reasoning," involves transcending the greatest good principle in arriving at a standard of justice under which an equality of right and respect for the dignity of every individual is preserved. Actually reached by very few people, stage six, for Kohlberg, offers an ideal endpoint reached when the assumptions of basic rights, reciprocity, and equality are applied most logically, consistently, and comprehensively.

Applications

Kohlberg's theory has been applied to the description, prediction, and changing of attitudes and behavior. Kohlberg studied a large sample (in Chicago) from childhood to adulthood and found an evolution of moral reasoning in the exact sequence suggested by his theory. Studies of moral reasoning in a variety of Western and non-Western cultures have shown the expected relationship of higher levels of reasoning among the older and the more mature adolescents and adults, although the postconventional stages are seldom found in non-Western cultures. Since each person goes through the sequence at his or her own pace and may become arrested at less mature stages, within any group there are individual differences in stages of reasoning. High-level moral reasoners everywhere have been shown to be aware of more of the ethical considerations involved in such social issues as capital punishment and euthanasia.

The most important application of the theory has been the prediction and influencing of moral behavior. Helping a stranger in distress ("altruism") is often considered by psychologists to represent such moral behavior. In numerous experiments (but not all) in which a collaborator pretends to be in distress, high moral reasoners are more likely to help than are those who reason at the lower stages. Being able to resist the temptation to cheat represents another such moral behavior. Again, students high in moral reasoning have been shown to be less likely than others to cheat on tests that experimenters have rigged to make cheating appear easy and hard to detect. Criminal acts, on the other hand, are usually considered bad moral behavior. Most studies have found low moral reasoners common among criminal and delinquent populations.

There is good reason to believe that raising one's level of moral reasoning will result in more moral behavior. Even without planning, the child's moral reasoning advances as his growing cognitive capacity makes it possible to reflect on the dilemmas posed by everyday social relationships. Whether to report a cheating friend or to tell a "white lie" to spare feelings are common problems of everyday life. Parents and educators can encourage this moral growth. As the child faces such situations, educators could encourage moral reflection by emphasizing the effects of various actions on the feelings of others. Suggestions made on a slightly higher stage than the child's own stage of reasoning may be particularly likely to stimulate growth. Problem-based courses in social studies or ethics and cross-cultural experiences can encourage moral reflection. Always, the moral educator must confront the child with problems and thoughts that promote a sort of creative tension. Children who come from authoritarian, punishment-oriented homes often lag in moral reasoning because they have been discouraged from questioning rules.

Crucial to the treatment programs designed by Kohlberg are group discussions of various social dilemmas, particularly ones emerging from the subject's own experience. One experimental program employed with delinquents involves a miniature "just society" in which the rules that will actually apply to the group emerge from such discussions of effects and consequences. The most effective of such programs involve discussions that continue on a regular basis for a period of time and a group composed of members who are on various levels of moral reasoning. Kohlberg has pointed out that this "just society" is radically different from most prisons, which employ a punishment-obedience orientation antagonistic to growth in moral reasoning.

Context

Kohlberg's theory emerged from the functional approach to social science, which treats individuals and social systems as mutually interacting parts of organic wholes. Most directly influenced by the American educator John Dewey, Kohlberg began to view children's growing capacity for thought as making possible their comprehension of progressively more complex social situations, provided that a cooperative environment presents such situations. Parents and educators could help, too, but as gardeners fertilizing a growing plant rather than as artisans carving a figure out of a soft piece of wood. Swiss psychologist Jean Piaget also had a direct impact upon Kohlberg's work. Piaget observed that children first view the rules of games as absolute and only later do they realize that it would be fair to change these rules if the players agree. This became the basis for Kohlberg's stages one and two and his investigations into those shifts in reasoning that occur later in development.

Kohlberg made two assumptions that were unusual in social science in 1969 when his work became known. First, his is a cognitive theory—it assumes that the thinking, reasoning process is of great importance in determining behavior. To do right, one must know what right is. This may seem obvious, but many behavioral psychologists of the era viewed a knowledge of behavioral traits as one's control over one's impulses as the only important factor in behavior. Kohlberg admitted that such factors as empathy and will power are also determinants of whether one acts on beliefs, but he insisted that reasoning is important as well. Second, he assumed that certain moral decisions are better than others and that the logical basis of these better decisions is the same in every culture. While the norms of a particular culture may affect the content of dilemmas, there are certain universally valid requirements of moral decision making. Kohlberg's views contrasted, therefore, with prevailing views of cultural relativism.

Kohlberg's theses of cognitive influences on moral behavior and of the cross-cultural generality of the sequence he outlined have been largely supported by research. An important qualification must be made concerning research support for the postconventional stages. An overwhelming body of evidence supports the thesis that people in varied cultures move through the first four stages in sequence. This same evidence suggests that only a small percentage of people in any culture ever reach the postconventional stages. This percentage grew even smaller as the testing and scoring of moral dilemmas became tighter and more reliable in the 1980's. While it can be maintained that the logical requirements of reasoning about the most difficult moral dilemmas require postconventional reasoning, the validity of the core theory does not rest on this assumption.

A criticism of Kohlberg's theory that has been given serious attention is that it is "elitist." It has been charged with bias toward Westerners and toward males. Well-educated males from Western cultures generally do best in solving the types of moral dilemmas presented by testing based on Kohlberg's ideas. This does not necessarily mean, however, that they are more moral. Psychologist Carol Gilligan has pointed out that a narrow focus on certain stages as defined by Kohlberg ignores an important dimension of growth in the moral reasoning of women. Women typically increase their concern for others in the context of the responsibility of close relationships. No matter how intense such concerns may be, they are simply relegated to stage three in Kohlberg's model. In his system, however, male administrators who can make "hard decisions for the good of the company" rate stage four.

1260   *Sociology*

Some of the force of the "elitism" criticism is arguably reduced by acknowl-
edgments that the sequence in reasoning outlined by Kohlberg is only one part of moral
development, and that stages five and six, absent from non-Western cultures, are not
the most crucial parts of the theory. At the very least, Kohlberg has shown that a
sequence of progressively adequate moral reasoning occurs in maturing children and
adolescents of many cultures and that such advances in reasoning play a part in
influencing moral behavior.

Bibliography

Blasi, Augusto. "Bridging Moral Cognition and Moral Action: A Critical Review of
the Literature." *Psychological Bulletin* 88 (July, 1980): 1-45. Blasi summarizes
studies that explore such behaviors as resisting the temptation to cheat and helping
strangers in a crisis. Mostly, high moral reasoners have been found to do better.

Gilligan, Carol. *In a Different Voice: Psychological Theory and Women's Development.* Cambridge, Mass.: Harvard University Press, 1982. An eloquent feminist
critique of Kohlberg's justice orientation. Gilligan argues that Kohlberg's scheme
minimizes the moral growth of women in responsibility for caring relationships.

Jurkovic, Gregory J. "The Juvenile Delinquent as a Moral Philosopher: A Structural-
Developmental Perspective." *Psychological Bulletin* 88 (November, 1980): 709-
727. A review and summary of the many studies that mostly support the thesis that
juvenile delinquents are deficient in moral reasoning.

Kohlberg, Lawrence. *Essays on Moral Development.* San Francisco: Harper & Row,
1981-1984. 3 vols. The most comprehensive compilation of Kohlberg's writings
available. Articles are organized according to the three areas of Kohlberg's interest.
Volume 1 is entitled *The Philosophy of Moral Development: Moral Stages and the
Idea of Justice*; volume 2 is *The Psychology of Moral Development: The Nature
and Validity of Moral Stages*; and volume 3 is *Education and Moral Development:
Moral Stages and Practice.*

_____ . "Moral Stages and Moralization: The Cognitive Developmental
Approach." In *Moral Development and Behavior: Theory, Research, and Social
Issues*, edited by Thomas Lickona. New York: Holt, Rinehart and Winston, 1976.
A concise review and defense by Kohlberg of his theory. Incorporates Kohlberg's
major revisions of the early 1970's.

Modgil, Sohan, and Celia Modgil, eds. *Lawrence Kohlberg: Consensus and Controversy.* Philadelphia: Falmer Press, 1986. This volume contains constructive criticisms by some thirty scholars of every aspect of Kohlberg's theory. The reviews of
applications to education are particularly valuable.

Papalia, Diane, and Sally Olds. *Human Development.* 3d ed. New York: McGraw-Hill,
1986. Like most developmental psychology textbooks, this contains a description
of Kohlberg's theory. Includes a helpful chart outlining his stages. Most such general
texts describe the Kohlberg theory of 1969, before his revisions.

Thomas E. DeWolfe

Cross-References

Cognitive Development: Piaget, 278; Delinquency Prevention and Treatment, 476; The Family: Functionalist versus Conflict Theory Views, 739; Moral Development: Piaget, 1262; Parenthood and Child-Rearing Practices, 1336; Personality: Affective, Cognitive, and Behavioral Components, 1356; Personality Development: Erikson, 1362; Personality Development: Freud, 1368; Socialization: The Family, 1880; Values and Value Systems, 2143.

MORAL DEVELOPMENT: PIAGET

Type of sociology: Socialization and social interaction
Field of study: Development, personality, and socialization

The moral development of the individual begins when, as a child, the person internalizes rules and principles of right and wrong presented by a parental figure. Swiss psychologist Jean Piaget proposed an influential model of moral development, linking it to the child's level of cognitive understanding.

Principal terms
COGNITIVE: a term referring to all of the processes of the mind, including thinking, reasoning, knowing, remembering, understanding, and problem solving
DEVELOPMENT: orderly changes in an organism that include physical, mental, social, and personality changes
MORAL DEVELOPMENT: the onset and growth of an individual's ability to determine right from wrong, resulting in appropriate ethical behavior
MORAL RULES: obligatory social regulations based on the principles of justice and concern for the welfare of others
MORALITY: a system of rules handed down by cultural and/or societal consensus
SOCIAL JUSTICE: the sense that rights for society's individuals stem from reciprocity and equality among the members of the society as dictated by the social rules
SOCIAL ORDER: the way in which a society or culture functions, based on the rules, regulations, and standards that are held and taught by each member of the society

Overview

Every society has ideas about the rightness or wrongness of certain behaviors; these standards are called morals. Not all societies have the same morals, but some actions (such as murder and theft) seem to be universally considered wrong. Each individual learns these standards from their parental figures and teachers, as well as from peers. Moral development is the way in which these standards change for the individual as a function of time and experiences.

Swiss psychologist Jean Piaget was among the first to develop a theoretical model of cognitive and moral development. The central tenet of his ideas on moral development is that moral development is linked to a child's cognitive development; at certain ages, a child thinks in a certain way, and moral reasoning cannot develop faster than cognitive growth. Piaget devised a pair of related scenarios involving two boys, John and Henry, that he used to gauge a person's level of moral reasoning.

A little boy named John is in his room when he is called to dinner. He goes into the dining room. Behind the door on a chair is a tray with fifteen cups on it. John does not know this. He goes in, the door knocks against the tray, and all fifteen cups are broken. Another little boy named Henry tries to get some jam out of the cupboard one day when his mother is out. He climbs onto a chair, but he cannot reach it; in his attempt, he knocks over a cup. The cup falls and breaks.

When asked which of the above two boys is more naughty, most adults would immediately reply that Henry is the more guilty. Conversely, a child between the ages of six and ten usually will say that John is the more guilty. The differences between the two scenes consist of both the amount of damage done and the intentions of the two children. It is obvious that children and adults do not view the situations in the same way. According to Piaget, moral judgments are related to a person's stage of cognitive development. A person cannot progress to higher stages of moral development until the person has also progressed to higher stages of cognitive understanding.

Piaget states that to have moral maturity, a child must have both a respect for social rules (customs, morals, and laws) and a sense of social justice regarding equality and reciprocity among individual members of society. The development of morality includes several stages. The first stage, the premoral period, occurs through four to five years of age; the child has little awareness of rules or regulations. In games, very young children play for fun and have no understanding of rules or strategies for winning. The children follow their parents' judgments about what is right and wrong but have no cognitive understanding or internalization of these rules. In addition, the child during this stage has cognitive limitations such as egocentrism (believing that everyone views events from the same perspective as the child) and realism (confusing internal, subjective perceptions with objective reality). The child, being dependent, fearful, affectionate, and admiring of the adult, believes that the adult's rules are sacred and are to be obeyed absolutely. This feeling of adult sovereignty leads to the next stage of moral development, known as heteronomous morality or moral realism. This exists between the ages of six and ten. Children experience a period of moral absolutes and believe in punitive "imminent justice." The child thinks that behaviors are totally right or wrong and, egocentrically, thinks that everyone else feels the same way. Imminent justice may follow any transgressions—falling down and scraping a knee is seen as punishment for violating a social norm. Children during this stage think that John, with his fifteen-cup breakage, is more guilty than one-cup Henry because of the amount of damage done. They are not cognitively capable of making moral judgments based on intention; they understand only the consequences of the action.

Moral growth is dependent on the child's abandonment of egocentric viewoints and moral realism and instead developing a sense of individual self-concept. As children grow, they also learn about cooperative activity and equality among peers. The shift in moral development begins when socialization with peers demonstrates to the child that there are different points of view. In game playing, the child and a peer may take reciprocal turns, change roles, and cooperate in rule changing. Children realize that if they and their peers can change rules, then the previously unalterable rules seem less divine and more human. This occurs around age ten and signifies the shift into a new stage, called moral relativism or autonomous morality. The child learns that rules can be challenged. The child is also on an equal status with peers, which lessens feelings of inequality toward adults. The child learns to take the other person's perspective and in doing so loses egocentrism. When this occurs, the child is also able to realize that some actions should be judged on intentions rather than results. The child also realizes that punishment occurs only if the incident is witnessed by a human.

In Piaget's theory, the context of the social world is instrumental in moral development. The child must experience interactions with peers in order for the child to discard his or her egocentric viewpoint, to realize a sense of social justice, and to internalize society's standards while maintaining a sense of self. The parent begins the moral process, but society completes it.

Applications

Moral development involves the progression from lower to higher stages of reasoning; one cannot proceed to a higher stage of morality without the cognitive understanding that makes it possible. Thus, if a child thinks that John, who broke fifteen cups, is more guilty than Henry, who broke one cup, then merely telling the child that Henry's intentions were not as good as John's—and therefore that he is not as guilty—will not result in changing the child's perceptions. This can only occur if the child's understanding of the situation is actively challenged. Role playing is one way of achieving this. For example, the child who thinks that John is more guilty can be told to act out the two scenes, sequentially playing each of the two boys. If the child is asked questions about his or her feelings while going through each of the scenes, the child will gain empathy for each of the characters and will thereby gain a better understanding of intentions and actions. Once the child has the cognitive understanding of intentions, he or she is then able to reason at a higher level of moral development.

The first goal in trying to elevate a person's moral reasoning to a higher level, then, is to elevate the person's cognitive understanding of the situation. This can be done by citing similar examples within the person's own personal experience and relating them to the event at hand. For example, if a girl has accidentally broken something recently, then asking her if she remembers how she felt when that happened will remind her of the emotions she experienced at the time of the event. The child must then associate the remembered emotions with the situation at hand. This may be accomplished if one asks her questions such as, "Do you think that John might have felt the same way as you did when you broke the vase?" or, "How do you think John felt when the cups fell down? Have you ever felt the same way?" If one merely tells the child that John felt bad, she may or may not comprehend the connection, but if she is asked to reason through the situation by feeling empathy for John, the child is much more likely to progress to the next stage of moral reasoning. Such empathetic role playing can be effective in trying to change deviant behavior. If a boy is stealing, then having him play a role in a situation in which he is the one being stolen from is the quickest way to change his judgments of the rightness or wrongness of the behavior. Punishment may deter the behavior but does not result in a change in cognitive understanding or moral reasoning.

This type of role playing is most likely to aid the child from an understimulated home environment. The children whose social environments include many incidents of undesirable behaviors or who lack examples of positive behaviors must be stimulated in ways that appeal to their current cognitive understanding but that show them ways of thinking differently than current examples in their lives. Children cannot do better until they know better, and they cannot know better until they see alternative roles in action.

Context

The study of morality was once the domain of philosophers and essayists. With the work of Sigmund Freud and then Jean Piaget, however, in the early twentieth century, the study of morality and moral development in the social sciences began. Freud proposed, as part of his theory of psychosexual development, that children around four years of age assimilate the morals and standards of their same-sex parent. This process results in the beginnings of the superego (which, along with the id and the ego, compose the psyche). The superego is the storehouse for one's conscience. The child therefore has a rudimentary sense of right and wrong that is based, at first, on the morals of the parental figure. Freud's work was extremely controversial in the early twentieth century; moreover, his ideas on moral development did not lend themselves well to experimentation. Most work on moral development was an outgrowth of Piaget's work rather than Freud's.

Piaget is primarily known for developing a theory about the cognitive development of children. Piaget was working in the laboratory of psychologist Alfred Binet, who developed the first intelligence tests, when he began observing that children do not reason in the same way that adults do. He questioned Swiss schoolchildren about the rules by which they were playing a game of marbles. His concern with children's moral development was an outgrowth of his interest in, and observation of, their cognitive development. Psychologist Lawrence Kohlberg later elaborated on Piaget's work, proposing that there are three levels of moral reasoning, each of which contains two stages. Kohlberg's concept is the most frequently cited model of moral development.

An area of study sometimes called the study of "social cognitions" includes morals but also considers such issues as empathy, attribution, and motivation. The effect of emotions on cognitions (and their consequent contribution to moral judgments) is under study. For example, it has been shown that when people are in a good mood they are more likely to help another person than when they are in a bad mood. Expanding on this premise, research has demonstrated that the way people perceive an object or situation is closely linked to their psychological/emotional state at a given time. Even concrete perceptions can be changed by a person's state of being; people who are poor, for example, have been found to judge the size of a quarter to be larger than do people who are rich, thus influencing people's motivations and intentions.

As cognitive theories consider the interactive reactions between emotions and cognitions, it is likely that new methods of study and new theoretical predictions will change the way psychologists study such areas as problem solving, decision making, reasoning, and memory. Each of these areas is related to the study of moral development and could change the way researchers view the acquisition of morality. In addition, as American society changes, new issues will emerge that will strain old theories. Issues that are particular to new generations will result in new ways of thinking about morality. Abortion, fetal tissue use, and euthanasia are a few topics that were hotly debated in the 1980's and 1990's; these topics were rarely or never discussed thirty years previously. As society changes, so do the moral questions with which it struggles.

Bibliography

Coles, Robert. *The Moral Life of Children.* Boston: Atlantic Monthly Press, 1986. Coles investigates issues such as films and morality, social classes, psychological events, and personality and moral development. Presents a comprehensive overview of Freudian theory and moral development. This book is easily read and should generally be enjoyed by the high school student.

Duska, Ronald, and Mariellen Whelan. *Moral Development: A Guide to Piaget and Kohlberg.* New York: Paulist Press, 1975. Duska and Whelan look at the work of these two developmental psychologists and trace Piaget's influence on Kohlberg. The authors include the moral scenarios and stories used in their research. Also includes research findings and ways in which to apply the theories to everyday situations in teaching children. Easy reading for the high school or college student.

Rest, J. R. *Moral Development: Advances in Research and Theory.* New York: Praeger, 1986. Various influences on moral development—cultural, emotional, religious, and experiential—are related. Rest includes a moral dilemma test and presents results of its use. Advanced reading, but recommended for its inclusion of the test.

Rich, J. M., and J. L. DeVitis. *Theories of Moral Development.* Springfield, Ill.: Charles C Thomas, 1985. Presents a range of psychologists' theories on moral development, including those of Freud, Alfred Adler, and C. G. Jung. In addition, it places moral development within the framework of higher education and relates it to the life span. Sections of the book would be difficult for a novice to follow, but in terms of a summary review of theoretical positions, the book is a handy and valuable reference.

Shaffer, D. R. "Moral Development." In *Social and Personality Development.* Monterey, Calif.: Brooks/Cole, 1979. All the major aspects and theories of moral development are discussed by Shaffer in this chapter. Includes research both supporting and arguing against each of the theoretical outlooks as well as definitions of relevant terms and easy-to-read graphs and tables. Highly recommended as an elementary text for general reading and for exploring research potential.

Donna Frick Horbury

Cross-References

MULTINATIONAL CORPORATIONS AND
THE THIRD WORLD

Type of sociology: Major social institutions
Field of study: The economy

Multinational corporations play a central role in the economies of the Third World. While profits realized through multinational investments have demonstrably enriched the industrialized world, considerable controversy exists over the manner and extent to which multinational investments can favorably contribute to Third World development.

Principal terms

DEPENDENCY PARADIGM: a theoretical perspective that views multinational corporations in the Third World as agents of foreign domination

FOREIGN JOINT OWNERSHIP VENTURE: in the Third World, refers to economic projects in which multinational and domestic investors share in ownership, management, economic risks, and profits

FOREIGN STOCK OWNERSHIP VENTURE: a multinational investment overseas that is decisively subordinated to the local owners and in which minority stock holdings usually reflect other forms of commercial cooperation

MODERNIZATION PARADIGM: a theoretical perspective that views multinational investment in the Third World as favoring development, providing capital resources, and spreading modern ideas and practices

MULTINATIONAL CORPORATION: typically, a private corporation principally headquartered in one nation which has branch offices and significant economic activities in one or more other nations

TECHNICAL/SERVICE CONTRACT: an established agreement between multinational corporations and foreign customers in which the former sells specific financial, managerial, or technological services to the latter

THIRD WORLD: a contemporary term for the developing countries as defined through their engagement in the early and intermediate phases of industrialization

WHOLLY OWNED SUBSIDIARY: in the Third World, an economic firm that is entirely owned by a foreign multinational corporation while operating under the auspices of a local, host economy

Overview

The overall benefits of multinational investment in the Third World have been the subjects of considerable controversy. Some scholars argue that multinational corporations provide a reliable and necessary influx of resources that can assist the development of Third World nations. Others assert that multinational operations essentially exploit the Third World, causing distortions in national development while taking out more wealth than they bring in. Such debates notwithstanding, the percentage of global economic activity being carried out by multinationals has continued to grow, and the Third World is a primary target for such investments.

Multinational corporations have a tremendous interest in the Third World. The potential for accumulating profits is greatly enhanced by the generally lower wage rates found in developing nations. The cheaper price of labor in the Third World is the result of lower levels of accumulated wealth, frequently coupled with widespread unemployment. In many cases, authoritarian state policies actively impede the effectiveness of labor organizations, thus depressing wage rates still further.

Third World nations often provide multinationals with lucrative access to vital raw materials. Typically lacking sufficient investment capital of their own, developing countries frequently invite multinationals to invest in such ventures as local mining, agricultural, and fishing operations, with the aim of sharing in the revenues generated by these extractive industries. A substantial share of the strategic raw materials that fueled industrial development in the advanced countries—such as sugar, cotton, and petroleum—are produced in the Third World. These products have been most commonly commercialized by multinational corporations.

Multinational investments in the Third World also stimulate the creation of new markets for goods produced in the advanced countries. Developing countries rely heavily upon important equipment, spare parts, and managerial/technical services from foreign suppliers in order to develop their own new industries. Multinational corporations are deeply involved in the marketing of such products, either through commercial sales and trade ventures or by means of internal distribution processes through which multinationals bring manufactured goods into their own operations in Third World countries.

Some additional Third World attractions for multinationals serve to reveal the disadvantages that their investments may exhibit for host countries. Many corporations produce in the Third World to evade environmental or safety regulations that exist in their home countries. This practice exposes Third World peoples to dangerous working conditions and the ever-present threat of environmental contamination. In many cases, developing countries entertain such risks in order to attract badly needed capital. These risks are often exacerbated by corrupt Third World officials who permit abusive and counterproductive investments in return for bribes and other personal rewards.

Multinational corporations frequently enjoy an additional incentive to invest in those Third World countries where they can avoid paying taxes to state authorities. Third World countries frequently offer multinationals substantial exemptions from paying taxes on profits. Moreover, this is sometimes coupled with home country exemptions that permit tax free profits on multinational investments in particular countries, typically as part of a foreign policy designed to assist Third World development.

In some cases, however, multinational corporations that wish to operate in the Third World meet local resistance. Multinational investments can pose serious challenges to a variety of interests in the host country, including those established local businesses and the local labor force. When multinationals gain a foothold in the Third World, their competitive power is frequently overwhelming to the local competition. Whether the state comes to the aid of these local businesses depends upon their relative political strength. The same is true for Third World workers, who quickly discover that their multinational employer is far more powerful than any local business owner. In many cases, labor organizations put forth demands that the state restrict and regulate the operations of multinationals in order to guarantee reasonable wages, safe working conditions, and environmental protection for their surrounding communities.

In the worst-case scenario, mounting local resistance leads multinationals to threaten the political sovereignty of the host country. Eager to protect their substantial investments, multinationals generally use their power to cultivate the loyalty of a Third World regime, rewarding and encouraging them to resist demands that are contrary to the multinational's interests. If the regime refuses to or is unable to cooperate, the multinational may seek to cultivate a change of government to a more "friendly" regime.

The infamous "banana republics" of Central America were those countries that experienced intense meddling in their internal political affairs on the part of multinationals. Firms such as Standard Fruit Company, United Fruit Company, and others actively opposed governments that they perceived to be hostile and abetted political regimes that protected their banana investments from the demands of exploited workers and frustrated local business interests. In these and countless other examples, multinationals have become a symbol of foreign interventionism, particularly when multinationals succeed in winning the backing of their powerful home governments in times of crisis. When governments have proved to be unusually problematic, multinationals have, on various occasions, been able to win military intervention by their home governments' armed forces to protect the "property" of their citizens.

Applications

Types of multinational investments in the Third World can range from very high to very low control over local operations. The most common examples of investments include wholly owned subsidiaries, foreign joint ownership ventures, foreign stock ownership ventures, and technical/service contracts. Each form of investment has a corresponding set of advantages and disadvantages for both the multinational investor and the host country.

When multinational corporations fully assume the risk of investing in wholly owned subsidiaries located in the Third World, virtually all of the profits from such ventures flow back to the home country. Control over decision making resides firmly in the hands of the multinational, while local authorities typically have little or no leverage over operations. Third World nations that host such subsidiaries seek to benefit from the generation of local employment, the introduction of new technologies, and the payment of taxes on the part of multinational investors.

Wholly owned subsidiaries tend to engender the highest degree of resistance on the part of local interest groups, primarily because of the lack of local participation in operational decision making and the absence of adequate recourse when abuses are alleged. Many observers have pointed out that "inappropriate technologies" are frequenty utilized by multinationals—that is, technological methods that offer little benefit to the larger local economy, environment, and/or labor force. With profits flowing out of the country and inappropriate technologies being employed, the local benefits from such investments rapidly begin to dissipate. In some cases, political pressure begins to mount for the nationalization of such firms, a process that involves the confiscation of the multinational's holdings, usually in accordance with some form of negotiated compensation.

In joint ownership ventures, multinational corporations form partnerships with local private or public (governmental) entities, whereupon investment resources and risks are shared along with the profits that result from successful operations. For multinational corporations, jointly owned firms add an extra measure of political security, providing them with a degree of local support in defense of the operations in times of political turmoil. During the 1980's, for example, joint ventures on the part of large oil companies resulted in considerable local defense efforts, even on the part of revolutionary, leftist governments. In countries such as Nicaragua and Angola, revolutionary governments were steadfast in their armed defense of multinational holdings when civil strife led to threatened attacks upon their investments.

A reduced amount of multinational control is observable in stock ownership ventures in which multinational investors provide international capital for projects for which local capital is insufficient to initiate or maintain operations. In addition to investing needed capital in exchange for profitable returns, multinational involvement in such operations can offer important advantages to host countries, including preferential access to international markets. These benefits are generally in proportion to the magnitude of the investment that is furnished by the multinationals. The risk of local political resistance to the investment is greatly diminished, since the multinational presence is far less visible.

At the lowest end of multinational involvement is the technical/service contract, a form of investment that is becoming increasingly preferred by multinationals doing business in the Third World. Through a contractual agreement, multinationals essentially provide a variety of marketing, technological, managerial, or financial services on a payment-for-services-rendered basis. This is attractive to both partners for a variety of reasons. For example, it preserves a large degree of local control over economic assets and strategic, operational decision making in the developing country, while it practically eliminates risks for the multinationals. Although technical/service contracts involve a very minimal fixed investment, they can involve large sums of money in an ongoing collaboration between multinational and foreign firms. This, in turn, offers substantial profits to the multinational and immunity from the risks of nationalization. Like other forms of investment, however, technical/service contracts can create a strong local dependence upon the multinational investor.

Although multinationals operating in the Third World have learned to share or even avoid outright ownership in order to minimize their risks abroad, many have also experienced growing political resentment in their home countries. So long as unemployment remains uncomfortably high in the more developed countries, workers feel betrayed when multinationals shift their production to Third World sites in order to capitalize on lower wage rates. The worldwide trend toward more open markets with fewer restrictions on commerce and investment nevertheless makes such shifts increasingly likely.

Context

The role of multinational corporations in the Third World has been systematically considered by the sociology of development. Sociological literature concerning the Third World became largely dominated by the modernization perspective during the 1950's and into the 1960's. Influenced heavily by the Weberian tradition, modernization theorists conceptualized development as a progressive rationalization of social life whereby the modern ideas and practices of the industrialized West became promulgated throughout the developing world.

The modernization perspective postulated that a proliferation of modern institutions would create the necessary conditions for promoting sustained economic growth in modern industries. An inflow of external resources from the developed world would provide the catalyst for the systematic industrialization of developing areas at a level sufficient to promote an expanding rate of productive investments.

Modernization theorists therefore saw multinationals as a necessary reservoir of external resources. Multinational investments, they argued, could provide a medium for the transfer of modern technologies to backward Third World areas. At the same time, increasing contact between "modern" multinationals and "traditional" developing areas would promote the spread of modern values. With growing trade between developed and developing nations, the essential goods necessary to sustain newly developed industries could be guaranteed, and such ties were viewed as mutually beneficial to both trading partners. In short, intensive Third World contacts with multinational corporations were seen as being indispensable to a national strategy designed to modernize through industrialization.

By the 1960's, considerable political turbulence occurred in response to the numerous economic failures experienced by nations that had been heavily penetrated by multinationals. This led a new generation of theorists, particularly among Third World scholars, to question the modernization perspective. The resulting critique of multinational investments began to reveal the negative consequences of over-reliance upon external resources. This critical stance soon mushroomed into a full-fledged, alternative development approach that became known as the dependency perspective.

Dependency theorists showed that multinational corporations generally took more resources out of developing countries than they put in. Numerous studies revealed that technologies introduced by multinational investments were frequently inappropriate to local conditions, with the result that these so-called "modern" practices often interacted unfavorably with the existing level of technological development. In some cases, a negative, destructive effect on productive, indigenous practices was the most evident result. Moreover, it was shown that the intensifying commerce that was encouraged by modernization strategies resulted in highly unequal trade relations. While Third World nations paid increasingly higher prices for imported goods, the prices tended to fall for the more basic, raw material commodities that they were encouraged to produce for export.

In view of the deepening economic crisis that developed in many Third World nations through the 1970's and afterward, the sociology of development literature became greatly influenced by the critical dependency perspective. Since then, most contemporary sociological approaches remain attentive to the numerous social problems that potentially surround multinational investments in the Third World.

Bibliography

Barry, Tom, Beth Wood, and Deb Preusch. *The Other Side of Paradise: Foreign Control in the Caribbean.* New York: Grove Press, 1984. A good overview of the high degree of multinational penetration in the Caribbean. The authors provide a critical introduction to the various mechanisms of multinational control.

Berberoglu, Berch. *The Political Economy of Development: Development Theory and the Prospects for Change in the Third World.* Albany: State University of New York Press, 1992. An excellent primer on all aspects of the development process. The author offers a concise overview of development theory and the various models of development, followed by several case studies designed to illustrate the complexities of Third World development.

Bruyn, Severyn T. *The Social Economy: People Transforming Modern Business.* New York: Wiley, 1977. A seminal work in the field of socioeconomics. The author devotes considerable attention to exploring the possibilities for a favorable relationship between multinational corporations and host countries of the Third World.

Deere, Carmen Diana, et al. *In the Shadows of the Sun: Caribbean Development Alternatives and U.S. Policy.* Boulder, Colo.: Westview Press, 1990. A well-researched overview of the problems faced by Third World countries in a region heavily penetrated by multinational corporations. The authors provide a critical analysis of multinationals along with an ambitious array of alternative government policies that could promote genuine development in the Caribbean.

Gereffi, Gary, and Donald L. Wyman, eds. *Manufacturing Miracles: Paths of Industrialization in Latin America and East Asia.* Princeton, N.J.: Princeton University Press, 1990. This anthology of fourteen interdisciplinary studies provides an excellent, comparative approach to multinational investment in the Third World. State policies that have maximized the benefits of multinational investments in East Asia are highlighted, and various theories are advanced to explain why multinationals have failed to produce similar development successes in Latin America.

Manley, Michael. *Up the Down Escalator: Development and the International Economy: A Jamaican Case Study.* London: Andre Deutsch, 1987. A fascinating case study of one Caribbean nation's struggle to confront multinational investors, written by a former president of Jamaica. The author illustrates the pressures that multinationals exert upon Third World economies, the numerous problems that result from unequal trade, and the costs and benefits that are incurred when multinationals are challenged.

Petersen, Kurt. *The Maquiladora Revolution in Guatemala.* New Haven, Conn.: Center for International Human Rights at Yale Law School, 1992. A revealing case study of a development strategy based on the encouragement of multinational investment in assembly industries. The author develops a sophisticated analysis of how the maquiladora revolution resulted in many negative social consequences for the Guatemalan economy.

Sachs, Wolfgang, ed. *The Development Dictionary: A Guide to Knowledge as Power.* Atlantic Highlands, N.J.: Zed Books, 1992. A very useful anthology of twenty essays, aimed at treating the key concepts within the sociology of Third World development. The collection emphasizes the need to reexamine critically the Eurocentric bias within the development literature. A more culturally sensitive and environmentally sound approach to Third World studies is advocated

Villamil, José J., ed. *Transnational Capitalism and National Development: New Perspectives on Dependence.* Atlantic Highlands, N.J.: Humanities Press, 1979. Although somewhat dated, this collection of fourteen articles remains valuable because it offers an excellent overview of the political, economic, and military implications of multinationals operating in the Third World. The case studies, which emphasize Africa and Latin America, are well-developed in their theoretical approach.

Zeitlin, Maurice. *The Large Corporation and Contemporary Classes.* New Brunswick, N.J.: Rutgers University Press, 1989. A highly analytical work consisting of a series of essays written from a Marxist perspective. The author seeks to show how social class forces impinge upon corporate behavior. The effects that multinationals have had on workers in countries such as Chile and Cuba are examined.

Richard A. Dello Buono

Cross-References

Agrarian Economic Systems, 60; The Agricultural Revolution, 67; Capitalism, 191; Corporations and Economic Concentration, 360; Industrial and Postindustrial Economies, 940; The Industrial Revolution and Mass Production, 946; Industrial Societies, 953; Modernization and World-System Theories, 1241.

THE NATION OF ISLAM

Type of sociology: Major social institutions
Field of study: Religion

The Nation of Islam is an African American religious movement that advocates the return to Islamic religious practices as a means to escape racial inequality and oppression. It proclaims an activist nationalism and millenarianism as it fights for the economic, political, educational, and social uplifting of African Americans.

Principal terms

DEIFICATION: an act of reverence and idealization by which one is said to possess the qualities of a divine being; the attributing of godlike holiness to a person

ENDOGAMY: the allowing of marriage and procreation only for people within the same tribal, religious, class, or ethnic group

ISLAM: a religion of belief in one God, Allah, founded by the prophet Muhammad, with the Qur'an (Koran) as its bible

MILITANT: one who aggressively (not necessarily violently) pursues a cause, be it religious, political, or ideological; militancy can lead to bigotry and fanaticism

MILLENARIANISM: a belief in and anticipation of a coming period of justice, prosperity, joy, and salvation; a perfect new world is envisioned following the overthrow of an oppressor

MISCEGENATION: racial intermarriage, especially sexual intercourse and procreation between blacks and whites or between whites and other people of color

MUSLIM (MOSLEM): one who believes in, practices, or follows Islamic religion

NATIONALISM: devotion to the pursuit of economic, territorial, and political independence by an ethnic group from a nation or by a nation from foreign domination

ORTHODOX: conforming to established, traditional, and generally acceptable religious practices and beliefs; may also be applied to acceptable behavior and attitude in general

SEGREGATION: rejection of racial, class, or ethnic integration; especially an officially imposed physical separation and isolation of a powerless or minority group from a powerful or majority group

Overview

The Nation of Islam (also referred to as the Black Muslim movement, the World Community of Al-Islam in the West, and the American Muslim movement) began as a millenarian religious movement in Detroit, Michigan, in 1931. It was founded by

Wallace D. Fard (also called Wallace Fard Muhammad, Farrad Mohammad, F. Mohammad Ali, Professor Ford, or simply Farad), who is believed to have immigrated to the United States from Saudi Arabia in 1930. Reported to be a descendant of the Koreish tribe of the prophet Muhammad and of the Mecca royal dynasty, he quickly built a mosque in Detroit and began spreading his salvific message as he sold silk materials from house to house.

The great urban migrations of African Americans from South to North left in their wake a black population suffering from severe economic, social, and political deprivation. Their sense of hopelessness ignited in them a focus on religious matters with sociopolitical overtones. As the one channel open to them for free association, unapologetic expression, and self-leadership, religious activities became a focus of social, political, and economic undertakings. Under these conditions, two precursors of the Nation of Islam were born: the Moorish Science Temple and the Universal Negro Improvement Association. Both involved nationalistic fervor.

The Moorish Science Temple was founded in Newark, New Jersey, in 1913 by Noble Drew Ali, formerly Timothy Drew. Establishing a strict moral code for its members, Ali taught that peace on earth would come only when each race on earth had its own religion. The Moors initiated the move for a distinctly black religion with nationalistic overtones. Though they were loyal to the United States flag, it was their belief that through divine intervention the rule of the oppressors would come to an end. The followers preferred to be called Moors rather than Americans. A more aggressively political and nationalistic group called the Universal Negro Improvement Association (UNIA) grew out of the ashes of the Moorish Science Temple when Ali died.

Marcus Garvey founded the UNIA between 1914 and 1916 and quickly rose to prominence with a "back to Africa" philosophy. The idea was to move all blacks to Africa as their home. Toward this, the UNIA began a large monetary and commercial enterprise, sent its representative to the League of Nations, and formed a governmentin-exile in Liberia. When Garvey was deported from the United States in 1927, the movement began to fade. The fading of this group and the economic disaster wrought by the Great Depression created a vacuum that the Nation of Islam, adopting Garveyite and Moorish principles, filled.

Within a few years of its inception, the Nation of Islam, through the leadership of Fard, formed an impressive organization, running an elementary school, a Muslim Girls Training school, a University of Islam, an Islamic security force called the Fruit of Islam, and vast business holdings. Fard had begun to rebuild the black family, educate and protect African Americans, and work toward the black economic independence and self-sufficiency that Garvey had earlier sought. By the time Fard mysteriously disappeared in 1934, Elijah Muhammad (formerly Elijah Poole) had assumed leadership; after internal strife, he moved the headquarters of the Nation of Islam to Chicago and rebuilt the membership of the movement. From the Chicago Temple, the Nation of Islam disseminated its religious, political, and social doctrines.

As stated in some of its publications, such as *Muhammad Speaks* and *The Final*

Call, the Nation of Islam holds that Allah is not a spiritual being, since the concept of God-in-Spirit "enslaves the minds of the ignorant" to focus on life after death instead of life here on earth. Allah's presence on earth is as material as his promises and activities. Apart from teaching African American Muslims their preslavery history in order to instill in them a sense of pride and teaching a belief in a divine promise to inherit the political leadership of the earth when their oppressors are overthrown, the Nation of Islam adheres to strict moral codes in prayer rituals, body cleansing, and diet. Members of the Nation of Islam are forbidden to eat pork, smoke, take drugs, gamble, or drink alcohol. Miscegenation and interracial marriages are not allowed; endogamy is encouraged, and male members are always reminded to protect their women. Though divorce is permitted, it is frowned upon, and adulterers are severely punished.

Economic self-sufficiency is one of the points most strongly emphasized by the Nation of Islam. It has economic holdings in many states of the United States. As early as 1973, after it had received huge financial support from Libya, Qatar, and Abu Dabhi to further Islamic interests in the United States, the Nation of Islam bought the Guaranty Bank and Trust Company of South Chicago. In 1985 Louis Farrakhan, one of the ministers of the Nation of Islam, received a five-million-dollar loan from Libya to promote People Organized and Working for Economic Rebirth (POWER). POWER aims at developing an economically independent African American population. Some products bearing the label "Clean and Fresh" have been sold and marketed by POWER.

One of the political demands of the Nation of Islam from its inception has been its interest in the creation of a separate nation for African Americans in North America. This was tied to a demand for complete freedom, for justice to be equally applied to all, for release of all imprisoned Muslims, an immediate end to police brutality, creation of segregated schools (that would allow equal education), and the free teaching of Islam without hindrance or suppression. These demands were published in every issue of *Muhammad Speaks* until 1975, when Wallace D. Muhammad (now Warith Deen Muhammad) made changes in the general doctrine and interpretation of the Nation of Islam. Leading a splinter group, Louis Farrakhan reintroduced these demands, found in every edition of *The Final Call*.

Applications

Knowledge of the beliefs and activities of the Nation of Islam is valuable in a number of areas. The Nation of Islam is an important religious movement in that it is significant in the lives of a large number of African Americans. It has been studied both as a religion and as a social movement. Knowledge of its tenets and its stands on sociopolitical issues helps both scholars and laypersons to understand the thinking of a different mindset and to recognize the attractions that religious movements, particularly those based on a millenarian worldview, have for people.

One of the most illustrious members and ministers of the Nation of Islam was Malcolm X (born Malcolm Little and also known as El Hajj Malik El-Shabazz). His own life is a testimony to the influence of the Nation of Islam on the life of an African American. From a life of stealing, crime, drugs, and pimping, which had garnered him a jail term at the Norfolk Prison Colony, Malcolm X was converted to the Nation of Islam. He gained a new identity, a new feeling of pride and usefulness, and the urge to study and learn about his ancestral history and the history of the society in which he lived. In his own words:

> [I]t was in prison that I first heard the teachings of the Honorable Elijah Muhammad. His teachings were what turned me around. . . . [I]n 1946, I was sentenced to 8-10 years in Cambridge, Massachusetts as a common thief who had never passed the eighth grade. And the next time I went back to Cambridge was in March 1961, as a guest speaker at the Harvard Law School Forum.

Association with the Nation of Islam changed his life, and he became one of the greatest African American leaders of his time. His new knowledge of himself and belief in the doctrine of the Nation of Islam made him change his ways and "clean himself up and stand up like a man should before his God."

Knowledge of how the Nation of Islam has combated drug addiction through its brotherly and caring attitude toward drug addicts could be useful to contemporary drug programs and to the role religious bodies might play in them. In his 1964 autobiography, Malcolm X discusses the steps the Nation of Islam took in reclaiming drug addicts. He alludes to a report in *The New York Times* of some clinical agencies seeking help from the Nation of Islam concerning programming for drug addicts. The Nation of Islam introduced a six-point process of therapy for the drug addict.

The first step of the Nation of Islam's approach is to make the addict admit that he indeed is an addict, for true therapy cannot begin until he admits the seriousness of his drug condition. It may take a long period of persuasion by patient Muslim former addicts to convince the addict of his enslavement to drugs, but usually the patience pays off.

Once the addict admits his problem, the second step sets in. The Muslims try to explain to him the root of his problem. He is an addict because he is trying to escape the reality of his black presence in white America. The realization of perceived cultural inferiority leads to the third step, in which the addict is shown a way to save himself from drugs and an inferiority complex by joining the Nation of Islam. Thus the Islamic religion itself becomes a way to overcome addiction. The fourth stage involves exposing the addict to the social activities of the Nation of Islam. Through watching the clean and proud habits of members of the Nation of Islam, he soon develops a feeling of pride in himself; he respects and feels affection for himself and others. His self-image and ego built up through Islamic fraternity, the addict moves to the fifth step—that of voluntarily initiating a break from his drug habit. He goes "cold turkey"; that is, he undergoes the physical torture and mental agony that accompany a break with drugs. Here the brotherhood of the Muslim former addicts is of paramount importance. They must watch and care for him around the clock as withdrawal sets in. When the ordeal ends they feed him, clothe him, and help him get on his feet again.

This act of charity and selflessness makes him loyal to the Nation of Islam and to those who helped him to regain himself. Finally cured, a sixth and final step is undertaken. The new member of the Nation of Islam is officially an ex-addict; he accepts as a responsibility the task of going to places where drug addicts socialize so as to attempt to "salvage" his drug-using friends.

The importance of this aspect of the practices of members of the Nation of Islam to the entire populace must not be overlooked. When one saves a drug addict from addiction, one is, in a sense, helping to save the society at large. As Malcolm X noted, African American drug addicts are often poor people who, to survive and maintain their drug habits, must steal, go into prostitution, and even kill. They are also health risks, as they contract and transmit a number of diseases directly or indirectly related to their drug use; among these are hepatitis, tuberculosis, and acquired immune deficiency syndrome (AIDS). To reclaim an addict is to reclaim society.

Another example of how the Nation of Islam works in society may be seen in its political involvement. In 1984, Louis Farrakhan actively supported Jesse Jackson's campaign to be the Democratic Party's candidate for president of the United States. For the first time he registered to vote, and he led thousands of other African Americans and members of the Nation of Islam to register to vote. He also preached that putting African Americans in political leadership is the key to a peaceful coexistence and to preventing the world from destruction. Farrakhan also vowed to "lead an army" of African Americans to Washington, D.C., to meet the president to ask for a self-governing African American state or nation should Jackson be shut out of leadership.

Finally, the Nation of Islam uses its standing among African Americans in a number of arenas, ranging from business dealings to the impact of international affairs on individual citizens. For example, when under the leadership of Warith Deen Muhammad, the Nation of Islam in conjunction with a Chicago firm signed a twenty-two-million-dollar contract with the Defense Department. Later, when in 1986 President Ronald Reagan issued an executive order banning U.S. citizens from visiting Libya, Louis Farrakhan and the Nation of Islam challenged the order on the grounds that it violated their freedom of religion, speech, and travel.

Context

The Nation of Islam developed in the early twentieth century from the need of a people on the fringe of culture and power in the United States to find an outlet to voice their religious, economic, social, and political concerns. Because religion is one area of the life of a people in which one's liberty is not threatened through special-interest legislation, African Americans have used it to pursue things of special interest to them. One readily recalls how most African American leaders of thought have been people connected with religious activities—Martin Luther King, Jr., Jesse Jackson, and Andrew Young come immediately to mind. These people used Christianity in the pursuit of civil rights and racial equality. The Nation of Islam has used a different religion, Islam, to pursue similar interests. What is innovative in its appearance is its more radical approach—its advocation of secession from the United States and its promise of a new world in which anti-black, oppressive American political institutions would fall.

The Nation of Islam offers pride in religion and in themselves to African Americans. It is the first distinct religion established by African Americans that shares no exact doctrines and origins with Christianity, seen by some as the religion of the former slave master and therefore regarded as a symbol of oppression. Radical African Americans have viewed the Bible as a tool of enslavement, of "chaining" the African American mind to a spiritual heaven that rewards the oppressed after death while the oppressor uses the gun to build an empire of material wealth here on earth. The Nation of Islam brings a focus on heaven that begins on earth. To the "Lost-Found" members of this religion, the Nation of Islam, through its educational, social, economic, and political programs, not only promises a black millennium but also, in many ways, seems to take positive steps to initiate it.

The birth of the Nation of Islam has made sociologists examine millenarian religious movements closely. The Nation of Islam has shed light on the apparent survival of such movements even when their prophecies are not fulfilled and on the power such movements have in the spiritual and material uplifting of the economically poor and the politically and socially disadvantaged. It has encouraged sociology to examine miscegenation and segregation from a minority viewpoint; before the emergence of the Nation of Islam, sociology had analyzed these issues mostly from the perspective of the cultural majority.

Bibliography

Baldwin, James. *The Fire Next Time*. New York: Dial Press, 1963. This book is a treatment of race relations in general in the United States with special focus on the manner in which it adversely affects the African American. The Nation of Islam is discussed within this context.

Lee, Martha F. *The Nation of Islam: An American Millenarian Movement*. Lewiston, N.Y.: Edwin Mellen Press, 1988. An interesting book that studies in detail the Nation of Islam from the angle of millenarianism. Lee analyzes both the myths and facts about the movement and its leaders and shows the changes it has undergone through the decades. Two appendices give the doctrines and positions of the movement as found in *Muhammad Speaks* and *The Final Call*, official publications of the movement. Highly recommended.

Lincoln, C. Eric. *The Black Muslims in America*. Rev. ed. Boston: Beacon Press, 1973. Tracing the root of the Nation of Islam to the great migrations of African Americans from the rural South to the urban North and the Great Depression, the book focuses on the movement to the 1970's. Contains good notes and an index.

Marsh, Clifton E. *From Black Muslims to Muslims: The Transition from Separatism to Islam, 1930-1980*. Metuchen, N.J.: Scarecrow Press, 1984. A brief history of the African American Muslim movement from its beginning to 1980. A good and easily readable book, its shortcoming is that it has not been revised to include events after 1980.

Norton, Philip. *Black Nationalism in America*. Hull, Humberside, England: Department of Politics, University of Hull, 1983. Published under the Hull paper series in politics, this work discusses the significance of the African American Muslim movement. It treats it as a historical phenomenon, as a political activity, and as an aspect of race relations in the United States.

Williams, Lena. "Move to Heal Black Muslim Rift Appears to Be Under Way amid Pressures." *The New York Times*, November 19, 1986, B6. In this article Louis Farrakhan discusses his activities in the Nation of Islam. He also talks about Elijah Muhammad, Warith Muhammad, the World Community of al-Islam in the West and the Nation of Islam in general. Discusses Farrakhan's rift with Warith Muhammad; relations with Jews, Christians, and Orthodox Islam; and the controversy surrounding Elijah Muhammad's estate.

X, Malcolm. *The Autobiography of Malcolm X*. With the assistance of Alex Haley. New York: Ballantine Books, 1973. While focusing on Malcolm X, the book is also an illumination of the lives of African Americans in a prejudiced society and of the activities of the Nation of Islam. It is interesting for its discussions of both religion and sociopolitical awareness. Fascinating reading even for those who may disagree with Malcolm X.

I. Peter Ukpokodu

Cross-References

Inequalities in Political Power, 972; Islam and Islamic Fundamentalism, 1022; Millenarian Religious Movements, 1213; Political Influence by Religious Groups, 1394; Poverty and Race, 1472; Racial and Ethnic Stratification, 1579; Social Movements, 1826; Socialization: Religion, 1894.

THE NATION-STATE

Type of sociology: Major social institutions
Field of study: Politics and the state

The nation-state is the fundamental political unit of international relations in the modern world and the highest expression of social integration and communal identity. It serves as both a potential source of internal or domestic unity and a potential source of conflict in international relations.

Principal terms
CITIZENSHIP: membership accorded to individuals within a particular nation-state which guarantees certain rights and requires certain responsibilities
EQUALITY: the condition in which states, as sovereign subjects of international law, are considered to be legally equal
INDEPENDENCE: the quality of being autonomous, owing allegiance to no higher authority
INTERDEPENDENCE: the condition in which a state depends on other states for elements of its livelihood
IRREDENTISM: a claim made by people in one country for rightful ownership of territory in a neighboring country where their ethnic co-nationals live
NATIONALISM: devotion to one's nation as distinct from other peoples and nations, including a desire to protect and defend the nation from external infringement
SELF-DETERMINATION: the right of a people to their own independent nation-state
SEPARATISM: a movement by a people to obtain independence from an existing sovereign state
SOVEREIGNTY: that characteristic of nation-states which accords them equality and independence, and marks them as the highest legal entities in international relations
XENOPHOBIA: fear of foreign peoples

Overview

The nation-state is one of the most important social and political institutions of human interrelations. National units determine their own domestic legal codes and foreign policies; establish internal mechanisms to protect, promote, and sustain life and property; and strive to preserve their national culture, to protect their borders from military incursion, and to promote the social well-being and economic prosperity of their citizens. Nation-states alone can impose restrictions on the movements of people across borders, establish immigration criteria, and impose and ensure the enforcement of regulations on commerce. Only nation-states can legally declare war on, accord recognition to, or enter into treaties with other nation-states without seeking permission from some other source.

The modern nation-state emerged after the Protestant Reformation of the sixteenth century and the religious wars of the seventeenth century in Europe, but the concepts of the nation, the state, and the city-state actually originate in ancient history. The Greek city-states, for example, faced many of the same problems that are faced by contemporary nation-states concerning questions of citizenship rights, regulation of citizen behavior, immigration, commercial relations, foreign policy, and war. The modern nation-state, however, is a product of more recent struggles. Most students of the nation-state trace its modern roots to the Peace of Westphalia, which ended the Thirty Years War between Catholic and Protestant princes in Europe in 1648. The treaties that constituted the Peace of Westphalia accorded rulers the right to determine the official religion of their nation without outside interference. The signatories to these treaties accorded formal recognition of one another's sovereignty, independence, and equality within recognized territorial boundaries. Virtually all of the nation-states at this time were monarchies or principalities. This situation gradually changed as the sovereignty of the state, after centuries of revolution and internal evolution, came to be vested in the people as a whole, and as democratic forms of government emerged. Still, in almost every other respect, the modern state is very much rooted in the Westphalian principle of sovereignty.

The term "nation-state" is often used interchangeably with the terms "nation" and "state." Each term, however, has a slightly different meaning or connotation. The term "nation" usually refers to a group of people who have a common tradition, cultural heritage, and shared history. Nations often consist of people from a single racial or ethnic group who share a language and religion. Their common religious, linguistic, cultural, and historical bonds give these peoples a sense of oneness that distinguishes them from other people and causes them to protect the nation and its ancestral lands from foreign intervention. The essence of the idea of nationhood lies in this shared sense of unity.

The term "state," however, has a very specific definition in terms of modern international law. A state consists of a government that is recognized by other governments and that has control over a specific territory and population. The state, in short, may or may not be coterminous with the nation. It may control a territory in which a single nation or people lives or it may have jurisdiction over a territory inhabited by many nations or peoples. In the former case, one may rightly call it a nation-state. Such has been the case with many of the states in Europe, which were nations long before the modern state came into being. In the latter case, there may be no sense of nationhood at all, but instead a tremendous degree of ethnic discord. The state may exist under such circumstances, but the nation cannot. Yugoslavia, once a recognized state, was probably never a nation in the strict sense of the term, and it has fallen victim to the national differences between Slovenes, Croats, and other groups, which sought self-determination, independence, and sovereignty apart from the dominant Serbs.

The state, whether or not it corresponds to a unified national population, has the authority to extend citizenship and to determine under what conditions aliens may travel through or reside in its territory. It may also determine under what conditions aliens may seek asylum or citizenship. These important functions of the state have direct consequences for people. The state also determines what rights its citizens will enjoy and what duties they will be responsible for performing. Duties include obeying the laws of the land, paying taxes in support of public programs and policies, and serving in the country's defense during times of war. Most states consider the education of citizens to be vitally important, and through a variety of means, including public education, ceremonial occasions, and political events, they attempt to inculcate patriotic values.

Applications

The practical effects of the nation-state can be found in three fundamental areas, including the problem of national self-determination, which often leads to war or revolution; the role of the state in socialization of its citizens; and the question of immigration and asylum law.

As noted previously, one of the problems faced by people in many countries is the lack of correspondence between the state and the nation. Many states in Africa have no sense of nationhood, because they are composed of many different, and often conflicting, ethnic groups. Yet many nations around the globe lack the international recognition they need from other governments to have a state. The Kurds of Iran, Iraq, Turkey, and Syria are in such a situation. They have every characteristic of a nation but lack a unified state to represent their national interest. It is possible, then, for a state not to be a nation and a nation not to be a state. The lack of correspondence between the state and the nation is a source of much of the regional conflict and revolution throughout the world. Where the nations and states are roughly cotermi- nous, however, one usually finds a much higher degree of social cohesion and stability.

Thus, there is genuine merit in the search for self-determination and in the quest to build the nation-state. The problem is that much political violence is often unleashed in the quest for self-determination, as different ethnonationalistic groups pursue their separatist or irredentist aims, or their internal struggle for control of the state. Even when separatist struggles are successful and a new nation-state is born, as happened in the early 1990's in Eritrea, the question of the new state's economic viability often arises. How small can a nation-state be and still survive as an effective political and economic entity? The breakup of larger states, such as the Soviet Union, into smaller nation-states ultimately raises these practical considerations. As was the case in the former Soviet Union, people often choose freedom and national self-determination over the benefits gained by being a small but politically dependent part of a larger political unit.

If ethnonationalistic demands for self-determination cause much conflict within states, nationalism as an expression of people's unity can also at times be a cause of international conflict and war. Many of the international conflicts of the twentieth century, including the two world wars, can be attributed, at least in part, to nationalistic sentiments. Too much of an emphasis on national distinctiveness and national superiority can drive a people to dominate other peoples. The history of the world is marked by countless examples of this impulse, and it is unlikely that this impulse will be eradicated despite international efforts at cooperation in the United Nations and other international organizations. Whether nationalism continues to be a source of international conflict, and whether ethnonationalistic impulses continue to be a source of domestic conflict, will depend in part on how nation-states educate their young.

Political socialization is a process in which all states engage. The principal means by which states attempt to socialize people is civic education. Children are taught the history of their nation, they are encouraged to celebrate its national holidays, they learn about important heroes and leaders, and they are taught about the struggles their ancestors endured to establish the nation. Often the media, if they are controlled by the state, are also used to present positive images of the state and its government to the people. Even when the media are not state-controlled, powerful images of national pride are conveyed to the public as the media cover the drama of national events, elections, and the daily workings of government. Such education is an important part of socializing an effective and loyal citizen body. To the extent that such education belittles other peoples, countries, or cultures, however, it can support national hostility and thus promote a brand of nationalism that is prone to conflict. Even within a nation-state, and especially in one whose population has been formed by diverse immigrant elements or indigenous peoples, the question can arise whether the educational process should emphasize the common tradition of the nation or the diverse constituent cultural elements. Should it aim at the assimilation of different cultures into a common national tradition or should it support efforts to establish and promote cultural diversity, autonomy, or even separation? The controversy surrounding multicultural education in the United States is only one example of how education and socialization are often driven by these questions, which ultimately are questions about nations and nationalism.

Finally, every nation-state must be concerned about the interests of its citizens, ensuring that their employment, education, health, and social welfare needs are met and that their rights and liberties are protected. States must also determine the mechanisms by which one attains citizenship. Usually, this is done by virtue of blood ties—that is, having parents who are citizens or being born within the territory of the state. Defining the citizen body is an important task of the nation-state. Determining how to treat aliens, immigrants, and refugees is another. Aliens may gain entry to the country as immigrants or refugees seeking asylum from persecution abroad. The state determines which of these will be eligible for citizenship and defines a process of naturalization through which naturalization can be achieved. The liberality or restrictiveness of the immigration and naturalization policies adopted by states is influenced by the general political culture of the state, its openness to outsiders, its tradition of immigration, and its economic situation. Some countries and peoples have very parochial cultures and xenophobic reactions to alien influences. Others are more open.

Even in the most open societies, however, popular opinion can excite restrictive and even xenophobic reactions to alien influences. Others are more open. Even in the most open societies, however, popular opinion can excite restrictive and even xenophobic responses during times of national exigency or economic decline.

Context

Nation-states arose as expressions of the common traditions of peoples and the desire of those peoples to protect themselves from external incursion. Aristotle observed, in his *Politics*, that states emerged when households and families found that they could not adequately ensure their own survival and protection. Groups of families gradually coalesced into states, which were more self-sufficient and were able to provide for the protection of ancestral lands. As nations grew and expanded, however, they often clashed with one another over land and resources. The nation, formed in part to ensure protection and promote internal cohesion and harmony, could also be a source of international conflict. Nations can also, however, cooperate to seek mutually desirable goals. Throughout history, nation-states have engaged in both international conflict and international cooperation.

Nation-states still serve many important social, economic, and political functions. They continue to command the loyalty of their citizens. They promote internal harmony, economic prosperity, social stability, political independence, and the physical preservation of the nation. In many parts of the world, national sentiment remains one of the most powerful sources of conflict within and between nations. Therefore, separatist and irredentist claims continue to cause revolutions and wars. Many large states break apart because of such pressures. As modern states have grown in size and complexity, they have, paradoxically, become less independent and more interdependent. Very few modern states are able to provide their people with all the necessities and luxuries of modern life. To achieve economic prosperity, they must engage in international commerce. To resolve internal ethnic disputes, many states must rely on external support, foreign intervention, or international diplomacy. To cope with the degradation of the environment, the depletion of the ozone layer, the management of fisheries and ocean resources, they must cooperate with one another to find solutions. In this sense, then, nations are increasingly interdependent.

The increased interdependence of states has led many commentators to suggest that the nation-state has outlived its usefulness, that it is an anachronism of a conflict-ridden past that deserves to be swept away. The contemporary experience of nations suggests, however, that nation-states, though often reformulated, remain a very stubborn and persistent institution. The Soviet Union crumbled, but it became smaller nation-states. Yugoslavia died, but Croatia and Slovenia were born. Czechoslovakia became two republics. The Ethiopian government succumbed to the separatist claims of Eritrea, but the Ethiopian state survived, though truncated in territorial scope, and the new nation-state of Eritrea was born. The European Community may seek a broader European identity, but the nations of Europe persist in their unique identities. This abbreviated litany provides only a few examples of the continuing capacity of nation-states to survive. It would be imprudent to predict the quick demise of the nation-state. For many peoples throughout the world, national aspirations remain strong calls to action that provide the motivation for personal sacrifice to a common cause.

Bibliography

Akzin, Benjamin. *State and Nation*. London: Hutchinson University Library, 1964. A brief, readable introduction to the terminological distinctions, literature, and theory of nations, states, and nationalism. It examines nations, single and multiple ethnic states, integrationist and pluralist states, secessionist questions, and the problem of nationalism in developing countries.

Armstrong, John. *Nations Before Nationalism*. Chapel Hill: University of North Carolina Press, 1982. A very scholarly, analytical, historical treatment of the emergence of nations from early times to the nineteenth century, this book examines the religious, ethnic, linguistic, and social origins of the nation.

Horowitz, Donald. *Ethnic Groups in Conflict*. Berkeley: University of California Press, 1985. For the more intrepid reader, this scholarly book provides useful insights into the workings of ethnic conflict, irredentist and separatist claims, and assimilationist and pluralist strategies for overcoming tensions produced by ethnic diversity.

Kohn, Hans. *Nationalism: Its Meaning and History*. Rev. ed. Princeton, N.J.: D. Van Nostrand, 1965. This classic, beautifully written work traces the history of nationalism and provides a representative sample of readings from primary sources that illustrate the meaning and potency of nationalism as a source of identity for peoples in different times and places.

Ronen, Dov. *The Quest for Self-Determination*. New Haven, Conn.: Yale University Press, 1979. Tracing the right of self-determination to the American and French revolutions, this book examines the history of the development of this right, the various forms it has taken, and several contexts in which it has been asserted.

Suhrke, Astri, and Lela Garner Noble, eds. *Ethnic Conflict in International Relations*. New York: Praeger, 1977. A useful anthology of case studies in ethnic conflict and its national and international implications. Comparative case studies include Cyprus, Northern Ireland, Lebanon, Eritrea, the Kurds in Iraq, the Kazakhs in China, and Muslims in Southeast Asia.

Tivey, Leonard, ed. *The Nation-State: The Formation of Modern Politics*. New York: St. Martin's Press, 1981. A collection of essays devoted to such issues as the origin of the nation-state, the varieties of nationalism, the relationship between socialism and nationalism, the experience of nation-state in Asia, Africa, Europe, and the future of the nation-state.

Robert F. Gorman

Cross-References

Authoritarian and Totalitarian Governments, 153; Democracy and Democratic Governments, 483; Legitimacy and Authority, 1055; Political Socialization, 1407; Political Sociology, 1414; Revolutions, 1641; Socialism and Communism, 1873; The State: Functionalist versus Conflict Perspectives, 1972; War and Revolution, 2164.

NATIONAL HEALTH INSURANCE

Type of sociology: Major social institutions
Field of study: Medicine

National health insurance plans generally have four major goals: universal access to affordable health care services, equitable allocation of resources, high-quality care, and cost containment. Among the distinguishing features of systems are their degrees of reliance on government involvement in health insurance schemes and the nature of their financing arrangements.

Principal terms

ALLOCATION OF RESOURCES: a scheme under which limited or scarce resources (such as organs, prescription drugs, and inpatient care) are distributed; also called rationing

COST CONTAINMENT: a policy that attempts to prevent the rapid escalation of expenditures for health care

EGALITARIANISM: a system emphasizing equal political, social, and economic rights for all persons

EQUITY: a system emphasizing fairness and justice

POLICY: interests and principles reflecting those underlying values within society that constitute a common understanding by those in authority; a dynamic pattern or course of action

PRIVATIZATION: the location of power in the hands of regional authorities rather than the central government

UNIVERSALITY: the quality of being available to all, as in universality of access to health care

Overview

Worldwide, there are various national health insurance plans that strive for equity in health care by ensuring financial access to universal health care services. The ability of all citizens to share confidently and equally in a health care system without fear of runaway costs and regardless of ability to earn money and/or pay illustrates a strong commitment to egalitarianism.

Achieving an equitable, affordable system of acceptable quality health care, however, necessarily entails rationing and limiting certain choices that can be made by patients and health care providers. Shifting resources between groups of the population in order to achieve universal access also entails reducing or denying some services to one group in order to benefit another. Restricting freedom of choice means that patients cannot obtain all the health care they wish at any given time or place, that physicians are constrained in diagnostic and therapeutic regimes, and that hospitals are limited in the range of services that they offer. In order to achieve universal access to the health care system for all members of the community, financial barriers that impede access to the system must be removed, and private insurance plans and other privately funded arrangements must be eliminated.

Universality of access does not always guarantee an adequate system of health services. Organizational problems exist by virtue of the fact that such a system is shared, with funding provided by the national government as well as local authorities (privatization). The fact that funding comes from both sources often results in wide variations in coverage and discretion in administration. The shared funding, however, makes possible a uniform level of service, ensuring that poorer areas as well as urban centers receive a fair share of resources. Portability of coverage (the ability to move from place to place or job to job without the threat of losing insurance benefits) also aids the general welfare by preventing migrants or members of underprivileged groups from being dropped from the system.

Applications

Among the many countries that have national health insurance, three are representative of the multiplicity of insurance arrangements. These are Canada, the United Kingdom, and Germany.

Canada's system of health insurance is financed by general taxation and federal grants. The system is characterized by community access to health care; everyone has access to the same system at no cost and without class distinction. The general tax revenues (primarily income and sales taxes) spread the burden over all wage earners and include the entire population. In Europe, in contrast, coverage in many countries is linked to status. German sickness funds are defined by occupations, with regional funds for those with no occupation and private coverage for those with the highest incomes. Dutch compulsory coverage applies only up to a certain income level.

Theoretically, national health insurance in Canada was designed to minimize political and social inequities that served to bar access. In practice, however, it has given rise to long waiting lines for elective surgery and diagnostic procedures such as magnetic resonance imagery (MRI), lithotripsy, radiation therapy, and cardiac surgery. Supply constraints caused by limited hospital budgets leave little room for innovative practices. Most small hospitals provide only community services and have reduced the number of full-time positions. For sophisticated procedures such as cancer treatments, transplants, and cardiac surgery, patients must be transferred to large tertiary care centers where these procedures are performed. By necessity, therefore, the largest percentage of money is spent for in-patient hospital care.

Physicians in Canada maintain their autonomy because third-party insurer approval of procedures has been eliminated. Citizens have free choice regarding physicians. Physicians work privately and are not employed by the government, as they are in the United Kingdom. Patients are free to get second or third opinions from physicians of their choice. What is centralized in the Canadian system is the administration of insurance, which saves costs by eliminating paperwork and red tape, and by deferring cost containment measures to provincial governments.

"Medical necessity" is the requirement for reimbursement. Prescription drugs and dentistry are not covered under the universal hospital and medical insurance plans.

Physicians are reimbursed according to a uniform schedule of fees negotiated at periodic intervals by an agency of the provincial ministry of health and the provincial medical association. Hospitals are not reimbursed directly but are supported through budgets negotiated annually with the ministry of health. Salaries of hospital physicians are paid from those budgets, as are the costs of diagnostic services and prescription drugs provided to in-patients.

Physicians cannot "extra-bill" patients for fees above those negotiated by the provincial government in return for covered services. Those services not considered "medically necessary" are charged to the patient in full in any amount. In some provinces, physicians have the option of not participating in the public insurance plan. They may charge whatever fees they wish but must choose whether to work privately or under the public plan; they cannot do both. Additionally, no private insurer can sell coverage for services already covered under public plans.

Long-term care is not part of the universal health insurance program in Canada as defined by the government, and it remains largely a provincial matter. The flexibility given to the provinces by the Canada Health Act of 1984 has created much variation among the provinces in terms of ensuring long-term care at different levels. Moreover, each of the Canadian provinces has the option of having a different health insurance plan. Differences are relatively minor, however, and private insurance is used to equalize discrepancies in coverage. Supplementary insurance coverage exists for out-of-pocket expenses.

Because it is government controlled, the Canadian health care system is also highly politicized, and the government must answer for every weakness within it. The Canadian system, however, enjoys a generally high level of popularity among citizens, each of whom shares an interest in correcting problems within the system because each has a personal stake in it.

Instituted in 1883, the German health care system represents a middle ground in the approaches taken by Western countries to provide health care in order to protect their citizens against the economic consequences of illness. Characterized by comprehensive medical benefits and free choice of physician unrelated to one's ability to pay, the German system combines government-mandated financing by employers and employees with private care by physicians, controlled hospital expenditures, and administration by nonprofit insurance organizations.

The insurance organizations, known as "sickness funds," establish and collect revenue and turn it over to regional associations composed of ambulatory-care physicians that reimburse physicians for their services on the basis of a negotiated fee schedule. Each sickness fund is a self-governing and self-sustaining body. Membership is compulsory and is based primarily on occupational status. More than 90 percent of the population is covered by the statutory health insurance scheme. The sickness funds that operate within a certain geographic area also negotiate a daily rate with local hospitals. Regardless of a patient's diagnosis, the same per diem rate is paid to a hospital. For patients covered by private insurance, the federal government has imposed price regulations for hospitals' and physicians' services. There is a sharp distinction between ambulatory physician care and hospital care. Ambulatory-care physicians are reimbursed on a fee-for-service basis, and rates are established through a schedule negotiated with the sickness fund. Hospital-based physicians are paid by the hospital on the basis of specialty and seniority. Only private patients who are not covered by sickness funds or public assistance have to make additional payments for hospital services. Dental and prescription drug coverage is included. The German system inspired the national health insurance plans of Japan and Korea.

Health insurance in the United Kingdom came into existence in 1948 with the advent of the National Health Service (NHS). As contributory health insurance was replaced with direct provision of health care by the government, the welfare state was born. Aimed at providing comprehensive health services first to all who were in need and later to the entire population, it resulted from compromise among ministers, civil servants, and pressure groups, including the medical profession, hospitals, and insurance committees, and grew out of wartime conditions, economic constraints, political considerations, and a basic commitment to structure a more egalitarian society. Funding generally comes from three sources: general taxation (the largest source), national insurance contributions, and individual insurance plans. The NHS has three aims: quality of care, economy, and equity. It provides a package of uniform benefits to everyone at low cost but offers no choice of hospital, physician, payment method, or level of expenditure. Ninety percent of all costs are paid out of the general revenue. Hospitals are publicly owned, and specialists are either part-time or full-time salaried hospital staff. Long waiting lists are the norm. General practitioners are paid a yearly fee that is negotiated jointly by their representatives and the government. Dentists are paid on a fee-for-service basis, pharmacists are paid according to a schedule negotiated with the government, and prescription drugs are provided at a small charge.

British health care costs remain among the lowest per capita in Europe, primarily because financing is under parliamentary control rather than in the hands of insurance companies or reimbursement boards. Government policy has been to control expenditure from within while encouraging the development of private payment systems. This has led to a fear that the government might abandon the NHS. Although the current system has wide public support, there has been ongoing debate in the 1980's and 1990's about privatization.

Other systems, such as that of France, are characterized by nonuniform coverage in which government reimbursement is not total and patient copayment varies according to type of care, institution, and total amount to be paid. Although it was originally intended to be a general, national, comprehensive system that would bring together private medical insurance and national health insurance, the French system was never unified.

Government involvement in Belgian health care is limited to regulations and partial funding with increasing reliance on the private sector and decreasing comprehensive public insurance arrangements. In Denmark, basic health care services are provided free of charge to all citizens by the public health sector. This includes all hospital services and primary health care services. Only 5 percent of insurance is not publicly financed. Patients in the public sector may choose a physician and make a new choice every year. In Greece, patients are unable to select a physician or hospital. Hospitals are founded and operated only as state hospitals by the government. Access is difficult, and health services are not competitive. Italian health care is competitive, with private institutions operating within the National Health Service, which was established in 1978. Citizens have the right to choose a physician. Spanish health care is publicly financed, but private funding and private health care also exist. Under the Spanish free enterprise system, the state is limited exclusively to dictating policy. The Swedish system is also characterized by public ownership but is organized by county councils. In-patient care is provided by salaried physicians, ambulatory care is provided by hospital-based clinics, and salaried physicians are employed by county councils, enterprises, and corporations. National health insurance in Sweden covers health care costs marginally; the main burden is assumed by county income taxes. A small portion of the cost is paid by the patient at the time of illness. It is evident, therefore, that a wide divergence in health care plans exists.

Context

When national health insurance was first introduced, the primary concern was to make the available medical resources more accessible. Insurance was not universal; although it was usually compulsory for certain segments of the population, it excluded some members and their dependents. Limited in scope, coverage proceeded to include larger population groups in subsequent years either by expanding the health insurance organization or by creating a national health service, as in the United Kingdom.

Although the package of benefits offered was usually limited initially, consisting primarily of physicians' services, the range of benefits gradually expanded to become comprehensive, including, for example, hospital care (acute and extended), nursing home care, dental coverage, prescription drugs, diagnostic services, and rehabilitation. Equity in health care was the underlying issue. A specific goal was to diminish economic inequalities in access to care by lowering financial barriers and restructuring the social strata that had formerly kept certain segments of society from utilizing health care facilities. Equal availability in all regions of the country eventually resulted as health care resources became more widely developed.

Cost-containment mechanisms brought about by concern over steadily rising expenditures, limiting benefits, services, and utilization were reduced and abolished in favor of cost-sharing, utilization control, and the formulation of a comprehensive system. The emerging approach represented a broader application of the equity principle by improving the development and distribution of health care resources.

Since national health insurance was introduced, there has been a general increase in the quantity and quality of resources. Development of new and different resources as a result of technological advances and better-qualified health care workers have been evident in all the countries studied. Because health care is being viewed as an entitlement by all segments of the population, and the once-forgotten underprivileged members of society recognize that they, too, may share in health care benefits, health education is assuming an important role: persuading citizens to use health services wisely and to assume an increased responsibility for their health.

Bibliography

Andreopoulos, Spyros, ed. *National Health Insurance: Can We Learn from Canada?* New York: Wiley, 1975. A reprint of a 1974 symposium on national health, this book contains graphs and tables, but it is somewhat dated in its discussion of expenditures.

Bennett, Arnold, and Orvill Adams. *Looking North for Health: What We Can Learn from Canada's Health Care System.* San Francisco: Jossey-Bass, 1993. A series of articles by diverse authors written in lay language, the book provides a multifaceted comparison of the Canadian and American health care systems. The articles present the perspectives of physicians, hospital administrators, government officials, and business executives. Highly recommended and informative.

Blanpain, Jan, with Luc Delesie and Herman Nys. *National Health Insurance and Health Resources: The European Experience.* Cambridge, Mass.: Harvard University Press, 1978. A clear, detailed resource that discusses health care systems in Germany, England and Wales, France, The Netherlands, and Sweden. It also focuses on government policies in those countries. Contains tables, an index, and a separate bibliography.

Casparie, A. F., H. E. G. M. Hermans, and J. H. P. Paelinck, eds. *Competitive Health Care in Europe: Future Prospects.* Aldershot, England: Dartmouth, 1990. A compilation of papers from a three-day seminar in 1988, this book contains a brief overview of the health care systems in Belgium, Denmark, France, Greece, Italy, Luxembourg, The Netherlands, Portugal, Spain, and the United Kingdom, illustrating their similarities and differences in the light of the then-impending European single market and its implications for health care. It is valuable as a quick reference tool for comparative study.

De Geyndt, Willy. *Managing Health Expenditures Under National Health Insurance: The Case of Korea.* Washington, D.C.: World Bank, 1991. A working paper with tables and graphs, this short study introduces the Korean health insurance plan and compares and contrasts it with that of Japan.

Gray, Gwendolyn. *Federalism and Health Policy: The Development of Health Systems in Canada and Australia.* Toronto: University of Toronto Press, 1991. A detailed historical development of health care systems in Australia and Canada with comparisons. Carefully researched and written, it is valuable for its contextual analysis. The concept of federalism as it emerged in both countries is illustrated throughout.

Ham, Christopher. *Health Policy in Britain: The Politics and Organisation of the National Health Service.* London: Macmillan, 1982. Describes organization and structure of the British National Health Service, with chapters on formation, decision making, implementation, and policy making. Valuable as a detailed history but provides relatively little information on current status. Well documented and thorough.

Organization for Economic Cooperation and Development. *Health and Pension Reform in Japan.* Paris: Author, 1990. A working paper with graphs and charts which illustrates the health care system in Japan, focusing on economic considerations.

Sass, Hans-Martin, and Robert U. Massey, eds. *Health Care Systems: Moral Conflicts in European and American Public Policy.* Dordrecht, The Netherlands: Kluwer, 1988. This book contains a series of essays dealing with the micro- and macroallocation of health care and rationing in countries such as Germany, France, and The Netherlands. Certain articles assume controversial positions and make conflicting recommendations. The chapter on the moral and public policy issues in the German health care system is especially noteworthy.

Marcia J. Weiss

Cross-References

Health and Society, 852; Health Care and Gender, 858; Health Maintenance Organizations, 864; The Medical Profession and the Medicalization of Society, 1159; Medical Sociology, 1166; The Medicalization of Deviance, 1178; The Institution of Medicine, 1185.

NEW TOWNS AND PLANNED COMMUNITIES

Type of sociology: Urban and rural life

New towns and planned communities have served as major agents of social change throughout history. Because the structure of communities has a social and economic impact upon everyone who lives within them, societies have put considerable effort into planning their communities.

Principal terms

CITY BEAUTIFUL PLAN: a city plan that emphasizes the preservation of a locale's natural beauty, building in conformity to it

CITY PLANNING: a development plan focusing on all or part of a city rather than on a larger area

CLASSICAL ARCHITECTURE: architectural forms that borrow heavily from the architecture of ancient Greece and Rome

GARDEN CITY: a town or city, usually with a controlled population of from ten to fifty thousand, that preserves its natural attributes and fosters the cultivation of gardens

GENTRIFICATION: a process through which a run-down neighborhood is rehabilitated

GRID DESIGN: a city plan in which most streets intersect at right angles

SOCIAL ENGINEERING: a process by which government or industry impinges upon a populace in order to achieve specific social ends, such as racial integration

SOCIAL STRATIFICATION: the hierarchical ranking of groups of people according to race or other arbitrary factors

SPOKES-AND-HUB DESIGN: a city plan in which streets radiate at angles from a central area

Overview

City planning dates to the time shortly after ancient humans ceased to be essentially hunters and gatherers and established themselves primarily in one place. Villages grew, then cities. The ancient cities of Babylon, Nineveh, Jerusalem, Cairo, Athens, and Rome arose according to plans that have dominated city planning since earliest times.

Classical Greek and Roman cities essentially had two main thoroughfares—one running east-west, the other north-south—each often a mile or more long. These two thoroughfares intersected, creating the city's center, a public square, an open space that became the heart of an ancient city. Smaller streets usually ran parallel to the main streets, creating the grid pattern that currently exists in many modern cities. The growth and development of Roman cities and towns was controlled by strict zoning regulations.

Medieval cities largely offered their inhabitants security from invaders. The comfort of the masses, who lived in crowded, unsanitary conditions that led to epidemics, counted for little. Streets in these cities were mere passageways, small arteries through which waves of invaders could not move easily. These small streets led usually to a central square where people gathered both to socialize and to gather information.

With the beginning of the Renaissance in the fourteenth and fifteenth centuries, new urban concepts emerged, often in refurbished portions of existing cities. Narrow streets gave way to boulevards. Elaborate buildings were erected, and efforts were made to beautify the areas surrounding them with gardens, parks, and impressive approaches.

The first major city in the United States that was planned from scratch was Washington, D.C., which, upon completion, replaced New York as the nation's capital. Pierre Charles l'Enfant's design proposed superimposing diagonally upon a great rectangle main thoroughfares, all leading to the capitol. L'Enfant, who emphasized the need for open space, had learned much from Baron Georges-Eugène Haussmann's spokes-and-hub plan for the reconstruction of Paris.

L'Enfant's plan for Washington was greatly distorted in its execution, partly because of bureaucratic tangles, which helps to substantiate the statement that Heikki von Hertzen made when he was developing Finland's most celebrated planned city, Tapiola, in the 1950's: "The most dangerous enemy of community planning is bureaucracy."

Landscape architect Frederick Law Olmsted did much to emphasize the need for green areas in urban communities and to encourage the city-beautiful notion in the United States. Olmsted designed a number of company towns in New England, modeling them after early New England towns with tree-lined streets and broad commons. He is best known, however, for urging New York's commissioners to buy land while it was still available in order to create Central Park.

Olmsted's concepts were exemplified in 1908, when his Forest Park Gardens became operative. His concept was also evident in Sunnyside Gardens (now Queens), a quarter-hour commute from Manhattan, and in Radburn, New Jersey, near Paterson, which opened in 1929. Most of the more successful and celebrated planned communities—Reston, Virginia; Greenbelt and Columbia, Maryland; Westlake and Laguna Niguel, California; and scores of others—adopted Olmsted's mandate that communities set aside considerable public space for parks.

One of the most widely acclaimed European planned communities is Finland's Tapiola, six miles from Helsinki. Set in a spectacular evergreen forest beside the Gulf of Finland, Tapiola integrates all classes of people and provides employment for large numbers of its residents. Heikki von Hertzen, a banker, planned the community according to the garden-city plan. All the buildings in Tapiola are heated by a single central heating plant. Tapiola emphasizes people and nature over machines and industry, although bowing slightly to the latter.

There are separate roads for automobiles and bicycles, and there is an elaborate system of footpaths for pedestrians. Major roads lead around Tapiola; vehicular traffic within it is minimized. Because no dwelling is more than 250 yards from a food store, driving is unnecessary.

More than 90 percent of Tapiola's housing, consisting of single-family homes and walk-up apartments, is owner-occupied. A thirteen-story office building dominates the landscape and has a noted restaurant atop it. Cultural life in Tapiola is so lively that people travel there from Helsinki for concerts, plays, and other events.

Dramatic increases in world population have spurred the development of new towns and planned communities in Europe. Along with Tapiola, the most successful are Stockholm's satellite cities—the most celebrated are Vallingby, Farsta, and Taby—in Sweden, and Bijlmermeer in The Netherlands. Many of the successful cities owe a great deal to Welwyn Garden City, built in pre-World War I Britain, which allowed one acre of open space for every fifty inhabitants and which is a model for planned communities.

Applications

The movement toward new towns and planned communities greatly accelerated in the United States at the end of World War II when returning veterans were marrying in unprecedented numbers. They needed housing in a country that had virtually suspended residential building from 1941 until 1945.

The first major effort to meet this need was launched by William Levitt, who built communities in the Northeast. In four years, he turned a potato patch within commuting distance of Manhattan into Levittown, a community of 17,500 single-family homes, schools, shops, and parks. Although Levitt's houses looked alike, he eventually solved that problem by means of creative landscaping. Levitt's cookie-cutter communities served one major socioeconomic group: young Caucasian returning war veterans. Blacks were excluded from Levitt's communities.

Many planned communities focus, although not always exclusively, on a specific group, such as adults over fifty and retirees (Del Webb's various Sun City communities, Lake Havasu City, Leisure World, and Green Valley, Arizona), members of a religious sect (Utah's largely Mormon communities or Amish communities in Pennsylvania, Illinois, and other states), well-educated people (Westlake or Irvine, California), or so-called Yuppies (many urban districts that have undergone gentrification). One planned city, Soul City, North Carolina, was launched in 1969 as a haven for blacks escaping discrimination in other southern communities.

Perhaps the two best planned communities in the eastern United States are Columbia, Maryland, and Reston, Virginia. Both are close to Washington, D.C., although neither was established as a bedroom community. Part of the concept of these and similar communities is that most residents will also work in them.

During 1963, John Wilson Rouse, a mortgage banker with a vision, quietly bought half of Howard County, Maryland, an area slightly smaller than Manhattan Island. Rouse's philosophy was that the United States can build privately financed model communities if it can convince business people of their profitability. Rouse built seven villages around a central business area, aiming to attract a final population of about 110,000, nearly twice that of Howard County in 1963.

The emphasis of Rouse's plan was to put humans at the center of everything he proposed. For example, he convinced representatives of the Protestant, Catholic, and Jewish faiths to share religious facilities so that more money could be spent ministering to people. Costing more than $2 billion to build, Columbia committed 20 percent of its acreage to open space, including parks, lakes, golf courses, and bike paths. Rouse persuaded The Johns Hopkins University Hospital to set up a satellite hospital there and to offer a health care plan.

More than thirty corporations opened operations in Columbia, providing employment for many of the residents, a full 15 percent of whom were black. Ethnic diversity was an aim of this planned community, whose architecture was traditional (favoring colonial houses) but whose social outlook was untraditional, demonstrating how social engineering often becomes part of city planning.

Shortly before Rouse bought his land, Robert E. Simon, Jr., bought eleven square miles of fox-hunting country less than twenty miles northwest of Washington, D.C., in Fairfax County, Virginia. Simon got the entire property for $13 million, about $1,900 an acre. He and his architects planned a cosmopolitan community that would accommodate 75,000 people. It would be integrated in terms of both race and economic level.

The community was to consist of seven villages with a broad variety of residences, from single-family homes to high-rise apartments. Simon's plan devoted 23 percent of the land to open space, including the impressive Lake Anne, which became a central point in the community. A large industrial park offered employment for many of the inhabitants.

Simon's plan became mired in red tape. Many of the early inhabitants still worked in Washington and had to commute much of the distance over small country roads because Simon could not gain permission to open a Reston exit from the superhighway that served nearby Dulles Airport. Chartering buses to transport people to their jobs helped. Nevertheless, Reston was running at a deficit. Ultimately, it was taken over by Gulf Oil, one of its large lenders, and was run successfully, but not according to the philosophy on which the town was originally based.

In California, a unique planned community was developed thirty-five miles south of Los Angeles in Orange County. The Irvine family held in one piece the 88,000 acres that James Irvine, Jr., owned at his death in 1947, a legacy from his father, who had bought the land for thirty-five cents an acre.

The Irvine holding, twice the size of San Francisco and six times the size of Manhattan Island, became the largest planned community in the United States. It began when the Irvine Company gave the University of California one thousand acres on which it built the Irvine campus of the university, a facility for 27,000 students. Carefully planned residential areas stretched out from the University, their development controlled by the Irvine Company, which leased rather than sold the land to its occupants.

Architect William Pereira planned three tiers of development for the Irvine Ranch, envisioning an eventual population of half a millon largely upper middle-class residents, in eleven discrete communities, all served by the 622-acre Newport Center. Irvine Ranch, which is more socially stratified than towns such as Columbia or Reston, has a 2,600-acre industrial park that is adjacent to Orange County's John Wayne Airport on the development's northern perimeter. Nearly two hundred corporations have located there, creating some 150,000 jobs. Initially, a major impediment to the development of Irvine Ranch was the Irvine Company's insistence on holding title to the land and leasing it to residents.

The growth of planned communities stalled somewhat in the 1980's, largely because of the economic downturns of that decade. Nevertheless, brisk real estate markets in the Southwest led to an acceleration in the building of such communities in the early 1990's.

Context

From earliest times, the need for new towns grew out of the socioeconomic needs of people. As agrarian society diminished and the industrial and postindustrial ages dawned, it became increasingly important to establish communities that were designed to meet the social, economic, and physical needs of those who would inhabit them.

In many societies, particularly those of eastern Europe, the Middle East, and Asia, government is expected to provide for these needs. In societies more attuned to a free-enterprise, capitalistic economy, planned communities usually develop through a combination of private initiative and governmental subsidies.

During the New Deal, U.S. president Franklin Delano Roosevelt established the Resettlement Agency, under whose auspices three planned communities were established—Greenbelt, Maryland; Greenhills, Ohio; and Greendale, Wisconsin—all of which were modeled after the garden-city, city-beautiful concept.

Growing social concerns in subsequent decades focused attention on planned communities designed to solve specific social problems, such as overcrowding, or to provide for the special needs of minority groups or the aging. In the late 1940's and early 1950's, returning servicemen were beginning families. Their most immediate need was to have their own individual housing.

The racial uprisings of the late 1960's highlighted the shame of America's urban ghettos and underlined the need for a kind of urban renewal. When urban renewal dispossessed people from their homes and replaced their buildings with dwellings they could not afford to live in, great injustices ensued.

This situation, combined with the country's refusal to give long-term care to many mental patients, has resulted in the homelessness that afflicts thousands of people in cities today. Planned communities intended to meet the needs of the homeless are slowly appearing in some urban areas.

The graying of America has intensified the need for special-interest communities to serve the aging population, particularly its less affluent members. The danger is that in meeting this need, society may isolate the elderly, which would have a negative social impact on most levels of society.

Finally, the cost of housing in many areas, particularly the West Coast, is currently so high that middle-class young people cannot afford to live apart from their parents. Many retirees or people nearing retirement are faced with having children in their late twenties and older living at home, many having returned there after costly divorces. The housing question is politically charged and involves serious financial commitments from the public and private sectors. Unbridled growth also creates long-term problems that cannot be ignored. Usually, when a planned community springs up, arable land is diverted from agriculture, which, over time, can lead to significant food shortages. Every aspect of urban and suburban expansion touches directly on nearly every important aspect of human existence, making it imperative that growth be achieved thoughtfully, conscientiously, and intelligently.

Bibliography

Breckenfeld, Gurney. *Columbia and the New Cities.* New York: I. Washburn, 1971. Breckenfeld provides an excellent overview of planned communities. He goes into detail about governmental involvement in their development. His main focus is on Columbia, Maryland, although he discusses at length a number of the sixteen new towns that the Office of Housing and Urban Development has helped to finance.

Campbell, Carlos. *New Towns: Another Way to Live.* Reston, Va.: Reston, 1976. Campbell puts the planned community of Reston in historical perspective. He details the philosophy of its builder, Robert E. Simon, Jr. He also shows how Gulf-Reston, Incorporated, made a going concern of the community, but at the expense of the developer's basic social philosophy.

Hardy, Dennis. *From Garden Cities to New Towns: Campaigning for Town and Country Planning, 1899-1946.* New York: E&FN Spon, 1991. Hardy is particularly strong in discussing Britain's leadership in the garden-city movement. The book has a broad focus, discussing new towns in Europe and the United States as well as in Britain. Hardy shows interesting progressions in urban planning.

Hertzen, Heikki von, and Paul D. Spreiregen. *Building a New Town: Finland's New Garden City, Tapiola.* Cambridge, Mass.: MIT Press, 1971. The authors provide a strong background for new towns. They then focus on Tapiola, perhaps one of the most successful planned communities in contemporary society. The book is detailed and readable.

Hiss, Tony. *The Experience of Place.* New York: Alfred A. Knopf, 1990. Hiss combines anthropological and sociological points of view. The first section, "Experiencing Cities," is especially relevant. The second section, "Encounter the Countryside," however, has much to offer those who would make new towns conform to nature.

Kelly, Barbara M. *Expanding the American Dream: Building and Rebuilding Levittown.* Albany: State University of New York Press, 1993. Kelly provides a compelling history of the rapid development of Levittown in the mid-1940's. She then shows how its developer, William Levitt, worked to overcome the sameness of his houses by, as he put it, letting planting become more important than planning. The result is a much-improved community.

Van Der Ryn, Sim, and Peter Calthorpe. *Sustainable Communities: A New Design Synthesis for Cities, Suburbs, and Towns.* San Francisco: Sierra Club Books, 1986. One of the best studies of the environmental impact of new towns. The contributors are much concerned with urban ecology. They are also concerned with the sociological aspects of community development.

Walter, E. V. *Placeways: A Theory of the Human Environment.* Chapel Hill: University of North Carolina Press, 1988. Walter's understanding of how people perceive space and react to it is remarkable. His whole thesis has to do with how humans live as members of a natural environment. This book, which is at times utopian, is extremely thought-provoking.

R. Baird Shuman

Cross-References

Aging and Retirement, 47; Cities: Preindustrial, Industrial, and Postindustrial, 253; The Concentric Zone Model of Urban Growth, 322; Industrial Societies, 953; Suburbanization and Decentralization, 2010; Urban Planning: Major Issues, 2109; Urban Renewal and Gentrification, 2116; Urbanization, 2129.

NUCLEAR AND EXTENDED FAMILIES

Type of sociology: Major social institutions
Field of study: The family

A nuclear family is commonly defined as consisting of two generations, parents and children. An extended family also includes other generations (such as grandparents) or other relatives. The family may be described both in terms of its organization and its activities. In addition, families—both nuclear and extended—can be discussed in terms of the types of boundaries that form around them.

Principal terms

CONSANGUINE: related by blood; having the same ancestry

FAMILY LIFE CYCLE: a framework for studying the family incorporating a series of stages, typically based on children's ages

HALF-RELATIVES: people having one common progenitor; for example, the biological child of two previously married persons would be the half-brother or sister of children brought to the family

SOCIALIZATION: the processes through which individuals learn the values and norms of the society in which they live

STEPRELATIVES: people related by the remarriage of a parent rather than by blood

Overview

The concept of "family" is most successfully defined through an analysis of the boundaries that outline family. A boundary signifies who is included and who is not included in the family. The boundary may be a legal relationship such as marriage or adoption. When the boundary is legal, the family members and society at large accept it as constituting a legal bond that lasts until another legal act negates the original contract. A biological or consanguine boundary also exists. The strongest consanguine boundary concerns birth parent and child, but it also includes grandparents, cousins, uncles, and aunts. In addition, there may be a boundary consisting of a psychological or emotional relationship. This is a boundary of attachment, according to which a person is considered part of a family even though not legally or biologically related. Children in foster families are an example. Finally, there is the physical boundary, or the actual place of residence of the members.

Family is easiest defined when legal, biological, emotional, and physical boundaries coincide. When this does not happen, complex family structures develop. The number of family configurations that can be produced is vast. A lack of congruence in the family boundary not only leads to difficulty in defining the family but may also lead to boundary ambiguity for the individual members.

Family has been given many meanings; it has become a "sponge" term, according to sociologist David Popenoe, absorbing numerous definitions and variations. Aca-

Sociology

demic disciplines, organizations, religions, and professional and lay individuals typically construct a definition of family that is representative of their own group's values.

Types and sizes of families may be classified according to the diameter of their boundaries. The nuclear family is the smallest unit and consists of two generations: the parent or parents and child or children. The extended family consists of three or more generations living together. Another variation is a family consisting of a combination of nuclear families.

The historical view of nuclear families is that of a unit comprising mother, father, and child or children. In this definition of nuclear family, all boundaries most often agree. According to the 1990 U.S. Census data for children under age eighteen, 79 percent of white children, 37.7 percent of black children, and 66.8 percent of Hispanic children lived with both parents. The average sizes of these nuclear families were 3.12, 3.46, and 3.83 people, respectively.

When two generations, rather than the presence of both mother and father, is the defining criterion for nuclear family structure, another nuclear family form emerges— that of the single-parent family. Single-parent families exist because of divorce, separation, the death of a spouse, or parents never having been married. Census data report that divorce (38.6 percent) is the most common cause of single parenting, followed by parents never having married (30.6 percent), separation (20.3 percent), and one partner being widowed (7.1 percent).

Reconstituted or blended nuclear families occur through remarriage or through the first marriages of single parents. Statistical data from the U.S. Bureau of the Census shows that 64.9 percent of divorced women and 22.6 percent of widows remarry. Fourteen percent of all U.S. children under eighteen live in stepfamily arrangements. This new legal boundary may create a family in which not all persons agree on the psychological/emotional boundary. It introduces steprelatives and half-relatives as a new and complex set of relationships. Marriage and family experts Robert H. Lauer and Jeanette C. Lauer suggest that stepfamilies may not have "clear-cut" boundaries. For example, views such as "He is not my 'real' brother" may be voiced by stepsiblings.

The physical boundary or common residence is usually included in the definition of family. This simply means that the parent(s) and child(ren) are living together. Child custody is sometimes awarded jointly, in which case a child may have two physical boundaries and nuclear families—one at the home of a father and one at the home of a mother. Since the number of times a person divorces and remarries is not limited, a child may have more than one set of family networks and interrelationships to work through in one lifetime.

Extended families live together for as many specific reasons as there are families. There are advantages to extended families. Jean Treloggen Peterson of the University of Illinois includes the following in a 1993 list of advantages of extended families. They provide an ability to coordinate short-term recurring labor needs. They enable the organization of ways to meet the family's short-term, recurring child care needs or the needs of other dependents. They permit flexibility—that is, the ability to change membership and organization almost literally overnight. They provide an ability to pool resources and to draw on those pooled resources on a daily and recurring basis to achieve some economies of scale. According to the 1990 U.S. Census, extended families make up about 4 percent of American households.

Applications

Families, nuclear and extended, not only "are," as defined by their boundaries, but also "do," or function within those boundaries. Families share resources, goals, history, values, experiences, rituals, love, and commitment to one another. In addition, families provide for the socialization and nurturance of children with continuing interactions and affection; for the emotional, intellectual, social, physical, and religious development of members of all ages; for food, nutrition, and health; for clothing needs; and for shelter and environment.

The quality of the "doing" or functioning in nuclear or extended families varies. The difference in how well a family functions is related to a number of family characteristics. In *Secrets of Strong Families* (1985), Nick Stinnett and John DeFrain describe six qualities that impact on how well families function. These include commitment, appreciation, communication, time, spiritual wellness, and coping ability. This list of qualities describes a family that typically functions very well. A family that has trouble functioning would be deficient in at least some of these qualities. Most families exist on a continuum somewhere between the extremes, with varying degrees of these qualities being present at different periods in the family life cycle.

According to Stinnett and DeFrain, commitment is a dedication to seeking the welfare and happiness of the other family members. Commitment implies caring for someone or an attachment to them, and it suggests that because of that attachment responsibilities will be fulfilled. Lauer and Lauer believe that families that are committed to their members are more willing to work together to solve problems. Sociologists Mary Ann Lamanna and Agnes Riedmann agree that persons who feel a commitment to one another want to work problems out. They also suggest that persons who are committed have more fun together and have communication that is more open. Lauer and Lauer also suggest that sharing fun and creating family memories or history builds or deepens commitment.

Appreciation is the second characteristic that is prevalent in families that function well. Stinnett and DeFrain found that showing appreciation often was a characteristic that kept families "doing" at a functional level. Appreciation helps to build self-esteem. Some suggestions from Stinnett and DeFrain for promoting appreciation include creating a positive environment in the home, developing individual styles for showing appreciation, and accepting appreciative comments gracefully when they are given.

Good communication is an integral part of successful functioning. Sociologist Stephen J. Bahr in *Family Interaction* (1989) describes positive and negative communication skills. Persons practicing positive communication send clear and congruent messages, listen, show empathy, express support, and negotiate. Criticizing, complaining, disagreeing, ignoring others, refusing to talk, and saying one thing while meaning another are all negative communication tactics that are present in some families. Poor communication is associated with marital dissatisfaction and with general family unhappiness.

One of the things that effectively functioning families do is spend time—quality and quantity—together. In a survey by family specialist Dolores Curran on what makes a family healthy, family professionals ranked different family traits. Three of the top fifteen traits pertained to family time. Trait number five was, "The healthy family has a sense of play and humor." Trait number nine was, "The healthy family has a balance of interaction among members," and trait number fourteen was, "The healthy family shares leisure time." Although families may believe that spending time together is important, they also think that finding the time is getting harder. Consultants Mark Mellman, Edward Lazarus, and Allan Rivlin report that lack of time together is seen by many Americans as a threat to the family. In their study of family values, 54 percent of the families surveyed believed that spending more time together would strengthen family values.

Almost without exception, when studies concerning families that function well are conducted, there is mention of shared religious convictions. The presence of religious values, rather than the specific religion, is the determining factor. Religion has great impact on the lives of Americans, from how many children are born into a family to how people cope with trouble. A religious heritage in many ways forms a subculture, as people group themselves with others of similar faith. Bahr quotes the results of a 1985 Gallup Poll, which found that 80 percent of Americans believe that religion is important to them and that 90 percent list a religious preference. Bahr also reports a connection between religion and satisfaction with family life. Among religious youth, less teen drug abuse, less delinquent activity, and less premarital sex has been noted.

According to Pauline Boss in *Family Stress Management* (1988), the meaning one brings to a stressor is important in how one copes with stress. In the last of Stinnett and DeFrain's characteristics that help a family function, coping ability, the ability to view a problem as an opportunity to grow, helps to keep a family functioning. The ability of family members to learn to manage everyday stress and to find the resources to help them in times of greater trouble is very important in keeping a family functioning.

While the preceding information can be applied to all nuclear and extended family forms, generally original research has focused on traditional nuclear families. In research focusing on single-parent families, Leslie N. Richards and Cynthia J. Schmiege identified five strengths, including parenting skills, managing a family, communicating, growing personally, and providing financial support. Providing financial support is a problem far more often for single mothers than for single fathers. When single mothers could successfully provide the finances they saw it as a source of pride. Single fathers, however, seemed to view financial provisions as a given.

Context
In Western Societies, the nuclear family has been the chosen family form since the

mid-1600's. The extended family predated the nuclear style in such societies as the ancient Hebrew, Greek, and Roman societies. Both nuclear and extended families existed among the European colonists in North American from the early seventeenth century. When people began to emigrate from Europe to North America, it was typically the nuclear family or single men that came rather than an extended family. Although families with eight or nine children were common in the colonies of North America, the average family comprised about six persons. As white Americans moved west, it was typically the nuclear family that pulled up roots and left to make a new beginning.

The process of children growing up and leaving home is a significant part of what has been called the "family life cycle." Joan E. Norris and Joseph A. Tindale suggest that leaving home serves at least two notable purposes: It provides more freedom for the parents who remain and less parental authority over the young adults who leave. It is important to realize that this physical separation of parents and children by no means ends the reciprocal support system that usually exists. It represents rather a renegotiating of intimacy and separateness.

The prevailing economic climate influences when many young adults leave home. In a robust economy, they leave earlier than during periods when it is hard to find employment or the job outlook is uncertain. Thus, although Norris and Tindale note that independent living by both parent and child generations is "normative," they also note that economic situations in particular may have strong effects on behavior. Children may remain at home longer or may move back with their parents—sometimes bringing their own children with them, creating an extended family. Extended families are also formed when one's elderly parents move in. Again, economic factors are found to be important in decisions regarding elderly parents moving in with their middle-aged offspring.

The extended family, even with its advantages and even when it is functioning very well, appears to be a result of necessity more than a desire to live as three generations for some intrinsic value. According to Norris and Tindale, this was also true in early America. As the baby boom generation reaches old age, the over-sixty (and over-seventy-five) population will increase significantly, and the number of families living as extended families can be expected to increase. This will particularly be true if economic conditions are conducive to older children remaining at home.

That defining the nuclear family has been reduced to an analysis of "boundaries" demonstrates the dynamics of the family since early American history. In early America remarriage because of divorce was minimal; however, blended families did exist because of the remarriage of widows and widowers. They were relatively rare; even more rare were never-married single parents. Two hundred years has brought about considerable change in family forms. Debate over why these changes have occurred and over the impact of these changes on individual family members by age groups, on the functions of a family, on the existence of the family itself, and on society in general has pervaded the study of the family since the early 1970's. Also debated— both among sociologists and the general public—has been the approach that society should take to these changes. On one hand, some urge increased acceptance and toleration of all forms of families, including providing desperately needed help for poor, single-parent families. Others advocate actively trying to stop or reverse the changes that have occurred. Regardless of the many forms the family can take, the family has been a fundamental human institution since before history began, and it will continue to be centrally important for the foreseeable future.

Bibliography

Bahr, Stephen J. *Family Interaction.* New York: Macmillan, 1989. An introductory college-level text on the family. Includes author and subject indexes. Interesting reading that discusses research and some of its applications and ramifications.

Boss, Pauline. *Family Stress Management.* Newbury Park, Calif.: Sage Publications, 1988. Presents theory for understanding both normative and catastrophic stress; includes suggestions of ways to apply the concepts. Includes charts.

Curran, Dolores. *Traits of a Healthy Family.* Minneapolis, Minn.: Winston, 1983. Intended for the lay audience. Very interesting report of clinical research with many applications. Challenges readers to work toward improving the health of their own families.

Lamanna, Mary Ann, and Agnes Riedmann. *Marriages and Families: Making Choices Throughout the Life Cycle.* 2d ed. Belmont, Calif.: Wadsworth, 1985. College-level text for a marriage and family course. Includes case studies, photographs, charts, appendices, and index.

Lauer, Robert H., and Jeannette C. Lauer. *Marriage and Family: The Quest for Intimacy.* 2d ed. Madison, Wis.: Brown & Benchmark, 1993. College-level text. Chapters contain summaries, self-tests, and areas for personal journal entries.

Leslie, Gerald R., and Sheila K. Korman. *The Family in Social Context.* 6th ed. New York: Oxford University Press, 1985. A comprehensive look at the family. Includes photographs, a subject index, and an author index.

Mellman, Mark, Edward Lazarus, and Allan Rivlin. "Family Time, Family Values." In *Rebuilding the Nest: A New Commitment to the American Family,* edited by David Blankenhorn, Steven Bayme, and Jean Bethke Elshtain. Milwaukee, Wis.: Family Service America, 1990. One article in a good collection of editorial essays concerning the condition of the American family.

Norris, Joan E., and Joseph A. Tindale. *Among Generations: The Cycle of Adult Relationships.* New York: W. H. Freeman, 1993. A concise report on research relevant to the interaction between generations. Written for the lay audience.

Peterson, Jean Treloggen. "Generalized Extended Family Exchange: A Case for the Philippines." *Journal of Marriage and the Family* 55 (August, 1993): 570-584. A valuable report on extended families with a discussion of original research. Includes a reference list.

Popenoe, David. "American Family Decline, 1960-1990: A Review and Appraisal." *Journal of Marriage and the Family* 55 (August, 1993): 527-542. Article expresses the author's opinions, based on research, concerning the changes in and the condition of the family. Popenoe's article is followed by three responses.

Richards, Leslie N., and Cynthia J. Schmiege. "Problems and Strengths of Single-Parent Families: Implications for Practice and Policy." *Family Relations* 42 (July, 1993): 277-285. Includes a review of previous research along with a report on original research. Includes graphs and references.

Stinnett, Nick, and John DeFrain. *Secrets of Strong Families.* Boston: Little, Brown, 1985. Interesting book written with the lay audience in mind. Excellent combination of research and real-life examples. Chapters include practical suggestions for improving family functioning.

Diane Teel Miller

Cross-References

The Elderly and the Family, 627; The Family: Functionalist versus Conflict Theory Views, 739; The Family: Nontraditional Families, 746; Inheritance Systems, 989; Parenthood and Child-Rearing Practices, 1336; Remarriage and "Reconstituted" Families, 1629; Residence Patterns, 1635; Socialization: The Family, 1880; Two-Career Families, 2077.

ORGAN TRANSPLANTATION

Type of sociology: Major social institutions
Field of study: Medicine

Advanced biomedical technology enables physicians to transplant a variety of organs, ranging from eye corneas to hearts, into people whose organs are failing them. This technology has profound sociological and ethical ramifications; for example, choices must be made regarding whose lives are to be prolonged and what sources of organs are to be utilized.

Principal terms
ALLOGRAFT: an organ or tissue transplant that is obtained from a donor other than the transplant recipient
AUTOGRAFT: an organ or tissue transplant that is obtained from the same person who will be its recipient
GENERAL ANESTHESIA: a process in which a drug called an anesthetic causes the loss of feeling throughout the body and renders a patient unconscious during surgery
GRAFT: a piece of living tissue or an organ that is moved from one place to another on a person's body or from a donor to another person
IMMUNE SYSTEM: the body mechanism that combats disease caused by microbes or other outside threats; it is composed of white blood cells that consume microbes (phagocytes) and cells that make antibodies (lymphocytes)
LOCAL ANESTHESIA: anesthesia that deadens feeling in only a part of the body, allowing a patient to remain conscious during surgery
ORGAN: a body part made of several tissues and specialized to perform a necessary body function (for example, the heart)
TISSUE: a single type of cell organized as a group to carry out a specific function; the combination of several tissues for a specific function produces an organ
XENOGRAFT: an organ or tissue transplant that comes from an animal donor rather than from a human

Overview

The fact that medical technologists developed the means to transplant vital organs from one person's body to another has created a number of interrelated medical, sociological, and ethical concerns. A date often cited as central to the development of these issues is December, 1967, when South African physician Christiaan Barnard performed the first human heart transplant. The world press heralded the achievement, but many observers were disturbed. Ethicists raised the specter of doctors "playing God" in making decisions about who would be eligible for the benefits of the new technology; conservative religious groups decried the "defiling" of the body of the organ donor. Gradually, over the course of decades, organ transplants and organ donation became accepted as standard procedures. Many individuals carry donor cards on their person stating that their organs may be removed after their death for transplantation; California, for example, sends people such cards along with their driver's licenses to fill out and carry if they desire.

Organs for transplantation come from a variety of sources: from relatives who donate them to loved ones, from the very recently deceased bodies of people who have willed their healthy organs to society, and even—in some countries—from needy people who wish to sell them. The availability of useful transplantable organs is very limited compared with the huge number of people who seek organ replacement surgery.

The supply and demand problems associated with organ transplants have led to several present and potential societal concerns. First, it is necessary for doctors to decide who is to get the available organs, a problem fraught with ethical dilemmas. A second problem is related to the worldwide issue of poverty and concerns the fact that in some countries it is legal to sell, rather that donate, one's organs for transplantation. Organs such as kidneys can be transplanted from a living person because people have two and can survive with only one; yet the danger always exists that the remaining organ will become damaged, thereby threatening the person's life. Many social scientists argue that the conditions of dire poverty that would drive a person to sell body organs must be alleviated. A third issue—one that has become less important since the first days of transplantation, however—is the question of how to address the opposition of some religious groups who feel that organ removal constitutes defilement of the human body. Finally, the medical community has had to confront the possible specter of "organ-napping": the stealing of organs from living or recently deceased people to supply a feared organ black market. Before addressing these issues, it is helpful to explore the origins of organ replacement and the capabilities of modern procedures for carrying it out.

The earliest instances of procedures that could be called organ transplantation (or grafting) may have occurred in India in the third century B.C.E. There, physicians of antiquity reportedly used pieces of skin transplanted from a patient's cheek or neck to repair severe nasal injuries. It was not until the sixteenth century that skin grafting procedures spread to Italy and then throughout Europe. It was quite rare for a sixteenth century patient to undergo such surgery, however, because it was extremely painful (the terrible pain often lasted for months), and anesthesia and painkillers were nonexistent. Moreover, the risk of death was very high. The absence of sterile techniques—microbial causes of disease were unknown—swelled the number of patient deaths.

Two nineteenth century medical breakthroughs set the scene for the development of modern organ transplantation methodology. They were the first use of general anesthesia, by the American dentist William Morton (1846), and the beginnings of the use of sterile techniques in surgery by British surgeon Joseph Lister (1877). These life-saving breakthroughs led surgeons to attempt to transplant organs between people;

however, most late nineteenth century and early twentieth century transplantation efforts failed miserably.

The obstacle that was still unsurmounted was the body's defense against bacteria and other foreign cells, the immune system. It was this obstacle that, until the middle of the 1960's, effectively limited tissue transplantation to blood transfusions, corneal transplants, and skin grafts from twins. At that time, better understanding of the immune system and the ability to type all tissues (in a fashion similar to blood typing) enabled surgeons to begin to transplant many body organs (such as livers, kidneys, and hearts) with some success. The success of such operations, however, as evaluated by one-year and five-year survival rates, was still very low.

The development of drugs that suppress the action of the immune system, called immunosuppressants, made successful organ transplantation possible. The first widely used immunosuppressant drug was cyclosporine, developed in 1969 and widely used beginning in the early 1980's. Cyclosporine nearly tripled the success and survival rates of most types of organ transplants attempted. Transplantation efforts burgeoned. Perfection of its use, and the subsequent development of other immunosuppressants, led to the prolongation of life for many thousands of people, worldwide, by organ transplantation. Cyclosporine is still one of the main immunosuppressant drugs utilized in transplantation.

Organs and tissues that doctors are now able to transplant include cornea, bone, skin, blood vessels, bone marrow, kidneys, livers, hearts, and lungs. The surgical procedures involved vary greatly in difficulty, have widely varying success rates, and differ as to whether use of allografts (grafts received from others), autografts (those from other parts of the patient), or xenografts (from animals) are mandated.

Cornea and bone allografts, carried out quite easily, are almost always successful. Bone marrow and skin transplants, though widely successful, require autografts and utilize very complicated transplantation procedures. Liver, kidney, heart, and lung transplants require allografts and have lower long-term success rates. In addition, these organs must have been freshly removed from donors and require meticulous tissue typing of donors to assure reasonable hope of success.

Applications

For a discussion of the sociological and ethical aspects of organ transplantation, it is helpful to divide transplantable organs into three groups based on the ease of obtaining them, the relative facility of their transplant actualization, and their operation success rates. Bone and cornea transplants, representing the first group, are successful virtually all the time; the cornea (the transparent membrane in front of eye lens) has been replaceable since the 1940's. The surgical technique is routine and can be performed under a local anesthetic; it can restore sight to those whose has been lost or impaired from scarring or clouding of the cornea. Bone transplants are also relatively simple to perform and long lasting, either as autografts or as allografts. Cornea and bone allografts are relatively easy to procure and to store for long time periods before their use.

Other types of organ transplants are more difficult. Skin is perhaps one of the most difficult, overall; permanent skin transplantation cannot be done unless it involves grafts from another part of the body of the patient needing the surgery (autografts). Because of the difficulty of these transplants, and because of the need for extensive skin grafts for severe burn victims, temporary grafts from human cadavers or of synthetic or animal skin are used. These allografts are necessary to prevent excessive loss of body fluids until sufficient amounts of the patient's own skin, "harvested" as autografts or grown in the laboratory, can enable the completion of the permanent grafting process.

Because of their natures, bone, cornea, and skin grafts do not lead to the major sociological issues associated with some other transplants. In the first two cases, the reason is the relative plenty of these donated body parts and the comparatively low cost of the medical procedures involved. In the case of skin grafting, the need for autografts and the easy availability of cadaver, animal, and synthetic skin are the reasons.

More problematic are kidney, liver, lung, and heart transplants. These operations are always allografts, with the most successful type being kidney replacements. Kidney replacement surgery is deemed so successful that tens of thousands of such operations are now carried out yearly. Fortunately, because every human possesses two kidneys and only requires one for survival, most donors will live normal lives unless the remaining kidney fails. Many times the replacement organ comes from a relative or a close friend. Kidneys from people who have specified that their organs may be used for medical purposes after their death are another significant source. Total kidney availability from friends and from all other donors, however, does not meet the need for the organs. Adding to the need for kidneys for transplantation is the fact that many recipients experience transplant rejection (sometimes several times) and need multiple kidney replacements.

Heart and liver allografts are yet another story. As no one can live without these "one per person" organs, transplants must all be allografts from people who will them to society for such use after death. Hearts can be used as an example. These organs must be transplanted very soon after death. Because of this organ's instability and because of the difficulties of surgical implantation, heart transplants are less often successful than kidney transplants, and the successes involved are often of shorter duration. The sociological issues involved include the unwillingness of many potential donors even to think of donating their organs after death because of a religious or personal abhorrence of defiling the body by removing organs; this is considered a problem by some because the available pool of organ donors could be larger if such objections could be overcome.

Another issue involved in organ transplantation is exemplified by the case of a kidney transplant received in 1982 by a Massachusetts toddler, Jaime Fiske. Her father was a hospital administrator who actively sought a kidney for Jaime through medical channels. Controversy arose because the child's father was deemed to have unfair access to organs, compared with the general public. To solve any similar contemporary and future problems, the federal government passed the Uniform Anatomical Gift Act, in 1987. This law was designed to make organ transplants fairer by requiring all transplant centers to ignore possible biases about who should receive their available organs. It is not clear whether the hoped-for "total fairness" can ever be attained, but many inequities are said to have been addressed by its enactment.

Another sociological and psychological aspect of organ replacement that is rarely considered is the personal feelings of the vital organ recipient. Too often, transplantation success lasts for less than a year; when the new organ fails, another transplant is needed. Despite the fact that the transplant recipient has had his or her life prolonged beyond original expectations, psychological problems can be profound. Some recipients, for example, report going through hell while awaiting a new organ. Others, after a transplant operation, continually expect the worst, living in constant fear of organ rejection and death while in apparent good physical health.

Context

There is often said to be a lag between the development of technology (particularly in the twentieth century) and the societal acceptance and widespread use of the technology. Organ transplantation represents a clear example of the relationship between technology and social change. The medical establishment has had to grapple with new ethical issues and answer criticism from the society at large. Government has had to frame new legislation to define what constitutes criminal activity in this area. Two related social problems involving transplantation technology are the determination of who is to receive a given organ and the source of the organs to be used. It has been strongly argued that, initially, rich people and those well connected to the biomedical community had unfair access to organs. Legislation was passed in the late 1980's to ensure a more uniform and unbiased dissemination of the organs in question. This has in a large part addressed problems of fair organ dissemination.

The high cost of organ transplantation is another issue; it is inextricably related to the high costs of health care generally. The dissemination, in the late 1980's and early 1990's, of large numbers of transplant organs caused increases in per capita medical costs because of the high costs of transplants (about ten thousand kidneys a year for example at $30,000 or more per kidney), most of which are funded by health insurance. Among the many social implications of the high cost of health care is the argument that employers began to hire temporary or part-time labor rather than attempt to pay for health insurance for their employees. Some have said that this has helped destabilize 1990's society, as many individuals found themselves out of work and unable to pay for the things they need.

The possibility of a black market for illegally obtained organs is a fear that some observers have. Worst-case scenarios have been envisioned involving organ-napping rings supplying dealers with surgical parts for desperate buyers able to afford them. Efforts to prevent this possibility have included government legislation and the policing actions of medical associations. The repercussions that would be faced by any biomedical personnel caught in the act of aiding in the transplantation of black-market organs are also expected to be a strong preventive. It is hoped that this problem will not occur except in extremely rare and isolated cases.

Bibliography

Kittredge, Mary. *Organ Transplants*. New York: Chelsea House, 1989. This useful, well-illustrated book covers organ transplant history (the various types of transplants, their costs, their shortcomings, and efforts in progress in the 1980's), organ typing, and patient viewpoints. Ethical issues and the outlook for the future are also discussed. Sources of additional information include organizations that can be contacted and additional readings.

Lee, Sally. *Donor Banks: Saving Lives with Organ and Tissue Transplants*. New York, Franklin Watts, 1988. This brief book describes organ transplants and organ banks. Topics include blood banks; eye banks; replacement of hearts, livers, and kidneys; and the utilization of bone and skin grafts. Problems associated with obtaining adequate numbers of organs and tissue supplies are enumerated. Several striking photographs, some information sources, and a glossary are included.

Leinwand, Gerald. *Transplants: Today's Medical Miracles*. New York: Franklin Watts, 1985. This interesting book covers the history of organ transplantation from medieval times to the late twentieth century. Includes the development of organ transplants, ways to decide who is to get a particular organ, legislation and its shortcomings, and efforts directed toward the future. A useful glossary and valuable references are also included.

Miller, George W. *Moral and Ethical Implications of Human Organ Transplants*. Springfield, Ill.: Charles C Thomas, 1971. This book by the pastoral care director of a Florida hospital contains a history of modern transplants, moral and ethical transplantation concerns, a description of the costs of many transplants, and the results of questionnaires sent to others. Some technical background and an ethics bibliography are included.

Simmons, Roberta G., Susan D. Klein, and Richard L. Simmons. *Gift of Life: The Social and Psychological Impact of Organ Transplantation*. New York: John Wiley & Sons, 1977. This insightful professional book includes chapters that cover the psychological and social problems of transplant recipients, views of donors and families of donors, transplantation methodology, financing, and delivery of transplants. A very extensive bibliography and a glossary are included.

Sanford S. Singer

Cross-References

ORGANIZATIONS: FORMAL AND INFORMAL

Type of sociology: Social structure
Field of study: Key social structures

A formal organization consists of a group of people working cooperatively toward a common goal under the supervision of those vested with authority. Informal organizations refer to loosely coupled, loosely defined, unauthorized relationships that tend to occur between individuals and groups within a formal organization. These concepts help to explain how organizations work, both on paper and in practice.

Principal terms
> ACCOUNTABILITY: the responsibility for one's own actions and those of subordinates
> AUTHORITY: the probability that a set of commands from a given source will be obeyed by a set of individuals
> BUREAUCRACY: a concept of formal hierarchical organizations elucidated by Max Weber
> CENTRALIZATION/DECENTRALIZATION: in centralization, authority is in the hands of very few people; in decentralization, authority is distributed among many individuals
> DIVISION OF LABOR: a structure in which tasks that become too complex for any one person to accomplish are subdivided
> HIERARCHY: a pyramidal structure with one or few individuals at the top having supervisory authority over others in subordinate positions
> LINE EMPLOYEES: those directly responsible for carrying out the objectives of an enterprise, supervising others below them and reporting directly to those above them in the hierarchy
> SPAN OF MANAGEMENT: the number of people reporting to a manager
> STAFF EMPLOYEES: workers who assist and advise line managers and do not have direct authority over other personnel

Overview

Formal organizations exist in all facets of life. Churches, governments, schools, factories, and retail establishments are all examples of formal organizations. Definitions of the term vary, but most would agree that a formal organization consists of a group of individuals, has interrelated parts in terms of activities and functions performed, has members who cooperate to achieve common goals, and is united by members who exercise authority and leadership. According to sociological theory, formal organizations develop when a task is too complex to be completely performed by one person. Thus, formal organizations are based on the division of labor. As more workers are involved in an organization, workers tend to specialize, each doing his or her own task. As organizations grow, departmentalization—in which work is divided, and like activities are grouped into departments—occurs.

As an example, a very simple retail-sales operation may be performed by one person—the shopkeeper—who orders goods, staffs the sales counter, takes inventory, monitors payments and billing, and cleans the shop. In a slightly larger retail operation, separate individuals specialize in buying, selling, cash management, cleaning, and maintenance. In large department stores, staffs of individuals under separate managers handle such departments as accounts payable, accounts receivable, buying (perhaps even specialized into clothing buyers, housewares buyers, jewelry buyers), and advertising. In the latter type of organization, each department typically has a manager who oversees the work of a number of people within that department.

Formal organizations tend to be structured in a pyramidal fashion; often, such organizations use charts to depict the pattern of organization, which is a hierarchy. Those in authority delegate responsibility to those below them, and departments of individuals assigned to similar tasks are formed. In organizational diagrams, workers may be shown as having "line" authority over others (if the others report directly to that person), or they may hold "staff" positions (those which advise and assist a "line" position). Individuals are usually placed in staff positions for their expertise and in line positions through promotion from a position lower in the hierarchy. Formal organizations conduct their relationships through a structured flow of communications. Information generally flows up or down, following the same lines that are shown on organizational charts. In addition, added structure—in the form of controls such as the use of authority and power, assignment of responsibility, and accountability—exists to ensure that quality work is accomplished.

Authority in an organization typically gives an individual the right to issue instructions to others and to see that the orders get carried out. When authority is widely dispersed, decentralization exists; when authority is in the hands of a few, authority is considered to be centralized. Authority may take several forms, including line authority (the right to require certain kinds of performance from subordinates) and staff authority (the right to advise—not give orders—based on expertise).

Formal organizations tend to be relatively permanent, and one of their functions is to retain that permanence. In fact, some critics of formal organizations point to such organizations' ability to resist or withstand change. Formal organizations adapt to change very slowly and are difficult to down-size.

Formal organizations may be designed by product, territory, matrix, or function. An organization may set up its organizational structure to reflect its different products (for example, a department store may have an electronics division, an automotive division, and a housewares division). Another organization may have a structure based on the regions that it serves (churches, for example, often have regional organizational structures such as synods and parishes). Matrix organization is more complex. In matrix organization, which is common in the aerospace industry, functional managers have authority flow, which is vertical, and project managers (who have project team members with various functions) have authority that flows horizontally. This intersection of authority flow, if diagrammed, creates a matrix. Finally, organizations may divide labor by function (a large corporation, for example, might have an accounting department, a sales department, and an advertising department).

Informal organizations tend to spring up within formal organizations. Since communication is structured and closely controlled within formal organizations, people in such organizations—by virtue of their desire for "belonging"—tend to form unsanctioned networks of communication and friendship. These networks become organizations in themselves, with shared values, norms, and communication patterns. Thus, informal organizations, in contrast to the formal organization within which they exist, are loosely defined, flexible, and loosely organized. They may have no explicitly agreed-upon goals, but they may have much unsanctioned power within the organization by virtue of their "control" over their members. Informal organizations arise to satisfy social needs, provide a sense of belonging and identification, supply informal information on acceptable and unacceptable behavior, offer a sympathetic ear, contribute to creativity, perpetuate cultural values, and provide informal channels of communication.

Informal organizations can be viewed positively or negatively. From the management point of view, informal organizations are positive when they reinforce standards of conduct, help morale, and provide additional means of communication. Informal organizations become troublesome from a management perspective when they perpetuate rumors, provide resistance to change, and oppose management's efforts.

Applications

Much information gained from the study of formal organizations is applied directly in such areas as management training. One major application of formal organizational theory is in the division of labor. Most large organizations specialize by setting up departments organized by function, product, region, or matrix. Hierarchical organization is common in many organizations, and most large organizations can produce an organizational chart showing reporting relationships, areas of line and staff authority, and responsibilities of each department or division.

Some major dilemmas are revealed by examining the actual practice of formal hierarchical organizations. One problem with formal organizations is related to communications. Most research reveals the need for free-flowing communication for creative decision making. In a formal organization, with only hierarchical and structured flow of information, many opportunities for good communication and creative decision making are lost. This fundamental dilemma was described in a 1962 study by Peter Blau and W. Richard Scott, who noted that "the very mechanism through which hierarchical differentiation improves coordination—restricting and directing the flow of communication—is what impedes problem-solving."

Management consultants Tom Burns and G. M. Stalker dealt with this dilemma when suggesting changes in the electronics industry in the 1960's. In *The Management of Innovation* (1961), they pointed out that success in an industry affected by rapid technological change requires social and administrative innovation as much as technical prowess. For this reason, Burns and Stalker made numerous recommendations, shifting away from the formal bureaucratic model of organization. These recommendations included reducing emphasis on hierarchy, encouraging lateral organizational communication, discouraging vertical communication, and creating ad hoc centers of authority built around technical expertise rather than assigned positions of authority in a hierarchy.

Another dilemma facing formal hierarchical organizations stems from the tension between bureaucrats and professionals in such organizations. Bureaucrats rise through such systems by promotion; by the time they get near the top, they may or may not have the expertise to make decisions to guide their segment of an organization. Their authority stems from, and their loyalty is owed to, those to whom they report. A bureaucrat's decision-making standards are thus centered on the organization itself.

Professionals, on the other hand, have a body of expertise from which to draw when making decisions. A professional has a professional code of ethics and a responsibility to other professionals in the same field. To make the distinction clearer, true bureaucrats do what their superiors tell them to do, while professionals tend to trust their professional expertise, even if such an approach leads to conflict with superiors. The final judgment of whether a bureaucrat's decision is right or wrong is left to management (those above that person in the hierarchy); judgment of a professional's decision making should be left to a jury of professional peers.

Organizations run by professionals and organizations run by bureaucrats can thus be very different. When a professional is hired in a bureaucratic organization and is expected by the organization to act as a bureaucrat, the resulting dilemma often becomes obvious; the tension created by differing standards can be difficult to resolve. College faculty members who move into college administration, or professional sociologists or social workers who attain management positions in social-welfare agencies, are commonly confronted with such difficulties.

One primary area of importance in terms of applications is the debate over whether managerial control through a rigid hierarchy of authority is the best way to run an organization. William Ouchi's "Theory Z," more recent efforts related to "total quality management" (TQM), and Burns and Stalker's findings, all raise questions about the utility of hierarchical organizational structures. Research into informal groups has suggested that their potential for enhancing communication, improving work quality, and increasing organizational efficiency may be greater than the gains to be made through increased efforts to understand and reproduce hierarchical formal organizational structures.

Further study of the area of informal organizations could lead to possible solutions for some of the problems noted above. An understanding of informal organizations may, for example, help to explain why a company or agency works as it does instead of how it is supposed to work "on paper." Many management-training programs fail to incorporate this sort of information, however; many such programs fail to acknowledge that there may be informal communication and loyalty networks that are not adequately tapped within a given formal organization.

Strategies that suggest involvement of workers across all levels of the hierarchy

(TQM, for example) have the potential to harness the power of the informal organization if such strategies do not become overly institutionalized (and do not come to be perceived by workers as tools of management). Informal organizations also have the potential to solve some of the communication problems of formal organizations by helping to circumvent the controlled "upward or downward" flow of information characteristic of formal organizations.

Context

Much of the work on which formal organizational theory is based stems from Max Weber's studies of bureaucracy. Some of the characteristics of bureaucracy noted by Weber—specialization/division of labor, hierarchical organization, and communication up and down a reporting structure—are characteristic of formal organizations. Weber, however, stressed that he was describing bureaucracy as an "ideal type" and not as something actually observable in practice. This approach has led to much criticism of his work and also has caused many scholars to call for work that goes beyond his perspective.

Robert K. Merton, a later theorist, called for a balanced description of bureaucracy, including a delineation of its dysfunctions as well as its functions, in the 1940's. Others, including 1960's scholars Peter Blau and W. Richard Scott, have pointed out that specific elements described by Weber may be in conflict with one another. For example, hierarchy of authority promotes discipline and makes possible coordination, but a hierarchical structure also discourages subordinates from accepting responsibility.

In the late 1940's, Philip Selznick cautioned that analysts needed to examine informal networks and structures as well as formal ones, despite the fact that most sociological analysis of the time was primarily concerned with formal organizations. One earlier study of informal groups was conducted by F. J. Roethlisberger and William J. Dickson and was based on workers at an electric plant in the 1930's. Roethlisberger and Dickson found that informal groups in a production setting tended to adopt certain norms of behavior. These norms included informal rules that discouraged members from turning out either too much or too little work and from informing on other workers. The study provided much of the information in use today regarding informal groups.

From the 1950's to the 1970's, many sociologists focused on developing typologies of organizations, since it was obvious that any one model of the "generalized" formal organization was too broad. Everett Hughes, James Thompson and Arthur Tuden, Herbert Simon, Peter Blau and W. Richard Scott, and Amitai Etzioni all contributed variations of typologies of organizations. The work of many later critics of this approach has tended to focus more on informal groups, the "power" of individuals within organizations, resistance within organizations, and other related topics.

Bibliography

Blau, Peter, and W. Richard Scott. *Formal Organizations*. San Francisco: Chandler, 1962. One of the standard works of organizational theory. Provides basic information on formal and informal organizations, relevant research and theory, and a discussion of dilemmas facing formal organizations.

Eldridge, J. E. T., and A. D. Crombie. *A Sociology of Organisations*. New York: International Publication Service, 1975. Provides an excellent history of sociological thought regarding organizations; also includes chapters involving typologies of organizations, missions of organizations, organizational cultures, and critiques of current sociological theory regarding organizations.

Grusky, Oscar, and George A. Miller, eds. *The Sociology of Organizations: Basic Studies*. New York: Free Press, 1970. This compendium of classics in organizational sociology makes numerous foundational works (by such individuals as Max Weber, Talcott Parsons, and Amitai Etzioni) accessible. The chapter introductions are useful analyses of the materials used and highlight debates among the writers.

Hicks, Herbert G., and C. Ray Gullett. *Organizations: Theory and Behavior*. New York: McGraw-Hill, 1975. A readable overview of sociological and management perspectives on organization theory and practice. Good annotated bibliography and case studies with each chapter. An excellent balance of theory and applications.

March, James, and Herbert Simon. *Organizations*. New York: John Wiley & Sons, 1958. Discusses assumptions underlying classical organizational theory. Illustrates how the rules governing formal organizations limit the ability of the individual or group to deal creatively with decision-making situations.

Roethlisberger, F. J., and William J. Dickson. *Management and the Worker*. Cambridge: Harvard University Press, 1939. Describes the often-cited study of informal organizations based in the Hawthorne plant of Western Electric. Emphasizes the power of informal organizations within a production setting.

Zey-Ferrell, Mary, and Michael Aiken. "Introduction to Critiques of Dominant Perspectives." In *Complex Organizations: Critical Perspectives*, edited by Mary Zey-Ferrell and Michael Aiken. Glenview, Ill.: Scott, Foresman, 1981. A useful critical overview of mainstream organizational sociology. Includes a helpful and thorough bibliography.

M. C. Ware

Cross-References

Bureaucracies, 172; Industrial Societies, 953; Industrial Sociology, 960; Social Groups, 1806; Statuses and Roles, 1978; Traditional, Charismatic, and Rational-Legal Authority, 2064; Workplace Socialization, 2202.

ORGANIZED CRIME

Type of sociology: Deviance and social control
Fields of study: Forms of deviance; Social implications of deviance

Organized crime pertains to criminal activity involving multiple offenders operating in a structured manner for purposes of sustaining large profits from an illegal enterprise. Various forms of organized crime are prevalent throughout society and collectively account for much of the economic losses attributable to crime in the United States.

Principal terms

CORPORATE CRIME: organized crime committed by a group of individuals for corporate gain in the otherwise legitimate marketplace

CRIME ORGANIZATIONS: syndicates or "families" whose members are organized on the basis of ethnic traditions or kinship ties for purposes of committing organized crime; the most commonly cited example is the Mafia

CRIMINOGENIC MARKET STRUCTURES: economic conditions that promote organized crime in the legitimate marketplace or that contribute to the creation of an illegitimate marketplace

ETHNIC GROUP: a group that shares a common heritage and cultural or subcultural background

SUBCULTURAL VALUES: traditions, beliefs, interests, and behavior patterns associated with a particular population or segment of society

WHITE-COLLAR CRIME: crime committed by high-status individuals, in the course of their occupations, for personal gain

Overview

Crime is a complex and multifaceted problem; the study of crime seems to produce more questions than answers. This perception clearly applies to organized crime—debate begins with the fundamental issue of how to define it. Presidential commissions, special task forces, government agencies, and prominent criminologists have offered a variety of definitions. Many of the difficulties originate from the ambiguous nature of the key term "organized." Though some definitions may state that a simple plurality of two or more individuals qualifies as organized, most crime analysts conceive of this activity as being much broader in scope. Yet even if agreement existed as to the precise number of individuals minimally required to satisfy the definition, there would remain a variety of ways to focus on organized crime.

Criminologist Howard Abadinsky, in his book *Organized Crime* (1990), notes the many different slants that exist. Some definitions stress the kinds of illegal activities that represent organized crime. An example of this perspective is one which states:

> Organized crime consists of two or more persons who, with continuity of purpose, engage in one or more of the following activities: (1) The supplying of illegal goods and services, i.e., vice, loansharking, etc.; (2) Predatory crime, i.e., theft, assault, etc.

Another definition, also cited by Abadinsky, shifts the focus to the roles and interpersonal relationships within organized crime:

> An organized crime is any crime committed by a person occupying, in an established division of labor, a position designed for the commission of crime providing that such division of labor also includes at least one position for a corrupter, one position for a corruptee, and one position for an enforcer.

Debating whether to stress an organization's activities or its makeup may not be very fruitful in the long run. Close examination of such definitions reveals that they steer one in more or less the same direction. They are misguided to the extent that they confine the analysis of the topic to stereotypical crimes (such as gambling, narcotics, and racketeering) committed by stereotyped organizations (such as secret criminal groups and societies) that rely primarily on violence to sustain their operations. It is an image of organized crime that conjures up visions of gun-toting gangsters who are bound by a sinister code of enforcement. This is indeed one level of the problem. It is essential to recognize, however, that this image is actually a perspective on crime organizations rather than on organized crime itself.

A more expanded view, one that targets organized crime, requires the avoidance of loaded terms such as "enforcer" or biased phrases stipulating that organized crime depends upon the "use of violence to maintain discipline." Criminologist Dwight C. Smith, Jr., raised this issue in his book *The Mafia Mystique* (1975). There, and in more recent works, Smith argues that organized crime is a broad concept that encompasses crime at many levels. The common denominator is that of being a business enterprise for illegal profits.

Smith is not alone is his assessment. Criminologists Peter Reuter, Jonathan Rubenstein, and Simon Wynn, for example, reached similar conclusions in their study of the sanitation and vending machine industries, two enterprises often linked to racketeering. They found that these were legitimate businesses more often than not. When they were illicit in nature, they typically represented the work of small, transient operators. Reuter observed in another study that some traditional criminal activities, such as gambling and loansharking, were operated as illicit businesses responsive to market forces rather than as rackets controlled by a criminal organization.

Thus, the essence of organized crime is that it entails an ongoing illegal enterprise necessarily involving multiple participants. As such, organized crime may be found both on the street and in the corporate suite. It is not limited by ethnicity, race, or social class. Though organized crime includes criminal organizations such as the so-called

Mafia, it is not limited to them. Organized crime may also refer to the illegal activities of otherwise legitimate organizations. Although white-collar and corporate crime are often considered distinct from organized crime, a convincing case has been made that all fit within an overarching pattern that can be called organized (some experts prefer the term "organizational") crime.

Given the breadth of included activities, it may very well be that the costs of organized crime constitute the lion's share of the annual crime bill in the United States. Arriving at accurate figures on the overall costs is difficult. Nevertheless, estimates by law enforcement officials contend that crime syndicates, or families, typically reap profits in excess of $50 billion each year from narcotics, gambling, and various rackets. Not included in this figure are their earnings, legitimate and illegitimate, from real estate, hotels, motels, restaurants, and other outwardly legal ventures. The cost of organized crime committed in the American business sector may be added to this: The U.S. Congress has projected, for example, that it will cost the public between $300 billion and $473 billion by the year 2021 to recover from organized crime (corporate and white-collar crime) committed in the savings and loan industry during the 1980's.

Applications

The study of organized crime must include a search for causes that explain its existence throughout different levels of society. Historically, the problem has been linked to the activities and characteristics of ethnic subcultures, principally Italian or, more specifically, the Sicilian Mafia. Not only has organized crime been found among other ethnic groups (such as Jewish, Irish, Hispanic, Asian, and African American people), but also it has been, and continues to be committed by white, middle-class, fully assimilated Americans. The common thread that runs throughout organized crime is not ethnic or racial, but economic. Organized crime is the product of criminogenic market structures in which there is a demand for illicit goods and services or in which there exist opportunities for illicit profiteering in an otherwise legitimate marketplace. In either case, the crimes are made possible and encouraged by ineffective measures of control. The following examples, one involving a criminal syndicate and the other a corporate concern, illustrate the market-force character of organized crime.

When laws are passed that restrict broadly desired goods or services, a market structure is created that may promote organized crime. The passage of the Volstead Act in 1919 prohibited the sale and distribution of alcoholic beverages, a widely desired commodity. "Prohibition" was an attempt by moralists to control the social problems associated with alcohol abuse. The law not only failed to control these problems but also provided tremendous opportunities for organized crime syndicates that sprang mainly from Italian, Irish, and Jewish street gangs. Prohibition proved to be so lucrative that it provided a financial base for other opportunities in racketeering, vice, and legalized gambling (as in Las Vegas) when the Volstead Act was repealed in the early 1930's. The continued involvement of criminal syndicates in casino gambling, for example, is evidenced by periodic prosecutions for "skimming," the pocketing of millions of dollars prior to reporting earnings for tax purposes. The traditional syndicates have also branched out into the legitimate business sector wherever controls are weak, unenforced, or nonexistent.

International secrecy laws in banking allow organized crime syndicates to launder stolen securities. These are then used to meet the demands created by a criminogenic market structure in which legitimate avenues of credit are unavailable to a business. For a certain fee, the businessperson may "rent" the stolen securities and use them for collateral to obtain a loan.

As the traditional Italian-dominated syndicates have turned increasingly to brokering their services and investing their capital in outside ventures, other groups have started to dominate their customary activities, principally the drug trade. Beginning in the 1970's, Hispanic groups such as the Herrera family and the Medellín cartel of Colombia gained a large share of the U.S. market. Other groups, notably the African American El Rukns and Asian American Triad members, also moved into drug distribution as well as loansharking, gambling, prostitution, and extortion. Though it is costly and widespread, organized crime committed by criminal organizations may pale in significance when compared with the organized crimes that occur in the corporate world.

By the time Prohibition had enriched crime syndicates, the oil industry was an established monopoly which used ruthless tactics that would now be clearly criminal. During the period when ethnic gangs were running petty protection rackets, Standard Oil reigned supreme through price manipulations and covert rebate deals with the railroads. Though antitrust laws are now in place to protect against unfair monopolistic practices, the large oil companies continue to engage in activities that could be considered highly organized crime.

Oil is critical to the industrialized world. Manipulation of the supply and demand relationship poses the potential for immense profits and is, thus, a criminogenic market structure. The energy "shortages" of the 1970's were times of crisis for the public but opportunities for profiteering by major oil companies. Sociologist James W. Coleman describes this phenomenon in his book *The Criminal Elite: The Sociology of White-Collar Crime* (1989). In one instance, Coleman states, the major oil companies exploited market forces by reducing their sales volume to "smaller major" companies. The object was to cut the supply to independent dealers who bought oil from the smaller major companies. The effect was bankruptcy for many of the independents and a reduction of suppliers to the public. Through an illegal conspiracy to restrain trade, the large oil companies increased their portion of the retail market.

Profiteering by the oil refining industry has made it perhaps the largest single violator of environmental law. Environmental pollution abounds, as do price-fixing, restraint of trade, and other examples of organized crime by corporations because laws that are supposed to police these criminogenic market structures are deficient. Most contain loopholes and provide inadequate penalties that do not deter. Furthermore, agencies charged with enforcing the laws are comparatively understaffed and underfunded. They are often little match for the legal and financial resources of organized corporate criminals.

Context

Few Americans had ever heard the word "Mafia" prior to 1900, let alone considered the concept of organized crime. Anyone having an interest in the topic had to rely on the words of European scholars. One of the first American sociologists to explore this subject was Donald Cressey. He played a principal role in the government's *Task Force Report on Organized Crime* (1967) and subsequently wrote a book entitled *Theft of a Nation* (1969). Cressey's vision of organized crime parallels that held by the government, the media, and much of the public. It casts organized crime as a nationwide conspiracy dominated by Italian Americans, as depicted in such popular films as *The Godfather* (1972). This view of organized crime is actually an examination of criminal organizations that downplays the role of other ethnic groups and ignores the idea that the Mafia and illegal corporate activities may both be considered organized crime.

The failure of sociologists to include illegal corporate behavior within the concept of crime goes beyond Cressey's influence. A few decades before Cressey's work, Edwin H. Sutherland, often hailed as the "father of American criminology," was the first to term corporate-related offenses "white-collar crimes." He went on to describe them as offenses committed by syndicates whose members were typically of lower class ethnic origins, be they Italian, Jewish, or Irish.

Beginning in the 1970's, the basis for equating white-collar crime, corporate crime, and syndicate crime with organized crime appeared in Smith's work *The Mafia Mystique* (1975). Smith denies that organized crime is a national conspiracy controlled by ethnic groups who depend on violence. Instead, he maintains that organized crime springs from the same criminogenic economic forces that operate in both the legitimate and illegitimate marketplace. This perspective has prompted some criminologists to replace the phrase "organized crime" with "organizational crimes" in an effort to further stress the broad scope of the problem.

Analyzing organized crime in the above manner has far-reaching implications. To begin with, sociologists and criminologists will necessarily have to focus less on ethnic and subcultural values and more on criminogenic market structures—their nature and the conditions that nurture them. What, for example, are the common factors that pertain to the legal and illegal drug trade that prompt restraint of trade in the former case and a marijuana distribution network in the latter? Finally, public policy regarding control will require the vigorous application of effective laws to both syndicate and corporate organized criminals. Perhaps more important, long-term controls will rest upon strategies designed to neutralize the crime-producing aspects of any marketplace.

Bibliography

Abadinsky, Howard. *Organized Crime*. Chicago: Nelson-Hall, 1990. Though Abadinsky treats organized crime in conventional terms, he gives an interesting account of its history in New York and Chicago. He then moves on to nontraditional forms (non-Italian gangs or syndicates) and concludes the ten-chapter book with a discussion of the activities (and the social, political, and legal responses to) criminal organizations.

Calavita, Kitty, and Henry N. Pontell. " 'Heads I Win, Tails You Lose': Deregulation, Crime, and Crisis in the Savings and Loan Industry." *Crime and Delinquency* 36 (July, 1990): 309-341. In this article, Calavita and Pontell provide an easily readable and detailed account of organized crime in the savings and loan business. It clearly documents how deregulation and protectionism created a criminogenic market structure for the unlawful risk-taking that eventually derailed the industry.

Coleman, James W. *The Criminal Elite: The Sociology of White-Collar Crime.* 2d ed. New York: St. Martin's Press, 1989. This book presents an excellent analysis of corporate and white-collar crime. Coleman cites examples ranging from false advertising to international violations of civil liberties, using actual cases. He then offers an overview of the difficulties of controlling the problem, such as litigation issues and pitfalls in enforcement. Coleman concludes with a discussion of possible reforms.

Cressey, Donald. *Theft of a Nation.* New York: Harper & Row, 1969. Cressey's book mirrors the government's version of organized crime presented in its 1967 *Task Force Report on Organized Crime.* It is a primary example of the popular view of organized crime as an entity dominated by approximately two-dozen "families" and a commission of members having an Italian American heritage.

Smith, Dwight C., Jr. *The Mafia Mystique.* New York: Basic Books, 1975. The pioneering work in which Smith analyzes organized crime from an economic, entrepreneurial viewpoint. The book is very interesting and is written as an informative perspective rather than as a textbook.

Henry W. Mannle

Cross-References

Crime: Analysis and Overview, 373; Decriminalization, 456; Gangs, 792; Victimless Crime, 2150; White-Collar and Corporate Crime, 2179.

PARADIGMS AND THEORIES

Type of sociology: Sociological research
Field of study: Basic research concepts

A paradigm refers either to an exemplar or to a set of convictions shared by members of a scientific community, whereas a theory is a conceptual structure created to correlate, systematize, and explain a set of facts. Sociologists use paradigms and theories to make sense of the data they have gathered about human social behavior.

Principal terms
ANOMALY: an observational, experimental, or theoretical discovery that appears to contradict the accepted scientific paradigm
MIDDLE-RANGE THEORY: a sociological theory based on a limited set of assumptions that goes beyond the description of social phenomena to explain them through an empirically verifiable set of ideas
NORMAL SCIENCE: the research activities of scientists after the establishment of a paradigm that help to articulate and consolidate it by solving its remaining problems
PARADIGM: in the exemplary sense, a scientific achievement embodying experimental results and theoretical interpretations that serve as a model of how puzzles are to be solved; also the constellation of beliefs, values, methods, theories, and laws shared by members of a scientific community
SCIENTIFIC REVOLUTION: a historical event during which a scientific community abandons a traditional paradigm in favor of a new one whose worldview, methods, and logical structure are incompatible with the paradigm it replaces
THEORY: systemically organized knowledge, well established and justified, that enables scientists to analyze, explain, and predict the nature and behavior of a specific group of phenomena

Overview

From the inception of their discipline, sociologists have collected information about human behavior and tried to understand it in theoretical terms. Unlike physical scientists, however, whose theories are readily verifiable (or falsifiable), social scientists have generated theories that seemed unavoidably contaminated with ideological bias and other errors. Indeed, critics have argued against the scientific nature of the social sciences by pointing out that no truly general social laws or theories have been produced with, for example, the predictive power of the theory of gravity in astronomy. Nevertheless, sociologists have not been able to resist theorizing about their data; instead of grand theoretical systems, they have developed what sociologist Robert K.

Merton has called "middle-range theories" consisting of limited sets of assumptions from which highly specific verifiable hypotheses are derived.

According to Merton, the word "theory" has been much too loosely used by sociologists, encompassing everything from day-to-day working hypotheses through more elaborate speculations to comprehensive and unified systems of thought. Merton uses the term "sociological theory" to refer to logically interconnected sets of propositions from which empirical uniformities can be deduced. He chose this middle way between rigorous empiricism and grand theorizing because he, like many sociologists, believed that no general theory of sociology was possible, only special theories at a low level of generality. Early sociologists believed that they had discovered some basic social laws—for example, laws of social evolution—but modern critics such as the philosopher of science Karl Popper have shown that the evolution of human societies, just as the evolution of plants and animals, is a unique historical process, so these "laws" of social evolution are nugatory. Social scientists, confined as they are to unique human phenomena, cannot discover a universal theory of social behavior.

Despite these problems, social scientists cannot restrict themselves solely to collecting "social facts," because such facts never speak for themselves. In no science do facts ever exist independent of a social context. In gathering facts the sociologist must decide which are relevant, and these decisions are colored by the values, views, prejudices, and social group of the observer. The scientist necessarily filters his or her facts through certain conceptual schemes. The historian of science Thomas S. Kuhn, whose analysis of science has strongly influenced modern sociologists, showed that science does not consist of a detached search for truths about the natural world. Rather, scientists are part of a community whose shared commitments (or "paradigms") focus their activities on those variables that make sense in the light of the paradigm's conceptual structure.

Although Kuhn did not invent the term "paradigm," he gave it a new interpretation. In his seminal work *The Structure of Scientific Revolutions* (1962), Kuhn based his analysis primarily on the physical sciences, but social scientists found his arguments easy to adapt to their interests. Like many social scientists, Kuhn opposed the positivist interpretation of scientific development, which viewed science as growing in a continuous and progressive ascent to the truth. Kuhn, on the other hand, saw science changing discontinuously throughout its history, and he was skeptical about any conceptual scheme's approach toward absolute truth. As a paradigm holds sway in a scientific community for a time, it helps scientists make sense of the phenomena they observe and solve the particular puzzles that crop up, but it may also blind scientists to phenomena and puzzles that fall outside the purview of the paradigm. Nevertheless, anomalies do arise during this period, which Kuhn calls the period of "normal science." Initially, these anomalies may be ignored or handled through ad hoc explanations, but they accumulate, and when a creative scientist devises a new paradigm that explains everything the old paradigm explained along with the accumulated anomalies, then a scientific revolution is under way.

The Kuhnian paradigm and its allied analyses stimulated much new work in the social sciences. Some sociologists thought that paradigms might reveal how the subjects and methods of sociological research are generated, but others showed that paradigm guidance is at best a partial explanation of problem selection, since it could not explain why and how sociologists select problems that challenge the dominant paradigm. Even more problematic was the issue of whether sociology, with its plurality of approaches, methods, traditions, and ideologies, could actually have anything akin to a Kuhnian paradigm. According to Robert K. Merton, no paradigm yet proposed has come close to unifying sociology. In fact, he argues that it would be dangerous for sociologists to adopt a single paradigm as a panacea for the problems that plague their discipline. A pluralism of models of the human social condition is better than a totalitarian paradigm that might change the everyday life of human beings for the worse. Because of this danger, Merton viewed sociological paradigms broadly as the foundations upon which a house of interpretations can be built. He has made propaedeutic use of paradigms in his sociological work, and these interpretive paradigms have helped sociologists uncover the array of hidden assumptions underlying various types of sociological analysis.

The sociologist who has done the most to adapt Kuhn's vision of physical science to the study of sociology is Robert W. Friedrichs. His work on paradigms in the social sciences won for him the prestigious Sorokin Award of the American Sociological Association. Friedrichs had become fascinated by Kuhn's view of revolutionary science as the competition of worldviews, and this perspective reminded him of the intellectual pluralism within sociology. He therefore proposed a paradigm for sociology that recognized, even legitimized, the variety of assumptions, methods, and theories in his discipline. He saw the paradigm as a way to reconcile the many worldviews in sociology and to rescue their proponents from the defensiveness they felt about their science vis-à-vis the physical sciences. Friedrichs' adaptation of Kuhnian analysis revealed that sociology was a young science, with typical adolescent problems and opportunities. Furthermore, the less mature sciences such as sociology go through paradigm-anomalies-crisis-revolution-new paradigm stages already pioneered by the more mature sciences such as physics. For Friedrichs and other sociologists, Kuhn had fabricated a conceptual scheme that allowed them to see the organization, practice, and future of their discipline in a new light. In this way Kuhn became an esteemed figure in sociology, even an "oracle" for its professional nature and destiny.

Applications

Throughout the history of their science, sociologists have used theories and paradigms because these conceptual frameworks have helped them practice their trade. Even before the term "sociology" was coined by Auguste Comte in the nineteenth century, various peoples used theological or philosophical conceptual frameworks to describe the customs and institutions of their societies. These frameworks have been studied by, for example, the modern theologians who have used "the Jewish-Christian apocalyptic paradigm" to understand how such institutions as the church functioned during the patristic age. The Protestant paradigm of the Reformation has helped some social scientists understand how ascetic Protestant groups provided a value orientation that encouraged work in business and science. Max Weber's theory of the role of ascetic Protestantism in the development of modern capitalism is well known and has given rise to a substantial scholarly literature both supporting and attacking his thesis. Merton's theory that Calvinist sects significantly influenced the quantity and character of scientific discovery in the seventeenth century also has had a great influence on social scientists and historians of science.

Émile Durkheim's theory of suicide is the classic example of what Merton calls a middle-range sociological theory and how such a theory can be applied. Durkheim (who, along with Weber, helped found modern sociology) tried to go beyond the simple description of suicide rates in nineteenth century Europe to derive specific hypotheses that enabled him to elucidate the role that regulation and integration play in leading various people to commit suicide. For example, he discovered that social cohesion, which provides emotional support to group members subjected to acute anxieties, should, through its absence, form an important part in the genesis of suicide. Since Catholics have greater social cohesion than Protestants, Durkheim predicted lower suicide rates among Catholics than among Protestants, a prediction that was empirically verified. He also developed a theoretical concept, anomie, to help understand his data. Anomie, at the personal level, describes alienation and purposelessness experienced by an individual; at the social level, it signifies a pathological condition for a society whose basic values have been badly eroded. Such events as the sudden death of a spouse or an economic depression often create anomie, which, Durkheim predicted, would lead to high suicide rates. He tested these hypotheses using government data and found that widows and widowers did indeed have higher suicide rates than married people and that suicide rates were higher during depressions than they were during periods of economic stability. Despite these accomplishments, Durkheim's theory was criticized for not being genuinely scientific, since it explained only certain empirical data and could not explain all variations in suicide rates.

Paradigms, which have much broader applicability than Durkheim's middle-range theory on suicide, perform several useful functions in modern sociology. For example, they have a notational function, since they help sociologists arrange pivotal ideas in a pattern that reveals their interrelations. This can help sociologists describe and analyze particular problems, such as how a reference group (such as a family or peer group) influences behavior (dress, speech, or, in the case of a social analysis of the American soldier in World War II, the desire for combat). Paradigms have also been important in the emergence of a special field of sociological inquiry—the sociology of knowledge. Proponents of this field of sociology argue, in simple terms, that "you are what you know," and that what one knows is determined by one's social group. Knowledge, according to these sociologists, is not purely objective but involves bargaining. Room for such negotiations exists because human experience, no matter how extensive or profound, ultimately gives only glimpses of reality or tantalizing fragments of a missing whole. In his paradigm for the sociology of knowledge, Merton emphasizes how social class, cultural values, and occupational role influence such mental constructions as the ideas, beliefs, and theories of even those sciences such as physics and chemistry that were traditionally seen as insulated from such influences.

In addition to the use of paradigms in the sociology of knowledge, where they have helped focus attention on such core problems as the impact of moral beliefs and religious and political ideologies on all intellectual debates, paradigms have been used more concretely—for example, in studies on deviant social behavior, racial discrimination, and racial prejudice. Merton's paradigm of deviant behavior is well known. He has argued that the disjunction between culturally defined goals and the means available to achieve them generates the anomie that tends to produce socially disruptive persons. Like many of the embryonic theories of sociology, Merton's paradigm of deviant behavior has defects that restrict its usefulness as an explanatory or predictive model. Some critics have even claimed that it is little more than an elaborate classification scheme and that its predictions (for example, that much deviance should occur among those deprived Americans who experience social hindrances to monetary success most keenly) tend to be platitudinous. Merton has replied that his paradigm provides a systematic approach to the analysis of social sources of deviant behavior and that it shows specifically how some cultural structures pressure certain people to engage in nonconforming conduct.

Context

Despite the prolific writings about sociological theory, no consensus exists that even one of the many proposed sociological theories fully satisfies the criteria of rigor, generality, and predictability characteristic of a truly scientific theory. With this assessment in mind, it is easy to see why the history of sociological theory has largely developed between the extremes of classificatory frameworks and grand explanatory systems. Most common are those sociologists who temper their generalizations with meticulous observations and show how these observations can be made relevant in the light of certain general ideas.

Since the 1960's, the discussion of theories in sociology has been deepened by the application of Kuhn's analysis of science. Although the term "paradigm" was used by philosophers, sociologists, and others prior to the 1960's, Kuhn's popularization of the term through his phenomenally successful *The Structure of Scientific Revolutions* helped create an influential series of studies by sociologists. Kuhn's attack on traditionalists who saw science progressing only through the accumulation of factual information and his assertion that the scientific community plays the major role in accepting (or rejecting) new paradigms fit in well with modern sociological analyses. Kuhn's work provided the means for sociologists to explain their disagreements over the nature of the problems, methods, and explanations in the social sciences (since they were comparable to the less intense disagreements about these matters in the physical sciences). Kuhn had shown that even the physical sciences consisted of knowledge manufactured or shaped through the agency of either explicit or tacit philosophical, religious, social, cultural, and political forces.

The Structure of Scientific Revolutions has become the most widely read academic publication of the twentieth century (it has sold about a million copies and been translated into sixteen languages). It is now the *vade mecum* for many social thinkers about how science develops. It has also generated a large body of criticism. Early reviewers pointed out the ambiguity involved in Kuhn's many uses of the term "paradigm" (one critic enumerated twenty-one different meanings). In the second edition of his book Kuhn responded to these criticisms by distinguishing two families of meaning for "paradigm." The past achievements of such scientists as Copernicus, Isaac Newton, and Albert Einstein provide paradigmatic models about how problems in particular sciences are to be solved (the exemplary meaning), but scientists also work in communities which serve as the producers and validators of scientific knowledge (the sociological sense).

Other critics attacked Kuhn's notion of the essential incommensurability of rival paradigms. Since he emphasized that each paradigm represents a radically new way of viewing the world and doing science in it, many commentators took this to mean that scientific theories cannot be rationally evaluated or compared to see which is superior. Indeed, Kuhn compared a scientist's conversion to a new paradigm to religious conversion. This seemed to some critics to say that science is irrational and subjective. If no rational basis exists for choosing one paradigm over another, then the choice of one worldview seems arbitrary and subjective, a matter of psychology and sociology more than of physics or astronomy. In his later writings Kuhn clarified his position on these matters. Theories may be incommensurable, he states, but this does not make them incomparable. Different paradigms are like different languages: Some meaning is lost when one language is translated into another, but much of the original can be found in a good translation.

Kuhn's book appeared in the 1960's, a time of great social turmoil, and some sociologists, seeking to understand the book's rise to prominence among academics, have pointed out that influential sectors of various intellectual communities, including social scientists, are well served by his ideas. Kuhn appealed to conservative scholars because he emphasized the resistance of paradigms to change, but his treatment of revolutionary change in science appealed to radical scholars who could cite Kuhn to justify their claim that proponents of traditional paradigms are in the grip of irrational forces that prevent them from adopting new ideas. Several sociologists have written that the use of paradigms in the social sciences seems to be increasing rather than decreasing despite their controversial nature. Kuhn's thesis has greatly increased the influence of the social sciences on how activities in the physical sciences are interpreted; the sociology of science has become an important subfield. His ideas have also influenced the way in which paradigms are understood and used in the social sciences.

Bibliography

Friedrichs, Robert W. *A Sociology of Sociology*. New York: Free Press, 1970. This work, which has been highly praised by prominent scholars and leaders of the profession and which won for its author the Sorokin Award of the American

Sociological Association, is generally regarded as the definitive account of how external factors influence sociological analysis. Friedrichs adopted Kuhn's thesis to make intellectual diversity an important part of normal sociological science. He offers his analysis of sociological as a paradigmatic solution to the problem of the conflicts and diversity in his discipline.

Hoyningen-Huene, Paul. *Reconstructing Scientific Revolutions: Thomas S. Kuhn's Philosophy of Science.* Chicago: University of Chicago Press, 1993. This book, translated from the original German edition of 1989, is the authoritative philosophical study of Kuhn's body of work. Previous scholars have given various interpretations of Kuhn's ideas, but Hoyningen-Huene goes beyond these interpretations to bring all of Kuhn's thinking about science into focus through rigorous philosophical analysis. Besides tracing Kuhn's own intellectual evolution, Hoyningen-Huene discusses the meaning of paradigms, paradigm shifts, normal science, and scientific revolutions. An extensive bibliography of primary and secondary sources. Index.

Kuhn, Thomas S. *The Structure of Scientific Revolutions.* 2d ed. Chicago: University of Chicago Press, 1970. Kuhn's book, originally published in 1962, is regarded as a landmark in the intellectual history of the twentieth century. Its stimulating account of the nature of science introduced an array of ideas that has remained at the center of discussion for a variety of scholars, and his approach has become the basis for much new thinking in the social sciences. A second edition, with a postscript appeared in 1970.

Merton, Robert K. *Social Theory and Social Structure.* Glencoe, Ill.: Free Press, 1949. Merton has been called the most influential scholar in American sociology. He is particularly well known for his contributions to the sociology of science. This book consists of a collection of Merton's writings, organized to reveal the interplay between social theory and social research. He devotes much of the book to middle-range sociological theories. The extensive footnotes contain abundant references to the literature; includes indexes of names and subjects. A second edition was published in 1957, a third in 1968.

Sperber, Irwin. *Fashions in Science: Opinion Leaders and Collective Behavior in the Social Sciences.* Minneapolis: University of Minnesota Press, 1990. Sperber's purpose in this book is to clarify the role of fashion in modern society by showing its pervasiveness even in academic and scientific institutions. An important part of the book is his critical analysis of Kuhn's influence on modern sociology in general and on the sociology of science in particular. He uses the concept of fashion to show how Kuhn's own thought became popular and prominent among academics. He also analyzes the ascendance of Robert Friedrichs' model of dialectical pluralism in American sociology. Includes endnotes with extended discussions and many references to the literature, a bibliography, and an index.

Robert J. Paradowski

Cross-References

Ethics and Politics in Social Research, 675; Experimentation in Sociological Research, 721; Hypotheses and Hypothesis Testing, 915; Logical Inference: Deduction and Induction, 1093; Sociological Research: Description, Exploration, and Explanation, 1920; The History of Sociology, 1926; Sociology Defined, 1932; The Sociology of Knowledge, 1946.

PARENTHOOD AND CHILD-REARING PRACTICES

Type of sociology: Major social institutions
Field of study: The family

Parenthood involves the total responsibility for the emotional, social, economic, and cognitive well-being of a child. Parents may follow a number of approaches to rearing a child, and various theories and studies have examined the outcomes of those approaches.

Principal terms
AUTHORITARIAN PARENTING STYLE: an approach that stresses the child's obedience and the parent's power and authority
AUTHORITATIVE PARENTING STYLE: an approach that involves two-way communication between parent and child and that deemphasizes arbitrary parental power
BONDING: forming a close, emotionally intimate relationship with a child
DEMOCRATIC CHILD REARING PHILOSOPHY: a belief that a child is a unique, basically good individual deserving of respect
PERMISSIVE PARENTING STYLE: an approach that allows children to set their own boundaries except in cases where their safety would be jeopardized

Overview

Until the 1960's, the American view of the institution of the family was virtually monolithic. The "typical" mid-twentieth century American family was a nuclear family consisting of a mother, a father (who were also husband and wife), and a number of children (two to four children was widely considered an average and "normal" number). Societal changes began to alter this picture in the 1960's, however, and the changes have continued and expanded.

It is no longer universally assumed that marriage will involve parenthood; this is attributable to many factors, including the wide acceptance of birth control and an increase in women pursuing careers rather than devoting their lives only to motherhood. Moreover, parenthood itself no longer conforms to the image of a previous era. The number of single parents has increased dramatically, primarily because of increases in the divorce rate and in unmarried pregnancies. Many divorced people remarry, creating new families; the number of people who have become stepparents has therefore also increased. Parenting also occurs in other family situations, such as in adoptive families and foster families.

Parenthood is not restricted to a particular age group beyond the requirement that a biological mother must have begun menstruating but not yet gone through menopause (which generally occurs when a woman is in her late forties or early fifties). Teenage pregnancy has increased tremendously since the 1960's. Teenage pregnancies that are not terminated most often result in adolescent girls becoming single mothers or giving their babies up for adoption. The overall number of teenage pregnancies, according to some reports, had begun to stabilize by the early 1990's, but there continued to be a rise in the number of early teenage pregnancies. Compared with earlier decades, more unwed teens—perhaps 95 percent—were electing to keep and rear their children.

Sociologists have studied the differences in the ages at which married people from working-class and middle-class backgrounds become parents. According to a study by Lillian Rubin published in 1976, working-class couples have their first child an average of nine months after marriage. Professional middle-class couples, on the other hand, have their first child an average of three years after marriage. For many working-class couples, the early birth of a child often creates considerable financial and psychological stress, and parenthood is undertaken in the midst of this surrounding tension.

Some women, particularly well-educated and professional women, are marrying at a later age and planning their children for later years. According to a 1989 Census Bureau report, 25 percent of women ages thirty to thirty-four were childless. Most of them, however, hoped to have children; they did not intend to remain childless.

The number of children living with both their biological parents has decreased. It has been estimated that, beginning in the 1990's, more than 50 percent of all children will have lived in a single-parent home before they turn eighteen. This fact is attributable primarily to divorce, birth outside marriage, and the death of one parent. Although the mother is still the most frequent single parent, the number of single fathers is steadily growing. In divorce proceedings, fathers are more frequently given custody of older children (and male children) than of very young children.

Parents have various reasons for having children. A 1979 study by Lois Wladis Hoffman and Jean Denby Manis defined some of those reasons. Most common was a desire to have someone to love and nurture. This reason was given by some people in all parenting situations and at all ages. Indeed, as sociologists David B. Brinkerhoff and Lynn K. White state, "The parent-child bond is the strongest family relationship, and it stays strong until old age." The second most frequently given reason was the stimulation that children bring to life situations. Development of self was the third reason. The fourth reason involved giving parents a sense of achievement and creativity. The fifth reason centered on religious beliefs. The final reason was the belief that children would confer economic benefits on the parents. The decision to become a parent is rarely based on only one of these factors; it usually involves a combination of these reasons.

The expected outcomes or goals of parenthood are similarly varied. A broad goal is to rear to adulthood an independent, self-reliant, self-confident, happy, socially and intellectually competent individual. Another major goal is to have a satisfactory parent-child relationship. These goals are more likely to be reached when the parent is secure in her or his role. According to child psychologist Bruno Bettelheim, "the security of the parent about being a parent will eventually become the source of the child's feeling secure about himself." These goals are achieved through the child-rearing practices that are implemented in the home.

Applications

Child rearing involves a long-term commitment lasting from a child's birth to his or her late adolescence. After the child-rearing process is finished, however, the parent-child relationship still exists. Parenthood does not end when a child has grown to adulthood. Ellen Galinsky has proposed six stages of parenthood that reflect the commitment over time that is required for parenting. Image making is the first stage. This takes place during pregnancy and is a time of contrasts of both high hopes and intense worries. Most important, it is a time of imagining and planning the life the parents will have with the child.

Nurturing, the second stage, is concerned with reconciling differences between the image and reality of the child and parenting. It is a time of bonding and getting to know the infant child. Change and adaptation are key concepts during this time. The third stage is authority. This stage develops gradually as the child grows. During this time the child's own identity and self-concept is being formed. It is a time of establishing the parent-child power distribution, and thus the parent's philosophy of parenting becomes a crucial issue.

The fourth, or interpretive, stage begins around elementary school age and continues into the early teen years. The important task during this time is to interpret for the child the family's values in relationship to his or her ever-widening circle of relationships. Increasingly in this stage the parent(s) must decide how involved to be in the child's world. Patterns of separateness and connectedness form.

Redefining the parent-child relationship is the overarching task of the fifth stage, that of interdependence. It is a transitional time when teenagers are evaluating parents and when the parent is losing control and the child is assuming responsibility for his or her own decisions.

The last stage is that of departure. This is a crucial time of evaluation for the parents as they examine what kind of "job" they have done. During this stage, parents adjust their image of what it will be like for the children to be gone after years of thinking about it. It is also a time of redefining a relationship with an adult child. Not the least of the tasks during this stage is dealing with the physical reality of separation from the child. Fortunate parents during this stage will experience moments with adult children that "validate" the total parenting process.

Educators Fred O. Bradley and Lloyd A. Stone, in their book *Parenting Without Hassles* (1983), describe three models of child rearing: democratic, autocratic, and anarchistic. The models describe basic philosophies of parents that affect the approach to parenting. One's child-rearing philosophy is influenced by one's own upbringing and by education about the process of human growth and development as well as about what makes a good or effective parent.

The concept of childhood control is at the root of parenting philosophies. A parental view of a child as a unique individual who is basically good, deserving of respect, and (with guidance) able to develop to his or her own potential leads to a democratic philosophy and environment of child rearing. In democratic family living, children are seen as individuals with needs and desires. There is mutual parent-child respect, and there are identified boundaries. In addition, parents and children each have responsibilities and work cooperatively to solve problems.

On the other hand, a perception of the child as a person who is basically evil and needs to be controlled and dominated is the basis of an autocratic philosophy. The autocratic mode of parenting historically has been the prevailing philosophy and has only in recent history been challenged. Finally, perception of the child as completely capable of making independent decisions and benefiting from the absence of rules is the heart of an anarchistic philosophy.

Two classifications of child-rearing practices that correlate to democratic, autocratic, and anarchist family living have evolved from the research of sociologists Ronald L. Simons, Les B. Whitbeck, Rand D. Conger, and Janet N. Melby (1991). They identified constructive and destructive parenting practices. Constructive techniques incorporating warmth, reasoning, and clear communication can be seen as related to democratic living, whereas destructive practices (including coercion and hostility) may be related to life in an autocratic home; feelings of rejection may be connected with the anarchistic style. Democratic and constructive parenting are associated with positive outcomes for the children in the areas of intellectual, social, and moral development. Children reared according to the destructive parenting strategies that are sometimes found in autocratic homes stand a greater chance of living with negative consequences such as academic failure, substance abuse, and delinquency.

From these opposing philosophies and atmospheres develop parenting styles of three varieties. These parenting styles, first identified by Diana Baumrind in 1973, are authoritarian, authoritative, and permissive. These styles can be viewed as forming a continuum with authoritarian and permissive at opposite extremes and authoritative in the middle of the continuum. Parents' approaches to child rearing may be located anywhere on the continuum.

Authoritarian parents value obedience as being of utmost importance. They use power to make the child's behavior conform to their expectations. Communication is from the top down. Children have a "place," and authoritarian parents believe it is their responsibility to keep children there. Warmth and nurturance may be lacking.

In the middle of the continuum are authoritative parents. They set boundaries and limits, but the limits are not arbitrary: They are based on reasoning that may have included the child in the initial boundary decision. Bruno Bettelheim suggests that effective parents consider any situation not only from their own point of view but also from the perspective of the child. After considering both positions, the effective parent will integrate the two and make a decision. Authoritative parents are seen as warm and nurturing. Compliance is achieved through two-way communication and reasoning, and the use of power is reserved as a last resort.

Children reared in a permissive atmosphere are left to make their own decisions concerning limits and boundaries. Concern for the child's safety is the only circumstance in which permissive parents intercede in the child's decisions. Autonomy of the child is valued above compliance. Because permissive parents may ignore the needs of the child, this parenting style generally relates to the classification of destructive parenting.

A review of children's characteristics during and after being reared according to these different styles shows that authoritative parenting results in more positive outcomes. Children reared in authoritative homes are found to be self-reliant, self-controlled, cheerful, socially comfortable with peers and adults, curious, purposeful, and achievement oriented. In contrast, children from authoritarian homes are moody, distrustful, unhappy, aimless, fearful, easily annoyed, and aggressive at one extreme and sulky at the other. Children from permissive families show aggression, noncompliance with adults, a lack of self-control, and impulsive and domineering behavior. Childhood development expert James Garbarino has stated that children can survive different parenting and intellectual atmospheres and that what children need the most and cannot develop successfully without is acceptance. Child development specialist Urie Bronfenbrenner concurs: "A child needs the enduring irrational emotional involvement of one or more adults in care and in progressively more complex joint activity with that child."

Context

The study of parenthood has been a relative latecomer to the areas of sociology and psychology concerned with family structures and relationships. Sociology was for many years primarily concerned with the roles of married men and women as husbands and wives rather than as parents. In psychology, too, the emphasis was on married people's adult relationships. Child psychology was (and is) its own separate area.

Among the factors that helped create a need for examinations of parenthood were the post-World War II baby boom of the late 1940's and early 1950's and the expanding types of parenting experiences (including stepparenthood and single parenthood) of the 1970's and 1980's. Researchers in both sociology and psychology began to examine such things as the complex interrelationships between parenting styles and personality development. Among the most influential early writers in this area—both in the social science community and among the general public—were Bruno Bettelheim and Benjamin Spock. Diana Baumrind's categorization of authoritarian, authoritative, and permissive parenting styles, published in 1973, was also influential among psychologists.

The number of children per American family has decreased since the nation's early years, and the number of children that live with two biological parents has also decreased. Yet despite the changes in society and in the institution of the family that have occurred since the 1950's, Americans still value parenthood and view children positively. Parenting situations and styles vary according to a parent's own background, personality, current lifestyle, attitudes toward parenting itself, and education. D. F. Alwin documented a societal shift from a more autocratic parenting mode in the 1950's and 1960's to a democratic mode in the 1970's and 1980's.

Many professionals agree on the desirability of parenting education in a modern, complex society. Americans are trained or educated for most adult roles; parents, however, are left to their own resources unless they actively seek resources elsewhere. Training, such as parenting classes, does exist. Some hospitals and social service agencies (as well as some high schools) provide such services. Support groups are available; they usually center on one particular issue or problem involving child rearing. Another source of parenting education is the proliferation of books on library and bookstore shelves.

Bibliography

Bettelheim, Bruno. *A Good Enough Parent*. New York: Alfred A. Knopf, 1987. An extended essay sharing the insight and understanding of the author on rearing children. Covers a wide range of parenting concerns.

Bigner, Jerry J. *Parent-Child Relations*. 3d ed. New York: Macmillan, 1989. An introductory college text concerning parenting. Parenting theories are discussed, characteristics of each childhood life cycle is presented, and social issues related to parenthood are included. Research is synthesized for each area.

Bradley, Fred O., and Lloyd A. Stone. *Parenting Without Hassles*. Salt Lake City, Utah: Olympus, 1983. Written for the lay audience, this is a "how-to" book. Emphasis is on democratic living and its benefits to the parent and child.

Bronfenbrenner, Urie. "The Parent/Child Relationship and Our Changing Society." In *Parents, Children, and Change*, edited by L. Eugene Arnold. Lexington, Mass.: Lexington Books, 1985. The compiled reports of a conference with the same name. Societal change in general is included; food and family, an area often overlooked, is discussed.

Galinsky, Ellen. *The Six Stages of Parenthood*. Reading, Mass.: Addison-Wesley, 1987. A comprehensive look at each of the six stages of parenthood. Many practical examples are interspersed. The questions asked of interviewed parents are included in the appendix. An index is included.

Garbarino, James, Robert H. Abramowitz et al. *Children and Families in the Social Environment*. 2d ed. New York : Aldine de Gruyter, 1992. A collection of essays that place children both in families and in a realistic societal context. The chapter entitled "The Ecology of Childbearing and Child Rearing" is a synthesis of research related to the transition to parenthood.

Hanson, Shirley M. H. "Single Custodial Fathers." In *Dimensions of Fatherhood*, edited by Shirley M. H. Hanson and Frederick W. Bozett. Beverly Hills, Calif.: Sage Publications, 1985. Hanson's emphasis is on the single father in this anthology concerning many aspects of fatherhood.

Jaffe, Michael L. *Understanding Parenting*. Dubuque, Iowa: Wm. C. Brown, 1991. An introductory college text providing an overview of the parenting process.

Emphasizes the relationship between parents and children. Social issues such as children with special needs, family violence, and divorce are included.

Diane Teel Miller

Cross-References
Child Abuse and Neglect, 218; Day Care and the Family, 450; Delinquency Prevention and Treatment, 476; The Family: Functionalist versus Conflict Theory Views, 739; The Family: Nontraditional Families, 746; The Feminization of Poverty, 754; Nuclear and Extended Families, 1303; Socialization: The Family, 1880; Values and Value Systems, 2143.

PARTY POLITICS IN THE UNITED STATES

Type of sociology: Major social institutions
Field of study: Politics and the state

The contesting of democratic elections in the United States occurs through a process whereby candidates are nominated by, and usually campaign with the help of, one of the two major political parties, the Democrats and the Republicans. Since the 1960's, campaigns have relied increasingly heavily on television as a campaign tool.

Principal terms
DEMOCRACY: a type of political system characterized by the free and open election of government leaders
PARTISAN REALIGNMENT: a lasting change in the coalitions that support a political party, often though not always resulting in a shift in the party's relative dominance
PARTY IDENTIFICATION: a relatively stable allegiance to a particular political party; the percentage of people identifying with American political parties has been decreasing since the 1950's
POLITICAL PARTY: an association of individuals who share certain broad policy concerns and who field candidates for office in elections
POLITICAL SPOT ADVERTISEMENTS: television commercials used as a campaign tool that often emphasize a candidate's image rather than substantive policy issues
SPLIT-TICKET VOTING: voting for candidates of different political parties on the same ballot; split-ticket voting has been increasing since the 1960's

Overview

Political parties in the United States are the chief means by which regular democratic elections are structured and carried out. Political parties nominate candidates, prepare platforms or policy positions on which to run candidates, and then assist in the actual campaigns of persons running for office. Parties are involved in races for office ranging from the highest level, such as president of the United States, to the local level, such as mayors and members of city councils. Political parties began to be somewhat marginalized in the campaign and election process in the 1970's and early 1980's as television became a more powerful force in the campaign process. Since that time, while parties are in some ways less powerful than they were in the pretelevision era, they have regained power and influence in the campaign and election process.

While the United States Constitution does not provide for or discuss political parties, the nation saw the creation of political parties in the early days of the republic. Patterned somewhat on the early struggle for the ratification of the Constitution, the earliest parties, the Federalists (who supported a strong central government) and the Jeffersonian Republicans (who favored a more decentralized national government) came into being and contested elections largely in a two-party system until the dissolution of the Federalist Party in the 1820's.

This initial party system, made up of the Federalists and the Jeffersonian-Republicans, collapsed because the Federalists split internally over issues of personality and policy, and declining public support. The election of 1824 was quite unusual in that five viable candidates ran for president. In the election itself, Andrew Jackson led in both the popular vote and electoral vote but lacked enough electoral votes to gain election. Thus the election was thrown to the House of Representatives, where each state delegation cast one vote. In a choice between the top three finishers— Jackson, John Quincy Adams, and Henry Clay—the House selected Adams, who had won Clay's endorsement. Adams became president and named Clay as his Secretary of State, thus enraging Jackson. This election created a violent split in the Jeffersonian-Republican party between the supporters of Jackson and the supporters of Adams. By 1828, Jackson's support for a more democratic nomination process triumphed, as did his bid for the presidency.

The second party system, begun in 1828 with Jackson's win, saw competition between the Jacksonian Democrats and a new political party called the Whigs until the time just prior to the Civil War, when tensions were high regarding the institution of slavery. At this time, the new Republican Party was born and absorbed the Whigs. In its first election (in 1856) it advocated a policy that called for admission of the new state of Kansas as a free state and supported congressional authority over slavery in the territories. Thus, the new Republican Party was largely an antislavery party. In 1860, the Republicans nominated the winning Abraham Lincoln for president. The Republican Party emerged after the Civil War as the dominant party and remained so until Democrat Franklin Roosevelt's election in 1932.

In the midst of the Great Depression came the election of 1932, and the Republicans nominated incumbent Herbert Hoover for president. The Democratic Party, still the minority party, nominated Franklin Roosevelt. The American people largely blamed Hoover and the Republicans for the Depression, so they elected Roosevelt and put their faith in the Democratic Party to affect change.

The coalition of people who elected Roosevelt in 1932 was substantially the same coalition that elected Democrats to high office through the 1960's, and perhaps somewhat longer. Sometimes called the New Deal Coalition, after Roosevelt's New Deal program, this collection of urban workers, blacks, Jews, intelligentsia, and ethnic Americans, coupled with the traditionally Democratic South, dominated the American political system for many years. Considerable debate has taken place over whether the New Deal coalition fractured in the 1970's, thus setting the stage for (or actually creating) another partisan realignment. Perhaps the main difference was that by the 1970's, and certainly by the 1980's and 1990's, most voters were viewing candidates as individuals rather than as representatives of political parties.

After the 1960's, fewer voters cast their votes along straight party lines, and more frequently split their votes between the parties. In addition, around this same time, the mass media became very important in the nominations, campaigns, and elections of candidates to the highest offices. New campaign technology, revolving largely around television, but also strongly influenced by sophisticated polling and direct mail solicitations, moved politicians away from the parties and toward more candidate-centered campaigns.

Applications

One of the chief purposes of political parties is the selection of candidates and the contesting of elections. Since 1952, there have been numerous significant and often interrelated changes in the nomination and election processes.

The years between the 1890's and 1950's were a transition period from party domination of nominations and campaigns to a more candidate-centered process. The Populists and Progressives of the late nineteenth and early twentieth centuries helped weaken the role of political parties by pushing for changes such as the direct primary, the direct election of senators, and the secret ballot. The development of radio and then television enabled voters to hear and then see political information from nonparty sources. The spread of the automobile and a more mobile American society weakened ties to local party organizations. These changes allowed the creation of the first candidate-centered campaigns—campaigns not necessarily sanctioned or aided by the political parties.

Presidental campaigns were the first to be altered by the new technology. Because presidential campaigns cover a wider constituency, command greater financial resources, and present the biggest prize, they were the first to adopt newer forms of campaigning; lower-level campaigns then followed. The decades after the 1950's saw the lessening of the role of political parties in most campaigns and the rise of candidate-centered campaigns run by professional consultants. Significantly, the use of professional consultants and advisers and new technologies required ever-greater sums of money.

From the 1950's to 1980's, the number of people identifying themselves strongly with a particular political party declined 10 percent, while those refusing any political label increased 15 percent. There was also an increasing number of split-ticket voters. From the 1970's on, at least two-thirds of Democrats and independents and one-half of Republicans split their votes for various candidates between the two major parties. Thus, party identification faded as a strong determinant of the voting choice of many citizens. At about the same time, new technologies such as television and the use of sophisticated computers for public opinion polling became widely accessible.

The confluence of television and presidential campaigns began in the 1952 election in which Republican Dwight Eisenhower ran against Democrat Adlai Stevenson. While the Democrats paid very little attention to the new technology of television, the Republicans had already discovered its power in the forms of commercial advertising. Thus, the Republicans created a detailed marketing strategy for Eisenhower which made use of television. Democrats, on the other hand, saw television as an extension of the stump speech, dedicating 96 percent of their television time to traditional speeches. Republicans spent $1.5 million on political spot advertising—the first televised political commercials. A new form of campaigning was born.

Thus, mass media replaced the political parties as the primary link between the candidates and the voters. Party organizations could no longer guarantee delivery of the vote and thus almost withered away at the local (ward or precinct) level. Candidates could bypass the parties and take their case directly to the people. The political consultants hired by the candidates were interested not in informing the public about the policy concerns of the day but in selling the candidates by creating a positive image of the candidate (and a negative image of the opponent) in the minds of the voters.

With this new reliance on television to sell the candidate came an increased need for vast sums of money to finance it. This need, coupled with the ability to circumvent party leaders and go directly to the people via television, increased candidates' reliance on special interests to fund their campaigns and decreased the need to have solid party backing to run for office. Thus, the modern candidate must be a successful fund-raiser. In the past, politicians had to work their way up through the party organization, but since the advent of television campaigning, politicians need only target and attract votes using specialized and expensive polling and advertising.

The technologies that are now used to such a great extent in political campaigns are very expensive. The average candidate spends roughly 50 percent of his or her time raising money, and then spends about 50 percent of the money on political spot advertising. Thus, the costs associated with running for elected office, especially for the U.S. Congress, are extraordinary and increasing at a fast rate.

In 1984, incumbents running for re-election to the U.S. House of Representatives spent an average of $276,000, a 388 percent increase over 1974. Some candidates spent far more. Challengers rarely have the financial resources to compete in the same spending league as the incumbents. On average, challengers to the House of Representatives spent $119,000 in 1984. In this election, only three (out of 144) challengers defeated incumbents; in 1990, as in most years, 96 percent of the incumbents were re-elected to the U.S. House. The near inability of challengers to defeat incumbents is attributable in large part to the extraordinary sums of money needed to fund campaigns. Incumbents have far greater success in raising the necessary funds. This disparity in funding levels of campaigns and in outcomes has led some to argue that Congress is being bought by the highest bidders or that Congress is beholden to the special interest groups that provide such a large portion of its campaign funds. The chief reason that so much money is collected and spent is the changed nature of campaigning—its reliance on television and other technologies.

Context

The decline of political party organizations occurred simultaneously with the decline of party identification and the increasing irrelevance of the parties to many voters. Traditionally, political scientists spoke of three factors as composing one's vote choice: party identification, candidate image, and political issues. Since the age of television began, candidate image became more important, so that by the 1970's, candidate image was the single most important factor in most voters' choices.

Some argue that this portends a dissolution of the political parties in the United States, a dealignment from political parties. In this analysis, parties are said to be of declining importance because of weakening party loyalties and the destruction of party organizations. This view was especially popular in the 1970's and very early 1980's. Popularized by William Crotty and Gary Jacobson in their book *American Parties in Decline* (1980), this thesis asserts that political parties are dying institutions that no longer command the loyalty of the electorate. The parties, they argued, are weak as well as financially bankrupt.

Others have seen a rejuvenation of the political parties. Led by the Republican Party, the parties began efforts to strengthen their role in elections. By the late 1980's, both parties were providing services such as surveys, data processing, and campaign schools; they even began to advertise on their own behalf.

Republican efforts started in 1977 in an attempt to rebuild a party seriously damaged by Watergate and the presidential defeat in 1976. The party established a direct-mail fund-raising program to bring in small donations from a large number of individuals. Success with that program allowed the party to provide many useful services to Republican candidates. By 1980, a stronger Republican Party emerged. The Democratic Party saw what the Republicans were doing and began to emulate it, although it was not until the middle to late 1980's that the Democrats began to raise large sums of money and put the funds to use to serve Democratic candidates. These activities have helped both parties become more powerful players in campaigns and elections; however, whether these services and tactics will truly rejuvenate the parties is the focus of some debate. Some observers believe that truly rejuvenated local parties are necessary before the parties can regain a larger share of influence in the process of campaigning.

Bibliography

Diamond, Edwin, and Stephen Bates. *The Spot: The Rise of Political Advertising on Television.* 3d ed. Cambridge, Mass.: MIT Press, 1992. This is a classic study of political commercials, recounting the rise of the political spot from the early 1950's. The authors examine the impact of the spot ad on voter's decisions. Also included is a detailed examination of the role of spot ads in the 1988 presidential campaign.

Jamieson, Kathleen Hall. *Packaging the Presidency: A History and Criticism of Presidential Campaign Advertising.* New York: Oxford University Press, 1984. Interesting and clearly written, this book examines in detail the role of all forms of presidential campaign advertising from 1952 through 1980. Includes some photographs.

McCubbins, Matthew D., ed. *Under the Watchful Eye: Managing Presidential Campaigns in the Television Era.* Washington, D.C.: Congressional Quarterly Press, 1992. This collection of essays deals with the role of television in presidential elections. Particularly useful is the chapter by Matthew McCubbins on "Party

Decline and Presidential Campaigns in the Television Age."

McGinniss, Joe. *The Selling of the President, 1968.* New York: Pocket Books, 1970. This is a landmark study of Richard Nixon's first successful campaign for president. Exceptionally well written and very interesting. The author, a journalist, takes the reader into the heart of Nixon's campaign. The book is a classic in the study of the history of political advertising.

Maisel, L. Sandy. *Parties and Elections in America: The Electoral Process.* 2d ed. New York: McGraw-Hill, 1993. This work is one of the best comprehensive undergraduate textbooks on American political parties and the electoral process. This lengthy volume includes many useful tables and charts. It is interesting and well written.

Nimmo, Dan, and James E. Combs. *Mediated Political Realities.* 2d ed. White Plains, N.Y.: Longman, 1990. This book examines the role of television, radio, newspapers, film, and magazines in popular culture and politics. Particularly useful is chapter 2, which deals with presidential campaigns.

Patterson, Thomas E. *The Mass Media Election: How Americans Choose Their President.* New York: Praeger, 1980. A comprehensive examination of election news coverage and its impact on voters. It examines the mass media election and how people respond to it. The book is based on a major panel survey conducted before, during, and after the 1976 election.

Rubin, Bernard. *Political Television.* Belmont, Calif.: Wadsworth, 1967. An early examination of the role of television in politics. Particularly useful is its detailed examination of the 1960 election between John Kennedy and Richard Nixon.

Sorauf, Frank J., and Paul Allen Beck. *Party Politics in America.* 6th ed. Glenview, Ill.: Scott, Foresman, 1988. A classic work on American political parties. This work covers topics such as party organization, the party as an electorate, political parties in the electoral process, the party in government, and the role and theory of political parties.

Lisa Langenbach

Cross-References

Democracy and Democratic Governments, 483; Political Action Committees and Special Interest Groups, 1387; Political Influence by Religious Groups, 1394; Political Machines and Bosses, 1400; Political Socialization, 1407; Political Sociology, 1414; Power: The Pluralistic Model, 1484; The Power Elite, 1491.

PATRIARCHY VERSUS MATRIARCHY

Type of sociology: Sex and gender
Field of study: Basic concepts of social stratification

Considerable controversy surrounds the concepts of patriarchy and matriarchy. Mainstream social science once generally accepted the universality of male domination throughout human history. Theorists often appealed to biological determinism, arguing that patriarchal social institutions were fundamentally rooted in the species. A longstanding, dissident view, however, argues that matriarchy historically preceded patriarchy. Many contemporary theorists now question the universality of patriarchy.

Principal terms

COLONIALISM: a geopolitical phenomenon in which one nation's power is imposed upon foreign territories, typically for the political, economic, and/or military benefits of the colonizer

ETHNOCENTRISM: the tendency to view one's own culture as universal and essentially superior, promoting a view of other cultural practices as inferior, incompletely developed, or pathological

MATRIARCHY: an institutionalized system of female dominance that is thought by some theorists to have characterized early periods of human history

MATRILINEAL DESCENT GROUPS: a form of kinship structure in which family ties are organized around females, with all children becoming members of their mother's descent group

MATRILOCALITY: often associated with primitive agricultural societies, matrilocality refers to family residence patterns revolving around matrilineal kinship groups, including women, their unmarried sons, daughters, and sons-in-law

PATRIARCHY: an institutionalized system of male dominance that is expressed in social practices and corresponding social ideologies

PATRILINEAL DESCENT GROUPS: a form of kinship structure in which family ties are organized with respect to males, making all children members of their father's descent group

PATRILOCALITY: a family residential pattern that revolves around the male who lives with his wife, his unmarried daughters, and his sons and their wives and children

SOCIALIZATION: a social process through which humans learn the norms that prevail in their society and systematically internalize them as a guide to their own behavior

SOCIOBIOLOGY: a scientific attempt to explain social-level phenomena in terms of biological variables; this approach is frequently criticized by the social scientific mainstream as analytically flawed

Overview

The concept of patriarchy refers to the institutionalized domination of women by men. Virtually every society in the present epoch exhibits patriarchal forms of social organization. As a pervasive and readily observable form of social stratification, patriarchy can be expressed in a variety of ways, depending upon the larger social structure in which it is situated. Whether it is tied to the ownership of property, access to political power, or the acquisition of social status, patriarchy directly affects the relative opportunities of men and women to acquire social rewards.

Matriarchy as a scientific concept refers to a social setting in which women exert a pervasive dominance over men. Various anthropological conceptions of matriarchy have envisioned a social system in which females exert primary decision making over family relations, with influence over the familial descent being traced exclusively through the maternal line, taking on the name of the maternal clan (matrilineality). In this system, males take up residence at the homestead of the female spouse (matrilocality). These kinship characteristics form the basis of a pervasive female dominance that permeates all other social institutions of the matriarchal society.

A longstanding tradition in the social sciences argues that matriarchy was the first form of social stratification. Numerous ethnographic studies of indigenous cultures reveal female-centered aspects such as myths and religious beliefs as well as matrilineal patterns of kinship and matrilocal family residence patterns. Such practices are viewed by some theorists as the cultural remains of full-fledged, matriarchal societies that preceded these indigenous cultures.

Traditionally, however, most social scientists have assumed patriarchy to be universal throughout human history. A widely shared view is that all societies were more or less patriarchal, differing only in terms of the extent to which gender stratification had become fully developed. In fact, many scientists argue that matriarchy is little more than a myth created by those who are resentful of patriarchy. Citing studies from biology and even psychology, some go so far as to argue that patriarchy is universally rooted in the "natural" condition of the species. The recent development of sociobiology has, in its most extreme expressions, attempted to explain the alleged universality of specific human behaviors that typify patriarchy by reference to genetic origins.

Contemporary theorists have generally become critical of these extreme positions, arguing that the social sciences have failed to investigate adequately the supposed universality of patriarchy. Among these are numerous radical theorists who have proved to be particularly receptive to theories of matriarchy. Many Marxist social theorists, for example, have argued that a matriarchal era was part of early human history, just as a "primitive communist" or nonstratified era characterized an even earlier epoch.

Marxists maintain that a pervasive ethnocentrism among social scientists has largely prevented a serious consideration of the available evidence concerning the matriarchal era. This ethnocentrism takes the form of "projecting" Western, patriarchal relations of power and authority upon qualitatively different social relations that characterize the so-called "primitive" or indigenous societies. Consequently, the ethnocentric bias serves to justify patriarchy ideologically, making institutionalized male domination, like class society itself, appear to be an inevitable or "natural" part of human society. Some versions of radical feminist theory likewise argue that matriarchy once existed. Feminists who promote such views, however, assert that it is erroneous to view matriarchal societies simply as a "female version" of patriarchy. Rather, matriarchal systems are seen as more egalitarian and less alienated from nature, with greater respect for ecological integrity and social harmony. In such a view, a return to a matriarchal society would constitute the most desirable alternative for the future of humanity.

Still other theorists argue that both matriarchy and patriarchy are forms of exploitative societies. In their view, however, egalitarian societies also once existed that conformed to neither variety of domination. This idea lends support to the possibility of creating a future society that is free of gender-based domination. This latter position forms part of a perspective that is most commonly promoted by socialist theorists.

Applications

The debates that surround patriarchy and matriarchy frequently rage over the historical universality of male dominance, the social causes of patriarchy, and the potential for a nonpatriarchal future. Many radical social theorists are inclined to accept theories of an ancient matriarchy, because to do so is to reaffirm the tremendous malleability of human nature and the historically particular aspects of patriarchal systems. Conservative theorists, in contrast, are unyielding in their defense of the universality of patriarchy. They contend that the earliest social institutions, like those of modern societies, are rooted in certain fixed, "natural" characteristics of the species; for example, the superior strength of males, the maternal instinct, and so forth.

Illustrative of those who support the universal patriarchy thesis is Steven Goldberg, who, in *The Inevitability of Patriarchy* (1973), argues that male dominance is physiologically based in the hormonal structure of human beings. From Goldberg's perspective, socialization simply expresses, rather than creates, the traits of male aggression and female nurturance. This sociobiological view directly contradicts the views of cultural anthropologists such as Margaret Mead, who argues in *Sex and Temperament in Three Primitive Societies* (1963) that socialization is the source of gender-based traits. Mead shows how differing gender identities observed within distinct societies are so markedly diverse as to defy any possibility of a biologically determined sexual identity. Gender identities are instead seen as the product of lifelong socialization processes in which humans are taught the "proper" way to behave in accordance with their socially defined gender status.

More sophisticated analyses have attempted to frame the debate concerning the universality of patriarchy in the context of larger social and historical processes. One such study, done by Eleanor Burke Leacock (*Myths of Male Dominance*, 1981), demonstrates the pervasive influence that colonialism had upon the rise of patriarchy among certain indigenous peoples. Leacock focused upon the Montagnais-Naskapi, an Inuit (Eskimo) people of the Labrador Peninsula in what is today part of Canada. She uses a variety of sources of data, including archival records from the seventeenth century collected by French explorers and French Jesuit missionaries, to show that prior to colonization, the hunting, fishing, and gathering culture of the Montagnais-Naskapi was basically egalitarian. The small amount of gender inequality that did exist appears to have been to the advantage of women, as is indicated by their matrilocal residential patterns. All accounts point to the prominent role that women played in decision making prior to the consolidation of French colonial control.

During the course of the seventeenth century, the influx of the French fur trade into the area gradually undermined the preexisting social relations of the Inuits. The introduction of more advanced technologies and imported goods were accompanied by mandated changes in social organization. For example, only men were permitted to engage in official transactions with the French. At the same time, an ideological offensive was unleashed by Jesuit missionaries, who systematically worked to convert the Inuits to Christianity, extolling the moral superiority of patriarchal relations of exclusive monogamy, preaching the immorality of divorce, and promoting the establishment of absolute male authority within the family. All such values were previously unknown to the indigenous society and, in many cases, they provoked a concerted resistance on the part of the Inuits. Leacock ultimately chronicles how all these economic and ideological changes mutually reinforced one another, creating a rapid process of social change that, in less than a century, led to the imposition of patriarchal relations that mimicked the normative values of the colonizer.

The empirical evidence of nonpatriarchal societies in the precolonial context contradicts the notion of universal male dominance. In such societies, decision making was essentially collective and widely dispersed. Under colonialism, the intrusion of commodity relations resulted in the creation of the nuclear family and the progressive separation of the "public" and "private" spheres of everyday life. Just as women become excluded from a public sphere dominated by patriarchal, colonial authority, the once-strong presence of the tribal collectivity gradually withered until it disappeared in all but its ceremonial forms. The striking change that occurs during the colonial period, therefore, is the marked decline in the status of women relative to men. Colonialism consciously and explicitly allocated formal public authority to men, a process that was reinforced by the patriarchal ideology that was being propagated by Christian missionaries. Evidence from other studies suggests that this process also took place in Africa and elsewhere where European colonialism was imposed.

Context

One of the earliest expressions of matriarchy was made by J. J. Bachofen in *Das Mutterrecht* (1861), or *The Mother-Right*. Bachofen argued that one's paternity was not generally known in primitive, nonmonogamous cultures, and hence the observance of "mother-right"—that is, the belief in the apparently magical powers of the woman to give birth—led to the formation of kinship clans based on one's relationship with the known mother. Prior to Bachofen, evidence of matriarchal practices within indigenous societies was interpreted to signify aberrant cultures that were doomed to extinction.

The publication of L. H. Morgan's *Ancient Society* (1877) offered a more comprehensive theory, which viewed the early development of matriarchies as a "normal" stage in the orderly evolution of human societies. Morgan's work was bolstered by his direct contact with Iroquois Indians, whose agricultural working units were based on maternal lineage. Since Iroquois society was dominated by agricultural activity, the matrilineal clan was of the highest social importance, and it was not until Western cultural contact occurred that the shift to patrilineality was effected. Morgan came to realize that once exposure to European colonizers took place under highly unequal terms, it elevated the importance of those activities that were controlled by men. This in turn caused a relative devaluation of the role of women, paving the way for a transition to patriarchy.

While Morgan's work emphasized the great technological discoveries or "inventions" that marked humanity's climb into civilization, he successfully wove the hypothetical existence of prehistoric matriarchies into his larger scheme of unilinear evolution. Unfortunately, once evolutionary theories declined in popularity among anthropologists, who increasingly favored more particularistic approaches, Morgan's assertions concerning matriarchies suffered a similar fate.

The work of Friedrich Engels and other Marxists breathed new life into matriarchal theories, because the Marxists critically accepted Morgan's view, reinterpreting it in their system of historical materialism. Engels' *The Origin of the Family, Private Property, and the State* (1884) asserted that the overthrow of mother-right was the "world historical defeat of the female sex," in which women were progressively reduced to instruments of economic production (and biological reproduction) in societies based on private property. Yet Engels further argued that patriarchal domination could itself be overthrown with the abolition of capitalist private property, the socialization of industry, and the eradication of the coercive family structure that is ruled by men.

Robert Briffault's *The Mothers* (1927) clarified the need for theorists to see primitive matriarchies in terms distinct from modern patriarchies, not because women did not rule, but because the nature of their domination was qualitatively different in societies without private property. Margaret Mead's classic *Sex and Temperament in Three Primitive Societies* (1935) further popularized the debate concerning gender-based stratification by arguing that sex roles are socially produced rather than biologically rooted.

The lasting significance of Mead's work rests in her explanation of gender-based differentiation in terms of culturally organized processes of socialization, a conceptual plateau that is tolerant of conscious social reform. Perhaps for this reason, her work has been relentlessly scrutinized and criticized by conservative social scientists ever since its initial publication. Part of this backlash dovetailed with the growth in popularity of sociobiology in the 1970's. Certain advances in genetic research during that decade encouraged new allegations to be made in favor of the biological determination of gender relations. Since then, the polemical dispute between sociobiology and cultural anthropology has remained intense, with each side seeking to establish its scientific jurisdiction over gender differentiation, a phenomenon that ultimately makes matriarchy or patriarchy possible.

Bibliography

Briffault, Robert. *The Mothers: The Matriarchal Theory of Social Origins.* Abridged ed. New York: Macmillan, 1931. A classic treatise, first published in 1927, that argues that a primitive matriarchy preceded modern patriarchy. The author argues that matriarchy gave way to patriarchy in conjunction with the shift from primitive hunting and gathering systems to more advanced forms of agricultural production.

Eisenstein, Zillah R., ed. *Capitalist Patriarchy and the Case for Socialist Feminism.* New York: Monthly Review Press, 1979. A very useful collection of essays that explore the relationship between patriarchy and capitalism. Attention throughout is given to the role that feminism can play in understanding and resisting patriarchal oppression. The authors share the belief that women's equality is tied to the struggle for socialism.

Engels, Friedrich. *The Origin of the Family, Private Property, and the State, in the Light of the Researches of Lewis H. Morgan.* New York: International Publishers, 1972. A classical Marxist study of the family. Engels reinterprets L. H. Morgan's theory of matriarchy through a dialectical materialist framework in which the transition to patriarchy is decisively tied to the rise of private property.

Goldberg, Steven. *The Inevitability of Patriarchy.* New York: William Morrow, 1973. The author's sociobiological approach views patriarchy as the expression of inherent traits that are rooted in the human species. Males are seen as dominant because of their hormonal predisposition to be aggressive, while females are seen as nurturing and passive because of their hormonal makeup. Sociobiological views such as Goldberg's have been widely discredited in the social sciences because of their ahistorical and uncritical posture toward the countervailing, anthropological evidence.

Leacock, Eleanor Burke. *Myths of Male Dominance: Collected Articles on Women Cross-Culturally.* New York: Monthly Review Press, 1981. In this important and highly readable series of essays, a contemporary anthropologist critically evaluates the various theories of matriarchy and patriarchy. She argues throughout that the notion of male domination as a universal phenomenon, thought to be rooted in biological or psychological structures, is in reality a cultural myth. Her principal contribution is to show how colonialism spread European patriarchal systems to North American Inuits (Eskimos), displacing the indigenous, matriarchal structures that were once prevalent.

Mead, Margaret. *Sex and Temperament in Three Primitive Societies.* New York: William Morrow, 1963. This classic study by a renowned anthropologist serves to critique those who root gender-specific behaviors in the biological constitutions of men and women. Her support of cultural socialization theories of gender identity inspired many subsequent theorists to question biological theories of gender differentiation and patriarchy.

Morgan, Lewis Henry. *Ancient Society: Or, Researches in the Lines of Human Progress from Savagery, through Barbarism to Civilization*. Chicago: Charles H. Kerr, 1877. One of the most famous statements of the evolutionary anthropological approach to the origins of humanity, Morgan's book postulates a materialist analysis that argues that the human species gradually worked its way up out of savagery, through barbarism, and into civilization. The earliest stages of kinship formation are viewed as female-dominated by Morgan, giving rise to the theory that all human cultures may have once been matriarchal.

Reed, Evelyn. *Woman's Evolution from Matriarchal Clan to Patriarchal Family*. New York: Pathfinder Press, 1975. Written by a noted socialist theorist, this book continues the tradition pioneered by Lewis H. Morgan and Robert Briffault in arguing that primitive, matriarchal clans were the original form of social kinship. Reed's thesis is that the incest taboo, which is widely seen as the basis for social kinship, actually emerged out of a female-imposed prohibition on cannibalism.

Zaretsky, Eli. *Capitalism, the Family, and Personal Life*. Rev. ed. New York: Harper & Row, 1986. A widely read study of the relationship between patriarchy and capitalism. The author explains how the development of capitalism led to the separation of the "private" and "public" spheres of social life, leading to the decline of women's power and status within industrialized capitalist societies.

Richard A. Dello Buono

Cross-References

Communal Societies, 297; The Family: Functionalist versus Conflict Theory Views, 739; Gender Inequality: Analysis and Overview, 820; Gender Inequality: Biological Determinist Views, 826; Gender Socialization, 833; Inheritance Systems, 989; Residence Patterns, 1635; Social Change: Evolutionary and Cyclical Theories, 1773; The Women's Movement, 2196.

PERSONALITY: AFFECTIVE, COGNITIVE, AND BEHAVIORAL COMPONENTS

Type of sociology: Socialization and social interaction
Field of study: Development, personality, and socialization

Personality is the individual's relatively distinct and consistent manner of perceiving, thinking, feeling, and behaving. This pattern of existence is sometimes used to infer the fundamental essence of the individual functioning in the physical, psychological, and social worlds.

Principal terms

AFFECT: emotion; the term denotes emotion as distinct from behavioral or physiological effects and emphasizes the fact that affect can be rated according to valence (a positive or negative value) and intensity

BEHAVIOR: overt forms of action and doing that are observable and measurable

COGNITION: the processes through which sensations are transformed, reduced, elaborated, stored, recovered, and used; includes perception, thinking, forming and retrieving memories, and generating patterns of action

MOTIVATION: the reasons, intentions, or purposes behind psychological processes; motivation may include plans, strategies, and goals

SELF: one's essential nature, which provides one with direction and identity

SELF-CONCEPT: a set of cognitions or thoughts regarding the self

SELF-ESTEEM: the affective or emotional appraisal of value regarding the self

SOCIALIZATION: the process by which individuals learn and internalize the elements of their culture and through which the personality develops socially

UNCONSCIOUS: influences that may alter one's experiences and behavior, but of whose presence one is unaware

Overview

Personality refers to an individual's unique manner of perceiving, thinking, feeling, and behaving. Personality is held to be those nonphysical characteristics of the individual that are relatively distinct and consistent. Personality has been extensively investigated in the social sciences, primarily by psychologists. The personality is also of interest to sociologists, however, because although a personality is unique to an individual, it is strongly affected by social forces. People do not live in isolation; to a certain extent, individuals and their personalities are inextricably interwoven with the society in which they exist.

Personality research has generally centered on the investigation of how the self characteristically functions. Various researchers have developed and explored a number of theories of personality based on observations of characteristic patterns of psychological functioning known as personality types or patterns. Psychological functioning usually refers to perception, thinking, feeling, and behaving. The first two of these functions correspond to what is often termed the cognitive component of personality, while the third and fourth respectively correspond to the affective and behavioral components.

The cognitive personality components involve thinking, or cognition. Cognition may be either verbal or imagistic. It includes reasoning, logic, problem solving, decision making, and memory. Cognitive components process stimuli from the world outside the self (they may be either present or remembered stimuli) and extract information from them. They involve analyzing events mentally. Some psychologists consider perception to be an aspect of cognition.

Affective components include emotions such as joy, fear, surprise, sadness, disgust, anger, acceptance, and anticipation. These emotional experiences are noncognitive and nonbehavioral appraisals of the value of certain stimuli. These appraisals of stimuli have valence—they may be considered either positive or negative. Thus, one may refer to positive emotions (such as joy) or negative emotions (sadness). Emotions can also vary according to their intensity. To the extent that someone experiences a strong emotion, he or she characteristically responds either by approaching the stimulus or avoiding the stimulus. Based upon these functions, motivation can be viewed as an affective component. The study of motivation is concerned with why people are driven to do certain things; approach to and avoidance of stimuli are directly related to motivation in that they affect one's intentions, reasons, purposes, plans, and goals.

The behavioral component includes all physical actions that an individual makes; it is the "doing" component of personality. The behavioral component is always observable and measurable, whereas the cognitive and affective components are not observable except by the individual experiencing them. They are therefore measurable only through self-report and behavioral inference. The earliest studies of cognition and personality involved self-observation and self-report. As the twentieth century progressed, however, the trend was toward observation of behavior. The behaviorist school of psychology, dominant in the mid-twentieth century, held that the only valid scientific study of humans was the direct study of observable behavior—all else, it was argued, could only be conjecture. By the later decades of the century, however, the severe limitations of such an approach to studying the human mind and personality caused many researchers and theorists to move away from the strict behaviorist approach.

Personality patterns or types always involve all three components as well as the relatively distinctive ways that individuals combine them. Relatively speaking, no two individuals think alike, are identically motivated, or behave alike. An analogy could be drawn between the three personality components and the three primary colors. The personality itself would be the painting that is created in an artist's own distinctive style but that nevertheless is composed of subtle variations of the three primary components. Just as artists, although unique, may be grouped according to style (Impressionist, surrealist, abstract), so personalities have been grouped by social scientists and clinicians according to types, such as healthy (or "hardy") and pathological (for example, neurotic, psychotic, and narcissistic).

It is important that, in defining the components of personality and categorizing personality patterns and types, a central issue of personality is not overlooked. This is the fact that the most fundamental question of any personality theory has to do with the very nature of the self. The question of "who we are" as humans is not a simple one, and it tends to be resistant to strictly scientific inquiry. Attempting to answer this basic question requires the integration of the philosophical and the scientific approaches to psychology.

There are many referents to "self" in personality theories, such as "self-concept" and "self-esteem." Self-concept generally refers to how and what one thinks of oneself; self-esteem corresponds to how one feels about oneself—how one values oneself. Yet, although such definitions may be offered, they do not say what "self" is: To what do words such as "I" and "self" really refer? This fundamental issue in personality is often not explicitly stated, so one is left wondering what assumptions the theory in question might be making about human nature. A related problem is that of reductionism in the study of personality. Reductionism is the tendency to state that a complex phenomenon is nothing more than the sum of its perceived constituent parts. (For example, a mob could be viewed simply as a number of people "acting out"; love could be seen as a sociobiological drive that allows the human species to survive.) In personality theory, various forms of reductionism have stated that the self is nothing more than the physiological structures of the brain and body or that it consists only of the mind and its cognitive processes. Other theories maintain that humans are active agents that direct processes in life. The crucial point is that every personality theory makes assumptions, either implicitly or explicitly, about human nature that affect the theory's interpretation of personality.

Applications

Knowledge gained from the study of personality assists in understanding and predicting the social behavior of people. It also allows researchers to examine how socialization affects the development of personality. Socialization refers to the social development of the self; to social learning such as customs, conventions, and culture; and to experiences leading to an increased understanding and acceptance of others. Three areas in which evidence suggests that personality and socialization may be related are gender differences in personality, self-awareness of minority-group members, and the Type A personality pattern.

The differences between the two sexes, obvious anatomical differences aside, are relatively quite small when compared with the significant amount of overlap among individual members of both genders regarding a large number of psychological functions. The differences that have been observed in some studies are based on averages. Females generally seem to show more well-developed verbal abilities or verbal intelligence than men do, although no differences exist for overall intelligence. Males tend to exhibit more well-developed mathematical and spatial manipulation than females do. Females seem more likely to experience fear, anxiety, and timidity than males, and males have a tendency to experience greater anger in response to frustration.

According to many psychologists and sociologists, the causes of these observed differences (observations that are troubling to some and are not universally accepted) lie in the socialization process rather than in any innate differences between the sexes. It is not difficult to see that formal institutionalized education can reinforce conditions that lead to gender differences in verbal and mathematical abilities. For example, teachers who stereotypically expect males to be "smarter" in mathematics and expect females to excel in verbal tasks may unwittingly be reinforcing those possibilities by supplying greater attention and rewards for males in math class and for females in verbally oriented classes. If indeed gender differences are created in this way, then these differences are more reflective of social conditions than of "self" conditions. The positive aspect of this situation is that self-awareness or self-influence can lead both to changes in self and to social change.

Self-awareness has an important influence on personality development. If one thinks of oneself as an angry and aggressive person, for example, then one will think, feel, and act accordingly. At young ages, people's self-awareness (and therefore their self-influence) is less powerful than biological and social forces. In other words, before a person is old enough to be fully self-aware, social feedback has strong influences on the person's self-concept and level of self-esteem. Research in this area has suggested that there may be a tendency for minority individuals to display more self-rejection and experience lower self-esteem than nonminority individuals. (Research in this area is not without its problems, however, such as the production of results according to how questions are phrased by researchers or how questions are interpreted by subjects.) Exposed to prejudices, stereotypical thinking, and discriminatory practices, minority group members may experience a sense of self that is distorted and invalid. Negative self-concept and low self-esteem are channeled into negative and self-defeating behavior.

The Type A personality (or behavior) pattern is associated with an increased risk of developing coronary heart disease. It has been argued that this increased risk is attributable to the increased intensity and frequency of stress-related experiences that the Type A individual creates or finds. It has been suggested that the Type A person has trouble connnecting his or her level of self-accomplishment to an appropriate level of self-esteem. Since most individuals are motivated to experience high levels of self-esteem (to feel good about themselves), Type A individuals must perform and accomplish at high and constant levels. This leads to experiences of frustration, anger, cynicism, aggression, and a sense of "time urgency" that leads to rushing to get things accomplished and ultimately to low self-esteem.

Through therapy and counseling, the Type A person may change behaviorally, becoming less time urgent and learning progressive muscle relaxation, may change cognitively, focusing less on time and accomplishment while reappraising frustrations or failures, and may change affectively by shifting perception to sources of high self-esteem that are not conditional. In these ways, the negative and potentially unhealthful aspects of the personality pattern may be adjusted.

Context

It can be argued that the study of personality goes back at least to the time of the Greek physician Hippocrates (460-377 B.C.E.), with his conception of four bodily fluids or humors—blood, black bile, yellow bile, and phlegm—accounting for the temperament of an individual. It can certainly be argued that conceptions of the self, couched in terms such as the "soul," were examined long before that. The move to the systematic study of self and personality by psychologists is often said to have been initiated by Wilhelm Wundt at the University of Leipzig in Germany. In 1879, he first began to formally explore conscious experience by introspection or self-examination. Although personality was not yet formally approached, the groundwork was being laid. In 1893, William James of Harvard University published the text *Psychology*, which, although it did not contain a chapter on personality, contained chapters on personality's component parts. Prominent chapters included "The Self," "Conception," "Memory," "Perception," "Reasoning," "Emotion," and "Will." About this time in Vienna, Sigmund Freud was developing a theory about conscious and unconscious mental processes. He discovered these processes while working with individuals troubled by emotional, anxiety-based problems. Personality became an area of systematic study in American universities in the mid-1930's.

From then to the present, a wide variety of theories and research areas in personality have been developed. The theories have often focused on one of the component parts of personality—for example, the cognitive models of George A. Kelly or Albert Ellis, the social learning model of Albert Bandura, the behavioral models of John Dollard and Neal E. Miller and those of B. F. Skinner, the biological or dispositional approach of Hans Eysenck or Gordon Allport, and finally the affective or motivational models of personality that also address the self, such as those of Abraham Maslow, Carl Rogers, and Victor Frankl.

These theories have all attempted to describe and explain the processes that account for personality. They have accounted for systems of therapy which have assisted countless individuals in times of personal suffering. The study of personality, particularly humanistic theories that focus on self-potential and the movement toward growth, has had a great impact upon institutionalized education. Studies of personality have also had an impact on social policy in general. The future of the study of personality lies, to a great extent, in the formulation of holistic theories that can do justice to affect, cognition, and behavior while recognizing the fundamental importance of the concept of the self.

Bibliography

Carson, Robert, and James Butcher. *Abnormal Psychology and Modern Life.* 9th ed. New York: Harper Collins, 1992. A well-written work on personality processes that become established as psychological disorders. All disorders are presented with descriptions of cognitive, affective, and behavioral symptoms.

Engler, Barbara. *Personality Theories: An Introduction.* 3d ed. Boston: Houghton Mifflin, 1991. A good introductory text that presents major theories in personality as well as some biographical information on the theorists. Presents information on philosophical assumptions that can be used as a way of evaluating different theories.

Hogan, Robert. *Personality Theory: The Personological Tradition.* Englewood Cliffs, N.J.: Prentice-Hall, 1976. A more advanced book on theories of personality, though still very accessible and readable. Material is presented regarding certain root ideas in personality which every theory needs to address; among them are socialization, motivation, and explanation.

James, William. *Psychology.* New York: Henry Holt, 1893. A very interesting introductory work in psychology of great historical significance. The early work of James, a founder of the discipline of psychology, is quite readable and interesting.

Pervin, Lawrence. *Current Controversies and Issues in Personality.* 2d ed. New York: John Wiley, 1984. A very good collection of essays examining the different issues, both philosophic and practical, which affect and are affected by personality theory. A good source for a more advanced and dynamic understanding of personality.

Tloczynski, Joseph. "Is the Self Essential?" *Perceptual and Motor Skills* 76 (June, 1993): 723-732. An examination of the concept of the self. A more advanced reading but one that is useful for understanding the concept for reductionism as well as the philosophical bases of personality theory.

Joseph Tloczynski

Cross-References

Cognitive Development: Piaget, 278; Interactionism, 1009; The Looking-Glass Self, 1099; Moral Development: Kohlberg, 1255; Moral Development: Piaget, 1262; Personality Development: Erikson, 1362; Personality Development: Freud, 1368.

PERSONALITY DEVELOPMENT: ERIKSON

Type of sociology: Socialization and social interaction
Field of study: Development, personality, and socialization

Erik Erikson's psychosocial theory proposes that personality development is a consequence of how well the individual successfully resolves life's crises that result from the new skills and possibilities that physical maturation brings and from the increasing societal demands placed on the maturing individual. In Erikson's theory, there are eight stages of personality development that unfold throughout the life span.

Principal terms
  CORE PATHOLOGY: a strong, negative resolution of a particular psychosocial crisis
  CRISIS: the normal set of strains and stresses that result from an individual's attempts to adjust to society's demands
  EPIGENETIC PRINCIPLE: the idea that growth unfolds according to a plan in which each aspect of that plan has its own special time of development and builds upon earlier developmental aspects to eventually form a functioning whole
  PSYCHOSOCIAL: the interaction between individual desires and abilities and societal expectations and demands
  RADIUS OF SIGNIFICANT RELATIONSHIPS: the normal realm of important social relationships that characterize each stage of development
  VIRTUE: a gain in character strength and personality maturity that results from successfully resolving a psychosocial crisis

Overview

Erik Erikson's psychosocial theory emphasizes the adjustment of the individual to his or her particular society. Erikson proposed that this adjustment process inevitably leads to conflicts between society and the person that each individual must work to overcome in order to develop a healthy personality. The personality becomes increasingly more complex as the person moves through a sequence of eight such conflicts or, in Eriksonian terminology, "crises" in each stage of development. The person will also expand the variety and depth of intimacy of his or her social relationships throughout these developmental stages. If an individual resolves a crisis in a more positive way (rarely will resolutions be completely positive or negative), then that person will increase his or her ability to function effectively in society and will be able to build on that virtue (character strength), increasing the likelihood of successfully resolving a future crisis. In contrast, negative resolutions will lead to the development of core pathologies that will impair both adaptation to society and the ability to resolve future crises successfully.

Erikson divides the entire life cycle into eight critical stages of development. The ages for each stage are approximate, although the sequence of these stages is seen to be the same for all cultures. These eight developmental stages will be briefly described, identified by the crisis that typifies that stage.

"Trust versus mistrust" (birth to one year) is Erikson's first psychosocial stage. In this stage, infants, if successfully resolving the crisis, learn to trust others and themselves. Trust develops from the dependability and consistency of the primary caregiver's (usually the mother) interactions with the infant.

"Autonomy versus shame and doubt" (one to three years) is the second psychosocial stage. Children become more independent physically and psychologically and are determined to assert that control over their behavior. If parents and/or other caregivers are harshly punitive in the inevitable clash of wills with the toddlers, a sense of shame and doubt in this newfound autonomy may result.

"Initiative versus guilt" (three to six years) is the third psychosocial stage, corresponding roughly to the remainder of the preschool years. Children use initiative—an active mental investigation of the world—and identification with their parents to develop a sense of who they are. Guilt may result if children engage in actions that bring strong disapproval from their parents (such as sexual play).

"Industry versus inferiority" (six to puberty) is the fourth developmental stage. Here teachers begin to play an important role. Children develop a sense of industry when they are able to master various skills (such as school work) and a sense of inferiority when they feel incompetent in relation to others. It is Erikson's belief that teachers have an important responsibility in fostering a child's sense of industry during this time of life.

"Identity versus identity confusion" (adolescence), the fifth stage of development, is the time in life when individuals are supposed to develop a strong sense of who they are as unique people. Lack of good role models may lead to a poorly formed sense of identity. The ability to choose a path in life and to resist roles forced on them by peers, parents, and other significant figures are crucial in the formation of adolescents' identities.

In "intimacy versus isolation" (young adulthood), Erikson's sixth psychosocial stage, the main developmental task is to form close, deep, and enduring relationships with others. Spouses, colleagues, and other partners in society are greatly influential in a person's life during this stage. Isolation results when an individual is unable to form intimate relations with others.

"Generativity versus stagnation" (middle adulthood), the seventh of Erikson's stages, is the time in life in which individuals are assuming important roles in the community. People may believe they are making worthwhile contributions to their families and community (generativity) or may feel as if their contributions are of little worth (stagnation). Caring about others, those close to you and those not so close to you, is what energizes the adult's generative concerns. Generativity is what provides for the continuity of society from one generation to the next generation.

"Integrity versus despair" (later adulthood) is the eighth and last of Erikson's psychosocial stages. In facing their own mortality, people can gain a sense of meaningfulness and wholeness in relation to their humanity (integrity) or look back on their lives with a sense of regret and gloom (despair). It is also the task of the older adult to look to the present and future for meaning in living. Personality development continues throughout the life cycle.

Applications

Erikson's psychosocial theory has stimulated researchers to investigate the numerous conclusions and implications of his ideas. Research has been particularly plentiful in regard to two of his most crucial psychosocial stages: trust versus mistrust and identity versus identity confusion.

During the first psychosocial stage of development, infants seek the warmth, nurturance, and comfort they receive from their parents, according to Erikson. As infants' needs are met through the consistent and dependable nurturing they receive, they develop a sense of confidence in getting their needs met as well as a sense that they are valued. Furthermore, a trusting relationship leads to greater faith in the future: An infant in a trusting relationship develops an increasing ability to delay gratification. Erikson proposed that the capacity to trust leads to the virtue of hope, giving the person the strength and determination to resolve future crises, particularly the ability to form deep, long-lasting relationships with others.

A number of studies have looked at the developmental consequences to infants who have strong feelings of doubt and fear—mistrust—in their earliest relationships. Mary Ainsworth demonstrated in 1979 that parental lack of responsiveness to an infant's crying can contribute to an insecure attachment relationship with the infant that will last far beyond the first year of life. Furthermore, some of her research found that mothers who were quick to respond to their infants' cries early in the first year of life had infants who cried less later in that first year. It appears, therefore, that early mistrust, stemming from lack of parental responsiveness, can contribute to maladaptive social interactions later in life.

Another factor that can contribute to a sense of mistrust is a high turnover rate among caregivers. Carollee Howes, in studies done in the 1980's, has documented not only the high caregiver turnover rate in both in-home and out-of-home day care but also the consequences of this inconsistency in caregiving. Howes found that the greater the changes infants and children experienced in daycare, the worse their adjustment to the first grade. Furthermore, she reported that low-quality day care was associated with low self-control, less task orientation, and more problems in peer interactions, particularly high levels of hostility, in early childhood.

Jay Belsky, in a series of studies published in the 1980's, concluded that the damaging effects of low-quality day care are most profound during the first year of life—Erikson's first psychosocial stage. Belsky says that research indicates that those infants less than one year old who receive more than twenty hours a week of day care are much less likely to develop secure relationships with their mothers. He argues that mothers are much more attentive to their baby's communication attempts than babysitters, and thus the probability of an infant's needs not being met is greater when the infant is in the care of a day care worker. Belsky has further linked "excessive" day care during the first year of life with greater emotional and behavioral problems in later childhood, including high levels of disobedience and aggressiveness.

Erikson's emphasis on the importance of the development of trust during the first year of life appears to be well-founded in the light of such research. Most research is also in agreement with Erikson's notion that the quest for identity formation is a key developmental task during adolescence. What occurs during this stage was seen by Erikson to have the greatest impact on the adult personality.

James Marcia has expanded Erikson's theory of identity development. Marcia has presented a theory proposing that adolescents resolve their identity crisis in four main ways, which he termed "identity statuses." "Identity diffusion" refers to people who have yet to explore meaningful identity options (no crisis) and show no personal investment in an identity. "Identity foreclosure" people also fail to experience an identity crisis, but they have a commitment to an identity. Unfortunately this commitment is not self-chosen; rather, the individual is simply living out the desires of significant people in his or her life. "Identity moratorium" is the status in which individuals are in the midst of an identity crisis. They have not yet made a commitment to an identity, but they are working toward that personal investment. The last status, "identity achieved," refers to people who have gone through an identity crisis and have developed a personal investment in an identity.

How adolescents resolve their identity search has been found to be closely linked to parenting styles. Marcia found that parents who are involved with their children's lives, setting limits but allowing adolescent input into those limits, are most likely to foster identity achievement in their children. Parents who set limits without adolescent input into those limits are most likely to engender identity foreclosure. Identity diffusion was seen to be the most likely result of permissive parenting, where adolescents received little guidance or discipline.

Erikson has also written about the importance of culture in identity development. He examined at length the task of minority youth in integrating into the mainstream culture while struggling to maintain their unique cultural identities. No matter what the minority culture may be, the availability of successful minority role models to the adolescent appears to be the crucial factor in the formation of a prosperous self-identity.

Another important factor in identity formation may be a difference in gender paths. Carol Gilligan has proposed that identity is more closely linked to independence and achievement in males, as opposed to relationships and strong affective bonds in females. Research has tended to support Gilligan's ideas in regard to identity, generally finding that female self-identity is strongly linked to a sense of caring and connectedness with others. Those females who wish to integrate motherhood and successful careers may have an especially complex task of establishing an identity, according to Gilligan.

Context

Born in Germany in 1902, Erik Erikson is one of the most intriguing figures in psychology. His biological father, whom he never met, was Christian, and his adoptive father was Jewish, causing him problems of acceptance in both Christian and Jewish circles. Upon graduation from high school he wandered around Europe, hoping to be an artist and seeking his own identity. (The name "Erikson" is Erik's creation; Homburger is his given surname.) Erikson eventually settled upon teaching as a career in 1927 in Vienna. It was there that he met Sigmund Freud, entered the Psychoanalytic (Freudian) Institute, began a personal analysis with Freud's daughter Anna, and was graduated in 1933 with training in both child and adult psychoanalysis.

With the cloud of Nazism lowering over Europe, Erikson and his family moved to the United States in 1933. That year he became Boston's first child psychoanalyst. In subsequent years Erikson held a diversity of positions, including posts at Harvard University, the Menninger Foundation, and the University of California at Berkeley, where, in 1950, he wrote *Childhood and Society*, his first significant book. His research studies have run the gamut from examining the child-rearing practices of the Sioux in South Dakota, to investigating the identity crises of adolescents in India, to studying combat crises of American soldiers in World War II. Erikson's breadth of cross-cultural experiences has placed him in a unique position to write about personality development throughout the life span.

Erikson accepted many of the basic concepts of Freudian theory, including the importance of the unconscious and much of the psychoanalytic methodology. While he did not intend for his psychosocial theory of development to replace Freud's theory, there are important differences between Erikson's and Freud's theories. Freud's theory stops with adulthood, whereas Erikson's theory extends into old age. Even more significant is the nature of the two theories: Freud emphasized the role of biology in development; Erikson underscored the importance of socialization—the interrelationship between individuals and their cultures. It also should be pointed out that while Freud's ideas were primarily based upon his experiences with patients in Vienna, Erikson's theory has a much broader cross-cultural appeal, given the remarkable range of settings that engaged the interests of Erikson.

Some of Erikson's most intriguing writings are found in his "psychohistories"— studies of historical figures using the methods of both historical analysis and psychoanalysis. Erikson's best-known studies are of Martin Luther, the religious reformer (published in 1958), and Mohandas (Mahatma) Gandhi (published in 1969), a book that won a Pulitzer Prize and the National Book Award in 1970. In these psychohistories Erikson emphasized the importance of examining a person's statements in the light of both the person's developmental stage and what was happening in the world around the person at that time. He also pointed out that psychohistorians must be particularly aware of the risk of projecting their own biases into their interpretations of the figures being studied.

Erikson is highly regarded in academic circles. His theory of development and concepts of identity formation and crisis are attractive to many sociologists and psychologists alike and seem destined to influence personality research and theory for many years to come. Erikson's keen observations, range of cultural experiences, and compassion for the human condition make him an enduring figure in the study of personality development.

Bibliography

Coles, Robert. *Erik H. Erikson: The Growth of His Work*. Boston: Little, Brown, 1970. Coles, a noted psychiatrist, presents a unique view of the life and work of Erikson from the perspective of a former student and colleague. Particularly notable is the reprinting of Erikson's letter of resignation from the University of California, Berkeley, stemming from Erikson's refusal to sign a loyalty oath.

Erikson, Erik H. *Gandhi's Truth on the Origins of Militant Nonviolence*. New York: W. W. Norton, 1969. This Pulitzer Prize-winning book is an outstanding psychohistorical analysis of the life of Mohandas Gandhi, the great Indian leader and reformer. The book was stimulated by Erikson's visit (for the purpose of giving a seminar on the life cycle) to Ahmedabad, India, the city of Gandhi's first ascent to prominence, where Erikson became acquainted with people who had known Gandhi.

_____. *In Search of Common Ground: Conversations with Erik H. Erikson and Huey P. Newton*. Introduced and edited by Kai T. Erikson. New York: W. W. Norton, 1973. Conversations between Erikson and Newton are recorded and edited by Erik Erikson's oldest son, a noted sociologist. The depth of both Erikson's insight into ethnic and minority concerns and his compassion for the human condition are revealed in this engaging book.

_____. *The Life Cycle Completed: A Review*. New York: W. W. Norton, 1982. In this book Erikson focuses his attention on the later stages of development. Highlighting the problems of adulthood and aging, he elaborates on the need for personal growth through the whole of the life cycle.

Newman, Barbara M., and Philip R. Newman. *Development Through Life: A Psychosocial Approach*. 5th ed. Pacific Grove, Calif.: Brooks/Cole, 1991. The authors present an introduction to developmental psychology that closely follows an expanded Eriksonian theoretical framework. The book is written in an accessible style appropriate for a high school or college level audience. A unique feature is the selection of many Picasso paintings and drawings to illustrate the text.

Paul J. Chara, Jr.

Cross-References

Cognitive Development: Piaget, 278; Interactionism, 1009; The Looking-Glass Self, 1099; Parenthood and Child-Rearing Practices, 1336; Personality: Affective, Cognitive, and Behavioral Components, 1356; Personality Development: Freud, 1368; Socialization: The Family, 1880.

PERSONALITY DEVELOPMENT: FREUD

Type of sociology: Socialization and social interaction
Field of study: Development, personality, and socialization

Sigmund Freud (1856-1939) is generally regarded as having proposed the first comprehensive theory of human behavior, a component of which addresses the processes of socialization and the development of the personality throughout childhood. One of Freud's major contributions is the notion that experiences in early childhood have a significant and lasting effect on the personality of the adult.

Principal terms

ANAL STAGE: the stage of psychosexual development in which the anus is the primary source of pleasurable sensations

EGO: the part of the personality that deals with reality, thus bridging the gap between the unconscious mind and the outside world

EROGENOUS ZONE: a part of the body that is capable of producing pleasurable sensations when touched

FIXATION: the process whereby a person remains at a particular psychosexual stage because of some inadequacy in the satisfaction of the needs specific to that stage

ID: the part of the personality that is the source of the basic instincts; the id exists within the unconscious mind

IDENTIFICATION: the process of taking on the characteristics of another person

OEDIPUS COMPLEX: an important event associated with the phallic stage, characterized by attraction to the parent of the opposite sex; sometimes called the "Electra complex" in girls

ORAL STAGE: the stage of psychosexual development in which activities associated with the mouth are the principal source of pleasure

PHALLIC STAGE: the stage of psychosexual development in which the genitals provide the main source of bodily pleasure

SUPEREGO: the "moral" part of the personality; contains the individual's conscience

Overview

Few if any scientific theories can match Sigmund Freud's "psychoanalytic theory" in terms of overall impact on thought in the Western world. This complicated explanation of human personality and behavior has contributed ideas and language that have become not only part of psychiatry, psychology, and the social sciences in general, but also part of everyday life. For example, Freud's most fundamental principle was his notion that the major determinants of human behavior lie outside conscious awareness. Today there are virtually no social or behavioral scientists who do not acknowledge the existence of the unconscious (in at least some form), and its role in influencing behavior has been embraced by popular culture as well.

Trained as a physician, Freud specialized in neurology. Early in his career he became fascinated by cases of hysteria, a condition in which physical symptoms (often severe, such as paralysis of a limb or loss of vision) occur without any underlying organic cause. On the basis of his work with hysteric patients, Freud concluded that this disorder results from unconscious psychological conflict that is expressed in bodily form. Freud found that he could often make the symptom disappear by encouraging the patient to talk freely about anything that might come to mind ("free associate"). These experiences with hysteria served as the impetus for the development of his theory of personality, with the role of the unconscious serving as its cornerstone. As his medical practice began to focus more and more on emotional disorders, Freud's theory evolved, and he further developed his techniques for exploring the unconscious mind.

Freud believed that the nature of the human mind is biologically determined and that its operation is governed by powerful instincts. There are two categories of these: the life instincts, such as the sex drive, which tend to sustain human beings and to promote the continued existence of the species; and the death instincts, such as aggression, which tend to be destructive. How these instincts are expressed is determined by the operation of three distinct parts of the personality. Each of these components represents a particular type of force operating within the personality. Freud's approach is often called a "psychodynamic" theory. The most basic of these is the id, the source of all the psychic energy that drives the personality. In other words, the instincts reside here; consequently, all needs spring from the id. A feeling of hunger, for example, would be prompted by the action of the id.

The id works completely within the realm of the unconscious mind and is incapable of making contact with the external world. A hungry person's id, therefore, can generate only an image of food; alone, it does not possess the ability to generate a strategy for actually satisfying the hunger. This is where the second component of the personality, the ego, is important.

The ego acts as a bridge between the unconscious mind and the outside world. Its job is to find a realistic way to satisfy the needs generated by the id. When the id prompts feelings of hunger, the ego leads the television-watcher who wants a snack to search through the refrigerator or causes the hungry automobile traveler to start noticing the billboards advertising restaurants that lie ahead at the next freeway exit. The id and ego often clash, however, because when the id "wants" something, it wants it immediately. Unable to appreciate the limitations imposed by reality, the id needs to be reminded, for example, that lunch must wait until the traveler gets to that next freeway exit where a restaurant can be found. The id is the only part of the personality present at birth; a baby's inability to delay gratification when he or she needs to eat or to eliminate thus provides a concrete illustration of the id at work. The ego, on the other hand, develops as a result of experience with the external world.

The third component of the personality, the superego, provides yet another basis for conflict. A major function of the superego, which emerges between the ages of three and five, is to act as the person's conscience. It appears as the child is socialized into the culture's value system, primarily by the parents. The hungry driver can again be used as an example. His id is making him hungry, and his ego finds a fast-food restaurant offering the double cheeseburger that will quiet his id. The superego may intervene, however, to remind him that he has vowed to eat nothing but salads for lunch until he loses a few pounds, and it has the ability to make him feel guilty if he breaks his promise.

Freud's theory proposes that conflict (which in turn leads to anxiety) is inevitable, since it is actually built into the structure of the personality. At best, the three components will be equal in strength, thus minimizing conflict. Since one of the most powerful instincts is the sex drive, and because a person is often taught strict rules governing sexual behavior, many psychological problems stem from an individual's sexuality. They often involve guilt, although the unconscious may disguise it in some way (such as hysteria). Much of Freud's work, then, deals in some way with sexuality; how that sexuality develops served as the framework for the application of his ideas to an analysis of personality development.

Applications

Freud believed that the power of the sex instinct makes it the driving force behind the development of the personality. It is important to remember that Freud conceptualized sexuality very broadly; his notion included the desire for sexual intercourse, but it also extended to other activities that support life, such as eating. Freud's work with his patients led him to conclude that their problems often stemmed from experiences they had had early in life, and this idea plays a major role in his theory of psychosexual development.

Psychosexual development takes place as the child progresses through a series of stages, the first three of which are especially important to the developing personality. In each of these stages a different part of the body is particularly sensitive to stimulation and serves as a strong source of pleasure for a limited period of time—to be replaced eventually by a different focus of bodily pleasure. The enjoyable sensations that surround these "erogenous zones" are the forerunners of adult sexuality.

The initial stage of development is the oral stage, in which the main activities of the infant are focused on the mouth. This stage lasts through the first year of life, a time in which nursing, biting, and then chewing dominate the infant's behavior. These behaviors satisfy the tensions generated by the oral needs, which are unique to this period of development. If these needs are not satisfied sufficiently or consistently, or if they are gratified excessively, the individual may become "fixated" in this stage. For example, a mother who nurses her baby unpredictably may create an oral fixation in the child, as might a mother who weans her baby too soon. Such a fixation has a direct impact on the individual's personality.

The second two years of life constitute the anal stage, in which the primary source of pleasure shifts to the anus. During this time the child's physical development allows him or her to gain control of the anal sphincter muscles, thus permitting toilet-training. The child becomes able to defecate voluntarily when the bowel is full, reducing the tension that has been created. The child eventually derives pleasure from this biological act. Fixation at this stage generally results from unsatisfactory experiences associated with toilet-training.

The third stage of psychosexual development, the phallic stage, spans ages three to six. Here the child discovers that manipulating his or her own genitals is pleasurable. Parents who shame or scold a child excessively for playing with the genitalia risk creating a phallic fixation in their child.

As suggested earlier, an oral, anal, or phallic fixation reveals itself in the particular personality characteristics of the adult. For example, an orally-fixated person who was nursed inadequately may try to compensate by overeating or smoking (both of which involve the mouth) as an adult. An adult with an anal fixation resulting from parents who used harsh punishment whenever the child "had an accident" during toilet-training might be disorganized or messy, traits that could be signs of rebellion against those parents. Finally, a man fixated in the phallic stage might be excessively concerned with proving his masculinity.

One particularly significant type of conflict must be dealt with at this stage of development, and successfully resolving this issue is critical to the development of the superego. Freud believed that during the phallic stage all children are sexually attracted to the parent of the opposite sex. The young boy thus sees his father as a rival and experiences anxiety over the possibility of retribution from him—especially because the father is more powerful. Freud referred to this situation as the Oedipus complex, and it is eventually resolved as the boy learns to repress his feelings for the mother; the boy instead begins to identify with the father. This process of identification leads the boy to take on some of the father's personality characteristics, including those that reflect morals, values, and rules that the superego can use to govern behavior.

In young girls this conflict is called the Electra complex, and Freud believed it to be somewhat more complicated than the Oedipus complex. (Some critics argue that Freud offered a less satisfactory explanation of these events in girls.) Nevertheless, the fundamental dynamics and the eventual outcome of the process for a girl parallel what happens with the boy: She must deal with her sexual feelings for the father, eventually repressing them and identifying with the mother. Freud believed that the differences between the Oedipus and Electra complexes lead the process of psychosexual development to produce stronger superegos in boys.

Following the phallic stage, sexual feelings disappear until about the age of twelve or so. Freud described this stage as a period of latency, and it is relatively uneventful from a psychosexual standpoint. When the person reaches puberty, the newly developed sexual maturity signals the beginning of the final stage of psychosexual development, the genital period, characterized by typical sexual desire for the opposite sex.

Context

Psychology had been in existence as a separate scientific discipline for only a few years when Freud began developing his ideas in the late 1800's, and psychoanalytic theory offered that field's first comprehensive statement on the operation of the human personality. As such, it served in a sense as a model for other personality theories that followed Freud's. Some later theorists in the psychoanalytic tradition suggested modifications of some basic Freudian notions (such as placing less emphasis on sexuality); other psychologists, with different theoretical perspectives, presented ideas that could be interpreted as direct challenges to Freud. In either case, Freud must be recognized as having done much to foster the development of this area of psychology.

Generally speaking, the different theoretical perspectives that emerged to address personality processes have almost always been linked to the treatment of psychological disorders, so Freud's work had a major impact on the development of the field of clinical psychology (and psychiatry) as well. Freud's ideas about personality evolved as he developed and refined psychoanalysis directly through his work with patients. Although his therapeutic techniques have fallen into disfavor in some circles, they are still practiced today and sometimes include "modernized" derivations of the more traditional psychoanalytic methods. Even many of the treatment strategies associated with other theoretical positions reflect a Freudian influence. More important, Freud removed much of the mystery surrounding mental disorders by suggesting that they are outgrowths of personality processes that exist in everyone. As a consequence, Freud played a vital role in revolutionizing the treatment of mental illness.

Some of Freud's ideas have become permanent fixtures in the social and behavioral sciences, destined to endure independently of psychoanalytic theory itself. Foremost among these is his belief that childhood experiences shape the personality of the adult. Given that virtually nobody disputes this notion today (even thinkers representing theoretical positions very different from psychoanalysis), it may be hard to accept that there was a time when this principle was not taken for granted; nevertheless, Freud was the first to make such a claim. Perhaps equally important is his contention that unconscious processes are a powerful force within the personality; as indicated earlier, almost all social and behavioral scientists now accept at least some variation of this basic theme. His other durable contributions include his views on the instincts that drive certain behaviors and his suggestion that sexual issues are central to human psychology.

Modern theorists and laypersons alike continue to be fascinated by the inner workings of the mind. Freud's influence can be detected in literature, art, music, humor, and everyday conversation in addition to the social sciences and psychiatry. In fact, the widespread nature of his impact might be his most impressive accomplishment.

Bibliography

Bootzin, Richard R., John Ross Acocella, and Lauren B. Alloy. *Abnormal Psychology: Current Perspectives.* New York: McGraw-Hill, 1993. Many textbooks in abnormal psychology, developmental psychology, human sexuality, and other areas contain (usually in no more than a few pages) accessible and reasonably complete discussions of basic Freudian theory. This text offers a very readable presentation that is especially thorough for this type of source.

Freud, Sigmund. *A General Introduction to Psycho-Analysis.* Translated by Joan Riviere. New York: Liveright, 1935. This volume comprises a series of lectures presented at the University of Vienna between 1915 and 1917. Intended for the layperson, the book is a good starting point for the reader desiring original material. There have been several translations of this work (also available as *Introductory Lectures on Psychoanalysis*).

Gay, Peter. *Freud: A Life for Our Time.* New York: W. W. Norton, 1988. Several biographies of Freud are interesting at least in part because they address controversies that have resulted from disagreements among Freud's biographers. This book, published more than three decades after the first biography, addresses some of the questions surrounding certain "facts" about his life. Contains some rare photographs.

_____, ed. *The Freud Reader.* New York: W. W. Norton, 1989. This volume of readings is a representative collection of Freud's writings on a broad range of topics. It includes some of Freud's famous case material as well as an excerpt from his autobiography. The editor provides an extended, useful introduction that establishes a cultural and historical context for the book.

Hall, Calvin S. *A Primer of Freudian Psychology.* 1954. Reprint. New York: Octagon Books, 1978. Written by a noted Freud scholar, this work stands as one of the most authoritative and frequently cited books about the theory of psychoanalysis. While this source may make challenging reading for some, it nevertheless remains a classic.

Hall, Calvin S., and Gardner Lindzey. *Theories of Personality.* 3d ed. New York: John Wiley & Sons, 1978. Textbooks on personality generally include entire chapters dealing with Freud, and this classic text contains one of the best. Recommended for the reader who is interested in a somewhat more complete presentation than would be found in an abnormal or developmental psychology text.

Jones, Ernest. *The Life and Work of Sigmund Freud.* 3 vols. New York: Basic Books, 1953-1957. Written by a well-known English psychoanalyst who was a colleague of Freud, this biography represents an "insider's" perspective. This impressive and detailed three-volume work is the so-called "authorized" biography, the contents of which were subject to the approval of Freud's family. It is standard material nevertheless.

Steve A. Nida

Cross-References

The Authoritarian Personality Theory of Racism, 159; Deviance: Biological and Psychological Explanations, 532; Gender Socialization, 833; Interactionism, 1009; Personality: Affective, Cognitive, and Behavioral Components, 1356; Personality Development: Erikson, 1362.

PLURALISM VERSUS ASSIMILATION

Type of sociology: Racial and ethnic relations
Field of study: Patterns and consequences of contact

American society comprises many groups—ethnic, racial, and religious—with distinctive heritages, values, languages, and lifestyles. This diversity brings both tensions and strengths to society. Pluralism promotes the maintenance of the separate identities of the groups, while assimilation stresses the merging of groups into a single, shared culture. The latter generally involves the adaptation by minorities of the culture of the society's dominant group.

Principal terms
BICULTURALISM: acknowledging joint allegiance to two cultures—in this context, to one's native culture and to the larger American society
BILINGUALISM: fluency in two languages, such as English and the language of one's heritage
ETHNIC GROUP: a set of people identifiable by their shared cultural background
ETHNOCENTRISM: the tendency to use one's own cultural background as a reference point for reacting to life's experiences and judging all other groups
ETHOS: the distinguishing character or set of beliefs of an ethnic group
LOBBY: a political pressure group working on behalf of a particular cause
MINORITY GROUP: a group of people that has less social or economic power than the dominant (majority) group

Overview

The Great Seal of the United States and several American coins carry the Latin motto *E pluribus unum,* or "One composed of many"—a social paradox that lies at the heart of the controversy over pluralism and assimilation.

These two terms represent contrasting views on the question of whether American society should perpetuate its diverse cultural and ethnic patterns or, rather, should blend homogeneously into a single culture with a common set of social practices. Those who favor pluralism want the distinctive features of the multiple social subgroups to flourish; those who favor assimilation think that all subgroups should move toward merger with the United States' traditional culture, which uses the English language and historically has been most heavily influenced by European—particularly British—social patterns. Pluralists fear that assimilation leads to a crushing social conformity, while assimilationists fear that pluralism leads to the social disintegration of the nation.

The terms used in this debate have many variants. Approximate synonyms for pluralism include "multiculturalism," "ethnicity," and "ethnocentrism." The term "segregation," though it carries many negative connotations because separateness was once legally enforced on African Americans, also describes extreme pluralism, since absolute pluralism would keep ethnic identities separate and intact. Hardly any theoretical academicians favor this extreme. In the twentieth century, however, some members of racial and ethnic subgroups fiercely defended their own social patterns and unique attributes, effectively accepting self-segregation as an ideal. The idea that blacks, for example, comprise a "separate nation" follows the Black Muslim teachings of Malcolm X.

Assimilation—also sometimes called "depluralization," "amalgamation," "acculturation," and "Americanization"—is nearly synonymous with what in the 1960's was promoted as social integration. This was a process by which minorities (especially African Americans) could move into the dominant culture and enjoy its socioeconomic advantages. The Civil Rights movement of the 1950's and 1960's, led by leaders such as Martin Luther King, Jr., had advocated assimilation as a means to achieve a just society that de-emphasized ethnic differences and removed class and racial barriers to progress. Most white liberals and social planners supported social integration. Yet by 1990 the various experiments (and many failures) at making it work—notably compulsory busing as a means of achieving educational assimilation—had created widespread skepticism that social unity could be achieved. Some observers had come to doubt that a single society with common customs was even a worthy goal. Meanwhile, the economic gap between middle-class white Americans and the poorer classes—containing high percentages of black and Hispanic people—had widened.

Through most of the nation's history, Americans have viewed their country as a cultural "melting pot," and a pattern of cultural assimilation has been taken for granted. Second-generation immigrants—often white Europeans—generally drifted away from their cultural heritages, learned English, and moved into the social and economic mainstream. The myth grew that the United States had an amalgamated culture. Beginning in the late 1960's and early 1970's, however, vocal minorities launched the "new ethnicity" movement to gain respect for their native cultures and ethnic identities and to question the traditional patterns of assimilation. Hispanic Americans joined in, as that group grew numerically in the Southwest and in many American cities. American Indians found leaders to voice their protests against the cultural majority. The black ethnocentrism of the 1970's had rediscovered the African heritage and promoted black pride. In 1977, Alex Haley's immensely popular book *Roots: An American Saga* (1976) was turned into a television miniseries; the book and series helped give African Americans a sense of collective identity—a shared story of suffering and survival to replace old cultural insecurities and negative images. By the late 1970's, many subgroups of Americans were vocal about expressing their own unique identities as well as their own grievances and political demands.

The traditional American ethos came under fire from feminists, gays, and other groups, including people with disabilities. They claimed that the dominant American culture had discriminated against them and had never let them assimilate; therefore, the way to meet their goals was to emphasize their differences. Increasing attention was paid to the idea that the American melting pot, rather than creating a unique society by melting many cultures into a new, synthesized culture, actually involved forcing other cultures to acculturate to the ways of the dominant culture, which was largely of Anglo descent. The term white Anglo-Saxon Protestant (WASP) became an increasingly pejorative tag. Among the political ramifications of this perception was the fact that the U.S. Congress was increasingly seen as a club of privileged white males that did not represent the American people. President Bill Clinton, after his 1992 election, vowed to make his administration "look like America," thereby acknowledging the popular appeal of social pluralism.

One clear irony of the movement toward pluralism in the late 1980's and 1990's was that, in the 1960's, assimilation had been essentially a liberal movement aimed at social reform. Yet by the early 1990's, the idea seemed conservative and, to many liberals, an outmoded idea. The new liberal position was to accept and respect ethnic and cultural diversity.

Applications

Pluralism and assimilation in their pure forms do not exist. They are concepts that represent opposite poles of people's thinking about an ideal society. Social reality exists somewhere between the two poles. Pluralism emphasizes the division of Americans into many groups according to various characteristics, such as ethnicity, and emphasizing diversity and separateness. Assimilation stresses the commonalities of Americans. Thus the pluralist focuses on the "many" in *E pluribus unum*, while the assimilationist focuses on the "one."

Many field studies by sociologists have studied the views of Americans toward pluralism and assimilation at given times and places. One 1990 study was carried out among working-class ethnic groups in Pontiac and Hamtramck, Michigan, by Wallace E. Lambert and Donald M. Taylor, social psychologists at McGill University. The study interviewed Polish Americans, Arab Americans, Albanian Americans, and African Americans, as well as middle-class whites with no distinctive non-Anglo traditions. Each group except the whites had its traditional culture and "heritage" language. (Linguists recognize characteristic features in "black English," the spoken dialect of some African Americans.) All these ethnic groups, including middle-class whites, expressed varying degrees of preference for pluralism over assimilation. The researchers thus concluded that "conventional wisdom about assimilation being a fundamental American ideal may be out of date or wrong." Significantly, all the ethnic groups in this survey wanted their children to become bicultural and bilingual, thus having what the parents regarded as the best of both worlds—the native culture and American society at large. Lambert and Taylor also monitored one pilot program in which a group of elementary schoolchildren received part of their instruction in English and part in Arabic, their heritage language. Post-tests showed that the bilingually educated students equaled or surpassed students who studied only in English.

Beginning in the 1970's, some ethnic groups in the United States pushed for bilingual education to meet the practical needs of their children. Some liberal educators even favored recognizing "black English" as a respectable academic medium, though most black parents thought their children needed to learn the language that was used by society at large. By 1990, the demand from blacks for their "right-to-language" was seldom heard, but cultural pluralism combined with an increase in the Hispanic population by then had had the effect of making some areas of the country (such as south Florida) effectively bilingual, with English and Spanish coexisting in the culture.

One troubling revelation in Lambert and Taylor's 1990 study in Michigan was that "competing ethnic prides" generated widespread intergroup prejudices, distrust, segregation, and social tension. In an earlier study (1981), Lambert had already supported what others had observed by documenting increasing racial and ethnic conflict in the United States, with "ethnic specificity," intergroup violence, "mutual distrust and suspicion, exaggerated ethnocentrism, and own-group isolation" being common features of the society.

Some positive practical effects of assimilation are illustrated by Gordon D. Morgan, a sociology professor at the University of Arkansas, who argued in 1981 for the "oneness of America." Morgan notes that by 1981 a significant group of African Americans had been able to move into the social and economic mainstream—often with government help, intervention, and support to overcome the "disability" of race—and had thereby made great gains for themselves. Government-supported social services such as better prenatal care and Head Start for youngsters had helped in the process, and considerable social equalization had occurred. Younger, more educated blacks especially were able to interact with whites and others in meaningful ways as they chose, Morgan maintained, and being black had lost much of its social stigma and all of its legal significance.

Context

Except for American Indians, the United States is a "nation of immigrants," so every American has a "first" culture demanding some degree of recognition. Thus, despite the "melting pot" myth, pluralism was not really new in 1970. African Americans had always been mostly segregated, because of white racist policies, and maintained their own social patterns. Forced onto reservations in the eighteenth and nineteenth centuries, American Indians had also held on to vestiges of their heritages. Neither of these groups had been able to participate in the American dream of upward mobility. American Jews, though often economically successful, had also faced discrimination and traditionally maintained a social separateness. Every large American city had its "Little Italy" or "Chinatown"; ethnic sections and suburbs had always existed, proliferating as new groups of immigrants such as Middle Easterners and Asian Indians settled in the country. Separate religious sects such as the Mennonites and the Amish had also refused assimilation. Though many other Americans paid only lip service to the "hyphenated" part of their self-definitions, a widespread sense of heritage persisted among large numbers of individuals.

As Joane Nagel, a sociologist at the University of Kansas, noted in 1993 in *The Chronicle of Higher Education*, "Ethnicity will never go away. It's constantly reinvented and revitalized. The idea of assimilation, of once and for all settling the race question, is very unlikely. Ethnicity has this dynamic quality." Corresponding with the rise of the "new ethnicity," a huge body of sociological writings on pluralism existed by the early 1990's. The academic contexts for this complex subject are not purely historical or sociological. Rather, the topic cuts across every feature of American life, with special relevance to education, religion, economics, business, health care, and politics.

James A. Crispino's study of Italian Americans, published in 1980, is instructive in showing that, despite the "new ethnicity" of the 1970's, this group continued to be assimilated. It seems likely that for white Europeans this pattern, which has always been the norm, may persist. More generally, as Lambert and Taylor noted in 1990, it appears that types of social assimilation that concurrently respect pluralism may be the most workable. Thus the confrontational either/or approach that is often taken can be misleading, since pluralism combined with assimilation will probably prove to be the future norm. In one sense, that combination has always been the true norm, though the United States has liked to stress its unity and ignore its problematic divisions.

The 1990 census showed a mosaic of racial and ethnic groups in the United States, with African Americans comprising 12 percent of the population; Hispanics, 9 percent; Asian Americans, nearly 3 percent; and American Indians, Eskimos (Inuits), and other native peoples, 0.8 percent. The projection is that by 2050, racial and ethnic subgroups will make up nearly half of the country's population. In such a context, voices such as Gordon Morgan's ("America is not a good place for cultural pluralism and ethnicity to flourish. . . . Cultural pluralism seems to have very little future in America in the long run") seem distinctly out of touch with reality. Rather, it appears that "managing" pluralism so as to take full advantage of diverse cultural strengths while avoiding ethnic splintering of the country will be the greatest social challenge of the twenty-first century.

Bibliography

Coughlin, Ellen K. "Sociologists Examine the Complexities of Racial and Ethnic Identity in America." *The Chronicle of Higher Education* 24 (March, 1993): A7-A8. Discusses the difficulty of defining racial and ethnic groups, noting diversity within traditionally labeled groups. Includes a bibliography of sources covering the years 1985 to 1992.

Crispino, James A. *The Assimilation of Ethnic Groups: The Italian Case*. Staten Island, N.Y.: Center for Migration Studies, 1980. This case study of Italians in Bridgeport, Connecticut, indicates continued assimilation during the 1970's, despite the general "ethnic revival" of that decade. Includes a long bibliography.

Dinnerstein, Leonard, and Frederic Cole Jaher, eds. *Uncertain Americans: Readings in Ethnic History*. Rev. ed. New York: Oxford University Press, 1977. Historically organized groupings of essays and excerpts by various representatives of "deprived minorities," emphasizing the "harsher aspects" of ethnic experience in the United States from the colonial era through the 1970's. Includes accounts by American

Indians, African Americans, European Americans, and Hispanics.

Fuchs, Lawrence H. *The American Kaleidoscope: Race, Ethnicity, and the Civic Culture.* Hanover, N.H.: Wesleyan University Press, 1990. A massive book by a liberal Brandeis University professor of American civilization and politics. Traces the historical origins of the American "civic culture" and of the ethnic factions and conflicts within that framework. Fuchs expresses hopes of strengthening the whole while paradoxically reinforcing the freedom of ethnic expression. Heavily documented, carefully indexed.

Gomez, Rudolph, et al., eds. *The Social Reality of Ethnic America.* Lexington, Mass.: D. C. Heath, 1974. Selected essays from the 1960's and early 1970's by representatives of four minority groups: African Americans, American Indians, Japanese Americans, and Mexican Americans. Aimed at the beginning student in ethnic studies who wants to understand basic facts about these groups—their lifestyles, heritages, and social problems.

Gordon, Milton Myron. *Assimilation in American Life: The Role of Race, Religion, and National Origins.* New York: Oxford University Press, 1964. A specialist in intergroup relations, Gordon studied twenty-five organizations representing American cultural subgroups and found these organizations to be generally promoting pluralism in the 1960's; he predicts the continuation of pluralism but hopes for a balance with assimilation.

Lambert, Wallace E., and Donald M. Taylor. *Coping with Cultural and Racial Diversity in Urban America.* New York: Praeger, 1990. This study based on fieldwork among diverse urban residents in Michigan examines group attitudes, finding general support for pluralism (and opposition to assimilation) among all ethnic groups. Includes methodological explanation and bibliography.

Morgan, Gordon D. *America Without Ethnicity.* Port Washington, N.Y.: Kennikat Press, 1981. Reacting to the formation about 1970 of the Black Caucus of the American Sociological Association, an academic sociologist sketches in this brief, coherently reasoned book the background of the rise of cultural pluralism in the United States and argues against the trend, advocating assimilation.

Ringer, Benjamin B., and Elinor R. Lawless. *Race—Ethnicity and Society.* New York: Routledge, 1989. An interesting book rather heavy with sociological jargon. Argues that the lingering effects of historical racism and the cultural biases of "dominant whites" in the United States still operates against persons of color, even though a widespread belief during the 1980's was that past injustices were made right during the 1960's and 1970's and that modern society is "color blind."

Wurzel, Jaime S., ed. *Toward Multiculturalism: A Reader in Multicultural Education.* Yarmouth, Maine: Intercultural Press, 1988. Essays and excerpts through the 1980's, selected with the aim of giving the reader a multicultural perspective. Assumes that society is multicultural and that thoughtful awareness will help Americans acquire the skills necessary to deal with ethnic diversity.

Roy Neil Graves

Cross-References

Annihilation or Expulsion of Racial or Ethnic Groups, 92; Assimilation: The United States, 140; Cultural and Structural Assimilation, 405; Ethnic Enclaves, 682; Ethnicity and Ethnic Groups, 689; Immigration to the United States, 928; "Middleman" Minorities, 1200; Minority and Majority Groups, 1219; "Model" Minorities, 1233; Race and Racial Groups, 1552.

THE POLICE

Type of sociology: Deviance and social control
Field of study: Controlling deviance

The police are the institution authorized by society to use coercive force and other means to control deviance. The effectiveness of this institution depends not only on professional ability but also on community support.

Principal terms

ALIENATION: the withdrawal of a person or a group from the mainstream of society; police brutality, for example, may provoke a racial minority to regard the country's criminal justice system as an oppressive foreign power

BUREAUCRACY: the civil service in modern governments; typically a bureaucracy is a large-scale organization, marked by centralized control and differentiated functions

CIVIL SERVICE: the organized civilian rather than military employees of government, appointed to their positions and paid (in contrast to amateurs or unpaid volunteers in public service)

COMMUNITY: any stable group, such as a neighborhood or professional association, that provides its members with primary personal relationships based on common values

CRIME: a punishable offense according to the laws enacted by society

DEMOCRACY: a form of government based on the freely given consent of its members; it is characterized by majority rule, protection of the rights of all its members, and effective control over the exercise of power

ETHOS: the governing ideals of a group, consisting of values that determine the thought and behavior of its members

FORENSIC: the scientific research, investigative techniques, and other skills used in legal proceedings

MODERN STATE: a politically organized society that holds sovereignty or the ultimate authority to rule

PROFESSION: a vocational group whose practitioners need higher education and advanced training; a profession typically has clearly defined entrance requirements, certification of competence, and procedures for internal control

Overview

In its current use, the word "police" refers to the institution within a country's criminal justice system that is responsible for maintaining public order, protecting property and persons from illegal actions, and investigating crimes. Its many earlier definitions included a much greater variety of duties, such as regulation of weights and measures, public sanitation, and fire protection. In continental European usage from the seventeenth to the nineteenth century, the term encompassed all aspects of public order that lay outside the purview of the military. The term, as referring to the enforcement of law, was first used among English-speaking people in the early eighteenth century; they adopted it from the French. In his 1800 book on the police of the River Thames, Patrick Colquhoun was the first author to use the term in its modern sense, applying it to the Marine Police, an agency that he helped establish which was entrusted with the task of preventing, detecting, and punishing crime in London's harbor.

In contrast to earlier, informal police administration, such as London's parish watchmen in the early nineteenth century, modern police are a complex, professional bureaucracy. A typical contemporary police force is organized hierarchically, like other major civil services, with a chain of authority, standardized procedures, and a distinctive ethos. At the top of the administrative pyramid of a typical large urban American police force is a chief or a commissioner who directs the work of numerous bureaus and divisions.

Standardized procedures are designed to help ensure against the corrupting influences of partisan politics, arbitrary conduct by leaders as well as the rank and file, and other abuses of policing. Recruiting, promotions, and disciplinary action are conducted according to civil service regulations. Other procedures are standardized by legislation, judicial orders, and agreements among professional police associations. A professional ethos of shared values appropriate to policing, such as honesty, loyalty, obedience, and emotional restraint, is inculcated by education and training as well as by the discipline to which police are subjected.

Modern police also aspire to the character and prestige of a profession, such as the legal, medical, and teaching professions. This is especially true in the higher levels of administration. The skills required to manage a large urban police force are attained through higher education, often in one of the hundreds of college-level criminal justice programs. Other opportunities for professional training are offered at state and metropolitan police academies and at the facilities of the Federal Bureau of Investigation (FBI) in Quantico, Virginia. Police today are more specialized than ever before. The complexity and sophistication of crime require the police to create units that are highly trained for certain tasks, such as those dealing with auto theft, terrorism, or corporate fraud. In several of the specialized fields—for example, forensic investigation—formal training at the university level may be required.

While sharing these common characteristics, modern police differ greatly from country to country. The police in the United States are predominantly armed civil servants, organized in several thousand autonomous districts that vary widely in size, from a sheriff and one or two deputies in rural counties to forces of thirty thousand or more in the largest metropolitan centers. Working within a heterogeneous society prone to violence, American police are regarded ambivalently by the general population and are more or less alienated from significant minorities. State and federal police, such as the FBI, who have narrowly defined roles, are more highly regarded. The police in Britain are also civil servants, but they are generally unarmed and enjoy a higher level of community support. They are organized in some forty semi-autonomous districts under the authority of the home secretary, who ensures uniform administration and standardized procedures. The Scandinavian countries, the Low Countries, the Irish Republic, Canada, Australia, and New Zealand have forces similar to the British. Most countries in continental Europe, Latin America, Asia, and Africa have mixed forces composed of civil servants and soldiers. Typical of their military components are the French *gendarmerie* and the Italian *carabinieri*. Their police administrations are highly centralized and standardized under a minister of the interior of the national government.

The techniques of police work are determined both by the kinds of crime the police are required to combat and by the resources that society puts at their disposal. In what has been called the reactive mode of operation, citizens make complaints of burglary, assault, or other crime, and the police come to the scene. In the proactive mode, the police initiate investigations of drug traffic and other illegal behavior. Modern science has greatly enhanced these techniques. The police of most industrialized countries use electronic computers to search records, sort through fingerprint files, compare modus operandi material and psychological profiles, and answer questions concerning suspicious automobiles or missing persons. The rapid evolution of technology has not only improved the effectiveness of the police in the field but also strengthened command and control within police forces.

Applications

It matters greatly how the police of a multicultural, democratic society are organized and how they operate. The Rodney King case in Los Angeles, as well as similar incidents in the 1980's in Detroit and Miami, indicate that, unless the police are sensitive to cultural differences and respectful of human dignity and civil rights, the society they serve is likely to experience serious conflict.

On March 3, 1991, Rodney King, a black man, was beaten by several white police officers at the conclusion of a high-speed automobile chase. Videotaped by an onlooker, the beating was shown on national television and prompted an outraged public to demand that the officers be charged with felonious assault. Their apparently egregious brutality resonated in the public mind, creating widespread sentiments among whites as well as blacks that what happened to King was not an isolated instance of abuse but rather typical. He differed from other victims of police brutality only by his misfortune having been videotaped.

The trial of four of the officers by the state of California was moved from Los Angeles to suburban Simi Valley. On April 29, 1992, an all-white jury acquitted the men. This verdict was widely perceived as a miscarriage of justice, triggering massive riots among blacks in Los Angeles. Fifty-eight persons were killed, and property damage totalled billions of dollars. In August, 1992, the federal government indicted the four officers for violating King's civil rights. This time the case was tried before a racially mixed jury in Los Angeles. In April, 1993, it convicted Laurence Powell and Stacey Koon and acquitted Timothy Wind and Theodore Briseno. In August, 1993, Powell and Koon were sentenced to thirty-month prison terms. The sentence was widely perceived to be light; there were protests, but no violence occurred.

The King case and similar incidents elsewhere have brought the issue of police brutality to the nation's attention, demonstrating that the institution of the modern police must be anchored in democratic values or it will be subject to abuses of its power, ranging from relatively benign intimidation of citizens to lawless, brutal violence. The abuse of police power necessarily leads to public fear and mistrust of the police and to reluctance to cooperate with them or to fund them. In addition, qualified young men and women who might otherwise join the police may look elsewhere for a career.

Effective policing requires community cooperation. Where the community is hostile, weak, or indifferent, the police will find it difficult to operate. The police will not receive adequate funds or suitable recruits from the community. Members of a hostile community can obstruct the work of the police by sheltering or shielding suspects and by refusing to give information or testimony. They will also violate the law with greater frequency, as a way of defying and showing contempt for an institution they fear or despise. The police, in turn, will be sorely tempted to use force to establish their authority and to resort to intimidation (perhaps even torture) to gain information, thereby adding to the alienation that obstructed their work in the first place.

The problems of modern policing can be addressed partially by reforming the institution. Departments need to be mindful of democratic values when selecting leaders and recruits, when framing their rules and regulations and demanding compliance with them, and when educating and indoctrinating their personnel to induce willing compliance. The fruit of such reform will be a democratic ethos that requires of the police not only obedience, loyalty, honesty, courage, and commitment to enforcing the law but also self-restraint, sensitivity to the diversity of human needs and cultural values, courtesy and respect for human dignity, and humane concern for suffering and hardship.

The police, however, cannot be reformed without a certain amount of reformation in society itself. Few if any serious reforms can take place solely at the initiative of, and under the power of, the police themselves. O. W. Wilson, for example, needed the full support of Mayor Richard Daley in order to reform the Chicago police in the 1960's. Robert Peel needed the backing of the Duke of Wellington and the approval of the House of Commons in order to create the London Metropolitan Police in 1829. Moreover, he could not have secured such support unless there was consensus among influential social leaders that reform of the police was necessary. If any society wishes to enjoy more effective policing and a greater degree of public safety, it must take the steps necessary to make the bureaucratic, professional, and specialized police sensitive to ethnic and racial differences, respectful of human dignity, and soliticitous of civil rights. The public and its political leadership must understand the mission of the police in a multicultural, democratic society and the inherent limitations of the institution.

Context

The size and complexity of the police have grown with the modern state. Previously, communities policed themselves. In the Anglo-American tradition, the first police was the medieval "watch" that required citizens to assist the town constable. On the European continent, the police developed from the military as well as from the watch. By the nineteenth century, the watch was obsolete, and new systems emerged. In the United Kingdom, Robert Peel created for Ireland a military-style colonial police that was copied throughout the British Empire and in the Philippines when the islands came under American control.

A second system, Peel's greatest achievement, was the London Metropolitan Police (LMP), established in 1829. Administered by the Home Office through two appointed commissioners, the LMP was largely shielded from political influences. Peel instilled in the LMP a civil (in contrast to a military) ethos in order to win community support. During the nineteenth century, the urban and county police forces were reformed on the LMP model, consolidated, and brought under the supervisory control of the Home Office. In the twentieth century, centralization was accelerated, regional crime squads and other specialized units created, women integrated into the force, and a measure of democracy introduced.

A third system evolved in the United States. The federal, democratic, and pluralistic characteristics of the nation strongly influenced its policing. The constitution of 1787 assigned primary responsibility for police to the states, which in turn delegated it to local units of government. In the nineteenth century, both rural and urban police forces were caught up in patronage politics as well as in social, ethnic, and racial conflicts. At the century's end, American police were widely regarded as ineffective, brutal, and corrupt.

Reform of the police has been a major objective of progressive reformers since the late nineteenth century. With assistance from the FBI, urban police in the United States were gradually freed from political influence, professionalized, and better coordinated. The states also created police units, such as highway patrol units, and the federal government established numerous policing agencies to serve special needs as diverse as protecting the president and interdicting drug traffic. While the federal and state role in policing has grown during the twentieth century, American police continue to be largely local and independent.

On the European continent a more centralized, military-style police developed. At the beginning of the nineteenth century Joseph Fouché, Napoleon's police chief, created a national *gendarmerie*, soldiers detached from the army for police duty. By mid-century Paris, like London, had a civil urban police, but they were armed and less dependent on community support than the LMP. In the twentieth century French policing grew more specialized (for example, in riot control) and less military. Women were integrated into the lower echelons. The French model was widely adopted by other European, Asian, and Latin American nations in the nineteenth century and by many Third World countries in the twentieth. The trend toward more specialized, centralized, and professional police can be expected to continue in the future.

Bibliography

Bayley, David H. *Patterns of Policing: A Comparative International Analysis*. New Brunswick, N.J.: Rutgers University Press, 1985. On the basis of contemporary and historical information, the author constructs several general propositions about how the police function. The subjects of his comparative analysis are the police of the United States, Sri Lanka, Singapore, The Netherlands, Norway, India, France, and Great Britain.

Cramer, James. *The World's Police*. London: Cassell, 1964. Brief descriptions of most of the world's police forces, enhanced by many illustrations and a bibliography.

Dunham, Roger G., and Geoffrey P. Alpert, eds. *Critical Issues in Policing: Contemporary Readings*. Prospect Heights, Ill.: Waveland, 1992. A comprehensive collection of readings from the work of a variety of experts and specialists. Besides an introductory survey of the history of the police, the book includes such topics as police deviance, community-based policing, the use of force, hazards of police work, and minorities in policing.

Fogelson, Robert M. *Big City Police*. Cambridge, Mass.: Harvard University Press, 1977. A history of police reform in the modern United States. Crime statistics, Fogelson believes, are too inexact to measure the effectiveness of the police. Nevertheless, he contends that twentieth century attempts to reform the police have bettered conditions within the institution but have not improved its enforcement of the law. This book contains a wealth of information based on solid research.

Johnson, David R. *American Law Enforcement: A History*. St. Louis: Forum Press, 1981. A useful textbook focusing on the crime-fighting function of the police. It includes a good brief description of the federal government's role in policing. It also treats the response of municipal and state police forces to changing patterns of crime and to demands of reformers for greater efficiency and professionalism.

Powers, Richard Gid. *Secrecy and Power: The Life of J. Edgar Hoover*. New York: Free Press, 1987. This lengthy work offers the general reader a well-balanced, carefully researched, and fascinating exploration of the life and work of the single most influential policeman in U.S. history. The FBI became Hoover's surrogate family, the author contends, in which he indulged a mania for social control that extended to the most trivial details of the organization.

Stead, Philip J. *The Police of France*. New York: Macmillan, 1983. A sympathetic history of the French police since the seventeenth century, this work deals mainly with its institutional characteristics. The author also concentrates on developments since World War II. The general reader will find this work a useful introduction.

Charles H. O'Brien

Cross-References

The Courts, 367; Crime: Analysis and Overview, 373; The Criminal Justice System, 380; Gangs, 792; Juvenile Delinquency: Analysis and Overview, 1036; Prison and Recidivism, 1519; Uniform Crime Reports and Crime Data, 2090.

SURVEY
OF
SOCIAL
SCIENCE

ALPHABETICAL LIST

CATEGORY LIST

CATEGORY LIST

SOCIOLOGY